Admiralty
Manual of Navigation
VOLUME I

B.R. 45 (1)

Revised 1964

LONDON
HER MAJESTY'S STATIONERY OFFICE

Consolidated Edition 1970
incorporating Changes 1 to 4
Reprinted 1977
including the 1972 International
Regulations for preventing collision
at sea.

HER MAJESTY'S STATIONERY OFFICE

Government Bookshops

49 High Holborn, London WC1V 6HB
13A Castle Street, Edinburgh EH2 3AR
41 The Hayes, Cardiff CF1 1JW
Brazennose Street, Manchester M60 8AS
Southey House, Wine Street, Bristol BS1 2BQ
258 Broad Street, Birmingham B1 2HE
80 Chichester Street, Belfast BT1 4JY

Government Publications are also available
through booksellers

ISBN 0 11 770768 6

Andrew

Pitcher

R.F.A AD.1979

RECORD OF CHANGES

CHANGE NO.	A.F.O. P SERIES	DATE OF INSERTION IN THIS COPY	INITIALS

Changes 1 to 4 have been incorporated.

ADMIRALTY

1st January 1964

DND 109/61

B.R. 45 (1), *Admiralty Manual of Navigation*, Volume I, 1964, having been approved by My Lords Commissioners of the Admiralty, is hereby promulgated.

B.R. 45 (1) dated 1955 is hereby superseded.

By Command of Their Lordships,

NAVIGATION AND DIRECTION DIVISION

(131873)

A 2

Preface

The *Admiralty Manual of Navigation* consists of four volumes:

Volume I is a practical guide for seamen officers covering the syllabus laid down for examination in Navigation and Pilotage for the rank of Lieutenant, but omitting the study of nautical astronomy and meterology.

Volume II is the textbook of nautical astronomy and off-shore navigation completing the above syllabus. This volume also covers the syllabus of meteorology for officers qualifying in Navigation.

Volume III is based on the navigation syllabus for officers qualifying in Navigation and deals with advanced subjects and mathematical proofs not included in Volumes I and II. It will be unnecessary for seamen officers in general to study this volume. (*Out of print.*)

Volume IV is intended to provide data on certain navigational equipment and techniques used by H.M. ships and details of the handling qualities of various classes of H.M. ships. It is not available for the Press or public.

Thanks are due to the Hydrographic Department, the Naval Meteorological Branch, the Admiralty Compass Division, the Astronomer Royal, the Institute of Navigation, and various instrument manufacturers. Acknowledgement is also due to Messrs. Hutchinson and Co. (Publishers) Limited, for the use of extracts from *On the Bridge*, by Vice-Admiral Sir James A. G. Troup, K.B.E., C.B.

PUBLISHER'S NOTES TO 1977 IMPRESSION OF VOLUME I

1. The International Regulations for Preventing Collisions at Sea, 1972, are reproduced in this impression; see Chapter XV.

2. The International Association of Lighthouse Authorities' new Maritime Buoyage System 'A' (IALA System A) is due to be introduced in the Dover Strait and vicinity from April 1977 and will be progressively introduced in the N.W. European Area thereafter. Details of IALA System A will be found in:

Notice to Mariners No. 514(P) of 1976.

Notice to Mariners No. 1276 of 1976 with accompanying page L70 showing symbols and abbreviations.

NP 735. *IALA Maritime Buoyage System 'A'*.

The above publications are obtainable from the Hydrographer or from Admiralty Chart agents.

Contents

CHAPTER I

Position and Direction on the Earth's Surface

NAVIGATION is the art of finding the position of a ship at sea, and conducting her safely from place to place. That part of navigation which is concerned with the open sea and with observations of heavenly bodies is fully dealt with in Volume II.

The main purpose of Volume I is to describe pilotage, which is the art of conducting a ship in the neighbourhood of dangers, such as rocks and shoals, and in narrow waters. Pilotage calls for a knowledge of charts, *Sailing Directions* and other publications, and also of artificial aids to navigation such as buoys, lights, fog signals and radio aids. But first, in order to appreciate their uses and limitations, some knowledge of the Earth and the units of measurement concerned with it is necessary.

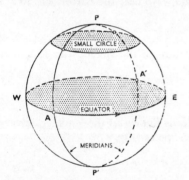

FIG. 1a. The Earth: Observer above the Equator

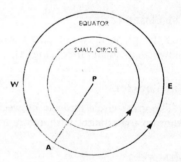

FIG. 1b. Observer directly above the North Pole

THE EARTH

Although the Earth is not a perfect sphere, it may be considered so for the purposes of navigation, as the errors which result rom this assumption are usually negligible. The departures from the spherical shape are explained fully in Volume III.

THE POLES OF THE EARTH

In Fig. 1a, *P* and *P′* are the extremities of the Earth's axis of rotation, and are called the 'poles'.

(131873)

EAST AND WEST

The direction towards which the Earth rotates is called 'east'; the opposite direction is called 'west'.

NORTH AND SOUTH

The two poles are distinguished arbitrarily. The Earth, when viewed from above the North Pole (P), rotates in an anti-clockwise direction (Fig. 1b). Alternatively, the North Pole may be regarded as that pole which lies to the left of an observer who is facing east. The opposite pole is called the South Pole (P'). The north-south direction is clearly at right angles to the east-west direction. The axis $P'P$ if projected would lie very nearly in the same direction as a star known as the Pole Star or *Polaris*.

THE GREAT CIRCLE

A sphere is formed by rotating a circle about a diameter. Any section of a sphere by a plane must therefore be a circle. If the plane passes through the centre of the sphere, the resulting section is the largest that can be obtained and is known as a 'great circle'. It is important because it gives the navigator the shortest track between any two places which lie on it, since the great-circle track is the nearest approach to a straight line which can be drawn on the surface of a sphere. It is also the path taken by a radio wave near the Earth's surface.

THE SMALL CIRCLE

If the plane does not pass through the centre of the sphere, the section is known as a 'small circle' (Fig. 1).

THE EQUATOR

The great circle midway between the poles is known as the 'equator'. Every point on the equator is therefore 90° from the poles (Fig. 1).

MERIDIANS

These are semigreat circles joining the poles, and are perpendicular to the equator. In Fig. 1a, PAP' is one meridian; $PA'P'$ is another on the other side of the Earth.

Latitude and Longitude

To find the position of any point in a plane, it is sufficient to know its shortest distances from two lines in that plane, preferably at right angles to each other (Fig. 2a).

When the point lies on a sphere, the same method holds in principle, but the distances from the two axes must be measured in angular and not linear units.

The corresponding axes on the Earth's surface are the equator and the meridian through Greenwich (Fig. 2b). The equator is selected because it is conveniently situated for the purpose: it is midway between the poles and its plane is at right angles to the axis of spin. The Greenwich meridian is selected by international agreement and is known as the 'prime meridian'. Distances from these axes are measured in the directions governed by the Earth's rotation – North, South, East and West.

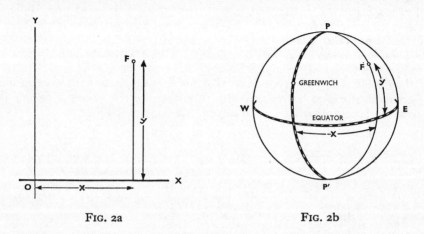

FIG. 2a   FIG. 2b

LATITUDE

In Fig. 2c, *PFP'* is the meridian passing through a place *F* and meeting the equator at *L*. The angular distance *FL* is called the 'latitude' of *F*. The angle *FCL* thus measures the latitude of *F*. The latitude of a place is therefore the angular distance of that place N. or S. of the equator. The angle is measured at the centre of the Earth in the plane of the meridian through the place. It is expressed in degrees, minutes and seconds, from 0° to 90°.

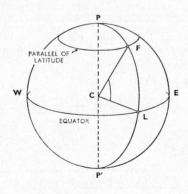

FIG. 2c

PARALLEL OF LATITUDE

Places having the same latitude as *F* clearly lie on a small circle, the plane of which is parallel to the plane of the equator. This small circle is called a 'parallel of latitude'.

LONGITUDE

In Fig. 3a, *PFP′* is the meridian through *F* meeting the equator in *B*. The meridian through Greenwich meets the equator in *A*. The angular distance *AB* is called the 'longitude' of *F*. The longitude of a place is thus the angular distance, expressed in degrees, minutes and seconds, between its meridian and the meridian of Greenwich. The angle is measured at the centre of the Earth in the plane of the equator.

Longitude is named '*E*.' or '*W*.', depending on whether the place is east or west of the Greenwich meridian.

Longitude cannot be greater than 180° east or west, because the plane of the Greenwich meridian bisects the Earth (Fig. 3b). For this reason, longitude is always measured along the shorter arc, e.g. *AB*, and not *AWEB*.

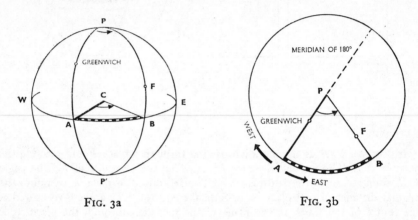

FIG. 3a   FIG. 3b

Position

The position of a place can therefore be described in terms of latitude north or south of the equator and longitude east or west of the Greenwich meridian. St. Thomas' Church tower, Portsmouth, for example, is in latitude 50 degrees, 47 minutes, 24 seconds north of the equator, and in longitude 1 degree, 6 minutes, 10 seconds west of Greenwich.

The position is recorded thus:

$$50° \ 47' \ 24''N.$$
$$1° \ 06' \ 10''W.$$

DIFFERENCE OF LATITUDE

The 'difference of latitude' between two places *F* and *T* in Fig. 4 is the difference between the latitudes of *F* and *T*; that is, the length *FM* along the meridian through *F*, cut off by the parallels of latitude through *F* and *T*.

If the two places are on the same side of the equator and have the same name – both are *north* in Fig. 4a – the difference is found by subtracting the latitude of *T*, the smaller one, from the latitude of *F*.

If *T* lies on the side of the equator opposite to *F*, and the two places have opposite names, *north* and *south* (as in Fig. 4b), the difference of latitude is the sum of the separate latitudes.

The expression 'difference of latitude' is used whether the latitudes have the same names or not. It is always referred to as the *dee-lat*, an abbreviation which is conveniently written 'd.lat'.

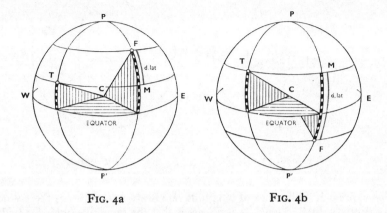

FIG. 4a   FIG. 4b

The rule for finding the d.lat may be summarized thus:

Same names – subtract,
Opposite names – add.

If a ship is steaming from F to T, it is necessary to put a name to the d.lat in order to indicate whether she is moving north or south. In Fig. 4a she would be moving south, and the d.lat would be marked S. In Fig. 4b she would be moving north, and the d.lat would be marked N.

For example, a ship steaming from Portsmouth (50° 48'N.) to Gibraltar (36° 07'N.) would change her latitude by 14° 41'S., because she herself is moving south. Thus:

From Portsmouth	50° 48'N.
To Gibraltar	36° 07'N.
d.lat (*same names: subtract*)	14° 41'S.

A ship steaming from Suva, in Fiji (18° 09'S.), to Honolulu (21° 18'N.) would change her latitude by 39° 27'N., because she herself is steaming north. Thus:

From Suva	18° 09'S.
To Honolulu	21° 18'N.
d.lat (*opposite names: add*)	39° 27'N.

DIFFERENCE OF LONGITUDE

The 'difference of longitude' between two places F and T (Fig. 5) is the difference between the longitudes of F and T – that is, the length BD cut off along the equator by the meridians through F and T, or the angle at the pole between the meridians of the two places.

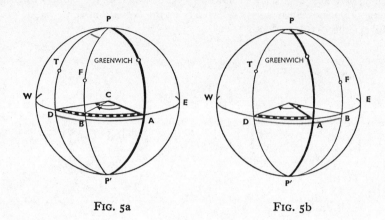

FIG. 5a   FIG. 5b

The expression 'difference of longitude' is always referred to as the *dee-long*, conveniently written 'd.long'. It is apparent that the same rule holds for finding the d.long as for finding the d.lat, namely:

Same names – subtract,
Opposite names – add.

For example, a ship steaming from Sandy Hook, New York (74° 00′W.), to the Bishop Rock Light in the Scillies (6° 27′W.) would change her longitude by 67° 33′E., because she herself is moving east. Thus:

From Sandy Hook	74° 00′W.
To Bishop Rock	6° 27′W.
d.long (*same names: subtract*)	67° 33′E.

A ship steaming from Malta (14° 31′E.) to Gibraltar (5° 21′W.) changes her longitude by 19° 52′W., because she herself is moving west. Thus:

From Malta	14° 31′E.
To Gibraltar	5° 21′W.
d.long (*opposite names: add*)	19° 52′W.

Should this sum exceed 180°, a small adjustment is necessary, as the following example will make clear.

Suppose that a navigator wishes to take his ship from Sydney (151° 13′E.) to Honolulu (157° 52′W.) (Fig. 6). By rule, the d.long is 309° 05′W., because he would go back to the Greenwich meridian and then onwards, proceeding west all the time. But in practice he would obviously go the shorter way, which is east. The number obtained from the rule must therefore be subtracted from 360° if it exceeds 180°, and its name must be reversed. Thus:

| From Sydney | 151° 13′E. |
| To Honolulu | 157° 52′W. |

| d.long (*opposite names: add*) | 309° 05′W. |
| | 360° |

| d.long | 50° 55′E. |

When positions are defined by their latitude and longitude, therefore, the position of one place relative to another can be defined by means of a d.lat and a d.long.

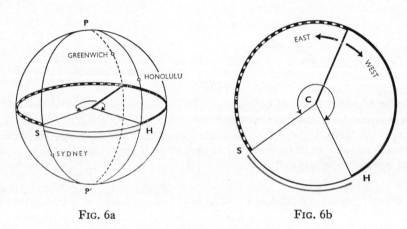

FIG. 6a   FIG. 6b

UNITS OF MEASUREMENT

Angular Distances between Two Places

Since it is agreed to consider the Earth as a sphere, the distance between places on the Earth's surface is conveniently expressed in angular measure.

The length of the great-circle arc FT in Fig. 7, for example, is ($R \times$ angle FCT), R being the radius of the sphere and the angle FCT being measured in radians. Because R is constant, the length FT is proportional to the size of the angle FCT. For this reason, it is customary to refer to the shorter arc of the great circle joining two points as the 'angular distance' between them.

The most convenient unit for measuring distance on the Earth's surface is therefore based on an angular unit, and the unit of distance selected is the length of a great-circle arc which subtends an angle of one minute at the centre of curvature.

Linear Measurement of Longitude

It can be seen from Fig. 6a that the distance on the Earth's surface between any two meridians is greatest at the equator and diminishes uniformly until it is zero at the poles, where all the meridians meet. The linear distance of a degree of longitude on the surface of the Earth therefore varies in accordance with its latitude and cannot be taken as a standard measure of length. For instance, the distance on the Earth's surface representing 30 degrees of longitude at latitude 60°N. is 902½ nautical miles, whereas at the equator it is 1,800 nautical miles.

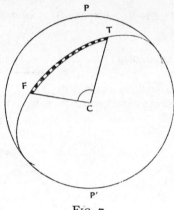

FIG. 7

Linear Measurement of Latitude

On the other hand, the distance which represents a degree of latitude is approximately the same anywhere on the Earth's surface. For instance, the actual distance between 30 degrees and 60 degrees south is approximately the same as that between 0 degrees and 30 degrees north.

THE NAUTICAL MILE

This is a standard fixed length. The term 'nautical mile' in British publications today is the British Standard Nautical Mile of 6,080 feet (1,853·18 metres), although the International Nautical Mile of 1852 metres is now used by most other countries.

Except on charts, where the symbol M is adopted, the nautical mile is always denoted by ′, which is the symbol for a minute of arc. Thus 10′·8 means 10·8 nautical miles. (The symbol is placed before the decimal point, and not after the final figure—e.g. 10′·8 and not 10·8′—in order to ensure that no error is made in the position of the decimal point.)

If, for example, the angle FCT in Fig. 7 happened to be 56° 25′·5, the length of the great-circle arc FT would also be 56° 25′·5 in angular measurement, or (56×60)+25·5 minutes of arc—i.e. 3,385·5 nautical miles.

THE SEA MILE

This is the length of one minute of arc, measured along the meridian, in the latitude of the position; its length varies both with the latitude and with the figure of the Earth in use. The sea mile is used for the scale of latitude on large-scale Admiralty charts, as distances are measured using the latitude graduations of the chart borders.

Distances given in the *Admiralty Distance Tables* and in *Ocean Passages of the World* are in sea miles.

THE KNOT

In navigation the unit of speed is one nautical mile per hour, and that unit is called a 'knot'. If a vessel steams through the water a distance of 8 × 6,080 feet in one hour, she is said to be 'steaming at 8 knots', or simply, 'steaming 8 knots'.

The term knot is derived from the old method of finding a ship's speed through the water by means of a log and line. Pieces of coloured rag, tied in knots, were equally spaced along the line, and the number of knots paid out over the stern during a given interval of time (measured by a sandglass) indicated the ship's speed in nautical miles per hour.

THE STATUTE MILE, OR LAND MILE

This is an arbitrary unit introduced by Queen Elizabeth I, who decreed that it was to be 8 furlongs of 40 perches of $16\frac{1}{2}$ feet – making 5,280 feet in all.

The nautical mile being 6,080 feet and the statute mile 5,280 feet, 7 nautical miles are approximately equal to 8 statute miles. More accurately, 13 nautical miles are equivalent to 15 statute miles.

> *Note:* The arithmetical labour of converting nautical miles into statute miles may be avoided by using the Traverse Table, which is explained in Volume II. If this table is entered for an angle of 30° and the figure against that angle in any latitude column is treated as the number of nautical miles to be converted, the distance given at the top of the column will be the corresponding number of statute miles.

SEA MEASUREMENTS

1 fathom	= 6 feet, or 2 yards
1 cable	= 608 feet, or roughly 200 yards, or 100 fathoms
10 cables	= 6,080 feet, or 1 British standard nautical mile, or roughly 2,000 yards
1 British standard nautical mile	= 6,080 feet, or roughly 2,000 yards, or 1,853·18 metres
1 International nautical mile	= 1,852 metres
1 league (obsolete)	= 3 nautical miles
1 knot	= 1 nautical mile per hour

COURSE AND BEARING

Direction

Before a navigator can take his ship from, say, Scapa Flow to Bergen, he must first ascertain the direction in which Bergen lies from Scapa Flow, so that by steering in that direction he may arrive at Bergen. Direction is thus determined by the point on the horizon towards which a person is aiming or a vessel is moving. It is thus essentially a line.

The cardinal directions are North, South, East, and West.

Bearing

To the navigator of a ship in mid-ocean, the horizon is a circle drawn about the ship as centre, and there is nothing to distinguish one point on that circle from another.

In order to proceed in a particular direction it is therefore necessary to refer to some datum line or fixed direction.

The angle between this datum line and the direction in which it is required to proceed is called the 'bearing' of the point towards which, the ship is proceeding.

True Bearing

The most convenient datum is the meridian through the ship's position, because that is the north-south line. Bearings measured from this datum are known as 'true bearings'.

In Fig. 8a, *FP*, the meridian through *F*, gives the direction of true north. *FT*, the great circle joining *F* to *T*, gives the direction of *T*. The angle *PFT* is the true bearing of *T* from *F*.

If *T* is close to *F*, the small area of the Earth's surface traversed by *FT* may be considered flat, and no appreciable error will be introduced if the great circles are drawn as straight lines, as in Fig. 8b.

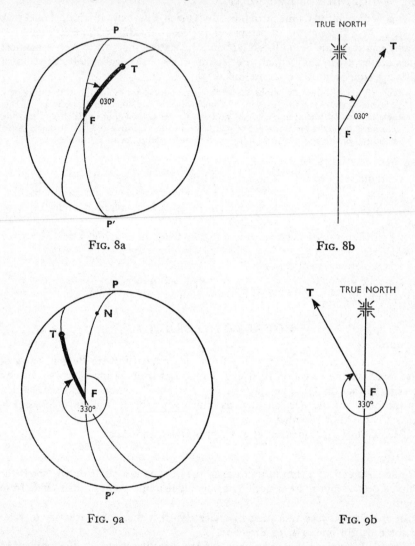

Fig. 8a

Fig. 8b

Fig. 9a

Fig. 9b

To obtain a true bearing, the angle *PFT* is always measured clockwise from 0° to 360°, and it is always written as a three-figure number. The method of distinguishing true bearings from magnetic or compass bearings is described later. In Figs. 8a and 8b, *T* would be said to 'bear' 030° from *F*. In Figs. 9a and 9b, *T* bears 330° from *F*; and the point *N*, which lies on the meridian through *F* and is therefore due north of *F*, bears 000°.

Position of Close Objects

It is often convenient to indicate the position of an object by its bearing and distance from a known or key position. A shoal, for example, might be described as being 229°, 7 miles from a certain lighthouse, and a cruiser 078°, 10 miles from a flagship.

True Course

The direction in which a ship moves in still water is the direction of her fore-and-aft line. The angle between this fore-and-aft line and the meridian through her position is called her 'true course'. The bearing of the ship's head is thus the same as her course.

THE COMPASS

The navigational compass is an instrument that gives the necessary datum line from which courses and bearings can be measured. There are three kinds of compass – gyro-compass, magnetic compass and gyro-magnetic compass.

The Gyro-Compass

This instrument, which is described in Chapter VIII, is essentially a rapidly spinning wheel or gyroscope, the axis of which is made to point approximately true north. Thus, in the gyro-compass the navigator has an instrument which will indicate the direction of the true north by pointing along the true meridian. Bearings taken with a gyro-compass are therefore true bearings, and are always referred to in three-figure numbers. To enable this to be done, the outer rims of the gyro-compass repeaters, with which bearings are taken, are graduated clockwise from 000° to 360°.

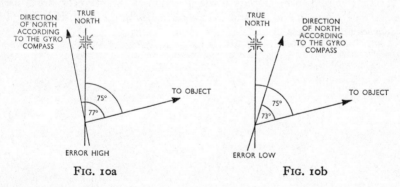

FIG. 10a   FIG. 10b

ERROR OF THE GYRO-COMPASS

For a number of reasons, the gyro-compass will not always point exactly to the true north. It may settle a degree or two on one side or the other of the true meridian, and if it does so, the compass will be said to read 'high' or 'low'. The methods of finding the error of the gyro-compass are described in later chapters.

If the gyro bearing of an object is 077°, while its true bearing is known to be 075°, then it can be seen in Fig. 10a that the gyro is reading 2° *high*; similarly, if the gyro bearing is 073°, as in Fig. 10b, the gyro is reading 2° *low*. In order to obtain the true bearing, a gyro error *high* must be *subtracted* from the gyro bearing, and a gyro error *low* must be *added* to the gyro bearing. The suffixes G and T may be used to denote Gyro and True compass courses or bearings.

The Magnetic Compass

This instrument, which is described in Chapter IX, may be considered as a bar magnet freely suspended in the horizontal plane. Being thus unrestrained, it turns and settles with one end pointing approximately to the north. It will not, as a rule, point to the true north, because the Earth's geographical or true poles do not coincide with the magnetic poles to which the ends of the compass needle are attracted.

The direction assumed by the compass needle, when affected solely by the Earth's magnetic force, is known as a 'line of total force'. The vertical plane passing through a line of total force is termed the 'magnetic meridian'. Thus such a needle is said to lie in the 'magnetic meridian'. Owing to the irregularity of the Earth's magnetism, the magnetic meridian, although a semigreat circle, does not necessarily pass through the magnetic poles.

The Gyro-Magnetic Compass

This instrument, which is described in Chapter X, uses a magnetic compass to seek north, and a gyroscope for stabilisation. It indicates magnetic north, but when the correct variation and deviation are set on the compass console, it transmits true north to repeaters.

Variation

The angle between the true meridian and the magnetic meridian at any place is called the 'variation' at that place.

Variation is said to be easterly if the direction of the magnetic north lies to the east of the true meridian, and westerly if it lies to the west. It is expressed n degrees and minutes of arc.

In Fig. 11, the variation at F would be about 20° west.

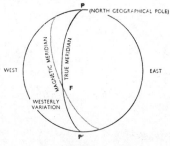

FIG. 11

In practice, the navigator obtains the variation either from the navigational chart which he is using or from a special 'isogonic' chart on which all places of equal variation are joined by what are known as 'isogonic lines'. An isogonic chart is reproduced in Chapter IX. On ordinary charts the variation is given for a certain year, together with a note of any annual change which it is undergoing. The Navigator must always allow for this annual change.

The variation in the Solent, for example, is given on Admiralty Chart No. 394 as being 8° 25′W. in 1959 and decreasing about 8′ annually. In 1964, therefore, it will be 5 × 8′ (or 40′) less, which gives 7° 45′W.

Graduation of Magnetic Compass Cards

Magnetic compass cards used to be divided into four quadrants by the cardinal points, North, East, South, West. Each quadrant was further divided into eight equal parts, the division marks being called 'points'; each point had a distinctive name – North, North by East, North North East, and so on. There were thus thirty-two points in the whole card. In the days of sail a ship was normally steered to the nearest point or half point. Later, since a steam ship was able to steer with more accuracy, the card was also marked in degrees from 0° to 90°, from North and South to East and West. A point is thus 11¼°, and the term 'point' is still used with that signification. Modern compass cards are marked from 0° to 360° clockwise from compass north, since there is no longer any reason for retaining the rather confusing older style.

Magnetic Bearing

By 'magnetic bearing' is meant the angle between the direction of the place or object in question and the magnetic meridian at the place of observation. Thus, in Fig. 12 the magnetic bearing of T from F is the angle between the great circle FT and the magnetic meridian through F.

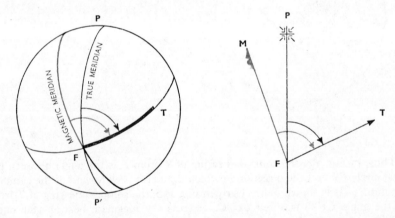

FIG. 12

Magnetic bearings were easily distinguished from true bearings when the former were described with reference to the cardinal points. In the new style both are now given in three figures, and so magnetic bearings are distinguished by the suffix M (for magnetic). In Fig. 12 the magnetic bearing of T from F (that is, the angle MFT) is about 085°M., whereas the true bearing (the angle PFT) is about 065°. The difference between these two angles is the variation.

The magnetic bearing of a place or object is therefore – to enlarge the definition – the angle between the magnetic meridian and the direction of the place or object measured clockwise from 0° to 360° from magnetic north.

Deviation

If a magnetic compass is put in a vessel, the presence of iron or steel will cause the compass needle to deviate from the magnetic meridian. The angle between the magnetic meridian and the direction in which the needle actually points is called the 'deviation'.

The direction in which the compass actually points is known as 'compass north' to distinguish it from magnetic north and true north. If compass north lies to the east of the magnetic meridian, the deviation is said to be easterly; if west, it is said to be westerly.

Compass Bearing

By 'compass bearing' is meant the angle between the direction of compass north and the direction of the place or object in question. Compass bearings are measured in a similar manner to magnetic bearings; they are given in three figures, from 0° to 360°, measured clockwise from compass north, followed by the suffix C (for compass).

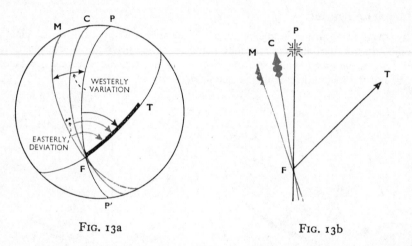

FIG. 13a   FIG. 13b

Thus, in Fig. 13a the compass bearing of T from F is the angle between the great circle FT and the direction in which the north-seeking end of the compass is pointing. As is shown more clearly in Fig. 13b, the compass bearing of T from F (the angle CFT) is about 055°C. whereas the magnetic bearing (the angle MFT) is about 065°M., and the true bearing (the angle PFT) is about 045°.

The angle MFC is the deviation (about 10° east), and the angle PFM is the variation (about 20° west).

It should be borne in mind that whenever a navigator uses a magnetic compass on board a ship he obtains a compass bearing, and he must correct it for both deviation and variation in order to arrive at the true bearing. *The deviation used must be that for the ship's head at the time of the observation.*

Change in Deviation

The magnetic compass is usually placed on the bridge, which is generally nearer to the bows than to the stern. The iron and steel in the ship are therefore not symmetrically situated in relation to it, and every time the ship alters course that iron and steel will change position relatively to the compass card, and so will attract or repel the needle by a different amount. The deviation will therefore change for every alteration of course.

DEVIATION TABLE

The actual amount of this deviation for any direction of the ship's head can be found by 'swinging ship'. The deviation can be reduced, if necessary, by placing permanent magnets and soft-iron correctors at the compass, as described in Chapter IX. It is not possible, however, to correct the entire deviation in this way; and the amounts which remain can be shown conveniently in the form of a table, as follows:

DEVIATION TABLE

SHIP'S HEAD POINTS (DEGREES)	BEARING OF DISTANT OBJECT		DEVIATION
	Magnetic (from chart)	*Compass (observed)*	
N. (000°)	236°M.	238½°C.	2½°W.
N.N.E. (022½°)	236°M.	239°C.	3°W.
N.E. (045°)	236°M.	239°C.	3°W.
E.N.E. (067½°)	236°M.	238½°C.	2½°W.
E. (090°)	236°M.	237½°C.	1½°W.
E.S.E. (112½°)	236°M.	236½°C.	½°W.
S.E. (135°)	236°M.	235½°C.	½°E.
S.S.E. (157½°)	236°M.	234½°C.	1½°E.
S. (180°)	236°M.	233½°C.	2½°E.
S.S.W. (202½°)	236°M.	232¾°C.	3¼°E.
S.W. (225°)	236°M.	232½°C.	3½°E.
W.S.W. (247½°)	236°M.	233°C.	3°E.
W. (270°)	236°M.	234°C.	2°E.
W.N.W. (292½°)	236°M.	235°C.	1°E.
N.W. (315°)	236°M.	236°C.	NIL
N.N.W. (337½°)	236°M.	237½°C.	1½°W.

The normal method of correcting the compass is by swinging the ship through successive angles of 22½°, and the deviation table is usually made out for these intervals.

The deviation for a direction of the ship's head lying between any two of the headings given in the table can be found by simple interpolation. Thus, if the deviation is required for 260°C., the table shows that it is between 3°E. (the deviation for W.S.W.) and 2°E. (the deviation for West); the actual amount is just under 2½°E.[1]

---

[1] In practice a standard compass should never have deviations of this size; they should always be less than 2° if the compass has been properly corrected.

Deviation Curve

If the above deviation table is arranged in the form of a graph – the deviation being plotted against the compass direction of the ship's head – a deviation curve is obtained. This is shown in Fig. 14.

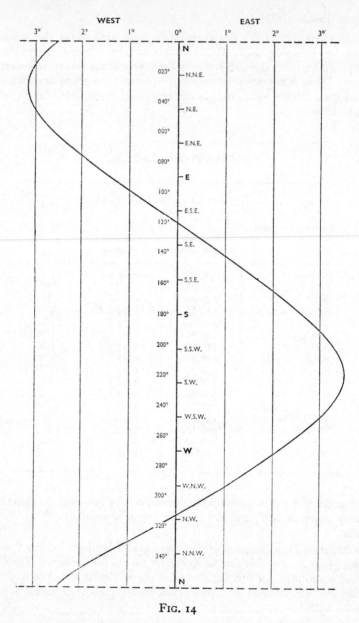

Fig. 14

Conversely, if a deviation table for every ten degrees is required, it can be made out from the deviation curve.

The deviation curve has a slight advantage over the deviation table in that the deviation for any intermediate direction of the ship's head can be found by inspection.

The Ship's Course

The course of the ship is, strictly speaking, the direction in which she is moving through still water – the direction, that is, of her fore-and-aft line; and her course-angle is the angle between that direction and the direction of true, magnetic, or compass north. It is customary, however, to speak of the course-angle as 'the course'. All that has been said about the bearing, which is also an angle, may equally be said about the course.

TRUE COURSE is the angle between the direction of true north and the ship's fore-and-aft line, measured clockwise from 0° to 360°. (Angle *PFB* in Fig. 15.)

MAGNETIC COURSE is the angle between the magnetic meridian and the ship's fore-and-aft line, measured clockwise from 0° to 360° from magnetic north. (Angle *MFB* in Fig. 15.)

COMPASS COURSE is the angle between the direction of compass north and the ship's fore-and-aft line, measured clockwise from 0° to 360° from compass north. (Angle *CFB* in Fig. 15.)[1]

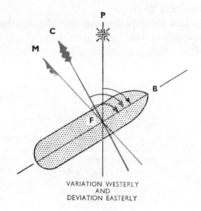

VARIATION WESTERLY
AND
DEVIATION EASTERLY

FIG. 15

Correction of Courses and Bearings

In practice, the navigator is faced with the problem of finding, for example, the true bearing when he has taken the compass bearing, or of finding the compass course when he has worked out his true course. He must, therefore, apply the necessary corrections for variation and deviation. The first of these is found from the chart for the year in question. The second is found from the deviation table

---

[1] In considering the alterations in a ship's course, it must always be remembered that the ship herself turns round the compass, and also that, beyond adjusting itself for deviation, the compass needle does not move. The bowl of the compass is fixed in the ship, and a mark called the 'lubber's point' is indicated on it in order to show the fore-and-aft line.

or curve *for the compass direction of the ship's head*, and it is essential to bear this in mind when correcting a compass bearing. The compass bearing of an object may be 203°C., but if the compass direction of the ship's head is 072°C., then the deviation applied to 203°C. must be taken out for 072°C.

To Find the True Course from the Compass Course

In Fig. 16, *FB* is the direction of the ship's head; the compass course is the angle *CFB*; the magnetic course is the angle *MFB*; and the true course is the angle *PFB*.

In Fig. 16a the magnetic course is less than the compass course by the amount of the westerly deviation; and the true course is less than the magnetic course by the amount of the westerly variation. Therefore, to find the true course, the westerly deviation and variation must be subtracted from the compass course.

In Fig. 16b the magnetic course is greater than the compass course by the amount of the easterly deviation, and the true course is greater than the magnetic course by the amount of easterly variation. Therefore, to find the true course, the easterly deviation and variation must be added to the compass course.

In Fig. 16c the magnetic course is greater than the compass course by the amount of the easterly deviation, and the true course is less than the magnetic course by the amount of the westerly variation. Therefore, to find the true course, the easterly deviation must be added to the compass course and the westerly variation subtracted from it.

Since no restriction has been placed on the size of the angle *CFB* beyond the fact that it is measured from compass north, the rule for converting a compass course into a true one therefore suggests itself.

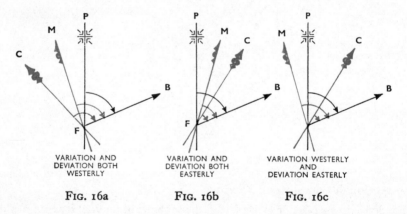

VARIATION AND DEVIATION BOTH WESTERLY

VARIATION AND DEVIATION BOTH EASTERLY

VARIATION WESTERLY AND DEVIATION EASTERLY

FIG. 16a   FIG. 16b   FIG. 16c

Consider *easterly* deviation and variation as *plus* and *westerly* deviation and variation as *minus*, and add them to or subtract them from the compass course accordingly. For purposes of this calculation, compass course is always measured as an angle between 0° and 360° from compass north.

EXAMPLES

1. *A ship is steaming 210°C. by magnetic compass. Her deviation table shows that the deviation is 3°E., and the chart shows that the corrected variation for her position is 12°W. What is her true course?*

Compass course	210°C.
Easterly deviation	3°+
Westerly variation	12°—
True course	201°

2. *Again, suppose the ship is steaming 315°C. by magnetic compass. Her deviation table shows that the deviation is 5°W., and the chart shows that the variation is 8°E.*

Compass course	315°C.
Westerly deviation	5°—
Easterly variation	8°+
True course	318°

To Find the Compass Course from the True Course

To do this, the signs in the above rule must be reversed; that is, westerly variation and deviation must be considered as positive, and easterly variation and deviation as negative. There is, however, a small complication. Before the navigator can find his compass course he must know the deviation. But he cannot take out his deviation until he knows his compass course. He therefore takes out an approximate deviation for his magnetic course, and, if necessary, a second and more accurate one when he has found what is really an approximate compass course.[1]

EXAMPLE

A navigator has worked out his true course as 208°. The variation is 12°W. What course must he steer by compass?

True course	208°
Westerly variation	12°+
Magnetic course	220°M.

and if he enters the deviation table on page 15 for that course it is seen that the approximate deviation is $3\frac{1}{2}$°E.

Magnetic course (as above)	220°M.
Easterly deviation	$3\frac{1}{2}$°—
Compass course	$216\frac{1}{2}$°C.

If he now enters the deviation table with this approximate compass course he obtains a deviation of 3°·4, and a more accurate compass course would be 216°·6C. But since he would tell the quartermaster to steer to the nearest degree – i.e. 216°C. it would not be necessary to trouble about one-tenth of a degree.

---

[1] If the compass is closely corrected, the deviation should not be large enough to make this second approximation necessary.

To Lay off a Compass Course or Bearing on the Chart

All charts have what are known as compass 'roses' printed on them. When there are two concentric rings the outer ring represents the true compass, and the inner the magnetic compass, as shown in Fig. 17. Some small-scale charts have only the true compass rose; others have also an indication of the amount of magnetic variation.

On the east-west line of the magnetic rose is written the variation, the year for which it is correct, and its rate of change.

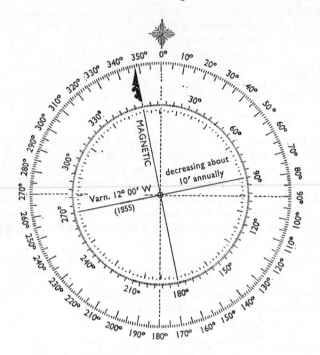

FIG. 17. Compass Rose printed on Admiralty Charts

Before he can use this magnetic rose for laying off a compass course, the navigator must apply both the deviation and the change of variation. This can be done conveniently in one step by combining the deviation with the change of variation and then applying the result as an error to the magnetic rose.

EXAMPLE

In 1960 the compass bearing of an object is 157°C., the deviation 3°W.; and the variation from the chart is 12°W. in 1955, decreasing 10′ annually.

The change in variation during 5 years is 50′, which may be taken as approximately $\frac{3}{4}$°. The error to be applied to the magnetic rose on the chart is therefore $3°W. - \frac{3}{4}°E.$, or $2\frac{1}{4}W.$ – that is to say, compass north lies $2\frac{1}{4}$° to the west of magnetic north. This may be taken into account by placing the parallel ruler (with which the bearing is laid off) on the magnetic rose in the direction of 157°C., and then slewing it *anti-clockwise* through $2\frac{1}{4}$°, since, in order to pass from magnetic north to a compass north to the west of it, the movement must be anti-clockwise. The reading on the magnetic rose (that is, the adjusted magnetic course) is thus $154\frac{3}{4}°$M.

To check this, apply the rule for correcting courses and bearing.

Compass bearing	$157°$C.
Westerly deviation	$3°—$
Magnetic bearing	$154°$M.
Easterly change in variation	$\frac{3}{4}°+$
Magnetic bearing adjusted to chart	$154\frac{3}{4}°$M.

In effect, this method of applying an adjusted deviation to the compass course or bearing and then using the magnetic rose saves the navigator the trouble of making calculations on paper, because he has merely to add or subtract two small quantities and slew his parallel ruler by that amount. The rule to be followed is as follows:

If the combined deviation and change of variation is *westerly*, the ruler must be slewed *anti-clockwise*; if *easterly*, *clockwise*.

Should it be required to know the compass course to steer in order to steam along a certain line on the chart, the above procedure must be reversed. By placing the parallel ruler along this line and running it to the nearest magnetic rose, a magnetic course is obtained for the variation used in the rose, and to this course must be applied the deviation corrected for any change of variation.

EXAMPLE

Suppose that in 1960 it is required to steer a course which, as read off the magnetic rose, is 068°M.; and that the deviation is 3°E., and the variation 12°W. in 1955, decreasing 10' annually. What is the compass course?

The change of variation in 5 years is again 50'E. The error to be applied to the magnetic rose is therefore $3\frac{3}{4}°$E. That is, compass north lies $3\frac{3}{4}°$E. of magnetic north; the compass reading is less than the magnetic, and the parallel ruler must be slewed that amount anti-clockwise, thereby giving on the magnetic rose a reading of $064\frac{1}{4}°$C.

To check this by rule:

Magnetic course by chart	068°M.
Easterly change in variation	$\frac{3}{4}°—$
Magnetic course	$067\frac{1}{4}°$M.
Easterly deviation	$3°—$
Compass course	$064\frac{1}{4}°$C.

(Note that in this example the rule applied is the reverse of the one used in the example on page 20 since we are now converting Magnetic to True.) To facilitate these conversions, a small Compass Comparison Disc, Pattern No. 69B, is supplied to ships, as shown in Fig. 18.

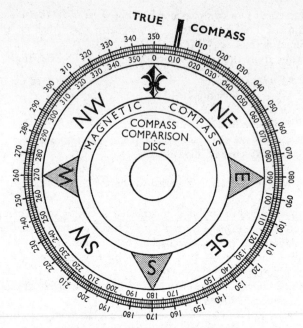

Fig. 18. Compass Comparison Disc

Aid to Memory. – These rules may be remembered by the following aid to memory.

COMPASS TO TRUE ADD EAST   C AD E T

————————→

To Check the Deviation

Suppose that a compass bearing is taken of an object the true bearing of which is known. Then, if the variation is also known, the deviation can be found and compared with that obtained from the deviation table or curve.

The true bearing of the Sun, for example, can be found by methods which are explained in Volume II. Suppose it is 230°, as shown in Fig. 19, the compass bearing at the same moment being 235°C. and the variation 12°W. Then:

True bearing of Sun	230°
Westerly variation	12°+
Magnetic bearing of Sun	242°M.
Compass bearing of Sun	235°C.
Deviation	7°−, and therefore easterly

Relative Bearings

Bearings of objects are frequently given, not with reference to the true, magnetic or compass north, but to the fore-and-aft line of the ship. They are then said to be 'red' or 'green', according to whether the object (and therefore the bearing) lies to port or to starboard. These are known as 'relative bearings'.

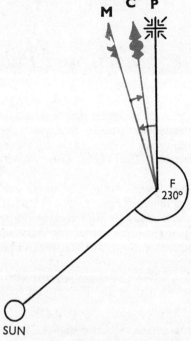

FIG. 19

In Fig. 20 the bearing of X is Green 30, that of Y, Red 140. If the ship herself is steaming 045°, then the true bearing of X is 075° and of Y, 265°. Alternatively, X could be said to be 30° on the starboard bow, and Y 40° on the port quarter.

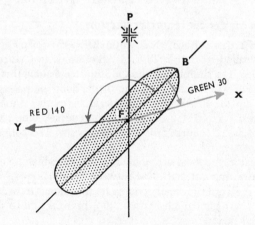

FIG. 20. Relative bearings

The expressions 'on the bow', 'on the beam', and 'on the quarter', without any specified number of degrees or points, mean respectively 45° or 4 points, 90° or 8 points, and 135° or 12 points from the ship's head.

CHAPTER II

Admiralty Charts and Publications

THE HYDROGRAPHIC Office of the Admiralty was instituted in 1795, solely for the production of navigational charts. Its twenty-five departments now contain technical branches dealing with – in addition to the Admiralty charts – such matters as *Sailing Directions, Tide Tables, List of Lights, Notices to Mariners,* etc.

Attached to the Chart Branch are several naval assistants and experienced surveying and navigating officers. Their duty is to study the daily flow of hydrographic information which comes through correspondence, foreign notices, and other channels. They pay particular attention to matters of navigational urgency that require announcement by Notices to Mariners and immediate correction of the chart plates.

The Hydrographic Department produces approximately six thousand different charts and diagrams, which may be grouped into the following categories:

(a) Navigational charts, on which the ship's track is plotted.

(b) Non-navigational charts, which cannot be used for plotting the ship's track.

(c) Diagrams.

(d) Plotting sheets.

NAVIGATIONAL CHARTS

Charts drawn on the Mercator Projection

A line on the Earth's surface which cuts all the meridians and parallels at the same angle is called a 'rhumb line'. If, therefore, two places on the Earth's surface are joined by a rhumb line and the ship steers along this line, the direction of the ship's head will remain the same throughout the passage. This direction is determined by the angle from the meridian to the rhumb line, measured clockwise from 0° to 360°, and is called 'the course'. The rhumb line itself is often spoken of as 'the course'. On the Earth's surface a continuous rhumb line would appear as a spiral.

To the navigator, the most useful chart is one on which he can show the track of his ship by drawing a straight line between his starting-point and his destination, and then measure the steady course he must steer in order to arrive there. The Mercator chart (first published in 1569) permits him to do this, because it is so constructed that:

(a) rhumb lines (or courses) on the Earth appear as straight lines on the chart;

(b) the angles between these rhumb lines, on Earth and chart, are unaltered. It therefore follows that:

(c) the equator, which is a rhumb line as well as a great circle, appears on the chart as a straight line;

(d) the parallels of latitude appear as straight lines parallel to the equator;

(e) the meridians, within the limits of the chart, appear as straight lines perpendicular to the equator (*see also* Volume II);

(f) a straight line joining two points does not represent the shortest distance between them (unless they both lie on a meridian or on the equator). The shortest distance, being a great circle, would appear as a curve (Fig. 21).

The Mercator projection is not a true geometric projection, but is mathematically constructed to fulfil the condition imposed above.

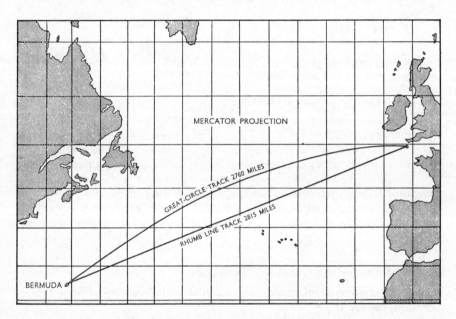

FIG. 21. Mercator Projection of the North Atlantic Ocean

SCALE ON A MERCATOR CHART

Since the equator is shown on the chart as a straight line of definite length, and the meridians appear as straight lines perpendicular to it, the longitude scale is fixed by that length and is constant in all latitudes. On the Earth, however, the meridians converge, and therefore land masses on a Mercator chart will be increasingly distorted in an east–west direction proportional to their distance from the equator, until at the poles their size would be infinite (Fig. 22).

In order to preserve the correct shapes of the land (this property is called 'orthomorphy'), the parallels of latitude, which are equally spaced on the Earth's surface (Fig. 23), must be increasingly spaced towards the poles on the Mercator chart, until at the poles the latitude scale becomes infinite.

This distortion, as is explained in Volume II, is governed by the secant of the latitude. On a Mercator chart, Greenland (in 70°N.), for example, appears as broad as Africa at the equator, although the latter is really three times as broad as Greenland. (The secant of 70° is 3.) Thus the varying latitude scale, which governs the distortion of distances in all directions, will measure correct *distances* for all places situated in its *own* latitude. This scale is therefore known as the 'scale of latitude and distance'.

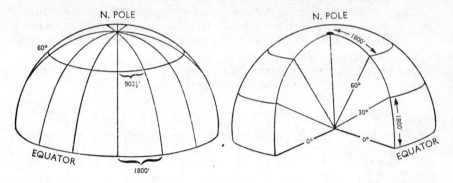

FIG. 22. Linear measurement of longitude   FIG. 23

It must be remembered that the Mercator projection does not show the correct relation between distances measured in different parts of the chart, unless they are in the same latitude; and therefore it is not possible to take off distances from the margin at random. Nor, as should now be clear, is it possible to use the longitude scale for measuring distances, except at the equator.

The Mercator projection is used for all Admiralty charts having a natural scale[1] smaller than 1/50,000 – a scale, that is, of less than one-and-a-half inches to one mile.

Charts drawn on the Gnomonic Projection

(A full description of this projection, which is a true geometrical projection, is given in Volume II.)

The chart is drawn on a flat surface, touching the Earth at one point, usually the central point of the chart, which is known as the 'tangent point'.

Lines are drawn from the centre of the Earth, through points on the Earth's surface, until they reach the flat surface of the chart. Hence:

(a) great circles appear as straight lines on the chart, and rhumb lines appear curved;
(b) meridians are straight lines converging to the poles;
(c) parallels of latitude are curves;
(d) the farther a point on the chart is away from the tangent point the greater will be the distortion.

On gnomonic charts and plans drawn since 1943 the inner border lines are not rectangular, but are actual meridians and parallels. Thus no error will result if longitude is read from the border.

---

[1] The natural scale is the ratio of a length measured on the chart to a corresponding length measured on the Earth's surface.

This projection is used for:
(a) great-circle sailing charts;
(b) polar charts (since the distortion near the poles of a Mercator projection renders the latter method quite unusable);
(c) charts of a natural scale larger than 1/50,000 – a scale, that is, greater than one-and-a-half inches to one mile.

HARBOUR PLANS

These plans are a special form of gnomonic chart, the small area of the Earth concerned being treated as flat.

The latitude and longitude of the 'observation spot', or some prominent object, is given under the title; and on an ungraduated plan the position of any other point can be laid down by noting its difference of latitude and longitude from the observation spot, these differences being measured on the separate scales of latitude and longitude shown on the plan. The form of graduation used on a gnomonic chart is different from that on a Mercator chart. (This difference can be seen on Admiralty Chart D 6697, which shows standard patterns of borders, graduations and scales.)

TO CONSTRUCT A SCALE OF LONGITUDE ON A PLAN

If a scale of longitude is not given, it can be found from the following construction:

From the zero on the scale of latitude draw a line making an angle with it which is equal to the latitude of the place – 45° in this case – as shown in Fig. 24.

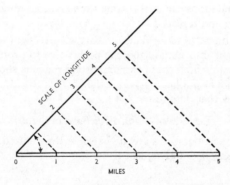

FIG. 24

From each division on the scale of latitude drop a perpendicular to this line. The intersections of these perpendiculars with the line mark the scale of longitude.

Distortion of Charts

The original work of a chart may be either engraved on a copper plate or drawn in ink on an enamelled zinc plate. In either case it is then transferred to a zinc printing plate, from which the charts are printed by a lithographic process.

Charts are liable to slight distortion at certain stages in the process of reproduction. Any distortion may be observed by checking the dimensions of the
original plate, shown in one corner of the chart.

In a given measured distance, the effect of distortion clearly decreases as the
scale increases and will have the least effect on large-scale charts. Moreover, the
original plates of large-scale charts are brought up to date before the plates of
small-scale charts. For these reasons, and for other reasons which will be given
later, the *largest-scale chart available should always be used.*

(The process of reproducing charts is described in Volume III.)

Information shown on Charts

NUMBER OF THE CHART. – This is shown in the right-hand bottom corner and
(since 1947) also in the left-hand top corner.

TITLE OF THE CHART. – This is shown in the most convenient place, so that no
essential navigational information is obscured by it.

DATE OF SURVEY OF THE CHART. – This is given under the title.

DATE OF PUBLICATION. – This is shown outside the bottom margin of the chart,
in the middle thus:

> Published at the Admiralty, 30th May, 1960.

DATE OF NEW EDITIONS. – When a chart is revised throughout and modernized
in style, a new edition is published, the date of the new edition being shown thus:

> *New edition, 2nd January, 1961*

This is printed on the right of the original date of publication. All large and
small correction notations are at the same time erased, and all old copies of the
chart are cancelled and replaced.

DATE OF LARGE CORRECTIONS. – When a chart is corrected (not revised throughout) from important information too comprehensive to promulgate or to insert
by hand, the date on which these corrections are made is shown on the chart to
the right of the date of publication; or, if the chart is already marked with a new
edition date, below that date, thus:

> *Large corrections, 14th February, 1961*

All small correction notations are at the same time erased, and all old copies
of the chart are cancelled and replaced.

DATE OF SMALL CORRECTIONS

(a) When a chart is corrected from information promulgated in Admiralty or
Fleet Notices to Mariners (other than Temporary or Preliminary – *see below*),
the year, if not already shown, and the number of the notice, are entered in the
bottom left-hand corner of the chart, thus:

> *Small corrections, 1961 – 302.*

Charts in stock at the Hydrographic Supplies Establishment and the Admiralty
Chart Depots are corrected by hand from such information. When received in
a ship or establishment, therefore, the charts need to be corrected only for
subsequent notices affecting them.

(b) Prior to 1954 when a chart was corrected from information which was considered of no importance from the standpoint of safe navigation and which was therefore not promulgated in Admiralty or Fleet Notices to Mariners, the year, if not already shown, and the date of the correction were entered on the chart, in one of two ways, in the bottom left-hand corner below the margin and in sequence with the notations referred to in the preceding paragraph, e.g.: –

Small corrections 1952 – | **5.20** |

or *Small corrections 1952* – (*VI.12*) –

These indicate that the chart received minor corrections on 20th May, 1952 and 12th June, 1952, respectively, which would appear on late printings.

In such cases copies of the chart held by ships and establishments were not usually replaced, though in exceptional cases, e.g. when new compass roses were inserted, new copies of the charts might be supplied. It should be particularly noted that the absence of the corrections represented by 'square' or 'bracket' dates from a chart does not in any way invalidate it for navigation.

(c) Since 1954, in order that more attention may be given to New Editions, Large Corrections, and corrections by Notices to Mariners, and for other reasons, the making of minor corrections to chart plates as in (b) has been discontinued. Information of no importance to safe and convenient navigation is instead recorded for inclusion in the next New Edition or Large Correction; or for promulgation in later Notices to Mariners should change of circumstances alter the importance of the information. In consequence the small correction date enclosed in a rectangle does not appear later than 1953 on navigational charts.

(d) The date of Temporary and Preliminary notices is inserted in pencil below the permanent small-correction notations, thus:

(T) and (P) 1961 – *301*.

Charts in stock at the Hydrographic Supplies Establishment and Admiralty Chart Depots are *not* corrected from these notices; when charts are received from one of these sources they will therefore have to be corrected in pencil from the relevant notices.

(e) When it is necessary to bring the compass roses of a chart up to date a new copy is printed and the date of modernization is printed chronologically with the notations of the small corrections, thus: (**v.20**).

DATE OF PRINTING. – This is shown in the right-hand top corner thus: 135.60, which indicates that the chart was printed on the 135th day of 1960.

METHOD OF PRINTING. – The type of plate used is indicated by letters at the bottom right-hand corner of the chart.

DIMENSIONS OF THE CHART in inches, between the inner lines of the graduation, are shown in brackets in the bottom right-hand corner. They are useful for checking the dimensions of the chart should distortion be suspected. If a very accurate chart is required, a 'dry proof' may be demanded. This is obtained by a different printing process and is less liable to distortion; but, for reasons given in Volume III, it is not suitable for normal use.

SCALE OF THE CHART

(a) The natural scale is shown beneath the title.

(b) On some large-scale charts a scale in appropriate units is shown, to supplement or to replace the normal latitude scale by which distances are measured. In order to make the nature of this scale clear, it is headed: 'Scale of Latitude and Distance'.

STANDARD ABBREVIATIONS AND SYMBOLS used on Admiralty charts are shown on Chart 5011, which is kept in the Folio (H.92) containing miscellaneous charts and diagrams. Extracts from this chart are reproduced in Fig. 25 (a–d).

THE UNITS USED FOR DEPTHS are stated in bold lettering below the title of the chart. On modern charts, soundings under eleven fathoms are given in fathoms and feet. Depths are given below Chart Datum, which usually approximates to Mean Low Water Springs. This ensures that there will never be less water underneath the ship than is charted, and thus a margin of safety is provided. Underlined figures on banks – e.g. 4 – denote the number of *feet* the bank dries above Chart Datum, irrespective of the unit used for soundings.

Figures shown thus $\frac{\cdot}{25}$ indicate 'no bottom at 25 fathoms' (where the fathom is the unit used on the chart for soundings). This incomplete information is only inserted in charts when more details are not available.

FATHOM LINES. – On most charts all soundings of, and below, certain depths are enclosed by lines of different characters, so that the mariner will know that, if his track crosses that line, he will be in less than a certain depth. Details of the different fathom lines are shown on Chart 5011.

HEIGHTS are given in feet above Mean High Water Springs. The heights of small islands are shown in brackets close beside the object to which they refer. This is to avoid confusion with the soundings.

TIDAL INFORMATION for various ports on the chart is printed in a table in a suitable position on the chart.

TIDAL STREAM INFORMATION

(a) All information about tidal streams, whether in tables, or in notes giving the times of slack water and the rate of the tidal streams, is given in some convenient place on the chart and referred to by a special symbol – e.g. ◇ – at the position for which the information is given.

(b) This information may be shown by means of tidal stream arrows on certain charts when sufficient data for constructing tables are not available. Reference to these arrows is made in Chapter XII.

Colours Used on Charts

Lights, radio beacons, and sometimes tidal stream 'diamonds', are distinguished by a magenta overprint to facilitate identification.

On some charts, areas of sea below certain depths are distinguished by a blue wash, or by a blue wash line following the appropriate fathom line. This system is coming more and more into general use, especially on the larger-scale charts.

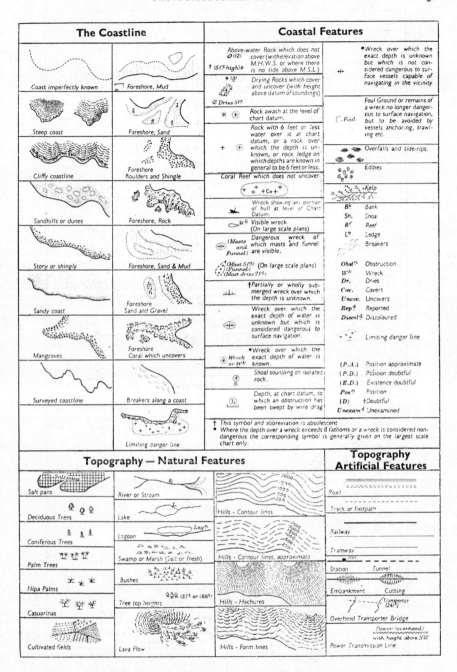

FIG. 25a. Extracts from Admiralty Chart 5011
(Explanations of symbols and abbreviations as shown on the charts
issued by the Hydrographic Department, Admiralty)

Lights

☆ ✶	Position of light	F.	Fixed	Vi.	Violet
Lᵗ	Light	Occ.	Occulting		
Lᵗ Ho.	Lighthouse	Fl.	Flashing	Bl.	Blue
		Qk. Fl.	Quick Flashing	G.	Green
		Int. Qk. Fl.	Interrupted Quick Flashing	Or.	Orange yellow or amber
☆ Bⁿ	Light beacon	Gp. Int. Qk. Fl.	Group Interrupted Quick Flashing		
	Light vessel			R.	Red
Lᵗ V.	Light vessel			W.	White
		Alt.	Alternating	obscᵈ	Obscured
Lᵈᵍ	Leading	Gp. Occ. (2)	Group Occulting	(U)	Unwatched
		Gp. Fl. (3)	Group Flashing	occasˡ	Occasional
		† Fl. (S-L)	Flashing (Short and Long flashes)	irreg.	Irregular
(Fish g)	Fishing	† Gp. Fl. (S-L)	Group Flashing (Short and Long flashes)	Provˡ	Provisional
				Tempᵡ	Temporary
		F. Fl.	Fixed and Flashing	Extingᵈ	Extinguished
		F. Gp. Fl. (4)	Fixed and Group Flashing	Lᵣ	Lower
		Gp. Fl. (B)	Group Flashing ·—···	vertˡ	Vertical
		Gp. Fl. (PM)	Group Flashing ·——·—··	horˡ	Horizontal
		Air Gp. Fl. (AB)	Air light group flashing ·— —··		
		Fog Detʳ. Lᵗ.	Fog Detector Light		

Example of abridged description of light.   ☆ Gp. Occ. (2) W. R. 5 sec. 130 fᵗ 12 M. (U).
All lights are white unless otherwise stated.
Alt (Alternating) signifies a light which alters colour.
The number in brackets after the description of Group Flashing or Group Occulting Lights denotes the number of flashes or eclipses in each group. The characteristics of the Lights which exhibit groups of flashes representing letters of the Morse Code are shown by the appropriate letters in brackets.
Occasional Light (or Fog Signal) is one which is given only when a vessel is expected or in answer to vessels signals or at other irregular times.
The elevation given against a light is the height of the focal plane of the light above Mean High Water Spring Tides, or above Sea Level in cases where there is no tide.
The visibility of lights is given in nautical miles, assuming the eye of the observer to be 15 feet above the sea.
Bearings of lights are given from Seaward.

Buoys and Beacons

○ •	Position of buoy or beacon	H.S.	† Horizontal stripes
	Light buoy	V.S.	† Vertical stripes
Bell Bell Bell †	Bell buoy	Cheq.	† Chequered
Gong Gong Gong	Gong buoy		
Whis. Whis. Whis.	Whistle buoy		
	Can buoy	W.	White
	Conical buoy	B.	Black
		R.	Red
	Spherical buoy	Y.	Yellow
	Spar buoy	G.	Green
	**High Focal Plane or Pillar buoy	Or.	Orange
	Spindle buoy	Gy.	Grey
	Buoys with topmarks	Bl.	Blue
	Barrel buoy		
	Light float		Floating beacons
	Firing Danger Area buoys		† Fixed beacons
	Wreck buoy	○ Bⁿ	Beacon, in general
	Telephone or Telegraph buoy	Bⁿ Tower ○ Bⁿ Tower	Beacon tower
	Mooring buoy	Y	Perch
	Mooring buoy with telegraphic & telephonic communications	Refl.	Reflector

**When exceptionally it is necessary to distinguish the markings more definitely the following variations will be used for horizontal, vertical, or chequered buoys:—

The position of a Light Vessel, Buoy, or Beacon is the centre of the Base, and is usually indicated by a small circle.

In the case of two-colour buoys each colour is indicated below the appropriate symbol, the colours being shown in alphabetical order.

† This symbol and abbreviation is obsolescent.

‡ The abbreviation Bⁿ is normally shown with each fixed beacon symbol.

• For Automatic Bell Buoys period and number of strokes shown thus:-Bell (2) 90 sec.

Fɪɢ. 25b. Extracts from Admiralty Chart 5011 (continued)

Radio and Radar

o	W/T	†Radio Telegraph Station
o	R/T	†Radio Telephone Station
(o)	RⁿBⁿ	Radiobeacon
	W/T Bⁿ	†Radiobeacon
(o)	RⁿD.F.	Radio Direction Finding Station
o	W/TDF	†Radio Direction Finding Station
o	Radio Mast / Radio Tⁿ	Mast or lattice towers of a radio station forming a conspicuous landmark
(o)	Rⁿ	Coast Radio Station which transmits on request ("QTG") for the use of ships D.F.
(o)	Ra.	Coast Radar Station
(o)	Racon	Radar Responder Beacon
	Ra Refl.	Radar Reflector / †Radar Reflector
	Ra. (conspic)	Radar Conspicuous Object
(o)	Ramark	Radar Beacon (continuous)

† This symbol is obsolescent

·NOTE:—Outer circles are in magenta

Fog Signals

Fog Sig.	†Fog Signal Station
Fog W/T	†Radio Fog Signal
Explos.	Explosive Fog Signal
Sub. Fog Sig.	†Submarine Fog Signal
S.B., Sub. Bell	†Submarine Bell (wave action)
S.F.B.	†Submarine Bell (mechanical)
S.O.	Submarine Oscillator
Nauto.	Nautophone
Dia.	Diaphone
Gun	Gun
Siren	Siren
E. F. Horn	Electric Fog Horn
Bell	Bell
Whis.	Whistle
Reed	Reedhorn
Gong	Gong
⊙〜〜〜	Submarine Sound Signal connected to the shore

† This abbreviation is obsolescent

Harbours

Prohib⁴ Anch⁹	Anchorage Prohibited	⚓	Anchorage
(fishing stakes symbol)		Whᶠ	Wharf
(fishing stakes symbol) Fishing Stakes		⑥	Berth numbers
Fish Traps	Fish Traps	▫ Dⁿ	Dolphin
Ldg	Landing place	o Bollard	Bollard

Depth Contours

Fathoms
1	† ....
2	....
3	....
4	... ...
5	....
6	--- --- ---
10	-·-·-·-·-
20	-··-··-··-
50	-···-···-
100	--·--·--
200	--··--··
500	--·--·--
1000	---·---·-
2000	----··----
3000	---···---
5000	----···----

NOTE:—A blue tint is shown on many charts to emphasize the shallow water areas. Normally the tint is inserted between the H.W. line and the 3 fathom line, and a ribbon of tint added on the shoal side of the 6 fathom line, but on some charts other fathom lines may be so tinted. Examination of the chart will reveal the limiting depth of the tint.

† This symbol is obsolescent

Soundings

⑩ E.D.	Doubtful sounding
127 (with bar)	No bottom found
Dredged to 20 fᵗ (1948)	Channel or area dredged to depth indicated, at Chart datum (with date of year of dredging)
3	Drying height
7 (underlined)	Depth, at chart datum, to which an area has been swept by wire drag
127	Soundings taken from older surveys or smaller scale charts
5₃	Sounding in fathoms and feet
④ R	Shoal sounding on isolated rock

Buildings

	City; Town
	Village
Cas.	Castle
Ho.	House
Vᵃ	Villa
Fᵐ	Farm
✚ Ch.	Church
Cath.	Cathedral
R.C.	Roman Catholic
⊕	Temple
✚ Ch.	Chapel
⚲	Mosque
⊠	Shinto Shrine
ᶜ	Moslem Tomb
Ft	Fort
Tⁿ	Tower
⚙	Windmill
o• Chⁿ	Chimney .
•.. Water Tⁿ	Water Tower
O O	Oil Tanks
O O	Gasometers
▫ Oil Derrick	Oil Derrick

FIG. 25c. Extracts from Admiralty Chart 5011 (*continued*)

Tides and Currents

H.W.	High Water		*I.S.L.W.*	Indian Spring Low Water
L.W.	Low Water		*H.W.F.&C.*	†High Water Full and Change
M.T.L.	Mean Tide Level		*L.W.F.&C.*	†Low „ „ „ „
M.S.L.	Mean Sea Level		*Estab.ᵗ*	†Establishment
H.W.O.S.	†High Water Ordinary Springs		*Equin.ᵗ*	†Equinoctial
L.W.O.S.	†Low „ „ „		*Q.ᵗ*	†Quarter
Sp., Spr.	Spring Tides		†	Current, with rate
Np.	Neap „			Flood stream with rate
M.H.W.S.	Mean High Water Springs			Ebb „ „ „
M.H.W.N.	„ „ „ Neaps		*Vel.*	Velocity
M.H.H.W.	„ Higher High Water		*Kn.*	Knots
M.L.H.W.	„ Lower „ „		*H.ᵗ*	Height
M.L.W.S.	„ Low Water Springs		*H.h.*	Hour
M.L.W.N.	„ „ „ Neaps		*m.*	minutes
M.L.L.W.	„ Lower Low Water		*ord.*	†Ordinary
M.H.L.W.	„ Higher „ „		*Fl. fl.*	†Flood

Ⓐ Ⓑ Ⓒ   Positions for which information regarding tidal streams is given on the chart

†Black dots on the Tidal Stream arrows indicate the number of hours after High or Low Water at which the streams are running.

† This symbol and/or abbreviation is obsolescent

Control Points

△	Triangulation point
● ▫	Fixed point
•810	Height of summit
+Obs.ⁿSpot	Observation spot
⊼ B.M.	Bench mark
▫ See View	View point
Astr.ᵗ	Astronomical

Miscellaneous

St.ⁿ Sta.	Station		*Sem.*	Semaphore
C.G.	Coastguard		*St.ⁿ.Sig.St.ⁿ*	Storm Signal Station
L.B.	Life Boat		*F.S.*	Flagstaff
L.S.S.	†Life Saving Station		*Sig.*	Signal
R.S.	†Rocket Station		*Obs.ʸ*	Observatory
Sig. St.ⁿ	Signal Station		*Off.*	Office

† This abbreviation is obsolescent

General Remarks

MERIDIANS. Charts are generally drawn on the True Meridian if not, a True Meridian is given on the chart.

LONGITUDES are referred to the Meridian of Greenwich.

CHART DATUM. The reduction level for soundings, where appropriate, is stated either in the Tidal Information Table, or, on older charts, in the title.

SOUNDINGS are generally shown in Fathoms and Feet in depths of less than eleven fathoms, and in Fathoms elsewhere. Some older charts, however, show fractional parts of fathoms in the shoaler areas, and certain large scale charts show soundings in Feet. The unit used is stated in the title of the chart.
The position of the sounding is the centre of the space occupied.

DRYING HEIGHTS. Underlined figures on Rocks and Banks which uncover, express the heights in Feet above the datum of the chart, unless otherwise stated.

HEIGHTS. All heights (except those expressed in underlined figures as above) are, unless otherwise stated, given in feet above Mean High Water Springs, or, in places where there is no tide, above the level of the sea, and are shown thus .125.

Heights are enclosed by brackets in the case of islets, the tops of artificial features (e.g. chimneys) and where the figures are removed from the object.

SCALES. The Natural Scale is the proportion which any measurement on the chart bears to the actual distance represented thus $\frac{1}{25,000}$
A Sea Mile is the length of a minute of Latitude at the place, and a Cable is assumed to be a tenth part of a Sea Mile.

DECCA CHARTS. A ‡ shown on certain charts against Adjoining and Larger Scale Chart numbers indicates that a Decca latticed version of that number is published.

DIMENSIONS OF PLATE. The figures in brackets in the lower right-hand corner of a chart, thus:-(38·43 x 25·49) are the dimensions of the plate in inches between the innermost graduation or border lines.

DATE OF CHART CORRECTIONS. For the method of dating charts for corrections see the introductory chapter in the Admiralty Sailing Directions.

NAMES. Names shown in brackets are generally obsolete names to read with the Admiralty Sailing Directions of an earlier date.
Brackets are also used to denote names which are being changed and occasionally to indicate conventional names

FIG. 25d. Extracts from Admiralty Chart 5011 (*continued*)

To Describe a Particular Copy of a Chart

When describing a particular copy of a chart, state in the following order:

(1) the number of the chart;
(2) title;
(3) date of publication;
(4) date of the last new edition;
(5) date of the last large correction;
(6) number (or date) of the last small correction.

To Distinguish a Well Surveyed Chart

Bear in mind the following points:

(a) the survey should be reasonably modern;
(b) soundings should be close together and regular, with no blank spaces;
(c) fathom and contour lines should be shown;
(d) there should be plenty of contour lines and other detail;
(e) all the coastline should be completed, with no dotted line indicating lack of information.

Degree of Reliance

The degree of reliance to be placed on a chart depends on the character of the original survey and on the completeness of the reports of subsequent changes. Moreover the number of soundings which can be shown clearly is governed by the scale of the chart. A scale of one inch to the mile, for example, only permits each sounding to occupy an area representing 8 acres of actual ground. Even the closest sounding may not detect sharp inequalities of the bottom. The remarks on 'The Use of Charts as Navigational Aids', included in the introduction to each volume of *Sailing Directions*, should be carefully studied in this connection.

Hints to Remember when Using Charts

(a) Always use the largest-scale chart, because:

(1) any errors are reduced to a minimum;
(2) if the chart is distorted, these errors will have the least effect;
(3) more detail is shown;
(4) the plate from which the largest-scale chart is made is corrected before the plates of small-scale charts.

(b) Transfer positions from one chart to another by bearing and distance from a point common to both charts, and check by latitude and longitude. This is most necessary as a check against mistakes and because the graduations on the two charts may differ.

(c) Always obtain a fix as soon as possible after the ship's position has been transferred from one chart to another.

(d) Always use the nearest compass rose, because:

(1) there will be less effect of distortion, and the correct variation will be used;
(2) an error will be avoided if the chart used is drawn on the gnomonic projection.

(e) Remember the change of variation printed on each compass rose.

(f) Keep only one chart on the chart table, to avoid the error of measuring distances off the scale of a chart underneath the one in use.

(g) Make certain whether the units used for soundings on the chart are fathoms or feet.

(h) When measuring distance by the latitude scale, measure roughly the same amount on each side of the mean latitude of the track being measured.

(i) The surface of the chart can best be preserved – and plotting will be most clear – if a 'B' pencil and a soft rubber are used. In wet weather, it is a good plan to place a towel along the front of the chart-table when working on the charts, and to remove dripping headgear.

THE ARRANGEMENT OF CHARTS

The Chart Folio

Outfits of charts required by ships and establishments are normally supplied in limp canvas folios. The charts in each folio are arranged, as far as possible, in geographical sequence.

The folios are numbered and arranged geographically to cover the world. The approximate limits of standard Admiralty chart folios are shown on Index Chart X.6051, which is contained in NP Item 133, the *Hydrographic Supplies Handbook* (H.51). Pasted on the outside of each folio are:

(a) The 'folio label', which shows the folio and serial numbers, the date of original issue from the Hydrographic Supplies Establishment, subsequent dates of issue from Chart Depots, and the names of ships and establishments to which issued. On this label is also inserted the number of the last *Notice to Mariners* for which the folio was amended.

(b) The 'folio list', which shows the numbers and titles of the charts contained in the folio, and the titles of the appropriate volumes of *Sailing Directions* and *List of Lights*, which are automatically supplied with the folio.

A column is left blank in the folio list for the insertion of the consecutive numbers of the charts as arranged in the folio, in order to facilitate, in conjunction with the Index (NP Item 133a) the extraction of charts from the folio, and their re-insertion.

Duplicate folio lists are supplied and kept together in a buckram envelope.

On the back of each chart is a 'chart label' on which is printed the chart number and title; space is available so that the folio number, th serial number of the folio, and the consecutive number of the chart can be inserted in pencil.

THE SCHEME OF CHART FOLIOS

The ordinary chart folios are divided into three categories:

(1) The *complete folios*, which together provide for the whole world, are numbered from 1 to 100.

(2) The *abridged folios*, which contain selections of charts from one or more folios, are intended primarily to provide for passage through the areas covered by the complete folios, including entry into the more important harbours in those areas, and for most of the requirements of Royal Fleet Auxiliaries. These folios are indicated by red figures on Index Chart X.6051, and are numbered between 101 and 199. In most cases the

'abridged folio' number corresponds to the 'complete folio' number, e.g., Folio 105 is the abridged version of Folio 5.

(3) *Local and special folios* provide for local services in the vicinity of dock-yard ports, or for special requirements not covered by the above. These are numbered in the 300 series and include folios of such charts as wreck charts and Consol and Loran lattice charts.

SHIPS' BOATS' CHARTS

A set of small-scale ocean charts is supplied in a waterproof wallet for use in a ship's boats. This wallet also contains some drawing instruments and sunset and sunrise tables.

YACHTSMEN'S CHARTS

Small charts are being produced in a convenient size for yachtsmen.

Hydrographic Supplies Handbook (H.51)[1]

This book (a new edition of which is published from time to time) contains information relating to the supply and correction of Admiralty charts and publications, chronometers and watches. The more important contents are:

(a) General information, including a list of Chart and Chronometer Depots.
(b) Charts: remarks on their arrangement and correction.
(c) Navigational publications. Remarks on *Sailing Directions*, *List of Lights*, *Admiralty List of Radio Signals* and *Tide Tables*.
(d) Notices to Mariners, their arrangement and contents.
(e) Outfits of charts and publications: information relating to their supply, upkeep, etc.
(f) Air charts and maps: reference to their supply.
(g) Chronometers and watches: remarks on their supply, replacement and repair.
(h) Disposal of chart outfits, etc.
(i) Lists of chart and map folios, and the contents of certain ones.
(j) Lists of navigational publications, with their scale of issue.
(k) Establishment of chronometers and watches.
(l) Index Chart X.6051, showing approximate limits of Admiralty Chart folios.

Chart Correction Log and Folio Index (NP Item 133a)

As the number of a chart gives no clue to its geographical area, the Chart Correction Log and Folio Index enumerates the folios in which a particular chart may be found and provides space for the insertion of the consecutive number and for logging the Notices to Mariners that affect each chart.

Catalogue of Admiralty Charts and Other Hydrographic Publications (H.D.374)

This catalogue, published annually, is supplied to major ships. It contains a list of miscellaneous charts and diagrams, a list of navigational charts arranged in

---

[1] *See* also *Queen's Regulations and Admiralty Instructions.*

geographical sequence, a numerical index to charts, and a list of *Sailing Directions* and other publications of use to mariners. In addition, there are Index charts giving the limits of all charts and the areas covered by the *Sailing Directions*. The limits of charts are also shown on the Index charts at the beginning of each volume of the *Sailing Directions*.

Confidential, Restricted, and Special Purpose Charts

Confidential and certain Restricted charts are contained in folios numbered in the 700 series. These include 'Fleet' charts, Telegraph charts, Radar and Range-finder Calibration charts, Air Operational charts, Sonar charts, Submarine charts, Practice and Exercise Area charts and Wreck charts. Other Restricted and Special Purpose charts are contained in folios in the 300 series, previously mentioned.

The folio and serial numbers of confidential chart folios and the copy numbers of any confidential H.D. (Hydrographic Department) publications held on charge should be recorded in the *Register of Confidential Charts and other H.D. Publications* (H.402).

Most Fleet and Special Purpose charts are identified by a prefix letter. Where the basic chart is a sales chart (1–4000) the appropriate letter is placed before the basic chart number. Thus L12 is a Consol Lattice on basic chart 12; L(D1) 2450 and L(D5) 2450 are Decca Lattices for chains 1 and 5 on basic chart 2450. Charts in the series 5000 are miscellaneous, e.g. Index, Instructional and Loran, the latter prefixed by L. Classified charts are mainly in the 6000 series with a prefix letter, e.g. F6688 – a Fleet navigational chart.

A *Catalogue of Confidential Fleet and Restricted Charts and Other Hydrographic Publications* is issued to all ships carrying Fleet chart[1] folios. It contains a list of the prefix letters mentioned above; a catalogue of all special charts not included in H.D.374 (in addition to some which are therein); a list of Fleet, Operational and Special chart folios; a list of Hydrographic publications; and a numerical index of the charts contained in the catalogue.

PLOTTING DIAGRAMS

These are listed in H.51 and are supplied in a special folio (H.413).

AIR CHARTS

Particulars of all air charts for the use of aircraft are contained in the *Catalogue of Admiralty Air Charts* (H.D.339), which, together with *Admiralty Air Notices*, from which they are corrected, are supplied to aircraft-carriers. Reference to these is made in H.51. They are the responsibility of the Lieutenant-Commander (Operations).

MAPS

Maps are supplied for the use of aircraft and for shore operations. They are provided in folio form and as loose copies. Further details are given in the *Catalogue of Admiralty Air Charts*.

---

[1] Fleet charts show, in general, information which is not necessary for ships other than H.M. ships, e.g. fleet berths. The Fleet chart is sometimes on a larger scale than any basic sales chart of the same area, and so it is most important that the navigator should always ascertain what Fleet charts, if any, cover the area in which his ship is operating. Cases have occurred of ships being stranded because this precaution has been neglected.

TELEGRAPH CABLE CHARTS

These are special Fleet chart folios which show details of all submarine cables. Whenever a ship intends to anchor in a position which is not a normal anchorage, the appropriate Telegraph chart should be consulted to ascertain that there is no cable likely to be fouled by the anchor.

NON-NAVIGATIONAL CHARTS AND DIAGRAMS

A number of charts supplied to ships are marked 'Not to be used for Navigation'. The reason for this is either that they do not originally show all the navigational dangers – e.g. operational outline charts – or that they are not kept corrected by Notices to Mariners, etc. Only the basic set of Navigational and Fleet charts is so corrected. It may sometimes be necessary to plot the ship's position on one of these charts (e.g. on a lattice chart used with Radio Navigational Aids); if so, the position should then be transferred to a navigational chart. There are also a number of miscellaneous charts and diagrams, such as Instructional charts and Weir's Azimuth Diagram, which are numbered in the 5000 series. Mention has already been made of certain of these miscellaneous charts; others include:

Reference chart folios for Flag Officers;
Chart Atlas folio for instructional use and general information;
Ice charts;
Magnetic variation charts.

THE FOLIO CONTAINING MISCELLANEOUS CHARTS AND DIAGRAMS

A special folio, H.92 (or H.134, abridged set), is supplied to ships. This contains the majority of miscellaneous charts, diagrams and tables not found in the folios previously enumerated. A list of its contents is given in H.51.

SUPPLY, UPKEEP AND DISPOSAL OF CHART OUTFITS AND PUBLICATIONS

Full information is given in H.51, which should be studied by the officer responsible for the charts. The regulations which are at present applicable are described below. If the *Admiralty Manual of Navigation* is found to differ in this respect from H.51, the latter should be considered the authority, since it is amended at more frequent intervals.

First Supply[1]

Application for an outfit of chart folios and publications for a ship commissioning or re-commissioning in home waters should be made to:

The Hydrographer,
Admiralty Hydrographic Supplies Establishment,
Creechbarrow House,
Taunton, Somerset.

[1] *See* also *Queen's Regulations and Admiralty Instructions.*

For ships abroad, application should be made to the chart depot on the station; or, if there is none, the outfit will be sent from England. A list of all chart depots is contained in H.51. The officers making the application should state the date on which the outfit will be required and, if necessary, the address to which it should be forwarded. An indication of the service for which the outfit is required should be given. It is normally advisable to obtain it about fourteen days before the ship proceeds to sea. The Hydrographer confirms what service the ship is proceeding on, and arranges for the outfit to be supplied from the nearest Chart Depot.

> *Warning:* It is the responsibility of the Commanding Officer of the ship, and not that of the Hydrographer or the Admiralty, to ensure that adequate charts are held on board for the service on which the ship may be employed. For instance, a ship normally holding an Abridged folio may be required to enter some particular port for which adequate large-scale charts are only contained in the complete folio. The necessary charts must then be demanded from the Hydrographer to supplement the normal outfit.

State of Correction on Supply

The charts are normally supplied corrected up to date for *permanent* notices only, the date of the last correction being shown both on the folio labels and on the Issue and Receipt Certificate (H.62). The publications are not corrected upon issue, but they are accompanied by all necessary supplements, Notices to Mariners, etc.

To enable charts to be corrected for existing Temporary and Preliminary notices, the following are supplied with the outfit:

(a) A set of weekly editions of Fleet and Admiralty Notices to Mariners from No. 1 of the current year, plus earlier editions as required. In one of these will be found the latest monthly list of (T) and (P) notices in force.

(b) Any (T) and (P) notices which affect the outfit, published since the latest weekly edition.

Action on Receipt of the Chart Outfit

1. Check the folios by the Issue and Receipt Certificates (H.62).
2. Check the associated sets of navigational publications by H.51.
3. Check the charts in their folios by the folio lists.
4. Sign and return the receipt certificate on the duplicate copy of Form H.62.
5. Insert, in pencil, consecutive numbers of charts in folio lists, in duplicate folio lists, and in the folio index.
6. If not already complete, insert in pencil the folio, serial and consecutive numbers on chart labels.
7. Correct charts for any permanent notices published since the number shown on the form H.62.
8. Correct charts for (T) and (P) notices in force, starting preferably with the area in which the ship will be operating first.
9. Correct the navigational publications.

Action on Receipt of a Newly Published Chart

Its arrival should be noted in:

1. NP Item 133a Index,
2. the folio list,
3. the duplicate folio list,
4. the index chart in the appropriate *Sailing Directions*, where the area of the chart should be indicated,
5. the body of the *Sailing Directions*,
6. Catalogue of Admiralty Charts H.D.374.

The chart should be corrected for any (T) or (P) notice affecting it, and for any Permanent notice issued since the advertisement of the chart in Section II of Notices to Mariners.

Action on Transfer of Chart Folios and Publications

Combined Transfer and Receipt Certificates (H.11), supplied in book form, are used when chart folio and publications are transferred from one officer or ship to another, or to a chart depot.

Instructions for its completion and disposal are given on the form, each separate folio being listed thereon, but only the appropriate 'set' of publications. It is essential that the Hydrographer should receive a copy of this form immediately, in order that Notices to Mariners and replenishments may be diverted.

Subsequent Upkeep of Chart Outfits

Replenishments are supplied from the Hydrographic Supplies Establishment. They include the following:

(a) Daily Notices to Mariners, which are issued to ships when any navigational information needs to be promulgated urgently. Such notices should receive immediate attention. They are distinguished by the notation (H) and are reprinted in the weekly editions.

(b) Weekly Editions of the appropriate Admiralty and Fleet Notices to Mariners, as indicated on pages 42 and 43, with an additional copy of Section VI for the correction, by the Communications Department, of the second copy of the *Admiralty List of Radio Signals*.

(c) Charts. New charts, new editions, charts corrected by large corrections and those corrected by the small correction described at (c) on page 29 are automatically supplied. Receipt of those charts to which a ship is entitled can be checked by reference to the Weekly Edition of Notices to Mariners, which contains a list of new publications.

(d) Navigational publications. New publications and amendments are also supplied automatically, and their receipt can be checked as in (c).

(e) Worn or damaged charts and publications are replaced on demand, Form H.38 being used for charts and Form H.177 for maps and publications. These should normally be addressed to the Admiralty Hydrographic Supplies Establishment, as chart depots are authorized to deal with them only if the demand is urgent. Instructions for local purchase of charts or publications, which should only be made in emergency, are contained in H.51.

Disposal of Outfit on Paying Off

When the ship is ordered to pay off and recommission immediately, the outfit should be retained for the next commission.

When a ship is ordered to pay off and not recommission at once, the Hydrographic Supplies Establishment should be asked for instructions about the disposal of the outfit.

If the ship is in foreign waters, the outfit should be returned to the nearest chart depot, and the transfer reported to the Hydrographic Supplies Establishment.

NOTICES TO MARINERS

These promulgate information

(a) announcing the publication of new charts and navigational publications, etc.,

(b) for making all corrections to charts and sailing directions and *important* corrections to *List of Lights*,

(c) for making *all* corrections to *List of Lights* (separately from (b)), Radio Signals and NEMEDRI, and

(d) on navigational warnings (NAVEAMS, HYDROLANTS and HYDROPACS).

The information at (a) and (b) is first published in Daily Notices to Mariners which have a limited circulation except when they are urgent; each item in these notices is given a separate number, running consecutively from the beginning of each year. The navigational warnings are also published daily.

The daily items are republished in Weekly Editions which contain also the information at (c). In these editions, the numbers allocated in the daily notices are retained.

The needs of the Royal Navy are met by the supply of Weekly Editions and this is effected automatically from the Hydrographic Supplies Establishment. The supply of the notices commences as soon as the outfit of charts and publications has been drawn and ceases when the outfit is returned.

Notices are despatched so as to arrive in the shortest possible time, air mail postage being used when suitable. Those who fail to receive notices or receive them late should inform the Hydrographic Supplies Establishment.

The Weekly Complete Edition comprises all notices and is supplied to H.M. ships, R.F.A.s, merchant ships and authorities who have an interest extending beyond Home (U.K.) waters.

DETAILS OF CONTENTS OF WEEKLY EDITIONS. – Every edition bears a number which corresponds to the week in which it was published.

The editions have six sections:

Section I comprises numerical and geographical indexes for Section II.

Section II contains the daily notices published during the week. It starts with the notices giving information on the publication of new charts, new editions and large correction of charts, new navigational publications and new editions of existing navigational publications. Reference to these notices enables authorities to ensure that they have received new material to which they are entitled and, if not received, to demand them.

There is also published monthly a list of new sailing directions, etc., and supplements that are under revision or in the press.

> *Note:* Any information of value in the compilation of sailing directions and supplements under revision should be forwarded to the Hydrographic Department and attention drawn to points which in ordinary circumstances would not be considered sufficiently important to warrant the rendering of a Hydrographic Note (Form H.102).

Thereafter, this section contains notices giving the instructions needed to make corrections to charts and, if necessary, to *Sailing Directions* and *List of Lights*. (So far as the *List of Lights* is concerned, only important amendments are included in this Section (*see also* Section III).) Each notice is headed by its number and general description, followed by details of the information arranged under appropriate sub-headings; at the end are shown the serial numbers of the charts, titles of the publications affected and the authority for the information. The chart numbers are arranged in order of scale commencing with the largest-scale chart. When a chart is affected by only certain sections of a notice these sections are, if necessary, quoted in brackets after the serial number of the chart. Notices may be accompanied by reproductions of portions of the charts affected ('Blocks') showing the corrections referred to in the notices. Temporary and Preliminary notices are distinguished by the notation (T) or (P) printed immediately after the number of the notice.

A list of Temporary and Preliminary notices in force is published monthly, usually during the last week of each month. The list is arranged under geographical headings and enumerates the charts affected. (T) and (P) notices in force on the 31st December are reprinted in the Annual Summary of Notices to Mariners (*see* below).

> *Section III* contains all corrections for the week to the various volumes of the *Admiralty List of Lights, Fog Signals and Visual Time Signals*, including those contained in Section II.

> *Section IV* contains corrections to the NEMEDRI route book and the annual Notice to Mariners No. 18 (Areas dangerous due to mines).

> *Section V* contains navigational warnings, i.e. NAVEAMS, HYDROLANTS and HYDROPACS broadcast during the week.

> *Section VI* contains corrections to the *Admiralty List of Radio Signals*.

Other Editions of Notices to Mariners

Apart from the Daily Notices and the Weekly Complete Edition, there are the following:

(a) *Weekly Edition of Fleet Notices.* – This promulgates classified navigational, meteorological and hydrographic information. It is supplied to ships holding Fleet charts.

(b) *The Annual Summary of Admiralty Notices to Mariners.* – This is a collection of twenty notices (numbered 1 to 20) of a permanent nature and reprints of (T) and (P) notices and navigational warnings in force on the previous 31st December. The volume is published on 1st January each year.

Certain of the individual notices that comprise the volume (e.g. No. 3, 3a and 3b which concern official radio messages) are also published separately from the volume and supplied to those who are specially concerned with them.

(c) *Section IV* of the Weekly Complete Edition is also printed separately from the edition and is supplied to those whose interest in N.M.s is restricted to the correction of the NEMEDRI route book.

(d) *Section VI* of the Weekly Complete Edition is also printed separately from the edition and copies are supplied for the use of the communications departments in H.M. ships and radio operators of merchant ships.

Radio Navigational Warnings

Local Navigational Warnings for all parts of the world are broadcast from the country of origin. Particulars are given in Volumes I and V of the *Admiralty List of Radio Signals* where times, frequencies and other relevant information may be found.

For waters around the British Isles warnings of an urgent and temporary nature are broadcast from G.P.O. Coast Stations and promulgated to H.M. ships as WZ messages.

LONG-RANGE WARNINGS. – For certain specified areas the methods of promulgation are as follows:

East Atlantic, Mediterranean and Red Sea. – By NAVEAMS. Important warnings are re-broadcast from Washington.

West Atlantic. – By HYDROLANTS. Some important messages are re-broadcast as NAVEAMS.

Pacific Ocean East of 105°E (not including Gulf of Thailand). – By HYDROPACS.

'W' MESSAGES. – Other areas are covered by British Commonwealth Navigational Warnings issued in consecutive series with a monthly list of messages in force.

Long-Range and 'W' messages are reprinted in Section V of Admiralty Notices to Mariners Weekly Edition.

Long-Range warnings are also reprinted in *U.S. Notices to Mariners.*

CORRECTION OF CHARTS

All small but important corrections which affect navigation, and which can be made to the charts by hand, are promulgated in Notices to Mariners, and (with the exception of corrections from Temporary or Preliminary notices) should at once be made neatly in permanent violet ink on the charts affected. The notation of small corrections made is inserted as described on page 28. The recognized abbreviations shown on Admiralty Chart 5011 should be used.

If several charts are affected by a notice, the largest-scale charts should be corrected first.

Generally speaking, the amount of detailed information which should be inserted on a chart should conform to that already shown. This will vary according to the scale of the chart.

On Large-scale charts, always insert the abridged descriptions (as shown on Chart 5011) of all details of lights, light-buoys and fog signals; and the dates (year only) of obstructions, reported shoals, dredged channels, depth of water on bars or in shifting channels and irregularities of lights.

On Coastal charts, insert the abridged descriptions of only the principal lights and fog signals – i.e., those lights and signals that will assist in making a landfall.

Details of lights to be inserted are generally fully described in the Notices to Mariners. If they are not, particulars of such lights should be omitted[1] in the following order as the scale of the chart decreases:

1. Elevation.
2. Period.
3. Number in group.
4. Visibility.

Particulars of fog signals should be inserted in their appropriate positions, if there is sufficient space; otherwise they should be entered in a tabulated list under the title, or in some other convenient place. Inner harbour light-buoys and beacons should not be inserted on coastal charts. Against other light-buoys insert only the character of the light.

On Ocean charts, only lights which are visible 15 miles or over should be inserted, and details about them should be confined to character and colour.

INSERTION OF WRITING

If possible, insert writing clear of the water (unless the objects concerned are on the water), and take care not to obliterate any information already on the chart. When cautionary or tidal notices, etc., are inserted, they should be written in a convenient but conspicuous place, preferably near the title, where they will not interfere with other details.

ERASURES

Any details which have to be cancelled should, when necessary, be crossed through in permanent violet ink. *They should never be erased.*

BLOCKS

Notices to Mariners are occasionally accompanied by reproductions of portions of charts which are called 'blocks'. When correcting charts from such blocks the following points should be borne in mind:

(a) A block not only shows corrections, but may also cancel work already on the chart. The latter would invariably be mentioned in the text of the notice and the fact that a block accompanies a notice does not mean that the text of the notice can be disregarded.

---

[1] The colour is never omitted, except when the light is white.

(b) The boundary lines of a block are arranged for convenience of reproduction, and need not be followed when the block is cut for pasting on the chart, provided that paragraph (a) is considered.

(c) The new information shown on a block can sometimes be inserted on the chart by hand; the reason for printing the block in such an event is to avoid a long description of the new information in the text of the notice.

(d) Owing to distortion, the block will not always fit the chart exactly; therefore when a block is pasted on to the chart care should be taken that the more important navigational corrections fit as closely as possible. This can best be achieved by fitting the block while it is dry, and making two or three pencil marks round the edges to use as fitting marks.

Apply paste to the chart and not to the block, otherwise the block may suffer distortion.

Correcting Charts from Temporary and Preliminary Notices

These corrections should be inserted in pencil on the charts, together with the number of the notice – for example: NM $\dfrac{742}{1961}$ (T). The number should also be entered in pencil, in the manner described on page 29, in the bottom left-hand corner of the chart under the permanent small-correction notations.

Temporary corrections should be rubbed out when the notice to cancel them is received, but Preliminary corrections should be inked in when the notice is received reporting that the changes have been made.

Charts in stock at the Admiralty Chart Establishment, chart agencies and depots are not corrected from (T) and (P) notices; and charts received from any of these places should be corrected in pencil, as necessary, from the copies of such notices already held, or from those supplied with the chart.

Corrections from Radio Navigational Warnings

These warnings (see page 44) usually concern derelicts and drifting obstructions, the temporary extinction of lights, the displacement of important aids to navigation, ice reports, etc. They should be noted in pencil on the chart affected. Radio Navigational Warnings of a permanent nature and those relating to derelicts and drifting obstructions to navigation are re-issued as Admiralty Notices to Mariners, but other warnings are not re-issued in this way, except in special circumstances. When the warning is cancelled in the meantime or is considered unimportant from the point of view of safe navigation, a suitable annotation is made.

Corrections from Information Received from Authorities other than the Admiralty

Such information should be noted in pencil on the charts affected, but no charted danger is to be expunged without the direct authority of the Hydrographer. When an Admiralty Notice to Mariners is received confirming this information, the pencil corrections should be erased, and the necessary corrections should be inserted in the way already described.

PUBLICATIONS

Publications used by the Navigating Officer are divided into two categories:

(1) Publications supplied by the Hydrographer (H. and H.D. Series).

(2) Textbooks, reference books, handbooks and forms obtained from the C.B. Officer or Supply Department (C.B.s, B.R.s, and 'S' Series).

Sets of Navigational Publications

Navigational Publications (N.P.s) are made up into sets, details of which are given in H.51. All major war vessels are supplied with the 'Complete set for General Service'. In addition, the appropriate *Sailing Directions* and *List of Lights* are issued automatically with chart folios, as indicated at the bottom of each folio list.

State of Correction on Supply. – Navigational publications are not corrected on supply, but the latest supplements, summaries of notices, and any other amendments not issued as Notices to Mariners, are automatically included.

Meteorological Publications

A list of these publications, together with the scale of issue, is given in the *Meteorological Supplies Handbook* (W1). Ships with qualified Meteorological Officers are issued with a 'complete set'; those with a qualified Navigating Officer but no Meteorological Officer, with an 'abridged set'; and others with meteorological working charts only.

Aviation Publications

(a) The *United Kingdom Air Pilot* promulgated by the Ministry of Aviation, is distributed by the Hydrographer, Taunton, to Naval authorities, establishments and ships concerned. This book is in looseleaf form and contains information regarding aeronautical facilities in the United Kingdom. It is the responsibility of the Lieutenant-Commander (Operations). It is amended by *Notices to Airmen* (NOTAMS) and by monthly supplements which contain any new or reprinted sheets. A Check List is issued monthly to enable the holder to check that his copy of the book is up to date.

(b) Instrument Approach and Landing Charts are also distributed by the Hydrographer.

(c) Other basic aeronautical information, not necessarily applicable to the 'Air Pilot', is promulgated by 'Information Circulars'. These are distributed on behalf of the Admiralty by the Ministry of Aviation. (Correspondence relating to them should, however, be addressed to the Hydrographer.)

Navigational Publications

ADMIRALTY SAILING DIRECTIONS

The *Admiralty Sailing Directions*, also called 'Pilots', are published in about seventy-five volumes covering the world. They contain general information useful to the navigator, and the appropriate volumes are automatically supplied with chart folios.

The main contents of each volume conform generally to the following:

(a) A caution drawing attention to annual Notices to Mariners.

(b) Notation form for supplements and summaries of Notices to Mariners relating to the book.

(c) A caution against using the book without consulting the latest supplement, etc.

(d) A caution regarding the units of measurement and other standards used in the book.

(e) Advertisement to the edition. This states the latest Notice to Mariners embodied in the book.

(f) Information relating to Admiralty charts and publications, general navigation and meteorology.

(g) *Index chart.* – This shows the area covered by the volume, and the limits and numbers of all Admiralty charts (but not Fleet charts) for the area. The number of the chart is marked in the corner of the chart limits. A star and a number against the name of a place – for example, *2793 Cowes* – indicate that a plan of Cowes is given on Chart No. 2793. A number against the name of a place – for example, 1698 *Dover* – indicates that a separate plan of Dover, bearing that number, is published.

(h) *Chapter 1.* – Except in those volumes that are concerned with the British Isles, Chapter 1 opens with a brief description of the countries covered by the volume, their government, flora, fauna, trade and currency. Then follow, in all volumes, details of meteorology, tides, tidal streams, signals, cautions, life-saving, systems of buoys, communications, radio stations, dockyards, rat destruction, Standard Time, fuel supplies, and any directions not given in *Ocean Passages of the World*.

(i) Other chapters contain detailed descriptions of the area covered by the volume. The largest-scale charts of the area that is being described are shown at the top of each page, and the general charts of the area at the bottom.

(j) *Appendices.* – At the end of the book there are several appendices which generally give details of the following:

(1) Orders in Council concerning dockyard ports.

(2) A list of ports available for underwater repairs, with details of the largest dry dock, floating dock or patent slip at each port.

(3) A list of the principal ports, showing particulars of depths, etc.

(4) A table of reported radar ranges.

Discrepancies. – Should information given on charts and in the *Sailing Directions* differ, the information given on the largest-scale chart is to be accepted.

New Editions. – A new edition of each volume of *Sailing Directions* is published at intervals of approximately twelve years. The numbers of the Notices to Mariners affecting it, between the dates of going to press and of its issue to ships, are given in the notices announcing its publication, in order to enable the new edition to be corrected before being brought into use.

Supplements. – A supplement to each volume is generally published biennially, each supplement cancelling the previous one. The following instruction appears on the front covers of the supplements and in a cautionary note in the 'Pilots':

'Whenever reference is made to the Pilot, this Supplement must be consulted.'

Supplements should be retained intact inside the cover of the 'Pilot', their existence being noted in pencil on the flyleaf of the book. The last notice used in compiling the Supplement is stated in the advertisement. New and/or altered information appearing in the supplements for the first time is enclosed in square brackets; deletions from previous supplements are indicated by a horizontal line.

Summaries of Notices to Mariners. – When a volume of *Sailing Directions* is taken up for revision, no further supplement to that edition is issued, but subsequent notices affecting it are summarized each year and issued as a separate publication, until the new edition is published. Details should also be entered on the flyleaf of the book, as already described.

Correction from Notices to Mariners. – Notices to Mariners affecting *Sailing Directions* should be indicated in pencil in the margin or entered in manuscript in the appropriate place, as is convenient.

ADMIRALTY LIST OF LIGHTS, FOG SIGNALS AND VISUAL TIME SIGNALS

This publication, normally called the 'Lights List', is published in twelve volumes covering the world. The volumes are divided geographically, as indicated on the index chart on the back of each volume, and are published at intervals of about 18 months, at the rate of one volume every six weeks.

Contents :

(a) Index chart, showing the limits of the volumes (back cover).

(b) Introductory remarks on types of lights, fog signals, submarine sound signals, radiobeacons, radar reflectors, light-vessels, wreck-marking vessels and distress signals.

(c) Table of ranges for calculating the distance a light may be seen for different heights of eye.

(d) Luminous visibility diagram.

(e) Details of all navigational lights (except light-buoys[1]) and fog signals. The existence of radiobeacons is indicated where appropriate, but details of them are given in the *Admiralty List of Radio Signals* (Vol. II).

(f) Traffic and other signals, details of which will be found in *Sailing Directions*.

(g) Details of Visual Time Signals.

Types of Printing. – Different types of printing are used to distinguish various lights, as follows:

Bold type: the names and geographical ranges of lights showing 15 miles and over.

Roman type: shore lights other than the above.

ITALIC CAPITALS: the names of light-vessels.

Italics: floating lights other than the above.

Position. – The approximate latitude and longitude of lights are given, to facilitate reference to the chart.

Unwatched Lights. – The letter **U** after the name of a light indicates that it is unwatched and therefore should not be relied upon implicitly.

---

[1] Details of light-buoys may be found on large scale charts and in the *Sailing Directions*.

Elevations. – The elevation given in column 5 is measured between the centre of the lantern and the level of Mean High Water Springs or Mean Higher Water, whichever is given in the *Tide Tables*.

The height given in column 7 is that of the structure, measured from top to base.

With light-vessels, it is the height of the daymark above the waterline.

Geographical range. – The range given in column 6 is that at which an observer, with height-of-eye of 15 feet, would be able to see the light in clear weather. If the light is not of sufficient intensity to be seen from the limit of its geographical range, its luminous visibility is given.

Sectors. – The true bearing of sectors *from seaward* is given in column 8 (*see also* Chapter V).

Corrections. – Permanent and Temporary corrections to the volumes are promulgated in the Weekly Complete Edition of Admiralty Notices to Mariners, Section III. A list of the corrections, accumulated while the volume was in the press, is contained in Section III of the Weekly Edition announcing its publication. Important corrections are also repeated in Section II of the Admiralty and Fleet Notices to Mariners, for the correction of charts. All corrections should be noted in pencil.

Admiralty List of Air Lights (H.D.455)

This publication, supplied only to aircraft-carriers, contains world-wide details of all air lighthouses, airfield beacons and lighted obstructions. It is primarily for use in conjunction with air charts, but some of these lights are of use to surface navigation and, where appropriate, details are given so that they can be plotted on surface charts. The characteristic of many air lights is a flashed letter or group of letters. Some of these lights are also included in the *Admiralty List of Lights*.

Admiralty List of Radio Signals

This publication consists of five parts, the main contents of which are enumerated below.

Volume I – Communications

- (a) *Caution drawing attention to Annual Notices to Mariners.
- (b) *Preface, with explanatory notes on the volume, including the date of the latest correction embodied in the book.
- (c) *Directions for correcting the book.
- (d) *List of abbreviations used in the book.
- (e) International radio watchkeeping periods.
- (f) *Diagram to facilitate the comparison of Zone Time at different places.
- (g) *Lists of callsigns.
- (h) Long-distance ship-shore radio communications.
- (i) Small craft watchkeeping arrangements (Great Britain and Eire).
- (j) List of pilot vessels and stations equipped with radio.
- (k) List of coast radio stations.
- (l) Medical services and quarantine reports.

---

* Items with an asterisk prefixed are also to be found in one or more of the other volumes of the *Admiralty List of Radio Signals*.

(m) Epidemiological bulletins.

(n) VHF services.

(o) General radio regulations, distress signals, *International Morse Code and conventional signals, *abbreviations used in radio, *frequency and wavelength conversion table.

Volume II – Direction-finding Stations and Radiobeacons
General information and details of services of:

(a) Radio direction-finding stations.

(b) Radiobeacons.

(c) QTG Service and calibration stations.

(d) Radar stations.

(e) Codes and Regulations.

(f) Diagram for obtaining half-convergency.

Volume III – Meteorological Services

(a) Meteorological services and codes.

(b) Beaufort Scale and various conversion tables.

Volume IV – Meteorological Stations
List of Meteorological Observation Stations.

Volume V – Radio Time Signals, Standard Frequency Services, Standard Times, Radio Navigational Warnings and Position-fixing Systems

(a) Uniform time system, including diagram to facilitate the comparison of Zone Times at different places, table of Standard Times kept in different countries, and list of countries keeping Summer Time.

(b) Radio time signals.

(c) Standard Frequency Services.

(d) Radio navigational warnings (including Ice Reports) – general information and details of services.

(e) Position-fixing systems: Loran, Consol, Decca.

(f) Time zone chart.

System of Numbering Radio Stations. – The allocation of numbers to the various services is as follows:

Nos.   1–999 refer to Coast Stations (Vol. I).
    1001–1999 ,, ,, DF Stations (Vol. II).
    2001–2999 ,, ,, Fog Signals and Radiobeacons (Vol. II).
    3001–3999 ,, ,, Time Signals (Vol. V).
    4001–4999 ,, ,, Weather Bulletins and Storm Warnings (Vol. III).
    5001–5999 ,, ,, Navigational Warnings and Ice Reports (Vol. V).
    6001–6999 ,, ,, Standard Frequency Service (Vol. V).

The number of thousands is an indication of the service concerned, while the other digits remain the same throughout the book for any particular station. Thus, while Station 958G is Cape Race *Coast Radio Station*, 1958G is Cape Race *DF Station*, 2958G is Cape Race *Radiobeacon*, 4958G is Cape Race *Radio Weather Message Service*, and 5958G is Cape Race *Navigational Warning and Ice Signal Station*. Cape Race transmits neither time signal nor Standard Frequency Services, therefore there is no Station 3958G or 6958G.

---

* Items with an asterisk prefixed are also to be found in one or more of the other volumes of the *Admiralty List of Radio Signals*.

New Editions and Corrections. – Each volume, an annual publication, is produced separately and is accompanied by a supplement which contains corrections issued between the date of the volume's going to press and the date of the Notice to Mariners announcing its publication.

Corrections to all the volumes are promulgated in Section VI of the Weekly Complete Editions of Admiralty Notices to Mariners; important corrections affecting charts are also included in Section II of these editions. Corrections may also be promulgated in the form of Supplements.

Corrections should be made in the volumes by means of a marginal reference to the relevant edition of N.M.s, or, where convenient, by manuscript insertion in the text. It should be remembered that such notations are cancelled by the Supplement in which they are incorporated.

Supply to Ships. – Ships are supplied with two copies of Volumes I, II and V and one copy of Volumes III and IV, the second copy being for the use of the Communications Department. A second copy of Volume III is also supplied to ships in which a qualified Meteorological Officer is borne.

NEMEDRI ROUTE BOOK

This book, the full title of which is *North European and Mediterranean Routeing Instructions*, contains details of all areas dangerous on account of mines, and routes (with the special buoys marking them) to be followed through and between such areas.

Index charts, which show these details, are also included. The book forms part of the set of navigational publications and is supplied to ships carrying the chart folios for the appropriate areas covered by NEMEDRI.

It is normally corrected from Section IV of Admiralty Notices to Mariners, but urgent amendments are issued by NAVEAMS. In order to maintain the sequence of amendments, information that has been promulgated by NAVEAM will be repeated in Section IV, with an appropriate note. The last Weekly Edition of Notices to Mariners that has been embodied in the book is announced on the Contents page.

This book will be abolished as soon as the mining situation permits.

OCEAN PASSAGES OF THE WORLD

This book is supplied to ships in which a qualified Navigating Officer is borne. It contains information and cautions concerning ocean routes, together with an account of the relevant oceanic winds and currents. Charts are included which show routes, winds and currents for different parts of the world.

Much useful information is included which will not be found in the *Sailing Directions*, since the latter are concerned mainly with coastal waters.

DISTANCE TABLES

Admiralty Distance Tables are published in five volumes covering the world, and give the shortest navigable distances, in nautical miles, between various ports. For passage planning it is advisable to add about 5 per cent to the overall distance.

Each volume is divided into sections, as shown on the key chart in the back of the book.

Any two contiguous sections or volumes have a port common to both; this is marked in red on the key chart. This common port must be used as a stepping-stone when the distance is required between places in contiguous sections.

EXAMPLE

To find the distance from Devonport to Cromarty

Distance Tables, Volume I, will be required. Take out the Key Chart and it will be found that Devonport lies in Section A and Cromarty lies in Section C. The common port between Sections A and C will be found to be Dover.

From the index, Dover appears on pages 8 and 55.

From page 8, Dover to Plymouth	= 226'
From page 55, Dover to Cromarty	= 505'
Therefore Plymouth to Cromarty	= 731'

TIDAL PUBLICATIONS

Details of Tide and Tidal Streams Tables, and other tidal publications, are given in Chapter XII.

LECKY'S VERTICAL DANGER ANGLE AND OFF-SHORE DISTANCE TABLES

This book is supplied with the navigational publications, and its use is described in Chapter IV.

ASTRONOMICAL PUBLICATIONS

These publications are listed in the *Hydrographic Supplies Handbook* (H.51). They include Altitude and Azimuth Tables, Nautical and Air Almanacs, Astronomical Navigation Tables, and Azimuth Diagrams.

THE SHIP'S LOG (S.322)[1]

The Navigating Officer is to have charge of the Ship's Log (S.322), and should present it weekly for the Captain's inspection. He is responsible that it is correctly and neatly written up, in non-indelible pencil, and that it is initialled by the Officers of the Watch while the facts are fresh in their minds. Any alteration is to be initialled by the Officer of the Watch and sanctioned by the Captain.

The log in current use, which expires monthly, is to be kept in a cover (S.321A). The completed log is to be signed by the Navigating Officer and delivered to the Captain at the end of each month; or, if the Navigating Officer is superseded before this, he is to sign it and deliver it to his successor. The completed log is then to be kept in cover S.321B, which contains twelve monthly logs. It may be demanded for inspection by the ship's Administrative Authority at suitable intervals. Completed ship's logs are to be transmitted to the Head of the Record Office, Admiralty, in batches of twelve, on the expiration of two years from the first ship's log of the series.

A specimen log for a short sea passage is given on pages 54 and 55.

Instructions for completing the ship's log are given in *Q.R. and A.I.*, extracts from which are reprinted inside the cover, together with various relevant meteorological tables.

---

[1] *See* also *Queen's Regulations and Admiralty Instructions.*

H.M.S. *NONSUCH*   *Fri* day 17th of *November* 1961

Time	Log Reading	Distance Run Miles and Tenths	Mean Revs. Per Min.	True Course	Error of "A" Gyro	Error of "B" Gyro	Course by Auxiliary Compass	Variation	Deviation	Wind Speed in Knots	Wind Direction From	Weather and Visibility	Waves Direction From	Period in Seconds	Height in Feet	Corrected Barometric pressure in Millibars	Temp. Dry Bulb	Temp. Wet Bulb	Temp. Sea
0001																			
0100																			
0200																			
0300	1265.3	6.4	70.3	133°	NIL		143°	8°W	2°W										
0400	1280.5	15.0	142	230°	"		237°	8°W	1°E	9	230	bc 7	225	3	2	1009.4	52	51	50
0500	1292.1	11.5	110.2	260°	"		267	8 W	1 E										
0600	1305.4	13.3	124.9	260	"		267	8 W	1 E										
0700	1320.5	15.0	142	260	"		267	8 W	1 E										
0800	1331.9	11.2	107.6	Var	-		Var	-	-	10	220	bc 7	225	3	2	1005.7	53	47	51
0900	1344.1	12.0	114.1	Var	-		Var	-	-										
1000	1357.3	13.0	121.9	329°	NIL		336°	8½°W	1½°E										
1100	-	5.6	58.3	Var	-		Var	-	-										
1200										10	215	bc 8	225	2	2	1004.7	56	50	51

Zone time kept at Noon	Distance Run through the Water (Midnight to Midnight)	Position	Latitude	Longitude	Depending on	Ship's Berth and Anchor Bearings	Currents Experienced (Sea) Readiness of Ship for Sea (Harbour)
0	103.0	0800	50°27.2N	2°16.8W	Fix at 0755	S.Railway Jetty	
		1200				59 {'A' head 178½° ; House (conspic) 329° ; Weymouth B'water Hd 253°	1026 4 hours
		2000					

Time	Log Reading	Distance Run Miles and Tenths	Mean Revs. Per Min.	True Course	Error of "A" Gyro	Error of "B" Gyro	Course by Auxiliary Compass	Variation	Deviation	Wind Speed in Knots	Wind Direction From	Weather and Visibility	Waves Direction From	Period in Seconds	Height in Feet	Corrected Barometric pressure in Millibars	Temp. Dry Bulb	Temp. Wet Bulb	Temp. Sea
1201																			
1300																			
1400																			
1500										15									
1600					~~Fr. 15 210~~					15	210	c 7	220	2	2	1003	52	50	50
1700																			
1800										15	210	c 7	220	2	2	1002.3	49	45	50
1900																			
2000										15	210	c 6	215	2	2	1002	49	45	50
2100																			
2200																			
2300																			
2400										20	200	c 6				1000.5	47	45	49

From *Portsmouth*   to *Weymouth*   , or at

REMARKS	Initials of the Quarter-master	Initials of the Officer of the Watch or Day
0145 Port watch employed preparing for sea.		
0200 Guard boat hailed.		
0215 S.S.D. closed up — singled up.		
0230 Cast off — courses and speeds for leaving harbour. 0240 No. 6 buoy abeam 0.5c.		
0255 Dolphin Bns. φ 238° (gyro correct). 0252 { Horse Sand fort 110° / Spit Sand fort 190°		
0255 A/c 133°. 0320 A/c 230°. { No man's land fort 343°		ABC
0315 Nab Tr 133° 2·4		
0411 a/c 260 0402 { St Catherines Lt 266½		
0420 spoke Nieuw Amsterdam Ventnor pier 287		
0430 entered fog — speed 8 kts — started siren — placed lookouts Shanklin pier 353		
0515 fog lifted — speed 15 kts. 0530 { 50° 29' N / 01° 33.3 W [Decca]		
0615 144° Anvil Point 8·0		
0710 Sonar control room & ops. room closed up 0715 exchanged identities with H.M. S/m TATE		
0725 S/m dived 50°27'N 2°15'W. 0730 Commenced A/s exercise — Co & sp. as req. 0955 Portland Bill Lt 302° 7·8		JEF
0800 Both watches of hands employed cleaning ship.		
0900 Exercised action stations. 0915 Secured.		
0920 A/s exercise completed — course 270° speed 15. 0935 { Shambles Lt V 013° / Portland Bill Lt 325° 6·2		
0933 S/m surfaced bg. 100° 1,000 yards. 0935 A/c 020° 0955 A/c 329°		
1015 Speed 12. 1019 Speed and course as required for anchoring in Weymouth bay.		
1026 Came to starboard anchor in 7 fm. veered to 4½ shackles on waterline.		ABC

Ship's Draught			Leave granted to Ship's Company	Number on Sick List	A.B.C.D. State		Result of Daily Muster of Signal Publications
Occasion for Notation	Forward	Aft	Port watch and 1st Starboard 1600 – 0700	3	0200	3Y	Correct
On Sailing	13' 0"	16' 6"	C.P.O. and P.O. 1600 – 0730		0245	3X	
On arrival	13' 0"	16' 0"	Normal w/k leave		0430	3Y	
					0515	3X	Signature of Mustering Officer
					1030	4X	

1315 B.W. of hands employed washing ship's side and ~~painting mast~~.		
~~1415 HMS Carley anchored in S.11.~~		
1508 Lieutent A.H. Over joined from HMS Drake.		F
1730 H.M.S. Carley sailed		
		WAB
2100 Rounds Correct.		
		FJ

Fishing Vessel Log (S.1176)[1]

At sea this log is to be kept under the supervision of the Officer of the Watch. In it should be noted the fact of the ship's passing through or near any fishing fleet, with additional details as given in the instructions for this log. The object is to furnish evidence in the event of any claim by fishing vessels for nets or gear damaged by H.M. ships.

In addition, it includes descriptions of different methods of fishing, and methods of avoiding damage to the gear.

The log should be retained on board for reference until the ship is paid off, when it should be sent to the Secretary of the Admiralty (Naval Law Branch).

Areas in which fishing takes place are shown in the Fishery charts, which are listed in H.D.493. B.R.786, *The Fishing Fleets of Western Europe*, also shows areas in which fishing takes place, and in addition gives much useful information, together with illustrations, concerning methods of fishing and types of fishing vessels. It also contains a chapter on whales.

Record of Observations for Deviation (S.374a); and Tables of Deviation (S.387)

Details of these forms are contained in Chapter IX.

Pilotage Forms (S.21; S.454)[1]

Normally, the Navigating Officer – or, if no qualified Navigating Officer is borne, the Captain – performs the pilotage; and, subject to the conditions contained in B.R.2030 (*Information as to the Payment of Pilotage to Officers of H.M. ships and vessels*) this officer may claim payment for such pilotage on Form S.454.

Whenever a local pilot is employed, a Voucher for Payment of Pilotage (S.21) is to be completed and handed to the pilot, or he is to sign the Pilotage Account form; both should show the exact positions between which the ship was piloted. (For further details concerning pilotage *see* Chapter V.)

Tonnage

At various ports, both British and foreign, the rates for dock and harbour dues, and those payable to local pilots, depend upon the ship's tonnage. The figures quoted for this purpose are of three kinds: displacement tonnage, gross tonnage, and net (or register) tonnage.

Certificates showing gross and net tonnages are supplied to H.M. ships on completion or on re-measurement after structural alterations. They should be kept in the Ship's Book and the facts recorded in the Navigational Data Book.

(a) *Displacement tonnage* is the weight of water displaced by the ship and is equal to the weight of the ship and all that is in her: it therefore varies with her draught.

Displacement = volume of water displaced (in cubic feet) divided by 35 or 36, according to whether the water is salt or fresh respectively.

'Standard Displacement', used for warships, is that laid down by the Washington Treaty (1923) and is the displacement of the ship complete, fully manned, with engines, armament, ammunition, provisions, stores, equipment and fresh water for crew, but *without* fuel or reserve feedwater.

---

[1] *See also Queen's Regulations and Admiralty Instructions.*

(b) *Gross tonnage* comprises the internal capacity of the ship below the upper deck, with the addition of permanent closed-in spaces above the upper deck. It is reckoned in tons (for this purpose, 100 cubic feet are taken as the equivalent of 1 ton); certain factors are, however, included – e.g., double-bottom compartments, and shelters above the upper deck for passengers. Gross tonnage is used to classify ships for many purposes, e.g., the Merchant Shipping (Wireless Telegraphy) Act, 1919. In a warship the gross tonnage is usually equivalent to about 60 per cent of the standard displacement.

(c) *Net tonnage*

(1) This is properly referred to as 'Register tonnage' so far as registered vessels are concerned. It is obtained from the gross tonnage by making deductions on account of space occupied by propelling machinery, fuel, crew accommodation, etc. In a limited sense, it represents the cargo-carrying capacity and the liability for dues. The 'Register' is kept by the Registrar of Shipping (an official of H.M. Customs) at the particular port of registry.

Net tonnage is commonly used as a basis for the assessment of port dues throughout the world, and for light dues[1] for ships trading to Great Britain.

(2) The net tonnage for warships is specially computed and is shown on a slip of paper which is attached to the Suez Canal Special Tonnage Certificate. The slip is worded as follows:

'For the purpose of assessment of dock and harbour dues for the United Kingdom the net register tonnage of this vessel is......'

Notes:

(i) Revised net tonnage is also used for docking at Bombay.

(ii) Revised net tonnage is not to be used on Form S.21 for assessment of pilotage rates.

(iii) Revised net tonnage is not used for passage through the Suez Canal.

Passage through Canals

Special rules are applied when assessing tonnage for canal dues, the principal ones being the following:

(a) *Suez Canal.* – A special Tonnage Certificate for the Suez Canal is issued by the Ministry of Transport. It shows the net tonnage upon which dues will be charged when passing through the Canal.

(b) *Panama Canal.* – All warships, other than transports, colliers, supply ships and hospital ships, are required to present duly authenticated displacement scale and curves, stating accurately the tonnage of displacement at each possible mean draught; and dues are charged on the actual displacement at the time of transit.

(c) *Kiel Canal.* – Dues are based on the gross tonnage, as given in the Ship's Book, divided by 1·7.

---

[1] Light dues are levied upon vessels for the provision and maintenance of lighthouses, buoys, etc., which have been placed for the benefit of vessels navigating adjacent waters. Note also that the *Register Book*, published by Lloyd's Register of Shipping, gives the gross and net tonnage of most of the merchant ships of the world.

REPORT OF TURNING AND MANOEUVRING TRIALS (S.347)[1]

Trials, sufficient to obtain the necessary data to complete Form S.347, are to be carried out within 6 months of a ship's being commissioned.

One copy of this form is to be retained in the Ship's Book, one copy in the Navigational Data Book, and three copies are to be forwarded to the Admiralty.

For small ships, only one vessel of each class need carry out these trials. The Admiralty will subsequently promulgate one copy of the Form S.347 (which is then to be retained in the Ship's Book) to the other ships of the class.

NAVIGATING OFFICER'S WORKBOOK (S.548); and NOTEBOOK (S.548A)[1]

The results of all observations and calculations connected in any way with the navigation of the ship are to be kept in a book (S.548). In addition, all angles, bearings and other information connected with navigation are to be recorded in S.548A. These books are to be examined by the Captain whenever he may think fit to call for them and may be demanded at any official inquiry into loss or damage sustained by the ship. When the Navigating Officer is superseded, he should retain his S.548s until completion of his Advanced Course, but may dispose of his S.548As as he thinks fit. If, however, a ship is paid off before a case of collision or damage is settled, the relevant S.548A should be forwarded to the Secretary of the Admiralty (N.L. Branch).

NAVIGATIONAL DATA BOOK[1]

In order that the records of the performance of a ship under all conditions of wind and weather which are gained in one commission may be available for the next, a manuscript Navigational Data Book is to be kept by the Navigating Officer and is to contain the following information:

(a) *Dimensions and Tonnage*

All details of length, breadth, height and tonnage from ship's book. (Note which tonnage figure should be quoted for Pilotage dues.)

Heights of eye (6 foot man) for the various decks from which sights might be taken.

Tracing of end elevation (from astern) of ship's stern (particularly important in ships with proud propellers).

Tons per inch immersion.

Distance from Pelorus and Navigational radar aerial to stem and stern.

Distances at which buoys are in transit with base of jackstaff, etc. (Shadow diagram.)

(b) *Anchors and Cables*

Details of size, age, weight, capacity and all tests and ranging of anchors, cable and cable-holders.

A series of diagrams should give the position of each shackle within its cable after each ranging – to assist in maintaining even rate of wear.

Speed of weighing anchor in minutes per shackle.

(c) *Turning Trials*

From Report of Contractor's Turning Trials or of Ship's Turning Trials the following should be prepared:

Table and/or graph for taking station from the bow. (Template for use on a P.P.I. should also be prepared.)

---

[1] *See also Queen's Regulations and Admiralty Instructions.*

Losing Ground Diagram.

Amount of wheel for altering course.

Time taken to turn at rest.

Starting and stopping data.

(d) *Revolution Tables and Full Power Trials*

Tables and/or graphs for engine revolutions for speeds after various periods out of dock.

All available information on engine revolutions for speeds when various shafts are stopped or trailed.

(e) *Fuel Oil Capacity and Consumption Data*

This information should be obtained from the Engineer Officer and should include:

Consumption (in tons per hour)/speed.

Miles range/speed, allowing a small percentage of fuel remaining.

(f) *Shiphandling Characteristics*

General observations from experience.

Standard distances at which to reduce speed, stop and go astern when approaching an anchorage, buoy or alongside berth.

Effects of wind at various speeds ahead and astern.

Steerage way at various slow speeds.

Amount of leeway for various directions of relative wind.

Record of tricky berthing, with solution to each problem.

(g) *Replenishment*

Notes of experience gained.

Abnormalities of interaction.

Method of approaching the close-aboard position.

Diagram of ship's replenishment positions (on same scale as ATP 16 for R.F.A.s).

Distances usually maintained for various rigs.

(h) *Compasses*

Details of those fitted.

Record of each swing (magnetic).

(j) *Echo Sounder*

Details of fitting.

(k) *Bottom Log and A.R.L. Tables*

Details of fitting.

Table of errors of the log and all automatic tables after each log calibration.

(l) *D.G. Equipment and Ranging*

To include a record and report of each ranging, wiping and deperming.

(m) *Navigation Lights – Types and Positions*

To include Pattern numbers of lights and the situation of all mains and battery lights and switches.

(n) *Radio Aids*

List of all equipment fitted.

(o) *Steering Equipment and Positions: Orders for Steering Breakdowns*

Full details.

(p) *Conning Positions*
   To include brief description of all communcations (except for the Bridge), chart tables, and compasses available at these positions.

(q) *Navigational Communications*
   Full details of intercommunications, voicepipes and telephones.

(r) *Special Sea Duty Stations*
   Full details of all personnel, with their positions and tasks.

(s) *Catamarans, Fendering Positions and Mooring Spaces*
   All special features of the ship with regard to berthing – for example:
   Width of catamarans for berthing a carrier port side to.
   Proud propellers.
   Minimum length of catamarans, as dictated by frame-spacing.

(t) *Carriers only*
   Visibility diagram.
   P.I.M. table.
   Turning into wind graph.

(u) *Narrative of Ship's Movements and Passage Analysis*
   Distance-steamed table.
   An outline record of all passages, berths, disasters, exercises, and lessons learnt.

(v) *Engines*
   Maker, horsepower, economical speed range, maximum revolutions ahead and astern (with corresponding speeds), drills for connecting and disconnecting shafts (if appropriate) and blowing soot, work-up rates and special limitations.

(w) *Man Overboard*
   Diagram to show shiphandling action for various directions of relative wind.

(x) *Bridge*
   Large scale diagram of layout with explanatory notes.

This book may be required for examination by a Court Martial in the case of loss, stranding or hazarding of a ship. It is to be produced at inspections and transferred to successive Navigating Officers; and, on paying off, it is to be handed to the Superintendent of the Dockyard for safe keeping until the ship recommissions.

Bridge Plotting Forms (S.376)

These forms are supplied in pads. Each form consists of a skeleton spider's-web of 10-inch diameter (same as Type 978 P.P.I.) suitable for plotting the positions of ships in company.

Report of Grounding or Collision (S.232)[1]

Reports on Form S.232 are to be rendered after all collisions and groundings. Whether or not legal claims or proceedings are anticipated, they are to be rendered as follows:

---

[1] *See also Queen's Regulations and Admiralty Instructions.*

Original to be completed and forwarded by the Commanding Officer to:

Treasury Solicitor, 35 Old Queen Street, London, S.W.1.

Copy to be forwarded to:

Administrative Authority for transmission through Commander-in-Chief to Admiralty.

In the case of grounding:

A copy of the relevant portion of the chart is also required. The spot, as fixed by angles, should be marked on the chart, and a tracing made.

The tracing should contain as much of the adjacent coastline as will enable it to be laid accurately over the chart affected. In addition, the true meridian line and the details necessary to describe a particular copy of a chart (*see* page 35) should be marked on the tracing. Tracing paper is supplied in the small envelope H.137. The tracing should be forwarded with the report.

REPORT TO THE COURT BY NAVIGATING OFFICERS (S.1555)[1]

In the event of a Court Martial arising from loss, stranding or hazarding of a ship, the Court will direct one or more navigating or other competent officers of ships present to work up the ship's position and render a report on this form.

RADIO NAVIGATIONAL AIDS REPORT FORM (H.434)

This form, supplied with the navigational publications, is used for forwarding reports, as ordered, on the performance of the various radio navigational aids fitted in the ship.

TABLE OF MASTHEAD HEIGHTS

This confidential book contains various dimensions of British and Commonwealth warships. It should normally be retained by the Navigating Officer, so that it may be readily accessible at sea.

MANUAL OF SEAMANSHIP, VOLS. I, II, III AND MANUAL OF NAVIGATION, VOL. IV

The Navigating Officer should make himself thoroughly acquainted with these books, which contain remarks on the behaviour of ships under various conditions, the effects of rudders and propellers, the gaining and losing of speed, entering and leaving harbour, steering arrangements, etc.

REPLENISHMENT AT SEA (ATP 16)

This book serves as a general guide in all matters relating to replenishment of ships at sea. It describes various methods, together with the type of gear involved, and also includes remarks on manoeuvring and handling ships during such evolutions.

HYDROGRAPHIC REPORTS BY NAVIGATING OFFICERS[1]

Forms

The particulars of all information obtained which may affect charts and other navigational publications are to be forwarded to the Hydrographer on a Hydrographic Note (H.102). A duplicate of this, together with a copy of any tracings,

---

[1] *See* also *Queen's Regulations and Admiralty Instructions.*

etc., should be sent to the Commander-in-Chief of the Station. A preliminary report of urgent information is also to be made by signal to the Admiralty and to the Commander-in-Chief of the Station.

In each ship the Hydrographic Notes forwarded should be numbered consecutively, starting on the 1st January each year. A modified version of this form is used by the Mercantile Marine and other non-naval authorities.

General Remarks

Every opportunity should be taken to obtain information which may be of value to the Hydrographic Department for the correction of charts and other publications.

Ships can also be of great assistance in planning re-surveys by reporting on the adequacy or otherwise of existing charts and plans and the need for resurveys or new surveys in the light of new development and possible future strategy. The man on the spot is often in a better position to judge these matters than the Hydrographer. In this connection the views and requirements of harbour authorities and pilots are of great assistance. A short letter giving the reasons for survey or re-survey or for the proposed withdrawal of an obsolete chart or plan, the authority and if possible a priority 1, 2 or 3, bearing in mind that each harbour authority considers his own area of paramount importance, is all that is required.

The Captain of a ship employed on special service, such as an experimental cruise, or on a visit to an unfrequented place, is to forward a hydrographic report with his Report of Proceedings. This should contain all matters which may be of interest to the Hydrographer and which have not been included in a report on Form H.102. A copy is to be sent direct to the Hydrographer.

Officers rendering Hydrographic Notes should be guided by the instructions contained in Form H.102 and by the relevant articles in *Q.R. and A.I.* In addition, the following points should be noted:

(a) The Admiralty charts and navigational publications should be compared constantly with the conditions found actually to exist.

(b) Information, to be of value, must be as precise and up-to-date as possible. However, ships should not hesitate to forward information unavoidably obtained by a lower degree of accuracy, provided that full details of the method by which it has been obtained is given. The date of the information should invariably be given.

(c) The amount of useful information which can be supplied will generally be greatest when ships visit unfrequented places. Confirmation of matter already appearing in the *Sailing Directions* is very acceptable.

(d) The volume and page of the *Sailing Directions* affected must always be given, not only when some correction is made to a passage in the book, but also when information is entirely new and cannot be placed under any heading appearing on the relevant page.

(e) The number of the largest-scale chart affected should always be quoted. When any chart is specifically mentioned in the report, the date of the last new edition or Large correction is to be stated, together with the date or number of the last Small correction, as shown on the copy used.

(f) True courses and bearings are invariably to be given, measured in degrees (clockwise) from 000° to 360°.

(g) When photographs, sketches, tracings, etc., are sent in, they should be included as enclosures. (*See also* SKETCHES AND PHOTOGRAPHS, page 67.)

(h) Reports should be forwarded on separate sheets and arranged so that the subject-matter proper to each of the numbered sections can be used separately.

(i) When information is supplied which leads to the correction of an Admiralty chart or plan of a place in foreign waters for which a recognized hydrographic authority exists, credit will not be given, in the title of that chart or plan, to the ship or officer supplying the information, because reference to the national authority concerned is always made before chart action is taken.

(j) Since the value of the material supplied will depend principally on the extent to which it can be used for the improvement of hydrographic publications, officers should take care that all objects quoted, when fixing positions or for other purposes of reference, are recognizable with exactness upon the chart.

(k) When dredging operations or building work – such as that on breakwaters, wharves, docks and reclamations – are described, a clear distinction should be made between work completed, work in progress, and work projected. An approximate date for the completion of unfinished or projected work is valuable.

Information not required

(a) It may be assumed that the Hydrographic Department of the Admiralty is in possession of complete sets of the latest editions of charts and *Sailing Directions* issued by foreign countries. Tracings of foreign charts, therefore, are not normally required.

(b) Information about navigational aids in foreign waters is not usually accepted without prior reference to the Hydrographic Office of the country concerned, as these offices can generally be relied upon to publish notification of all changes of any navigational interest in their own Notices to Mariners, copies of which are received by the Hydrographic Department of the Admiralty.

(c) Confirmation of published reports of irregularities in radio signals is not required.

Information for Charts and 'Sailing Directions'

NEWLY-DISCOVERED DANGERS

The position and extent of any shoal or danger discovered, especially of one upon which a vessel has struck or grounded, should be determined, if practicable, by five horizontal sextant angles between well-selected objects; and a careful true bearing to one of these objects should be given. The least depth should be obtained whenever possible and, if there is shoal water, the nature of the bottom. (*See Q.R. and A.I.*)

SOUNDINGS

When soundings are recorded, the methods of sounding are always to be stated, as well as the dates and times and the tidal reductions used.

Soundings are to be reduced to the level of the datum of the Admiralty chart; or, when this is not known, to a level the tide will seldom fall below. Details of the datum used must be given.

In order that the Hydrographer can make use of echo-traces forwarded from ships, the following points should be noted:

(a) Mark the trace each time a fix is obtained by drawing a line along the curved edge of the scale, care being taken not to foul the stylus pen.

(b) Number the fix and note the time.

(c) Insert the recorded depth of all peak soundings.

(d) On completion of sounding, and before rolling up the paper, draw in the bottom trace and transmission line, and dry the paper, preferably in a dim light. This will ensure that when the trace fades the record will remain clear.

(e) Mark conspicuously all changes of phase.

(f) Insert the make and type of Echo-sounding machine and 'Transmission correctly set at x feet'.

'Add (subtract) y feet for increased (decreased) draught'.

'Speed set to suit 4920 ft./sec. sounding velocity'.

Also, mark the graduations of the scale at convenient intervals.

(g) It is recommended that an indelible pencil or ball-pointed pen should be used for all writing on the echo-sounding trace.

For further details of the above, *see* the remarks on Echo Sounding in Chapter VII.

Note: The remark 'Discoloured water reported' occurs on a number of charts. Experience has shown that more often than not, such remarks have no permanent significance. In order that this valueless information may eventually be omitted from charts, soundings confirming or disproving the existence of a possible danger should be obtained when passing through or near these areas, the results being forwarded to the Hydrographer.

HARBOUR WORKS AND PORT INFORMATION

When reference is made to piers or wharves, the depths at the outer end and alongside are the most important items of information that can be given (although all dimensions are useful).

The length and bearing of any extension should be given in such a way that they can be plotted with as great precision as the scale of the chart permits. The position of any new lights on them should be stated exactly, and the removal or continuance of any lights charted on the pier or breakwater before extension should be mentioned.

Information in Admiralty publications on matters such as docks, cranes, patent slips, and facilities for repairs; supplies of coal, oil, water and stores; time, weather, tidal signals, and pilots, should be checked for additions or corrections.

Where dredged channels exist, the date of the last dredging and the depth obtained should be noted.

LOCAL PUBLICATIONS

Many ports, even those of secondary importance, publish a guide book compiled by the local authorities, and these books frequently contain a plan of the harbour. Opportunity should be taken, when circumstances permit, of comparing the information in such publications with that given in the *Sailing Directions* and on charts; if the publications appear to contain useful material not already provided by the Hydrographic Department, a copy should be included with the Captain's report. Care should be taken to obtain the date and authenticity of the material in the book, if these are not given. On the charts or plans in these books it is important to note whether the datum for heights and soundings, the scale and the True North are given, and then to check them; or to supply them if they are not given.

A Port Officer sometimes has a large-scale manuscript plan of the harbour and approaches, which is merely his own enlargement of the plan published by the government. The value of such a plan can, however, be judged only by comparison with the Admiralty chart.

Town plans are not generally of importance, but these should be considered or forwarded if the chart is shown by them to need amendment for water-frontage or other matter of navigational interest.

CONSPICUOUS OBJECTS

Objects which are already noted on the chart or described in the *Sailing Directions* as conspicuous should always be observed for any changes in them that may have occurred; and the growth or erection of anything that may obscure them or detract from their value as marks should be noted. In many parts of the world, charts are still based on surveys made a considerable time ago, and so it should be remembered that conspicuous objects are particularly liable to change.

Any conspicuous or radar-conspicuous objects which are not at present shown on charts, but are of navigational interest, should be described as fully as possible for shape, colour and size (as appropriate); and their exact positions should be given with reference to objects that are shown on the chart.

When tracks are described or inserted on copies of charts, their value is greatly enhanced if they are accompanied by soundings or by a note of the observed least depth, reduced to chart datum.

CHANNELS AND PASSAGES

When reports are made on a discrepancy in the charting of a channel, or a passage between islands, and when information is supplied about one shore only of a strait, or about some island in such water, every effort should be made to obtain a connection by angle or bearing between the two shores. The absence of such a connection may have been the original cause of the discrepancy reported, and may cause serious difficulty in making proper use of the information supplied.

POSITIONS

Observations for positions of little-known places are always welcomed, especially if the reporting officer has reason to question the charted position. Full details of astronomical observations should be given, in order that their value may be assessed. When practicable, the position should be linked with some existing triangulation or known position. Care should always be taken to dispel uncertainty about the existence, extent and precise position of reported dangers and doubtful islands, and to obtain the least depth where appropriate. Careful examination of such objects is of the greatest importance, both in the general interests of navigation and for the maintenance of the reputation of the Admiralty charts for accuracy and completeness of information.

Whenever a search or examination is made, the state of the weather and light should be described fully if they are likely to have had any influence on the result.

It cannot be emphasized too strongly that, in general, the only effective method of obtaining evidence about the existence of reported dangers is to take positive soundings in the vicinity and, if possible, to obtain specimens of the bottom.

ORTHOGRAPHY

In some places – e.g. certain atolls in the Pacific Ocean – it has been found that native names reported as the names of islands are in reality only the names of localities on those islands, and that each island has either a different name or no general name at all. Officers should take pains to ascertain the precise local significance of any new native names that are reported, and great care should be taken to obtain the correct rendering of native names generally.

INFORMATION CONCERNING LIGHTS

If lights are observed to have characteristics different from those described in the *List of Lights*, as amended by the latest Notices to Mariners, every endeavour should be made to ascertain locally whether the alterations are permanent.[1]

TIDAL STREAMS

Observations of tidal streams should be obtained whenever possible. If only a general description can be given, care must be taken to avoid any ambiguity that might arise from the use of the terms 'flood' and 'ebb' streams. It is generally preferable to give the direction of the stream, e.g., 'east-going' or 'west-going'. The time of the change of stream should always be referred to high water; for instance, 'the north-going stream begins two hours after high water'. When the time of local high water is not known, the turn of the stream should be referred to high water at the nearest port for which predictions are given in the *Tide Tables*.

CURRENTS

In order that full value may be obtained from information on currents, it is essential that the ship's position should be checked by observations as frequently as is practicable, because the currents experienced during the course of, for example, a period of twenty-four hours, may vary considerably both in direction and in strength. Whatever the interval between sights may have been, the results, when used by the Meteorological Office, are converted to twenty-four hour values and are plotted in a mean position between the observed positions. Should the vessel have altered course between sights, a considerable error may be introduced by assuming that this mean position lies midway between the observed positions. It is necessary, therefore, that this mean position should

---

[1] *See* also *Queen's Regulations and Admiralty Instructions.*

always be obtained by estimation for half the time that has elapsed between sights.

If the following details are available they should invariably be included:

Date.
Positions between which current was experienced.
Mean position between observations.
Time elapsed between observations.
Direction (True).
Speed (knots).
Direction and force of the wind.

INFORMATION CONCERNING MAGNETIC VARIATIONS

The accuracy of the lines of magnetic variation shown on the Admiralty charts is important, not only for the ordinary purposes of navigation, but also for the determination of the secular change of variations; and such accuracy can only be secured if a sufficient number of observations is forthcoming. Every opportunity should be taken, therefore, to obtain observations at sea for magnetic variation, especially in those localities where the variation changes appreciably with a small change of position (*see* also *Q.R. and A.I.*). The procedure is described in Chapter IX.

INFORMATION CONCERNING RADIO SERVICES

Reports should be made of any irregularities in radio signals that have not already been announced. Any other information that may be useful for the *Admiralty List of Radio Signals* should be forwarded.

If radiobeacons are observed to have characteristics differing from those given in the *Admiralty List of Radio Signals*, as amended by the latest Notice to Mariners, endeavour should be made to ascertain locally whether these alterations are permanent.

Similarly, the permanence of any changes observed in the time or type of transmission of weather bulletins and storm warnings, navigational aids, warnings or time signals, should be verified.

ZONE TIME

Information should be supplied concerning the time kept locally, if it differs from that given in the latest edition of the Time Zone Chart (No. D.6085) or in the most recently published A.L.R.S. (Vol. V), or the *Nautical Almanac*.

ORIGINAL SURVEYS

Officers who undertake any original survey which may be used either for the production of a new plan or the correction of an existing plan or chart, should refer to the *Admiralty Manual of Hydrographic Surveying* and to the *Admiralty Manual of Tides*.

SKETCHES AND PHOTOGRAPHS

Illustrations derived from sketches and photographs form a very valuable adjunct to the *Sailing Directions*, and every opportunity should be taken of adding to them. The existing views in the *Sailing Directions*, or on charts, should be examined for possible improvements – for example, the addition of a conspicuous object.

Usually, a good sketch will be of more value to the Hydrographer than a photograph.

Sketches and photographs of navigational interest may be divided broadly into three classes:

(1) General views of a coast or anchorage, showing the principal charted features. These enable the mariner, when making land or approaching the anchorage, to identify these features more readily than can be done from a written description.

(2) Views of leading marks or anchoring marks.

(3) Sketches or photographs of special objects that cannot easily be described in words.

In the case of (1), and sometimes in the case of (2) also, a photograph will have to be taken from a considerable distance, and will usually give poor results unless enlarged or taken with a telephoto lens. Even when enlarged, the photograph will usually require treatment in order to emphasize the desired conspicuous features. This can be done satisfactorily only by the man on the spot, either when he is in a similar position on a subsequent occasion, or by his referring to an outline sketch made at the time the photograph was taken. Alternatively, a photograph may be used for the purpose of improving or correcting a sketch.

If an outline sketch is made in order to supplement a photograph, the names or descriptions of the conspicuous objects shown on it can conveniently be inserted against them, and it can then be attached to the photograph. The vertical scale on outline views should be $1\frac{1}{2}$ times or twice as large as the horizontal – i.e., the heights of objects should be exaggerated somewhat; but this should be done with discretion, especially if there are any objects, such as islets, in the foreground.

When no outline sketch has been made, the names can be inserted on the photograph itself, but when this is done a second print, without names, should be attached.

Always state, in the report and on the photograph or sketch itself, the exact position from which the photograph was taken or the sketch made.

Sketches and photographs forwarded with a view to reproduction should never be gummed or pasted to the pages of a report, but should be placed in an envelope which should be attached securely to the report.

NAVIGATIONAL FORMS

NAVIGATIONAL FORMS

CONTENTS OF SMALL ENVELOPES H.137 AND H.138

One of these is supplied with the set of Navigational Publications and contains various quantities of the following:

NUMBER	TITLE	REMARKS
H.102	Hydrographic Note	*See* previous remarks.
H.38	Demand form for charts	Used for Admiralty and Fleet charts, diagrams, and meteorological working charts, but not maps or publications. Only to be completed in original.
H.177	Demand form for publications and maps	Used for navigational and meteorological publications and maps. Only to be completed in original.
H.112	Instructions relating to the supply, use and care of chronometers and watches	*See* also *Q.R. and A.I.*
H.11	Transfer and Receipt Certificate for chart folios, etc.	Supplied in books of fifty. To be completed in triplicate in accordance with instructions given on the form. Used for chart and map folios and sets of navigational publications, but not chronometers and watches.
H.394	Transfer and Receipt Certificate for chronometers and watches	*See* also *Q.R. and A.I.* Used whenever chronometers or watches are transferred or received; and also as a return rendered on paying off and on supersession, showing the chronometers and watches held and transferred.
H.488	Record of observations for variation	
—	Tracing paper	Some tracing paper is supplied for use with Hydrographic Notes, reports of groundings, etc.

OTHER FORMS USED BY THE NAVIGATING OFFICER

H.62	Chart Depot Report of Issue or Receipt of chart folios, chronometers, etc.	Issued by chart depots only. Original to be forwarded to Hydrographer. Duplicate to be returned by the ship to the chart depot. Triplicate to be retained on board.
H.80	Supply Note for charts and publications issued by the Hydrographer	Need not be retained.
H.192	Supply Note for charts and publications 'for official use only' issued by the Hydrographer	To be receipted by the ship and returned.

CHAPTER III

The Ship's Position and Track

DEFINING AND PLOTTING A POSITION

TO PLOT A POSITION DESCRIBED BY ITS LATITUDE AND LONGITUDE

When a position is described by its latitude and longitude, it may be plotted on the chart by one of the following methods:

1. Place an edge of the parallel ruler along a parallel of latitude and move the ruler until one edge passes through the latitude of the position, as indicated on one side of the chart. With the dividers, measure the distance, at the top or bottom of the chart, from the nearest meridian to the required longitude, and lay this off from the same meridian along the latitude shown by the ruler. If more convenient, the ruler can be placed to the longitude, and the latitude then be set off with the dividers.
2. Alternatively, the latitude and the longitude may be marked in pencil with the aid of the parallel ruler only.

TO FIND THE LATITUDE AND LONGITUDE OF A CHARTED POSITION

The latitude of any position is determined either by using the dividers to measure the distance of the point from the nearest parallel, or by referring it to the scale at the side of the chart by means of the parallel ruler. The longitude is found in a similar way.

TO PLOT A POSITION DESCRIBED BY REFERENCE TO ANOTHER OBJECT

A position may also be described by reference to some object.

EXAMPLE

'*245° lighthouse 3 miles.*' (*This means that the bearing of the position from the lighthouse is 245° and the distance is 3 miles.*)

In order to plot the above position, one edge of the parallel ruler should be laid across the centre of the nearest compass rose so that it cuts the 065° and 245° markings on the true rose. The ruler should then be moved until one edge passes through the position of the lighthouse. A distance of 3 miles should then be laid off from this position, making certain that it is laid off in the correct direction, i.e., 245° *from* the lighthouse.

TO TRANSFER A POSITION FROM ONE CHART TO ANOTHER

Whenever possible, a position should be transferred from one chart to another by bearing and distance from a distinguishing feature common to both, such as a point of land or a light, and not by latitude and longitude, the graduations of which may differ on the two charts owing to one having been constructed on later and more complete astronomical data than the other. (*See* also page 31.)

70

Position by Observation

The Position Line

In order that the navigator may be sure that he is following his pre-determined course it is necessary for him to ascertain his position from time to time. This he does by observing landmarks or heavenly bodies and, from his observations, obtaining what are known as 'position lines'.

A position line is any line, drawn on the chart, on which the ship's position is known to lie. It may be a straight or a curved line. The methods of obtaining a position line are described in the next chapter.

The simplest form of position line is the line of bearing obtained from a terrestrial object the position of which is known.

Suppose, for example, that a lighthouse (L in Fig. 26) is seen to bear 065° at 1030. A line drawn through L in the direction of the reciprocal bearing, 245°, is the position line.

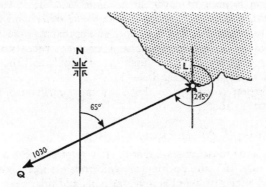

FIG. 26. The Terrestrial Position Line

Arrowheads on Position Lines

A position line obtained from a bearing of a terrestrial object, visually or by means of a navigational aid (e.g., DF bearing), is distinguished by a *single* arrow at the *outer* end.

A position line obtained from an astronomic observation or from the range of a terrestrial object is distinguished by a *single* arrow at *both* ends.

A position line that is *transferred* (*see* Chapter IV), is distinguished by a *double* arrow at *both* ends.

The Fix

If two position lines can be obtained at approximately the same moment, the position of the ship must lie at their point of intersection, which is the only point common to the two lines. A position thus obtained is called a 'fix', and it is important to remember that the term 'fix' is applied only to a position obtained by observations of *terrestrial* objects, regardless of whether the observations were made visually or by means of radio navigational aids. It is shown on the chart as a dot surrounded by a circle, with the time alongside it, thus: ⊙ 1100.

The fix is discussed further in the next chapter.

The Observed Position

It is desirable to distinguish between the position obtained by observations of terrestrial objects and that obtained by observations of heavenly bodies. For this reason, the position decided by the point of intersection of two position lines derived from astronomical observations, or derived from a number of such position lines, is known as an 'observed position' and is marked 'Obs.' It is shown on the chart as a dot surrounded by a circle, with Obs. and the time alongside it, thus: ⊙ Obs. 1100.

Position by Calculation

When it is not possible to obtain the ship's actual position by observations, a theoretical position can be worked up from the last observed position or fix.

Dead Reckoning (D.R.)

This expression is used to cover all positions that are obtained from the *course steered* by the ship and her *speed through the water*, and from no other factors. The D.R. position is therefore only an approximate position.[1] It is the position recorded by an automatic plotting machine when running on 'log'. (This machine is controlled by the ship's gyro-compass and the log, the latter giving the ship's speed through the water.)

The D.R. position is shown on the chart as a small cross with the time alongside it, thus: + 1000.

Estimated Position (E.P.)

This position is the most accurate that the navigator can obtain by calculation and estimation only. It is the position derived from the D.R. position adjusted for the estimated effects of 'wind across', currents and tidal streams; but it still remains an approximate position, because the exact influence on the ship's course and speed of these variable factors cannot usually be assessed.

The E.P. is shown on the chart as a dot surrounded by a small triangle, with the time alongside it, thus: △ 1000.

Summary of Positions on the Chart

A *Fix* is the ship's position found from reliable observations of terrestrial objects, obtained either visually or by a radio navigational aid.

The *Observed Position* is the ship's position found from reliable sights of heavenly bodies, as explained in Volume II.

The *Dead Reckoning Position* is the ship's position obtained by plotting on from the last fix, or observed position, the speed made good through the water along the course steered by compass.[2]

---

[1] The D.R. position, which is concerned with the speed made good through the water, allows for the amount that the ship's speed is reduced, or increased, by wind and sea, *but does not allow for leeway or drift.*

[2] In Air Navigation the term 'D.R. position' is normally used to describe the position obtained by calculations which include full allowance for tidal stream, current and wind, as applicable.

The *Estimated Position* is the best estimate of the ship's position worked up from the last fix, or observed position, and is found by allowing for every known factor that may have affected her movements.

TAKING COURSES FROM THE CHART

The course from one place to another on the chart is determined by placing an edge of the parallel ruler in such a position that it passes through the two places, and then moving the ruler so that one edge passes through the centre of the nearest compass rose; either a true or a magnetic course can then be obtained from the compass rose. It is a good plan to note the reciprocal reading of the compass rose, and to take a mean reading if there is any distortion.

If a magnetic course is required, allowance must be made for the change of variation, as explained in Chapter I.

Courses and bearings should always be referred to the compass rose nearest the ship's position, because on some charts the variation will differ appreciably with the position of each compass rose.

Plotting the Ship's Track

To Keep the Reckoning in Tidal Waters and To Find the Track

Plotting the ship's track from a known position is carried out in two steps.

1. By plotting the course steered and the speed made good through the water, thus arriving at the dead reckoning position.

2. By plotting on, from the dead reckoning position, the effect of:
   (i) current,
   (ii) tidal stream,
   (iii) wind and sea, other than that already considered in the speed made good through the water,

thus arriving at the estimated position.

Before describing the actual plotting on the chart, it is necessary to examine these various factors.

Currents. – Information concerning currents is given on Admiralty charts and on the special charts described in Volume II. Currents, which are permanent or seasonal movements of parts of the ocean, must not be confused with tidal streams, which are the horizontal movements of the sea caused by the periodic rise and fall of the tide.

Tidal Streams. – Information concerning tidal streams is given on Admiralty charts, in the *Sailing Directions*, in tidal stream publications, and in special tidal stream atlases. The various methods of estimating the direction and strength of the streams are described in Chapter XII.[1]

Wind. – The effect of wind will vary with every type of ship, and it is imperative that the navigator should collect as much information as possible concerning

---

[1] The direction of a current or tidal stream is always given as the direction in which the water is moving. It is said to set 150° – 2 knots, for example, and a ship that experiences such a stream for three hours will be set six miles in a direction 150°.

the effects of the force and direction[1] of the wind on the behaviour of his particular ship. Such data should be noted in the Navigational Data Book.

The wind affects a ship in two ways:

(a) The action of the wind on the hull and superstructure tends:

(1) to increase, or decrease, her speed made good through the water. This effect is allowed for in the dead reckoning, as already described.

(2) to blow the ship to leeward. This effect is frequently countered by the ship's tendency to turn up to windward. With an inexperienced or careless helmsman, the mean course steered may be 2 to 3 degrees to windward of the course ordered. If this occurs, the leeway may be more than counteracted, and it is possible that the track may be to windward of the course it is desired to steer. This 'boring to windward' is particularly noticeable in light craft running with the wind and sea on the quarter.

The effect of boring to windward can be gauged:

by noting the direction of the ship's head every 2 or 3 minutes, over a period of half an hour or more, and thus obtaining a mean course steered;

by comparing the track kept by an accurate automatic plotting instrument with the course that the helmsman has been ordered to steer.

(b) The wind causes a general drift of the surface water. This factor can be estimated only by experience and with a knowledge of the meteorological conditions which have obtained in the past forty-eight hours in the area through which the ship is steaming.

The *rate* of the surface drift approximates to 1/50 of the wind speed. The *direction* in temperate latitudes may be established by the following method. Stand with your back to the wind; then the direction of drift is 40° to your right in the Northern hemisphere, and 40° to your left in the Southern hemisphere.

Arrowheads

A single arrow is used on the course steered.
A double arrow is used on the ship's track.
A treble arrow is used on the tidal stream vector.

EXAMPLE

At 0900, the ship is known to be in latitude 57° 45′N., longitude 1° 40′W., steering a course 290° and making good a speed of 10 knots through the water. From the tidal stream atlas it is found that the tidal stream should be setting 260° at a rate of 2·5 knots. The wind is N.E., force 8. What is the ship's track?

First step: Plotting the course steered and the speed made good through the water.

---

[1] The system of naming the direction of the wind is exactly the opposite to that of naming tidal streams and currents. A northerly wind, for example, blows *from* the North, while a northerly or north-going current sets *to* the North.

In Fig. 27, the starting point A may be either a fix or an observed position; it is plotted on the chart in the manner already described.

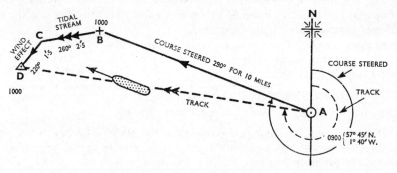

FIG. 27. Plotting the Estimated Position

Place the parallel ruler on the nearest compass rose so that its edge passes through the centre and also through 290° (the course being steered); and note, to ensure greater accuracy, that it also passes through 110° (the reciprocal of the course). Transfer this direction so as to pass through the starting point A, and draw a line of sufficient length to show the whole run; this will be the ship's course.

The log, or an estimate based on the revolution table and the effect of the wind, will give the distance steamed through the water between 0900 and 1000. In the example, the speed is given as 10 knots through the water, so measure off 10 miles from the scale of latitude corresponding to the latitude of A and lay it off from A along the course, thus obtaining the point B, which is the dead-reckoning position. Mark this point in the manner previously described.

If a magnetic compass is used, the compass course must be corrected for deviation and laid off from the magnetic compass rose, allowance being made for the alteration of variation since the year for which it is given on the chart, as explained in Chapter I.

Second step: Plotting on, from the dead-reckoning position, the effects of any current, tidal stream, or wind (other than that already considered in the estimation of speed made good through the water).

It is now necessary to consider the tidal stream, which is setting 260° at 2·5 knots, and the leeway and drift effect of the wind, which is blowing from N.E., force 8.

It is estimated, from leeway data obtained from the Navigational Data Book and from the use of the surface drift rule given on page 74, that the effect of this wind on the hull, and the effect of the surface drift of the water, will set the ship in a 220° direction at 1·5 knots.

From the 1000 D.R. position, B, lay off a line BC, 260°, 2·5 miles. This represents the amount the ship will be set by the tidal stream.

From C lay off a line CD, 220°, 1·5 miles. This represents the amount the ship will be set by the wind.

Note: The loss or gain of speed through the water caused by the wind has been allowed for in the dead reckoning, as already explained. The point D is called the 'estimated position' and is marked in the manner previously described.

At the end of one hour the ship would have reached B, if there had been no 'wind across' and no tidal stream. In point of fact she reached D. Over the ground, she therefore made good a course and speed indicated by AD, and it is important that this track should be drawn on the chart to ensure that the ship will not pass too close to any dangers.

In effect, the ship proceeds crabwise along this course made good (AD).

Until a reliable fix or observed position is obtained, the estimated position should not be discarded, even though subsequent checks, such as soundings, a single position line, or unreliable sights may cast doubts upon its accuracy.

To Shape a Course, allowing for a Tidal Stream

When the navigator knows the direction of the place he wishes to reach and the direction and strength of the current or tidal stream he will experience on passage, his problem then is to find the course to steer.

EXAMPLE

What course must a ship steer, when steaming at 12 knots, to make good a track 090° if it is estimated that the tidal stream is setting 040° at 3 knots?

Lay off the course to be made good (AB in Fig. 28). From A lay off the direction of the tidal stream, AC. Along AC mark off the distance the tidal stream runs in any convenient interval on a chosen scale. In Fig. 28 a one-hour interval has been allowed: thus, AD will be 3 miles.

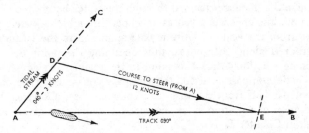

FIG. 28. To shape a course allowing for Tidal Stream

With centre D and radius equal to the distance the ship runs in the same interval (12 miles), and on the same scale, cut AB at E. Then DE is the course to steer.

This course is actually steered from A. AE is the distance made good in an 090° direction in one hour; it is marked with two arrowheads.

To reach a Position at a Definite Time, allowing for a Tidal Stream

EXAMPLE

What course must a ship steer, and at what speed must she steam, to proceed from a position A to an anchorage B in $1\frac{1}{2}$ hours, allowing for a tidal stream setting 150° at 3 knots?

Join AB, as shown in Fig. 29. This determines the course and distance to be made good in $1\frac{1}{2}$ hours: 090°, 15 miles.

From *A* lay off the direction of the tidal stream, 150°, and the set for 1½ hours, *AC* (4½ miles). Join *CB*.

Then *CB*, the course to steer, is 073°, and the distance the ship must steam in 1½ hours is 13'·4. The speed of the ship, therefore, should be 8·9 knots.

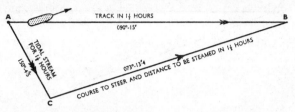

FIG. 29. To reach a position at a definite time, allowing for Tidal Stream

TO CLEAR A POINT BY A GIVEN DISTANCE AND TO FIND THE TIME WHEN AN OBJECT WILL BE ABEAM, ALLOWING FOR A TIDAL STREAM

EXAMPLE

A ship at A, shown in Fig. 30, steers so as to clear a lighthouse L by 5 miles, allowing for a tidal stream setting 140°. When will the lighthouse L be abeam?

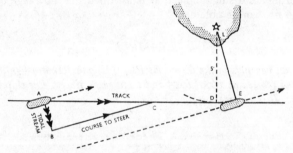

FIG. 30. To clear a point by a given distance

From *L* draw the arc of a circle, radius 5'. From the ship's present position draw a tangent to the arc. This is the course to be made good.

Find the course to steer, *BC*, by the method explained above. The light is abeam when it bears 90° from the course steered; that is to say, when the ship is at *E*, and not when she is in position *D* (the point at which she passes closest to the lighthouse). The time elapsed will be the time taken to cover the distance *AE* at a speed represented by *AC*, the speed made good.

TO FIND THE DIRECTION AND THE RATE OF THE TIDAL STREAM EXPERIENCED BETWEEN TWO FIXES

EXAMPLE

A ship is at A at 0100, as shown in Fig. 31, and steering 110° at 10 knots. At 0300 she fixes herself at B. What is the direction and rate of the tidal stream from 0100 to 0300?

Plot the ship's course 110° for a distance of 20′ from A. The difference between this dead reckoning position, C, and the observed position, B, at 0300 then gives the direction of the tidal stream CB (025°) and the distance it has displaced

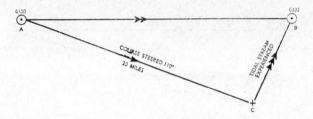

FIG. 31. To find the direction and rate of the Tidal Stream

the ship in 2 hours (7 miles). From these data the rate can be calculated. The tidal stream was setting 025° at 3·5 knots.

To Find the Course Made Good, using Three Bearings of an Object

If it has been impossible to obtain a fix and there is an unknown stream, the course which the ship is making good (but not the actual track) can be obtained by three bearings of a single object. It is assumed that no range of the object, and hence no fix, can be obtained.

EXAMPLE

In Fig. 32, bearings in the directions PL, QL, and RL of a lighthouse L are obtained and plotted at 1000, 1015 and 1040 respectively. The ship is steaming at 10 knots. It is required to find the course made good.

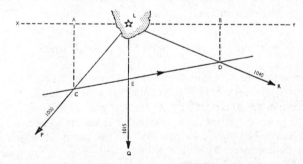

FIG. 32. To find the track, using three bearings of the same object

Through L draw XY in any direction and insert A and B on XY so that AL and LB represent the distances run at 10 knots in 15 and 25 minutes respectively – i.e., so that they are proportional to the time intervals between the bearings. Draw AC and BD parallel to the centre position line LQ. Join CD, which will then be parallel to the course made good (though not the actual track). (For the mathematical proof of this construction, *see* Volume III.)

This problem may also be solved by using a 'Douglas protractor'. If taut-wire measuring gear is available for measuring the distance run over the ground, the actual track can be determined. (Both these methods are described in Chapter VII.)

To Keep the Dead Reckoning or Plot during Manoeuvres (*for occasions when an automatic plot is not available*)

When the fleet is manoeuvring, alterations of course are frequently so numerous, and the distance run on each course so short, that the curves described by the ship while making the various turns form a large proportion of the plot, and it is therefore essential that allowances should be made for the turning circle and the loss of speed while turning, if the reckoning is to be accurate.

At any time during manoeuvres it may be necessary for the ship to shape a course for a particular position, and so it is essential that the reckoning should be kept in such a way that her position at any moment may be plotted on the chart with the least possible delay.[1]

Allowing for the Turning Circle

Before the various methods of allowing for the turning circle are considered, it is necessary to define the terms which will be used.

In Fig. 33, a ship steaming 000° puts the wheel over at the point A to alter course to 110°, and is steady on the new course 110° at point B.

The *Intermediate Course and Distance* are represented by the angle and distance from the position of the compass platform when the wheel was put over to the position when the ship is steady on her new course.

Angle CAB = the intermediate course

AB = the intermediate distance

The *Distance to New Course* is the distance from the position of the compass platform when the wheel was put over to the point of intersection of the new and original courses.

AC = the distance to new course

The *Advance* is the distance that the compass platform of a ship has advanced in the direction of the original course on completion of a turn. It is measured from the point where the wheel was put over.

AD = the advance

The *Transfer* is the distance that the compass platform of a ship is transferred in a direction at right angles to the original course.

DB = the transfer

---

[1] When ships form part of a squadron within easy visual touch of the flagship, **and** are unlikely to be detached during the manoeuvres it is advisable that they should also plot the flagship's track, for the following reasons:

   (a) The flagship's less frequent alterations of course and steadier speeds reduce the chance of errors.

   (b) The times recorded in the signal log give a valuable check on the times taken for the plot.

   (c) If the ship is detached unexpectedly, a range and bearing of the flagship will **at** once give the ship's position.

   (d) The alterations of course can often be plotted before it is necessary for the Navigating Officer to devote his attention solely to the handling of his own ship.

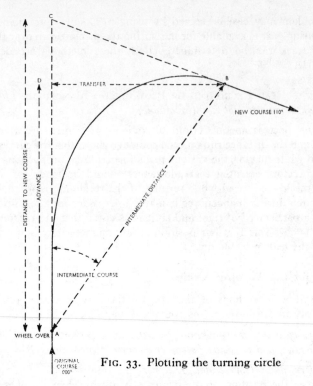

FIG. 33. Plotting the turning circle

In Fig. 34, a ship steering 000° alters course to starboard and turns through 360°. The wheel is put over at the point A: the ship has turned 180° on reaching point B, and 360° on reaching point C.

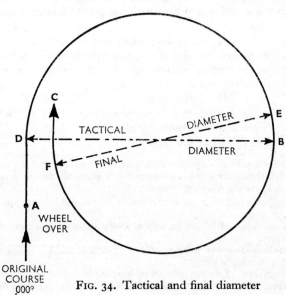

FIG. 34. Tactical and final diameter

The perpendicular distance between the ship's original course and her position when she has turned 180°, is called the *Tactical Diameter*.

$$BD = \text{the tactical diameter}$$

The *Final Diameter* is the diameter of the approximately circular path which a ship describes if the wheel is kept over.

$$EF = \text{the approximate final diameter}$$

The *length of the Arc* is the distance from point to point along the path actually described by the ship when turning.

All the above data for a ship can be obtained from turning trials.

METHODS OF KEEPING THE ACCURATE DEAD RECKONING ON A LARGE SCALE

There are various methods of allowing for the turning circle, other than the use of Automatic Plotting Tables:

1. Intermediate course and distance.
2. Distance to new course.
3. Drawing the turning circle with compasses.
4. Mid-time of turn.
5. Advance and transfer.
6. Using a protractor cut to represent the turning circle.

1. *Intermediate Course and Distance*

In Fig. 35, a ship is steering a course 000°. If the wheel is put over to alter course to 120° when in position *A* (at 0900), she will follow the curve *ADB* and will be steady on her new course, 120°, at the point *B*.

With data obtained from the turning trials, the point *B* can be plotted and the time taken to travel from *A* to *B* along the arc can be found.

During the turn from *A* to *B*, the ship will lose speed, so that when steady on the new course she will be moving at less than her original speed. It will not be correct, therefore, to continue plotting from the point *B*, unless some allowance is made for this loss of speed.

As an example, in the case of a cruiser the additional distance which must be travelled at the original speed to regain each knot of speed lost can be taken as 70 yards.

Suppose that a cruiser (in Fig. 35) with an original speed of 15 knots, loses 3 knots on the turn. She will then be moving at 12 knots when she steadies on the new course at *B*, and will have to regain 3 knots. This can be allowed for by making her cover an additional 3 × 70 (= 210) yards, at 15 knots; i.e., she may be plotted on *at 15 knots* from a position *210 yards 300° from B*. Her position on the plot will then be correct when she has regained her speed of 15 knots.

To obviate the additional plotting, a 'time correction' is provided which takes this additional distance into consideration. It consists of the time taken to turn plus the time taken to cover the additional distance at the original speed, and should be added to the time of 'wheel over' to give a time of arrival at *B* which will enable the ship to be plotted on from *B* at her original speed.

All subsequent positions can now be laid off along the new course and worked from the point *B*, the time interval being calculated from the corrected time.

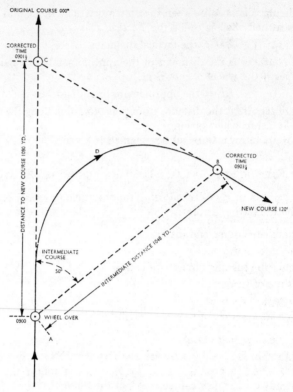

FIG. 35. Two methods of plotting a turn

From the results of turning trials of any ship, tables can be constructed to give the intermediate course and distance and time correction for any alteration of course, for different speeds and for different rudder angles.

The following is an example of such a table, constructed for a cruiser steaming at 15 knots, using 20° of rudder.

AMOUNT OF ALTERATION	INTERMEDIATE COURSE	INTERMEDIATE DISTANCE		TIME CORRECTION	
degrees	degrees	yards	miles	m.	s.
20	4·5	333	0·164	0	42
40	12·0	528	0·261	1	12
60	20·0	682	0·337	1	41
80	30 0	830	0·410	2	12
100	40 0	952	0·470	2	42
120	50·0	1,048	0·517	3	12
140	60·5	1,108	0·547	3	41
160	71·0	1,125	0·555	4	09
180	81·0	1,121	0·553	4	38

If this table is used, the point B in Fig. 35 is plotted 050°, 1,048 yards from A, and the corrected time of arrival at B is 0903¼ (odd seconds being ignored).

2. *Distance to New Course*

If this method is used for the turn shown in Fig. 35, the ship is plotting on her new course from the point C, where the new course laid back cuts the original course produced, although in fact she puts her wheel over at A, as before, and steadies on the new course at B.

If the time taken to travel the distance CB at the original speed is subtracted from the time correction previously described, then the time of arrival at the imaginary point C is obtained. This calculation is incorporated in another time correction, which again is added to the time of 'wheel over', so that the ship in this case may be plotted on from C at her original speed, although it is clear that the ship does not in fact pass through the point C at all.

The following is an example of a 'distance to new course' table constructed for a cruiser, speed 15 knots, using 20° of rudder.

ALTERATION OF COURSE	DISTANCE TO NEW COURSE		TIME CORRECTION	
degrees	yards	miles	m.	s.
20	244	0·12	0	31
40	377	0·186	0	52
60	480	0·237	1	08
80	618	0·305	1	21
100	800	0·395	1	29
120	1,090	0·538	1	25
140	1,616	0·797	0	51

If this table is used, the point C in Fig. 35 is plotted 1,090 yards along the original course 000°, and the time of arrival at this imaginary point is 0901½ (odd seconds being ignored).

This method has:

(a) the advantage of dispensing with the necessity to lay off an intermediate course. It involves only two simple corrections:

   (i) a distance to be plotted along the original course,

  (ii) a time correction to be added to the time of 'wheel over' in order to obtain the corrected time at the point C;

(b) the disadvantage that it cannot be used for alterations of course over 150° or so, because beyond this point the distance to new course becomes excessive.

3. *Drawing the Turning Circle with Compasses*

This method, shown in Fig. 36, is not as accurate as other methods, but may be used as an approximation.

Set the compass to half the tactical diameter; and, choosing by eye the point D, a little in advance of the point A where the wheel was put over, describe a circle with centre D. Draw the new course BC as a tangent to this circle, and write the actual time the ship steadied on this course against the point B.

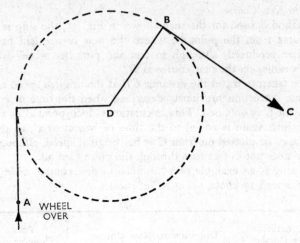

FIG. 36

4. *Plotting the Mid-time of the Turn*

Note the mid-time of the turn and plot the ship along the original course until this time. Plot the new course from this point.

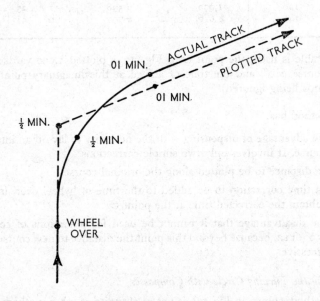

FIG. 37

This method, shown in Fig. 37, gives a close approximation, and the loss of speed is partly allowed for; but it should not be used when great accuracy is required.

5. *Plotting the Advance and Transfer*

This method of plotting can be seen in Fig. 33, the figures being obtained from the report of turning trials. The time of arrival at *B* is the time of 'wheel over' plus the same time correction as for Intermediate Course and Distance.

6. *Using a Protractor Cut to represent the Turning Circle*

This method has the disadvantage of requiring a large number of protractors for various speeds, rudder angles, and scales of plot.

> *Note:* Allowance for wind must also be made in large turns, because a ship turns more quickly into the wind than away from it.

Correction for Change of Speed

When speed is changed on a straight course, allowance must be made for the fact that the ship takes time to gather or lose way, however quickly the engines may respond to the revolution telegraphs.

For instance, in cruisers a distance correction of about 70 yards per knot of increase or decrease must be applied to the distance run, (+) when speed is reduced and (−) when speed is increased. The actual correction for any ship is found during turning trials, and should be noted in the Navigational Data Book.

Recording the Data

Whether the dead reckoning is being kept by hand, or by means of an automatic plotting table, it is important that an accurate record of all courses and speeds should be kept in the notebook, or on a specially prepared form. The layout of this record will vary according to the methods of individual Navigating Officers, and is immaterial, provided that sufficient data are retained to enable the ship's position to be worked up again should any doubt subsequently arise.

PLOTTING CHART

If the scale of the navigational chart is not suitable for keeping an accurate dead reckoning, a plotting chart may be used. Details of plotting charts are contained in the *Hydrographic Supplies Handbook* (H.51).

SPEED AND DISTANCE SCALES

There are several methods of calculating the distance run at varying speeds during a period of time:

(a) *The Mathematical Slide Rule* (shown in Fig. 38)

Let scale *A* represent time in minutes and scale *B* the ship's speed in knots. Keep the ship's speed on scale *B* set against 60 on scale *A*.

The distance run during any time interval can then be read direct from scale *B*. In Fig. 38 the slide rule is set for a ship's speed of 12 knots.

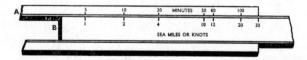

FIG. 38. Logarithmic slide rule used as a Speed and Distance scale

In order to find the ship's speed when the distance run is known, set the distance run on scale *B* against the time interval on scale *A*. The ship's speed can then be read off from scale *B* directly below the 60 on scale *A*.

(b) *The Speed/Time/Distance Slide Rule (Pattern Nos. 1435 and 1448)*

The instructions for this are given on the back of the rule, which gives direct readings for speeds up to 40 knots for periods between 15 seconds and 4 days. In addition, it provides a scale for converting departure into d.long, and vice versa.

(c) *A Speed/Time/Distance Diagram* or *Nomograph* is printed on the majority of plotting sheets; it can be used instead of the methods mentioned above.

CHAPTER IV

Fixing by Observation of Terrestrial Objects

IN CHAPTER III the methods of obtaining the ship's position by estimation were described. For the reasons given, such a position is liable to error, and it is therefore essential that the navigator should obtain the ship's position, whenever possible, by observations of terrestrial objects or heavenly bodies.

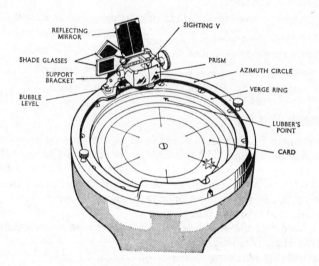

FIG. 39. Azimuth circle

Taking Bearings

The azimuth circle shown in Fig. 39 is designed so that the accurate alignment of the circle itself is not essential, and therefore a foresight is not fitted. The optical principles on which the instrument is designed are such that (provided the object is seen through the V) the correct bearing can be read, whether or not the circle itself is aligned so as to point at the object. A line is engraved on the face of the prism to facilitate the reading of the bearing. A bubble level is fitted to enable the azimuth circle to be kept horizontal while taking a bearing.

To take a bearing of an object at high altitude, the reflection of the object in the reflector should be sighted through the V sight, and the circle trained until the reflection is on the engraved line on the reflector. The bearing is then read on the engraved line on the prism. During this operation, care should be taken to keep the circle horizontal by means of the level. Instructions for checking the setting of the reflector and the prism will be found on page 316.

87

METHODS OF OBTAINING A POSITION LINE

A position line, as defined in Chapter III, can be obtained by:

1. a compass bearing of an object observed visually or by radar;
2. a relative bearing of an object observed visually or by radar;
3. a transit;
4. a horizontal sextant angle;
5. a vertical sextant angle of an object of known height;
6. a range by distance meter, when the height of the object is known;
7. a range by rangefinder;
8. a horizon range;
9. sounding;
10. an echo of the siren;
11. radio and submarine sound ranging (as described in Chapter V);
12. a radio position-fixing system (as described in Chapter VI);
13. a radar range (as described in Chapter VI);
14. taut-wire measuring gear (as described in Chapter VII);
15. an astronomical observation (as described in Volume II).

1. A Compass Bearing

When the compass bearing of an object is taken, the position line thus obtained is called a 'line of bearing'. The principle is described in Chapter III.

When a bearing of the edge of an object is taken, it is usual to distinguish the right-hand edge with the symbol >| or >|, and the left-hand edge with the symbol |< or |<. In this connection it is important to remember that a vertical edge gives the best bearing. When using an edge of land that is not vertical it must be realized that the waterline will only correspond to the charted edge of land at Mean High Water Springs.

The methods of obtaining bearings of objects by radar are described in Chapter VI.

2. A Relative Bearing

A line of bearing can also be obtained by noting the direction of an object relative to the direction of the ship's head.

If the lighthouse shown in Fig. 40 is observed to be 60° on the starboard bow (or Green 60) when the ship is steering 030°, it is clear that the true bearing of the lighthouse is 090°, and a line of bearing can be drawn on the chart.

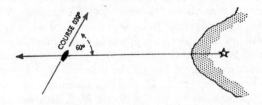

FIG. 40. Position line by Relative Bearing

3. A Transit

If an observer sees two objects in line, then he must be situated somewhere on the line (produced) which joins them, as shown in Fig. 41. This gives an excellent position line when the distance between the observer and the nearer object is not more than about three times the distance between the objects in transit.

A transit is usually shown by the symbol ϕ.

Note: If the bearing of the charted objects is taken when they are in transit, the error of the compass can be found. *See* page 98.

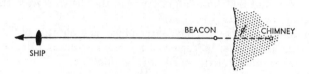

FIG. 41. Position line by Transit

4. A Horizontal Sextant Angle

Since all angles subtended by a chord in the same segment of a circle are equal, it follows that if the observer measures the horizontal sextant angle between two objects, he must lie somewhere on the arc of a circle which passes through them and which contains the angle observed.

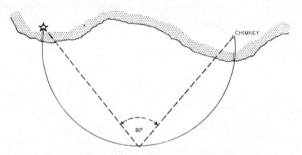

FIG. 42. Position line by Horizontal Sextant Angle

In Fig. 42, the angle between the lighthouse and the chimney has been measured by sextant and found to be 80°. A single horizontal sextant angle may be used as a 'danger angle' (*see* Chapter V).

5. A Vertical Sextant Angle of an Object of Known Height

If the angle subtended at the observer's eye by a vertical object of known height is measured, the solution of a right-angled triangle will give the observer's distance from the base of the object. The position line will then be the circumference of a circle whose radius is this distance.

The Danger Angle and Off-Shore Distance Tables ('*Lecky's Tables*') solves this triangle by using the height of the object and the corrected observed angle. The tables are divided into two parts, as described below.

PART I (*for use when the object is between the observer and the horizon*).

This covers heights up to 1,100 feet and distances up to 7·5 miles. It assumes that:

    (a) the observed angle is part of a right-angled triangle;
    (b) there is neither refraction nor curvature of the Earth;
    (c) the height of the observer's eye is zero;
    (d) the foreshore is vertically below the object.

Usually the error caused by these assumptions is negligible when the distance between the ship and the shore is greater than the distance from the shore to the point below the object.

The distance found is the distance of the object and not that of the foreshore.

The observed angle must be corrected for index error, and the height of the object must be amended for the height of the tide.

EXAMPLE

(*See Fig. 43.*) *A vertical sextant angle of a lighthouse, height 125 feet, is observed as:*

$$0° \, 25' \, 15''$$
Index error $\qquad\qquad 15'' +$

Corrected angle $\qquad 0° \, 25' \, 30''$

Part I of *Lecky's Tables*, entered with a height of 125 feet and an angle of 0° 25′ 30″, gives the distance as 2·78 miles.

The position line, therefore, is the circumference of a circle of radius 2·78 miles drawn with the lighthouse as centre.

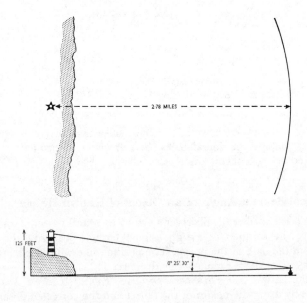

FIG. 43. Position line by Vertical Sextant Angle

PART II (*for use when the object is beyond the horizon*).

This covers heights up to 18,000 feet and distances of from 5 to 110 miles. The following corrections must be applied to the observed angle:

(a) the index error;

(b) a correction for dip, given on page 46 of the tables, which must always be subtracted from the observed angle;

(c) a correction for refraction, obtained by dividing the estimated distance in miles by twelve. The result of this division gives the refraction correction in minutes, which must be subtracted from the observed angle.

Note: If the estimated distance is found to be much in error, a second approximation will be necessary.

EXAMPLE

(*See Fig. 44.*) *A mountain 5,400 feet high is observed at a distance of approximately 24 miles. The vertical sextant angle is taken from a height of eye of 25 feet and found to be:*

	1° 57′ 20″
Index error of the sextant	40″+
	1° 58′ 00″
Dip correction	5′ 19″−
	1° 52′ 41″
Refraction correction	
$\left(\dfrac{24}{12} = 2′\right)$	2′ 00″−
True angle	1° 50′ 41″

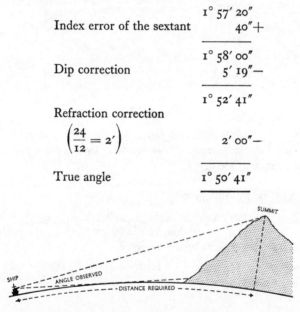

FIG. 44. Position line by Vertical Sextant Angle – object beyond horizon

Part II of *Lecky's Tables*, entered with a height of 5,400 feet and an angle of 1° 50′ 41″, gives the distance as 24·8 miles.

6. A Range by Distance Meter, when the Height of the Object is Known

This method is based on the principle of the vertical sextant angle.

There are three types of distance meter supplied to H.M. ships. They are described in Chapter VII. These instruments are useful because no calculation is involved, the range being obtained by a direct reading in every case. The position line is the circumference of a circle, the radius of which is the distance found by the instrument.

7. A Range by Rangefinder (the rangefinder is described in Chapter VII)

This method is useful for finding the distance of a single light at night, or the distance of an object unsuitable for a vertical sextant angle.

8. A Horizon Range

This method is most useful at night for finding the distance of a light when it first appears above the horizon or dips below the horizon. The distance of the ship from the horizon, and of the light beyond the horizon, can be found either from the geographical range table in the *List of Lights*, or from Table A in *Lecky's Tables*. These ranges, added together, give the distance of the ship from the light.

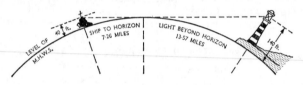

FIG. 45. Position line from Horizon Range

EXAMPLE

(*See Fig. 45.*) *A shore light 140 feet above the water is observed from the bridge to dip below the horizon. If the height of eye on the bridge is 40 feet, what is the distance of the light?*

The geographical range table gives:

Range of horizon from the light (140 feet high): 13·57 miles
  „   „   „   „   a height of eye 40 feet: 7·26 miles
∴ Distance from the light to the bridge is: 20·83 miles

If the above example is worked by Lecky's Table A, the distance is found to be 20·89 miles, because this table makes a different allowance for refraction.

Notes:
  (a) When the distance at which a light will come into view has been calculated it is also necessary to consider the intensity of the light. Information concerning this is given in the *List of Lights*.
  (b) This method of obtaining a range is useless in conditions of abnormal refraction.
  (c) As the height of a light is given above M.H.W.S. (*see* Chapter XII), the state of the tide must be taken into consideration if maximum accuracy is required.

9. Sounding

An approximate position line can sometimes be obtained from soundings. For example, it can be seen that the 100-fathom line at the south-western approaches to the English Channel is clearly marked on the chart. Thus, when a sounding of 100 fathoms is obtained in this vicinity, the ship must lie somewhere on this line.

Similarly, if a particular, well-defined fathom line is detected and identified, it will give a position line which may be used to clear some danger. A good example of this is given on page 144.

The nature of the bottom, which is found by sounding with the lead, can occasionally be used to give an approximate position line when the different formations are clearly defined on the chart. For example, in the channel leading up the River Plate, the 'Mud Wall' indicates the fairway. On one side the bottom is formed of sand and on the other side of stones.

10. An Echo of the Siren

If the echo of the siren from a cliff can be heard, it is possible to calculate the distance of the cliff and so obtain a position line. To do this, take the accurate time interval between the emission of the sound and arrival of the echo, then:

$$\text{the distance in feet of the ship from the cliff} = \frac{\text{the time interval in seconds} \times 1130}{2}$$

or, more approximately:

$$\text{distance in cables} = \text{time interval in seconds} \times \frac{9}{10}$$

THE TRANSFERRED POSITION LINE

Suppose, as shown in Fig. 46, that a lighthouse bears 034° from the ship at 1600 and that the ship is steaming 090° at 8 knots. What information is available about the ship's position at 1630?

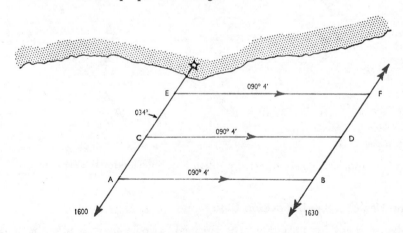

FIG. 46. The transferred position line

Draw a line *ACE* in a 214° direction from the light. This is the position line at 1600.

Suppose three lines, *AB*, *CD*, *EF*, are drawn, each in a direction 090° and each 4 miles in length (i.e., the ship's run in half an hour). Then, if the ship is at *A* at 1600, and is subsequently unaffected by wind or stream, she will be at *B* at 1630. Similarly, if the ship is at *C* or *E* at 1600, she will be at *D* or *F* at 1630.

Since *ACE* is the position line at 1600, *BDF* must be the position line at 1630. The original position line has, in fact, been transferred. The new line is known as the 'transferred position line', and will be parallel to the original position line. It is distinguished by two arrowheads at each end.

If the ship is set by wind or stream during the run, the point through which to draw the position line must be determined in two steps, as shown in Fig. 47:

1. Lay off, from any point on the original position line, the course and distance (*AB*) steamed by the ship in the interval.

2. From *B*, lay off *BK*, which is the direction and distance the ship is estimated to have been set, in the interval, by wind and stream. The position line is now transferred through *K*.

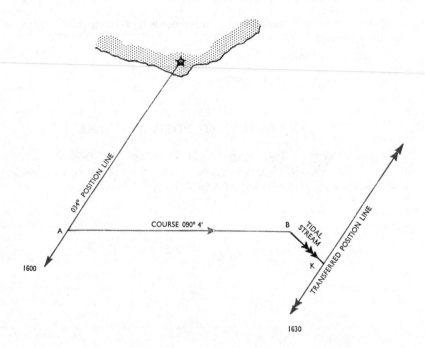

FIG. 47. The transferred position line, allowing for tidal stream

The Use of a Single Position Line

When two position lines cannot be obtained, a single one may often be of use in clearing some danger or making a harbour. For example, suppose that the course to be steered up a narrow and ill-defined harbour is 080°, as in Fig. 48.

The ship, steaming 180°, observes the time at which the lighthouse *L* bears 080°. The time taken to run the distance *AB* is calculated, allowing for wind and stream, and at the end of this time the ship alters course to 080°. It is clear that no matter where the ship was on the original position line *AL*, she will turn on to the transferred position line, *BK*, which will lead her into harbour.

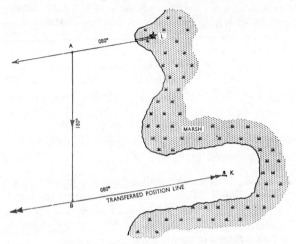

Fig. 48. The use of a single position line

FIXING THE SHIP

A fix is the position obtained by the intersection, at a suitable angle, of two or more position lines from terrestrial objects. Unless the position lines are obtained at practically the same time, one or more of them must be transferred, as described later.

The necessary combination of position lines to give a fix may be obtained from the following sources:

1. cross bearings;
2. a bearing and an angle;
3. a bearing and a distance;
4. a bearing and a sounding;
5. a bearing and a horizontal angle, from which a distance can be calculated;
6. a transit and an angle;
7. horizontal sextant angles;
8. two bearings of a single object, with a time interval between observations;
9. a line of soundings;
10. two or more ranges;
11. radio navigational aids (as described in Chapter VI);
12. bearings of a single object and a simultaneous taut-wire run (as described in Chapter VII).

Before these methods are dealt with in detail the following points should be noted and borne in mind:

Before Fixing. The navigator should identify all the objects he is going to use, and also make sure that they are marked on the chart. It is no use taking the bearing of one conspicuous object and then having to look about to select the others.

When taking cross bearings, the names of the objects should first be written down in the notebook. The bearings should then be observed as quickly as possible, care being taken that the object whose bearing is changing most rapidly is the last object to be observed. When anchoring, however, it is advisable to observe the most rapidly changing bearing first, as soon as the anchor touches the bottom. The reason for this is that the position required is that of the anchor.

The bearings should be written against the *names of the objects* in the notebook, and also the time of the fix. The time noted should be that at which the last bearing was observed, except when anchoring, when it should be that of the first one. The *time*, to the nearest minute, should also be written against all fixes on the chart.

Unless the bearings are taken almost simultaneously, it is impossible to obtain a satisfactory cut, especially if the first bearing is changing rapidly. The most favourable circumstances are when the first object is observed nearly ahead and the second nearly abeam.

To avoid phonetic errors, it is recommended that the person observing the bearings should also note them in the book and plot them on the chart.

When using a *magnetic compass*, remember that the deviation which must be used to correct the bearings is the deviation *for the direction of the ship's head when the observations were taken.*

Accuracy and rapidity in fixing are only obtained by practice, and it is essential that the navigator should make himself proficient in this art early in his career, for on occasions it may be essential to observe and plot three-bearing fixes at the rate of about one every minute.

CHOOSING OBJECTS

When a ship's position is fixed by three bearings, the objects chosen should, if possible, be so placed that their bearings differ by about 60°. The position lines will then make a good cut.

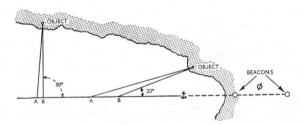

FIG. 49. Effect of a 5 degrees compass error at various angles of cut

When it is only possible to fix by two bearings, the objects selected should be such that the resultant position lines cross nearly at right angles, because the effect of any small errors in taking the observations and laying them off on the chart is least when the angle of cut is 90°, and gradually increases as the angle of cut decreases.

A cut of less than 30° should not be accepted as a reliable fix. Fig. 49 shows the difference in position caused by an error of 5° with a 90° cut and with a 20° cut, *A* being the correct and *B* the incorrect position. (*See also* Volume III.)

Always choose objects near the ship in preference to objects far away because:

(a) any error in the bearing of a nearby object has less effect on the accuracy of the final position than a similar error in the bearing of an object far away;

(b) long lines of bearing drawn on a chart are not so accurate as short lines on account of distortion.

When fixing by three bearings, the objects selected should not be so placed that the ship is on the circumference of the circle passing through them, for in such a case the three lines of bearing will always meet at a point, even when there is a large unknown compass error. This is clearly shown in Fig. 53.

If the ship is in a channel where it is possible that the two sides were surveyed separately, all the objects used in fixing her position should be on the same side of the channel.

1. Fixing by Cross Bearings

When lines of bearing are obtained from two different objects at the same time, the ship must be on both lines simultaneously. Therefore, if the lines of bearing cut at a suitable angle, her position lies at the point of intersection.

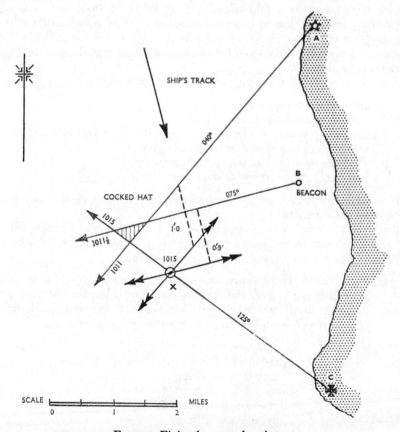

FIG. 50. Fixing by cross bearings

For example, in Fig. 50, assuming that the lighthouse bore 040° and simultaneously the church bore 125°, then if these two lines are drawn on the chart, their point of intersection must have been the ship's position at that time.

To avoid error, a third bearing (called a 'check bearing') should always be taken. This bearing should pass through, or close to, the point of intersection of the other two bearings. In Fig. 50 a check bearing of the beacon was 075°.

THE COCKED HAT

When three bearings are taken from a moving ship, the resulting position lines will not, as a rule, meet in a point; they will form a triangle, such as is shown shaded in Fig. 50. This triangle is known as a 'cocked hat'.

Since a position line indicates a line on which the ship lies at any one moment, the intersection of two or more such lines obtained at different times will obviously not show the correct position at either time. It is therefore necessary to transfer all but the last position line by amounts equal to the course and distance made good in the intervals from the last observation. The point where these transferred position lines then cut the other one is the position of the ship at the time of obtaining the last position line.

In Fig. 50, if it is assumed that the bearings of the lighthouse, beacon and church were taken, by a ship steaming at 15 knots, at 1011, 1012 and 1015 respectively, then the line of bearing through A must be transferred 1 mile in the direction of the ship's track; and that through B, 0·8 mile. When these adjustments are made the cocked hat disappears almost entirely, and the ship's position is fixed at X at 1015.

The causes of a cocked hat may be any of the following:

    (a) error in identifying the object,
    (b) error in plotting the lines of bearing,
    (c) inaccuracy of observation resulting from the limitations of the compass,
    (d) compass error unknown or incorrectly applied,
    (e) excessive time interval between observations,
    (f) inaccuracy of the survey or the chart.

If the cocked hat is large, the work should be revised to ensure that errors (a) and (b) are eliminated.

Error (c) should never be greater than $\frac{1}{4}$° and may generally be neglected.

Error (d) should be eliminated by taking every opportunity of checking the deviation or gyro error by any of the following methods:

    (1) *By a transit.* The compass bearing of two charted objects is observed when they are in line, and the true or magnetic bearing obtained from the chart; the difference between them will be the gyro error or deviation of the gyro or magnetic compass respectively. For example:

$$
\begin{array}{ll}
\text{charted true bearing:} & 079° \\
\text{gyro compass bearing:} & 081° \\
\therefore \text{ gyro error} = 2° \text{ high; or} \\
\text{charted magnetic bearing:} & 123°\text{M.} \\
\text{magnetic compass bearing:} & 120°\text{C.} \\
\therefore \text{ deviation} = 3°\text{E.}
\end{array}
$$

    (2) *By azimuth of a heavenly body,* as explained in Volume II.

(3) *By bearing of a distant object.* The ship is fixed by horizontal angles, as described later, and a compass bearing obtained of a distant object. This can then be compared with its bearing taken from the chart.

(4) *By reciprocal bearings with another ship whose compass error is known.*

(5) *By Douglas Protractor.* (This instrument is described in Chapter VII.) The bearings of the three shore objects are drawn on to the protractor, and the ship's position plotted. Then the amount by which the zero of the protractor is directed away from the North on the chart is the error of the compass. In the case of a magnetic compass, this error will be the algebraic sum of the variation and the deviation.

Error (e) can be eliminated either by making the observations again with shorter time intervals, or by applying the requisite 'run' to each bearing and transferring the position lines, as previously described.

Error (f) can be judged as described in Chapter II.

If it seems certain that the cocked hat is due to compass error alone, and the error cannot be ascertained by any of the methods described, then the cocked hat may be reduced and the compass error found as follows:

First, it will be evident that the error must have a definite sign; and, although this may be (+) or (−), it will be the same in each plotted bearing. Therefore,

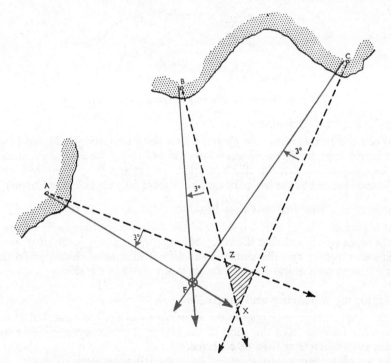

FIG. 51. Reducing the cocked hat and finding the compass error

if each position line is rotated by the same amount and in the same direction, a position can be found where they will all intersect. This position can usually be found by trial and error, in which case it will be found preferable to shift the bearing of the furthest object first, as this will have the greatest effect on the position of the fix.

In Fig. 51 the position lines have been rotated clockwise from the cocked hat XYZ to the point F, and the error has been found to be 3° low. (The theory of this is explained in Volume III, where a more accurate but slightly more complicated method is described.)

> *Note:* If the cocked hat is small, the position of the ship can usually be taken as its centre. If it is large and cannot be reduced by any of the methods described, the position of the ship should be taken as the corner of the cocked hat which will place the ship nearest to danger. This is not always the corner nearest to immediate dangers, but will depend on the ship's intended movements. It must be ensured that subsequent alterations of course for rounding marks, etc., will have a probable safety margin. For example, in Fig. 52, if the ship intends to steer as far to the northward as possible, her position should be taken as X. If, however, she intends rounding the rocks to the southward, it should be taken as Y, rather than Z, so that when she alters course she will ensure sufficient advance. As a further precaution, the course chosen from Y should be one which would also be safe had the ship really been at Z.

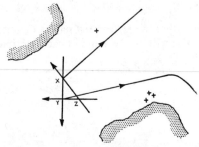

FIG. 52. Setting a safe course from a cocked-hat fix

The Hyperbolic Diamond

When two position lines are obtained by a radio navigational aid and plotted on a lattice chart, it will be evident – from a knowledge of the accuracy limitations of the equipment – that the ship's position lies not at a fixed point, but within a diamond formed by the lattice lines. This is more fully explained in Chapter VI.

Example of a Bad Fix by Cross Bearing

It is seen in Fig. 53 that the ship and the three chosen objects lie on the arc of the same circle, and that the three bearings will cut at a point whatever the unknown error is; and the chimney should not have been chosen when there was a beacon on a nearly similar bearing much closer to the ship.

2. Fixing by a Bearing and an Angle

It may happen that only one object is visible from the compass, but another object can be seen from the wing of the bridge. The sextant angle subtended by the two objects may then be observed.

To lay off a bearing and angle, either of the following methods can be used:

(a) Apply the angle to the observed bearing and thus obtain the bearing of the other object not visible from the compass. In Fig. 54, a hill bears 040° and the sextant angle to a church is 45°; hence the church bears 085°, and the fix can now be laid off by cross bearings.

(b) Through the hill draw the line of bearing 040°; from any point *A* on this line lay off an angle of 45°, on the side towards the church; lay the parallel ruler along the line *AH*, so obtained, and transfer it until one edge is on the church. The point where the edge of the ruler cuts the line of bearing from the hill is then the ship's position.

Note: It is advisable, when possible, to take a second angle as a check, and to select an object that is nearly at right angles to the line of bearing.

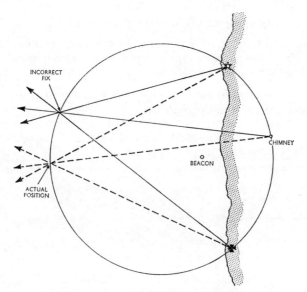

FIG. 53. Example of a bad fix by cross bearings
(unknown compass error 10° high)

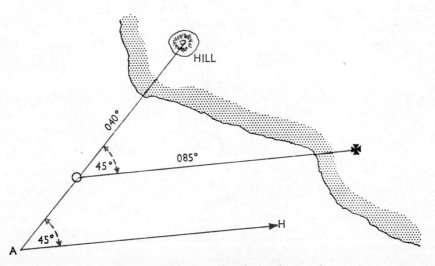

FIG. 54. Fixing by a bearing and an angle

3. Fixing by a Bearing and a Distance

When only one object is available, the ship can be fixed by a bearing and:

    (a) a range by rangefinder or distance meter (as explained on pages 91–2),
    (b) a vertical sextant angle (as explained on page 89),
    (c) a horizon range (as explained on page 92),
    (d) a radar range (as explained in Chapter VI),
    (e) a synchronised radio and sound signal (as explained in Chapter V).

4. Fixing by a Bearing and a Sounding (Fig. 55)

On approaching the land, an approximate position can be obtained, in places where the depth changes fairly rapidly, by observing a bearing and sounding at the same time. Remember that:

    (a) allowance must be made for the height of the tide before comparing the soundings with the chart;

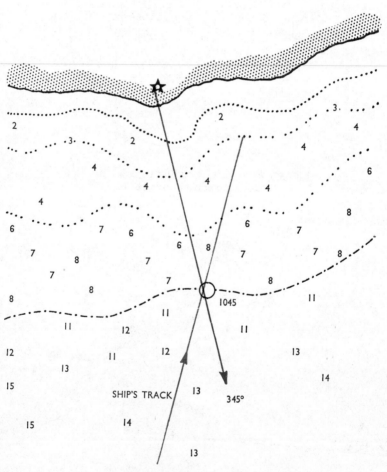

FIG. 55. Fixing by a bearing and a sounding

(b) the fix will not be reliable unless the fathom lines are very clearly defined;

(c) the fix will not be reliable unless the fathom lines are crossed as nearly as possible at right angles.

5. Fixing by a Bearing and a Horizontal Angle, from which a Distance can be Calculated

This method is most useful when the ship is passing a small island, when the compass bearings of the two extreme edges of the island would give too small an angle of cut. In such a case, the sextant angle between its edges should be observed, and the bearing of one edge. Then from the width of the island, as shown on the chart, its distance from the ship can be calculated.

EXAMPLE

The sextant angle between the extremes of an island 1·7 miles wide, as shown in Fig. 56, was found to be 7°, and at the same time the left-hand edge bore 085°.

To find the distance of the ship from the island, let R miles equal the distance. Then, since arc = radius × the angle in radians:

$$\frac{R}{1\cdot7} = \frac{360}{2\pi \times 7}$$
$$\therefore R = 14 \text{ miles (approximately).}$$

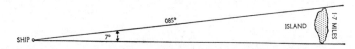

FIG. 56. Fixing by a bearing and a horizontal angle

6. Fixing by a Transit and an Angle

This is similar to a fix by a bearing and an angle, but since no compass is used, it has the advantage that any inaccuracy due to compass error is eliminated. This method is frequently used for fixing boats' positions when soundings are carried out during a survey.

7. Fixing by Horizontal Sextant Angles

This method fixes the ship's position by the intersection of two or more position lines; these are found by observing the horizontal sextant angles subtended by three or more objects. It is extremely useful for fixing the ship accurately when moored or at anchor, and for fixing the ship accurately at sea, when two trained observers are available.

The advantages of this method are:

(a) it is more accurate than a compass fix, because a sextant can be read more accurately than a compass;

(b) it is independent of compass errors;

(c) the angles can be taken from any part of the ship.

The disadvantages are:

(a) it takes longer than fixing by compass bearings;

(b) three suitable objects are essential;

(c) if the objects are incorrectly charted or incorrectly identified, the fix will be false and the error may not be apparent. For this reason, when a poorly surveyed chart is used, the ship's position should normally be fixed by compass bearings, because inaccuracies in the charted positions of objects will become apparent when simultaneous lines of bearing drawn on the chart do not meet at a point.

Theory: If A and B (Fig. 57) are two objects on shore approximately in the same horizontal plane as the observer, and the angle between them is observed, the ship must lie on the arc AOB bounding the segment which contains the observed angle. Similarly, if the angle between B and C is observed, the ship must lie on the arc COB. These arcs intersect at B and O. Therefore O must be the ship's position.

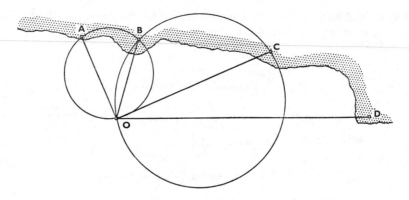

FIG. 57. Fixing by two or more horizontal sextant angles

To Plot the Fix

To do this it is not necessary to draw the circles: the three lines, OA, OB and OC may be drawn on tracing paper so that the angles at O are those observed. The paper is placed over the chart so that OA, OB and OC pass through A, B and C respectively; the position O can then be pricked through.

More convenient methods of plotting this type of fix are by Douglas Protractor or Station pointer, as described in Chapter VII.

A check angle should be taken, if possible, from the centre object to a fourth object. When a Station pointer is used, this angle can be plotted after the fix has been obtained – by holding the instrument steady and moving one of its legs to the check angle. This leg should then pass through the fourth object.

The fix shown in Fig. 57 would be written:

$$A \; 39° \; 12' \; B \quad 50° \; 47' \; C$$
$$B \quad 73° \; 49' \; D$$

CHOOSING OBJECTS

It is clear from Fig. 53 that if the lighthouse, chimney and church are on the arc of a circle passing through the ship, then she may be anywhere on the 'seaward' arc of that circle, and no fix is obtained in this case. To avoid this occurrence, the objects must be carefully chosen so that:

(a) they are either all on, or near, the same straight line, as shown in Fig. 58; or
(b) the centre object is nearer the ship than the line joining the other two, as shown in Fig. 59; or
(c) the ship is inside the triangle formed by the objects, as shown in Fig. 60.

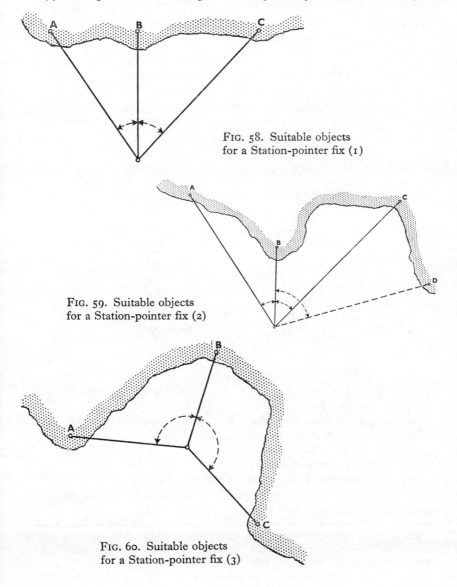

FIG. 58. Suitable objects for a Station-pointer fix (1)

FIG. 59. Suitable objects for a Station-pointer fix (2)

FIG. 60. Suitable objects for a Station-pointer fix (3)

In order to estimate the reliability of a station-pointer fix, further rules are given in Volume III; but those mentioned above are sufficient for ordinary navigational purposes.

8. Fixing by Two Bearings of a Single Object, with a Time Interval between Observations ('Running Fix')

If two position lines are obtained at different times, the position of the ship can be found by transferring the first position line to the time of taking the bearing for the second position line, as described on page 98. The point of intersection of the second position line and the transferred position line is the ship's position at the time of the second observation.

(a) To obtain a fix from two position lines obtained at different times, when the tidal stream is known.[1]

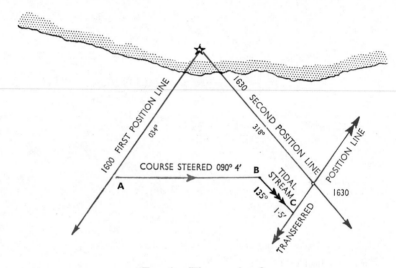

FIG. 61. The running fix

EXAMPLE

(See Fig. 61.) A ship is steering 090° at 8 knots. The tidal stream is estimated as setting 135° at 3 knots.

At 1600 a lighthouse bore 034°. At 1630 the same lighthouse bore 318°. Find the position of the ship at 1630.

A is any point on the first position line.

AB is the course and distance run by the ship in 30 minutes.

BC is the amount of tidal stream experienced in 30 minutes.

The point where the first position line, transferred and drawn through C, cuts the second position line is the ship's position at 1630.

---

[1] The accuracy of this fix will depend on the accuracy of the estimated run between bearings, and it is therefore essential to make due allowance for the wind and stream experienced by the ship during this interval.

(b) To obtain a fix from two position lines obtained at different times, when the tidal stream is unknown but a previous fix has recently been obtained.[1]

EXAMPLE

(See Fig. 62.) At 1700 a ship was fixed at A, and was steering 180°. At 1800 observed bearing of R was 090°. At 1836 observed bearing of R was 057°. Required the fix at 1836 and the stream experienced from 1700 to 1836.

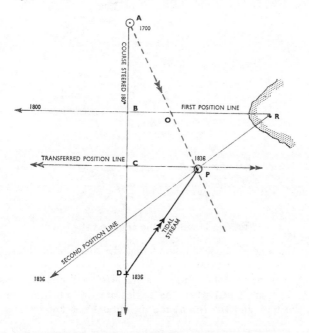

FIG. 62. The running fix with unknown tidal stream

Draw AE, the course steered, cutting the first position line in B. On the line AE insert C, such that BC is 36 minutes run at the speed given by AB. Transfer the first position line through C. The point P, where this cuts the second position line, is then the fix at 1836. AP is the course and distance made good between 1700 and 1836.

To obtain the tidal stream, plot D, the D.R. at 1836, along AE at the speed of the ship through the water. Join this to P, then DP is the direction and set of the stream between 1700 and 1836.

Proof: Since the triangles ABO and ACP are similar, AO/OP = AB/BC. AO and OP represent the speeds made good in 1 hour and 36 minutes respectively. The line AE could have been drawn in any direction which cuts the two position lines and, provided the proportion AB : BC remained the same, the transferred position line would always cut the second one at P. The tidal stream cannot, however, be found unless AE is plotted as described above.

---

[1] This method should only be used over a period, or in an area, in which it is certain that the strength and direction of the stream remain constant. Otherwise the fix will be inaccurate.

(c) *Doubling the Angle on the Bow* is a special form of running fix, which can
be plotted either in the way described in (a) above, or by a quicker method
resulting from the relation between the angles.

Suppose that the angle between the ship's head and the bearing of the light,
shown in Fig. 63, is measured as α° and the time noted. If the time is again

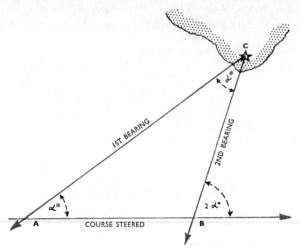

FIG. 63. Doubling the angle on the bow

noted when the angle is 2α°, it follows that the distance of the ship from the
object at the second observation is equal to the distance run by the ship during
the time between the two observations, since *ABC* will be an isosceles triangle.

If the bearings are taken when the angles are 45° and 90° from the ship's
course (on the bow and the beam) the fix obtained is known as a 'four-point
bearing'.

Doubling the angle on the bow cannot be used, in its simple form, if there
is any wind or stream across the course, i.e., if the track is not the course steered.
In this case, the observations must be plotted as a running fix.

A similar method, which gives the distance a ship will pass abeam of an object,

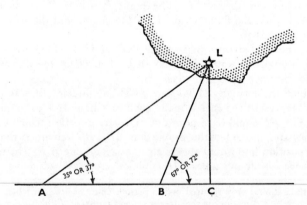

FIG. 64. To estimate the distance at which a ship will pass abeam of an object

is illustrated by the following example:

Take the time when the angle on the bow is 35° and again when it is 67°[1]; the distance run over the ground in the interval will be approximately the distance the ship will pass abeam of the object.

In Fig. 64, $AB = LC$, but only if the track is the same as the course steered.

9. Fixing by a Line of Soundings

When there are no objects suitable for observation, it is sometimes possible to obtain a fix by sounding. Although this method does not strictly conform to the definition of a fix, as previously given, in that it does not involve the intersection of two or more position lines, a positive indication of the ship's position can be obtained as follows:

Sound at regular intervals, noting the depth. The soundings must be corrected for the height of the tide. On a piece of tracing paper draw one or more meridians. Lay off the ship's track. Along this track plot the reduced soundings, on the scale of the chart in use. Place the tracing paper on the chart in the vicinity of the ship's estimated position, and, using the meridians as a guide in keeping it straight, move it about until the soundings on the tracing paper coincide with those on the chart.

The frequency at which soundings should be taken depends on the speed of the ship and the spacing and nature of the soundings on the chart.

Caution. – The approximate position found from a line of soundings should always be used with caution, because it is often possible to fit a line of soundings in several positions on a chart.

10. Fixing by Two or More Ranges

It may happen that ranges (but not bearings) can be obtained from two or more objects. If so, then the intersection of the range arcs will fix the ship's position. This method is used mostly when fixing by radar, as explained in Chapter VI, because radar ranges are generally more accurate than radar bearings.

Fixing Uncharted Objects and 'Shooting Up'

It sometimes happens, when coasting, that a conspicuous object is visible from the ship, but—although suitable for use when fixing—it is not shown on the chart. The position of such an object may be determined by:

(a) observing its bearing when it is in transit with other charted objects. Two or more such bearings drawn through the charted objects will then fix its position;

(b) obtaining a fix from charted objects, and simultaneously observing the bearing of the uncharted object. Two or more such bearings drawn from the positions of the fixes will then fix the position of the uncharted object.

It may happen that an object suitable for fixing is not clearly identifiable on the chart. One tall chimney, for instance, may be situated in a group of other chimneys all similarly marked on the chart. The one required may be identified by either of the two methods described above. This is called 'shooting up'.

Objects afloat may also be similarly 'shot up', as described in Chapter V.

---

[1]Angles of 37° and 72° give the same result.

CHAPTER V

Navigation in Pilotage Waters

AIDS TO PILOTAGE

Responsibility

The responsibility for lights, beacons, buoys, and the marking and removal of wrecks is shared by the various authorities listed below for the areas given, together with their adjacent seas and islands.

AREA	AUTHORITY
England Wales Channel Islands Gibraltar	*Trinity House*
Scotland Orkneys Shetland Islands Isle of Man	*Northern Lighthouse Board*
Northern Ireland and the Irish Republic	*Commissioners of Irish Lights*

Lights

DETAILS OF LIGHTS

These are given:

(a) On Admiralty charts, where they are distinguished by a magenta flare. Their abridged descriptions are printed in accordance with the rules given in Chapter II.

(b) In the *List of Lights* where additional information, not given on the charts, is included – e.g., details of the structure and the intensity of the light. The *List of Lights* is fully described in Chapter II.

(c) In the *Sailing Directions*, where only the height and description of the structure are given.

TABLE OF LIGHTS

ABBREVIATION	LIGHT	CHARACTERISTIC PHASES
F.	Fixed	A continuous steady light.
Fl.	Flashing	(a) Showing a single flash at regular intervals, the duration of light being always less than that of darkness. (b) A steady light with, at regular intervals, a total eclipse, the duration of light being always less than that of darkness.

TABLE OF LIGHTS—*continued*

Abbreviation	Light	Characteristic Phases
Gp. Fl.	Group flashing	Showing at regular intervals a group of flashes. These may be groups of equal flashes, e.g. Gp. Fl. (2); or groups of flashes unequally spaced, e.g. Gp. Fl. (1 + 2); or groups of one or two letters of the Morse code, e.g. Gp. Fl. (B) or Gp. Fl. (PM).
Occ.	Occulting	A steady light with, at regular intervals, a sudden and total eclipse; the duration of darkness being always less than, or equal to, that of light.
Gp. Occ.	Group occulting	A steady light with, at regular intervals, a group of two or more sudden eclipses.
F. Fl.	Fixed and flashing	A fixed light varied at regular intervals by a single flash of relatively greater brilliance.
F. Gp. Fl.	Fixed and group flashing	A fixed light varied at regular intervals by a group of two or more flashes of relatively greater brilliance.
Qk. Fl.	Quick flashing	A light which flashes continuously at the rate of more than 60 times a minute.
Int. Qk. Fl.	Interrupted quick flashing	A light which flashes at a rate of more than 60 times a minute with, at regular intervals, a total eclipse.
Gp. Int. Qk. Fl.	Group interrupted quick flashing	A light which shows groups of quick flashes, as defined above, separated by relatively longer periods of total eclipse.

Notes on Lights:

(a) All bearings referring to lights are given as true bearings *from seaward.*

(b) A number of lights change colour in sectors. The colours shown by such lights are given after their abridged description on the chart thus: **Fl. R.G. 6 sec.** The sectors are described in the *List of Lights* but are shown only on the larger-scale charts. Fig. 65 shows the appearance of the light given above, whose sectors are described as: 'R.055°–071° (16°), G.071°–091° (20°), R.202°–222° (20°)'. It should be clear that the colour of such lights does not change when viewed from a given position.

When altering course on the changing sectors of a light, alter on the correct compass bearing and do not rely on being able accurately to observe the change of colour, as this is often difficult to decide. Moreover variations in the atmosphere sometimes cause white lights to assume a reddish hue.

(c) Certain lights show differently-coloured flashes alternately. The description of their character is preceded by **'Alt.'** (for 'Alternating'), and followed by the colours shown, thus: **'Alt. Fl. R.G.'** Care must be taken to differentiate between such lights and those described in (b) above. Any of the lights (except fixed ones) given in the foregoing table may be preceded by 'Alt.'

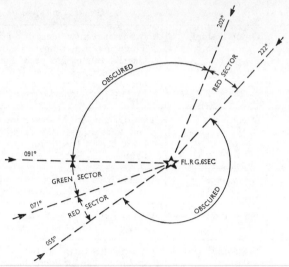

FIG. 65. Typical light sectors

(d) The geographical range given for a light – which is that for a height of eye of 15 feet in average local visibility – may be altered in practice by refraction, weather, the height of the tide and the difference between the actual height of eye and 15 feet. (The method of calculating the range of a light for own height of eye and for normal conditions, using the Geographical Range Table in the *List of Lights*, is described on page 92.)

The 'loom' of a light may often be seen at ranges considerably greater than that of its calculated range. This may sometimes appear sufficiently definite for obtaining a bearing.

(e) At short distances, flashing lights usually show a faint continuous light between flashes.

(f) Haze and distance may reduce the apparent duration of a flash.

(g) In determining the probability of sighting a light in haze, consider the intensity (*see* Luminous Visibility Table in the *List of Lights*).

(h) Lights placed very high – for example, on the Spanish coast – are often obscured by cloud.

(i) Where radar reflectors are fitted to lighthouses and light-vessels, this fact is indicated in the *Remarks* column of the *List of Lights*.

Exhibition of Lights

Lights are shown as follows:

IN CLEAR WEATHER

Lights under the jurisdiction of:

Trinity House   .   .   . ⎫
Northern Lighthouse Board   . ⎬ Sunset to Sunrise
Commissioners of Irish Lights ⎭

In Foggy or Hazy Weather

Lights under the jurisdiction of:

Trinity House . . .	May be shown during the day
Commissioners of Irish Lights	1 hour before Sunset to 1 hour after Sunrise
Northern Lighthouse Board .	According to the weather
Clyde Lighthouse Trust .	Shown during the day in fog

Fog Detector Lights

These are fitted for automatic detection of fog by day and night, additional to the main light. They sweep back and forth over a selected arc with a powerful bluish-white flash of about one second duration. On charts and in the *List of Lights* they are shown abbreviated as '& Fog Det^r. Lt.'

Air Lights

These, displayed primarily for the use of aircraft, are usually of a greater intensity than most navigational lights. They may have characteristics similar to navigational lights, or they can flash one-letter or two-letter morse groups in various colours.

Those that are likely to be visible from the sea are inserted in the *List of Lights* in geographical sequence with other lights, and their character is preceded by the word 'Air'. They should be used with caution, as any changes in the lights may not be promptly notified to the mariner. For further details *see* the *Admiralty List of Air Lights*, which is described in Chapter II.

Light-vessels

The following remarks refer to light-vessels off the coasts of the British Isles. Information concerning all light-vessels, British and foreign, is given in the *List of Lights* and the *Sailing Directions*.

(a) Light-vessels are painted red in England and Scotland, and black in Ireland. Names are painted in white letters on the sides of the vessels.

(b) The elevation given in the *List of Lights* is the distance from the waterline to the centre of the lantern.

(c) A white light is shown on the forestay, 6 feet above the rail, to show the direction in which the vessel is swung. This direction gives a useful indication, by day and night, of the direction of the tidal stream.

(d) When a light-vessel is off her proper station, the characteristic light is not shown nor is the characteristic fog signal sounded. In fog, she would sound the fog signal required for a vessel at anchor. By day, the black-painted mast-head mark should be struck. (The additional signals displayed, to indicate her state, are described in Chapter XV.)

(e) If for any reason the light-vessel is unable to show her usual characteristic light while on her station, the riding light only will be shown.

(f) If, in a fog, traffic appears likely to collide with the light-vessel, the ship's bell will be rung rapidly in the intervals between sounding the normal fog signal. If the normal fog signal is made by hand horn, the period of the signal is shortened as shipping approaches and may eventually be a continuous signal until there is no danger.

(g) 'JD' International ('You are standing into danger') may be hoisted by a light-vessel. If so, attention is called to it by the firing of a gun or rocket, repeated at short intervals until observed.

(h) Light-vessels make various distress signals, either for themselves or for other ships. Full details of these signals are given in the *List of Lights*.

(i) Light-vessels may be withdrawn for repairs without notice; and sometimes they are not replaced by relief vessels.

(j) Watch buoys are sometimes moored near light-vessels to give the latter a good indication of dragging. Such buoys are described later.

Uniform System of Buoyage Round the British Isles (Lateral System)

INFORMATION CONCERNING BUOYS (see table on page 116 *et seq.*)

(a) The best guide is the largest-scale chart of the place concerned.

(b) Details of buoys may be given in the *Sailing Directions*.

(c) Light buoys are not mentioned in the *List of Lights*.

(d) The term 'starboard hand' means that side of the channel which will be on the right hand of the navigator when he is going with the main stream or flood tide, or when entering a harbour or river from seaward.

The term 'port hand' means that side which will be on the left hand in the same circumstances.

The direction of the main flood stream round the British Isles is shown in Fig. 66.

(e) When trying to identify a buoy, the **shape** should be considered more important than the colour; but topmarks, lights or radar reflectors may give a misleading impression of shape in low visibility.

Uniform System of Buoyage (Cardinal System)

Certain countries use the Cardinal System in which the navigational marks are placed according to their bearing from the danger or channel. Details are given in the appropriate *Sailing Directions*.

Fog Signals

Information concerning fog signals is given:

(a) in full detail in the *List of Lights* or *Admiralty List of Radio Signals* (Vol. II), as appropriate;

(b) in brief detail in the *Sailing Directions*;

(c) in abbreviated form on the chart.

There are three types of fog signals:

1. Air fog signals.
2. Submarine sound signals.
3. Radiobeacons.

1. AIR FOG SIGNALS

Full details of these are given in the *List of Lights*.

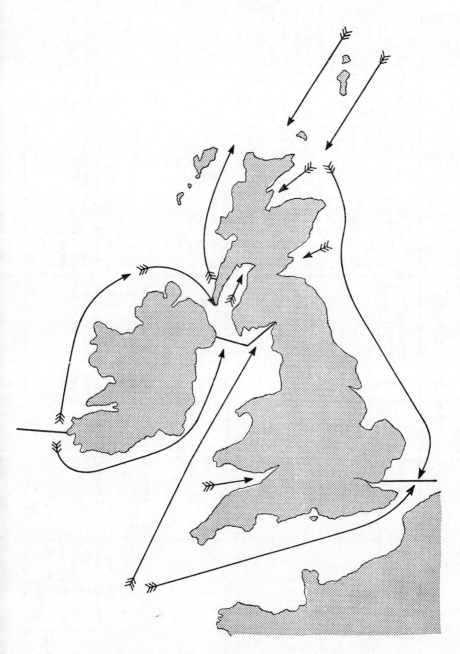

FIG. 66. The direction of the main flood stream around the British Isles

TABLE OF BUOYS

Buoy	Shape	Colour	Topmark (if any)	Light (if any)	Remarks
Starboard Hand	Conical	B. or B.W. Cheq.	Black cone, point upwards, or Black diamond (not at entrance to channel)	Fl. Gp. Fl. (3) Gp. Fl. (5)	Buoys of similar character may be distinguished, in addition to their topmark, by numbers, letters or names. If distinguished by numbers or letters, the numbering or lettering shall commence from seaward; odd numbers on the starboard hand and even numbers on the port hand.
Port Hand	Can	R. or R.W. Cheq.	Red can, or Red 'T' (not at entrance to channel)	Fl.R. Gp.Fl. (2) Gp.Fl.(2) R. Gp.Fl.(4) Gp.Fl.(4) R. Gp.Fl.(6)	—
Middle Ground	Spherical	To be left to starboard – B.W.H.S.	Outer end: black cone, point upwards. Inner end: black diamond	Lights will be distinctive and coloured red or white, the colour (white or red) and the rhythm to indicate the side on which the mark is to be passed	
		To be left to port – R.W.H.S.	Outer end: red can Inner end: red 'T'		
		To be left on either hand – R.W.H.S.	Outer end: red sphere Inner end: red St. George's Cross		
Mid-Channel	Usually Pillar, but may be any distinctive shape other than conical, can or spherical	B.W.V.S. or R.W.V.S.	Any distinctive shape, other than can, cone (point upwards) or sphere	Optional, but different from neighbouring lights at the sides of the channel	Marks the centre of the fairway. May be passed on either hand, but should preferably be left to port.

			Sphere painted black or red, or half-black and half-red horizontally	White or red with flashing character	
Isolated Danger	Spherical	Wide black and red horizontal bands separated by a narrow white band	—	White or red with flashing character	—
*Danger Area	Optional	Yellow, with Red St. George's Cross on top making R.Y.V.S. on sides. Letters 'DZ' on side	—	—	Marks any naval or military practice area. (See Note 3.)
Landfall	Optional	B.W.V.S. or R.W.V.S.	—	Flashing character	Placed near the entrance to channels off a shore with few prominent landmarks.
*Watch	Can	Red, with name of light-vessel in white letters followed by 'WATCH'	—	—	Placed near light-vessel to indicate when dragging.
Quarantine Ground	Optional	Yellow	—	—	—
Outfall and Spoil Ground	Optional	Yellow and black divided horizontally	—	Optional, but different from neighbouring lights in the vicinity	Marks the discharging ground for dredgers and sullage lighters
*Telegraph Cable	Optional	Black with 'TELEGRAPH' in white letters	—	—	Marks the shore end of telegraph cables.
*D.G. Range	Can	Blue and White Cheq.	—	—	Marks limits of degaussing range.
*Cable	Optional	Red or Black	Globe, or flag, or both	Two horizontal lights	Used by cable-ships to mark the ends of cables on which they are working. Should not be approached nearer than 500 yards.

E

TABLE OF BUOYS—*continued*

BUOY	SHAPE	COLOUR	TOPMARK (if any)	LIGHT (if any)	REMARKS
*Submarine Mining Ground	Optional	G.W.H.S. or G.W. Cheq.	—	—	Marks the limits of minefields or mining grounds.
Mooring	Cylindrical or Can	Any, usually black	—	—	—
*Aircraft Mooring	Elliptical (rubber) or Cylindrical or Can (steel and rubber)	Red	—	—	—
Spar	—	Any	—	—	Used to mark special positions or may be substituted for many of the standard buoys described.
*Wreck-marking	—	—	For details, *see* Fig. 68	—	—

* Not recognised by the *International Agreement for a Uniform System of Maritime Buoyage* (Geneva Conference, 1936).

Notes: 1. A 'Middle Ground', which is a shoal with a channel on each side of it, may be so long that it is necessary to have starboard and port hand buoys to mark the sides, in addition to the buoys mentioned in the table (*see* Figs. 67 and 68).

2. Any type of buoy may be lit. Light-buoys are not included in the *List of Lights*.

3. Danger Area Buoy is coloured Blue and White by international agreement. To improve its visibility, this has been modified (as detailed above) by U.K. authorities only.

4. A buoy seldom exhibits a fixed light, because it might be mistaken for a small vessel at anchor.

5. Foreign systems of buoys and topmarks are given in the appropriate *Sailing Directions*.

6. Where the shape of a buoy is optional, the shape should normally be in accordance with the rules for channel marking.

FIG. 69. ADDITIONAL BUOYS TO BE FOUND IN U.K. COASTAL WATERS

TABLE OF AIR FOG SIGNALS

Fog Signal	Operated by	Note Emitted	Remarks
Diaphone	Compressed air	Powerful low note	Distinguished by a 'grunt' at the end of the note.
Siren	Compressed air	Medium - powered high or low note, or combination	—
Reed	Compressed air	Low-powered high note	If the reed is operated by hand, the power will be small.
Tyfon	Compressed air	Powerful medium-pitched note from vibrating diaphragm	Similar to a ship's fog signal.
Nautophone	Electricity	High note, similar in power and tone to that of the reed	—
Electric Fog Horn	Electricity	Powerful medium-pitched note	Simultaneous emission of several sound frequencies.
Gun	Gun	—	An acetylene gun gives a bright flash.
Explosive	An explosion in mid-air	—	—
Bells	Mechanically or by wave action	According to the weight of the bell	When the bell is worked by waves the sound is irregular. Gongs are sometimes used.
Whistle	Compressed air or steam	Low power and low note	—

Points to remember when air fog signals are expected to be heard:

(i) Air fog signals are heard at greatly varying distances because the behaviour of a sound wave in air depends on the state of the air. Similarly the apparent direction of a fog signal can be misleading.

(ii) When an air fog signal is a combination of high and low notes, one of the notes may be inaudible at times.

(iii) Occasionally there are areas in the vicinity of a fog signal in which it is totally inaudible.

(iv) A station may not be aware that there is fog a short distance away, and so the fog signal will not be sounded.

(v) Some fog signals take some time to start up after signs of fog have been seen.

Mariners are therefore warned that fog signals cannot be implicitly relied upon, and the practice of sounding should never be neglected. Look-outs should be placed in positions where noises in the ship are least likely to interfere with the hearing of an air fog signal. Experience shows that an air fog signal, although not audible from the deck even when the engines are stopped, may be heard from aloft.

2. SUBMARINE SOUND SIGNALS

Full details are given in the *List of Lights* against the appropriate lighthouse or light-vessel and also in the *Admiralty List of Radio Signals* (Vol. II – under 'Radiobeacons'). Details of such signals on buoys are only given in the *Sailing Directions* and on the charts:

(i) *Oscillator* (chart abbreviation S.O.). – This is electrically operated and transmits a high note signal, usually in groups corresponding to letters of the morse code.

(ii) *Bells* (chart abbreviation S.B.). – These are fitted to buoys and operated mechanically or by wave action, in which case the sound is irregular.

In water, sound waves travel about four times as fast as they do in air (about 4,900 feet per second), and their progress is much less variable. They spread out in all directions, but are apparently diverted or deflected by shoals, land, breakwaters, and possibly by strong tides.

The range of submarine signals far exceeds that of air fog signals. Submarine oscillators (S.O.) have been heard at distances exceeding 50 miles, and submarine bells (S.B.) at distances exceeding 15 miles.

Ships fitted with receiving gear can find the bearing of a submarine sound signal with sufficient accuracy for safe navigation in a fog. Ships not so fitted can hear the signals from the hull below the waterline at distances which are well outside the normal range of air fog signals, though it is difficult to obtain a bearing.

3. RADIOBEACONS

Radiobeacons may be operated from stations near the coast, or in many cases from lighthouses or light-vessels. Details of all these are contained in the *Admiralty List of Radio Signals* (Vol. II), but only an indication of their existence is given in the *List of Lights* and on charts, against the appropriate lighthouse or light-vessel. Radiobeacons are designed mainly as aids to navigation during periods of fog or low visibility, but certain stations are operated irrespective of the state of the weather. The majority of stations, however, transmit signals at fixed times daily in clear weather, increasing the transmissions to a continuous service during fog.

Obtaining the bearing of a Radiobeacon. – The normal type of signal consists of a morse code signal, by which the station can be identified, followed by a characteristic signal group, which includes a long dash to enable ships fitted with direction-finding apparatus to obtain a bearing. In a few cases special apparatus has been installed which enables the bearing of the signals to be obtained by ships having only an ordinary radio receiver. One example of this, the rotating loop beacon, which is not at present operating in the U.K. (1963), is described in the *Admiralty List of Radio Signals* (Vol. II). Another example, the 'Consol' transmitter, is described in Chapter VI.

Instructions for the use and calibration of direction-finding apparatus are contained in Chapter VI. Details of routine and request DF calibration services are given in the *Admiralty List of Radio Signals* (Vol. II).

In addition to the normal radiobeacons, numerous coast radio stations provide a special service whereby ships equipped with DF apparatus can request transmissions. From these they can obtain bearings. These transmissions are known as the 'QTG' service. Selection of suitable stations is facilitated by including them in the *Admiralty List of Radio Signals* (Vol. II), at the end of each geographical section of the radiobeacons. For full details of the Coast stations, however, reference should be made to the *Admiralty List of Radio Signals* (Vol. I). Certain 'air radiobeacons' and 'radio ranges', primarily for the use of aircraft, are located on fixed sites and operated on regular schedules. Such services may be useful to shipping, and details of them are given in the *Admiralty List of Radio Signals* (Vol. II), after the 'QTG' services. They must be used with caution, since their operation may be changed or altered without notice to users other than airmen.

Obtaining the range of a Radiobeacon. – Stations are operated in conjunction with automatic submarine or air sound signals (normally at a lighthouse or light-vessel), in such a way that distance can also be determined, as described in the *Admiralty List of Radio Signals* (Vol. II).

Notes on Radiobeacons

Remember that serious dangers may arise from the misuse of radiobeacons, and particularly risk of collision with light-vessels operating such signals.

The vagaries of sound in fog are well known, and the mariner who, in thick weather, approaches a radiobeacon directly ahead on a radio bearing, relying on hearing the sound fog signal in sufficient time to alter course to avoid danger, is taking an unjustifiable risk.

Radiobeacons of themselves give no indication of distance off, and safety demands that every precaution should be taken.

Stations which distinguish between their fog and clear weather transmissions give automatic indication of the local visibility at the station.

NAVIGATION IN COASTAL WATERS

Preparatory Work

There are many points that the navigator should consider before the ship proceeds to sea, or makes a landfall after an ocean passage.

(a) He should make sure that the charts have been corrected up to date for all permanent and temporary Notices to Mariners and other navigational warnings, and that the largest-scale charts are provided for every part of the passage.

(b) He should make a study of the charts showing the environs for many miles around and all the lights which may be seen. Instances have occurred where a light has been sighted, but no corresponding light could be found on the chart, and the ship has either stopped or altered course the wrong way in the face of such a predicament. It subsequently transpired that the light was outside the limits of the chart in use and therefore not expected.

(c) He should consult the *Sailing Directions*, a description of which is given in Chapter II. The best plan is to go through the pages relevant to the part of the coast off which the ship will be navigating, inserting references, where applicable and necessary, to the supplements or other amendments. Then he should read this portion of the book in conjunction with the charts, Light List, tidal publications and local orders. This will give a very clear mental picture of what may be expected in the way of dangers, tidal streams, navigational aids, etc. It will also provide information on port traffic signals, signal stations and local weather signals, signals indicating depths of water over bars at harbour entrances, details of anchorages, berths, landing-places, and other local information.

(d) He should consider the possibility of meeting fog or low visibility when passing through narrow waters, and anticipate what action will then be required. Some examples of passages in fog are given later in this chapter.

(e) The speed at which the ship will proceed must be decided, and her intended track drawn on the chart, with the time on each course. These times are based on her speed and the estimated currents or tidal streams. Notes on leading lines, conspicuous objects, times of sunrise, moonrise, etc., and the time of turning of the tidal stream, should all be noted, together with the applicable items mentioned above, in the notebook.

(f) He should consider the ship's position at dusk and during darkness, with particular reference to possible dangers. By arranging the times of arrival and departure, it is often possible to avoid placing the ship in a difficult position, such as arriving at the harbour entrance or having to pass through a narrow, unlighted channel during darkness. It is a good plan to work out the arcs of visibility of all lights which may be sighted, as previously explained, and draw these across the ship's track. The approximate times of sighting can then be estimated for each light.

Method of Navigation

This will depend upon the degree of accuracy required.

In very confined waters the highest accuracy is required. This is obtained by keeping the ship on a predetermined track.

In more open waters it is sufficient to proceed from point to point, fixing the ship's position at intervals. The frequency and degree of accuracy of the fixes is dependent upon the deviation from the track that is permissible.

When leaving Portsmouth Harbour and proceeding to the eastwards, it would be necessary to use the former method until past the Nab Tower. Thereafter the latter method may be used, the fixing interval becoming greater and accuracy less essential.

Planning the Passage

Before navigating through very restricted waters, lay off, on the largest-scale chart:

    1. the tracks determined on;

2. the ship's turning arc (with radius representing that for normal wheel at the speed at which it is intended to proceed) at each alteration of course;

3. the points at which the wheel should be put over.

From the above information the following data can be entered in the notebook, as shown on page 138:

4. the various true (and magnetic) courses to steer;

Note: It is preferable to give the magnetic course, rather than the compass course, since the deviations of the standard and steering compasses are usually different and confusion could otherwise arise.

5. transits, clearing marks and leading marks and their bearings; one transit must be selected for checking the compass;

6. bearings of marks or transits used for obtaining the position at which to put the wheel over.

In more open water, the plan should be similar to the above, although it will not always be possible or even necessary to run on marks or to work out exact 'wheel over' positions for altering course.

CLEARANCE FROM THE COAST AND FROM OFF-LYING DANGERS

It is important that the present position of the ship should be known at all times. This entails constant fixing, together with intelligent forecasting. When coasting, the general rule is to pass sufficiently close to the shore to enable all prominent marks to be identified. The moment identification becomes difficult, a course diverging from the coast should usually be set.

To decide the distance from dangers and coasts at which the ship should pass requires experience, but the track chosen should be such that, if fog or mist should obscure the marks, the ship can still be navigated with the certainty that she is not running into danger. For this reason, avoid a course converging with the coast.

The following notes will serve as a rough guide when the track of a ship is laid off, but it should be borne in mind that the distances will have to be adjusted for the prevailing weather and tidal streams or currents likely to be experienced, and for the nature of the coast or dangers being approached and the probable opportunities for fixing the ship's position.

(a) When the coast is fairly steep, pass at a distance of 2 miles or over. At 2 miles objects can easily be recognised in normal weather.

(b) When the coast is shelving

(1) deep-draught ships drawing over 20 feet should pass outside the 10-fathom line;

(2) medium-draught ships drawing 10 to 20 feet should pass outside the 5-fathom line;

(3) light-draught ships drawing under 10 feet should pass outside the 3-fathom line.

When there are few lines of soundings on the chart, proceed with caution, following the lines of soundings on the chart where practicable.

(c) When there are dangers near the coast the position of which is not certain, pass at least 1 mile from them if there is sea-room, and if sufficient objects are available for frequent fixing. When tidal streams are strong, and in thick weather, increase this distance.

(d) Buoys and light-vessels should be passed at a distance of 5 cables, if there is sea-room. Course need not be chosen to pass close to buoys or light-vessels when there is deep water at a distance, particularly when radar and Decca are available for fixing.

(e) Where there are unmarked dangers out of sight of land, pass them at a distance of from 5 to 10 miles, depending on the time interval since the last fix and the tidal stream or current likely to be experienced. During dark hours these distances should be increased.

ALLOWANCE FOR THE HEIGHT OF THE TIDE

When the track will lead the ship into comparatively shallow water, such as the estuaries of rivers or the approaches to harbours, it is essential to consider the height of the tide in relation to the draught of the ship. An ample margin of depth should always be allowed.

It is sometimes convenient to mark dangers on the chart, or to shade inside a depth-line greater than the draught. For example, if a ship draws 20 feet, shade in the area inside the 5-fathom line, which will serve as a deadline. The margin of safety to be allowed cannot be laid down, but must depend upon circumstances.

PRESENCE OF OTHER SHIPPING

Consider the areas of dense shipping; if they cannot be avoided they should be crossed so that the least time is spent against the main stream of traffic.

PREPARATION OF PASSAGE CHARTS

It should be possible to prepare charts beforehand for a complete passage lasting several days and involving exercises and manoeuvres. Such a plan should be flexible enough to allow for alterations in the detailed programme without affecting the main issue.

The plan should include times for alterations of course round lights and headlands, all courses and speeds, and the time of anchoring. Gaps should be left for manoeuvring periods, an estimation of progress during these being made for continuity.

SELECTION OF COURSES TO STEER

Unless the intended track lies on a mark or a transit ahead or astern, or is designed to pass through a particular position, it may be an advantage to plan all courses to the nearest 5°. These are both easier to remember and to steer, and signalled alterations of course are often simplified.

TIME OF DEPARTURE AND TIME OF ARRIVAL

It is usually necessary to arrive at the final destination at a certain time, whether in order to save daylight, to catch a tide, or for operational reasons. Moreover the ship must not normally exceed economical speed on passage.

The time of arrival and speed having been decided, the time of departure must be calculated. This is most conveniently done by working back from the destination and the required time of arrival, in order to make due allowance for tidal stream and currents on passage. The distance from the final destination should be clearly shown on the track at convenient intervals, such as every 50 or 100 miles.

Circumstances nearly always tend to make a ship late rather than early, and it is therefore a wise precaution to plan the whole operation at one knot less than economical speed before taking the other factors into account. For long passages, an alternative allowance in hand of one hour per day will normally be sufficient.

It should be remembered that, when speed has to be adjusted in order to arrive at the correct time, there are two factors to be counteracted:

(1) the time already lost or gained when the decision to adjust speed is made;

(2) the time the ship will continue to lose or gain if stream and weather remain unchanged.

Fixing the Ship

(a) Fix frequently, in order to ensure an accurate continuous record. Times should be shown against all fixes on the chart, and both times and bearings should be entered in the notebook. Many fixes may prove unnecessary, but the sudden advent of thick weather will enhance the value of a fix taken shortly beforehand.

(b) Fixing at regular intervals of time facilitates the estimation of speed made good.

(c) The line joining a series of fixes, if-prolonged, indicates the course the ship will make good. This line should always be projected on the chart, to ensure that it does not lead into danger.

(d) Remarks on the choice of objects for fixing are to be found in Chapter IV.

When NOT to Fix

On occasions when only mountain summits, or distant or inconspicuous marks, are visible, a fix may give a position widely different from the ship's estimated position.

If there is no reason to mistrust the estimated position, a fix in these circumstances should be treated with caution.

'The route east from Gibraltar reveals on the Spanish side an engaging view of a series of mountain-tops each a little higher or lower than its neighbour. They look as if they should be used for navigation, but the writer has consistently failed to get any value from them. If objects are distant or difficult to distinguish, they must either be unmistakably "shot up" (see Chapter IV) or left alone'.[1]

Calculating the Distance that an Object will Pass Abeam

It is a help to be able to determine, with a simple mental calculation, the distance a ship will pass an object abeam on a certain course, and how much the course must be changed in order to pass the object a desired distance away.

One mile subtends an angle of one degree at a distance of 60 miles. Two-and-a-half cables subtend an angle of one degree at a distance of 15 miles.

---

[1] This extract, and those appearing on page 141 *et seq.*, are taken from *On the Bridge*, by Vice-Admiral Sir James A. G. Troup, K.B.E., C.B., by permission of Hutchinson & Co. (Publishers) Limited, London.

EXAMPLE 1

A light is sighted right ahead at an estimated distance of 15', and it is desired to pass 4' from the light. What alteration of course is necessary?

1° at a distance of 15' is equivalent to ¼ mile. The alteration required is therefore 16°. Alter course to bring the light 16° on the bow.

EXAMPLE 2

A light is sighted 10 degrees on the bow at an estimated distance of 12', and it is desired to pass 4' from the light. What alteration of course is necessary?

At 12' the estimated offing per degree is 12/60 = 1/5 mile. To pass 4' off, therefore, alter course 10° outwards from the present course to bring the light 4 × 5 = 20° on the bow.

Notes:
(i) Allowance must be made for any tidal stream or current.
(ii) When rounding a point which is very close to the ship and it is desired to keep at a constant distance from it during the turn, put the rudder over an amount corresponding to the tactical diameter required, a little before the point is on the beam; and subsequently continue to adjust the rudder angle so that the object remains abeam throughout the turn.

The Vertical Danger Angle

A vertical sextant angle can be used with advantage to ensure the safety of the ship in the vicinity of dangers. If the danger is close to high land or a lighthouse, proceed as shown in the following example:

EXAMPLE

It is required to pass 5 cables clear of a rock which is distant 3 cables from a lighthouse, shown in Fig. 70. The height of the light is 150 feet above mean high water springs.

With centre the lighthouse and radius 8 cables, describe an arc of a circle. Find the actual height of the light above sea-level by allowing for the difference between the height of the tide and the height of mean high water springs.

Lecky's Tables, or the masthead angle tables in *Inman's Tables,* will give the angle subtended between the light and sea-level from any point on the arc of the circle. Set this angle on a sextant, and so long as the reflected image of the lantern appears below the water-level, the ship is outside the circle and in safety.

If the height of the tide is not allowed for, and the height of the light, as printed on the chart, is used, the ship will actually be further from the light than is estimated, except in the unlikely event of the sea-level being above mean high water springs.

RANGEFINDERS

A rangefinder will give a position line, as described in Chapter IV, which can be used in a similar way to the vertical danger angle. In the above example

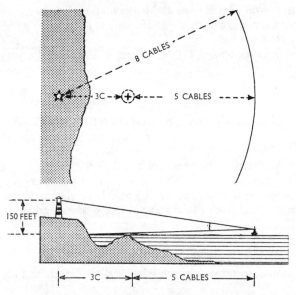

FIG. 70. The Vertical Danger angle

(as shown in Fig. 70), if the range of the lighthouse always exceeds 1,600 yards the ship will pass not less than 5 cables from the rock. A rangefinder is most useful at night, when one light may be the only visible object to assist the ship in avoiding a danger.

The Horizontal Danger Angle

The horizontal angle between two objects on shore may be used in a similar way. The objects should be chosen so as to lie approximately at the same distance on each side of the danger to be cleared. A mark should be made on the chart at a distance outside the danger at what it is considered safe to pass, and lines should be drawn from the objects to this mark.   The angle thus formed is measured, and if the angle subtended by the objects is less than that measured, the ship is outside the danger and in safety.

In Fig. 71, the horizontal danger angle for a clearance of 5 cables from the

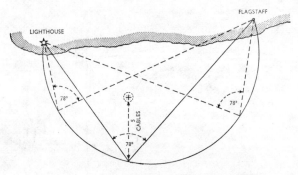

FIG. 71. The Horizontal Danger angle

F*

rock is plotted as 78°. So long as the horizontal angle between the lighthouse and the flagstaff remains less than 78°, the ship is outside the danger circle, and must pass clear of the rock.

When the angle subtended by the objects is less than the angle set on the sextant, the flagstaff will appear 'the wrong side of' the lighthouse.

NAVIGATION IN CONFINED WATERS

Altering Course

When course is altered it is necessary to allow for the turning circle and to decide on the point at which the wheel should be put over so that the ship, when steadied on her new course, may be exactly on the predetermined line.

This point is found from the 'distance to new course' table, as explained in Chapter III.

Turning on to a Predetermined Line

This is a simple matter if there are suitable shore objects and no tidal stream.

EXAMPLE 1

In Fig. 72 a ship steaming a course AB wishes to alter course and make good a course CD of 280°.

The distance to new course laid back from *CD* will give the point at which the wheel should be put over. If through this point a line is drawn parallel to the new course, it will be seen to pass (fortuitously) through the lighthouse: thus if the ship puts the wheel over when the lighthouse bears 100°, she must be somewhere on the line *LL'* and will fetch up somewhere on the line *CD* when steadied on the new course of 280°.

The ideal circumstances in the above example are seldom found in practice; but often there is an object available which allows the principle of the transferred

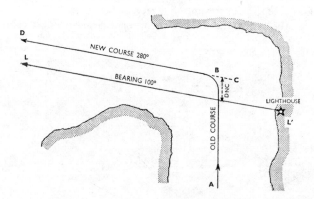

Fig. 72. Turning on to a predetermined line by a bearing

position line to be used in conjunction with the above method – as, for instance, if an anchorage is approached on a line of bearing or a transit. The alteration of course to the approach course can then be made on a bearing of the approach object.

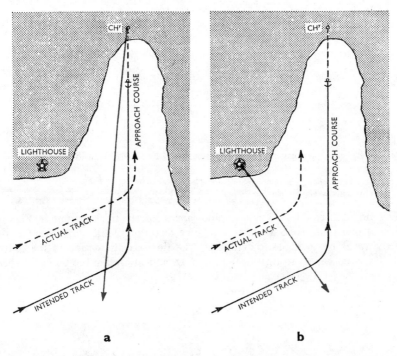

FIG. 73. Comparison of errors when turning on to a predetermined course

Fig. 73a shows the small error introduced on reaching the approach course, by using a bearing of the approach object to determine the point to put the wheel over.

Fig. 73b shows the large error which may occur if the object selected is not approximately parallel to the approach course.

EXAMPLE 2

In Fig. 74, a ship steaming 10 knots is steering a course AB. She wishes to turn on to line CD on a course of 003°. There is no tidal stream.

Lay back a distance *EF* equal to the distance to new course for the alteration of course, thus obtaining the position for putting over the wheel. Note the accurate time that a charted object *O* bears 003°. When this occurs the ship must be somewhere on the line *OG*; therefore work out the time the ship will take to steam from *OG* to *HK* (e.g., if the distance is one mile, the time interval will be 6 minutes). After 6 minutes put the wheel over; the ship should steady up somewhere on the line *CD*, as required.

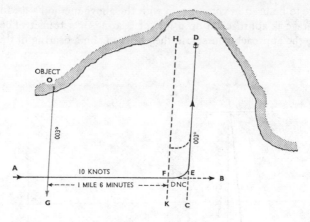

FIG. 74. Turning on to a predetermined line by time and bearing

To allow for a Current or Tidal Stream when Altering Course

The previous examples made no allowances for the tidal stream. In Fig. 75, a ship *A* is making good a course *AB*. The direction of the ship's head shows the allowance being made to counteract the tidal stream setting to the south-east. The ship wishes to turn to the line *CD*, and in finding the point *G* where

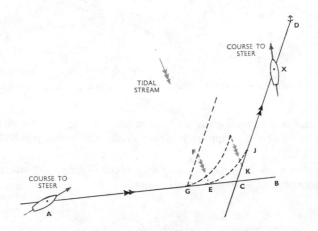

FIG. 75. Turning on to a predetermined line, allowing for tidal stream

the wheel must be put over, it is necessary to make allowance for the tidal stream experienced during the turn. When making good the course *CD*, the ship will again have to make allowance for the tidal stream and will steer the course shown at *X*. Thus the actual alteration of course will be the difference between the direction of the ship's head at *A* and at *X*.

Lay back from *C* the distance to new course for an alteration of course found from the difference of the ship's head at *A* and at *X*. This gives the point *E*.

From E lay back, in the direction of the tidal stream reversed, the distance that the tidal stream carries the ship during the elapsed time for the turn to the new course. This gives the point F.

Through F draw FG parallel to the new course CD. The point G will then be the position of the ship when the wheel must be put over, and the ship will arrive on the line CD at K.

Transits

When possible, choose a track so that two objects in transit may be seen ahead or astern; in other words, arrange that the ship may steam along the position line resulting from this transit. If the two objects are seen to remain in transit, the ship is following the chosen track; whereas if they are seen to be not exactly in line with each other, it is obvious that the ship is to the right or left of the correct track.

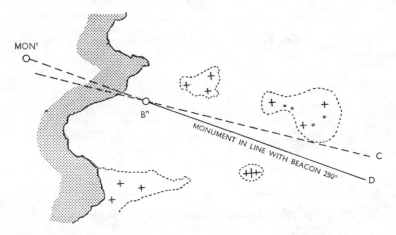

FIG. 76. Transit, leading marks, leading line

The value of a line of transit is proportional to the ratio of the distance between the objects in transit to the distance between the ship and the nearer object. The larger this ratio, the better the transit. If possible, the ratio should not be less than one-third.

Marks are said to be 'open' when they are not exactly in transit. Thus, in Fig. 76 a monument and a beacon are in transit to an observer D (or the monument is said to be 'on with' the beacon); but to an observer at C the monument is said to be 'open to the right of' the beacon.

If the objects are observed to be open, the correct line should be regained with a bold alteration of course (*see also* Fig. 77).

Leading Marks and Leading Lines

Many harbour plans show two marks which, being kept in transit, lead the ship clear of dangers, or in the best channel. Such marks are called 'leading marks', and they are shown on a chart by a line drawn through them called a 'leading line' (Fig. 76). The line is generally shown as one straight line, but sometimes as two parallel lines close together. The line is full, or double, for a part of its length, and then becomes dotted or single. This signifies that it is advisable to keep on it only as far as the full or double line extends, the dotted or single portion being drawn to guide the eye to the objects which are to be kept in transit. The names of the objects and their true bearings *from seaward*, when in transit, are generally written along the line drawn through them.

FIG. 77a. Monument 'on with' beacon

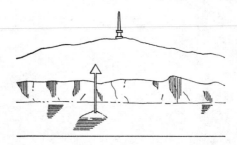

FIG. 77b. Monument 'open to right of' beacon

When the objects are in transit, a bearing of them should be taken and compared with that given on the chart. This ensures that the two objects seen in transit are the correct objects, and also checks the error of the compass.

The navigator must accustom himself to respond with the correct wheel order immediately the marks get out of alignment.

The rule is 'Follow the front mark'. For instance, in Fig. 77b, course must be altered to *port* to bring the marks back into line again.

Line of Bearing

If no transit marks are available, a line of bearing should be used (Fig. 78). The track is drawn on the chart to pass through some well-defined object – either ahead or astern, but preferably ahead of the ship – and the bearing of this line noted. Provided the bearing of the object remains at the bearing noted, the ship must be on her track. If the bearing changes, the ship will have been set off the track, and an alteration of course will be necessary to regain the line of bearing.

It is often possible when steaming on a line of bearing to observe some uncharted object, such as a telegraph pole or gap in the trees, which appears in transit with the object through which the line of bearing has been drawn. Such a 'home made' transit is often of great assistance in keeping the ship on the line.

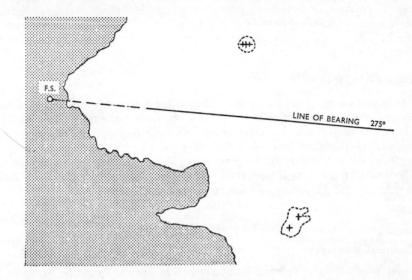

FIG. 78. Line of bearing

When laying off a line of bearing, choose an object which is not too far away. The closer the object is to the observer, the easier it is to detect by the change of bearing when the ship is being set off the line. For example, if the object is one mile distant, the bearing will alter one degree if the ship is set about 35 yards off the line; whereas if it is 10 miles distant, the ship will be set about two cables off the line before the bearing changes one degree.

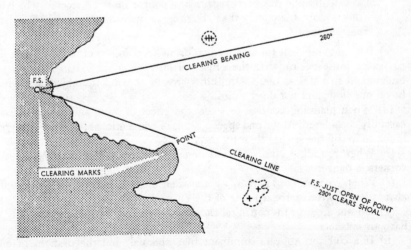

FIG. 79. Clearing marks, clearing line, clearing bearing

Clearing Marks

These are two marks shown on the chart (*see* Fig. 79), the straight line through which, called a 'clearing line', runs clear of certain dangers. When navigating near a danger, take care not to go inside the transit line of the clearing marks. So long as the ship is outside this line (that is, so long as the marks are kept open), she is safe from the danger.

Clearing Bearings

When no clearing marks are available, draw a line of bearing on the chart through some conspicuous object so as to pass at a certain distance from a danger. This line of bearing is called a 'clearing bearing', and provided the bearing of the object is kept either 'less' or 'more' than the clearing bearing, according to circumstances, the ship will be clear of the danger. In Fig. 79, the bearing of the flagstaff must be kept more than 260° but less than 290°, if the wreck to the northward and the shoal to the southward are to be cleared.

NOTES ON PILOTAGE

General Remarks

(a) When turning to bring leading marks in line, or to get on to a line of bearing, the wheel should be put over in good time. It should be remembered that if it is put over too soon, it can be quickly eased; but if too late, more wheel will not always be effective. Moreover the use of excessive wheel reduces the ship's speed, and this may be inconvenient, particularly if in company.

(b) When steering on a mark in a cross-stream, it should be clear that the course steered will differ from the correct bearing to be maintained – i.e., will differ from the course to be made good. If the correct bearing is not maintained, there are two factors to be considered:

   (1) The ship is off the line and must regain it by a bold alteration.
   (2) When the line has been regained, a course must be steered which will meet, more adequately than the original one, the stream which is being encountered.

(c) It is not sufficient for safe navigation to keep an object 'dead ahead'. The navigator must ensure that the object is *on the correct bearing*. It must be understood that unless there is no cross-stream or wind the object will *always* be on one bow, and not dead ahead.

(d) When planning courses to steer, the effect of wind and stream must be carefully considered. At normal speeds, ships of conventional build are influenced much more by the stream than by the wind.

(e) When rounding points of land or shoals, allow plenty of room – cutting corners is dangerous.

(f) When navigating in narrow waters where there is likely to be much traffic, always keep to the starboard side of the channel.

(g) Do not attempt to 'cut in' ahead of another vessel when approaching the harbour entrance.

(h) If a collision appears imminent in a channel, and the draught of one's own ship would allow her to be navigated outside the buoys, this action should be taken if collision cannot otherwise be avoided. In certain circumstances it may even be better to ground than risk a collision.

MAKING A FLAT AND FEATURELESS COAST BY DAY

When it is necessary by day to make a flat coast which is known to have few prominent objects, time may be saved if a position 5 or 10 miles to one side of the required position is steered for. On sighting the coast, course is altered in the required direction, and while running nearly parallel to the coast objects may be picked out and a fix obtained. At night the loom of town lights may be helpful as also a DF bearing of a local radio station.

Notes on Tidal Streams and Currents

Full information on this subject is given in Chapter XII, where reference is made to various relevant publications. The following remarks may, however, be noted here.

The navigator should always consult the wind and current charts, tidal atlases, and other publications.

When navigating along the coast, indraught into bays and bights is common. Sometimes there is an indraught at one end of an open bight and an outdraught at the other.

Currents, tidal streams and tides are affected by the wind. This effect is, however, frequently exaggerated, the supposed wind effect on the current being in reality wind effect on the ship.

The wind often produces a marked effect on both the time of change of the tide and its height.

It should be appreciated that the turn of the tidal stream often varies at different distances from the shore, although the time of high water may be the same at these points.

Near the sides of channels of any width, where shoaling is gradual, the direction of the tidal stream is almost always rotatory.

Compasses

The errors and deviations of the gyro and magnetic compasses should be checked after each alteration of course (*see Q.R. and A.I.*). The method of checking compass error by transits and other means is explained in Chapter I.

Remarks on the Use of Buoys and Light-Vessels

When shore marks are difficult to distinguish because of distance or thick weather, buoys and light-vessels must often be used instead.

Except in narrow channels, do not trust buoys implicitly, or fix by them when charted shore objects are visible at no great distance, because the position of buoys may vary with the tide, or they may drag or break adrift. But remember that the buoys marking a shoal are frequently moved as the shoal extends, and there may not be information of recent alterations. Thus a fix by shore objects will not necessarily give a correct position relative to a shoal, because the latter may have extended, the new position being shown by the buoys.

Always check the periods of lights in order that powerful distant lights, lighthouses or light-vessels shall not be mistaken for close and weak lights (e.g. buoys).

Always compare the name, colour, topmark, etc., of each buoy with the details shown on the chart, to avoid the possibility of mistaking one buoy for another.

When a buoy is passed, it is easy to see at a glance in what direction the tidal stream is running. Similarly, the way in which a light-vessel is swung will indicate the direction of the tidal stream, unless the wind is so strong that the vessel is swung across the stream.

A ship passing near a light-vessel or buoy which has clear water on both sides should pass on the downstream side to avoid fouling it through underestimation of the strength of the stream.

When rounding a buoy, the wheel must be put over in good time. When turning away from a buoy, care must be taken not to swing the ship's stern on to it by steering to pass too close to it, and putting the wheel over too late. When in line ahead proceeding down a buoyed channel, do not pass too close to the downstream side of the channel if there is any cross stream, as ships astern may then have difficulty in maintaining the line without colliding with the buoys. Remember that there is a certain amount of slack chain in buoy moorings, especially towards low water, and that the buoy may take a sudden sheer in a strong stream.

The Record

A detailed record should always be kept by the Navigating Officer on every passage to obtain data about the ship's performance under different conditions, and to provide a basis – if not a detailed plan – for subsequent similar passages. This record will normally contain more navigational information than the ship's log.

Although there is no hard-and-fast rule for laying out the record in the navigator's notebook, the following method may be found convenient.

Monday, 11th January, 1960
PORTSMOUTH to DOVER

Time	Course	Speed	Remarks
			H.W. L.W. Portsmouth $\begin{cases} 0946 \ 11'\!\cdot\!8 & 0242 \ 2'\!\cdot\!6 \\ 2217 \ 11'\!\cdot\!6 & 1507 \ 1'\!\cdot\!9 \end{cases}$
1025	var.	var.	Weighed and proceeded from No. 6 berth in company with squadron (4 ships). Single line ahead.
1030	134°	10	Set Co. with Kickergill Tʳ. φ Fᵗ. Monckton astern 314° (Gyro 1° H).
1039		12	No Man's Land Fᵗ. |→5c. Inc: spd:
1045			S. Parade Pier →| φ Horse Sand Fᵗ. 356° (Gyro correct)
1047	114°		Warner |→ 2c. a/c. T. Stream 311° – 1 kt. s.m.g. 10 kts.

Monday, 11th January, 1960

PORTSMOUTH to DOVER—*continued*

Time	Course	Speed	Remarks
1110	120°		New Grounds |→ a/c.
1115	var.	15	Carried out manoeuvres in vicinity Nab T^r.
1145			Manoeuvres completed ⎧ Nab T^r. 011° ⎨ Yarborough Mon^t. 298° ⎩ Ventnor R°. Masts 264°
1146	090°	12	Formed single line ahead. Set Co.
1245	083°		Owers L.V. ←| 5c. a/c. T. Stream 250° 1·5 kts. s.m.g. 11·2 kts.

This shows an extract from a passage between Portsmouth and Dover.

Notes:
  (i) Any error in estimation of time on passage can readily be seen by comparing the actual times with the planned times shown on the chart, and adjustments of speed can then be made as necessary.
  (ii) The courses shown are true courses, any gyro error being shown in the *Remarks* column. Similarly, all transits are given with their true bearings. For instance, at 1030 a transit on 314° showed that the gyro compass was 1° high (i.e. the compass bearing was 315°), and that the gyro course to steer was 135°. A second transit observed at 1045 indicated that the gyro was correct. Frequently an error may be observed before – or on – proceeding, when the speed/latitude corrector has been set for the passage but the ship has not attained her speed.
  (iii) Except in narrow channels, marked on both sides, the distance of objects when abeam and the side on which they are passed should always be indicated. The following symbols are used: \|→ abeam to starboard; ←\| abeam to port.
  (iv) In the *Remarks* column may be inserted an indication of altering course and speed, if desired; though this should be clear from the entries in their respective columns. The advantage of the column method is that it facilitates the checking of what the present course and speed should be (since they will always be the last entries in their respective columns), and also the calculation of how long the ship was on any particular course or steaming at any particular speed. If these items are inserted among the remarks, they can be very easily obscured.
  (v) Other details concerning the arrangement of ships in company, manoeuvres, wind, tidal stream or current, soundings, alterations of clocks, etc., should all be entered in the *Remarks* column.

USE OF THE NOTEBOOK FOR A PREPARED PASSAGE

Previously prepared data are essential for passages in confined waters. In clear and thick weather the navigator is thus enabled to direct his whole attention to conning the ship, noting the soundings, and generally keeping a good lookout, none of which is possible if he finds it necessary to be continually poring over chart and reference books.

It may be desirable to make out the plan, using bearings of lights only, and information useful for radar assistance, regardless of whether there are other suitable landmarks available, thus enabling the same plan to be used by day or night.

The following is an example of the use of a notebook for this type of information, and shows the first part of the passage from Plymouth breakwater to Devonport.

Entering Devonport

Speed	Course	Remarks
15	020° (029½°M)	On Drakes Is. F.S.
		W.O. when Mount Batten Tᵣ. bg. 040° (049½°M) and reduce to 10 kts.
10	041° (050½°M)	On Mount Batten Tᵣ.
		W.O. when ⏐← Trinity Pier bg. 340½° (350°M) and reduce to 8 kts.
8	345½° (355°M)	On St. Peter's Ch. ϕ F.S.
	etc.	

This information can be shown in pictorial form in the notebook, if preferred, as in Fig. 80.

It should be realised that this is only a pictorial method of remembering certain marks, courses and bearings. The chart itself must be used if any deviation from the predetermined track is necessary.

In the example given, more information would be included than is shown, such as tides, tidal streams, special signals, etc., as found in the various publications. Furthermore, when that particular problem is plotted for a ship whose tactical diameter is 5 cables, it will be found that on arrival at Asia Buoy it will be necessary to reverse the port engine in order to negotiate the next turn. The timing of the passage would be worked out in detail, allowing for tidal streams, etc.

Pilots

The regulations concerning pilots in *Q.R. and A.I.* should be carefully studied. For remarks on tonnage and payment of pilotage, *see* Chapter II.

Movements in Dockyard Ports

The regulations concerning the responsibility for moving ships in and out of dockyard ports, the provision of berthing parties and the employment of tugs are contained in *Q.R. and A.I.*

NAVIGATION IN CANALS

All passages through canals must conform to local regulations. The navigator should read all the relevant publications, and enter in his notebook the tidal stream or current expected, the various local signals, and the marks to be expected.

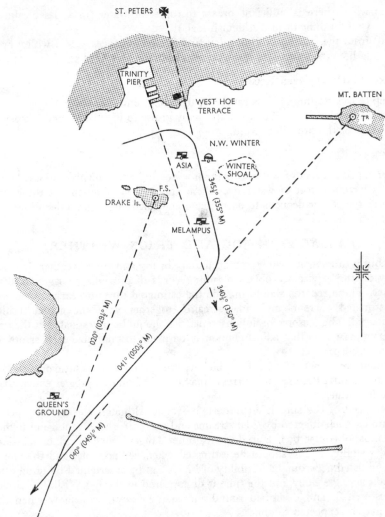

FIG. 80. Approach to Devonport prepared in pictorial form

In the Suez Canal it has been found that the water-level may be lowered as much as 1·5 feet when a ship proceeds at 5½ knots. This effect should be borne in mind when considering the draught clearance.

Notes on the handling of ships in canals and other restricted waterways will be found in the *Manual of Seamanship*, Vol. III.

NAVIGATION IN CORAL REGIONS

If the charts are inadequate, it is necessary to navigate by eye and with extreme caution. Place lookouts aloft and on the forecastle. Sound continuously.

Coral can best be seen:

(a) when the sun is high in the heavens;
(b) when the sun is astern;

(c) when there is sufficient breeze to ruffle the water (in a glassy calm it is often difficult to distinguish reefs);

(d) from the masthead. Under favourable circumstances, a reef with 3 or 4 fathoms of water over it can be seen from the masthead at a fair distance.

PASSING AN UNSURVEYED REEF

Keep to the weather side, because any detached pinnacles will then be shown by the sea breaking over them. Coral usually grows to windward, and is steeper on the side of the prevailing wind.

COLOUR OF REEFS

Reefs having 3 feet of water over them appear a light-brownish colour.

Reefs having 6 feet of water over them appear a clear green. As the depth increases the colour deepens to dark green, and finally becomes a deep blue.

PASSAGES IN FOG AND THICK WEATHER

The ability to navigate safely and accurately in fog and thick weather depends largely on the experience obtained from records of previous passages in clear weather. These records should include the estimated times on each course and the estimated currents and tidal streams, together with the actual results experienced. The reasons for any discrepancies should be investigated at the end of every passage, so that adjustments may be made to minimize such errors on subsequent occasions.

It should be remembered that in thick weather when there is little or no wind, estimates of tidal streams and currents may be relied on to a greater extent than in rough weather.

The speed of the ship is an important factor. Although at very low speeds the ship is much affected by tidal streams and currents, the advantage of higher speed must of course be balanced against other dangers, such as risk of collision.

The visibility in fog should be estimated whenever possible, and the ship's speed adjusted accordingly. Visibility of buoys can be ascertained by noting the time of passing a buoy and the time it disappeared in the fog. Visibility circles thus estimated, and described round succeeding buoys, will show when the latter may be expected to appear.

When it is seen that the ship is about to enter fog, always note the approximate bearing, distance and course of any ships in sight; and, if possible, obtain a fix.

Before Entering Fog

1. Reduce to a moderate speed see Chapter XV).
2. Operate radar.
3. Station lookouts. A good plan is to have two lookouts on the forecastle and two at the masthead, each with his own sector. Lookouts should be in direct telephonic communication with the bridge, or should be supplied with megaphones. Forecastle lookouts should be taught to indicate direction by pointing with the outstretched arm.
4. If in soundings, start sounding.
5. In the vicinity of land, have an anchor ready for letting go.
6. Order silence on deck.

7. Close watertight doors, in accordance with the ship's Standing Orders.

8. Start the prescribed fog signal.

9. Warn the engine room.

10. Decide if it is necessary to connect extra boilers.

11. Memorize the characteristics of air and submarine fog signals which may be heard. Remember that sound signals on some buoys are operated by wave motion and are thus unreliable.

12. Make sure that the siren is not synchronizing with those of other ships, or with shore fog signals.

13. Be prepared to take MF DF bearings of radiobeacons should other means of fixing be less reliable, and of other ships operating radio in the vicinity should radar not be working efficiently.

14. If in any doubt about the ship's position, alter course at once to a safe course, parallel to or away from the coast.

VISIBILITY

If there is better visibility from the upper deck or masthead than from the bridge, a relative bearing of an object sighted from either of these positions (and especially a beam bearing) will almost certainly improve the estimated position.

When fog is low-lying, the masts or smoke of ships in the vicinity may frequently be seen above the fog; hence the need for a lookout as high as possible.

SIREN ECHO

The formula for calculating the ship's distance off cliffs by siren echo is given in Chapter IV. These distances must be considered unreliable.

FOG SIGNALS

Remarks on these appear at the beginning of this chapter.

Classification of Passages in Fog

The following remarks on passages in fog are taken from *On the Bridge*, by Vice-Admiral Sir James Troup, K.B.E., C.B. Although there are modern and accurate methods of obtaining a position in a fog, and the point to point and inward bound types of passage have been made very much easier by them, the fundamental reasoning in these remarks holds good today.

'All passages in fog can and should be divided into one of three types, each requiring its own treatment:

    (a) Outward bound to the open sea.

    (b) Point to Point.

    (c) Inward bound.

'Under (a) – Outward bound – we would put a vessel sailing from the Straits of Dover or the Isle of Wight to Vigo, Gibraltar, or America.

'A ship bound from Dover to Plymouth in fog would come under (b) – Point to Point – somewhat loosely. A ship bound from the Isle of Wight to the Thames in fog must do point to point all the time.

'Ships bound for Falmouth from New York or for Weymouth from the Channel Islands are examples of (c) – Inward bound.

OUTWARD BOUND

'Outward bound being the easiest, we deal with it first. Almost regularly . . . a definite tonnage of shipping is lost due to failure to act upon the following elementary principle, "Outward bound, don't run aground".

'If we are approaching narrow waters, e.g. Dover Straits, we must know exactly where we are before getting there; but if a long passage has to be made, e.g., to Gibraltar from Dungeness, and if fog is met going down Channel, it is not going to matter much, if at all, either on the passage ·or when nearing Gibraltar, whether we get our last fix at Dungeness, Beachy Head, or even Ushant. More than one vessel bound, it might be, down Channel for America has been taken in towards the land to listen for a fog signal onshore, and has struck such rocks as the Manacles inside the Lizard. With 500 to 3,000 miles to go, a Captain may well argue as follows: "I shall be singularly unlucky if I carry this fog all the way, and if I have to go 2,000 miles in fog in the open sea I can only be 2½ per cent better off than if I go 2,050 miles from my last fix. A fix 2,000 miles from my destination is of little more value at the end of the passage than one obtained even farther away. Hence I shall not risk closing the land at the outset of my voyage; on the contrary, I shall keep out, and this will keep me clear of some of the traffic as well. If the weather improves, sights will give me an up-to-date fix; if the fog fails to lift, intense precaution will be as necessary on approaching my destination, whether I have come 500 miles or 2,000."

'No more need be said regarding the outward voyage, save to remark that if any good fix comes our way, possibly by sounding or DF, we seize the opportunity.

POINT TO POINT

'We mentioned Dover to Plymouth, and Isle of Wight to the Thames, as examples of point to point. Dover to Plymouth in fog was described as coming somewhat loosely under point to point. A ship so bound, after clearing the Varne Shoal off Folkestone, may sail ten miles or more off the land, until, in order to find Plymouth, the need arises to make Start Point or the Eddystone [Fig. 81]. In deciding whether to navigate in such a manner, or whether to hear each salient fog signal as he passes it, the Captain has to weigh well the advantages of either method. The Captain who has steamed down Channel far offshore all night has saved himself much anxiety regarding collision, and his vessel from all risk of grounding, but when he hauls in to make the Start he has a background of 200 miles DR and hence a considerable possibility of error. A man who hears each fog signal as he passes it is in a stronger situation as he approaches Start Point, having heard the Shambles Fog Siren only fifty miles "ago"; or as he approaches the Eddystone, having heard Start Point only twenty-five miles ago. Point to Point, if it can be carried out safely, is generally better navigation, yet it must be allowed that guidance from soundings or DF may render it unnecessary.

'The other example, namely, Isle of Wight to the Thames, needs few remarks. Point to point must be run all the way as the narrow waters are approached. Soundings, as we will learn, will often help us to see or hear the sea-mark we try to make. We *must* make it or stay to seaward. We can't pass eastward up the

Dover Strait without knowing where Dungeness is, and if we fail off Dungeness and go on, the Varne Shoal, Dover Breakwater or the Goodwin Sands will not excuse us; that's all.

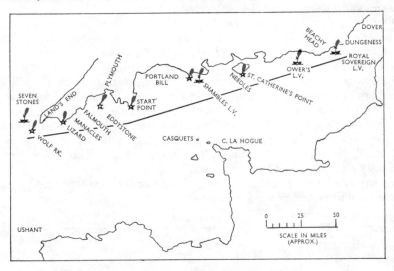

FIG. 81

'If the ship's past history has been satisfactory, the mind is sustained, in those short runs from one fog signal to another, by the knowledge that in clear weather the ship always has made objects on the correct bow – although (being temporarily blind) we insist on a safeguard. The important decision to make is which of the three methods should be adopted – on no account the middle course. The man who plays for a kind of half-hearted safety, steering somewhere between outward bound and point to point, five to seven miles off fog signals, doesn't "get there". If point to point has been selected, we give ourselves the best chance we can of hearing the fog signals by passing near them. There may be a sea-mark such as the Owers Lightship, which has deep water a mile or more inshore of it, an added reason for steering close to it. Provided the surroundings have been considered, and that our minds are prepared for the possibility, there is *sometimes* nothing disreputable about making such a fog signal ahead or on the "wrong" (outer) bow, for if seeing is believing, hearing, and hearing indubitably, is the next best thing.

INWARD BOUND

'In order of increasing difficulty, we have now to think of the ship coming in from the sea in fog. What should be in the Captain's mind as he approaches the land? We have no hesitation in replying: "I shall not grope or blunder in to narrow waters or near danger without adequate precaution." Having that decision ever in mind, the question will arise: "How far are we likely to be out of position?" If the vessel has only steamed a short distance from the departure fix, say thirty miles, and if the tides and currents are well known, it is reasonable to think that the ship will be not far distant from her estimated position. Yet, even in such a case, we should grasp at a precaution against being caught, unaware, out of reckoning. Knowledge of the probable difference between calculations and reality should be cultivated, and can only be gained by making passages and *thinking about them afterwards.*

'Our precaution may be a DF bearing; it is more likely to be got by sounding. Were we coming up Channel from Ushant to the Royal Sovereign Light Vessel off Beachy Head [Fig. 82,] we might well say to ourselves in that anxious hour before we hear the lightship's fog signal: "If we are ten miles to the west of our estimated position, we will run a few miles, during which we will get soundings of over thirty fathoms; if we are ten miles to the east, soundings of over thirty fathoms will be obtained for a very short time." (Note the trend of the thirty-fathom line.) "If we are late and astern of the estimated position, the ship will cross the twenty-fathom line later than expected; if we are early and ahead, the twenty-fathom line will be crossed sooner. This fathom line is obviously a good warning in these waters."

'In any one (or two) of these eventualities we correct our estimated position by the soundings, and proceed accordingly. . . .

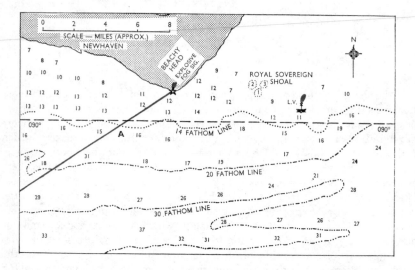

FIG. 82

'Another point to dwell upon is how the ship is heading compared to the trend of the land or danger line – whether steering parallel or at right angles to danger, or closing or opening it. Any of these measures may be necessary but the course parallel to danger has the merit that a slight alteration will turn the ship towards safety – a merit unshared by courses which close danger lines at or near right angles. It must be borne in mind that many ships, if steering directly or nearly so towards danger, will, even if the wheel is put hard over, close that danger by an "advance" of 500 yards or more before beginning to open from it.

'Having ensured that the ship is approaching on the safest available course, we must make the best plan for detecting the fog signal it is hoped to hear. . . .

It is suggested that, when groping for a fog signal which is being approached after a long D.R. run, it is seldom advisable to steer straight at it. Aim at ensuring that the fog signal is:

(a) somewhere ahead and,

(b) that you know on which side of the ship it is.

'We have seen the warnings which soundings would give a Captain approaching the Royal Sovereign Lightship; let us follow his fortunes a little farther, supposing him to be bound to the Thames from Ushant. He must know exactly where he is before he reaches the narrow waters east of Dungeness, and it is assumed that he has decided to make the Royal Sovereign Lightship. Now there is no great virtue about the fathom lines printed on the charts. The Captain, provided soundings are plentiful, is quite free to draw one in for his own use. In Fig. 82 a fourteen-fathom line has been inserted by the Captain, because he wants to steam on a line which will lead him safely a mile or two off the lightship. This line is somewhat irregular, but it should serve its purpose. If he passes two miles off the lightship, he thinks he should have a strong chance of hearing the fog siren. He next decided upon the maximum he is likely to be "out of position", i.e. the amount his reckoning may be wrong. This estimate is important and is gained by experience and by knowledge of the ship's performance in previous passages. He considers ten miles to be his maximum possible error. (The writer always hoped for an average error, including both distance and direction, of not more than one and a half per cent of the run, but seldom achieved such good results; he was generally within three miles of his estimated position after running one hundred.) A point "A" is then selected for which to steer. Point "A" has to be far enough to the westward to ensure that, even if the ship is out of position to the eastward the full ten miles, the vessel will cross the fourteen-fathom line westward of the lightship, so that the chance of hearing the fog signal will not be jeopardised. He has continued his fourteen-fathom line away to the westward to see whether, in the event of his being ten miles to the westward of his estimated position, this line will provide a precaution against dangers there. Aided by soundings, the Captain now approaches his fourteen-fathom line, correcting, if he can, his estimated position by the depths obtained.

'The point "A", in this approach, has a special merit, for a mariner approaching its vicinity has a chance of hearing Beachy Head fog signal further; the seaman will be prepared, in addition, to hear his own fog siren echoed off the cliffs. Should this echo be received, his knowledge of the approximate speed at which sound travels in air will give him an estimate of his distance off the land.

'At length, yet with little fear of any unexpected dénouement, he strikes his fourteen-fathom line and alters course sharply to 090°. When this alteration has been completed he feels happier, knowing he is steering parallel to his dangers. The lightship, he believes – even knows – to be ahead of him and on his port bow. Sounding is continued, and the fourteen-fathom line is followed by making turns of 20° to 40° in or out, according to the depth obtained. Perfect silence for a time longer than the fog signal's "period" is ordered on board from time to time. . . .

'Working eastward with this procedure, our Captain has run little if any risk, and he would be singularly unfortunate if he failed to hear the lightship.

'We have followed this case through its phases because it exemplifies well how much can be done with soundings. We note that every possible means was harnessed to his use by our Captain – soundings, fog signals, sirens, silence and even "safety first". He made his plan and, with a precaution against surprise from error in any direction, he worked it out. Having "got hold of" the Royal Sovereign, he may – if he has a visibility of 500 yards – be pictured leaving his fourteen-fathom line to starboard, and edging to port to obtain a sight of the lightship. Thereafter, with but a short run to Dungeness, he will be doing point to point, and he will know that, in a run of only twenty-two miles, he is unlikely to be much out of his course and will steer accordingly – always remembering, as he approaches Dungeness, that he must again take all reasonable precautions.

'In the example just described there was a safeguard for all four (there are only four) of the eventualities; ahead, astern, to starboard and to port of the reckoning. Many occasions arise when all four possibilities need not be, and cannot be, countered. A landfall can be envisaged in which we might unwittingly be fifteen miles east or west of our estimated position without endangering the ship, and yet it might be fatal to be three miles ahead of the reckoning. We must select the risks whose results would be distressing, and avoid encountering them without safeguard.'

ANCHORING

Choosing a Position in which to Anchor

In choosing a position in which to anchor the ship, numerous factors have to be considered, namely:

(a) The depth of water.

(b) The length and draught of the ship.

(c) Whether the bottom is firm or soft. The older types of anchor (e.g. Admiralty Standard Cast or Forged Head, Byer's, Hall's) will hold satisfactorily in firm sea-beds such as clay, soft chalk, sand, sand/shingle and heavy mud; but will drag in softer sea-beds, such as soft mud, shingle and shell. Modern anchors will hold satisfactorily in any kind of sea-bed except rock because they dig themselves in.

(d) Whether the anchorage is in a land-locked harbour or an open roadstead.

(e) The strength and direction of the prevailing wind. If possible, anchor near the weather shore and so have a lee with room to drag.

(f) The direction and strength of the tidal streams.

(g) The rise and fall of the tide.

(h) The proximity of adjacent ships.

(i) The proximity of landing-places.

(j) The amount of cable which will depend on the depth of water, type of cable, weather, length of stay, and to a certain extent the nature of the bottom. With wrought iron cable and an average holding ground the length of cable should be four to six times the depth of water; with the smaller modern forged steel cable, which is much lighter, six to eight times the depth of water. These figures are very approximate.

(k) The proximity of dangers. It is impossible to give any definite rule as to how near a danger a ship may be anchored, but an ample margin of safety should be allowed in expectation of bad weather and the ship dragging her anchors. At single anchor it is usual to allow a safety margin equal to the amount of cable to be veered plus the length of the ship plus one cable.

Always try to anchor stemming the wind or tidal stream, whichever is the stronger. It needs a strong wind to produce a greater effect on the ship than a tidal stream of $\frac{1}{2}$ knot.

Come to with the weather anchor, except in places where the stream is so strong that the ship will lie easier if the lee anchor is let go. If other ships are already at anchor, it is usually possible to observe, from their cables, which is the best anchor to use.

Anchoring a Ship in a Chosen Position

(a) Choose a conspicuous mark ashore – for example, the church in Fig. 83, the line of bearing of which, passing through the chosen position, clears all dangers. This is the line of bearing on which to approach. If a transit is available, use it in preference to a single object. When using a single object it is often found, on reaching the final course, that this object is in line with some tree or conspicuous mark, which can then be used for a transit. If no object at all is available for steering on, then the ship must be fixed all the way along her approach course; but such a situation rarely occurs.

The shortest route to an anchorage is usually chosen in preference to a long detour – unless a high degree of accuracy is required. A long detour is not justified solely on the grounds that a suitable mark ahead, on which to anchor, is not available on the short approach.

(b) From A, the position of the anchor, lay back AX, the distance from the stem to the standard compass. This distance can be obtained from the Navigational Data Book. X will be the position of the standard compass on letting go.

(c) From X lay off a position line to some conspicuous object – for example, the chimney – such that it makes an angle of nearly 90° with the line of approach. The instant of arrival at X is then found by observing the bearing of this chimney.

(d) The speed of the ship must be sufficiently reduced before anchoring so that when the engines are reversed on letting go the anchor, the way will be taken off the ship when the required amount of cable has been laid out. The distances at which to make this reduction of speed vary with different types of ships and should be shown in the Navigational Data Book.

(e) Suppose that the ship reduces speed at one mile and stops engines at four cables from the anchorage. From X lay back along the line of approach a distance of one mile, XZ. Then Z is the point at which to reduce speed. Lay back XY, a distance of four cables, and Y is the point at which to stop engines. The instant of arrival at Z (and Y) is found by watching the bearing of a suitable object near the beam in a similar way to finding the instant of arrival at position X.

(f) If there is a cross stream, the course must be adjusted to make good the correct line of approach. The effect of the cross stream will increase as the ship loses headway. This is particularly evident in heavy ships which may have to stop their engines as much as seven cables before letting go the anchor.

(g) Turn on to the line of approach as soon as possible, to give plenty of time to get the ship steady on the line of bearing. The Navigating Officer should take over the handling of the ship himself before turning on to this course.

(h) If the ship is set off the line of bearing, regain the line with a bold alteration of course.

(i) In ships with a long forecastle, if the ship's head is not the same as the bearing of the line of approach on letting go, the bridge may be at X but the anchor will not be at A.

(j) Have alternative objects and bearings ready in case the selected objects are obscured. It is as well to have a complete alternative plan prepared.

(k) Have all data, objects, bearings, etc., written down in the notebook, so as to avoid having to look at the chart unnecessarily.

The following is a suggested form of layout for the anchorage shown in Fig. 83, the objects to port and starboard of the approach course being shown to the left and right of the distance column.

Plan for Anchoring in No. 1 Berth, Church Bay

		H.W.	L.W.
CHURCH BAY	⎱	0236 11′·5	0850 2′·3
6th JUNE	⎰	1500 11′·2	2112 2′·0

E.T.A. 1700   Tidal Stream 160° 1 kt. (Springs).

From Co. 070°. When Church bears 004°, a/c 358° to keep Church bg. 000°.

Check compass on Lighthouse ϕ Windmill 294½°.

Windmill	Beacon	Distance (Speed)	Seamark	Chimney	Steer
288°		10 (10)			358°
		5	078°	036°	
		4	090°	042°	
		3	102°	050°	
	302°	2 (stop)		060°	354°
	291°	1		073°	
	277°	⚓		086°	

Anchorage: 10 fm. mud.

Port ⚓ 5 shackles.

Note: It will be observed that the Navigating Officer has chosen, as his mark for turning on to the final approach course, the object on which he will be finally steering, and not some other beam object such as the windmill (*see* also Fig. 73).

(l) When on the final approach do not con the ship, but give the quartermaster courses to steer. This will then leave more time for observing bearings, etc.

(m) Although buoys should not be relied upon, do not ignore them. They will often give a good common-sense indication of the ship's position.

(n) Be careful, if choosing an object such as a church or chimney, that it is not likely to be confused with other churches or chimneys in the vicinity (*see* also page 109).

(o) Consider the bearing of the sun during the approach, and the probable effect of dazzle on the observation of objects.

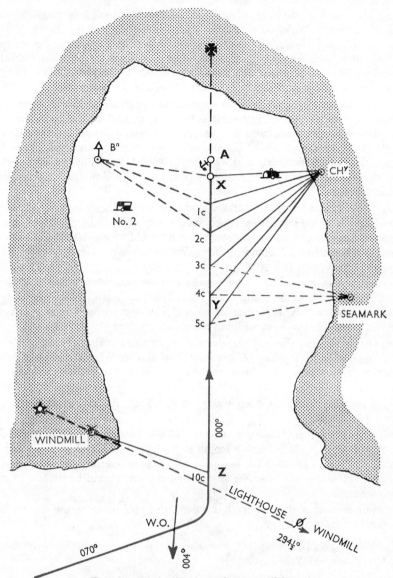

FIG. 83. Anchoring in a chosen position

(p) Submit the anchorage plan to the Captain in good time to make any alterations he may require; and ascertain that your suggestions on choice of anchor, amount of cable to be used, etc., are concurred in.

Information which the Captain particularly requires includes:

    (1) depth of water;
    (2) nature of bottom;
    (3) state of tide on anchoring;
    (4) rise and fall of tide;
    (5) tidal stream on anchoring.

(q) Keep the Captain fully informed of the situation during the final approach and, in particular, make sure that he hears your reports of the distance to go. It is not sufficient merely to report in a loud voice; the Captain may often have his attention diverted by signals, administrative matters, etc. The warning 'Stand by' should be given and then 'Let go' shortly before the final bearing comes on, to allow for delay in the anchor reaching the bottom.

(r) Make sure that a sounding is obtained at the moment of anchoring, both in order to check that sufficient cable is being used, and for the record (see (x) below). Leadsmen are placed in the chains when anchoring, mooring, and weighing, for obtaining soundings should echo sounding gear not be available. In addition, after anchoring and while weighing, they should be instructed to keep the lead on the bottom and report whether the ship is stopped, going ahead, or going astern.

(s) The Captain normally works the anchor flags. These are red and green hand-flags, denoting port or starboard anchor respectively. To avoid any chance of prematurely letting go the anchor, the flag should be exhibited steadily from a prominent position at 'Stand by' *for a few seconds only* before 'Let go', when it should be dropped smartly.

(t) As soon as the anchor is let go, the ship's position must be fixed. Since the ahead bearing and the beam bearing are already known, it is only necessary to obtain a check bearing of one other object. This should have been previously selected to make a good cut with the other two.

(u) On letting go, the engines are put astern to take the way off the ship. The duty of the Navigating Officer now is to observe what the ship is doing, either by beam bearings, by objects in the water, or by reports from the leadsmen in the chains.

(v) When anchoring in deep water, some cable should be veered before letting go.

(w) Anchor buoys. These are usually painted barricoes or blocks of wood which will support the necessary length of buoy rope. The buoy rope must be of sufficient length to reach the bottom at all states of the tide, so that, should it be necessary to slip the cable for any reason, the anchor can be readily located and recovered.

(x) The correct method of entering details of anchoring in the Ship's Log and notebook is as follows:

'Came to Port (Starboard) ⚓ with – shackles in – fathoms in No. – Berth (or in position –)'.

(y) The anchor bearings entered in the ship's log should be for the position of the anchor and not of the bridge on letting go.

Letting Go Second Anchor

If a gale should arise while the ship is riding at single anchor, the ship will normally yaw to an extent which will depend on her size and above-water design. At the end of each yaw, violent and sudden strains are brought on the cable, thus considerably increasing the chances of dragging.

In these circumstances some action is clearly required to prevent the ship dragging. Whether this can best be done by stopping the yaw, thus removing one of the contributory causes of dragging, or by putting out more weight of cable, is a controversial problem the solution of which varies with different ships and comparative sizes of cable.

There are two methods, based on the theories that:

(i) A second anchor dropped underfoot controls the yaw and thus reduces the sudden strains on the cable.

(ii) Two splayed anchors distribute the load between the cables, although they do not control the yaw.

In either method it is recommended that the second anchor should be let go when the ship has reached the limit of a yaw away from her first anchor. In the second method the amount of cable to be veered on the second anchor will depend upon circumstances, but at least four shackles will probably be required.

Without previous experience of a ship's behaviour, the first method may be adopted initially; then, if it does not prove successful, more cable may be veered on both anchors to conform to the second method.

Dragging

When selecting a transit or an object on shore (to watch its bearing) in order to see if the ship is dragging, it should be realized that it is not necessary for such objects to be marked on the chart. The object(s) should be chosen rather for position on the beam. Transits can be tested by walking along the upper deck to see if they open quickly enough to be of value.

The safest method of ensuring that the ship is not dragging is by fixing. Plot the position of the ship's anchor on the chart and draw a circle of radius equal to the length of cable veered plus the distance from stem to standard to give the 'bridge circle'. The fixes of the position of the bridge, by sextant angle and/or compass-bearing, will always lie within the plotted circle if the ship is not dragging.

Anchoring at a Definite Time without Altering Speed

It is always desirable to anchor the ship at the correct or advertised time; but a drastic increase or decrease of speed may not be possible or desirable, and it is therefore as well to plan the approach in such a way that the distance remaining to be steamed can be adjusted by alteration of course.

The following simple method of dealing with this problem enables the chart to be prepared beforehand; the navigator can see at a glance, whenever he fixes the ship's position, whether he is ahead or astern of time; and last-minute alterations of speed can be avoided.

EXAMPLE

A ship has signalled her time of anchoring at a position A, shown in Fig. 84, as 0800. She proposes to approach the anchorage on a course 180°. Her speed of approach will be 12 knots, and will not be altered until the engines are stopped at 3 cables from position A.

To prepare the chart, calculate the distance the ship will run in the 10 minutes prior to anchoring, making allowance for stopping engines 3 cables from A.

Lay back this distance *AB*, along the line of approach. *B* is then the position to be attained at 0750.

Since 5 minutes at 12 knots is equivalent to one mile, with centre *B* lay back 5-minute time circles. The chart is now prepared, and at 0710 the ship, steering 270° speed 12 knots, fixes her position at *F*.

At 0715 she is in position *E*, inside the 0715 circle. Similarly, at 0720 she is at *D*, inside the 0720 circle; but it is seen that at 0725 she will arrive at *C*, on the 0725 circle, at which time it will be necessary to steer the course *CB* in order to arrive at *B* at 0750.

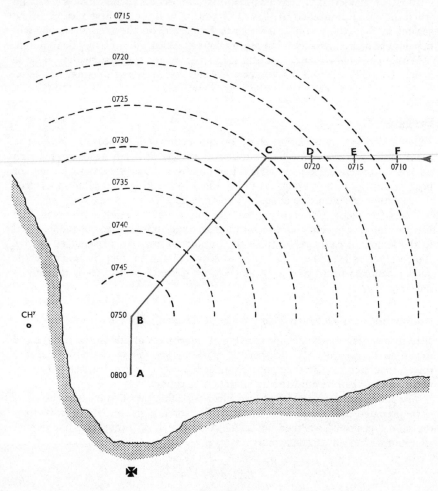

FIG. 84

Ensuring that the Anchor Berth is Clear

When approaching an anchorage, always make sure that the anchor berth and line of approach are clear of other ships. Check the position of any ship suspected of fouling the anchor berth by:

(a) fixing your own position and plotting the other ship by range and bearing;

(b) taking a bearing of the other ship when it is in transit with a charted shore object, and so obtaining a position line on which the other ship must lie. This should be done as early as possible and before altering to the approach course, so that a second position line may be obtained by observing a bearing of the ship in transit with another charted shore object. The position of the other ship will then be fixed, as shown in the following example.

EXAMPLE

A ship, shown in Fig. 85, steering 080° and intending to anchor in position Z by approaching the anchorage on a course 350°, suspects that a ship D is foul of her berth. At 1100 the ship is observed in transit with a chimney bearing 050°. At 1125 the ship is observed in transit with a flagstaff bearing 024°.

From these two lines of bearing, D's position can be plotted on the chart. The position of D's anchor must then be estimated, after allowance has been made for the wind and stream at the time.

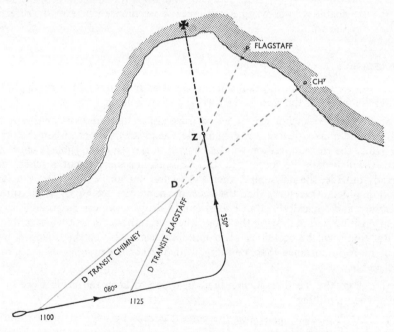

FIG. 85

Anchoring in a Poorly Charted Area

If there is no accurate chart of the anchorage, and the suitability of the berth is in any doubt, take careful soundings within a radius of at least 3 cables of the ship to make certain there are no uncharted rocks or dangers (*see* also *Queen's Regulations and Admiralty Instructions*).

MOORING

Mooring a Ship in a Selected Position

When mooring, the same principles apply as for anchoring, with the following exceptions:

(a) It is necessary, first, to decide the length of cable on each anchor when the ship has been moored. As a general rule, the amount of cable for a heavy ship is six shackles on each anchor. As explained in the *Manual of Seamanship*, Vol. II, one shackle of cable is usually required to go round the bows so that the mooring swivel may be shackled on. The distance between the two anchors when let go should therefore be $(6 \times 2) - 1$, or 11 shackles. If using cable with shackles of 15 fathoms, a shackle of cable equals 30 yards; therefore the distance of each anchor from the point A, in Fig. 86, should be $\frac{1}{2}$ (11×30), or 165 yards. This allowance does not vary appreciably with the depth of water.

(b) The direction of the line joining the anchors should coincide, if possible, with that of the previling wind or tidal stream; and each anchor should be sufficiently far from dangers, and from the anchors of other ships, to enable it to be weighed without inconvenience whatever the direction of the wind.

PROCEDURE

1. Reduce speed so that the cable on the first anchor is laid out straight and all way is taken off the ship as the second anchor is let go.

2. The second anchor can be let go from either the forecastle or the bridge. Given good marks, distant less than a mile, the precise moment when the bridge arrives at the correct position will be known; but, even if the cable is tautly laid out, it will usually be found that the eleventh shackle has not reached, or is already outside, the hawsepipe when the second anchor bearing comes on. It is recommended, therefore, that the second anchor be let go by a mixture of 'bearing' and 'shackles', in an endeavour to drop it as near as possible to the right position without giving the cable officer an impossible task when middling.

But there will be occasions when middling accurately in the assigned berth is of more importance than middling with the correct number of shackles on each cable.

3. Let go the weather anchor first, in order to keep the cable clear of the stem when middling.

4. The ship must *make good* the correct course between anchors while the first cable is being laid out.

5. Always avoid excessive strain on the cables.

6. In order to cant the ship in the right direction for middling, the whee may be put over about 2 or 3 shackles before letting go the second anchor, without having any appreciable effect on the berth.

7. Remember that the stem of the ship will fall well to leeward of the line of anchors when lying at open hawse.

EXAMPLE

A ship, shown in Fig. 86, is ordered to moor with 5 shackles on each anchor in position A. Stem to standard: 100 feet.

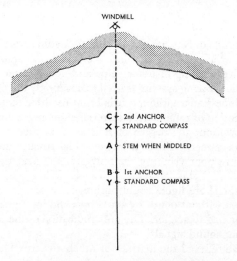

FIG. 86. Mooring in a chosen position

It is decided to approach with the windmill ahead on a line of bearing. This line of bearing will be the 'line of anchors' when the ship is moored.

From A lay off $AB = AC = \dfrac{(2 \times 5) - 1}{2} \times 30$ yards $= 135$ yards.

B and C will be the positions of the first and second anchors.

From B and C lay distances of 100 feet to Y and X.

Y and X are the positions of the standard compass at the moments of letting go the first and second anchor respectively.

CHAPTER VI

Radio Aids to Navigation

THE TERM 'Radio Aids to Navigation', or simply 'Radio Aids', is used to embrace all those systems which provide the means of fixing the ship's position as well as those which give warning of other ships and above-water obstructions. The term 'Radio Position-Fixing system' is used to cover only the former requirement and does not include Radar although it is often used for fixing the ship.

Before the invention of radio aids, a ship relied on an accurate reckoning from her last known position; the degree of reliance depended on the elapsed time and the correct assessment of speed, leeway, tidal streams and currents. When making a landfall in poor visibility the only aids to navigation were soundings and, by night, shore lights of reduced range. When visibility was further reduced by fog, the shore lights could no longer be seen. If the ship's position was not established without doubt by soundings and fog signals from lighthouse or light-vessel, she had to anchor. The only indication of the presence of another ship in fog was her sound signal.

Radio Aids have relieved the mariner of much anxiety. They have given him a means of discovering where he is with such accuracy that he can make a safe landfall and then proceed to his port no matter what the visibility may be. They show him the positions of other ships in a fog. But they must be used intelligently and the information derived from them must be superimposed on the fundamental teachings of navigation and pilotage and of the conduct of ships in narrow waters.

A position from a radio position-fixing system or radar must be related to the position by reckoning because human errors occur in reading an instrument whether it is a compass or a dial on a radio aid.

The influence of radar on the Rule of the Road is considered in Chapter XV

The Evolution of Radio Aids

Until 1939 the only radio aid in general use at sea was the Medium-frequency Direction Finding (MF DF) set. Many aids were produced during the Second World War and in 1946 the first International Meeting on Radio Aids to Marine Navigation (IMRAMN) was held at which different countries pooled their knowledge and attempted to lay down a policy for future developments.

Radio Aids may be divided into three categories: Ocean, Landfall or Coastal Navigation, and Pilotage. The degree of accuracy required of each is different. The table opposite gives the systems at present available in H.M. ships, which will be described later in this chapter.

Propagation of Radio Waves

Frequency and Wavelength. – Radio Aids make use of electro-magnetic waves similar to those of light, but differing in wavelength. For practical purposes the speed of such waves may be considered constant at approximately 300,000 km/sec.

CLASSIFICATION OF RADIO AIDS

FUNCTION	DISTANCE FROM NEAREST DANGER (*miles*)	ACCURACY REQUIRED	URGENCY	SYSTEMS AVAILABLE
Ocean Aid (O)	Over 50	±1 per cent of distance from nearest danger	15 minutes	1. MF DF (Adcock) (shore-based) 2. Loran 3. Consol 4. Decca
Landfall Aid (L) Coastal Navigation Aid (C)	Between 50 and 3	±½ mile to ±200 yards	5 minutes to ½ minute	1. MF DF shipborne and shore-based(L) *see Note* (i) 2. Loran (L and C) 3. Consol (L) *see Note* (ii) 4. Decca (L and C) 5. Radar, shipborne (L and C)
Pilotage Aid (P)	Less than 3	±50 yards	Instantaneous	1. Decca 2. Radar, shipborne, to U.K. specifications – *see Note* (iii)

Notes:

(i) Although MF DF does not strictly conform to the accuracy requirements given, it is included here to show the functions it may be considered to perform.

(ii) Consol cannot be used inside a range of 25 miles from the transmitter.

(iii) The U.K. specifications for Marine Radar (1957).

Waves may be defined either by frequency or length; frequency in kilocycles per second (kc/s) × wavelength in metres = 300,000, e.g., a frequency of 50 kc/s corresponds to a wavelength of 6,000 metres, a wavelength of 50 metres corresponds to a frequency of 6,000 kc/s. The table shows the arbitrary bandwidths into which radio waves are divided, and the systems described in this chapter.

WAVES FROM A TRANSMITTER

Radio transmission may be considered as consisting partly of a 'ground wave' which follows the surface of the Earth, and the remainder 'sky wave' which represents the rest of the energy transmitted in all directions in space.

Ground Waves. – By using low frequency (LF), a range of some thousands of miles can be reached thereby showing that the wave is bent to the curvature of the Earth. As frequency is increased the reception range is reduced until at very high frequencies communication is limited to a few miles. The range of reception not only depends on the power of the transmitter but also on the nature of the intervening ground; a signal that reaches 900 miles over the sea may not be heard at more than 100 miles over land.

Sky Waves. – Signals at frequencies between LF and VHF can be heard beyond the ground wave after an intervening interval (skip distance). Whereas the attenuation of the ground wave increases with frequency, the attenuation of these skip waves decreases.

Frequency	Wavelength	System
VLF 0–30 kc/s	Very long wave (more than 10,000 metres)	
LF 30–300 kc/s	Long wave (10,000–1,000 metres)	Decca: 80–150 kc/s
MF 300–3,000 kc/s	Medium wave (1,000–100 metres)	MF DF: 250–600 kc/s Consol: 200–500 kc/s Loran: 1,750–1,950 kc/s
HF 3–30 Mc/s	Short wave (100–10 metres)	
VHF 30–300 Mc/s	Metric (10–1 metre)	
UHF 300–3,000 Mc/s	Decimetric (1 metre–10 cm)	
SHF 3,000–30,000 Mc/s	Centimetric (10 cm–1 cm) 'S' band covers 10 cm 'X' band covers 3 cm	Radar: 9,000–10,000 Mc/s (shipborne)

Note: 1,000 kc/s = 1 Mc/s

Research has revealed that there is a belt of ionized gases extending from about 27 to 220 miles above the surface of the Earth, called the 'ionosphere', which refracts certain radio waves sufficiently to return them to the Earth.

The ionosphere consists of three main regions (Fig. 87); within two of which there is a layer of maximum ionization density. Generally speaking the ionization is at its densest over the sunlit portions of the Earth and at heights that vary with time of day, season and geographical position.

The regions and layers that most influence radio waves are, the 'D Region' at a height varying from 27 to 50 miles, the 'E Layer' varying from 50 to 90 miles, and the 'F layer' varying from 150 to 190 miles, above the Earth.

One effect of these regions and layers is to bend the sky waves. When this 'refraction' is sufficient to deflect the radio waves back to the Earth, the returning wave is called, inaccurately, a 'sky-wave reflection' or 'one-hop' wave. In some conditions sky waves undergo two or more reflections from an E or F layer and are called 'two-hop', 'three-hop', etc., with the suffix E or F as appropriate. Sky waves reflected by the D Region are normally so attenuated that multi-hop waves are not experienced.

Sky-wave reflections travel further than the ground wave and the same transmitted signal will be received at the receiver in the following order; ground wave, one-hop E, two-hop E, then F layer reflections. This sequence may be seen on a Loran indicator, described later. D Region sky-wave components affect the performance of Decca, but not Loran which works at a higher frequency.

EFFECT OF SKY WAVES

The density of ionization of the layers is less by night than by day so that the sky-wave effects experienced by a receiver vary.

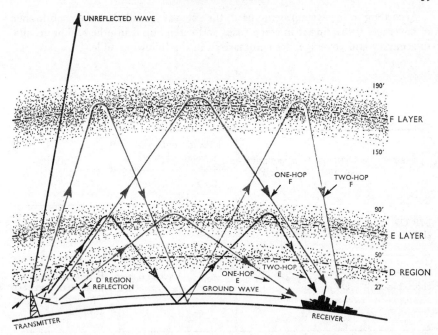

FIG. 87. Ground wave and sky wave paths

By day sky waves are attenuated and also reflected by the D Region, returning well within the ground wave; the attenuation is enough to prevent any serious interference from them. Any waves reflected from the E Layer are absorbed by the D Region before they can reach the Earth; no waves reach the F Layer.

By night sky waves are less attenuated by the D Region. Therefore reflections from both E and F Layers return to Earth; some within the ground wave, others beyond it. Thus the following sky-wave effects may be experienced:

NIGHT EFFECT (350–500 kc/s)

APPROXIMATE RANGE LIMITS (*nautical miles*)	SKY-WAVE EFFECT
0–75	Nil
75–350	Weak (mainly D Region reflections at shorter ranges).
350–500	Amplitude comparable with that of ground wave and causing difficulty in identification and serious interference.
500–limit of ground wave	Amplitude increasingly greater than that of ground wave.
Beyond limit of ground wave	Sky waves only received.

According to the system being used, the sky waves will affect the useful range of coverage, restricting it in some cases and extending it in others. The results, in accuracy and coverage, are summarized in the following table.

APPROXIMATE EFFECTIVE RANGES OF RADIO POSITION-FIXING SYSTEMS

System	General Method	Frequency (kc/s)	Range over sea (nautical miles) Day	Night	Remarks
MF DF shipborne	Loop type DF	250–600	300	25	
MF DF shore-based	Adcock DF	300–600	500	500 and over	Errors up to 4° experienced between 100 and 500 miles at night.
MF DF shore-based	Loop type DF	250–600	200	25	
Consol	Modulated C.W. Amplitude comparison	200–500	1,000	1,200	System cannot be used within 25 miles of station.
Loran	Pulse-time difference comparison	1,750–1,950	600	1,200	
Decca	C.W. phase comparison	80–150	300 300–1,000 (lower accuracy)	0–75 (as for day); 75–240 (poorer than by day); over 240 (liable to serious errors)	

Note: The range of shore-based, loop-aerial MF DF must be considered shorter than that of shipborne MF DF because the former relies on transmissions from ships which may not be as powerful as those from shore transmitters.

RADIO POSITION-FIXING SYSTEMS

1. MF DF

Principles

The principle of the medium-frequency direction finder is based upon the directive properties of a plane vertical loop aerial. The strength of a signal induced in such a loop by an arriving stream of electro-magnetic waves from a distant transmitter depends upon the aspect of the loop to the stream. As the loop is rotated about a vertical axis, so the strength of signal varies from a maximum to zero. The rate of change of signal strength is greatest near the minimum position which is the position normally used in direction finding. The method of indicating this minimum position may be aural, through headphones, or visual by the aid of a meter or cathode ray tube.

Instead of rotating the aerial, it is possible to use a system of fixed aerials consisting of two loops at right angles to each other. The direction of arrival of the waves is then determined by a *radio-goniometer* which is normally located in the DF office. This simple aerial can be sited in a position less liable to errors from induced secondary fields from the hull and superstructure.

Limitations of Frequency

The loop direction finder provides the best results when the radio waves are horizontal, i.e., ground waves. To obtain the greatest range and stability, the lowest possible frequencies should be used.

Since a number of merchant ships and small craft are fitted only with MF receivers and transmitters, the lower frequencies of the MF band have been selected.

The aerials are not yet immune from sky-wave effects so that inaccurate bearings are obtained when ground and sky waves are present or in the region where sky wave prevails.

The Track of a Radio Wave

Radio waves normally travel along great circles. If they cross the coast they may be deflected as much as five degrees according to the angle of crossing. This coastal refraction is zero when the waves cross at right angles and increases with the angle of incidence. The waves are always bent towards the coastline when they pass from land to sea. Greater errors may be experienced when radio waves pass over hilly country. These errors are best avoided by siting the transmitters on the coast and by the ship selecting stations so that the intervening distances between her and the stations do not pass over the land.

SHORE-BASED MF DF

Procedure

The ship asks for a bearing then transmits her call sign for one minute; the shore station takes the bearing and passes it to the ship. The only equipment required by the ship is a MF transmitter and receiver; she must, of course, know the geographical position of the station.

Some DF stations are grouped together under one control station so that a ship may request her position or simultaneous bearings from the group. A ship may obtain a fix from two or more independent stations; or a running fix from two bearings of the same station.

A radio DF station is indicated on charts by the abridged description R°.D.F. The older form W/T DF may still be found.

A list of DF stations is given in the *Admiralty List of Radio Signals*, Vol. II, together with the procedure and regulations governing their use. All bearings given are true, and may be obtained when the ship lies within the calibrated sectors. Variable errors may be experienced within these sectors, in which case the sub-sectors affected are designated as 'unreliable'.

Reciprocal Bearings

The minimum signal indicates either the bearing of the transmitter or its reciprocal. A 'sense-finder' in many installations removes this ambiguity. Without this indication a shore station may not be able to determine the correct bearing of the ship. Should a bearing that is evidently the reciprocal be signalled to a ship, it must not be reversed and plotted because the calibration error, applied by the station to the reciprocal bearing, is probably not the same as that which should be applied to the reverse bearing. In this case the corrected reciprocal bearing must be requested from the station. Certain DF stations, particularly those with extensive arcs of coverage, are equipped to furnish the two corrected true bearings for any observation; ships may choose whichever is applicable.

Range and Accuracy

The table on page 160 shows that there is a large difference between the night ranges of the loop-type and Adcock systems. This is due to the fact that the Adcock system uses aerials that can obtain bearings equally well from sky and ground waves. It can take bearings of ship and aircraft transmissions, but, unfortunately, it cannot be used afloat.

Generally speaking, bearings within the reliable, calibrated sectors of a DF station should be accurate to within two degrees for loop aerials, and less than two degrees for Adcock-type aerials. This is equivalent to about five per cent of the range. Bearings are classified as follows:

    Class 1: accurate to within 2 degrees
    Class 2: accurate to within 5 degrees
    Class 3: accurate to within 10 degrees
    Class 4: unreliable.

The class of bearing should be reported by both ship and shore DF operators. Instructions to radio operators for obtaining the best results from DF stations are given in the *Admiralty List of Radio Signals* (Vol. II).

Advantages and Disadvantages

The bearing is determined by skilled personnel. Personal error is reduced.

The instruments, being fixed geographically, are less liable to derangement than shipborne sets.

The ship has to transmit a radio signal. A reduction in signal traffic is always desirable, and in time of war radio silence may be enforced.

SHIPBORNE MF DF

Sources of Bearings

The bearing of a Coast radio station, which normally engages in radio communications with ships, can be taken. A coast radio station which transmits on request for the use of ship's DF is indicated on charts by the abridged description R°. Details of these stations may be found in the *Admiralty List of Radio Signals* (Vol. I).

Radiobeacons are established round the coast, often at lighthouses and lightships. They are sometimes arranged in groups of two or three working on the same frequency, with interlocked time schedules. Transmissions occur at advertised intervals in clear weather and more frequently in fog; they consist of a combination of identifying letters and long dashes. A radiobeacon is indicated on the chart by the abridged description: R°. B^n. The older form – W/T B^n. – may still be found. Further information on radiobeacons will be found in the *Admiralty List of Radio Signals* (Vol. II).

SUBSIDIARY USES OF SHIPBORNE DF

A ship may obtain the bearing of another ship with which she intends to effect a meeting; she may also establish a position line (DF bearing) from a ship whose position is known when her own position is in doubt. Shipborne sets are used to help locate a ship sending distress signals on 500 kc/s.

DF Installations in H.M. ships

H.M. ships are normally fitted with fixed, crossed-coil equipment incorporating a sense-finding attachment. The incoming signals are affected by the hull and superstructure of the ship – in a way analogous to the error introduced into a magnetic compass by a steel ship – so that the aerial should be sited amidships and symmetrically in relation to the nearest ship structure. The remaining errors can be discovered by 'swinging' or calibrating in a similar manner to that employed when adjusting compasses; but since it is only the above-water part of the ship that causes errors, the ship should be calibrated for different draughts (not normally necessary in warships). In addition, the errors may vary with frequency; calibration should therefore be carried out at the frequencies most used and the sense-finder checked at the same time.

The error is mainly quadrantal, having maxima on the bows and quarters and minima fore and aft and on the beams. It can be corrected electrically or mechanically (cams), or from tables or curves. Usually a combination of these methods is used.

The bearings obtained by DF are relative. True bearings can be ascertained after applying the necessary correction to the relative bearing. In some equipments a gyro repeater is incorporated so that true bearing can be obtained directly.

RESPONSIBILITY

The Navigating Officer chooses the stations from which bearings are required, considering in his choice the range, time of day, land error, etc. The Communications Officer is responsible for the operation of the set and the Electrical Officer for its maintenance.

Nomenclature

The first letter indicates the type of Aerial:

A = Adcock	F = Fixed Frame Coil
L = Loop	R = Rotating Frame Coil

The second letter indicates the System:

A = HF or MF	H = HF
M = MF	

The number indicates the Mark of equipment.

Example: F.M. 12 = MF DF, fixed frame coil, Mk. 12.

Calibration

The first calibration of a DF set in a new ship, or of a new type of set is carried out by officers from the Admiralty Surface Weapons Establishment (A.S.W.E.). Subsequent calibrations are conducted by an electrical officer of the ship, port, base or dockyard.

Facilities

H.M. ships normally employ a transmitting vessel. Details of these facilities and calibrating berths are published in current Fleet, Port and Station Orders. An alternative method is to observe bearings of a shore transmitting station. Certain radiobeacons listed in the *Admiralty List of Radio Signals* (Vol. II) provide special transmissions for calibration purposes.

Application for Calibration

A ship requiring calibration should apply at least two days before, or include it in the trials programme. To avoid delays during calibration, instrumental tests (laid down in the appropriate handbook) should all be completed beforehand.

Occasions when Calibration is Required

Initial Calibrations are carried out on new sets or when any alteration is made to an existing set.

Check Calibrations are carried out

(a) after any structural or rigging alterations have been made in the vicinity of the DF aerial;

(b) when results from the set are unsatisfactory and the errors cannot be attributed to any cause so far listed;

(c) at intervals of approximately one year.

Time Required

The normal maximum time required for MF calibration is:

Initial calibration: 3 hours.
Check calibration: $1\frac{1}{2}$ hours.

CONDITIONS DURING CALIBRATION

(a) All aerials, boats, cranes, guns, etc., particularly those near the DF aerial should be in the normal sea stowage position.

(b) Visual bearings should be taken from the position of the aerial. If the aerial is far from the bridge, a portable bearing plate (provided by the calibrating staff) is used. Communications with the DF office must be available.

(c) When calibrating from a shore station, the ship should lie from 3 to 5 miles distant and well clear of any land.

If a transmitting vessel is used, the ship should anchor so that the transmitting ship may safely circle the ship at a radius of not less than $7\frac{1}{2}$ cables.

In either case the berth should be clear of traffic so that no ship may pass between the transmitting and calibrating ships.

Procedure when Calibrating

Simultaneous visual and DF relative bearings are taken of the shore station or transmitting vessel. The rate of swing when calibrating on a shore station should not exceed 6° per minute. On completion, the required electrical or mechanical corrections are made; and a correction curve or table is made out, if necessary.

Choice of Station

When using either shore or shipborne DF, the following considerations govern the choice of a station:

(a) *Ship's distance from Shore Station.* – The accuracy of bearings varies with the time of day and type of equipment, while the maximum range increases at lower frequencies. If the effective ranges of DF sets given on page 160 are taken to give an accuracy of about 2°, then at greater ranges the accuracy will be less. Moreover, the conversion of great-circle into mercatorial bearing by the convergency method (described later) is an approximation which holds good only up to a range of about 1,000 miles. At greater ranges the 'Intercept Method' (described in Volume III) should be used.

If an accurate position is required the range should not exceed 100 miles, even though first-class bearings may sometimes be obtained up to the maximum effective range of the set.

For loop-type aerials the range is further restricted at night, as shown in the table on page 160. The maximum range at which certain radio-beacons may normally be used by day is given in the *Admiralty List of Radio Signals* (Vol. II).

(b) *Path of signal between ship and station.* – This should be as much over the sea as possible. If the path has to cross the coast, choose a station where the path crosses the coast as nearly as possible at right angles. Avoid hilly country.

(c) *Calibrated sectors.* – Ensure that the bearing obtained is within a reliably calibrated sector.

Errors of Shipborne Sets

If bearings are suspected to be in error, the following points should be considered before deciding that a set needs re-calibration:

(1) Coastal Refraction (Land effect).

(2) Sky-wave (Night) effect. Serious errors may occur at ranges greater than 25 miles (for loop-type systems) and between 100 and 500 miles (for Adcock systems) for bearings taken between one hour before sunset and one hour after sunrise.

(3) Class of bearing.

(4) Possibility of a reciprocal bearing.

(5) Accuracy of gyro and repeater, or method of converting relative to true bearing.

(6) Temporary structural changes, such as movement of armament while bearings were being taken.

(7) Use of radio (transmission) during DF operation.

(8) Incorrect application of convergency or incorrect plotting of the bearing (described later).

Plotting DF Bearings

Radio waves follow a great-circle track. Great circles appear as straight lines on Gnomonic charts but they cannot be used for plotting DF bearings because true bearings are maintained only at the point of contact (tangential point) on which the particular projection is based. A specially-constructed compass rose with unequal graduations would be required for each DF station and each position of a ship using its own DF set. This is obviously quite impracticable.

This subject is further explained in Volume III.

Convergency

A true (or great-circle) bearing, unless it coincides with the equator or a meridian, is represented on a Mercator chart by a line which curves towards the poles. Meridians are represented by parallel straight lines. It follows that a true bearing will cut successive meridians at different angles. This difference, when two

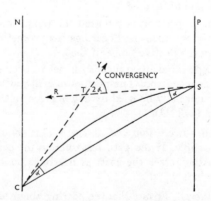

FIG. 88. Convergency and half-convergency

particular meridians are considered, is called 'convergency'; it depends on the differences of latitude and longitude, and on the mid-latitude between the points of intersection. In Fig. 88, *S* is a shore radio station and *C* a ship plotted on a Mercator chart. The curved line *CS* is the great-circle line of bearing between *C* and *S*; *CY* and *SR* are tangents to the great circle. The straight line *CS* is the mercatorial line of bearing (or rhumb line) between *C* and *S*.

The angle *YTS* is therefore the convergency and is equal to (*TCS* + *TSC*). Since these angles are equal, each of them is equal to half-convergency. (This is described more fully in Volume III.)

To obtain the mercatorial bearing when a true bearing has been observed by the DF set, it is only necessary to apply *half-convergency* to the true bearing and then to lay off the resultant (mercatorial) bearing from the station. Regardless of whether the bearing is obtained by the ship or the shore station, or whether in North or South latitudes, the rule for obtaining the mercatorial bearing is:

Apply half-convergency to the great-circle bearing towards the equator.

Convergency can be found by the following methods:

(a) By calculation from the approximate formula:

Convergency in minutes = difference of longitude in minutes × sin mean latitude (see also Vol. III).

(b) From the traverse table:

Enter the d.long as the distance and the mean latitude as the course; the resulting departure is then the convergency in minutes.

(c) From the convergency scale in the *Admiralty List of Radio Signals* (Vol. II) in the introduction to Radio Direction-finding stations.

Half-convergency can be obtained direct from Diagram 5061, to be found at the end of the *Admiralty List of Radio Signals* (Vol. II). Instructions for its use are given in the diagram.

EXAMPLE 1

FIXING THE SHIP BY SIMULTANEOUS BEARINGS FROM TWO SHORE DF STATIONS

In Fig. 89, a ship's D.R. is 48° 45′N., 25° 30′W.: DF bearings are taken from Malin Head 244¾° and Ushant 277½°. What is her position?

Malin Head	Lat. 55° 22′N.	Long. 7° 20½′W.
D.R.	Lat. 48° 45′N.	Long. 25° 30′W.

Mean Lat.   52° 03′N.   d.long 18° 09′·5 = 1089′·5

Convergency = 1089·5 × sin 52° = 859′ = 14° 19′

Half-convergency = 7° 10′

The true bearing signalled by Malin Head was $244\frac{3}{4}°$; therefore the **Mercatorial** bearing is $237\frac{1}{2}°$.

D.R.	Lat. 48° 45'N.	Long. 25° 30'W.
Ushant	Lat. 48° 26½'N.	Long. 5° 05½'W.

Mean Lat.	48° 36'N.	d.long 20° 24'·5 = 1224'·5

Convergency = 1224·5 × sin 48° 36' = 919' = 15° 19'

Half-convergency = 7° 40'

The true bearing signalled by Ushant was $277\frac{1}{2}°$; therefore the Mercatorial bearing is 270°.

Laying off $237\frac{1}{2}°$ and 270° on the chart from Malin Head and Ushant respectively, the intersection which is the ship's position is:

$$48° 27\frac{1}{2}'N., 25° 05'W.$$

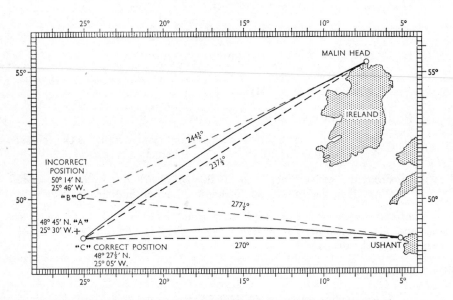

FIG. 89. Error in a DF fix when half-convergency is not applied

Fig. 89, drawn on Mercator's projection, shows the error involved if true bearings are laid off uncorrected for half-convergency. The solid lines are great circles. The red lines are the true bearings laid off as signalled, their intersection B in 50° 14'N., 25° 46'W. is approximately 110 miles from the correct position. The dotted lines are the Mercatorial bearings intersecting at C.

Position A is the D.R. from which the half-convergency was calculated. If the error in the ship's assumed position is very great, the value of half-convergency must be re-calculated using the Lat. and Long. of C, and a more accurate fix obtained.

Although this method is not completely accurate, it can be used for all practical purposes up to 1,000 miles range.

EXAMPLE 2

FIXING THE SHIP BY ASTRONOMICAL OBSERVATION AND A DF BEARING OF A RADIOBEACON

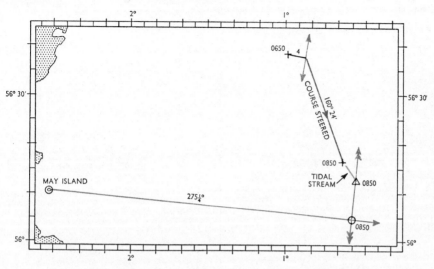

FIG. 90. Fixing by astronomical observation and DF bearing

In Fig. 90, ship's course is 160°; speed 12 knots. Tidal stream between 0650 and 0850 setting 140° – 2½ knots.

At 0650 in D.R. 56° 40′N., 1° 00′W., a sun sight gave an intercept of 4′ 'towards' 100°.

At 0850 the ship obtained a DF bearing of 276° of May Island Radiobeacon. What was the ship's position at 0850?

May Island	Lat. 56° 11′N.	Long. 2° 33′W.	
0850 E.P.	Lat. 56° 13′N.	Long. 0° 32′W.	

Mean Lat.   56° 12′N.   d.long 2° 01′ = 121′

Convergency = 121 sin 56° 12′ = 100

Half-convergency = 50′

The Mercatorial bearing of the radiobeacon is 275¼°.

From plotting on the chart, as shown in Fig. 90, the ship's position at 0850 is 56° 05′N., 0° 35′W.

The mathematical explanation of the above examples is given in Volume III.

2. HYPERBOLIC POSITION-FIXING SYSTEMS

All radio navigation systems which use fixed reference points on the Earth's surface must use either bearings or distance from these reference points as the basis of operation. So far, in DF, we have considered a system which uses bearings. Now let us consider how we can measure distance.

Construction of a Hyperbolic Pattern

Consider two transmitters, A and B in Fig. 91, 300 miles apart. If radio frequency pulses are transmitted simultaneously from A and B they will be received at the same instant by a receiver located at any point P on the right bisector of the base-line AB. The perpendicular bisector of the base-line is the locus of all points for which the time interval between receipt of pulses is Zero.

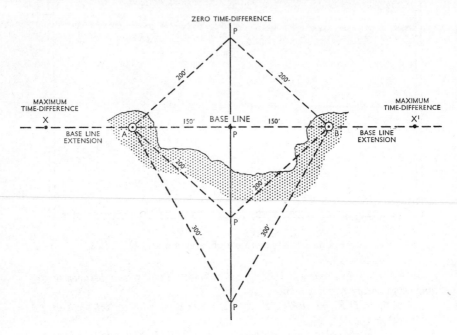

FIG. 91. Construction of a hyperbolic pattern (1)

Now consider a receiver situated at X on one extension of the base-line AB. B's signal now has to travel 300 miles further than A's before reaching the receiver. But if the receiver cannot differentiate between signals from A and B, there is no means of telling which of the two has arrived first and the receiver may be at X'.

Since radio waves travel at a speed of about 162,000 nautical miles per second, the unit of time used for convenience when measuring time-differences is one-millionth of a second, or one microsecond (abbreviation: μs). The base-line extension is therefore the locus of all points where the time-difference in the reception of signals simultaneously transmitted by A and B is 1800 μs[1], which is approximately the time taken by radio waves to travel 300 nautical miles.

Now suppose that the time-difference is 600 μs, which corresponds roughly to a distance of 100 nautical miles. In Fig. 92 it is seen that the receiver may be situated at any point Q which is 100 miles nearer A than B, or at any point R nearer B than A. The loci of all such points are two hyperbolae ST and UV

---

[1] This figure is taken for convenience; 1854 μs is a more accurate estimate.

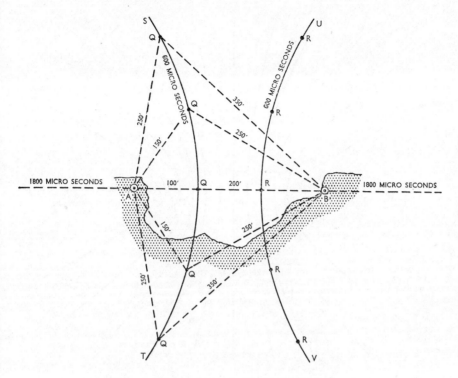

FIG. 92. Construction of a hyperbolic pattern (2)

with the stations A and B at the focal points. Both these hyperbolae are lines of constant path-difference equivalent to 600 μs of time. Similar hyperbolae can be drawn for any other time-difference. Fig. 93 shows hyperbolae drawn at intervals of 300 μs.

Ambiguity from Simultaneous Transmissions

It is clear from Fig. 93 that there is ambiguity in the observer's position because he may be on either one of a pair of similarly numbered position lines. Near the zero line this ambiguity would be hard to resolve in practice.

STAGGERED TRANSMISSIONS

By arranging for the pulse from A always to be received before that from B, the ambiguity is avoided. The difficulty of achieving an accurate delay in the transmission of B is overcome by using the pulse from station A – known as the 'master' – to trigger off the transmitter at station B – known as the 'slave'.

Since it is inconvenient in practice to work with such a small time-difference, the required separation is effected by imposing a further delay to the slave's signal. This consists of an accurately fixed time delay, plus a further small

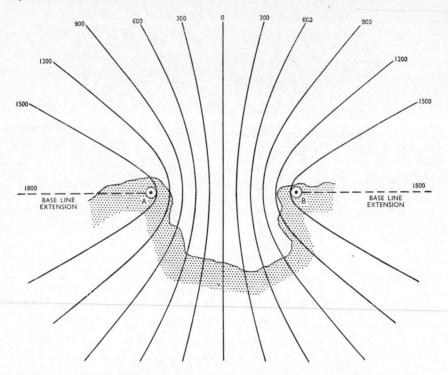

FIG. 93. Hyperbolic pattern: simultaneous transmissions

amount called the 'coding delay'. The effect of this is shown in Fig. 94, in which, for simplicity, the stations A and B are shown only 3 miles apart.

Consider two points C and D on the base-line, symmetrically situated on either side of the mid-point E. Suppose that, along the base-line, it takes:

20 μs for A's signal to reach B
7 μs for A's signal to reach C
13 μs for A's signal to reach D
7 μs for B's signal to reach D
13 μs for B's signal to reach C
10 μs for A's and B's signal to reach E, and that there is a time delay of 50 μs.

(1) The time-difference at C will be $(20 + 50 + 13) - 7 = 76\,\mu$s.
   The time-difference at D will be $(20 + 50 + 7) - 13 = 64\,\mu$s.
   Thus it is seen that the ambiguity which would arise from identical readings (Fig. 93) has been obviated.

(2) Similarly at any point X on the base-line extension and $x\,\mu$s from A, the time-difference would be:

$$(20 + 50 + 20 + x) - x = 90\,\mu\text{s},$$
and at any point Y on the base-line extension and $y\,\mu$s from B, the time-difference would be:

$$(20 + 50 + y) - (20 + y) = 50\,\mu\text{s}.$$

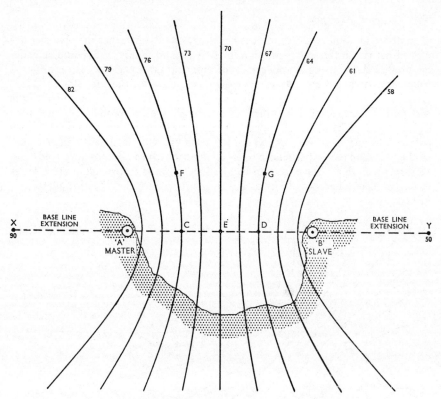

FIG. 94. Hyperbolic pattern: staggered transmissions

(3) Now, on the centre line at E the reading will be:

$$(20 + 50 + 10) - 10 = 70\,\mu\text{s}.$$

(4) Consider two points F and G symmetrically situated with respect to the centre line, so that it takes:

> 8 μs for A's signal to reach F
> 14 μs for A's signal to reach G
> 14 μs for B's signal to reach F
> 8 μs for B's signal to reach G

Now it will be found that:

> the time-difference at $F = (20 + 50 + 14) - 8 = 76\,\mu$s, and
> the time-difference at $G = (20 + 50 + 8) - 14 = 64\,\mu$s.

Ambiguity has again been avoided by the use of the time delay, and the figures confirm that the same values will be observed at F and C and at D and G.

There is now a single line for each time-difference, and these hyperbolae can be numbered as shown in Fig. 94 with the lower numbers near the slave station.

If a chart is overprinted with such a pattern, an observer provided with a suitable receiver can ascertain that he is situated somewhere along a particular position line.

THE LATTICE PATTERN

In order to obtain a position, it is necessary to establish that the observer lies on at least two intersecting position lines. A second family of hyperbolae could be produced by using another pair of transmitters operating on a different frequency, or at different time intervals, from those of the first station. More economically, as is done in practice, a second 'slave' station can be added to the first pair. By arranging for suitably different delays or frequencies, the three signals can now be observed separately and a position obtained from the 'lattice pattern', as shown in Fig. 95, where the position R is fixed at the intersection of the interpolated hyperbolic curves denoted by the numbers 59·5 (red) and 18 (green). A third 'slave' station can be incorporated to provide a third series of hyperbolae. Charts overprinted in this manner are called 'Lattice charts'.

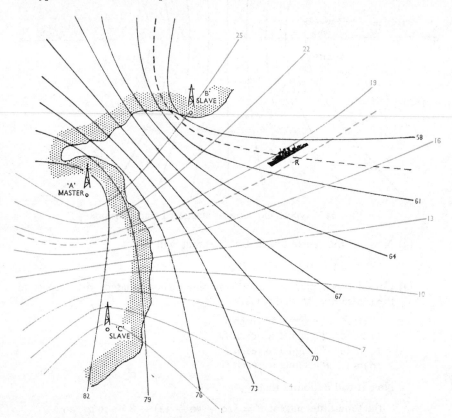

FIG. 95. Typical lattice chain (one 'master' and two 'slaves')

Systems using the Principle of Hyperbolic Position Lines

The system, so far described, that uses the measurement of the difference in the time of arrival of two signals, is used in the LORAN system and is known as the 'pulse method'.

Similar hyperbolic patterns can be drawn for the measurement of the difference in phase of the C.W. transmission as used in the DECCA NAVIGATOR system.

A hyperbolic pattern is also involved in the CONSOL system, although the principle is fundamentally different.

These three systems will be considered in detail later.

Coverage and Accuracy of Hyperbolic Position-fixing Systems

(a) COVERAGE

The coverage area of a system of this kind depends fundamentally on the propagation characteristics of the radio frequency used; but, with this limitation, the coverage area for a given accuracy varies as the square of the base-line length, so that it is important to use as long a base-line as is practicable. This is normally limited by considerations of equipment and suitable terrain.

In practice, the coverage of a pair of stations is limited to two sectors of approximately 120° about the 'normal' and situated on either side of the base-line. In order to obtain all-round coverage it is the practice to employ a four-station chain, with the master in the centre and three slaves whose bearings relative to the master are spaced approximately 120° apart.

(b) SPACING OF LATTICE LINES

Position-line accuracy varies over the coverage area. The spacing of the hyperbolic lattice lines for equal measurements of path-difference is not constant, but increases as the observer moves away from the 'normal' towards the extensions of the base-line joining a pair of stations; and hence the accuracy falls off in these directions. The greater the spacing, the lower the accuracy.

(c) THE DIAMOND OF ERROR

At distances which are large compared with the station separation, the position lines approximate to radial lines, through the mid-point of the base-line joining two stations. Hence, in a 3-station chain at these ranges, the position lines will tend to cut at an acute angle. In such circumstances, while the position line accuracy may still be reasonably high, the accuracy of the fix in a direction towards and away from the ground stations may well be rather low.

It may be said, very approximately, that the position line accuracy varies inversely as the distance from the ground stations, and the radial accuracy (i.e., the accuracy outwards from the centre) varies inversely as the square of this distance.

Fig. 96 shows the possible 'diamond of error' resulting from this. It is assumed that the limits of possible error for the system in question are $\pm \cdot 02$ lanes at position X, near the stations, and $\pm \cdot 04$ lanes at Y. It is seen that, even if the limits of possible error remain constant, the positional accuracy will decrease away from the stations. It is inaccurate, to a degree depending on the system in use, to plot the position as the actual cut of hyperbolae obtained from the reading of the instrument. The diamond of error should be determined from a knowledge of the particular system's capabilities, and the ship plotted at the most dangerous corner of the diamond, in accordance with normal navigational practice. (*See* Chapter IV, under 'The Cocked Hat'.)

(d) SPEED AND PATH OF RADIO WAVES

It should be clear that the success and accuracy of any hyperbolic system depend upon a knowledge of the exact path along which radio waves are propagated and the speed at which they travel between transmitting stations and

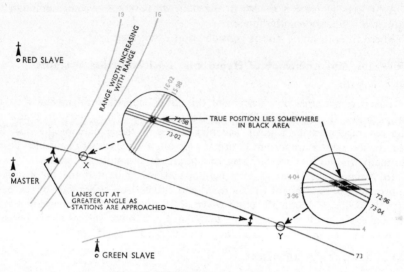

FIG. 96. The Diamond of Error

receiver. It has previously been explained how, in different circumstances, the path of the waves may be a straight line, a bent line due to refraction, or a number of lines resulting from ground-wave and sky-wave effects. It has also been explained how the speed of radio waves can be altered as they pass over different media and through different atmospheric conditions.

Variable errors are introduced by the vagaries of sky-wave reflections, while systematic errors are caused by the varying speed of radio waves and by the effect of reflections from such features as hills or cliffs. At ranges where sky waves are relatively stable, a reliable correction can be computed so that the sky waves may be used for obtaining positions. These corrections may be plotted on charts printed with ground-wave lattice lines, as, for example, in the Loran system.

(e) Synchronization of Transmitting Stations

Exact synchronization between the transmitters of a station pair is essential. This can normally be achieved by a monitoring system which observes and corrects any inaccuracies in transmission or coding delay times. In certain circumstances, when unavoidable inaccuracies occur, users are informed that the system is unreliable, either by signal or by special identification coding of the received signals used in the system, e.g., blinking of Loran pulses.

(f) Receiver Accuracy

This must be checked by some form of calibration – e.g., Loran alignment check and Decca zero reference check.

(g) Accuracy of Charts and Tables

Although the charts and tables supplied are of a high accuracy, there are areas near the base-line extensions where the normal methods of interpolation are no longer accurate. Moreover, in the vicinity of land, it is possible that errors may be detected in the computed values for lattice lines, for the reasons given in (d). The sky-wave corrections, also mentioned in (d), may also be in error, since they are computed for average conditions only.

Advantages and Disadvantages of Hyperbolic Systems

ADVANTAGES

Great inherent accuracy compared with great-circle bearing systems.
The system can handle an infinite number of observers at the same time.
No transmission is required to be made by the observer.

DISADVANTAGES

The relatively high cost of maintaining the transmitting stations and the number of men required to man them.
Special receivers are required by the observer (except in the case of Consol).
Ambiguity concerning the observer's position exists in some systems.
Interference from sky waves sometimes gives incorrect readings.
Necessity for special charts or tables.

Interference

Interference in received signals is usually caused by atmospheric conditions, mutual frequency transmission or sky wave. Low frequencies are particularly susceptible. Filter circuits are fitted to Loran and MF radio receivers to reduce it.

Cathode ray tube presentation enables an operator to read signals through this interference to a certain extent, even though it may be greater than the pulse he is trying to observe. Meter presentation may give no indication of a faulty reading.

At ranges where the amplitudes of sky and ground waves are comparable there will often be mutual interference between the two. In Consol, an incorrect 'count' of signals may result from this: in Decca it may cause 'lane slip'. It will be explained later how sky waves can be employed to extend the useful range of Loran; but the sky wave must be recognized otherwise a ground and sky wave may be matched together and provide an incorrect result.

3. CONSOL

This system was originally devised in Germany during the Second World War under the title of 'SONNE'. It has since been developed in the United Kingdom and is now known as 'CONSOL'.

Description

Consol provides long-distance navigational aid for ships and aircraft. The system requires automatic transmitting beacons on the ground, and a standard MF radio receiver in the ship or aircraft.

The position lines obtained are shallow hyperbolae which, for practical navigational purposes over the ranges involved, may be considered as great-circle tracks, owing to the short base-line between the transmitting aerials. Bearings can therefore be plotted on a Mercator chart after applying half-convergency.

The radiation patterns determining the system of position lines rotate uniformly during the transmission cycle, during which the system radiates complementary dot and dash signals. The required position line can be determined by making a count of the dot and dash characters heard during the transmission cycle. By reference to tables it is possible to establish that the observer is located on one of a number of alternative position lines situated between 10° and 15° apart in two coverage sectors of about 140° on either side of the line of the transmitting aerials.

Should the observer be in doubt about which position line he is on, he can take a DF bearing of the station. Normally the ship's estimated position dispels any doubt.

The Transmitter

The shore station transmitter consists of three vertical aerials, about 300 feet high, equally spaced in line about 1½ to 2 miles apart, which is roughly three times the wavelength in use. (The system operates in the MF band between 200 and 500 kc/s.) These aerials transmit the same medium frequency continuous wave. Variations in intensity of signals are heard at the receiver as a result of differences in the combined amplitudes of signals simultaneously received from all three aerials.

Operation

(a) The Equisignals

The two outer aerials radiate C.W. signals of equal amplitude but opposite phase; their amplitude is one-quarter of that of the centre aerial's signal. If the phase of the current fed to the outer aerials A and C (Fig. 97) is respectively

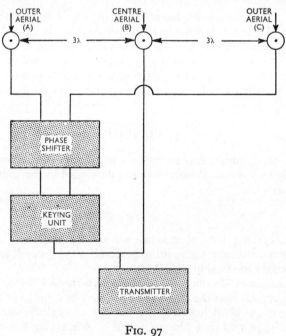

Fig. 97

90° ahead and 90° behind that fed to the centre aerial B, then at all points equidistant from A and C (i.e. along the perpendicular bisector of the line AC), the received signal would be of the amplitude of B's signal alone because the other two, being 180° out of phase, cancel out. Similarly, at every point where the difference in paths travelled by signals from the two outer aerials is equal to a whole number of wavelengths, so they will be 180° out of phase and B's signal alone will be heard. Elsewhere the amplitude of the received signal will depend on the difference in distance travelled by the waves from the outer aerials. From the explanation of hyperbolic position lines it will be appreciated that this produces a pattern of hyperbolae (Fig. 98) in which the lines represent all positions where only B's signal will be heard. In between these lines the amplitude of the received signal will gradually increase to a maximum and decrease to a minimum in the centre of alternate sectors.

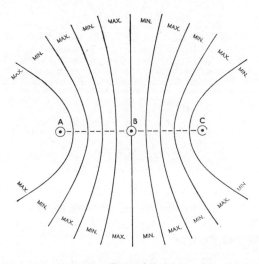

FIG. 98

The distance between aerials is small compared to the range at which the system is used (i.e., the minimum range is about twelve times the aerial spacing), so the hyperbolae may be considered as straight lines passing through the centre aerial. They are approximate great-circle tracks.

In the receiver is a beat frequency oscillator which produces a very faint, slightly wavering note from a signal of B's amplitude, called the *equisignal*. The Consol pattern therefore produces alternate sectors of strong and weak signals, separated by the equisignals.

(b) The Dot and Dash Pattern

If the phase of the current fed to the outer aerials is suddenly changed by 180°, the amplitude of a signal received anywhere in the coverage other than on an equisignal line will be changed so that strong signal sectors become weak ones, and vice versa. This is called *keying*.

During the keying cycle the aerials may be keyed at intervals of, for example, one-eighth and three-eighths of a second so that in what was a weak-signal sector there will be heard signals lasting one-eighth of a second between periods of three-eighths of a second's silence, i.e., dots; and in what was a strong-signal sector weak signals lasting one-eighth of a second will come between audible signals lasting three-eighths of a second – i.e., dashes.

Fig. 99 shows the alternate sectors of dashes and dots. It also shows the *ambiguous sectors* on either side of the base-line extension where, for approximately 40°, the same characters will be heard. These sectors cannot be considered as part of the normal coverage.

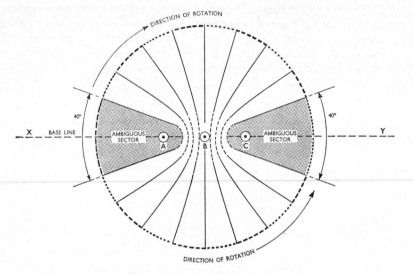

FIG. 99. Rotation of a Consol pattern

(c) ROTATION OF THE PATTERN

So far, an observer can determine whether he is on an equisignal line or in a dot or dash sector depending on the amount by which signals from *A* and *C* are out of phase with that from *B*, and the regular reversal of phase imposed on the signals from *A* and *C*.

If, superimposed on the keying cycle, the phase of the current to *A* and *C* is gradually changed by equal and opposite amounts, the whole pattern can be made to rotate. The pattern is shifted at a fixed rate of one sector's width in the period of the keying cycle of 30 seconds so that by the end of the cycle the position of the equisignal will have rotated to the position initially held by the one ahead of it, and the dot and dash sectors will have been exchanged. Each keying cycle starts with the same phase relationship between the aerial currents, so that the pattern of sectors is always the same. Since the gradual change of phase relationship and keying repeats in the same sequence and with the same rate, the rotation of the pattern is always the same in each cycle of operation. The pattern is symmetrical about the base-line, but the two halves rotate uniformly in opposite directions (Fig. 99).

There exists a relationship between the time, measured from the beginning of the keying cycle to the moment at which the observer hears the equisignal, and the observer's position in the sector. If he can determine exactly when he hears the equisignal, then his angular position in the pattern sector is known and a position line will have been obtained.

(d) CYCLE OF OPERATION

One complete transmission cycle consists of the callsign of the station followed by a long continuous note from which a DF bearing may be taken if required. Then the keying cycle begins, during which dots, equisignal and dashes are heard while the pattern rotates. The whole cycle is repeated continuously about every minute throughout the hours of service of the station.

Procedure for obtaining a Position Line

Select the station from the coverage diagram (D.6658) and obtain all the details about it, both from the *Admiralty List of Radio Signals* (Vol. V). Having identified the callsign, count the number of dots and dashes separated by the equisignal. If in a dot sector the dots are heard first. In each cycle a total of 60 characters should be heard, but in practice this is rarely possible because the moment of change from dot to dash is masked by the *twilight zone* in which the equisignal lies. To interpolate the equisignal, which is the centre of the twilight zone, the count must be corrected to allow for the characters lost. This is done by counting both dots and dashes, subtracting the sum of the two from 60, and adding half the difference to whichever is heard first. This gives the number of characters that occur before the equisignal, assuming that an equal number of dots and dashes is lost.

For each count of dots or dashes there will be a number of alternative true bearings from the station, each situated in a different sector of the pattern. The correct sector can be determined from the ship's estimated position or by DF. The corrected count can then be plotted on the special Consol chart (supplied by the Hydrographer).

If Consol charts are not available, the Consol tables in the *Admiralty List of Radio Signals* (Vol. V) must be used. Having obtained the true bearing for the ship's sector from the tables, half-convergency must be applied to it before the bearing can be plotted on a Mercatorial chart. Half-convergency can be obtained from tables that follow the Consol tables or by calculation as for radio direction-finding.

Since the accuracy of the bearing may be $\pm 0 \cdot 2°$, it will be found expedient at long range to lay off the two adjacent whole-numbered bearings and then to interpolate.

EXAMPLE

An observer in E.P. 58°N., 23° 30'W. obtains a count of Bushmills Consol station (55° 12'N., 6° 28'W.). The count consists of 44 dots and 12 dashes.

$$44 + 12 = 56$$
$$60 - 56 = 4$$
$$4 \div 2 = 2$$
$$\text{Corrected count} = 44 + 2 = 46 \text{ dots}$$

From the chart the approximate bearing of the ship's E.P. from Bushmills is 287°.

Reference to the Consol table for Bushmills dot sectors shows that the nearest bearing for 46 dots is 294°·2. From the appropriate half-convergency table for an observer in latitude 58° and longitude 23° 30′W, whose difference in longitude from Bushmills is 17°, the half-convergency is 7°·1 (to be subtracted from the true bearing). The mercatorial bearing is 287°·1.

Receiving Equipment

(a) THE RECEIVER

Consol signals can be received on a normal communication receiver for C.W. MF transmissions with narrow band characteristics. An output meter may sometimes materially assist in reducing the twilight zone.

Automatic volume control must not be used because a.v.c. compensates for fading and the difference between dots and dashes is primarily one of amplitude in the received wave. A.V.C. tends to reduce the change in the strength of the signal when keying takes place and broadens the twilight zone or it may displace the equisignal.

A MF DF receiver can be used for the count, subject to certain conditions. If a loop aerial, or goniometer, is turned to the position of minimum signal, as is the practice when taking DF bearings, large errors may result at certain ranges owing to sky-wave effects. Consol may be used beyond the normal range of MF DF, which is limited to ground-wave reception only for accurate bearings.

The aerial should be turned to the position of maximum reception or within 45° of this position if there is too much interference.

(b) THE AERIAL

If possible, a single vertical wire should be used.

(c) MF DF RECEIVERS

If the bearing of the station is not known to within 10°, a DF bearing must be obtained. Beyond the normal range of DF reception this bearing may be inaccurate but it will be sufficiently accurate to solve any sector ambiguity.

Coverage

Useful coverage is confined to two sectors of about 140° on either side of the base-line (Fig. 99). Outside these limits are two sectors in which ambiguity can arise, and where the accuracy is so low that the system is unreliable.

Sky waves may be used by night, thus extending the coverage.

APPROXIMATE OPERATIONAL RANGE (N. MILES) OF CONSOL IN LAT. 50°N.

	OVER SEA	OVER FLAT LAND
BY DAY	1,000	700
BY NIGHT	1,200	1,200

Consol should not be used within 25 miles of the station because the equisignal there tends to swamp so much of the keying cycle that interpolation of the dots and dashes in the twilight zone becomes inaccurate.

4. LORAN

This is a LOng RAnge Navigation radio aid developed in the United States of America from a British wartime short-range aid known as 'Gee'.

Principles

The transmitting stations are grouped in 'chains' of three: a master and two slaves. The observer must be provided with a special receiver in which the received signals are displayed on a cathode-ray oscilloscope which is essentially an electronic clock for measuring in microseconds the difference in time of arrival of the pulses from two stations. A fix is obtained by separate measurement of two pairs of stations, not necessarily of the same chain.

Special Loran lattice charts or Loran tables must be used for plotting the position of the fix.

Loran Transmissions

Each transmission pulse lasts about 40 microseconds and recurs at regular and accurately controlled intervals, called the pulse recurrence interval (pulse repetition frequency in British radar). The pulse recurrence interval (P.R.I.) varies for each station and lasts between 29,000 and 40,000 μs.

The transmissions of corresponding master and slave pulses are separated, for reasons previously explained, by a fixed time interval which consists of the time for a signal to travel from the master to the slave, plus one-half the P.R.I., plus an additional short time called the coding delay. The observer needs to measure the difference between the times of arrival of the two pulses so that there is no need for absolute synchronization of the receiver time-base with the times of transmission.

At all points in the coverage area the time interval between a master pulse and the next slave pulse is greater than that between slave pulse and the next master pulse. This provides a positive method of identifying the signals although their appearance is similar. In the measuring process the time difference is always measured from the master pulse and the time delay of one-half the P.R.I. is automatically removed.

The lines of constant time difference for each pair of stations are all pre-computed taking into consideration the curvature and eccentricity of the Earth, the time for the master pulse to reach the slave station, and the coding delay. The navigator follows a methodical measuring procedure, then he goes directly to the chart or tables to determine the line corresponding to the measured time difference.

Arrangement of Station Pairs

A master station controlling two slaves is called 'double pulsed' because it transmits two entirely separate sets of pulses, one for each slave. Pairs of Loran stations are situated up to 600 miles apart. Their positions can be found in the Loran

Coverage Chart or the Index of Loran Charts supplied with each folio of Loran charts; also in the coverage charts of the *Loran Tables* and at the back of the *Admiralty List of Radio Signals* (Vol. V).

Reception of Signals

On the face of the Loran c.r. tube a spot sweeps from left to right at a constant speed. The spot is deflected upwards to give a vertical line on the trace whenever a Loran pulse is received.

Suppose that the spot completes the trace 25 times per second; then the length of the trace represents one-twenty-fifth of a second, or 40,000 μs. If pulses are received from a station whose P.R.I. is 40,000 μs, they will appear at the same place on each trace, i.e. stationary. If the P.R.I. is less than the trace length – for example, 39,900 μs – then each pulse will appear 100 μs to the left of the previous one and will seem to be drifting to the left. Similarly, if the P.R.I. is *longer* than the trace length the pulse will drift to the *right*. To synchronize the receiver with pulses from a selected station, the trace length must match the P.R.I. of the station.

For convenience the trace on a Loran indicator is divided into two equal halves (Fig. 100). The upper half is called the 'A' trace and the lower half the 'B' trace. The spot traces out the pattern from the left of the 'A' trace. The dotted paths between the two traces are swept at a much higher speed and are invisible.

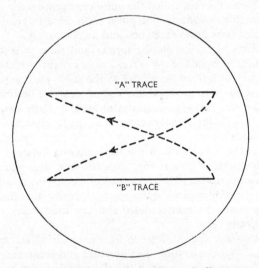

FIG. 100. The trace on a Loran indicator

Since the time of triggering the trace has no direct connection with the time at which the Loran signals arrive, the pair of pulses appear anywhere on the traces. The receiver is provided with a 'left-right' switch which temporarily changes the sweep recurrence rate, thereby making the pulses drift to left or right until the master pulse is in the correct position for measurement.

In this position (Fig. 101) the master pulse is near the left side of the 'A' trace, the slave pulse will then be on the 'B' trace because the interval between the master and slave pulses is always more than half the P.R.I. which is the time represented by each trace. Should the slave pulse appear on the 'A' trace, the master pulse will be on the left of the 'B' trace or on the 'A' trace to the right of the slave.

Time-difference Measurement

The time difference to be measured is the horizontal distance between the master and slave pulses (Fig. 101). The fixed delay of one-half the P.R.I. (represented by the heavy portion of the trace in Fig. 101) is thereby cancelled out. The other two components of the slave pulse delay are allowed for in the computation of the lattice lines.

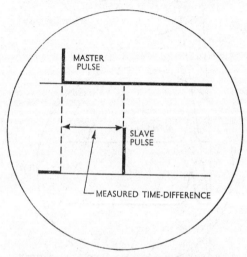

FIG. 101. Time difference measurement

To obtain accurate measurement, portions of the trace are electrically magnified. When the entire recurrence interval is displayed (Sweep speed 1), the portion to be magnified is raised to form a pedestal. The upper pedestal is fixed near the left end of the 'A' trace, whereas the lower pedestal can be moved along the 'B' trace by delay controls. To position both pulses on their pedestals, they are drifted by the left-right switch until the *master* pulse is on the 'A' *pedestal*; then the 'B' pedestal is placed under the *slave* pulse by operating the *delay* controls.

In Loran receiver DAS-2 there are four other sweep speeds providing three stages of magnification and one for signal matching when 'A' and 'B' traces are superimposed. In Loran receiver AN/APS-7A there are two other sweep speeds (Operations) providing two stages of magnification; the traces are superimposed in the last stage.

Identification of Loran Pairs

Since Loran stations do not transmit call-signs, they can only be identified by two distinguishing features: radio frequency channel, and pulse recurrence rate.

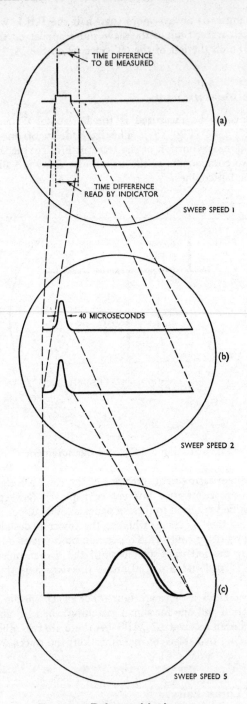

FIG. 102. Pulse-positioning process

Radio Frequency Channel

There are four frequencies, 1,950 kc/s, 1,850 kc/s, 1,900 kc/s and 1,750 kc/s which are designated the numbers 1, 2, 3 and 4 respectively and selected by the *channel* switch. These frequencies permit the use of E-layer reflections to increase the night time range of the equipment.

Pulse Recurrence Rate (P.R.R.)

The Basic P.R.R.s are described as H (high), L (low) or S of $33\frac{1}{3}$, 25 and 20 pulses per second respectively. The S basic P.R.R. is not yet in operational use. Each station has a Specific Pulse Recurrence Rate, numbered 0 to 7, in one of the groups. The rate for each pair of stations is described thus: 1H2, meaning

Frequency channel .   .   1
Basic P.R.R. .   .   .   H
Specific P.R.R. (station) .   2

The operator can select a particular pair of stations by frequency, then by selecting the basic P.R.R. All stations on this frequency and within range will appear on the indicator drifting across the scan at different speeds. The operator can then select a particular pair by making the sweep recurrence rate of the indicator the same as the P.R.R. of the selected pair whose signals now remain stationary and all the others, drifting across the scan, are ignored.

The system now provides for a possible total of sixty-four separate station pairs; and ninety-six pairs when the S basic P.R.R. is in operational use.

Taking a Reading with DAS-2

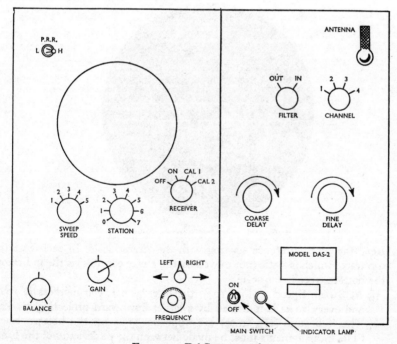

Fig. 103. DAS-2 controls

The following procedure applies to the reception of ground-wave signals on a DAS-2 receiver.

1. Switch on; allow 10 minutes to warm up. Indicator lamp shows red.
2. Carry out operating alignment check (page 198).
3. Select Loran pair from coverage chart and switch to appropriate Channel, P.R.R. and Station. (S basic P.R.R. is not available in this set.)
4. Switch Filter Out. (When In, signal strength is reduced and certain types of interference are eliminated.)
5. Select Sweep Speed 1; turn up Gain until pulses are a convenient height; turn Balance until pulses are of equal height; position master signal on the 'A' pedestal by the left-right switch (Fig. 102a), then position the 'B' pedestal under B signal by the Coarse Delay control.

   Note: If either signal is blinking on–off or sideways shifting, do not attempt to take a reading.

6. Select Sweep Speed 2; align slave with master by Fine Delay control; drift both signals to left by left-right switch and keep them there by adjusting the Frequency control (controls the sweep repetition rate) (Fig. 102b).
7. Select Sweep Speed 3; thence as for 6.
8. Select Sweep Speed 4; thence as for 6. (This step may be omitted.)
9. Select Sweep Speed 5. This superimposes one trace on the other. Use the Balance and Gain controls to get large, equal-sized pulses, then align their left edges with the Fine Delay control as in Fig. 102c.
10. Clear the trace of pulses by putting the Receiver switch to Off, and note the time which is the time of the observation. Do not now move any settings except the Sweep speed.

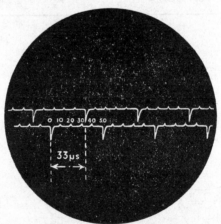

FIG. 104. DAS-2: Sweep speed 4

11. Read the time difference starting with the largest scale. In each case the top trace, which is static (not moved by the Delay controls) is the indicator; the bottom trace is the scale.

    (i) At Sweep Speed 4 (Fig. 104), the interval between markers is 10 μs and every 50 μs is indicated by a larger downward-projecting marker. The indicators (top trace) are opposite 33 μs on the bottom trace. (The measurements must be made between the peaks and not the bases of these markers.)

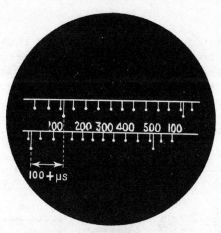

FIG. 105. DAS-2: Sweep speed 3

(ii) At Sweep Speed 3 (Fig. 105) each marker represents 50 μs and every
500 μs is indicated by a long marker. Counting as before, we now get
100 μs +. Adding the count from Sweep Speed 4 we have 133 μs.

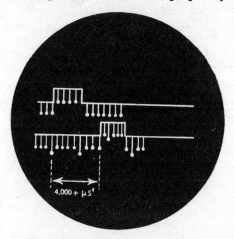

FIG. 106. DAS-2: Sweep speed 1

(iii) At Sweep Speed 1 (Fig. 106) each marker represents 500 μs and every
2,500 μs is indicated by a long marker. The count in this case is made
from the long marker on the lower trace that is immediately below the
left edge of the 'A' pedestal. There are eight markers before 'B' pedestal
giving a reading of 4,000 μs +. The total reading is therefore
4,000 + 100 + 33 μs or 4,133 μs.

Notes:

1. Sweep Speed 2 can be omitted because the markers on Sweep Speed 1 are
sufficiently accurate and clear.

2. If the total reading is about 2,500 μs or a multiple of it, all three long markers
(2,500, 500 and 50 μs) will appear close together on the trace at sweep speeds 4 and 3.
The 2,500 μs marker is the longest and the 50 μs marker the shortest.

AN/SPN-7A

This receiver has the same identification switches as DAS–2 except that the Basic P.R.R. switch has three positions H, L and S. The three station selector switches are grouped together in the order of the identification group symbol given in Loran charts or tables.

The signal controls have been improved. Receiver Gain and Amplitude Balance are mounted together concentrically. An Attenuator switch has been included for reducing the received signal strength when close to a transmitter (positions 1 and 2).

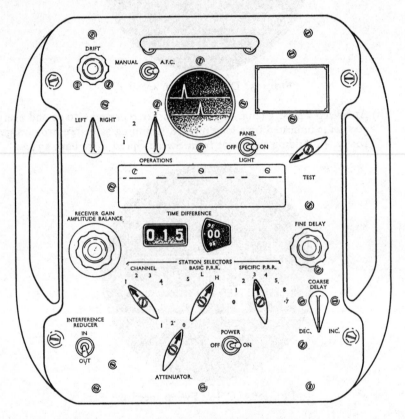

FIG. 107. AN/SPN-7A Controls

The Sweep Speed switch has been replaced by the Operations switch which has three positions only. Position 1 provides a slow sweep with pedestals. Position 2 expands the tops of the pedestals to the full width of the trace. Position 3 expands further the left-hand portion of each trace of position 2 and at the same time removes the trace separation.

A Manual–AFC switch has been included. In the Manual position proper adjustment of the Drift control will stop any drifting of selected signals by causing the sweep rate of the c.r.t. to synchronize with the P.R.R. of the received signal. In the AFC position not only are the two rates synchronized but the master signal is stopped and held at the left edge of the top pedestal in Operation 1, at the left edge of the trace in Operation 2, and in the centre of the c.r.t. in Operation 3.

The Time-Difference indicator, which consists of a counter mechanism to indicate the first three numbers of the time-difference reading and a dial to indicate the last two numbers, is automatically operated by the Coarse and Fine Delays. When the leading edges of the received signals are matched in Operation 3, the Loran time difference may be read directly from the indicator.

Taking a Reading with AN/SPN-7A

1. Switch on Power. Wait for 3 minutes.
2. Turn Test switch to OPR and Operation switch to 1.
3. Turn Receiver Gain fully counter-clockwise.
4. Centre Amplitude Balance control.
5. Turn Interference Reducer to Out.
6. Turn Manual–A.F.C. switch to Manual.
7. Set Channel, Basic P.R.R. and Specific P.R.R. for desired station pair.
8. Turn Receiver Gain to suitable level.
9. Drift signals along trace by Left–Right switch until one is on the A pedestal and the other on the B trace and to the right of the first.
10. Adjust the heights of the signals so that they are equal and adequate by the Amplitude Balance and Receiver Gain respectively.
11. Move pedestal B under signal B by Coarse Delay.
12. Switch to Operation 2 and align signals by Fine Delay.
13. Turn Manual–A.F.C. switch to A.F.C.

   Note: It is good practice to move the signals with the Left–Right switch to the right first and to turn up the Receiver Gain to look for weak ground-wave or first sky-wave signals before proceeding to the next step.

14. Switch to Operation 3; adjust Fine Delay so that B's leading edge is superimposed on A's; adjust Receiver Gain and Amplitude Balance until both signals are the same amplitude and about 1 inch high. Turn the Attenuator switch to 1 or 2 if the signal amplitude is too large.
15. Note the time of the observation and read the Time-Difference indicator.

Taking a Reading with AN/APN-9

1. Set the Amplitude Balance control at its centre position.
2. Set the Fine Delay control at its centre position.
3. Set the Drift control at its centre position.
4. Turn the Receiver Gain clockwise until the station rate identification (pilot light) illuminates. Wait at least 5 minutes for set to warm up.
5. Set R.F. Channel, P.R.R. (H or L) and Station (0 to 7) as appropriate.
6. Turn Function switch to position 1.
7. Rotate Receiver Gain clockwise until signals are clear.
8. Rotate Drift control until signals are stationary.
9. Operate Right–Left control until *both* signals appear on the *lower* trace with the left signal at the extreme left end.

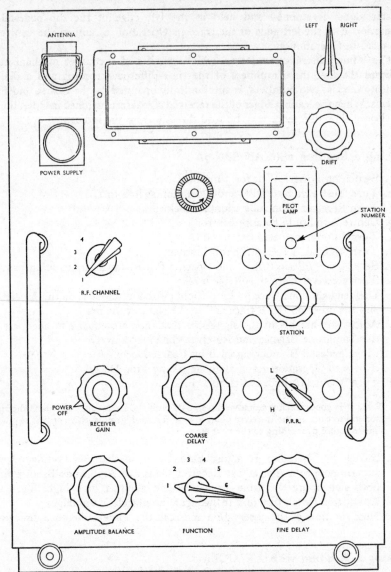

FIG. 108. AN/APN-9 Controls

10. Adjust **Coarse Delay** control until the variable delay marker is placed under the signal appearing to the right (Fig. 109).
11. Turn **Function** switch to position 2. Adjust **Receiver Gain** and **Amplitude Balance** controls so that signals are equal and sufficient. Adjust **Fine Delay** control so that one signal is directly over the other.
12. Turn **Function** switch to position 3. The traces are no longer separated. Adjust **Fine Delay** and **Amplitude Balance** until the signals are matched.
13. Note the Time. Do not now move any settings except the **Function** switch.
14. Turn the **Function** switch to position 4. A single trace, divided into 5,000 and 1,000 μs intervals, appears. If the **P.R.R.** switch is set to H the length

of trace will be three 5,000 μs. If it is set to L the length of trace will be,
four 5,000 μs. The position of the variable delay marker is measured from
the *right* of the trace. In Fig. 110 the reading is six 1,000 μs + about 750 μs
for the remaining interval.

15. Turn the Function switch to position 5. Two traces appear on the screen,
the upper divided into 10, 50, 100, 500 and 1,000 μs intervals, the lower
divided into 10 and 50 μs intervals. The cross hair for reading the time
difference appears on the lower trace and is always the 50 μs marker
approximately 40 to 70 μs from the left end (Fig. 111). The 1,000 μs
marker is the last complete 1,000 μs counted in the last step (Fig. 110).
The increment can now be read to the nearest microsecond as 762 (*to this
must be added 100 μs standard correction*, because measurement has been
made from the cross hair which is the second 50 μs marker from the origin
of the trace), giving a total of 6,862 μs.

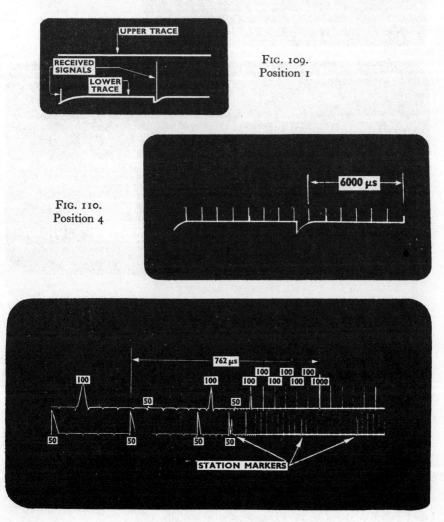

FIG. 109.
Position 1

FIG. 110.
Position 4

FIG. 111. Position 5

When the increment is small, for example 6,000 + 250 (approx.) μs, as shown in Fig. 112, the position of the last 1,000 μs marker when the Function switch is at position 5 may be misleading. The 1,000 μs marker always appears close to a 100 μs marker and the reading point of *both* is the beginning of that 100 μs marker. Reading to the left of this point, Fig. 113 shows that there are 25 μs to the position of the cross hair. The total reading is therefore 6,000 + 25 + 100 μs.

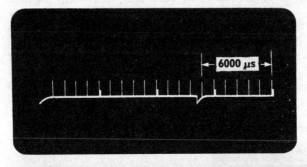

FIG. 112.
Position 4

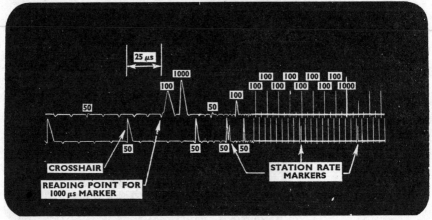

FIG. 113. Position 5

Notes:

1. The number of 50 μs markers on the lower trace between the cross hair and the first Station Rate Marker is a check that the set is functioning correctly for the selected station.

STATION RATE SWITCH SETTING	50-MICROSECOND INTERVALS
0	8
1	7
2	6
3	5
4	4
5	3
6	2
7	1

In Fig. 111 and 113 there are two 50 μs markers; the Station Rate setting is 6.

2. Position 6 of the Function switch separates the matched signals of position 3 when the navigator wishes to proceed along a Loran position line. Any deviation from the line will be shown by the signals separating laterally.

Plotting the Ship's Position

Having obtained the time difference from the receiver, the Loran position line may be determined from the appropriate Loran chart or from the tables. Interpolation is generally necessary because the position lines are computed for intervals of about 20 μs. The lines for each pair of stations are printed in a distinctive colour on the charts and the tables are printed in the same colour.

A second position line from another pair of stations is needed for a fix; one line being transferred if there is any interval between the observations.

If sky waves are used, special sky-wave corrections must be applied to the readings.

Ground and Sky Waves

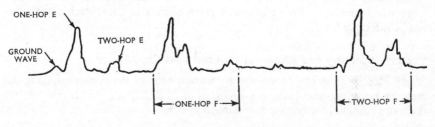

FIG. 114. Sky waves

A single transmitted pulse may appear on the receiver as a series of pulses similar to those shown in Fig. 114 (compare Fig. 87). The ground wave is received at diminishing strength out to a range of about 700 nautical miles (by day) over the sea, and much less over the land. Its useful range during the night is about 450 miles owing to an increase in atmospheric noise-level which swamps the Loran signals.

Sky waves are generally only received by night, and by making use of the first sky wave (one-hop E) the range of Loran may be extended to about 1,400 miles over the sea and slightly less over land.

Sky waves within 250 miles, multiple E-layer reflections and all F-layer reflections are unreliable and never used.

MATCHING PULSES

When two ground waves, no matter how weak, can be received, they should always be used in preference to sky waves. The letter G is used to indicate a time-difference reading of ground waves: e.g., 1406 G.

If no ground wave is received from either station of a pair, match the two one-hop E sky waves, write S after the time-difference reading and apply the sky-wave correction.

It may happen that a pair of stations has an unusually long base-line, or that land intervenes between a station and the ship making it impossible to receive two ground waves, or the ship may be within 250 miles of one station (where the sky wave is unreliable) and beyond the ground wave from the other station. In these circumstances a special correction is provided for matching a ground wave with a sky wave. The time difference must then be marked SG if the master sky wave is used, or GS if the slave sky wave is used. The distinction is important because the correction is added in the first instance and subtracted in the second.

SKY-WAVE CORRECTION

Loran lattice lines are computed on the charts and in the tables for ground-wave readings. When sky waves are matched, the sky-wave correction must be applied to S readings to convert them to G readings before they can be used on the charts or in the tables. The corrections are tabulated on the Loran charts at specific intervals of longitude and latitude in the same colour as the lattice lines to which they apply; they may be additive or subtractive. The correction can be obtained quickly using the ship's D.R. and interpolating on the chart or in the tables by eye. Corrections are not tabulated within 250 miles of the station from which the sky wave comes, and extrapolation to cover such areas must not be attempted.

Factors affecting the Range of Ground and Sky Waves

Signal identification can be assisted by a knowledge of the factors affecting the range of Loran signals. These are discussed in detail in the *Loran Handbook*, but the more common factors are summarised below.

EFFECT OF DISTANCE AND THE TIME OF DAY

The ranges of ground-wave signals have already been given.

The strength and number of sky waves vary with the time of day and seasonal and geographical conditions, but by night the train of sky-wave pulses may extend to more than half way along one of the traces at Sweep speed 1 (Operation 1). In the middle of the day only a ground wave of good signal-to-noise ratio is received; sky waves normally are not. As the evening progresses, the sky waves increase in strength while rising atmospheric noise-level gradually masks the ground wave. Eventually the one-hop E sky wave is the first visible pulse. Beyond about 1,200 miles only multiple-hop E and F layer reflections will be received; and although these have no operational use, it is possible that they may be mistaken for other reflections.

DIRECTIONAL EFFECTS OF RECEIVER AERIAL

The proximity of ship's structure or other aerials does not affect the accuracy of Loran signals but tends to produce arcs of poor reception so that an alteration of course to increase signal strength may sometimes be justified.

Identification of Ground and Sky Waves

The correct identification of ground and sky waves, which is the principal operational problem in Loran if satisfactory results are to be achieved, is fully covered in the *Loran Handbook* by description and photographs. A brief outline will be given here. Identification is assisted by an estimation of the distance between the ship and the stations, and a knowledge of the propagation properties of the Loran waves, so that when the receiver is switched on the operator knows roughly what to expect on the scan.

Sky-wave signals in general can be distinguished from ground-wave signals by two inherent characteristics:

(1) Fading, or variations in amplitude, which may be rapid or slow enough to be watched carefully for a few minutes. Ground waves always remain steady although they may flicker.

(2) Splitting, which consists of the pulse breaking into two or more humps (Fig. 115), which then fade independently. A source of error occurs at the climax of splitting if the left-hand hump has faded down into the noise and a reading is taken using the leading edge of the second hump. Again, it is essential to watch the pulse for a few minutes. The first sky wave is not always the strongest. To ensure that two one-hop E signals are in fact selected for matching, the gain should be turned up high and the scan to the left of the first easily-visible pulse should be studied very carefully at Sweep speed 2 (Operation 2).

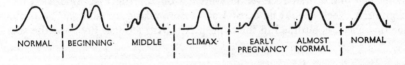

| NORMAL | BEGINNING | MIDDLE | CLIMAX | EARLY PREGNANCY | ALMOST NORMAL | NORMAL |

FIG. 115. Typical splitting of sky wave

Incorrect identification and consequent mismatching causes errors whose magnitude depends on the ship's position. A mistake of matching a ground wave with a sky wave, and calling both ground waves or both sky waves, will usually be great enough to be obvious if the estimated position is fairly good.

In general, a sky-wave correction is so small that if it is not applied to a sky wave when it ought to be applied, or if it is applied in error to a ground-wave match, the error will not be obvious especially when there is reason to doubt the estimated position.

SPILL-OVER SIGNALS

It sometimes happens that signals from another channel 'spill over' into the channel being used. Such signals are always distorted and often centre split. They do not fade and therefore should not be mistaken for sky-wave signals. They can be identified by turning the channel switch until the signals are strongest and least distorted.

GHOST SIGNALS

When the receiver is set to one specific recurrence rate, signals will appear from other basic P.R.R.s as stationary flickering ghost signals with the trace running through the base of the pulse (Fig. 116).

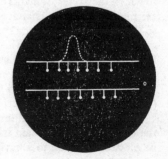

FIG. 116. Ghost pulse

BLINKING AND SHIFTING SIGNALS

When correct synchronization of a station cannot be maintained a distinctive signal known as *trouble blinking* is transmitted. The signal either blinks on and off or shifts from right to left every second. If either or both signals show trouble blinking do not take a reading from them.

INTERFERENCE

The possibility of interference to Loran signals was mentioned in the section on hyperbolic position-fixing systems. Further details of the type of interference to be expected, its appearance on the indicator and the use of the filter, are given in the *Loran Handbook*.

Operating Alignment Check

Whenever the Loran receiver is switched on for the first time each day, an alignment check should be carried out before taking a reading. The procedure for this check is outlined in the appropriate Instructional Book for the set.

Accuracy

The factors affecting the accuracy of the system are discussed in the section on the Hyperbolic Position-finding systems and in the *Loran Handbook*. Generally speaking the error should be within 0·5 per cent of the range from the mid-point of the base-line. This is ten times better than the accuracy of MF DF.

Loran Charts and Tables

Loran coverage extends over the North Atlantic and Pacific Oceans. British lattice charts for the former are prepared and supplied to ships by the Hydrographer. The charts are given the series letter L and are contained in a 300-series folio which also contains an index chart to show the lattice charts, the chains of stations with their station letters, frequency channels and pulse recurrence rates. A coverage chart is also included which shows the reliable ground- and sky-wave coverage to be expected from the chains.

The lattice charts are Mercator charts overprinted with lattice lines of a distinctive colour for each station pair. One chart may show two or three sets of lattices. Sky-wave corrections are given in the same colour as the lattice lines to which they refer; remarks on their use are included on the chart. No soundings are marked on these charts and they are not corrected by Notices to Mariners so that a position obtained should be transferred to the navigational chart.

Charts and Tables for the Pacific Ocean are prepared by the Hydrographic Office of the U.S. Navy. The Tables only can also be supplied to H.M. ships by the Hydrographer; they are NP 323–326 (U.S. Publication HO.221 Series). The charts are accompanied by a Catalogue of Loran Charts and Service Areas (HO. No. 1–L).

The Tables contain full instructions for their use and an index chart to show the coverage of each chain included. Loran lines obtained from the tables may be plotted direct on to a navigational chart or plotting sheet.

Publications

NP 304. – *Loran Handbook for Shipboard Operators* (*SHIPS 278*) is issued by the Hydrographer with the appropriate Loran charts and tables.

The *Instructional Book for Radio Navigational Equipment DAS and DAS-2* (*SHIPS 225A*) is issued with the set.

Operator's Manual for Radar Receiving Set AN/SPN-7A (*NAVSHIPS 91861*) is issued with the set.

Handbook of Operating Instructions for Radar Set AN/APN-9.

The *Admiralty List of Radio Signals* (Vol. V) contains a brief description of the system, followed by a list of the Loran chains in operation.

NOTIFICATION OF CHANGE OF SERVICE

These are promulgated in HYDROLANTS and HYDROPACS. Any permanent changes are also printed in Admiralty Notices to Mariners, Section VI, for inclusion in the *Admiralty List of Radio Signals* (Vol. V).

5. DECCA

This position-fixing system was developed in the United Kingdom during the Second World War by the Decca Radio and Television Company Ltd., London. This company operates the transmissions and provides the Admiralty, the Ministry of Transport, and other authorities and governments with special receivers for use in ships.

The system involves a number of fixed transmitting stations operating in the LF band on frequencies of about 100 kc/s. A Decca chain normally consists of a master station controlling the phase of three slaves, which are situated about 120° apart, at a radius of 60–100 miles from the master. This provides all-round coverage, and, because ground waves of this frequency band are not seriously attenuated by passing over land, the stations can advantageously be situated well inland. In the case of the English chain, for example, this enables the facilities of the system to be extended over the waters around England to a radius of at least 240 miles from London.

The transmissions from the chain are received by a special shipborne receiver, which measures the difference in phase of signals arriving from master and slaves. These are displayed on phase-meters called 'decometers', and the readings may be plotted on to Decca lattice charts, on which the lines of position are numbered in the same units as those shown on the decometers. The decometer indications are continuous, and depending on the position in the coverage, readings of the two appropriate decometers can be taken simultaneously whenever a fix is required. The third decometer can give some additional information, but usually its readings are disregarded in the wide sector around the base-line extension.

The lattice patterns are formed by hyperbolic position lines similar to those previously described. They are overprinted on ordinary Mercator charts. The slave stations are known as Red, Green and Purple slaves, according to the printed colour of the lattice lines derived from their transmissions. A very high degree of instrumental accuracy is obtained by the use of continuous wave (C.W.) transmissions, the phase of which, on arrival, can be measured to within

4°. Near the base-line between a pair of stations this may represent a distance as small as 10 yards, though it must be borne in mind that constant and variable errors due to operational causes exist in the system, which, in practice, does not normally give an accuracy as good as ± 10 yards. It is, however, considerably more accurate than any system employing pulse transmissions.

It is thus seen that the system fulfils the IMRAMN conditions for a coastal and pilotage aid (*see* page 157).

Description of the Decca System

PRINCIPLE OF OPERATION

Two stations, *A* and *B*, radiate in all directions C.W. signals which travel with the same known velocity. Consider first what happens on the base-line between points *A* and *B*, as in Fig. 117, assuming for simplification that the frequencies of the two transmissions are identical and that the stations are an exact number of wavelengths apart and that the signals start in phase, i.e., with zero phase-difference: they will arrive with zero phase-difference at a receiver situated at a point *P*, half-way between them, since they will have travelled equal distances, i.e., $BP - AP = 0$.

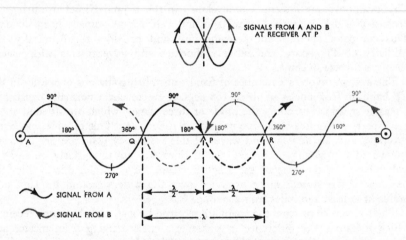

FIG. 117. Principle of phase comparison

Now consider points Q and R, situated half-a-wavelength $\left(\dfrac{\lambda}{2}\right)$ away from P.

At both these points it can be seen that the phase of each signal is 360°, so that the signal will again have zero phase-difference. The difference in the path can be expressed as:

$$\left(BP + \frac{\lambda}{2}\right) - \left(AP - \frac{\lambda}{2}\right) = (BP - AP) + \lambda.$$

i.e., the lines of zero phase-difference occur at intervals of half-a-wavelength; or, in other words, whenever the change in difference-of-path length is a whole wavelength (*see* Fig. 118).

A similar reasoning can be carried out for observation points lying outside the base-line. From this and from a previous explanation of hyperbolic position lines, it should be clear that lines joining positions of zero phase-difference drawn through such points as P, Q and R, in Fig. 117, every half wavelength along the base-line, will form a hyperbolic pattern with A and B as the focal points.

The areas between the lines of zero phase-difference in a Decca pattern are known as 'lanes', and it can be seen from Fig. 119 that the width of a lane is least along the base-line, where it is equal to half-a-wavelength at a frequency common to both stations.

It is essential that the signals from the two stations should be received separately in order to preserve their individual phase properties. Since the C.W. transmissions are simultaneous, this can only be achieved by transmitting on different frequencies: but these frequencies must have an exact common multiple. The transmissions are received by what are virtually separate receivers within the Decca Navigator receiving equipment. The frequencies of these signals are then multiplied up to their lowest common multiple, the so-called 'comparison frequency' on which the phase comparison is made.

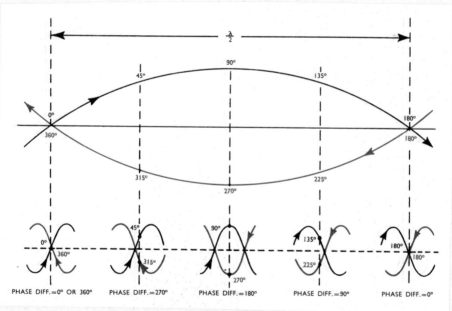

FIG. 118. Phase-difference

As the pattern is traversed by the Decca receiving equipment so the reading will be observed to alter steadily from 0° to 360° between the limits of each lane; the decometer, from which this reading is obtained, is therefore graduated in fractions of a lane instead of in degrees.

As a convention, the lattice lines are numbered in sequence, the first hyperbola being situated half-a-wavelength from the master station as shown in Fig. 119.

Thus the total number of lanes between any pair of stations is the length of the base-line divided by half-a-wavelength at the comparison frequency.

Now, in Fig. 117, the length of the base-line was considered, for convenience, to be equal to a whole number of lanes, but this is not necessarily the case in practice. To satisfy the convention stated above, the master station must be a position of zero phase-difference, and therefore at the position of the slave station there will usually be difference in phase corresponding to a fraction of a lane, unless the master and slave happen to be an exact number of half-wavelengths apart. The phase of the signal transmitted from the station B relative to that of A must be kept constant in order to maintain a fixed hyperbolic pattern. The stations must, therefore, be 'phase-locked', and this has to be done over an appreciable distance separating the stations, sometimes up to 100 nautical miles, the phase-difference being determined by this distance. Each slave station is fitted with equipment which receives the master signal, converts it to the slave frequency, and uses it to control the drive oscillator of the slave transmitter. Thus a constant phase relationship is maintained. To ensure that this relationship is maintained accurately, a monitoring station checks the transmissions.

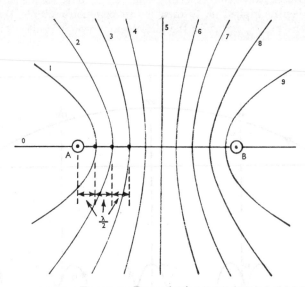

FIG. 119. Decca lattice pattern

THE DECOMETERS

A decometer is simply a phase-meter whose dial is graduated in hundredths of a lane-width; one revolution of the fractional pointer represents the extent of one lane. It will, therefore, indicate very accurately a receiver's position between two lattice lines, but it is unable to identify the particular lane in which it is situated. Since lane-width varies from less than a mile near the base-line to 3 miles or so at 300 miles range, this would cause a high degree of ambiguity, which a ship, entering the coverage area after an ocean passage, might well be unable to resolve.

Once the initial position has been established, however, the decometer, which is capable of continuous rotation, can integrate its movements in the lattice pattern by a set of counters geared to the fractional pointer.

In practice, each hyperbolic pattern on the chart is divided into 'zones' which are lettered from 'A' up to 'J' and then start again at 'A' should there be more than ten zones in a pattern. The zones are further subdivided into numbered lanes. To avoid confusion between different patterns on one chart, each pair of stations is allocated a different group of numbers. The correct zone and lane can be set on the decometer by means of a resetting knob, and its fractional pointer will automatically indicate the exact position within that lane without any further adjustment.

The master station operates three slave stations simultaneously, to produce three lattice patterns. These are coloured respectively red, green and purple on the chart; and the decometers, of which there are three at each receiver, are named accordingly to indicate the pair of stations and the lattice to which they refer. A set of decometers is shown in Fig. 120. The short pointer indicates fractions of a lane, the long pointer indicates the lane itself, while the zone letter is displayed in a small window in the face of the dial.

FIG. 120. A set of decometers

As a ship crosses the coverage area, the decometers, when once set up correctly, will continue to present her up-to-date position in the lattice, provided transmission and reception are continuous. Any break due to equipment failure or severe interference may cause an effect known as 'lane-slip', when the decometers miss or jump one or more lanes. Errors of this kind are unpredictable, and are most likely to occur at and outside the limit of the accepted coverage range. There, sky-wave component varying in amplitude and phase could be sufficiently large to take over temporarily the control of phase of the resultant field, so that the lane-slip would occur. The situation may be worsened by the presence of heavy atmospheric disturbances or interfering transmissions from other stations.

The Lane Identification Meter

The ambiguity of the system has been resolved in the QM5, QM9 and QM10 receivers by the addition of a fourth dial called a 'Lane Identification Meter' which enables the operator to set each decometer to the correct lane within a zone. He must still know which zone his ship is situated in, however, in order to set the correct letter on the decometer. Since a zone consists of about twenty or more lanes, this only requires that the D.R. position should be known within wide limits so that, except in unusual cases, no ambiguity should arise. Should lane-slip have occurred, the fact will be apparent from the lane identification meter as soon as the ship enters the L.I. coverage area, and the decometers can be reset accordingly.

Essentially, lane identification consists of transmissions from master and slave at much lower frequency than the normal. This lower frequency, which is used as a comparison frequency in the receiver, is actually obtained as a beat frequency of the two transmissions originating from the same station. Thus a very much coarser pattern is obtained in which the 360° phase change corresponds to a whole zone. Since this power frequency is a multiple of the pattern comparison frequency, a zone comprises a whole number of lanes. This is shown in Fig. 121.

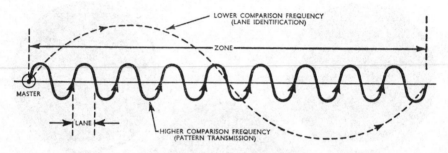

FIG. 121. Lane identification transmission (Green pattern)

The lane identification meter (Fig. 122), which measures phase-difference in the same way as the decometer, will indicate the position within a zone. If this meter is graduated in lanes, instead of fractions of a zone, it will then indicates directly the correct lane in which the receiver lies. It has three concentric scale (one for each pair of stations), coloured red, green and purple. Lane identification signals are transmitted from each pair in a fixed sequence at short intervals; and, as each one is received, a relay is closed, illuminating the appropriate coloured scale, while the pointer indicates the correct lane on that scale. The indication for each colour remains on the meter for about 5 seconds, which is ample time in which to obtain a reading.

Identification is made in two stages from the coarse to the fine pattern by providing an additional pattern of intermediate fineness because in certain conditions of sky-wave interference, the accuracy of the meter responding to the coarse pattern is inadequate for the required purpose. The indicator consists, therefore, of two separate components: the sector pointer and the 'vernier' pointer assembly. The former indicates the position to the nearest sixth of a zone, while the latter, working on an intermediate frequency, indicates the actual lane itself within that zone. The vernier indicator is basically a meter with a pointer revolving once as the receiver travels across the space between two adjacent boundaries of a lane (for example, one-eighteenth of the width of the zone for the green pattern) of the particular pattern which affects it; but, for compactness of display, the action is geared down six times mechanically, and the single pointer is replaced by an assembly of six pointers, which are read against the same scale as the sector pointer. The word 'vernier' is not used in this connection in its true sense, but merely to give a finer indication. A reading is effected by noting, on the illuminated scale, the lane number indicated by the particular vernier pointer which is enclosed by the arms of the sector pointer. Thus, in Fig. 122, if the red scale were illuminated on the meter, the correct lane reading would be between 7 and 8.

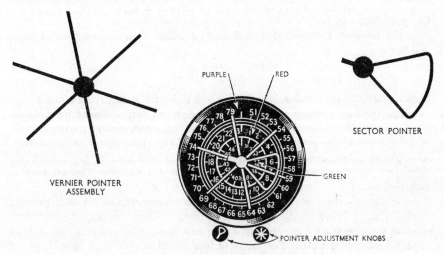

FIG. 122. Lane identification meter

Beyond 100 miles from the base-line, the centre of the sector pointer will not always coincide with the vernier pointer, owing to sky-wave interference; but as the vernier pointer indicates the exact lane, this will cause no inaccuracy. Near the limits of coverage at night, however, the arms of the sector pointer may coincide exactly with two vernier pointers, or the sector pointer may even enclose the wrong one.

The use of lane identification was approved by the Ministry of Transport in 1949, subject to strict compliance with the instructions contained in the relevant Data Sheets, which are promulgated by the Decca Navigator Company from time to time. Failure to follow the procedure laid down may result in misleading information being obtained.

Typical Chain Operation

Reference to the *Admiralty List of Radio Signals* (Vol. V), which gives details of the Decca chains in operation, shows that each station in a chain transmits on a different frequency. If the master and slave stations all operated on the same frequency, the receiver would be unable to distinguish between the incoming signals. In order to compare the phases, however, all the transmission frequencies are related harmonically, and each signal is separately converted in the receiver to a frequency which is the lowest common multiple of the master and slave frequencies. The relative phases can then be compared at this 'comparison frequency', which will be different for each pair. For example, if the Master (A) transmits on 60 kc/s and slave (B) transmits on 80 kc/s, the comparison frequency would be 240 kc/s.

So far as the receiver is concerned, apart from signal separation, the waves appear to have travelled from the transmitters at the comparison frequency, and it is upon this frequency that the number of lanes in a lattice depends. Remembering that one lane is half-a-wavelength wide along the base-line, and taking 240 kc/s as the comparison frequency of the AB pair, we obtain the following:

240 kc/s is equivalent to a wavelength of 1,370 yards

i.e., each lane will be 685 yards wide along the base-line.

If the distance between A and B is 85·5 miles, then the number of lanes will be:

$$\frac{85\cdot5 \times 2,000}{685} = 250$$

Both the width and the number of lanes will differ for each pair of a chain.

Thus, the four stations transmit continuously on four different frequencies. Phase comparison is made in the receiver on three comparison frequencies, to which (in pairs) the master signal and each of the three slaves are converted. The phase differences between the slave signals and that of the master are displayed on the decometers during the whole time that the receiver is switched on.

Lane identification is provided, at intervals of one minute on each pattern, during a short break in the normal transmissions. For this purpose the transmission frequencies are grouped in a different manner in order to produce the required coarser patterns. For the lane identification of a pair, in addition to the master and a slave, two transmitters – one at each section – are put in operation at fixed times every minute. These additional transmitters work on frequencies 'borrowed' from two of the remaining slaves. While this 'frequency borrowing' is taking place, transmissions from the stations normally operating on these frequencies are suppressed for about half a second.

The sequence of transmissions and suppressions is maintained to a rigid time schedule by automatic phase-locking circuits, and the sequence of events appears on the lane-identification meter in the following manner:

TIME (sec.)	LANE IDENTIFICATION	FREQUENCIES At Master At Slave	
0 to 0·5	Red		
15 to 15·5	Green	Master and Purple	Red and Green
30 to 30·5	Purple		

The last transmission is followed by a 30-second interval before the sequence starts again, so that the lane in each pair is identified once every minute. Since the time intervals are unequal (15 sec., 15 sec., and then 30 sec.) it is easy to recognize which L.I. transmission is on, and then check whether L.I. light sequence is correct.

In order to avoid false Red, Green, and Purple readings during the 'frequency borrowed' transmissions, the decometer circuits are cut off for this period; but, owing to storing elements in the circuit, the readings are maintained on the previous levels. This 'persistence' of the decometer readings is sufficiently long for them to be unaffected by the very short lane identification transmissions. The only effect on the decometers is a slight 'kick' of the pointers, which does not affect the accuracy of the reading.

The principle of operation of a Decca chain is explained further in Volume III.

The Receiver

The Mark V (QM5, QM9 or QM10) receiver, capable of operating with nine Decca Chains, is fitted in H.M. ships. The chain is selected by a switch on the lower right-hand side of the receiver case, which is marked with ten positions 1 to 9 and R.

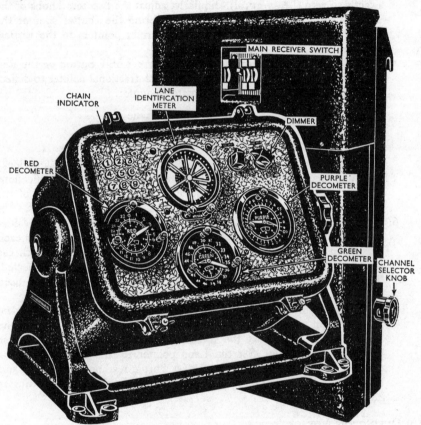

FIG. 123. Decca Receiver Mark V (QM10) and Decometer Unit

The Decometer Unit

Three decometers and one common Lane Identifier meter form the Decometer Unit which may be installed in any convenient place. All controls necessary for operating the receiver, once it has been switched on and switched to the correct chain, are contained in this Unit. An indicator shows the chain in use.

OPERATING PROCEDURE

This outline of operating procedure is extracted from the Decca Navigator Data Sheets, to which the reader must refer for greater detail.

(a) BEFORE SAILING

1. About half an hour before sailing ensure that the aerial is properly rigged and that power is from ship's supply.
2. Switch on the receiver.
3. Select the desired chain at the receiver. The number will then appear on the indicator to the left of the Lane Identification meter.
4. Press the REF knob of the Green decometer (Fig. 120) and, keeping it pressed, adjust all ZERO knobs (Fig. 120) to bring the fractional pointers exactly to zero (i.e., vertical). Similarly, adjust the two zero knobs of the Lane Identification meter (Fig. 122) to bring the central spot of the Sector pointer and any one of the six Vernier pointers to the vertical position (zero on the Red L.I. scale).
5. Holding the REF button depressed, press the TEST button on the Red decometer (Fig. 120). This should cause each fractional pointer to deflect clockwise by the following approximate amounts:

Red	0·20 Lane
Green	0·15 Lane
Purple	0·25 Lane

The L.I. Sector pointer should move approximately one Red Lane clockwise and the Vernier about one-sixth of this amount. The deflections indicate reception of the Master station and correct functioning of the equipment.

6. Carefully set all three decometers to the correct Zone and Lane values for the ship's position by pressing and turning the RESET knob on each decometer (Fig. 120). This should be done after the previous checks have been made, with the receiver switched on and the aerial connected. The receiver should not be switched off once the decometers have been set up.

   The lane numbers may be taken from the chart or from the Lane Identification meter using the procedure given in (d). In setting the Lane pointers, note that the fractional pointers always take up their position automatically. Set the Lane pointer to the *nearest* Lane: for example, if the chart shows the correct Purple reading to be 43·95 and the fractional pointer takes up a position at 0·01, the correct setting is 44·01.

(b) DURING THE VOYAGE

1. During the first hour, REF should be checked and the zeros adjusted if in error. This may be repeated occasionally during the voyage, taking care to check the Lane numbers before and after pressing the REF button.
2. Fixing by Decca consists simply in reading the two decometers that give the best cut and finding the intersection of the two indicated position lines. It is advisable to take the fractional reading first, then the Lane number and finally the Zone letter. When transferring the decometer

readings to the chart, reverse the process; identify the Zone, then the Lane, then interpolate between the Lanes.

3. To ensure that all transmissions (other than Lane Identification) are being correctly received, press the TEST button *without* pressing REF. This should cause the pointers to deflect clockwise as in (a) 5.

4. After switching the receiver to a new chain, immediately reference all decometers and the Lane Identification meter as in (a) 4. The ship's position should be transferred from the old chart to the new before plotting from the decometers.

(c) WHEN ENTERING THE COVERAGE OR WHEN FIRST SETTING UP WITHIN THE COVERAGE

1. Switch on; allow 15 minutes for warming up and then reference *all* meters.

2. Plot the estimated position of the ship on the Decca chart and, from this, set the Zone letter, Lane number and fraction on each decometer.

3. Observe the Lane Identification meter over several sequences of lights to check that the correct Red, Green, Purple sequence is being obtained. *Do not proceed with the setting up until regular and correct sequences are observed.*

4. Observe a group of three complete and, if possible, consecutive colour sequences of the following:

Red L.I. Vernier reading.
Red decometer reading.
Green L.I. Vernier reading.
Green decometer reading.
Purple L.I. Vernier reading.
Purple decometer reading.

Record these readings and also the difference between the L.I. Vernier and the decometer for each colour. *Do not reset the meters* but repeat the above procedure five times at intervals of a quarter of an hour.

5. Considering the record of the groups for each colour:

   (i) If this record over the last four groups shows that the difference between the readings of the L.I. Vernier and the decometer for any colour is consistent and less than half a Lane, you can consider *that* decometer to be correctly set.

   (ii) If there is a difference exceeding half a Lane and this difference is constant to within half a Lane over the last four groups, readjust the decometer by the appropriate whole number of Lanes. The decometer is now correctly set.

   (iii) If there is a difference which is *not* constant to within half a Lane over the last four groups, continue recording groups of sequences for that colour until it is. Then proceed as in (i) or (ii) as appropriate.

(d) USING LANE IDENTIFICATION TO CHECK DECOMETERS WHEN INSIDE THE COVERAGE

The Lane Identification meter is a valuable cross-check on decometer readings at any time and should be read and logged whenever the decometer reading is logged.

Do not reset any of the decometers on the evidence of a single disagreement between L.I. meter and decometer, particularly at night. To avoid unnecessary resetting of decometers the following procedure should be adopted:

1. Checking in Daylight

   In daylight the Lane Identification meter should give a very high percentage of correct readings everywhere within the approved coverage of the Chains. It should be possible to tell at a glance whether the Lane Identification meter agrees with the decometer reading and the difference between them should not exceed 0·5 of a Lane. If it does, and continues to do so on three successive readings separated by one minute, the decometer should be reset. If any doubt exists about the new setting, three groups of three readings should be made with five-minute intervals between groups.

2. Checking at Night

   At night there may be a higher percentage of disagreement between Lane Identification meter and the decometers, owing to sky-wave interference. It is recommended that groups of three sequences should be logged before any resetting action is taken. The interval between groups of readings depends on ship's speed, course, etc., but should not be less than five minutes and should be continued for at least one hour. If, when near the edge of coverage, the user has reason to suspect the whole number indicator on any decometer, e.g. if there is disagreement between the Decca fix and that obtained by another means, the procedure given in (c) above should be used to check the Lane number of that decometer.

HOMING TECHNIQUE

Homing is the reverse of fixing. Instead of reading the decometers in order to obtain the ship's position, it is possible to compute, from the lattice chart, particular readings at a position through which it is desired to pass. Alternatively, a number of readings may be computed in order to steer along a particular track. There are a number of variations of this technique, which are described below.

Lattice Homing

In this method, the course is selected to run parallel to one set of lattice lines, and the advance along the track is observed by the readings of the other decometer. The most accurate results are obtained when the lattice lines cut at right angles. The method may be used either on passage or for anchoring.

Fig. 124 shows a ship approaching her anchorage course from position *W*. It is required to anchor in position *Z*. The decometer readings at this position are:

Red: B 14·4
Green: H 33·4

An anchoring course parallel to the Red lanes is chosen, and this is clearly the line B 14·4. The Green lanes in this vicinity are about 3 cables apart, so it is decided to reach the anchoring course at Green lane H 36, which is about 10·5 cables short of the anchorage. The point at which to alter course is plotted

in the normal manner, making due allowance for tidal stream and wind. This
is point *X*, where the Red decometer reading will be B 13·9.

By plotting Decca fixes during the approach, the exact position at which the
ship arrives on the final course can be obtained. Notice that – provided the
wheel is put over when the correct Red reading is registered – the ship will

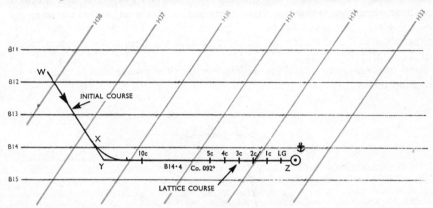

FIG. 124. Lattice homing

arrive at some point along the final course, whether or not she had previously
been set to port or starboard. Having turned to the final approach, it is only
necessary to ensure that the Red decometer continues to show B 14·4, while
the number of cables to go can be observed from the Green readings.

A previously prepared table will facilitate the operation.

APPROACH COURSE 092°

Red: B 14·4

Red increasing: a/c port

Red decreasing: a/c starboard

10 cables	Green: H 35·78 – Reduce to 8 knots.
5 cables	34·78
4 cables	34·53
3 cables	34·30
2 cables	34·06 – Stop.
1 cable	33·82
Let go	33·60
Final readings	{ Red: 14·4
	{ Green: 33·4

With these data, the navigator can remain at the Decca receiver, with the
Lattice Chart, and keep the Captain informed of the ship's progress.

When lattice homing is used in low visibility, particularly on much frequented
routes, there is a danger that more than one ship may be employing this technique
along an identical lane. This is particularly liable to occur in narrow waters,
where the choice of suitable lanes is restricted.

Diagonal Homing

Along any line drawn parallel to one diagonal of the lattice diamonds it will be seen that the values of the decometer readings increase or decrease together at the same rate. In the case of the long diagonal *AB*, in Fig. 125, the two readings both increase at the same rate, whereas along the short diagonal *CD*, the Red readings decrease, while the Green readings increase at the same rate. By choosing the appropriate course, a ship can be steered along a track parallel to either diagonal, and the course adjusted so that the decometer pointers rotate in the appropriate direction at the same rate. A study of the lattice chart will enable the navigator to decide which way to alter course should the rate of rotation differ.

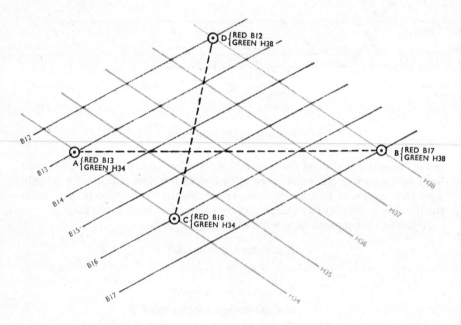

FIG. 125. Diagonal homing

Differential Homing

This method of homing, though less simple than the previous methods, has been devised so that any predetermined course, which does not lie along one of the lattice lines or one of the diagonals, may be followed. First, see which set of lattice lines are cut most nearly at right angles by the track. In Fig. 126 it is the Red lanes. Next, mark off equal intervals along the track where the Red readings have some convenient value – e.g., intervals of one lane.

Tabulate the predetermined Green readings at these points; then, as each Red reading appears on the decometer, record the time and the observed Green reading in the prepared table and, from a previous study of the lattice chart, alter course in the appropriate direction to regain the track. An estimation of tidal stream and current can readily be made from the observed readings. An example for the track *AB* in Fig. 126 is given opposite.

Time	Red Readings	Predetermined Green Readings	Observed Green Readings	Course
0810	B 17	35·4	35·6	310
0820	18	35·8	36·0	310
0830	19	36·2	36·3	300
0839	20	36·5	36·5	310
0848	21	36·8	36·8	315
0859	22	37·1	37·1	315
0908	23	37·4	37·4	312

If Observed Green is High, a/c to port.

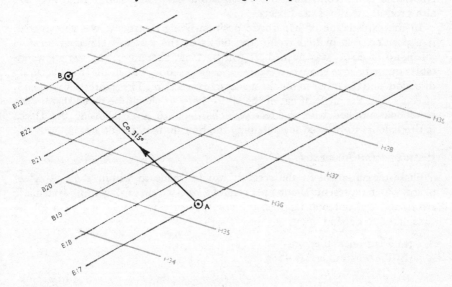

FIG. 126. Differential homing

Accuracy and Coverage

FIXED ERRORS

The accuracy of the system depends largely upon a very precise knowledge of the velocity of the radio waves concerned and of the actual tracks followed by the waves. Investigations into both of these factors are still being conducted; and where reliable data have been obtained, indicating systematic errors in the printed lattices, the results are promulgated by means of Decca Navigator Data Sheets. Instructions for applying such errors – which in a few areas may be as much as 0·6 of a lane-width – are also contained in these data sheets.

PHASE-LOCKING OF TRANSMISSIONS

It is essential for the accuracy of the lattice pattern that the correct phase-difference should be exactly maintained at the ground stations. The methods of ensuring this have been described. Information concerning any transmission failures is promulgated as described later.

VARIABLE ERRORS, AND THE DIAMOND OF ERROR

It has been previously explained that the presence of sky-wave component waves may cause variable errors at the receiver. In the case of Decca there is no means of distinguishing between the two waves, and this leads to an inaccuracy in the decometer readings which will vary with the range from the transmitters and with the time of day. At ranges greater than 75 miles, the accuracy at night is noticeably lower than it is by day, since sky-wave effect is normally only experienced during the night. Beyond a range of between 150 and 220 miles there is a serious danger of lane-slip. Instead of expressing errors in fractions of a lane, it is sometimes more convenient to know the expected error in cables, for various positions inside the coverage area of existing chains. Allowance tables containing this information have been compiled. These are also promulgated by Data Sheets.

In the explanation of hyperbolic position-fixing systems it was shown that, if a position was plotted within the limits of the system's expected error, a 'diamond of error' was formed. It will be clear, therefore, why the allowance tables quoted above show two errors for each position; one in the 'most accurate direction' and the other in the 'least accurate direction'. These directions depend, of course, on the angle of cut of the lattice lines. It should be noted that, in the handbook supplied with the receiver, chartlets are given showing the Decca lattice colours to be used for obtaining the best fix in different areas.

INSTRUMENTAL ACCURACY

Phase-measurement in the receiver can be made to within about $\pm 4°$ of phase, which represents about 2 per cent of a lane-width. Disregarding systematic errors and transmission failures, the accuracy of a fix from the system can be considered to depend upon:

    (a) Instrumental errors.
    (b) Propagation errors –
       (i) Sky wave;
       (ii) Coastal effects.
    (c) Lane-width.
    (d) Angle of cut of the hyperbolae.

Thus Decca errors are subject to many variables and cannot be summarized precisely. The following figures give a guide to the accuracy that should generally be expected:

BY DAY	BY NIGHT	ACCURACY
0–300 miles	0–75 miles	± 10 feet near base line; 1 mile at limits.
—	75–240 miles	Up to a maximum of about 5 miles, depending on sighting of slave stations.

COVERAGE

Although useful signals have been received at ranges greater than 1,000 miles, approval for use of the system has at present been restricted to within 240 miles from the centre of a chain. Beyond this range lane-slip is liable to occur, and positions obtained should be used with extreme caution.

Transmission Failures

Notification of any transmission failures, which might result in lane-slipping, is promulgated to shipping by signals broadcast from certain coast radio stations. Details of this service are contained in the *Admiralty List of Radio Signals* (Vol. V).

Decca Charts

Decca charts, produced by the Hydrographer, consist of Admiralty navigational charts overprinted with Decca lattices. They are given the series letter 'L' with the word 'Decca' in brackets after the number – e.g., L 1408 (Decca) – to distinguish them from other lattice charts. The chart folios are listed in H.51, and are numbered in the 300 Series. On the charts the zone letter and lane number are given against the hyperbola at the end of each lane. Hyperbolae may be printed at intervals of one lane or less, according to the scale of the chart.

Details of charts produced to cover Decca chains in foreign countries are promulgated in Data Sheets.

Publications concerning Decca

A handbook applicable to the receiver fitted is supplied to ships by the Decca Navigator Company. This contains all the instructions necessary for operating the receiver.

The latest information concerning the Decca system is at present made available to users in the form of Data Sheets, issued by the Decca Navigator Company. These may in due course be superseded by official information promulgated by the Hydrographer.

The *Admiralty List of Radio Signals* (Vol. V) contains a brief description of the system, together with details of the chains in operation.

B.R. 2917 (1), *Handbook for Receiver Outfit QM 5/9.*

RADIO NAVIGATIONAL AIDS IN GENERAL

Reports on Performance

If the results obtained from any radio navigational aid warrant the attention of the Admiralty being drawn to them, a report is to be rendered.

Typical circumstances which would merit a report are:

(a) Reliable results obtained at unusually long range.
(b) Failure to obtain satisfactory results when within the normal coverage.
(c) A consistent or unduly large error checked by other means of position-fixing.
(d) Unusually good, or bad, results obtained over a period of time.
(e) Unusual results being obtained, believed to be attributable to peculiarities of radio propagation or other technical reasons.

RADAR

This section describes the use that can be made of marine radar as an aid to navigation, and the complementary aids introduced on land marks and sea marks to help in their detection and identification; it also describes the techniques of 'parallel index' and 'blind pilotage'. Information on radar propagation, reflection, etc., and on the navigational sets and displays will be found in the *Radar Manual* and the *ND Drill Book*, Vol. I. The use of radar in fleetwork is contained in Chapter XIV.

Below are given some recommended practices for using radar as a navigational aid. It should be remembered that a visual bearing should be used in preference to a radar bearing, and that a radar range is less liable to error than a radar bearing.

Coastal Technique

(a) Fix by Radar Range and Visual Bearing

Fig. 127 shows a fix obtained by a visual bearing of a beacon from which a range has been obtained by radar. A radar range from the nearest land could also serve as a check.

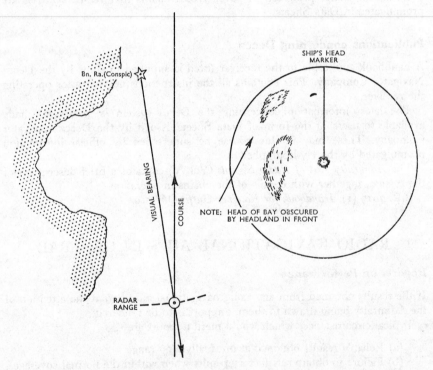

FIG. 127. Fix by radar range and visual bearing

(b) Fix using Radar Ranges as Position Arcs

This is normally the most accurate method of obtaining a fix, using radar information alone.

(1) *Short-range.* – Fig. 128 shows a fix obtained, in low visibility, by radar ranges of two conspicuous headlands *A* and *B*, and a buoy.[1] The P.P.I. shows the use that may be made of the heading marker as a check that the ship is safely clearing the rock; but it must be appreciated that in this case, if there is

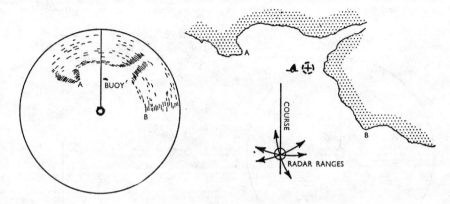

FIG. 128. Fix by radar ranges of three short-range objects

a strong tidal stream setting the ship to starboard, although the ship's head may still be pointing to the left of the buoy, the ship may yet be closing it on a steady bearing.

(2) *Long-range.* – At a great distance from the coast, land echoes from mountains may appear on the P.P.I. These may be the only visible echoes as the coast is approached and it is clearly desirable to make use of them to find the ship's position as early as possible. A study of the chart and an appreciation of the capabilities of radar will help to identify the echoes, but it cannot be expected that the position arcs obtained at great ranges will cut in a point. As shown in Fig. 129, they will probably do no more than indicate an area in which the ship is situated. Note that peak *E*, although higher than *D*, is in the latter's shadow area and is therefore not visible on the P.P.I. Any fix obtained in such circumstances should obviously be treated with reserve.

(c) THE RADAR STATION POINTER (Chart Misc. 5028)

This is a transparent plotting chart inscribed with radial lines from 0° to 360°; it enables the Navigating Officer to plot radar echoes to the scale of the chart in use. It will also assist in identifying the radar responses with charted features.

With the radar station pointer orientated correctly, and with the plotted radar echoes 'fitted' on top of the charted objects, the ship's position is at the centre of the diagram.

It can also be used for:

(1) determining errors in the orientation of the radar display;
(2) laying off sextant angles as an ordinary station pointer;
(3) plotting position lines.

---

[1] The position of the buoy should be established, as in visual pilotage practice, before reliance is placed on it.

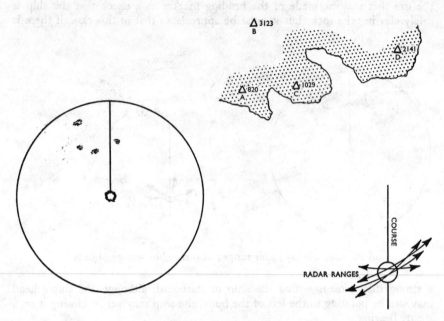

FIG. 129. Fix by radar ranges of long-range shore objects

Instructions and a table of approximate heights and distances at which echoes may be picked up by radar under normal conditions are printed on the diagram itself.

(d) Fix by Radar Range and Bearing

Fig. 130 shows a ship off a coast which is obscured by bad visibility. A fix has been obtained from a radar range and bearing of the headland *A*. In spite of the possibility of inaccuracy due to the beam-width, this bearing has been used, because ranges of the land at right angles to the bearing of *A* would be unsatisfactory owing to the poor radar response offered by the sand dunes. In practice, the bearing can be corrected approximately by applying half the beam-width of the set to the bearing obtained; in this case, it must be added.

Alternatively, a more accurate bearing will be obtained if the gain, or P.P.I. input, is reduced until the headland only just 'paints' on the P.P.I.

(e) Use of a Radar Range as a Clearing Line

When proceeding down a comparatively straight and featureless coast from which accurate fixes may be unobtainable, it is often possible to decide on a minimum range outside which no off-lying dangers will be encountered. Occasional ranges of the coastline abeam can then be obtained by radar, in order to ensure that the ship is not inside what is, in effect, a form of clearing line. (The navigator must be sure that he is getting echoes from the actual coastline, however; otherwise a large safety margin should be allowed.) This is shown in Fig. 131.

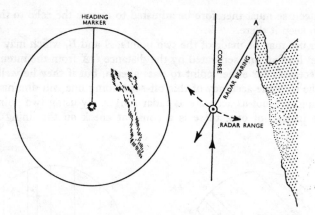

FIG. 130. Fix by radar range and bearing of a headland

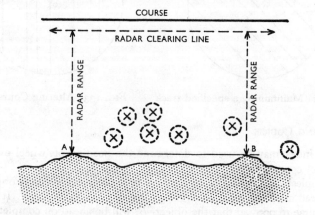

FIG. 131. Use of radar ranges to obtain a clearing line

Pilotage Technique

For operation in restricted waters it is essential to have a rotatable P.P.I. cursor engraved with parallel (index) lines, and, preferably, designed to overcome parallax error. It is advantageous to have the two larger display scales drawn on the display. The technique called 'Parallel Index', which uses these parallel index lines, can be employed in many ways.

> *Caution.* – It is most important that the centre spot of the P.P.I. should remain at the centre and that the ship's head marker should remain correctly lined up.

(a) MAINTAINING A SPECIFIED TRACK (Fig. 132)

If it is desired to pass at a specified distance, *OE*, off a radar-conspicuous object *D*, set the index lines parallel to the intended track, i.e. the charted track, draw the parallel through *E* in chinagraph pencil, and steer a course so that the relative track of *D* remains on the parallel index line *DE*. If the ship is set to starboard, the echo of *D* will move in from this line towards the centre of the

P.P.I.; the course must therefore be adjusted to restore the echo to the line *DE* and then to keep it there.

A similar use may be made of the two points, *A* and *B*, which may be treated as an off-set leading line separated by the distance *OX* from the intended track. It is not necessary for either point to pass abeam, but if they lie well ahead or astern of the ship the accuracy of this off-set leading line will diminish because radar bearings are not as accurate as radar ranges. By using two points for the off-set line instead of one, there is a constant check on the lining up of the P.P.I.

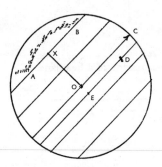

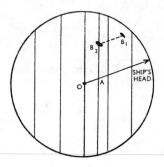

FIG. 132. Maintaining a specified track   FIG. 133. Altering Course (1)

(b) ALTERING COURSE

Parallel index may be used to determine the position of 'wheel over' for an alteration of course.

The simplest case is that of turning on to a radar-conspicuous object which will be ahead after the turn. In Fig. 133 the ship is steering 070°. It is desired to alter course to 000° so that the object, *B*, will be ahead on completion of the turn. Set the index lines parallel to the new course, mark the position *A* so that *OA* is equal to the 'distance to new course', and draw an additional parallel (if necessary) through *A* with a chinagraph pencil. The echo of the object will appear to move along the path $B_1 B_2$. Course should be altered when the echo reaches B_2.

Usually the navigator must choose a suitable radar-conspicuous object off the intended track on which to make his alteration of course; in fact, it is more accurate to do so. In Fig. 134 the ship is approaching harbour on a selected track parallel to the points *A* and *B*. Both *B* and *C* appear to be suitable marks on which the course alteration can be made. If *C* is chosen, the moment at which course should be altered is decided by the radar bearing, whereas if *B* is chosen it depends mostly on the radar range. *From this it is clear that, at the moment the alteration is made, the chosen object should be as near 90° from the future track as possible*; in this case *B* should be selected.

On the chart draw lines parallel to the new course through the edge of *B* and through the plotted position of 'wheel over', then measure the cross index ranges (C.I.R.).

On the P.P.I. cursor, at the scale to be used, mark the two parallel index lines for the two cross index ranges, then rotate the cursor to the intended new track.

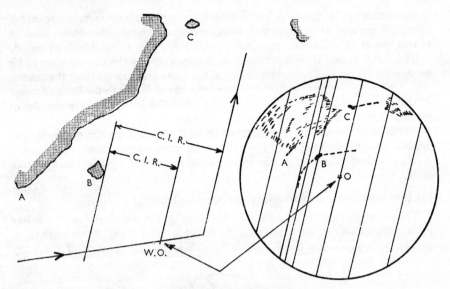

FIG. 134. Altering Course (2)

When the echo of B cuts the inner parallel, alter course; the echo should then appear to move as shown by the dotted track and coincide with the outer parallel at the end of the alteration of course. Subsequently the right edge of C may be used to continue the approach on the new course.

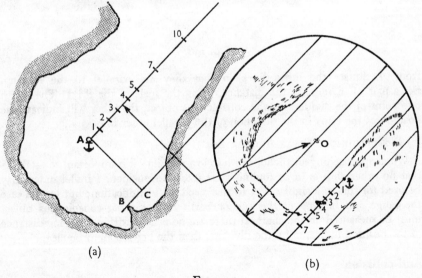

(a)

(b)

FIG. 135

(c) ANCHORING

It may happen that a ship is required to anchor by radar in a position that has no convenient radar ranging mark ahead. In Fig. 135a the approach course to the anchorage is shown. A line is drawn through the only radar-conspicuous object, B, parallel to the approach track, and the perpendicular drawn from A to this line at C. AC is the cross index range and BC is called the 'dead range'.

The P.P.I. cursor is then prepared as in Fig. 135b, on the display scale to be used, with the parallel index line drawn at the cross index range from the centre. The dead range is then marked, also the intervals of cables to the limit of range of the cursor. The cursor is then rotated so that the index lines are parallel to the approach track.

As the ship approaches, the distance to go is indicated on the cursor by the position of the echo of B. Fig. 135b shows the picture at $3\frac{1}{2}$ cables.

This method is subject to the inaccuracies introduced by any bearing error of B.

(d) IDENTIFICATION OF RADAR-INCONSPICUOUS OBJECT

The parallel index lines may be used to assist in the identification of a radar-inconspicuous object, such as a buoy. Select a radar-conspicuous object, A, in Fig. 136. From the chart, measure the bearing and distance of the buoy

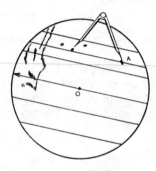

FIG. 136

from A. Rotate the index lines so that they are parallel to the bearing. Set a pair of dividers to the distance, using the scale of the P.P.I. Then with one point of the dividers on the conspicuous object, the other will indicate the position of the buoy in the direction of the parallel index line.

(e) ESTABLISHING A CLEAR ANCHOR BERTH

When approaching an anchor berth in low visibility it is important to establish that no other ship is in or fouling your intended position. Parallel index may be used for this in a similar way to that used for identification; but in this case the range and bearing of the anchor berth from a radar-conspicuous object must be measured on the chart. If there are no echoes within swinging distance of the position indicated by the dividers, then the berth should be clear.

Anti-collision

Another use of parallel index occurs in anti-collision work both in fog and in good visibility. If the parallel index is aligned with a few successive plots of another ship, the risk of collision can be rapidly assessed.

If the relative track of the other ship passes through the centre of the P.P.I., then that ship is on a collision course.

In Fig. 137, ship A is on a collision course; ship B will pass clear. The closest point of approach (C.P.A.) of B is the point Y and XY is the cross index range.

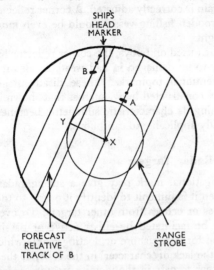

SHIP'S
HEAD
MARKER

B

A

Y

X

FIG. 137

FORECAST
RELATIVE
TRACK OF B

RANGE
STROBE

Increasing the Radar Response of Small Targets

Small targets, such as buoys, boats or visual beacons, are liable to give poor radar responses, owing to their unsuitable shape, the material of which they are made, or to the fact that they become lost in the sea clutter.

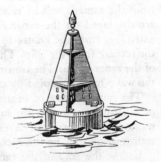

FIG. 138. Corner reflector assemblies fitted on buoys   FIG. 139. The radar buoy

(a) *The Corner Reflector.* – One method of improving this characteristic is to place on the target a corner reflector assembly. The reflector consists of three metal plates mutually perpendicular and mounted so that the axis of symmetry is horizontal. A radar beam striking the reflector from a wide range of angles of incidence will be returned nearly direct, without any scattering. Thus a group of these reflectors mounted together can be arranged in some suitable form so that a strong echo is returned towards any direction from which a beam arrives. Two of these corner reflector assemblies are shown in Fig. 138. The detection range of a buoy fitted with one of those reflectors is likely to be increased from about 2 miles to 5 or 6 miles; and, since its echo intensity is increased, there is now a better chance of seeing the buoy echo at close range through the sea clutter, provided the swept gain is correctly adjusted. A corner reflector assembly mounted on the mast of a wooden fishing vessel would be even more effective, on account of the added height.

(b) *The Radar Buoy.* – When used on buoys, the corner reflector has too great a windage area, and is likely to be damaged in bad weather; also it is liable to visual confusion with conventional topmarks. These disadvantages may be overcome by using a specially constructed buoy, such as that shown in Fig. 139. The buoy itself, while retaining its characteristic silhouette, becomes a form of reflector. The design is equally applicable to can buoys.

Positive Identification of Radar Targets

Although an important navigational mark may give a strong radar response, there are many occasions when it is difficult to identify it owing to the presence, on the display, of land echoes or echoes from other targets. To overcome this difficulty, identification may be facilitated by either active or passive devices. The active device can be used for either shore or floating marks which, because of the weakness of the echo, the lack of 'character' in the echo, or the possibility of confusion with land or other targets in the vicinity, require accentuating in some way on the radar screen. The passive device is suitable for targets which, although visible on the screen, are liable to be confused with other echoes.

Active Devices

(a) *The Ramark.* – This is a radar beacon which enables ships fitted with radar to obtain bearing indication of the beacon on the P.P.I. display. Signals from the ramark will be received when the radar aerial points towards it; they are displayed on the radar screen as a broken line, spread over about 2° and extending from the centre to the circumference of the P.P.I., on the bearing of the ramark from the ship. This line therefore 'flashes up' during each revolution of the radar aerial. The transmission sweeps over a range of frequencies to cover the wave-band occupied by different types of marine radar.

The ramark's line of bearing is 'coded' and consists of either dots or dashes, or a combination of both, so that positive identification can be obtained when more than one ramark is established in the same vicinity. In addition, the transmission may be 'time-coded' to a pre-arranged schedule.

Unless the *echo* of the ramark (or that of the lighthouse or other structure on which it is situated) is visible on the display, it will not be possible to obtain a range as well as a bearing.

These ramarks are at present in the experimental stage, and details of their establishment and service are promulgated as necessary in Admiralty Notices to Mariners. The ramark's transmission is independent of the reception of signals from radar transmitters, and it can therefore be used by any number of vessels simultaneously, with no chance of saturation or mutual interference. Moreover, in order to receive the ramark's transmissions, no ancillary device other than the radar set itself is required by a ship.

(b) *The Racon.* – This is the name given to a radar responder beacon which provides a direct indication of both range and bearing on a radar display. The beacon requires to be 'triggered' by a transmitter situated in the ship. At present there are no racons in operation for marine use.

Shore-based Radar

HARBOUR SUPERVISION

At a number of ports in different countries, radar installations have been set up on shore as an aid to traffic using the port. Although mainly useful in thick weather, such installations are also of assistance for informing vessels of the shipping situation at some distance from them. These installations normally consist of displays at the shore site showing, in one or more sections, the approaches to the port.

Information concerning their own positions and those of other vessels in the harbour approaches, and the relative position of navigational marks, can be passed to ships by radio. This enables traffic to use the port in conditions in which it would be impossible without such information to do so. It also provides the harbour authorities with an instantaneous check on the position of all buoys and other floating marks under their jurisdiction.

The system is intended solely to provide information, and does not attempt in any way to control the movements of vessels. This control remains, as is customary, in the hands of the master or captain.

FERRY OPERATION

In certain rivers, special radar equipment has been set up in order to facilitate the operation of ferries during thick weather. Depending on the local topography, the radar may be either shipborne or shore-based, with radio communication between shore and ferries. In some cases a definite degree of control is exercised from the shore.

BLIND PILOTAGE

Blind Pilotage is the name given to the operation of conducting the passage of a ship in pilotage waters, using any available means not denied the navigator by low visibility. It is therefore possible, and indeed usual, for the Blind Pilotage Position (B.P.P.) to be sited in a compartment from which there is no external view.

General Principles

To ensure success it is necessary to conduct the ship accurately along a pre-arranged track planned for either visual or blind conditions. In comparatively unrestricted waters, this is best done by constant fixing on the chart, using radar in conjunction with other aids as appropriate, e.g. MF DF, Decca and soundings.

In narrow waters and during the final stages of an anchorage it is clear that, just as in visual pilotage, the delays inherent in fixing are unacceptable. It is therefore necessary, for anti-collision and navigation in these conditions, to work directly from the P.P.I. or such other instruments as may be available – e.g. the decometers, if Decca homing technique is employed – using a prepared notebook. A cross-check between instruments should be made whenever possible.

In either case, the same organization is required and, whichever method is being employed, the following principles should be followed:

(a) The ship should be conned from the compass platform on recommendations from the B.P.P., and not from the B.P.P. direct, because it is only on the bridge that the 'feel of the ship' can be retained. Nevertheless, it will be advantageous if the conning orders can be heard in the B.P.P.

(b) It is desirable that the Captain should have easy access to the B.P.P., so that he can assess the validity of the navigational information used.

(c) It is most important that the Captain and the Navigating Officer together should study the prepared chart beforehand so that each is entirely familiar with the common blind/visual plan.

(d) The Navigating Officer should obtain and assess the data himself, whenever practicable; although certain information, such as soundings or asdic data, may reach him more appropriately through other operators.

(e) A chart with the intended track shown on it must be provided on the compass platform, both from a safety point of view and to enable the O.O.W. to plot chance visual bearings.

(f) It is most important that Blind Pilotage should be practised in clear weather, and visual checks plotted in order to assess the accuracy of the Blind Pilotage. Only thus can the necessary confidence in the system be established which will permit runs of some complexity to be conducted in safety under blind conditions.

Blind Pilotage Team and Equipment

Blind Pilotage requires a high degree of team-work in order that all relevant factors may be considered while assessing the ship's position and her future movements. It is essential that the Navigating Officer should be aware of every circumstance affecting the ship's passage, e.g. wind and tidal streams. A suitable arrangement of personnel and equipment, whereby this can be achieved, is described below.

(a) *Compass Platform.* – The Command cons the ship on recommendations from the Navigating Officer in the B.P.P. Chance visual bearings, fog signals heard, etc., are reported to the Navigating Officer. No special equipment is required, but clear and reliable two-way communication must exist between the compass platform and the B.P.P. *The conning intercom should on no account be used for this purpose.*

(b) *Blind Pilotage Position.* – The Navigating Officer conducts the pilotage and requires the following equipment in the immediate vicinity of the chart table:

(1) Compass repeater;
(2) Log (speed and distance), rudder and wind indicators;
(3) P.P.I. from H.D.W.S. radar;
(4) Appropriate radio aid presentation;
(5) Communication with the compass platform as in (a).

The following should also be provided in the B.P.P.:

(6) Echo Sounder, or direct communication with the E/S operator if the equipment is situated elsewhere.

(7) Reception only on conning intercom and/or a branch from the conning voice-pipe (not required if the B.P.P. is within an enclosed compass platform).

(8) Direct communication with DF and asdic compartments.

(c) *Anti-Collision Plot.* – It is neither necessary nor desirable to use an A.R.L. table for conducting Blind Pilotage, particularly in tidal waters. Some form of anti-collision plot must, however, be kept; the form of this will depend upon the equipment available.

The various methods are:

(1) A.R.L. table, which must be additional to the chart table used for pilotage, showing geographical position;
(2) Simple relative plot;
(3) Tracking direct on a fixed P.P.I. cursor;
(4) Relative track evaluation by echo plots or 'tails' and alignment of parallel track index.

Assessment of the Risk Involved in a Blind Pilotage Passage

Although normally the accuracy of Blind Pilotage is such that a ship can be taken to an open anchorage and anchored within 50 yards of the desired place, the degree of risk involved, particularly in restricted waters, must be carefully assessed. Congestion due to other shipping, and the consequences of failure of radar or other vital aids, once the ship has been committed to her passage, must be taken into account.

Technique of Blind Pilotage

A Blind Pilotage operation should be divided into two distinct phases of Preparation and Execution.

PREPARATION

(a) The track should be selected with particular reference to radar homing and ranging, especially by parallel index technique.

(b) Reliance on fixing by radar range and bearing on a single mark should be avoided.

(c) The Navigating Officer must decide carefully at what stage he will:

(1) change charts (bearing in mind that this involves a break of about 30 seconds);
(2) switch radar range scales (the track should be chosen, if possible, to avoid this being done at a critical moment);
(3) leave the chart and navigate at the P.P.I. from his prepared notebook.

(d) The determination of 'wheel over' position for altering course may be done either by observing the range of an object whose bearing is approximately at right angles to the new course, or by aligning the parallel index to the new track and turning, with due allowance for 'distance to new course'.

(e) For anchoring, ranges of an object ahead must be used instead of beam bearings, and these should be prepared in the notebook. The distance 'stem to radar aerial' should be substituted for 'stem to Pelorus'.

(f) The Navigating Officer should himself calibrate the radar displays and radio aid before starting the passage.

EXECUTION

(a) Throughout the passage the Navigating Officer should maintain a flow of information to the compass platform so that the Captain is kept fully in the picture and will be better able to concur or disagree with the recommendations from the B.P.P.

(b) As with all forms of fixing, it is most important to 'D.R. ahead' throughout. Procedure is greatly simplified if fixes are taken at the times shown against the D.R. positions; an immediate comparison is thus obtained.

(c) Use parallel index to keep on track.

(d) It must be appreciated that, whatever the technique employed, a drift off the line is likely to be detected less readily by radar than by visual methods.

(e) When anchoring blind it is necessary to work directly from the P.P.I. during the final stages. The Navigating Officer should move to the P.P.I. while there are at least 5 cables to go. The range strobe should be preset for the next 'distance to go' report (assuming an object ahead is being used); and the track should be checked throughout the approach. If there are no marks suitable for running a parallel index, he should pass the necessary fixing data to his assistant to plot on the chart and confirm that the ship is remaining on track.

Navigational Records

When carrying out a Blind Pilotage passage, the Navigating Officer will clearly be too busy to maintain a continuous written record. It is essential that such a record should be kept, however; and, in comparatively unrestricted waters, it is normally sufficient for this record to be kept on the chart itself by plotting fixes and noting the positions and times of alterations of course and speed and other relevant data. This procedure, involving thorough and methodical chart work, is in fact no different from that which should be practised during any pilotage passage.

In more restricted conditions, however, the Navigating Officer should pass a complete running commentary to the compass platform, as, for example:

'No. 7 buoy fine on port bow, 8 cables. Ship slightly to port of track. Steer 136 to regain'. A rating should keep a complete record of the commentary and all conning orders passed. In conjunction with the Navigating Officer's prepared notebook and the chart, this record should suffice for any analysis.

CHAPTER VII

Navigational Instruments[1]

I. SPEED AND DISTANCE RECORDERS

THE PITOMETER LOG

Two TYPES of bottom log are supplied to H.M. ships by the British Pitometer Log Co., Ltd., London.

Type D, for modern frigates, destroyers and above;

Type M.A.3, for old cruisers and carriers.

All pitometer logs are 'pressure-type' logs, i.e. they depend on the difference between the normal pressure (static pressure) of water resulting from the depth of the instrument protruding through the hull of the ship, and the pressure (impact pressure) due to the movement of the ship through the water. Description of the logs and operating instructions are given in B.R. 268(3).

TYPE D PITOMETER LOG

Description (Fig. 140)

Hull fitting. – This consists of a rodmeter, projecting about 3 feet below the hull when in the operating position, sited near the pivoting point of the ship. When housed, the rodmeter slides up through a watertight gland, withdrawal is prevented by stops, and the opening in the hull can be closed below the rodmeter by a sluice valve. The rodmeter is a hollow bronze rod of oval cross section, having a flat end containing one impact orifice facing forward and two cross-connected static orifices, one on each side. The impact and static orifices communicate with separate holes running lengthwise through the rodmeter to two cocks and thence by pipes to the Bellows-type Differential Unit and Controller.

Bellows-type Differential Unit and Controller (Fig. 141). – This consists of two metal bellows (**A** and **B**), connected to the impact and static orifices. The bellows act on a rocking arm (**C**) against a conical spring (**D**). When the ship is stopped, the pressure in both bellows is the same; but when steaming ahead the additional pressure from the impact orifice compresses the spring and, through link mechanism and gearing, drives a spindle carrying the pointer (**E**) of the Master Speed scale and the Control Arm (**F**) of the follow-up mechanism.

---

[1] The following instruments are described elsewhere as indicated:

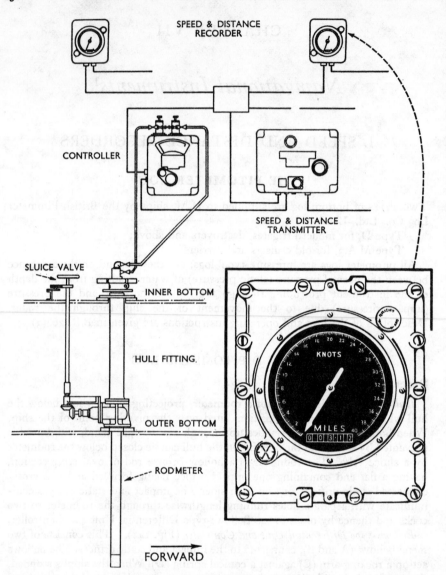

FIG. 140. Type D Pitometer Log

The pressure difference between the bellows varies as the square of the ship's speed, but the conical spring is designed to give equal spacing over the greater part of the Master Speed scale. However, a certain amount of non-linearity remains; it is calculated from speed trials after the log is first installed and a correction is made by introducing a cam into the follow-up drive within the controller so that the transmitted speed is linear throughout the range.

A percentage correction may be applied to the log speed by altering the length of the right-hand end of the rocking arm. A scale is provided.

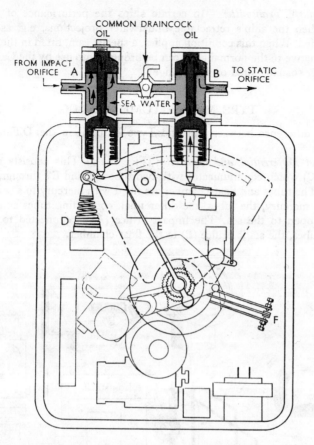

FIG. 141. Bellows-type Differential

Speed and Distance Transmitter. – The movement of the control arm in the Controller completes a circuit for the follow-up motor in the speed and distance transmitter which:

(a) drives the Speed Transmitter; this controls the speed Indicators and also provides the follow-up drive for the Controller;

(b) controls the position of the roller in a potter's wheel device in the distance transmission.

Speed is converted into distance as follows. A self-winding clock controls the speed of a motor which, through suitable gearing, drives the disc of the potter's wheel at a fixed rate (i.e. a certain number of revolutions in a fixed *time*). The potter's wheel converts *speed* (the position of the roller) into *distance* which is transmitted to the distance registers by impulses of 1/100 mile steps.

Speed Indicator and Distance Register. – These may be combined in one unit as shown in Fig. 140, or they may be separate. The Distance Register is a 5-dial cyclometer-type counter receiving impulses of 1/100 mile from the Distance Transmitter.

Cam Control Transmitter. – In certain ships the performance of the log is affected when the ship's retractable underwater projections, e.g. asdic dome, are protruded. When this condition applies, a special cam, fitted in the controller as an alternative to the normal cam, can be brought into use by the Cam Control Transmitter (usually sited on the Bridge).

TYPE M.A.3 PITOMETER LOG

The main difference between this and Type D log is in the Differential and Controller.

Mercurial Differential and Controller (Fig. 142). – This consists of a float-chamber (**C**) which communicates with two tubes (**E** and **E′**) through a smaller tube (**D**). The tubes and float-chamber are filled with mercury to a certain level. Above the mercury, the tubes, the differential, connecting tubes and rodmeter tubes are open to the sea. The impact orifice (**A**) is connected to the outer mercury tubes, the static orifice (**B**) to the float-chamber.

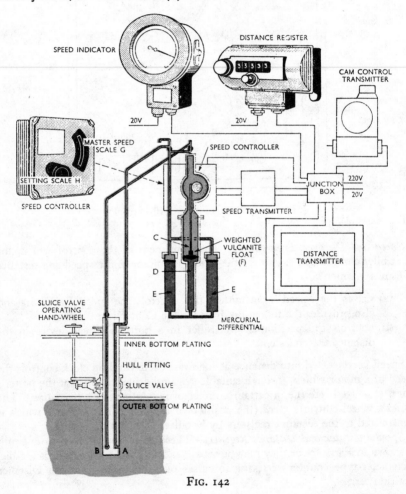

FIG. 142

A weighted float (**F**) rests on top of the mercury in the float-chamber, and carries a bronze rack which engages with a gear wheel which operates the pointer of the Master Speed scale (**G**) of the Controller. The follow-up and linear correction of the speed scale of this Controller is similar to that in Type D. The Differential and Controller are mounted in gimbals.

General Characteristics of Pitometer Logs

(a) There are no external moving parts, so there is little likelihood of the log being fouled by weed, waste or other obstructions.

(b) A direct indication of speed is obtained. The registration of distance is dependent upon the satisfactory working of an integrating mechanism.

(c) The log does not register speeds below 1 knot, except in special Pitometer logs for use in the Hydrographic Service.

(d) Once calibrated, it is not possible to adjust any error, except by fitting a new cam.

THE CHERNIKEEFF LOG

A full description of this log is given in B.R. 268(3).

Description

The general arrangement of the equipment is shown in Fig. 143.

(a) *The Impeller mechanism.* – An impeller is fitted on the lower end of a hollow vertical shaft, which can be projected about $1\frac{1}{2}$ feet below the hull of the ship. The impeller is rotated by the flow of water; it operates a submerged make-and-break mechanism, which works in oil inside the shaft. This mechanism transmits impulses electrically to the distance recorder, situated in some convenient position in the ship. The log thus primarily measures distance.

Water cannot enter the mechanism because oil inside the shaft is maintained at a higher pressure than that of the sea surrounding it, by means of an oil-injector operated by a handwheel. Owing to the very small clearance between the impeller shaft and its bearings, loss of oil to the sea is negligible.

If the impeller mechanism is not kept in order and perfectly clean, the whole installation fails. It is retracted into the ship by raising the shaft bodily; it can then be supported by a 'check tube'. A sluice valve can then be closed and the log shaft removed from its housing.

(b) *Transmission.* — The make-and-break mechanism, operated by the impeller, transmits impulses every 1/400 mile to the distance recorder. The electrical supply is normally obtained from the ship's L.P. system.

(c) *The Distance Recorder* (Fig. 144). – This consists of a dial with four pointers. The large red pointer indicates fractions (to the nearest 1/400) of a mile on the outer scale; one complete revolution of this pointer corresponds to one mile. The large black pointer indicates miles on the inner scale and completes one revolution every 100 miles. The scale of the small left-hand dial is 100 miles per division (1,000 miles for one complete revolution), while the scale of the small right-hand dial is 1,000 miles per division. The recorder shown in Fig. 144 registers 90·1 miles.

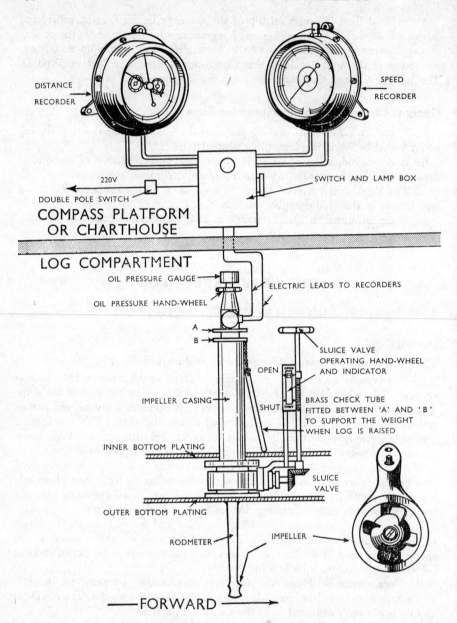

FIG. 143. Chernikeeff log assembly

The master distance recorder controls, by make-and-break contacts, the distance recorder repeaters, the master speed indicator, and the speed indicator repeaters.

When other methods are not available an indication of speed may be obtained from the distance recorder by the following procedure:

FIG. 144. Chernikeeff log: distance recorder

Note the number of divisions (miles) of the inner scale over which the red pointer moves in a period of 36 seconds. This will indicate the speed in knots. For example, if the watch was started when the red pointer was at zero, and in 36 seconds it reached the position indicated in Fig. 144, the speed at that moment, as indicated on the inner scale, would be 10 knots.

(d) *The Switch-box* (Fig. 145). – This contains a switch which controls the speed indicator. A speed table on the front of the box and a blue flashing lamp provide a secondary means of calculating the log speed. The time, in seconds, is taken between twenty-one lamp flashes, and the corresponding speed can be obtained from the table.

The flashes are made by the impeller make-and-break mechanism. Therefore, between twenty-one flashes, the log has run 20/400 mile, and if, for example, the time taken is 6 seconds, then the log speed is $\dfrac{20 \times 3,600}{400 \times 6}$, or 30 knots.

(e) *The Speed Indicator*. – The master speed indicator calculates the speed according to the number of 1/400 mile impulses received from the distance recorder in a fixed time. With a 5 second interval between successive counts, the impulses are counted for a period of 18 seconds and the speed, ½ knot for

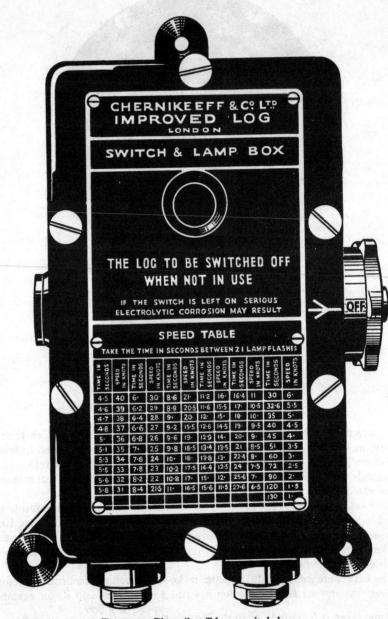

FIG. 145. Chernikeeff log : switch box

each impulse, indicated on the dial of the speed indicator. Thus changes of speed are indicated at 23 second intervals. The accuracy of the speed indicator depends on the accuracy of the impeller originating the distance impulses and the accuracy of the clock mechanism, the latter being enhanced by the short period of time involved and the fact that the clock error is not cumulative. Any number of speed indicators, without clock mechanism, can be controlled by the master speed indicator.

Calibration

The error of the log should always be determined by readings of the distance recorder. If the log speed is obtained from the speed indicator, any error found may be due to the indicator mechanism, and not to the log itself. The speed shown by the indicator should be noted every 18 seconds, and the mean speed for the run also obtained in this way, so that any discrepancy found may be rectified.

An error is corrected by removing the impeller and altering the pitch of its blades by the special calibrator supplied. Instructions for its use are contained in the handbook.

Possible Faults

The impeller may be fouled or damaged.

Readings will be unsatisfactory if the contacts in the submerged mechanism or in the various components of the speed indicator are faulty.

General Characteristics of the Chernikeeff Log

(a) The impeller is delicate and liable to damage or obstruction.

(b) A direct indication of distance is obtained; the registration of speed depends on the satisfactory working of an integrating mechanism.

(c) The log will register very low speeds, for example, the current while the ship is at anchor.

(d) Any error found by calibration can be easily removed.

(e) The Chernikeeff log may be fitted in vessels of all sizes, including small boats.

THE ELECTRO-MAGNETIC LOG

The Electro-Magnetic Log consists of a rodmeter, fitted in the hull of a ship in a similar manner to the rodmeter of a Pitometer Log, and a Master Speed and Distance Transmitter housing the electronic and electro-mechanical equipment. Connection between the rodmeter and the master speed and distance transmitter is by two screened cables.

An iron-cored coil mounted in a fibre-glass shell is fixed at the lower end of the rodmeter. The coil is supplied with alternating current and will, when moved through the water, produce a voltage in the water surrounding it. The voltage, proportional to the flux and the relative velocity of the rodmeter to the water, is picked up by two electrodes on the rodmeter and applied to the electronic circuits in the master speed and distance transmitter where it is converted into speed and distance. Various elements can be fitted in the master speed and distance transmitter and an associated ship's speed re-transmission unit to enable any kind of transmission for speed and distance, or pulse for distance, to be connected to remote indicators and other equipment.

OBTAINING THE ERROR OF THE LOG

Most logs have their errors, which should be found and recorded, as a percentage correction of the *log reading*, in the Navigational Data Book. If the error cannot be removed, this percentage correction must be applied to all subsequent log readings.

The percentage correction of the Pitometer or Chernikeeff log can be applied mechanically to the A.R.L. plotting table, if fitted.

Grid plotting has increased the requirement for accuracy in ship's automatic plotting tables. This accuracy is dependent on the compass and the bottom log. The log must therefore be calibrated accurately and checked very frequently. It should be calibrated at intervals not exceeding six months.

The information obtained from speed or endurance trials of H.M. ships is very valuable for estimating speed and endurance under operational conditions. Full value cannot be obtained, however, from Forms S.231 and S.346 unless the speeds are found by one of the accurate methods described below.

Log calibration consists of two operations carried out concurrently – first, calculating the speed of the ship as given by the log; and secondly, calculating the true speed of the ship. A comparison of these two will give the percentage log correction.

Since percentage log correction does not vary directly with speed, trials should be carried out over a wide range of speeds, in order to determine a series of log corrections. Subsequently the appropriate correction must be applied, according to the speed shown by the log.

Method 1. – From runs over a 'Measured Distance', with and against the tidal stream.

When the tidal stream is negligible, or can be assumed constant, two runs in opposite directions are sufficient. If the tidal stream is not constant, four runs are necessary – two in each direction. For each run, stop-watch times are taken as each transit is crossed, and thus speed over the ground can be calculated.

Method 2. – From equal runs on opposite courses, the ship being fixed by Decca.

Two or four runs will be necessary, as for Method 1. Runs are carried out on opposite courses over the same ground. The course should be chosen so as to cross one set of Decca lanes at right angles. The set of lanes chosen should normally be the most closely spaced in the trial area, and must be within good coverage from the Decca chain. At least five lanes should be crossed each way. The times of crossing the first and last lattice lines should be observed. Readings of two decometers should be taken every minute, in order that line as well as advance may be checked. The distance covered over the ground during the trial is the charted distance between the first and last lattice lines crossed, corrected as necessary if they were not crossed at right angles. (In neither method is it necessary to 'calculate the true speed of the ship *through the water*, as the formulae given on pages 239 and 240 use the calculated *ground speed*.)

Conditions during Calibration by any Method

In order to obtain high accuracy, the following requirements must be satisfied:

(1) Engine conditions should be maintained steady throughout each run, and to ensure that the terminal speed appropriate to these conditions has been reached, a straight run up to the 'measured distance' of at least five minutes' duration is necessary.

(2) When turning between runs, the rudder angle should not exceed 15 degrees. This limits the loss of speed during the turn to an amount which can be made up during the five-minute approach run.

(3) The rudder should be used sparingly during the run.

(4) Trials should be carried out in calm weather and in a wind of less than force 4, since the effect of wind and sea on recorded speed cannot accurately be estimated.

(5) The time interval between runs on the 'measured distance', when four runs are necessary, must be kept reasonably constant. If one run is made at 1000 and the second at 1020, then runs 3 and 4 should be made at 1040 and 1100 respectively.

(6) When four runs are necessary, the speed of all runs must be as nearly similar as possible, since the formula used in these circumstances is based on the assumption that the percentage error of the log remains constant over the speed range covered by the four runs.

Calculation of Log Speed

By the above methods it is possible to obtain a comparison of the speed through the water, as shown by the log, with that actually steamed by the ship. For logs which provide a direct measure of speed, the reading of the speed indicator should be noted every 15 seconds (or 10 seconds, for speeds over 20 knots); the mean thus obtained can be used to calculate the percentage log correction as shown below. The readings of the distance recorder should also be noted, so that any discrepancy may be detected and rectified.

For logs which primarily measure distance, the speed by log should be calculated from the time by stop-watch for a recorded distance through the water. A distance easily readable on the log, and covering approximately the whole time on the 'measured distance', should be used. This is more accurate than trying to read the distance through the water that coincides with the 'measured distance', since this would entail a reading of a fraction of a division on the scale. The speed indicators of these logs, if fitted, should be checked.

Calculation of Percentage Log Correction

It is necessary to carry out only two runs (one in each direction) if there is no tidal stream or if it can be considered constant for the duration of both runs. In this case, the percentage correction of the log is given by:

$$C = 100 \left(\frac{V_1 + V_2}{L_1 + L_2} - 1 \right) \qquad . \qquad . \qquad . \qquad . \qquad (formula \ 1)$$

An accurate correction can only be obtained under conditions of changing tidal stream if four runs (two in each direction) are carried out. In this case, the percentage log correction is given by:

$$C = 100 \left(\frac{V_1 + 3V_2 + 3V_3 + V_4}{L_1 + 3L_2 + 3L_3 + L_4} - 1 \right) \qquad (formula\ 2)^1$$

In both the above formulae:

C = Percentage log correction.

V_1, V_2, V_3 and V_4 = Ground speeds[2] measured on runs 1, 2, 3 and 4.

L_1, L_2, L_3 and L_4 = Mean log speeds measured on runs 1, 2, 3 and 4.

EXAMPLE 1

A ship steams over a measured distance of 1 nautical mile (of 6,080 feet), runs being made with and against the tidal stream, which is considered to be constant for the duration of the two runs. The time for the two runs is: –

Run 1: 3 minutes 38 seconds (= 218 seconds)
Run 2: 4 minutes 00 seconds (= 240 seconds)

$$V_1 = \frac{3600}{218} = 16 \cdot 5 \ knots$$

$$V_2 = \frac{3600}{240} = 15 \ knots$$

The average log speed, which is obtained as previously described, for the two runs is 16 and 14 respectively.

From formula 1:

$$C = 100 \left(\frac{16 \cdot 5 + 15}{16 + 14} - 1 \right)$$

$$= 100 \times 0 \cdot 05$$

$$= + 5 \ per\ cent$$

---

[1] It can be shown mathematically that the speed of any tidal stream is given by:

$$Speed = A + BT + CT^2 + DT^3 + ET^4 + \dots\dots\dots\dots$$

where A, B, C, etc., are constants and T is time from any chosen datum point).

Further, it has been found that, using only the first three terms, we get a very close approximation to the speed of the stream, i.e.,

$$Speed = A + BT + CT^2 \dots\dots\dots\dots$$

A stream which varies in this way is eliminated by four runs at equal intervals of time; and, taking a mean of the mean speeds so recorded (i.e., if V_1, V_2, V_3, and V_4 are the recorded speeds), then:

$$Mean\ of\ mean\ speed = \frac{V_1 + 3V_2 + 3V_3 + V_4}{8}$$

The use of this formula gives formula 2.

[2] Ground speeds must be measured in nautical miles of 6,080 ft per hour.

EXAMPLE 2

A ship steams over a measured distance of 1 nautical mile twice in each direction, to allow for a variable tidal stream. The results of the runs were:

Run 1 – Ground speed: 19·02   Log speed: 20·2
Run 2 – Ground speed: 24·08   Log speed: 21·1
Run 3 – Ground speed: 19·50   Log speed: 20·3
Run 4 – Ground speed: 23·70   Log speed: 20·8

From formula 2:

$$C = 100 \times \left(\frac{19\cdot02 + 72\cdot24 + 58\cdot5 + 23\cdot7}{20\cdot2 + 63\cdot3 + 60\cdot9 + 20\cdot8} - 1 \right)$$

$$= 100 \left(\frac{173\cdot46}{165\cdot2} - 1 \right)$$

$$= 100 \times 0\cdot05$$
$$= + 5 \text{ per cent}$$

Accuracy of Calculation

The accuracy of the calculations depends, obviously, on the accuracy with which the log speed and ground speed are recorded. It has been found in practice that the recording of stop-watch time when traversing a measured distance involves an error of about $\frac{1}{2}$ second maximum at high speeds, and slightly greater at low speeds. The ground speed may therefore be regarded as correct to within $\pm\frac{1}{3}$ per cent. For the log readings, when the speed is obtained by timing a predetermined distance through the water, the probable error is also about $\pm\frac{1}{3}$ per cent. Where log speed is obtained from a number of observations of the speed scale of the log, the accuracy of the result is dependent upon the size of the speed scale. If it is not possible to read more accurately than to 0·1 knot, the error will be of the order of $\pm\frac{1}{3}$ per cent at high speeds, and much greater than this at low ones.

The overall accuracy of the assessment of percentage log correction should normally be within ± 1 per cent.

THE DUTCHMAN'S LOG

This is another method of finding the speed of the ship at a given moment, when out of sight of land. The observation stations should be selected on the upper deck, one forward and one aft. The horizontal distance between the stations, which must be accurately measured from the plan of the ship, should be as great as possible. At each station a fixed open sight should be set up and trained accurately on the beam. If possible, each station should be in communication with a control position. Numerous floats should be prepared. The forward observation station must be sufficiently far aft to allow the floats to reach the water before they pass the line of sight. If arrangements can be made for another ship to drop the floats from a position ahead, so that the floats will pass the observing ship at about three-quarters of a cable on the beam, the observation stations can be nearly the whole length of the ship apart.

When all is ready, a float is dropped into the sea. At the moment the float passes his line of sight, the observer at each station gives a pre-arranged signal to the control position, where both times are noted to $\frac{1}{5}$ second. About five floats, dropped at short intervals, are required for each set of observations. The mean of the speeds obtained from the five observations can then be taken as the speed of the ship during the period covered by the observations. Great accuracy in observing and taking times is necessary in order to obtain correct results in a fast ship; for example, if the observers are 167 yards apart and the speed of the ship is 30 knots, an error of $\frac{1}{5}$ second in the elapsed time will produce an error of 0·6 of a knot in the speed obtained from one observation.

TO FIND THE SHIP'S SPEED BY ENGINE REVOLUTIONS

A 'Revolution Table' is obtained for each new ship as a result of trials. This gives the propeller shaft revolutions per minute required for each knot of the ship's speed in smooth water, when the draught is normal and the bottom clean. This table is a good guide for subsequent estimation of the speed through the water, provided that due allowances are made for variations in draught, the state of the ship's bottom, and the effect of wind and sea. As a rule, it is easier to estimate these allowances for a large ship than for a small one.

These tables can be compiled from the results of runs carried out in the same manner as those described for calculating log error. Copies of these tables should be kept in the Navigational Data Book.

TAUT-WIRE MEASURING GEAR

Taut-Wire Measuring Gear provides a method of measuring distance run over the ground, by means of a wire that is anchored to the sea bottom and paid out astern of the ship.[1]

The gear, originally designed for vessels locating faults in submarine telegraph cables, has been adopted in the Royal Navy mainly for use in surveying, mine-laying, and minesweeping operations.

Types of Gear

The following machines, manufactured by the Telegraph Construction and Maintenance Co., Ltd., Greenwich, are fitted in H.M. ships:

MARK 1 (Fig. 146). This is the machine found in the majority of vessels fitted with taut-wire measuring gear. It is supplied with 140 miles of wire.

MARK 4 (Fig. 147). This may be found in certain major war vessels, but is primarily for use in small craft. It is supplied with 20 miles of wire.

TAUT-WIRE GEAR MARK I

Components (Fig. 146)

Rollers. – One set of four rollers (two vertical and two horizontal) is fitted for guiding the wire on to the counter wheels. These rollers have been replaced in

---

[1] Taut wire gives a position line that is an arc of a circle described about the point of departure. The radius of this circle is the distance run over the ground.

later models by a bell-mouth lead-in. Another set of three rollers (two vertical and one horizontal) is fitted for guiding the wire over the stern.

After Leading Wheel. – This wheel guides the wire through the after rollers.

Tensionmeter. – The tensionmeter, or dynamometer, consists of a spring-loaded roller wheel by means of which the tension in the wire can be measured.

Cyclometer Wheel. – The cyclometer or counter wheel registers the amount of wire run off. It consists of a wheel 6·08 feet in circumference actuating a counter gear which registers to 1/1000 mile. Repeater counters should be fitted on the compass platform (near the log distance repeater) and in the chart house.[1]

Forward Leading Wheel. – This is similar to the after leading wheel and is provided to guide the wire from the counter wheel on to the dynamometer wheel.

Drum. – The drum carries 140 miles of 0·28 (22 gauge) bright steel measuring wire. It is fixed on a standard and does not revolve.

Drum Standard. – This carries the drum. A spindle, fitted to the standard, carries at its fore end a hand brake that passes through the centre of the drum; the unwinding mechanism is secured to the after end of this spindle. The brake is operated by a handwheel and is used to adjust the tension on the wire.

Unwinding Mechanism. – This consists of a revolving arm, called the flyer arm, secured to the after end of the spindle on the drum standard. The arm is fitted with a counterpoise weight at one end, and a special wheel called the *flyer* at the other end.

Davit. – A small davit is fitted for lifting the drum on to the standard.

To Prepare the Gear

1. Inspect the wire; run off and discard any that is rusted. A new drum is supplied well greased and covered.

2. Apply slight braking to prevent the wire from kinking while it is rove as shown in Fig. 146, taking care to keep it above the pins connecting the two sides of the dynamometer. The fore leading wheel is slightly offset from the counter wheel.

3. To the end of the wire secure a short stray line (a double thickness of codline is suitable). The stray line is secured to a 15 lb concrete clump sinker.

4. The sinker should be hove up close to the stern rollers and secured; any slack on the wire should be recovered by pushing back the flyer arm; the brake should then be adjusted to touch lightly.

5. Rope off the area between the flyer and the counter (unless a cage or guard rails are fitted) to protect the wire and personnel.

6. The master counter on the cyclometer wheel provides a check on the amount of wire run off the drum and should not normally be reset to zero before a run. If desired one of the repeaters can be set to zero.

Notes:

   (i) When the gear is idle the flyer should be left so that the oil hole in the lubricating ring is uppermost. The ring itself should be filled with waste to prevent the accumulation of dirt.

   (ii) Partially used drums are sometimes kept for use on short runs. A record must be kept of the amount of wire run off every drum held on board.

---

[1] The master counter is liable to wear out, and so, if there is a discrepancy between the master and the repeater, the latter should generally be considered the more reliable of the two. Steps should, however, be taken to check this when an opportunity occurs.

K*

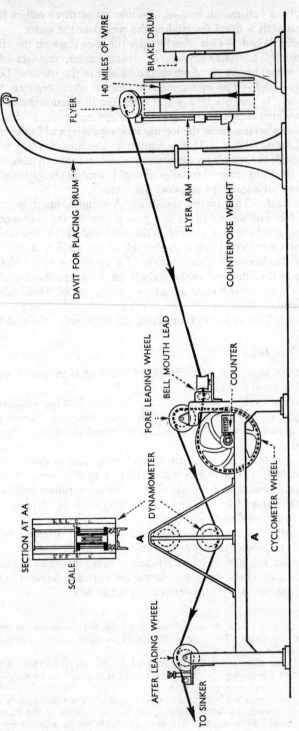

FIG. 146. Taut-wire Measuring Gear Mark I

To Run the Gear

1. Two men are required to start the gear – one to free the sinker, and the other to tend the brake. Unless an observer is required to read the counter during the run, only the brake operator is necessary.

2. Remove the waste from the oil ring and lubricate freely the flyer, and all gear with the exception of the brake straps, which need only a drop or two of oil.

3. Cut the tail which secures the sinker to the ship, and release the brake, allowing the wire to run out handsomely. Careful brake control is required so that the flyer arm does not overrun the wire and throw it off. If this occurs, the wire must be cut, another sinker bent on, and a fresh start made.

4. Adjust the brake so that the strain never exceeds 60 lb, nor falls below 30 lb, as indicated by the dynamometer. If, with the brake off, the strain is about 60 lb or fluctuates about that figure, as is likely to occur in a swell, speed must be reduced. The breaking strain of the wire is 200 lb.

Notes:
   (i) New brake linings are apt to be rough, making fine adjustment of the brake difficult. They should be well run in by carrying out practice runs.
   (ii) The brake tension should normally be maintained at about 38 lb, which is sufficient for depths up to 1,000 fathoms. Excessive tension is prevented at moderate speeds by control of the brake, but above a certain speed it can only be regulated by varying the speed of the ship. This critical speed will depend on the type of ship and the state of the sea.
   (iii) The gear is designed to run at speeds of about 12 knots or less, and such speeds are suitable for the majority of runs. Wartime experience in fast minelayers has shown, however, that the gear can be satisfactorily run at speeds approaching 30 knots, depending on the state of the sea, and that it is not necessary to reduce speed when streaming. This is a great advantage in cases where time is vital and where a reduction of speed may hazard the safety of the ship. A degree of skill is, however, required at the brake if success is to be achieved.
   (iv) A long drop for the sinker is desirable when streaming the gear, as this allows time for the flyer arm to gather momentum, so that when the sinker enters the water the sudden increase in tension is minimised.
   (v) The distance to be allowed for streaming the gear before starting the run must depend upon circumstances. In general, this distance should be three times the depth of water, with a further liberal allowance made for a second sinker to be streamed in the event of the wire parting. (This is more likely to occur while streaming than at other times.) In addition, the Navigating Officer requires time to check that his estimations of course, with allowance for the tidal stream, etc., are correct.
      Altogether, 3 miles will be the minimum distance to allow for the average run, but for high-speed runs in very deep water this may have to be increased to as much as 10 miles.

Procedure if the Wire should part during a Run

Note the reading and the exact time. Bend on a fresh sinker and stream again. Run for the required distance to allow the sinker to hold, then note the reading and the time again. The run between the two times must be estimated by the most accurate method available.

To Cut the Wire

When it is desired to cut the wire while the gear is running, choose a point where the run is horizontal, hold a piece of iron under the wire, and tap the wire quickly with a cold chisel. Alternatively, at moderate speeds, a pair of pliers may be used. At the same time increase the tension on the brake to about 45 lb so that the machine stops as soon as the wire is cut.

Precautions

(1) Always keep the brake-lever on: a heavy shower of rain on the brakes and straps will cause the flyer arm to be released suddenly and the wire will be thrown off.

(2) When the gear is idle, the drum should be kept covered in order to prevent the wire rusting. It rusts rapidly if not well greased.

(3) Should it be required to run the whole length of wire off the drum, the end that is fixed to the drum by a wooden peg should be examined beforehand, to ensure that it is not jammed. Otherwise the flyer arm will be bent or broken. To avoid the possibility of such an accident, it is always safer to cut the wire before the end is reached.

(4) If the sinker is hanging over the stern and not securely stopped before a run is started, it is advisable to lock one of the leading wheels, by means of a bar inserted through the spokes, in order to prevent the machine starting itself through vibration.

(5) No other ship should pass within half a mile astern of a ship running taut-wire measuring gear. Such a ship is distinguished by a special flag signal.

(6) A good deal of grease and oil is thrown off whilst the gear is working, so the deck should be covered with lime to protect it.

TAUT-WIRE GEAR MARK 4

This machine, shown in Fig. 147, is a simple version of the Mark 1. It may be placed in any suitable position on the vessel, so that the wire will have a clear run aft. It is often found advisable to place the gear on an elevated platform near the after rail.

The method of reeving the wire round the measuring sheaves is clearly indicated in the illustration. The wire is identical to that supplied with other types of gear, but is only 20 miles in length. The drum itself revolves to unwind the wire. Since no governor is fitted, as in the case of the flyer arm in the Mark 1 gear, it is difficult to prevent the wire overrunning and lying slack on the sea-bottom. Good brake control is therefore essential, and the brake linings must be well run-in to ensure smooth operation.

The weight of sinker and the tensions involved should be identical with those already described. In general, the instructions given for the Mark 1 gear apply equally to the Mark 4 machine.

The distance-indicator can be re-set by means of a vulcanite knob.

The method of discharging the empty drums and replacing the full drum calls for no special instructions. The charging lever provided is so arranged that the drum bore is brought into line with the bore of the side frames of the machine, so that the spindle may be readily reinserted. As the drums are wound according to which side of the ship the gear is fitted, it is important that a port drum should be placed in a port gear and a starboard drum in a starboard gear.

When not in use, a canvas cover should be provided for the machine.

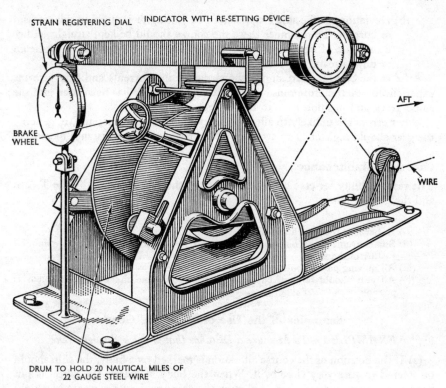

STRAIN REGISTERING DIAL   INDICATOR WITH RE-SETTING DEVICE

AFT

BRAKE
WHEEL

WIRE

DRUM TO HOLD 20 NAUTICAL MILES OF
22 GAUGE STEEL WIRE

FIG. 147. Taut-wire Measuring Gear Mark 4

CALIBRATION OF TAUT-WIRE MEASURING GEAR

Once installed, there is no means of altering the calibration of the gear unless the counter wheel is changed. Any error should be determined by several runs over a measured distance, and then applied, if appreciable, to the readings as a percentage of the distance measured.

Accuracy

The sources of error are:

(a) The circumference of the cyclometer wheel. This is 6·08 feet and is therefore only correct for latitude 48°, where 1 minute of latitude = 6,080 feet. This figure is used for the standard nautical mile, as explained elsewhere, for world-wide use; but if a 20-mile run is being carried out at the equator, for instance, where 1′ of latitude = 6,046 feet, then appreciable error will result. The taut-wire counter will register 20 miles when, in fact, 20 × 6,080 feet have been covered. This figure represents $\dfrac{20 \times 6080}{6046}$ or 20·112 nautical miles at the equator, which is an error of approximately 200 yards, or 0·5 per cent of the distance measured.

(b) Deviations of the ship's course, due to yawing or changes in tidal stream or current. To minimise these the course should be kept straight, either by the use of back transits (ashore or moored) or by running upstream or downstream.

A fix at the end of a run, and a knowledge of the currents and tidal streams experienced, are therefore most important when the gear has been used and the ship's track and position have to be verified.

Other errors are unlikely to affect ordinary navigational runs; and, in general, the gear should register to an accuracy of 0·2 per cent of the distance measured.

Care and Maintenance

The responsibility for care and maintenance of the gear is shared by the T.A.S. and the L. Branches.

Notes:

(i) In harbour the flyer arm should be kept unshipped.

(ii) Spare drums must be kept well covered and clear of the deck, to minimise rusting of the wire.

(iii) All moving parts should be kept clean and well lubricated.

(iv) All gear should be kept covered and protected from the weather as much as possible.

Examples of the Use of Taut-wire Gear[1]

EXAMPLE 1 – To Measure a Distance that is not a Straight Line

(a) If the position of the course alteration is marked by a buoy, the ship should be steered to pass very close to it. When the buoy is abeam, the wheel is put hard over and a reading taken. Although the ship turns on a wide arc, the bight of wire is soon pulled taut against the buoy mooring, so that the reading taken when the buoy was abeam may be accepted as the turning-point and as the initial reading on the new course.

(b) If the corner is not marked, the ship's track during the turn and for the next few miles must be plotted from turning data, the counter being read at the time of wheel-over, and again when sufficient distance has been run on the new course for the taut-wire run to be restarted.

EXAMPLE 2 – To Fix a Turning-point

A ship, shown in Fig. 148, runs taut wire from a known position at A, steering 135° for 40 miles[2]. On arrival at B, course is altered to 225°, and the procedure described in Example 1 (b) is carried out. On coming in sight of land at C, a fix is obtained. The distance run by taut wire from B to C is 30 miles. This includes the first half-mile on the new course, calculated from turning data. It is required to know the accurate position of the point B.

From Fig. 148, it can be seen that the intersection of arcs drawn with radius 40 miles from A, and 30 miles from C, gives the position of the point B.

---

[1] Other examples of taut-wire runs, mainly of use to the surveyor, are given in the *Admiralty Manual of Hydrographic Surveying.*

[2] The position of A can be most accurately determined by previously dropping a dan buoy, fixing its position by sextant angles, then starting the run when the dan is abeam on the correct course. The preliminary run up to the fix is required for the reason discussed on page 245.

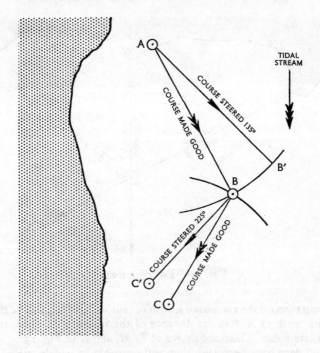

FIG. 148. Fixing a turning-point

EXAMPLE 3 – To Check the Speed/Revolution Table

If no measured distance is available, the speed/revolution table can be checked by carrying out runs with and against the tidal stream, using taut wire, and maintaining steady revolutions during the runs.

The taut-wire readings at the beginning and end of each run will give the distance covered over the ground. The average true speed through the water is obtained in the manner previously described for calculating the log error, and the mean revolutions for the runs are compared with this speed.

In order to obtain the best results, the stream should be constant up and down the runs, and the wind as light as possible.

EXAMPLE 4 – To Lay a Mark in a Predetermined Position (Fig. 149)

Select two (or, preferably, three) conspicuous shore marks, *A*, *B* and *C*, such that the angle subtended by them at the predetermined position is as nearly as possible 90° (or 60° for three marks). Calculate the distance from each shore mark to the intended position *X*.

Temporary dans should now be laid by taut wire in the following manner.

Each ship starts her run from an accurate departure fix, with the shore mark on a reciprocal of the course to be made good. She then steers the required course to *X*. The course can be checked by back bearings of the shore mark, though an accurate course is not so essential as a straight course for this method. The course made good should, however, be known.

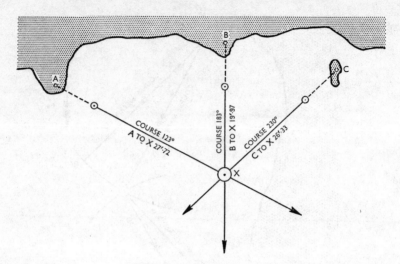

FIG. 149. Laying a mark (1)

Each ship runs off the calculated length of taut wire, which will be the distance from shore mark to X, less the distance of the fix from the shore mark. Each ship then lays a dan. These are shown at L, M, and N in Fig. 150.

When all dans have been laid, they will probably be widely spaced according to the accuracy of the courses made good.

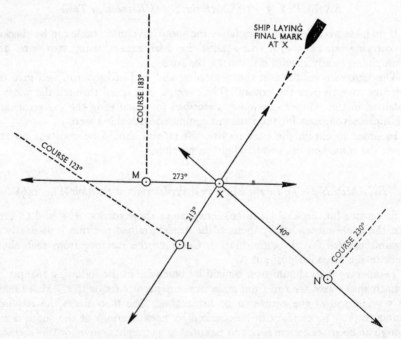

FIG. 150. Laying a mark (2)

The exact distance of each dan from its respective departure point is known, and the correct position X must lie, therefore, on the arcs of three position circles drawn through the three dans. In practice, these arcs may be assumed to be straight lines at right angles to the course made good.

The ship laying the datum mark then steams towards one dan on the correct course and lays the final mark at X when one of the other two dans comes on the correct bearing. The bearing of the third dan is used as a check. In Fig. 150 the ship steers 213° with L ahead and lays the final mark when M bears 273°, checking that, at the same moment, N bears 140°. For accuracy, allowance must be made for the distance between the bridge, from which the bearings are observed, and the position from which the dan is dropped, so that the bearings given above may require slight adjustment.

EXAMPLE 5 – Fixing the Position of a Mark Out of Sight of Land

The principles involved in Example 4 above can also be used in the following manner to fix the position of a mark.

Run taut wire, from a fix off-shore, on the estimated course to the mark. Record the distance by taut wire when the mark is abeam on the course made good, and thus obtain a position arc for the mark. This may be either plotted or calculated, as is convenient. Repeat the procedure from one or more widely divergent fixes, and the position of the mark will be the intersection of the arcs.

EXAMPLE 6 – Alternative Method of Laying a Mark in a Predetermined Position (Fig. 151)

A minimum of two ships is required, one to run taut wire, and the other to drop dan buoys. In Fig. 151, dan A is dropped before starting the run, and accurately fixed by sextant angles. The course and distance from A to B (the position for laying the last mark), is then determined from the chart. The gear is streamed so that it is running correctly on passing A, where a reading is taken.

The consort is stationed on the uptide quarter of the first ship, so that her dans will take up their final position on the track to be made good.

After running from A about half the visibility distance of a dan, the consort is instructed to drop the first intermediate dan. When it has been dropped, the leading ship obtains a range of this dan and notes the reading of the counter. From these readings and from a transit of A with the intermediate dan, the latter's position can be plotted. This transit serves as a check that the correct course has been maintained and, in the event of the wire parting, it is only necessary to restart the run from the last dan laid. Subsequent dans are dropped as necessary, until the position B is reached, where the ultimate mark is laid. The position of B can then be checked by another taut wire run to a land fix, on a course as nearly at right angles as possible to the initial run.

For a long run, if additional ships are available, this method may be modified as follows. Each successive dan is dropped by a different ship, which marks it until the next dan is laid. The previous one laid is then recovered, and the recovering ship rejoins the leader. This enables dans to be laid up to about 10 or 12 miles apart, the leader and marker burning searchlights, if required, to extend their mutual visibility.

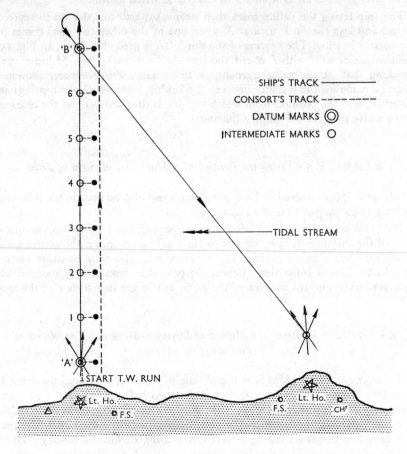

FIG. 151. Laying a mark: alternative method

EXAMPLE 7 – To Determine the Ship's Track, using Taut Wire and a Single Object

If a single shore object is available for observation while running taut wire, the ship's track can be obtained from three bearings of the object, and taut-wire readings taken at the times of the observations.

The method of obtaining the course made good from three such bearings is explained in Chapter III. If, now, the actual distance run over the ground between these bearings is known, then the track can be plotted by setting a parallel ruler to the course made good, and laying it across the three position lines in such a position that the two distances run are cut by the lines of bearing. There can be only one such position.

II. ECHO SOUNDING GEAR

Wire sounding machines, although still fitted in H.M. ships, are no longer used for sounding.

The echo sounding machine is now fitted in all ships and a number of boats, such as surveying boats. The earlier sets were sonic whereas Type 765 and later sets are supersonic and may be compared to an asdic set arranged to work vertically instead of horizontally.

This section gives a brief description of Type 765 and a summary of other sets. For further details of these sets and the operating procedures the relevant handbooks must be studied.

Basic Principles

A ship transmits an underwater sound impulse which travels outwards through the sea at uniform speed. On reaching the sea bed, part of the sound impulse is reflected and returns to the ship where its arrival is recorded graphically. The velocity of sound in sea-water is known; the interval between transmission and reception is proportional to the depth of water; therefore the depth can be determined.

In shallow water this interval is extremely short, for example the overall time is only about $\frac{1}{40}$ second in 10 fathoms. It is not possible to measure this by direct means, so the echo sounding machine provides a magnified time scale upon which these shallow soundings can be measured.

TYPE 765 SERIES

Outline of Operation

A constant speed motor in the *Recorder* drives a stylus across a slow-moving sheet of chemically-impregnated paper at a speed proportional to the speed of sound in sea-water. On each revolution of the stylus a transmitting cam on the stylus shaft opens a contact which triggers the *Contactor Unit* and a high energy current impulse is fed to the *Transmitting Transducer*. The transducer vibrates and emits a supersonic signal which is directed downwards through the ship's hull plating, then reflected from the sea bed and creates a vibration in an exactly similar transducer called the *Receiving Transducer*. The electrical impulse generated in the Receiving Transducer is amplified and rectified in the *Amplifier* and fed as a d.c. marking voltage to the recorder stylus which has now traversed the paper a distance proportional to the depth of water. The stylus produces a brown stain on the paper at the moment of transmission and again on receiving the returned echo. The depth can be read from a Perspex scale placed vertically in front of the paper.

Set variations

Each set is given two or three suffix letters, e.g. Type 765 AJT or Type 765 BK. The first indicates the system of power supply, the second the type of hull fitting, and the third whether a special recorder is fitted. Type 765 AJ indicates the normal arrangement; Type 765 BJS would be the set fitted in a ship with 230-volt a.c. supply and normal hull fitting, but the recorder would be designed for coastal survey.

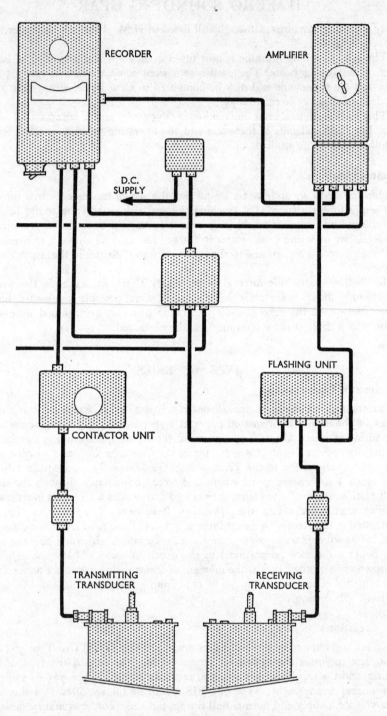

FIG. 152. Type 765 Series – Diagrammatic arrangement

Transducers

Transmitting and Receiving Transducers are identical. Each is mounted in a heavy cylindrical tank filled with fresh water and secured to the inside of the ship's plating. These 'Magneto-striction' transducers consist of a pack of thin nickel laminations with coils running through them and a parabolic reflector to concentrate the supersonic transmission. When the laminations in the transmitting transducer are subjected to a strong surge of current from the contactor unit, fed through the coils, they contract, start to vibrate and give off sound waves of 14·25 kc/s that are directed vertically downwards in a beam by the parabolic mirror. Some of these waves, reflected from the sea bed, enter the receiving transducer, are concentrated by the reflector on to the nickel laminations which vibrate and produce electrical oscillations in the surrounding coils. These oscillations are then amplified and rectified to produce the d.c. marking voltage for the stylus of the receiver.

When Magneto-striction transducers are used as receivers, the nickel laminations have to be maintained in a magnetised condition. This is done periodically by passing a heavy, unidirectional current, controlled by the Flashing Unit, through the windings of the transducer; the procedure is given in the handbook for the set.

Amplifier

Sensitivity is controlled by three pre-set controls inside the amplifier, adjusted by the Trials Installation Officer. Two external controls are mounted on the front panel:

(a) *Auto-Manual switch.* – This is a selector switch for automatic or manual control of sensitivity. It should be set to AUTO in depths of less than 30 fathoms and MANUAL in depths of over 30 fathoms.

(b) *Manual Sensitivity Control.* – When (a) is set to AUTO this control should be set to MAX. When (a) is set to MANUAL this control should be adjusted to give the best trace.

Recorder (Fig. 153)

As the stylus begins its traverse across the paper, the transmitter contacts in the recorder open, and the outgoing sound makes a transmission mark near the left edge of the paper. There is a slight delay, called 'contactor lag', between the opening of the contacts and the emission of the sound; the contacts are adjusted to allow for this. The transmission mark should normally be aligned to the depth of the transducers, as indicated on the scale, so that the returning echo will show the true depth below the surface. Should it be aligned to zero on the scale, the echo will record the depth below the keel. Whichever method is used, a notice must be fixed to the recorder stating whether the instrument is set to read depths below surface or below keel.

The transmission is controlled by an On–Off switch at the base of the recorder.

Gear change control gives a fast and slow speed of the stylus, thereby changing the range of soundings that can be obtained in one traverse over the paper.

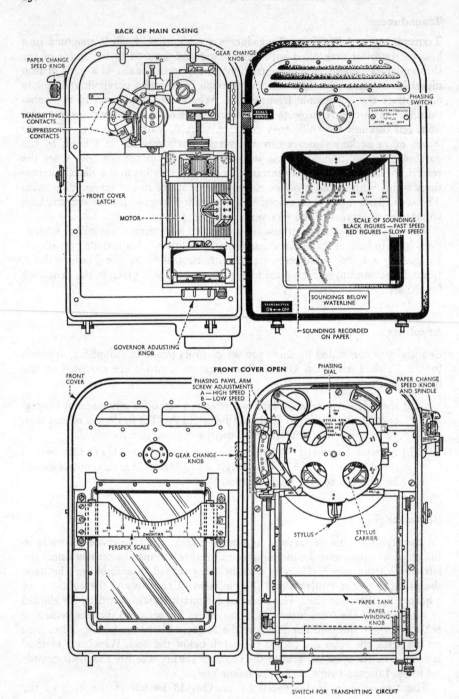

FIG. 153

PHASING

When it is desired to extend the range of the recorder without alteration to the scale or slowing up the movement of the stylus arm, the timing of the transmission relative to the position of the stylus can be advanced a known interval corresponding to a known depth. This is known as 'phasing' and the 'depth' by which the transmission is advanced is added to the depth shown on the scale to obtain the true sounding. A phasing switch on the outside of the recorder rotates the phasing dial mounted on the spindle on which the transmitting contacts are carried. A movement of the dial clockwise, i.e. counter to the rotation of the stylus, advances the moment of transmission by four specified 'depths', the amount being shown on the edge of the phasing dial that is visible through the large window in the front of the recorder.

If the phasing dial is turned when the recorder is switched off, *it must be turned clockwise* otherwise the transmission contacts will be damaged.

RECORDERS	PHASE		SCALE RANGE	
	High speed	Slow speed	High speed	Slow speed
	Zero		0– 30 fathoms	0– 300 fathoms
A.2935B	+ 20	or 200	20– 50 fathoms	200– 500 fathoms
A.2936B	+ 40	or 400	40– 70 fathoms	400– 700 fathoms
A.409	+ 60	or 600	60– 90 fathoms	600– 900 fathoms
A.381B	+ 80	or 800	80–110 fathoms	800–1,100 fathoms
	Zero		0–150 feet	0–150 fathoms
3608A	+ 100		100–250 feet	100–250 fathoms
5981A	+ 200		200–350 feet	200–350 fathoms
A.3588	+ 300		300–450 feet	300–450 fathoms
A.3589	+ 400		400–550 feet	400–550 fathoms

SCALES

The Perspex scales for recorders with 20 or 200 fathom phasing steps are engraved with two ranges:

0–30 fathoms in Black showing steps of 5 fathoms, further divided to show single fathom steps.

0–300 fathoms in Red showing 50 fathom steps.

PAPER

The roll of impregnated paper is housed in a tank, the hinged lid of which forms the contact surface over which the paper and stylus pass. The speed of the paper can be varied by the Paper Change Speed knob as shown in the following table. When the knob is out the speed is constant; when pushed in, the speed is related to the stylus speed.

If the bottom is uneven and a careful examination is desired, then the fast paper speed will give more separation of the traces. If the echoes are faint, e.g. at greater depths, a slow paper speed will help to accentuate the sounding. If running a line of soundings that require changes of scale, it is advisable to maintain a constant paper speed to assist subsequent analysis.

RECORDERS	SCALE RANGE	POSITION OF PAPER CHANGE SPEED KNOB	PAPER SPEED *In./Min.*	TIME MARKING INTERVALS	STYLUS SHAFT SPEED *Rev./Min.*
A.2935B	Fathoms 0–30	IN	0·4		206⅝
		OUT	0·2		
A.2936B	Fathoms 0–300	IN	0·04		20⅝
		OUT	0·2		
3608A	Feet	IN	0·992	60·5	246
5981A		OUT	0·496	121	
A.3588	Fathoms	IN	0·165	363	41
A.3589		OUT	0·496	121	
A.409	Fathoms 0–30	IN	4·41		205
		OUT	0·551		
A.381B	Fathoms 0–300	IN	0·441		20·5
		OUT	0·551		

Before operating the set, the paper must be drawn down by turning the milled knob until the stylus can traverse moist paper, otherwise no markings will appear on it.

SUPPRESSION

If the full transmission were recorded on the paper, shallow water echoes would be swamped by the marking due to the transmission pulse; so the length of the latter is restricted by a suppression slip-ring on the same shaft as the transmitter contact. A metal insert in the ring short circuits the suppression circuit as the stylus passes through o on the scale and only a thin transmission line appears on the paper.

ELECTRIC PENCIL

An electric pencil is provided for writing on the paper in the same manner as the stylus. If recordings of soundings and times inserted by the pencil are to be kept for any length of time, they must be emphasized in indelible pencil (or ball-point pen) otherwise the record will fade into illegibility.

To Operate the Set

Warning. – (1) Do not operate the gear change knob unless the Recorder is running.

(2) If the phasing is altered when the Recorder is stopped, the phasing disc *must be turned clockwise.*

NORMAL

1. Switch on main d.c. supply.
2. Switch on main a.c. supply.
3. Open front cover of recorder and turn the right-hand knurled knob until moist paper is drawn under the stylus. Close the cover.
4. Sharply rotate the gear-change knob to engage slow speed.
5. Rotate phasing disc until the figure o appears above the centre of the scale.
6. Pull out the paper speed control knob to give slow paper speed.
7. Switch on transmitter.

8. Set the amplifier switch to MANUAL and adjust manual sensitivity control until echo trace can be most clearly seen.
9. Read off depths on appropriate scale.

SHALLOW WATER OR GREATER ACCURACY

1. Sharply rotate gear-change knob to engage high speed.
2. Increase paper speed (if more separation of trace is needed).
3. In less than 30 fathoms set amplifier switch to AUTO and manual sensitivity control to MAX.
4. Read off depths on appropriate scale.
5. If the sounding obtained at slow speed was more than 30 fathoms, but within the limits of the high speed range, rotate the phasing disc clockwise until the echo appears on the trace.
6. Read off the sounding on the appropriate scale and add the phasing value.

AMBIGUITY IN READING DEEP SOUNDINGS

When the set is first switched on in deep water, a sounding may be obtained from the echo of an earlier transmission and give misleading results. To determine whether the recorded echo is a correct reading or not, the following action should be taken.

Switch off the Transmission On–Off switch at the base of the recorder; allow the stylus to complete four rotations; then switch on just before the transmitting contacts operate. Count the number of revolutions completed by the stylus before the echo appears on the trace. If an echo is received immediately after the first transmission, then the correct reading is that shown on the recorder. If no echo is received until after the second transmission, then the correct reading is the range of the echo sounder plus the depth shown on the recorder. If no echo is received until after the third transmission, then the correct reading is twice the range of the recorder plus the depth shown on the recorder.

An alternative method is to count the number of echoes received after the On–Off switch has been switched off. One echo shows that the recorded depth is correct; two echoes show that the range of the echo sounder must be added to the recorded depth; for three echoes add twice the range of the echo sounder. The paper drive must be turned manually to ensure that the stylus traverses well-separated paths on the paper.

Example. – An echo appears on the trace at 400 + 50 fathoms. The echo appears after the second transmission (or there are two echoes after the transmission is switched off). The range of the echo sounder is 1,200 fathoms. The correct sounding is 1200 + 400 + 50 = 1,650 fathoms.

REFLECTION ECHOES

In shallow water an echo may be received from a reflection of the original echo from the ship's hull and from the surface of the sea. (*See* Fig. 154.)

Interpretation of Soundings

Inconsistencies in the performance of echo sounding equipment should not be taken as an indication that they are inherent in the set itself. Many external factors influence the behaviour of the equipment, the more important of which are given below.

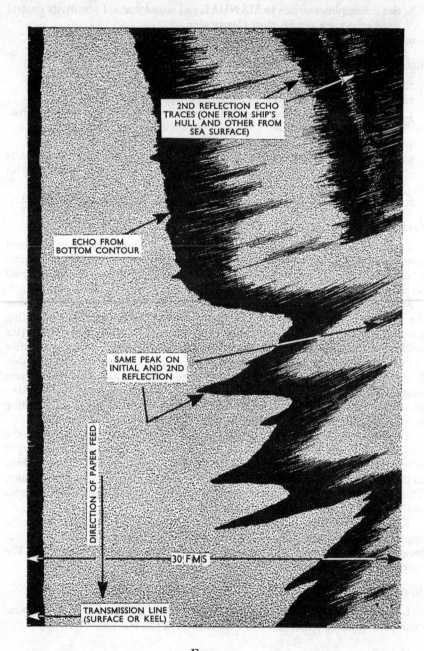

FIG. 154

FALSE SHALLOW ECHOES

Shoals of fish usually cause spurious echoes and may occasionally mask the bottom echo.

Dense layers of suspended matter in the water, or sudden changes of temperature and salinity may mask the bottom echo.

Strong eddies or weed may produce feathery echoes, but they are easily distinguished from the bottom echo.

WEAK ECHOES

These may be caused by some of the factors above and also by:

(a) Water noise interference due to:

(1) shape and condition of the hull;
(2) ship's speed;
(3) unsuitable siting of the transducers;
(4) sea and weather conditions.

(b) Aeration, influenced partly by (a), and also by:

(1) the application of wheel;
(2) stern way on ship, or the wake of vessels ahead;
(3) forward trim (in submarines and small craft).

VARIABLE ECHOES

Good and bad reflecting surfaces on the sea bed can account for considerable variations in echo strength. In general, hard sand, coral, chalk and rock are good; thick mud is bad. Rock, in stepped formation, can produce a confused trace in deep water on a steeply shelving bottom.

Errors and Adjustments

TRANSMISSION SETTING-ERROR

If the transmission line is set to the depth of the transducers, the recorder will show the depth of water below the surface. This practice is recommended for ships, such as warships where there is little change in draught, so that echo soundings may be related to the charted soundings. But it must be remembered that any alteration in ship's draught will affect the depth correction of the transducers.

SPEED ERROR

This is caused by the recorder running at an incorrect speed and varies with depth. If the recorder speed is too fast, the recorded depth will be too great, and vice versa.

The correct speed must be proportional to the velocity of sound in sea water, which varies with temperature and salinity. Naval echo sounding sets are adjusted for a speed of 820 fathoms/sec. (4,920 ft/sec.), which is the accepted rate for world-wide application, and they have a flexibility of adjustment to cover all likely velocities. For particularly accurate results, recorded soundings can be corrected by the *Tables of the Velocity of Sound in Sea-water* (H.D.282), but these tables are not required for normal navigational purposes.

The speed may be checked by either a tachometer (supplied to surveying vessels) or by timing the revolutions of the stylus with a stop-watch.

EXAMPLE

To check that a recorder for Type 765 is set for a sound velocity of 820 fathoms per second.

The scale is equivalent to $\frac{1}{4}$ revolution of the stylus.

Since the sound has completed a double journey, then for a velocity of 820 fathoms per second, an echo from a depth of 410 fathoms should take 1 second to go out and return, and the stylus should travel over 410 fathoms on the scale in 1 second to give a correct reading.

In slow speed the range of the scale is 300 fathoms. Therefore one complete revolution represents 1,200 fathoms.

If 410 fathoms on the scale is to be covered in 1 second, then 1 revolution of the stylus should take $\dfrac{1200}{410}$ sec., and in 1 minute the stylus should make $\dfrac{410}{1200} \times 60$ revolutions – i.e., a speed of 20·5 rev/min.

ECHO SOUNDING SETS

E/S TYPE	RECORDER PATTERN No.	STYLUS SPEED (*rev/min.*)	BASIC SCALE	PHASING AND MAX. DEPTH	VESSELS FITTED
762	A.1920B (110V) A.989B (24V)	533⅓ or 88⅔	0–60 ft/ fathoms	40 to 100 ft/ fathoms	I.M.S.
765	A.2935B, A.2936B A.409, A.381B	206⅔ or 20⅔ 205 or 20·5	0–30/300 fathoms	20/200 to 110/1,100 fathoms	General Service Navigational Set.
	3608A, 5981A A.3588, A.3589	246 or 41	0–150 ft/ fathoms	100 to 550 ft/fathoms	
771	AP.190528	164 or 27⅓	0–150 ft/ fathoms	100 to 900 ft/fathoms	Survey ships.
772	AP.190532 (24V) AP.190793 (12V)	273⅓ or 45⁵⁄₉	0–90 ft/ fathoms	60 to 540 ft/ fathoms	Survey boats and inshore survey craft.
775	Commercial K and H Type MS 26J	53⅓ or 5⅓	0–80/800 fathoms	80/800 to 450/4,500 fathoms	Survey ships.

III. RANGING AND STATION-KEEPING INSTRUMENTS

THE SMALL-BASE RANGEFINDER

Rangefinders are supplied for navigational purposes to all classes of H.M. ships down to and including frigates. They are classed as 'F.T. Type' rangefinders, and comprise a number of different types, of either 1 metre or 80 cm. base-length. All except one are now classified as obsolescent, but all types are regarded as interchangeable, and ships may be issued with any one of them until stocks are exhausted. The only ones continuing in service are:

Type F.T. 36 (or 37): 80 cm. – Pattern No. 10051

Type F.T. 37: 1 metre – Pattern No. 10080

This section gives a description of the instrument, together with general instructions for its operation and simple maintenance. The optical principles and laws involved are to be found in Volume III. An instructional handbook is supplied with each instrument. Copies of this handbook may be obtained, if required, from Messrs. Barr and Stroud Ltd., Anniesland, Glasgow.

The general arrangement of a rangefinder is shown in Fig. 155. An MB-type belt-and-socket mounting is supplied with some types; but when it is not supplied, the rangefinder is supported solely by taking its weight on the two handles.

The instrument may be used for ranges between 250 and 20,000 yards, though some types are supplied with a range scale whose maximum limit is 10,000 yards. The advantage of the higher limit is doubtful, as can be seen from the table given below.

Note: Type F.F.4, 18-inch – Pattern 3820, with range 0–300 yards, is issued to surveying ships.

Accuracy

The magnitude of errors which may be expected in range-taking is termed the 'uncertainty of observation'. The error varies as the square of the range, and is shown for different ranges in the following table:

RANGE	APPROXIMATE ERROR	
	1-metre base	*80-cm. base*
At 250 yards	0·25 yards	0·3 yards
„ 1,000 „	4 „	5 „
„ 5,000 „	100 ,	120 „
„ 20,000 „	1,600 „	2,000 „

Description

At the centre of the instrument are situated the right-hand eyepiece (for the observation of the range field), and the left-hand eyepiece (for the observation of the range scale). A focusing lever is provided for the former.

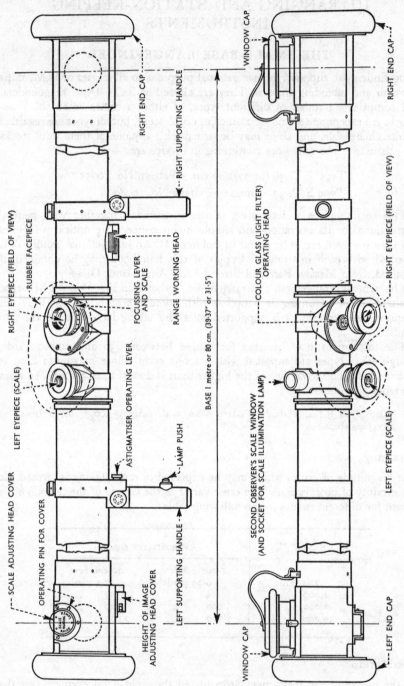

FIG. 155. Small-base rangefinder – general arrangements

Around the eyepieces is fitted a rubber facepiece, which serves as a cushion for the forehead, and protects the eyes. By the right eyepiece there is a small head, or pin, movement of which interposes a suitable coloured light-filter in the rangefinder beam.

At the front, opposite the left eyepiece, there is a window through which a second observer may read the range, if desired.

On the underside of the tube, by the right handle, is the working head, by the operation of which the ranges are determined.

By the left handle is situated the astigmatizer lever, by means of which spots of light, or irregularly-shaped objects, can be made to appear as long, vertical streaks in the field of view, thus facilitating ranging on such objects.

If illumination for the instrument is provided, a socket for one end of the electric leads, together with the lamp push, is contained in the left handle.

At the ends of the instrument are situated the windows, through which the beams of light from the object under observation enter the instrument. These windows are protected by leather caps or rotatable covers, which should be placed over them when the instrument is not in use.

Situated in recesses in the left enlarged end are the Height of Image and Scale Adjustment heads respectively. Both heads are protected by rotatable or hinged spring covers.

For the illumination of the scale at night, there is generally provided a lamp mounted in a case which is attached, by means of a bayonet joint, to the second observer-scale window. The lamp is permanently connected to a lead, which can be attached to a battery and to the switch in the left handle, as previously described.

The Field of View

The object is viewed through the right eyepiece and appears as an erect image, divided horizontally into two equal portions by a separating line. One half of this image is produced by each end of the instrument, and the two halves can be brought into coincidence by means of the range-working head.

The range scale is viewed through the left eyepiece, the correct range being the reading obtained when the two halves of the image are in coincidence, as shown in Fig. 156b.

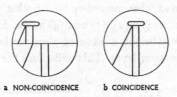

a NON-COINCIDENCE   b COINCIDENCE

FIG. 156

At the extreme high-range end of the scale there is engraved the 'Infinity' line, marked by a star. The small divisions on either side of the 'Infinity' graduation are provided for the purpose of facilitating adjustment, as described later. Each of these divisions is the equivalent on the scale of 10 yards at the 1,000-yards graduation.

To Determine the Range of an Object

By movement of the range-working head, the lower half of the picture in the field of view is displaced, relatively to the upper half, in a direction parallel to the separating line.

When the working head is rotated, the upper image follows the motion of the forefinger, and the lower image the motion of the thumb. When this is realized, the operator learns to work the head in the most natural manner to correct any want of alignment. Thus, if the upper image is towards the left of the lower, the operator pulls it towards the right by pulling the working head with the forefinger.

The best kind of object for rangetaking is one having a clear and distinct vertical edge, as, for example, a mast or a funnel; and whenever possible such an object should be chosen in preference to any other.

When observing small or ill-defined objects, greater accuracy of observation may often be obtained by using the astigmatizer, but this should not be used if satisfactory observations can be made without it.

To determine the range of an object in daylight, proceed as follows:

(1) Uncover the end windows.

(2) Locate the object and bring it into the field of view of the right eyepiece.

(3) Focus the right eyepiece upon the object by means of the focusing lever.

(4) By suitably directing the rangefinder, bring the images of the object on to the centre portion of the separating line of the right eyepiece.

(5) By rotating the small head or pin situated by the right eyepiece, interpose a coloured glass, if required.

(6) Place the forefinger and thumb of the right hand upon the working head, and rotate it until the images are in coincidence. The accuracy of the range determination depends upon the exactitude of the coincidence.

(7) When the coincidence is exact, read the range through the left eyepiece or, in the case of a second observer, through the scale window.

To determine the range of a light or other object at night, proceed as follows:

(i) Ship the lamp (if provided) and connect its leads to the battery and to the switch in the left handle. If the lamp gear is not provided, the scale can be illuminated when necessary by a pocket flashlamp.

(ii) Perform operations (1), (2), (3) and (4) as for daylight.

(iii) If the light is very bright, a coloured glass can be used, as before.

(iv) Raise the astigmatizer lever. This will cause the spot of light to appear as a streak.

(v) Perform operations (6) and (7), as described above.

(vi) Return the astigmatizer lever to its 'out' position.

The observer is recommended to bring the partial images of the object approximately into coincidence before they are astigmatized, otherwise some difficulty may be experienced in recognizing the corresponding portions of the same object when astigmatized, especially when there are several objects in the field of view. The object can be identified, however, by momentarily putting the astigmatizer 'out' and then returning it to the 'in' position.

Adjustments

1. HEIGHT OF IMAGE ADJUSTMENT

When the rangefinder is not correctly adjusted for Height of Image, an object in the field of view of the instrument may appear either 'duplicated' (as in Fig. 157a) or 'deficient' (as in Fig. 157b).

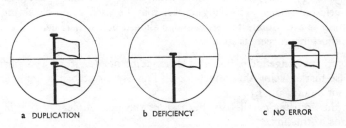

a DUPLICATION   b DEFICIENCY   c NO ERROR

FIG. 157

In the case of objects that are inclined to the separating line, a small amount of Height of Image error will affect the coincidence setting of the partial images, and therefore the accuracy of the scale reading. It is advisable, therefore, for the operator to form the habit of always testing Height of Image before commencing to make range observations. To test the Height of Image adjustment of the instrument, proceed as follows:

(1) Select any well-defined object and bring the partial images into alignment in the field of view. It is not necessary to know the actual range of the object.

(2) Elevate the rangefinder, so that the object is seen only in the lower half of the field.

(3) Gently and steadily depress the instrument, and thus cause the image to rise, in the field of view, up to the separating line.

If Height of Image is correct, the top of the object will appear in the upper half of the field at the instant that it disappears from the lower; that is, the separating line will have no apparent effect on the upward movement of the image. If the object appears too soon in the upper field, there is an error of 'duplication'; and if it appears too late, there is an error of 'deficiency'.

To Correct a Height of Image Error

(a) Expose the Height of Image adjustment head, and move it in accordance with the instructions engraved at the side.

(b) Check the adjustment by repeating the test described above.

(c) Replace the cover on the adjustment head.

2. SCALE ADJUSTMENT

If the range scale does not indicate the true range when a perfect cut has been obtained, then the rangefinder is said to have a scale error. Adjustment for this should not be made until any Height of Image error has first been removed. The mean of ten range cuts should be used to obtain the scale error.

A scale-error test may be carried out by one of the following methods, in order of preference:

(1) Infinity test on a celestial body or on the artificial infinity adjuster marks provided on the rangefinder box.

(2) Known range test on a terrestrial object.

In method (1) a star, or the Moon, when more than half full, are the most suitable celestial bodies. The astigmatizer may be used when observing a star. If the object is the Moon, its vertical edge should be used. If using the artificial infinity adjuster, proceed as follows:

Set up the rangefinder box at a distance of not less than 100 yards, with the base marks facing the rangefinder. (The exact distance is immaterial and need not be measured.)

Set the adjuster parallel to the base of the rangefinder by sighting along the ends of the box.

Direct the rangefinder so as to bring the adjuster marks on to the separating line in the range field.

Bring the mark at the *one end* of the adjuster, appearing in the one field, into coincidence with the mark at the *other end*, appearing in the other field, as indicated in Fig. 158. Take a series of readings to obtain the mean error.

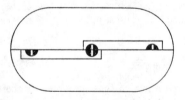

FIG. 158

It will be recalled that one division at infinity is equal to 10 yards at 1,000 yards on the scale. The permissible error of a 1-metre base instrument from the Uncertainty of Observation table given on page 263, is $4/10 = 0.4$ divisions at infinity; for an 80-cm base, it is 0.5 divisions at infinity. In taking the mean of a set of observations, readings below infinity should be subtracted from readings above infinity, and the remainder divided by the total number of readings.

In method (2), the object should have a well-defined vertical edge and be at the greatest possible range. This should be clear from the table on page 263 where it is seen that the greater error occurs at the greater range. Great care must be taken in ascertaining this range. The ship's position should be fixed by sextant angles and the ship should not be swinging appreciably.

When measuring the range on the chart, the scale of nautical miles should be converted to yards by using the table for the 'Figure of the Earth' in *Inman's Tables*, since the number of yards in a nautical mile varies with the latitude.

A good way (when possible) of testing the rangefinder is to take ranges of objects ashore on either beam, nearly or quite in line, each object being over 2,000 yards distant, and then to see if the total of the two rangefinder readings agrees with the distance between the objects according to the chart.

If the mean of the readings gives the true range within an allowance corresponding to the uncertainties of observations, the rangefinder is in adjustment.

To Correct a Scale Error

(a) Rotate the range-working head until the scale indicates 'infinity' or the known range opposite its index.

(b) Expose the scale adjustment head, and move the head in accordance with the instructions engraved at the side, until the images are in exact alignment.

(c) Take a new series of ten readings and find the mean of the observations.

When the adjustment is correct to within the allowance as previously stated, cover the adjustment head again.

THE WAYMOUTH-ROSS SEXTANT RANGEFINDER

This instrument (Pattern No. 10065) provides a means of obtaining:

(1) the range of an object of known height or length;
(2) the range of an object by the Horizon Method, using own height of eye;
(3) the height or length of an object of known range;
(4) the inclination of a ship of known length and range.

It may be used for ranges between 1,000 and 18,000 yards.

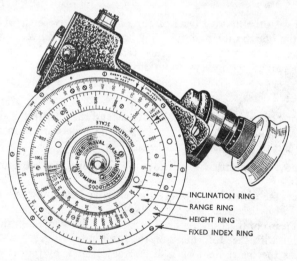

INCLINATION RING
RANGE RING
HEIGHT RING
FIXED INDEX RING

FIG. 159. Waymouth-Ross Sextant Rangefinder

Description (Fig. 159)

On the side of the instrument are one fixed and three independently rotatable concentric rings. These consist of:

(1) The outer fixed ring, which carries the height scale, the indices and an infinity mark.
(2) The height ring, graduated from 14 to 200 feet, which can be rotated relatively to the fixed ring. It also carries the range-scale index.

(3) The range ring, graduated from 1,000 to 18,000 yards, which is rotated by the working head at the centre of the rings. It also carries an infinity mark.

(4) The inclination ring, graduated from 5° to 90°, which can be rotated relatively to the range scale.

The telescope is fixed to the instrument and is focused by rotating the eye-piece. The object glass is split horizontally into two equal halves. One half provides the datum (which is capable of adjustment), and the other half can be moved by operating the working head. With one half object glass displaced, two images appear in the eyepiece – a real and a 'ghost' image. By displacement of images, as shown in Fig. 160, the angle subtended at the eye by a known height or length can be measured; the measurement thus obtained is indicated on the appropriate scale. A thumb lever near the handle is provided for use in

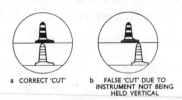

a CORRECT 'CUT'   b   FALSE 'CUT' DUE TO
                             INSTRUMENT NOT BEING
                             HELD VERTICAL

FIG. 160. Waymouth-Ross Sextant Rangefinder obtaining a 'cut'

conjunction with the divided head on top of the objective box, when obtaining a range by the horizon method. This method is described later.

The stowage box contains a leather carrying sling and supporting rod, a spray shade, two adjusting keys and a card of instructions.

Coincidence Test

The only error possible is that of coincidence, and the instrument should always be tested and adjusted for this before use. The procedure is as follows, care being taken not to touch the thumb lever:

1. Remove the knurled cap below the objective box, exposing the screw head.
2. Screw the divided head above the objective box upwards, i.e. in an anti-clockwise direction.
3. By means of the working head bring the infinity mark on the range scale in line with the 'Inf.' mark on the fixed index ring.
4. Focus the instrument on a distant object and, by means of the knurl-headed screw beneath the objective box, bring the two images into coincidence so that no ghost image is visible.
5. Loosen the two cheese-headed screws on top of the divided head, thereby releasing the scale, and screw down the mechanism as far as possible by means of the two projecting pins on the divided head. Excessive pressure should not be applied.
6. By means of the knurling, rotate the scale on the divided head until its zero is against the index line, care being taken that the mechanism does not rotate. Then tighten the two cheese-headed screws.
7. Replace the knurled cap below the objective box.

Adjustment for Smoothness of Operation

Should the motion of the working head become tight or loose, adjustment can be made by means of the small knurled nut at its centre.

The two slotted nuts are released by means of the keys provided, and the knurled nut tightened or slackened as necessary to obtain smooth working. The slotted nuts are then locked.

It is most important that the scales and working head should not be lifted while the nuts are slackened off, otherwise the mechanism will become displaced.

Operation

(1) *To find the range of an object of known height or length.* Set the height of the object against the black height index mark. By means of the working head, bring the upper edge of one image in line with the bottom edge of the other, as shown in Fig. 160a, taking care that the instrument is held exactly vertical. Alternatively, set the length of the object against the index, and, using the instrument horizontally, bring the right edge of one image in line with the left edge of the other. The range is then observed against the red pointer engraved on the height ring.

(2) *To find the range of an object by the Horizon Method.* By means of the divided head on the objective box, set own height of eye to the index line.

Set also the same height of eye on the height ring against the *green height* index mark.

Press the thumb lever upwards and hard home, and by means of the working head bring target's waterline in one image into coincidence with the sea horizon in the other image. The range is then read as before.

This method of obtaining ranges should not be used beyond the following limits:

Height of eye (feet)	Range (yards)	Height of eye (feet)	Range (yards)
20	5,000	80	9,000
30	6,000	90	9,500
40	7,000	100	10,000
50	7,500	110	10,500
60	8,000	120	11,000
70	8,500		

(3) *To find the height or length of an object of known range.* Obtain a 'cut' as described in (1) above. Then, taking care not to move the working head, rotate the height ring until the red pointer is set against the known range of the object. The black height index mark will then indicate the height or length (whichever is applicable) of the object.

(4) *To find the inclination of a ship of known length and range.* Set the target's length against the black height index mark, and the index of the inclination scale (90°) against the known range. Holding the instrument horizontally, bring the two images at the set base-length into coincidence. The inclination is read against the imaginary continuation of the red range index.

STUART'S DISTANCE METER

Stuart's Distance Meter (Pattern 498) is shown in Fig. 161. It provides a means of measuring the range of an object of known height at ranges between one-quarter of a cable and about 15 cables. Although the scale is graduated above this range, higher readings cannot generally be considered reliable.

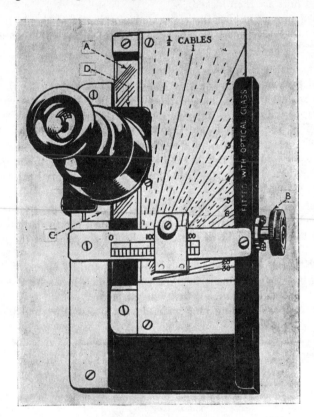

FIG. 161

Description

The instrument consists of a long curved lens (*A*), attached to a radial distance scale, which is graduated from one-quarter of a cable to 30 cables. Both this lens and the scale are mounted in a slide, which can be moved up and down inside the frame of the instrument. A pinion carried on the spindle of a milled knob (*B*) engages a rack to provide this movement.

A fixed wedge-shaped lens (*C*) is mounted, alongside the moving lens, on the frame of the instrument. A small telescope fitted with an interrupted thread can be inserted in the metal collar (*D*). The telescope should be focused after being fitted in the instrument. The object, when viewed, appears as a super-imposed image.

Across the movable distance scale is a fixed horizontal metal bar. This is the height scale; it is graduated from 0 to 220 feet. On this bar is a sliding pointer.

On the reverse side of the instrument is a blank table for inserting, in pencil, the required data concerning ships likely to be observed.

Operation

To obtain a range, set the height above the waterline of the target against the left edge of the sliding pointer. By turning the milled knob, bring the top of one image in line with the portion of the waterline which is immediately beneath the target in the other image.

The distance in cables is then read against the index mark on the sliding pointer.

> *Note:* When using a vertical angle between a masthead or other object and the water-line, the waterline immediately below the object should be observed. When keeping station in line ahead, this point cannot be seen, and some equivalent mark must be selected by eye. (Fig. 162.)

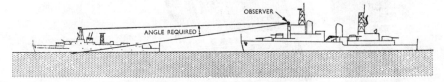

FIG. 162. Use of Stuart's Distance Meter

ALTERNATIVE USE

The instrument can also be used to measure the range of an object of negligible or unknown height. To do this, set own height of eye on the instrument and, by rotating the milled knob, bring the waterline of the object in one image up to the horizon in the other image. The error involved in this method is about 3 per cent of the range measured, but the method is of some value at ranges below the limit of the Waymouth-Ross instrument.

HUSUN MARINE DISTANCE METER (Pattern 703)

This instrument, shown in Fig. 163, may be used for obtaining ranges, between one and ten cables, of an object of known height. It is a sextant rangefinder, with index and horizon glasses enclosed in a case. Coincidence, as in Fig. 160, is obtained by rotating the working head (*A*) on the front of the instrument. In addition to moving the index glass, this rotates a cylinder. On the cylinder is engraved a curved line (*B*) which serves as a pointer.

The scales are situated on a slider behind a hinged window on the side of the instrument. The height scale, which is graduated from 30 to 150 feet, is set against an index on the frame. The range scale, graduated from 1 to 10 cables, moves with the height scale, and the correct range is read from this scale against the curved pointer.

MAINTENANCE OF RANGEFINDERS

Although built as strongly as possible, rangefinders contain a number of delicate parts, and great care must be taken not to impair their airtight and watertight properties. It is essential that optical instruments should be treated with care, and the external cleaning should be carried out only by personnel who understand the correct methods to employ. Dismantling and assembly of rangefinders

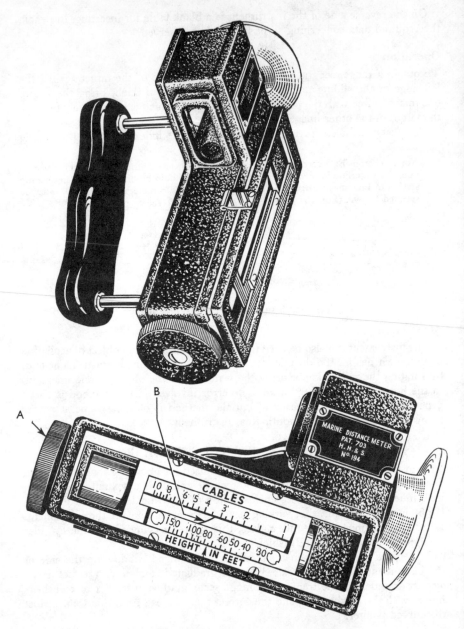

FIG. 163. Husun Marine Distance Meter

is a highly specialized job and conditions afloat are unsuitable for the work. All defective instruments should therefore be returned to S.N.S.O. for cleaning and repair in the Dockyards or by the makers.

If rangefinders are subjected to very strong sunlight there is a risk of the balsam in the eyepiece-prism combination becoming temporarily softened, thus allowing relative movement between the prisms. This movement will cause a scale error which may be beyond the scope of the scale adjustment. 'Stars' may also appear in the cement of the objectives. When the temperature (in sunlight) reaches, or is likely to reach, 90°F., the rangefinder should be kept in the shade, and whenever possible in its box.

Care of Instruments by Operators

Undue force should not be used on any working part which is stiff.

Optical glass surfaces should be cleaned with calico (Pattern 456) which must be clean and dry before use – it may be washed in methylated spirit. Optical glass is relatively soft, and must be wiped very lightly to avoid scratching.

External glass surfaces which have been subjected to spray may be found coated with salt crystals or grit. This should be washed off with soapy water and the surfaces wiped over with calico.

Chamois leather is provided for cleaning or drying external metal parts of the rangefinder.

Metal polish is never to be used for cleaning rangefinders.

If moisture is found to have collected on the inner surfaces of the optical parts, the instrument should be placed in a warm, dry place.

Neither the rangefinder nor its cleaning cloths should be stowed in the box unless they are quite dry.

IV. PLOTTING INSTRUMENTS

THE STATION POINTER

A station pointer, as shown in Fig. 164, is used for plotting the ship's position obtained by horizontal sextant angles. It consists of a graduated circle and three arms, the bevelled edges of the latter radiating from the centre of the circle. The centre leg, *OA*, is fixed, and its bevelled edge corresponds to the zero of

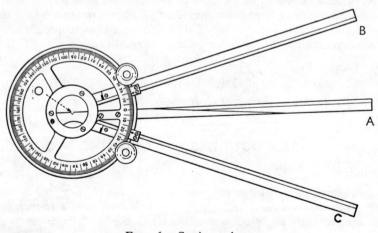

FIG. 164. Station pointer

the graduation of the circle, which is marked at every half-degree from 0° to 180° on either side. The two outer legs, *OB* and *OC* (called the 'left' and 'right' legs) are movable and can be clamped in any position.

Station pointers used in surveying are fitted with a vernier which will read to one minute of arc on each movable leg. These are supplied in different sizes, and are Hydrographic Office stores.

The centre of the circle is indicated by a small nick in the bevelled edge of the fixed leg. When the instrument is used, a sharp pencil point is essential in order that the mark made on the chart may exactly correspond with the centre of the instrument.

The bevelled edge of the right leg cannot be brought very close to that of the centre leg. For this reason, when the right-hand angle is very small – and consequently the right leg cannot be set to it – the left leg should be set to the small angle; and the right leg should be moved round and set to the sum of the right and left angles, measured from the fixed leg to the left. In these circumstances, the fixed leg should be directed to the right-hand object.

Testing

Station pointers should frequently be checked for accuracy. Chart 5007, *Diagram for Testing Station Pointers, Protractors, etc.*, is supplied for this purpose. The instrument should be placed on the diagram with the nick exactly at the centre of the radiating lines and the bevelled edge of the centre leg *OA* along the zero line. The movable legs should then be moved to coincide with the lines each side of the zero, and the error corresponding to the various angles read off, the sign + or − being given according to the direction in which these various angles must be applied to the observed angle. These errors should be tabulated and pasted in the lid of the box.

· While the instrument is being tested, it should also be noted whether the bevelled edge of each leg coincides throughout its whole length with one of the straight lines.

In certain circumstances, the station pointer becomes awkward to use. For instance, the charted positions of the observed objects may be hidden under the rim of the instrument, or the sides of a small chart table may prevent the arms of the instrument from being moved to the correct position on the chart. When this occurs, it is better to lay off the angles on a Douglas protractor.

Remarks on the use of the station pointer are contained in:

(a) Chapter IV.
(b) The handbook supplied with the instrument.
(c) The *Admiralty Manual of Hydrographic Surveying*.

THE DOUGLAS PROTRACTOR

Description

This instrument, shown in Fig. 165, is used as an aid to plotting, and for determining positions, tracks and bearings on charts. It consists of a 10-inch transparent square protractor, graduated all round in degrees from 0° to 359° in both directions, clockwise and anti-clockwise.

At the centre is a hole large enough to take the point of a sharp pencil. Pencil lines may be drawn on its underside, which has a matt surface. Thus, when the protractor is placed on the chart, matt side downwards, parallax is eliminated.

Methods of Use

(1) *To lay off a course or bearing.* – Align the centre hole and the required bearings on the inner scale with any convenient meridian. Adjust the protractor along this meridian until the ruling edge (which is the left-hand edge in Fig. 165) passes through the point from which the course is to be laid off. For example, to lay off a course of 040° from a point *A*, place the protractor on the chart so that the centre hole and the 40° mark on the inner scale are both on a meridian. Slide the protractor until point *A* is on the ruling edge; then rule the required course.

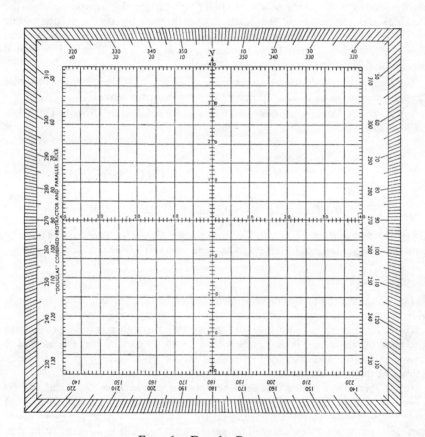

FIG. 165. Douglas Protractor

(2) *To read off a course or bearing.* – Place the ruling edge, or one of the lines parallel to it, along the course or bearing so that the centre hole is on a meridian. Where this meridian cuts the edge of the protractor, the figure on the inner scale will give the bearing.

(3) *To use as a parallel ruler.* – Align the protractor by one of its parallel lines on the bearing required and, by drawing pencil lines along the appropriate edge of the protractor, the latter can be transferred to the point required, with no chance of unperceived displacement.

(4) *To fix a position by angles.* – Lay off the observed angles on either side of the N.–S. line on the matt side of the protractor; then place it, matt side down, on the chart so that the pencil lines and the N.–S. line of the protractor run through the objects observed. The centre hole then represents the ship's position. The angles must be reversed – left for right, and right for left – when they are laid off.

(5) *To find the direction made good from a series of bearings of a single object.* – On one edge of the matt surface mark off, on the scale of the chart, the distance run through the water by the ship between the times of the bearings. Lay off the bearings on the chart in the ordinary way. Place the protractor over the bearings and adjust it until the bearings pass through the corresponding points on the edge of the protractor. Provided there is no *alteration* in the tidal stream, this edge will then be parallel to the course made good; but if there is any tidal stream or drift, it will not be the actual track.

(6) *To find the ship's position from a line of soundings.* – The protractor may be used for this, instead of tracing paper, as described in Chapter IV.

(7) *To obtain the compass error.* – This is also described in Chapter IV.

V. MANOEUVRING INSTRUMENTS

BATTENBERG COURSE INDICATOR

The Battenberg Mark 5 (Pattern No. 602) is designed for solving relative velocity problems based on P.P.I. presentation with own ship stationary at the centre.

Component Parts

(a) The frame is of aluminium with three handles at the back. The fixed outer ring is marked in degrees fron o to 359.

(b) A circular aluminium base-plate, rotatable through cut-away portions in the back of the frame, is engraved with continuous parallel black lines in one axis and interrupted parallel black lines in the other axis. Figures in black represent distance or speed.

(c) A rotatable Perspex disc is superimposed on the base-plate and can be clamped in any desired position. It is engraved with green concentric rings at radii of 10, 20 and 30 units from the centre, and with red rings for every intervening 2 units out to 36 units. The perimeter is marked in degrees from o to 359 in red and red radial lines mark every 10 degrees.

(d) Two metal speed-bars, pivoted about the centre, are engraved with figures from o to 35. Each bar has a movable slider which can be clamped in any required position. The milled screw heads are green and red.

(e) A circular distance/time scale is engraved on the back of the frame. The outer scale is marked in seconds from 15 to 60 and minutes from 1 to 60. The

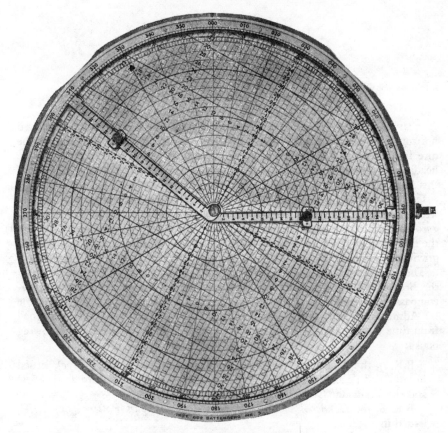

FIG. 166. Battenberg, Mark 5

inner rotatable scale is marked in miles from 0·1 to 40. By setting the ship's speed against the 60-minute mark, the distance covered in a specified time may be discovered. Conversely the speed or time may be found if the other two factors are known.

Examples of the use of the Battenberg for solving various relative velocity problems are given in Chapter XIV.

CHAPTER VIII

The Gyro-Compass

A COMPASS may be defined as an instrument which remains pointing in a fixed horizontal direction relative to an observer on the Earth, regardless of the direction in which the ship, aircraft or vehicle in which it is carried may be heading. It thus provides a datum from which courses and bearings, relative to this fixed direction, may be obtained.

One form of compass, described in the next chapter, is the magnetic compass which relies for its operation on the magnetism of the Earth. Another, the gyro-compass, described here, depends upon the Earth's angular velocity – i.e. the rate at which the Earth spins in space about its axis. Both types rely on gravity to define the horizontal.

There are several different kinds of gyro-compass in use; of these the Sperry, the Brown and the Anschütz are among the better known. The Sperry gyro-compass was altered by the Admiralty Compass Observatory in 1918 to become the Admiralty (Sperry-type) Gyro-Compass. This compass has been re-designed from time to time and the existing types are described in detail in the following books:

B.R. 9, the *Manual of the Admiralty Gyro-Compass* (*Sperry Type*), issued in 1953 and dealing with the Valve Follow-Up Compass (Pattern 2005 series) and the Contactor Compass (Pattern 1005 series).

B.R. 8, the *Handbook of the Admiralty Gyro-Compass Pattern 5005 series*, issued in 1958.

This chapter gives a summary of the theory of the gyro-compass; a description of those parts of the Pattern 5005 series for which special settings are required; follow-up, transmission and alarm systems; and the differences between the various series of compasses.

The Navigating Officer is responsible for the correct use of the gyro-compass equipment; i.e. when the compass is required and the settings to be applied to it.

The Electrical Officer has the gyro-compass equipment on his charge and is responsible for running and maintaining the compass, lining-up the repeaters and applying the settings required by the Navigating Officer.

THEORY OF THE ADMIRALTY GYRO-COMPASS

The gyro-compass consists essentially of a gyroscope, which has certain peculiar properties when its rotor is spinning. By the application of suitable controls use is made of these properties in such a way that the axis of this gyroscope seeks the true North and maintains itself in this direction.

Rigidity in Space

A 'free gyro', as defined in B.R. 8, is shown in Fig. 168. If the spin axis, X, of such a gyro is pointing in a certain direction in space, then, when the rotor

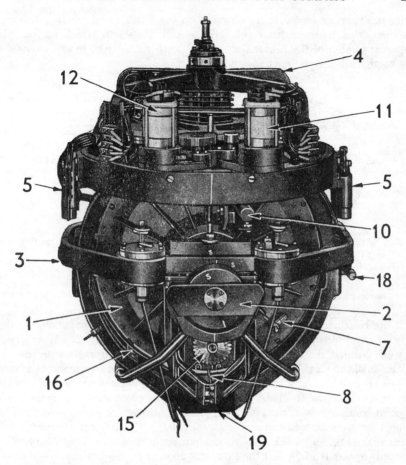

FIG. 167. The Admiralty Gyro-Compass A.P.5005 from south

1. Rotor Casing.
2. Compensator Weights.
3. Mercury Box Frame.
4. Spider Frame.
5. Athwartship Gimbal Bearing Housings and Oil Dashpots.
7. Air Valve.
8. Mercury Box Rod(s).

10. Level (SOUTH).
11. 1½-inch Magslip.
12. 1½-inch Magslip.
15. Latitude Rider.
16. Vertical Ring.
18. Mercury Box Clamping Bracket and Screws.
19. Lower Half Phantom Ring.

is spun at a sufficiently high speed, this axis will maintain the same direction, regardless of how its supporting frame is tilted or turned. This property is known as 'rigidity in space'.

APPARENT MOTION OF A FREE GYRO

Because of the rotation of the Earth, the spin axis of the gyro appears to move, although maintaining its direction in space. This motion is a combination of *drift* (about the axis Y) and *tilt* (about the axis Z): it is called 'apparent motion', since the heavens *appear* to an observer on the Earth to be moving, although we know that they are fixed and it is actually the Earth which moves. The apparent motion of the heavens above the northern horizon, to an observer in the northern hemisphere, is shown in Fig. 169.

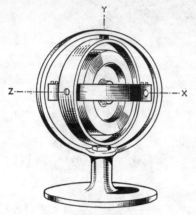

Fig. 168. A free gyro

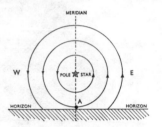

Fig. 169. Apparent motion of the heavens (observer looking northward)

If the North end of the axis of a free gyro were pointed at the star *A* in this diagram, it would appear to complete a circular path every 24 hours. If, however, it were pointed directly at the Pole Star, which lies approximately on the extension of the Earth's spinning axis, then it would appear to remain stationary.

The requirement of a compass is that it should continue to point in a fixed direction relative to an observer on the Earth. In practice, it cannot be made to point continuously at the Pole Star, primarily because it would be difficult to project the gyro axis on to the horizontal plane with sufficient accuracy. Only when at the equator would the gyro axis remain horizontal and stationary, since it is only at this latitude that the Pole Star appears on the horizon.

To fulfil the requirement, a settling position for the gyro is selected, such that the axis of spin lies horizontally in the true meridian – that is to say, aligned with a point on the horizon which lies in the direction of true North.

As already explained, the axis of a free gyro will not remain in this position except at the equator; it will wander off in a direction which varies in different latitudes.

Fig. 170 shows the apparent motion of the heavens, as seen by an observer looking northward in various latitudes. The arrows therefore also indicate the directions in which the North end of the axis of a free gyro would appear to wander. These movements may be summarized as follows:

    (i) If set *in the meridian*, the North end of the gyro axis will appear to *drift:*
        towards the *East*, in *North* latitudes,
        towards the *West*, in *South* latitudes.
    The rate of drift is zero at the equator and increases with latitude.
    (ii) If set *near the meridian*, in addition to any drift experienced, it will appear to *tilt:*
        upwards if set to the *eastward* of the meridian,
        downwards if set to the *westward* of the meridian.

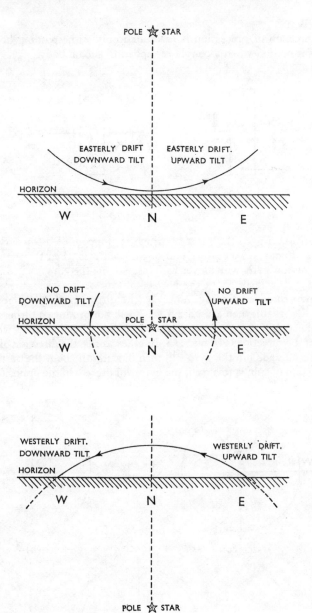

FIG. 170. Apparent motion of the heavens (observer looking northward)

The rate of tilting decreases from a maximum at the equator to zero at the poles. These two motions are the result of the gyroscope's rigidity in space. Before describing the controls required to maintain the direction of the gyro axis due North, it is necessary to examine the second property of the gyroscope.

Precession

The phenomenon of precession is associated only with spinning bodies and is the resultant motion when a couple is applied to such a body.

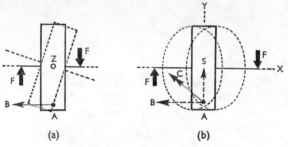

FIG. 171. Precession

Consider first a gyro the rotor of which is stopped. If a force F is applied, as shown in Fig. 171a, on either end of the spin axis, then the point A on the perimeter of the gyro will move, as expected, in the direction AB. In other words, the gyro will tilt about the horizontal axis Z.

If the gyro rotor is spinning, however (the direction of spin being indicated by AS, in Fig. 171b), then a similar force F will not produce a tilting movement. Instead, the point A will be accelerated in the direction AC, which is the resultant of the directions AB and AS. In other words, the direction of movement of A will be altered, and the gyro will turn in azimuth about the vertical axis Y. If the direction of spin is reversed, the gyro will precess in the opposite direction.

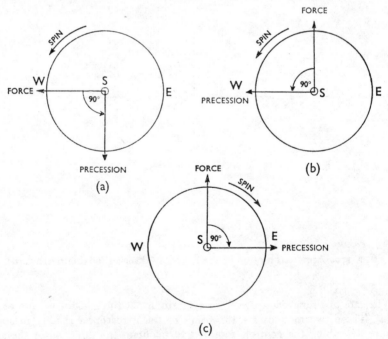

FIG. 172. Rule for precession (rotor viewed from south)

In a similar way, if a force is applied which tends to turn the gyro in azimuth, it will tilt. The theory of precession is given in B.R. 8, *Handbook of the Admiralty Gyro-Compass Pattern 5005 series.*

The rule for precession is, then: *rotate the line of action of the force 90° in the direction of spin. This will give the direction of precession.*

Fig. 172, which shows the forces in the plane of the rotor, illustrates this rule.

The Admiralty gyro-compass rotates anti-clockwise when viewed from the South end, as shown in Figs. 172a and b.

The Latitude Rider

If the gyro is started while its spin axis is lying in the meridian, it has been shown that, except at the equator, the North end of this axis will drift either to the East or to the West, depending on the hemisphere.

To prevent this drift away from the meridian, use is made of precession in the following way: a control is introduced to provide a rate of precession equal and opposite to the rate of drift. This control is provided by a device known as the 'latitude rider'.

The latitude rider consists of an adjustable weight, situated on the South side of the rotor-casing, as shown in Fig. 173. It may be screwed in or out to make the gyro either North-heavy or South-heavy, as required. When in its mid-position, the rotor and casing are perfectly balanced about the E.–W. tilt axis; this is the position required at the equator, where there is no drift to be counter-acted. This balance is achieved by a counter-weight on the North side of the rotor-casing.

The latitude rider has a scale marked in degrees, and is kept in position along its screw-thread by a bar notching into the latitude scale.

Setting the Latitude Rider

The following instructions should be observed for setting the latitude rider:

(1) The effect of an incorrect setting of the latitude rider is to introduce an error in settling of the master compass. The magnitude of this error is approximately 0°·2 per notch. One notch is equivalent to:

4° of latitude between latitudes 0° and 32°
5° of latitude between latitudes 32° and 52°
9° of latitude between latitudes 52° and 70°

(2) When a ship is on passage, the latitude rider should be kept set to within two notches of the correct latitude by alterations made when the weather permits. It must be noted that touching the sensitive element will inevitably disturb the gyro-compass, which will then wander until it resettles. Although the latitude rider can be shifted under penalty of a wander of about 2° in calm weather, the operation becomes more difficult in bad weather and should be postponed.

(3) A satisfactory method of making the adjustment is to lift the notch bar with a pencil, or similar tool, while the rider itself is turned with the free hand.

(4) In ships with more than one gyro-compass the settings should be altered on one compass at a time, allowing about 2 hours for each one to resettle after adjustment.

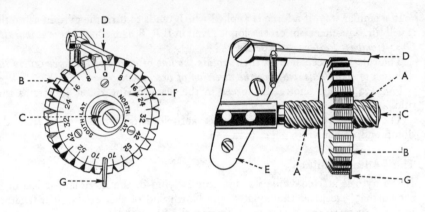

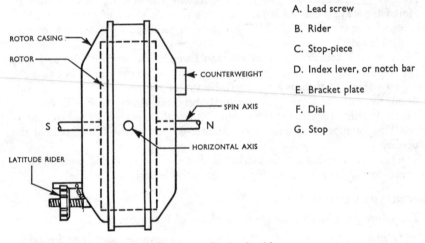

A. Lead screw

B. Rider

C. Stop-piece

D. Index lever, or notch bar

E. Bracket plate

F. Dial

G. Stop

FIG. 173. Latitude rider

Gravity Control

(a) THE UNDAMPED GYRO-COMPASS

By use of the latitude rider the gyro has been made to maintain its direction, pointing North, provided that the axis is not disturbed from the meridian. In practice, it is not always possible to start the gyro in the correct position, as the direction of true North may not be accurately known. Even if its axis should lie in the meridian, it may be disturbed and wander from this direction for a number of reasons. It is therefore necessary to devise another control which will cause the gyro to return to the meridian under all conditions, i.e. to make the gyro North-seeking. This is achieved by means of the gravity control.

From Fig. 170 it was seen that, in all latitudes, the North end of the gyro spin axis will rise if it is to the eastward of the meridian and fall if it is to the westward of the meridian. This tilt is used to cause precession in the required direction by introducing a control which makes the gyro top-heavy.

Consider, first, an imaginary bail weight (Fig. 174) on top of the rotor-casing. When the North end of the axis tilts up, the bail weight exerts a downward force on its South end. In accordance with the laws of precession, already stated, such a force will cause westerly precession of the North end of the axis, provided that the direction of rotation of the rotor is chosen correctly.

BAIL WEIGHT

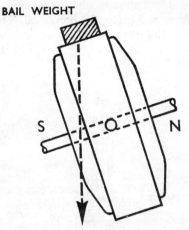

FIG. 174. Gravity control

When the North end of the axis tilts down, easterly precession will be caused.

Fig. 175 shows the path traced out by the North end of the spin axis of such a gyro.

Consider the gyro axis to be pointing in the direction of *A*. As the upward tilt increases, the torque caused by the bail weight – and consequently the rate of precession – increases. As the axis nears the meridian, the upward rate of tilt decreases (*see* Fig. 170), so that when the axis reaches the meridian at *B* the *rate* of tilt is zero, although the *angle* of tilt is a maximum.

Since the angle of tilt is a maximum at *B*, the rate of westerly precession is also a maximum; hence the North end moves to the westward of the meridian. From Fig. 170 it will be seen that here the direction of movement in tilt is downwards. This movement continues until the point *C* is reached. Here the axis is again horizontal, but, being to the westward of the meridian, downward

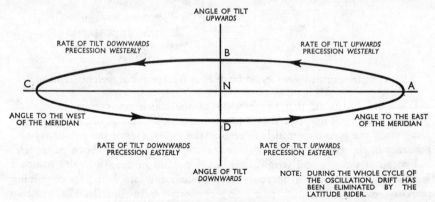

FIG. 175. Undamped gravity-controlled gyro (movement of North end of axis, viewed from South)

tilting movement causes the North end to fall below the horizontal. The top-heavy control now causes easterly precession towards the meridian.

The movement continues through D and back to A, where the cycle is recommenced. The North end will thus oscillate indefinitely, describing an ellipse about the meridian, above and below the horizontal. This motion is described as 'undamped', implying that the axis cannot settle in any fixed direction. In other words, the gyro is now *North-seeking*, but a further control is required before it becomes *North-finding*.

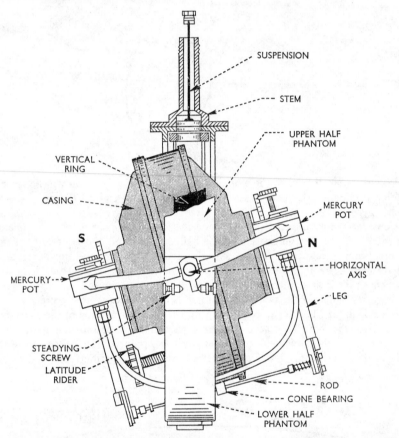

FIG. 176. Inner member, viewed from East (compensator weights removed)

It should be noted that the efficacy of the top-heavy control in causing precession depends upon the rate of tilt. It has been stated that this rate decreases away from the equator, until it is zero at the poles. Hence the sensitivity and accuracy of the gyro-compass are greatly reduced in latitudes above 70° or so.

Instead of using a bail weight, top-heavy control in the Admiralty compass is produced by the use of mercury. The system employs four pots containing mercury, each North–South pair being connected by a pipe. In Fig. 176 two of these pots are visible, the other two lie directly behind them. The complete unit, consisting of pots, framework and rods, is known as the 'mercury boxes'.

The mercury boxes are tilted, when the sensitive element tilts, by means of a mechanical contact at the 'cone bearing' on the bottom of the rotor-casing. Thus, if the North end of the axis tilts up, as shown in Fig. 176, gravity causes mercury to flow from the North to the South pots. This causes a thrust to be exerted on the South side of the cone bearing, which produces the same result as a top bail weight.

(b) DAMPING

The elliptical motion of an undamped gravity-controlled gyro, already described, consists of two oscillations, one in tilt and one in azimuth. These are interdependent, so that if the amplitude of one is damped out, the other will also disappear, and the axis will then settle.

In the Admiralty gyro-compass it is the oscillation in tilt which is damped out. This is achieved by introducing a precession in tilt which reduces any existing upward or downward tilt. To avoid the necessity of using further controls for this purpose, the mercury control is also made to provide the additional torque required.

As shown in Fig. 172a, a precession in tilt is produced by a force acting horizontally on the axis of spin. This requires a torque about the vertical axis. A control attached directly to the rotor-casing could not produce such a torque. However, if the control is attached (as described in B.R. 8) to the phantom – on pivots in line with the horizontal axis of the sensitive element – and suitable connection is made to the bottom of the casing, to the East or West of the vertical axis, then not only will the control produce a torque about the horizontal axis, but it will also produce one about the vertical axis.

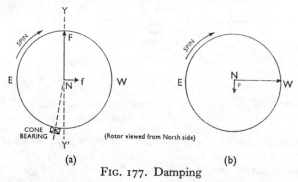

(a)   (b)

FIG. 177. Damping

Such a connection can be provided by displacing the cone bearing slightly to the eastward, as shown in Fig. 177a. The components (F and f) of a force on the South side of the cone bearing are shown in this diagram, while Fig. 177b shows the components (P and p) of the precession produced by such a force.

It can be seen that this small displacement of the cone bearing, which is about 1/10-inch from the vertical axis, results in unequal components of precession. Reference to Fig. 175 shows that only small amounts of tilt require damping; and, in practice, the amount of tilting experienced is about one-sixteenth of the displacement in azimuth.

Let us assume that the North end of the gyro spin axis is displaced to the eastward of the meridian and is pointing at A (Fig. 178). Owing to the Earth's rotation, the North end will rise and gravity will cause mercury to flow from the

North pot to the South pot. Accordingly, the South rod will thrust on the cone bearing. This will result in westerly precession (as with the undamped gyro) and in downward tilting precession, as shown in Fig. 177b. Thus it is clear that the cone bearing has in fact been displaced in the correct direction. The rates of both these precessions increase with tilt. As the North end approaches the meridian, the rate of downward precession increases, while the rate of upward tilt, due to the Earth's rotation, decreases. At some point B the two cancel each other, so that at this point the path of the North end will be horizontal. Between B and C the downward rate of precession exceeds the upward rate of tilt, so that the path crosses the meridian at a downward angle. As soon as the North end is to the westward of the meridian, the rate of tilt due to the Earth's rotation is downward; this combines with the downward rate of precession in reducing, still faster, the existing tilt. As the tilt is reduced, so the rate of westerly precession decreases, until the point D is reached. Here there are no effects due to the mercury boxes, which are now equally balanced, but the downward rate of tilt due to the Earth's rotation continues. (Note that ND is less than NA, owing to the effect of damping.) The path continues as shown, until, after one complete cycle – which is actually a spiral – the North end is displaced to the eastward of the meridian by an amount NA', which is approximately a quarter of NA.

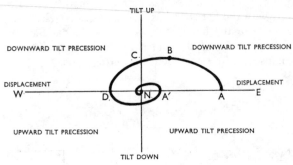

FIG. 178. Damped gravity-controlled gyro-compass (movement of North end of axis, viewed from South)

Provided that the initial displacement is not more than about 20°, the axis will be horizontal and in the meridian after three complete cycles. The rate of drift is cancelled out by the latitude rider. A North-finding gyro-compass has thus been achieved. The period of a complete cycle for the spiral is about 87 minutes, so that the gyro will take between 4 and 5 hours to settle. If started nearly in the meridian, it can be used for navigation in a correspondingly shorter time.

The following table shows the approximate minimum time that should be allowed if an error of ½° in the gyro-compass can be accepted.

Original displacement from Meridian	Gyro settled within ½° after
1°	½ hour
2°	1½ hours
4°	2 hours
16°	3 hours

SPEED ERROR

The Earth rotates through 15 degrees per hour. A point on the equator, there-fore, moves through space at a speed of (15 × 60) minutes per hour – i.e. 900 knots – in a W.–E. direction. In other latitudes the rotational speed of the Earth is (900 cos. latitude) knots. This movement is rotational about the Earth's axis of spin. This axis, when projected, we have considered to pass approximately through the Pole Star; the latter is therefore the only apparently motionless point in the northern part of the heavens. By means of the controls described, the gyro-compass has been made to settle with its spin axis lying horizontally in the meridian – i.e. with its axis at right angles to the Earth's rotational movement in space.

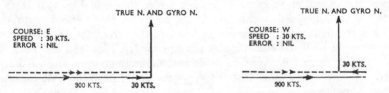

FIG. 179. Speed Error: ship on East-West course at Equator

Consider the gyro-compass in a ship at the equator steaming East or West at a speed of 30 knots. Its movement through space is then 930 or 870 knots respectively in an easterly direction. The gyro, therefore, experiences a slight change in the speed – but not in the direction – of its movement through space, and so it will still settle in the meridian (Fig. 179). A similar result is obtained in any other latitude.

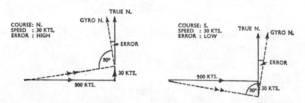

FIG. 180. Speed Error: ship on North-South course at Equator

Consider the ship steaming North or South at 30 knots. The gyro-compass will now be travelling through space in a direction which is the resultant of the Earth's and the ship's speeds. So far as the gyro-compass is concerned, the Earth now appears to be spinning about a different axis. It will therefore settle with its North end directed at a point on the horizon which is in line with a new, apparently motionless, point in the heavens. In other words, it will align itself to a false meridian. The result of this is shown in Fig. 180.

For intermediate courses, the resultant movement through space will differ less from the W.–E. movement of the Earth, so that the compass error will be less. At lower speeds the error will also be less. These facts may be summarized as follows:

COURSE NORTH:

North end of gyro-compass axis settles to *westward* of meridian – error *High.*

COURSE SOUTH:

North end of gyro-compass axis settles to *eastward* of meridian – error *Low*.

COURSE EAST OR WEST: gyro-compass settles – error *Nil*.

$$\text{Speed error} \begin{cases} \propto \text{cos Course} \\ \propto \text{Speed} \end{cases} \quad \cdot \quad \cdot \quad \cdot \quad \text{\textit{formula 1}}$$

In other words, speed error varies as the northerly or southerly component of ship's speed.

As already stated, Earth's speed $\propto$ cos latitude. The error resulting when a ship steams North at 30 knots in latitude 60° is shown in Fig. 181. Here the Earth's rotational speed is only 450 knots, so that a ship's speed of 30 knots causes a resultant which is clearly inclined further from the W.-E. direction than it would be if the ship were at the equator (*cf.* Figs. 180 and 181). The gyro-compass error will therefore be correspondingly greater. Thus, if Earth's speed decreases, it is clear that the error increases, provided that the ship's motion is unaltered.

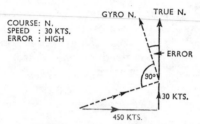

FIG. 181. Speed Error: ship on North-South course in Latitude 60°

Therefore,

$$\text{Speed Error} \propto \frac{1}{\text{Earth's speed}} \text{ or } \frac{1}{\text{cos lat.}} \quad \cdot \quad \cdot \quad \cdot \quad \text{\textit{formula 2}}$$

From formulae 1 and 2 an approximate formula is obtained which can be used when the ship's speed is below 50 knots. This formula is:

$$\text{Speed Error} = \frac{\text{Speed (knots)} \times \text{cos Course}}{5\pi \text{ cos lat.}} \quad \cdot \quad \cdot \quad \text{\textit{formula 3}}$$

where 5π, a constant, is the factor which gives speed error in degrees, if ship's speed is in knots.

Correction of Speed Error (5005 series)

The speed error is corrected in the Master Transmission Unit (M.T.U.) (Fig. 182) where the amount of correction required at any instant is computed automatically from the true course, latitude and ship's speed. The latitude (and ship's speed when the log is inoperative) must be set by hand. The correction is applied to the compass transmission and all outgoing transmissions are in terms of True Course. The magnitude of speed error in degrees for due north or south compass courses and for various latitudes and ship's speeds is given in B.R. 8.

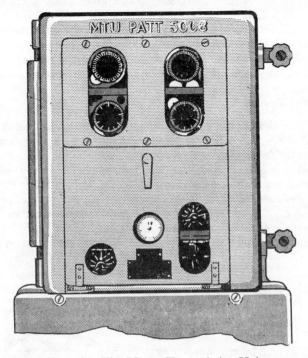

Fig. 182. The Master Transmission Unit

BALLISTIC DEFLECTION

An important consequence of the existence of speed error is that the settling position of the gyro-compass changes if there is any change in the northerly or southerly component of the ship's speed, such as occurs when the ship turns at high speed. If no special arrangements were made the gyro-compass would arrive at its new settling position after executing the usual spiral.

When a ship alters course or speed, the northerly component of its acceleration or deceleration causes mercury to flow into the South or North pots respectively; this is due to inertia.

The transfer of mercury which occurs under these conditions causes precession of the gyro in azimuth, known as 'ballistic deflection'. It will be recalled that a northerly component of speed causes the North end of the gyro axis to settle to the westward of the meridian. Similarly, a northerly component of acceleration of the ship causes the mercury boxes to become South-heavy. This results in ballistic deflection to the westward, which is the direction required in this case. It can be verified that easterly ballistic deflection will be caused when the acceleration has a southerly component; this corresponds to the easterly wander of the gyro axis when the ship's speed has a southerly component.

The amount of ballistic deflection depends on the amount of mercury transferred.

The construction of the mercury pots and their connecting pipes can be arranged so that the ballistic deflection resulting from a change of speed exactly equals the change-of-speed-and-course error.

It will be recalled, however, that speed error varies with latitude; therefore, it is necessary for the amount of ballistic deflection to be regulated accordingly. This is achieved by varying the free surface-area of the mercury in the pots, so that less mercury is required to flow in low latitudes, and vice versa.

Mercury Pot Domes

When a ship accelerates, the mercury flows to take up a 'false horizontal', which it maintains during the period of the acceleration. A system of domes in pots, which varies the free surface-area of mercury, governs the amount of mercury required to flow in order to attain this 'false horizontal'. This is shown in Fig. 183. The height of the domes is set according to the latitude. One dome of each pair is inverted, so that when their positions are altered, the centre of gravity of the system remains unchanged, and the correct balance of the mercury boxes is maintained. In Fig. 183a the domes are set for latitude 60°. The amount of mercury transferred (shown in solid black) is more than that in Fig. 183b,

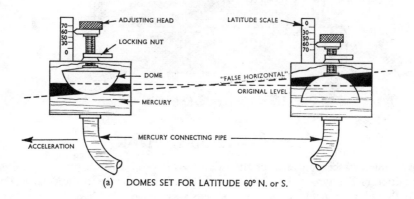

(a)   DOMES SET FOR LATITUDE 60° N. or S.

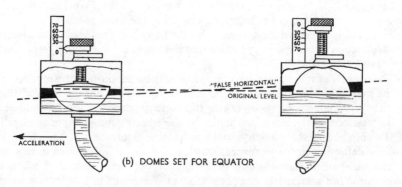

(b) DOMES SET FOR EQUATOR

FIG. 183. Mercury Pot Domes

where the domes are set for latitude 0°. Thus a greater precession will occur at the higher latitude, as required for correct ballistic deflection.

Settings. – The following instructions should be observed when setting the domes:

(1) The effect of having the mercury pot domes set for wrong latitude is that the compass will wander more after an alteration of course or speed.

(2) It is desirable that they should be kept set on passage, in the same way as the latitude rider, although the accuracy of the setting is not quite so important; it is, however, most important that all four domes should be at the same setting.

(3) To set the domes, ease the locking-nut at the foot of each dome shaft and turn the milled head through an exact number of half-turns up or down until the pointer is as nearly opposite the local latitude on the scale as possible. Each milled head should be turned through the same number of half-turns. When set, secure the domes in position by the locking-nuts.

(4) For latitudes between the equator and 30°, the pointer should be set to the line between 0 and 30. For latitudes 50°, 60° or 70°, the pointer should be set opposite the middle of the appropriate figure.

For intermediate latitude, one turn of the milled head is equivalent to:

$$5° \text{ of latitude between latitudes } 30° \text{ and } 50°$$
$$2\tfrac{1}{2}° \text{ of latitude between latitudes } 50° \text{ and } 70°$$

Therefore, by adjusting to half a turn, the domes can be set correctly to the nearest $2\tfrac{1}{2}°$ between latitudes 30° and 50°, or $1\tfrac{1}{4}°$ between latitudes 50° and 70°. On passage, settings should normally be altered for every 10° change of latitude above 30°. When a ship is remaining in one latitude the settings should be made to the nearest half-turn.

BALLISTIC TILT

It has been explained how change of speed or course produces ballistic deflection in azimuth towards the new settling position. Owing to the fact that the point of contact (i.e. the cone bearing) between the mercury boxes and the rotor-casing is offset to the East of the vertical axis, an unwanted tilt is introduced each time ballistic deflection takes place. This results in a small wander after alteration of course or speed.

If a ship accelerates in a northerly direction, the North end of the gyro axis will be precessed from its present settling position, S_1, towards the new settling position S_2 (Fig. 184).

Because of the eccentricity of the cone bearing, the path will be in the direction S_1T. Consequently, although the compass will have been precessed to its correct settling position in azimuth, the axis will have a downward tilt 'Ballistic Tilt'. Fig. 184 shows that the error will have its maximum value, 'the Ballistic Return', at V, about 22 minutes after the alteration of course.

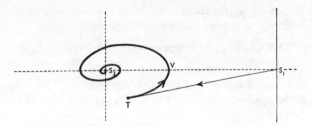

FIG. 184. Ballistic deflection and subsequent wander

MASTER COMPASS GENERAL DESCRIPTION
(5005 series only)

Sensitive Element

The Sensitive Element consists of the Rotor and Casing supported in the Vertical Ring, and the Compensator Weights that give the sensitive element equal moments of inertia about the two principal horizontal axes.

Phantom Ring

The Phantom Ring supports the sensitive element and is kept continually aligned with it so that the wire suspension of the sensitive element does not become twisted. It also carries the Stem, Slip rings, Azimuth gear and Compass card. It is through the azimuth gear that the phantom ring is aligned with the sensitive element and by means of which the magslips are rotated to transmit the compass heading. The card indicates compass course.

Mercury Boxes

The Mercury Boxes are suspended from the phantom ring. Any thrust caused by N.–S. out-of-balance of the mercury boxes is applied to the bottom of the casing by means of rods and pivot cups.

The Spider

The Spider is an iron casting which supports the phantom ring and sensitive element by means of the stem bearings. The spider is held in fixed relation to the fore-and-aft line of the ship and can rotate freely about the phantom ring as the ship changes course. Attached to the spider are the follow-up motor, which aligns the phantom ring with the sensitive element, together with the fine and coarse magslip housings and gearings.

The Gimbal Ring

This is an octagonal steel ring which supports the spider and gimbals the compass in the direction of the pitch axis. Dampers are fitted.

The Binnacle Ring

This is the outermost ring inside which the gimbal ring is pivoted in the roll axis. Dampers are fitted.

The Anti-Shock Mounting

This is not strictly part of the master compass, but is fitted in H.M. ships to protect the master compass from shock and vibration.

FOLLOW-UP AND TRANSMISSION
(5005 series only)

Master Compass Follow-up

The phantom ring is servo driven into alignment with the sensitive element. A pair of magslip transmitters are coupled to the azimuth gear to transmit the compass course to the M.T.U. follow-up servo system.

The Master Transmission Unit (M.T.U.)

The M.T.U. is servo driven to follow the master compass. It calculates and automatically applies a correction for speed and course error, using information obtained from the ship's log. It then supplies true course data in the form of 10 minute M-type transmission for navigational services only, together with 10° and 360° sector-value magslip transmission for the operation of retransmission units which feed the weapon control systems. Local latitude (and speed if log is inoperative) must be set by hand and the hand/log selector switch altered accordingly.

Compass Retransmission Units (C.R.U.)

These are conversion units which relay the compass transmissions in a number of different forms for various services. Their self-aligning servo systems may be operated from magslips in the M.T.U. or by the Admiralty Gyro-Magnetic Compass (*see* Chapter X).

Control Panel and Alarm System

The Compass Control Panel contains the gyro supply switch, gyro voltmeter and ammeter, and the alarm relays which indicate failure of the main and amplifier supplies and of the compass follow-up system. The relays operate on failure, light the red warning lamp, ring the alarm bell and extinguish the appropriate indicating lamp. When a fault is cleared the relays continue in the fault condition until reset by push-button to ensure that a temporary fault will be noticed.

The alarm system is operated from the 'maintained' 24 volt battery supply. As no alarm would be given if this supply were to fail, the presence of the 24 volt supply at the panel is indicated by a green lamp burning alongside the red alarm lamp at the main steering position.

ADMIRALTY GYRO-COMPASS (SPERRY TYPE)
(Series 2005 and 1005)

In these older compasses speed error is corrected in the compass so that the compass transmits True course.

Admiralty Speed Corrector

To correct the speed error, a correction is applied which moves the lubber ring in such a way that the lubber's point is put in error with respect to the fore-and-aft line of the ship. This error corresponds to the extent that the gyro axis is in error with respect to the true meridian.

The transmitters, which convey the direction of the ship's head to repeaters, are fixed to the lubber ring; when the latter is moved the correct course is transmitted to the repeaters.

The speed-corrector is mounted on the after side of the 'spider', which is a portion of the gyro-compass mounting fixed to the ship.

The dial, shown in Fig. 185, is graduated in tenths of a degree. Settings are applied by slackening the retaining screw A and turning the dial by means of the knob B until the required setting is aligned with the index C. The required setting is ascertained from an engraved table, fitted in the gyro room and on the pelorus stand. It is reproduced in B.R. 9. This table is entered for speed and latitude; the setting obtained represents tenths of a degree and is equivalent to $\dfrac{\text{speed (knots)}}{5\pi \cos \text{lat.}}$.

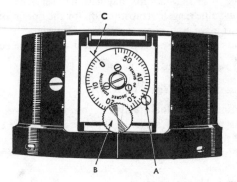

FIG. 185. The speed corrector

When this speed correction is applied, it can be seen that in practice the lubber's point is moved by an amount which differs with the heading of the ship. It will be recalled, from formula 3, that speed error varies as the cosine of the course; this factor is automatically applied by the 'cosine ring', which works in conjunction with the speed-corrector mechanism to modify the displacement of the lubber ring. (This is explained in more detail in B.R. 9.)

REMARKS ON SETTING THE SPEED CORRECTOR

(a) The speed correction may be applied without disturbing the sensitive element in any way.

(b) The extent to which it is kept set must depend upon circumstances and upon the convenience of the Navigating Officer, but it may be found useful to issue standard instructions to squadrons, in order to ensure uniformity within such limits.

(c) The result of an incorrect setting is that the ship's head will be wrongly indicated if the ship has any North or South component of speed. The direction of the error involved is summarized opposite.

Speed setting		Courses	Gyro error
Low	{	Northerly	High
		Southerly	Low
High	{	Northerly	Low
		Southerly	High

(d) The error in correction will have a maximum on North and South and will vary with the cosine of the course. The maximum extent of the error may be ascertained from the speed/latitude table. For example, in latitude 50°, if the setting corresponds to a speed of 5 knots less than actual speed, the maximum gyro error will be $\frac{1}{2}°$ high on North and $\frac{1}{2}°$ low on South.

(e) In general, the setting should be applied so that the compass is correct to within $\frac{1}{2}°$.

Follow-up and Transmission

In the 2005 and 1005 series, true course can be transmitted from the compass because the compass is corrected for speed error. M-type transmission in 10 minute steps is used for navigational purposes, and 2 minute steps for weapon control.

The follow-up system in the 1005 series includes Magnetic and Trolley contactors and the compass is known as the Contactor Compass. In the 2005 series a Valve Follow-up system is used and the compass is known as the Valve Follow-up Compass.

Alarm System

This is in principle the same as in the 5005 series except that an independent 20 volt alarm battery is fitted and there is, therefore, no need for a green indicating lamp at the steering position.

CHAPTER IX

The Magnetic Compass

THE magnetic compass is still the primary means of navigating many vessels and craft.

The purpose of this chapter is to explain the principles on which the magnetic compass works, to point out the rules which govern its satisfactory performance, and to enable officers to make the necessary preparations for its adjustment. In addition, a reference is made to degaussing and its effect on the compass.

The procedure for adjusting the compass, together with more specialized aspects of this subject, is covered in Volume III.

MAGNETISM AND TERRESTRIAL MAGNETISM

Natural Magnets

It was found in very early times that small pieces of certain iron ores had the property, when freely suspended, of settling with one axis in a particular direction, and had the further property of attracting small pieces of iron and steel. Such ores constitute natural magnets.

Artificial Magnets

Certain hard irons can be transformed into artificial magnets, having the same properties, by:

(a) contact with other magnets;
(b) electro-magnetism;
(c) being subjected to vibration while within the sphere of influence of another magnet.

These processes are also described in Volume III.

A compass-needle is essentially a specially constructed artificial magnet.

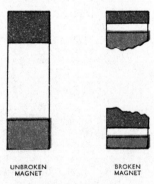

UNBROKEN
MAGNET

BROKEN
MAGNET

FIG. 186. Magnetic poles

Magnetic Poles

A small magnetized bar behaves as though its attractive property were located at two points near the ends of the bar. These points are called the 'magnetic poles'. The poles of a bar magnet are situated at about one-twelfth of its length from each end. By convention they are called 'red' and 'blue' poles.

A magnet possesses two poles. If a magnet is divided into smaller parts, each part becomes a complete magnet in itself (Fig. 186).

If two magnets are placed close together, it is found that the blue pole on one will attract the red pole (and repel the blue pole) of the other. Hence a fundamental law of magnetism: *Unlike poles attract: Like poles repel.*

Magnetic Field

It is assumed that 'lines of force' emerge from the red pole of a magnet and enter the blue pole. These lines, constituting the 'magnetic field' of the magnet, may be considered as the paths which would be followed by an isolated red pole, if such a thing could exist (Fig. 187). Alternatively, if a small magnetic needle were freely suspended in the magnetic field of a large magnet, it would set itself along the line of force in which it was situated.

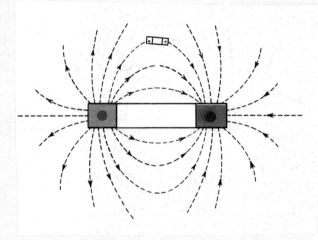

FIG. 187. Magnetic field surrounding a bar magnet

Effect of Heat, Rust and Vibration

Heat. – The effect of temperature on magnetic substances varies with the type of metal. For practical purposes it can be considered that normal atmospheric changes have no effect, and that soft iron loses all its magnetism when it becomes red hot.

Rust. – Considerable rust on magnets is found to decrease their magnetism.

Vibration. – As mentioned above when discussing artificial magnets, vibration assists iron to alter its magnetism, increasing or decreasing it according to circumstances.

Induction

A magnet will induce magnetism in a piece of iron or steel placed in its magnetic field. Since iron has a higher permeability[1] than air, the lines of force tend to concentrate in the metal (Fig. 188). This reduces the lines of force in the air space near it.

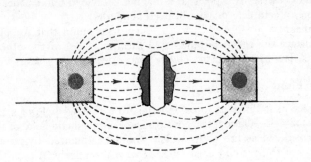

FIG. 188. Magnetic induction

Magnetic Screening (Fig. 189)

A region surrounded by iron and steel, such as an enclosed bridge or the steering position of a ship, contains only a part of the lines of force originating from an external source, because they tend to concentrate in the surrounding iron. Therefore the magnetic field of the Earth – which, as will be seen, is itself a magnet – will be reduced at a compass so placed. It is for this reason that the standard compass is situated in a position where it is possible for most of the

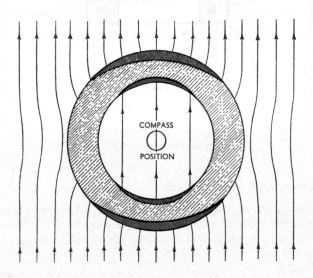

FIG. 189. Magnetic screening

---

[1] *See* page 303 for the definition of 'permeability'.

structure in its vicinity to be made of non-magnetic materials. This is impossible with between-deck compasses, which therefore suffer from an increase in period, and are liable to greater deviations than the standard compass.

Types of Iron and Magnetism

Iron and steel· may be divided into three magnetic types, according to the reactions of the metal to a magnetic field.

(1) *Hard iron* is the term used to denote those forms of iron and steel which are capable of becoming permanent magnets. These receive 'permanent magnetism'. (It should be noted that, as permanent magnets are made by artificial means, so they can be unmade; the term 'permanent' in this connection is therefore not strictly accurate.)

(2) *Soft iron* is the term used to denote those forms of iron and steel which are capable of becoming magnets when placed in a magnetic field, and of changing their magnetic condition with change of strength or direction of the field, or of their position in it. They do not retain magnetism on being removed from the magnetic field. These receive 'induced magnetism'.

(3) *Intermediate iron* is the term used to denote those forms of iron and steel which may be classified between the two extremes mentioned above. These receive 'sub-permanent magnetism'.

EXPRESSIONS USED IN CONNECTION WITH MAGNETISM

If there were a means of annulling the effect of the Earth's field and of producing magnetic fields of any amount, and if there were two iron bars of the same size and shape, composed of different magnetic materials, but not initially magnetised, then:

(a) If the two bars were placed in a magnetic field, magnetism would be induced into them. The one which received more induced magnetism would be said to have the greater *permeability*.

(b) If the bars were removed from the field, so that they were once more situated in a zero field, it would be found that they had retained a certain amount of magnetism. The one which retained the greater amount would be said to have the greater *retentivity*.

(c) Now suppose the bars were placed in a magnetic field of reverse direction, which could be increased in amount until the bars were once more demagnetised. The one requiring the greater field would be said to have been subjected to greater *coercive force*, or to have greater *coercivity*.

(d) It would be noticed that the magnetism produced in the bars would not vary exactly with the field producing it, but would lag behind it somewhat. (Retentivity was a particular case of this.) *Hysteresis* is the term used to denote this lag.

TERRESTRIAL MAGNETISM

Nature of the Earth's Magnetism (Fig. 190)

The magnetic field of the Earth is similar to that which would be produced by a short magnet situated near the Earth's centre, with its axis passing through the neighbourhood of Hudson's Bay in the North and South Victoria Land in the South. These points, although they are not the poles of the imaginary magnet described, are traditionally known as the Magnetic North (*blue*) Pole and the Magnetic South (*red*) Pole. They do not coincide with the true North and South Poles of the Earth, which are on the Earth's axis of spin.

The magnetic poles are not fixed, but are constantly moving in unknown paths, apparently completing a cycle in a period of many hundreds of years. A magnetic needle, freely suspended, will lie along the lines of force of the Earth's magnetic field. At the N. and S. magnetic poles it will rest vertically with opposite ends down at each pole respectively. To conform to the law that unlike poles attract each other, the North-seeking end of a compass needle or a magnet is called 'red'. At the magnetic equator, approximately half-way between the poles, such a needle would be horizontal whereas at any other place the needle will be inclined at what is known as the angle of dip (*see* below).

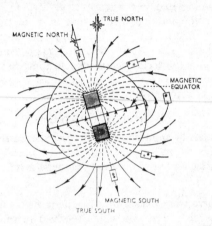

FIG. 190. Magnetic field surrounding the Earth

The irregularity of the Earth's magnetism can be seen in Admiralty Chart 5382 (part of which chart and of Charts 5383, 5378, 5379 and 5374 are reproduced between pages 306 and 307).

The Earth's Lines of Force

The direction assumed by a freely suspended magnetic needle, when acted upon by the Earth's magnetic force alone, is known as a 'line of total force'.

The vertical plane containing a line of total force defines the 'magnetic meridian'. Thus, such a needle is said to lie in the magnetic meridian. It should be realized that, owing to the irregularity of the Earth's magnetism (including the fact that the magnetic poles are not diametrically opposed), all magnetic meridians, although they are semi-great circles, do not necessarily pass through the magnetic poles.

Dip

The vertical angle between the magnetic needle and the horizontal (Fig. 191) is called the 'angle of dip'. This is zero at the magnetic equator, and 90° at the magnetic poles. Lines joining all positions of equal dip are known as 'isoclinal' lines; and these, with the magnetic equator (which may now be defined as the line joining all positions of zero dip), are analogous to parallels of latitude and the Earth's equator.

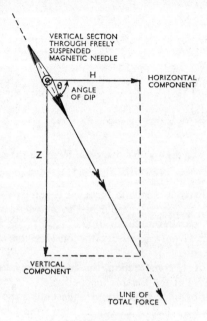

VERTICAL SECTION
THROUGH FREELY
SUSPENDED
MAGNETIC NEEDLE

H

HORIZONTAL
COMPONENT

θ

ANGLE
OF DIP

Z

VERTICAL
COMPONENT

LINE OF
TOTAL FORCE

FIG. 191. Magnetic dip

H and Z

The total force is divided into two components (Fig. 191):

(a) The vertical component, called Z, is shown on Chart 5378. On this chart the values of Z are expressed in dynes per unit pole, or 'oersteds'.

(b) The horizontal component, called H (also expressed in 'oersteds'), is shown on Chart 5379.

From Fig. 191 it can be seen that tan dip $= \dfrac{Z}{H}$. Curves of magnetic dip are given in Chart 5383.

THE MAGNETIC COMPASS

Since direction on the Earth's surface is measured by a horizontal angle, it is essential that the compass card should always lie horizontally. To ensure this, it is suspended so that the centre of gravity of the card, with its system of needles, is below the pivot, or point of suspension. This can be seen from Fig. 201.

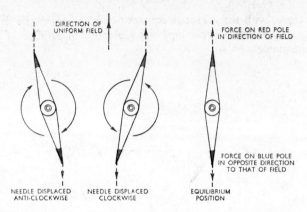

FIG. 192. Effect of the Earth's magnetic force on the compass needle

The effect of the Earth's magnetic force on a compass needle is to cause a 'couple', which tends to set the needle in the magnetic meridian. (A couple consists of two equal, parallel forces of unlike sense.) (*See* Fig. 192.)

For convenience, it is only necessary to consider the effect on the North-seeking end of the needle.

As a consequence of its construction, the compass needle is only directed by the horizontal force (H) of the Earth's magnetism.

Although the lines of total force are strongest near the magnetic poles (*see* Chart 5382), the directive force – as can be seen from Chart 5379 – is greatest near the magnetic equator; and as the latitude increases, so H decreases until, in the vicinity of the magnetic poles, it is zero, and the compass then becomes useless.

Variation

The Earth's magnetic field is very irregular and, in general, the magnetic and true meridians do not coincide. The horizontal angle between the magnetic and true meridians is called 'magnetic variation'.

Variation is called *westerly* when magnetic North lies to the West of true North, and *easterly* when it lies to the East of true North (Fig. 193).

As the magnetic poles move, so the variation changes. It is subject to three types of change:

(1) a continuous alteration, called 'secular' change;

(2) a seasonal fluctuation, called 'annual' change (*N.B.* This should not be confused with the annual alteration in the variation due to the 'secular change');

(3) a daily fluctuation, called 'diurnal' change.

Of these, (2) and (3) may be neglected in practical navigation, although in the United Kingdom the diurnal change, which increases with latitude, may be as great as 25'.

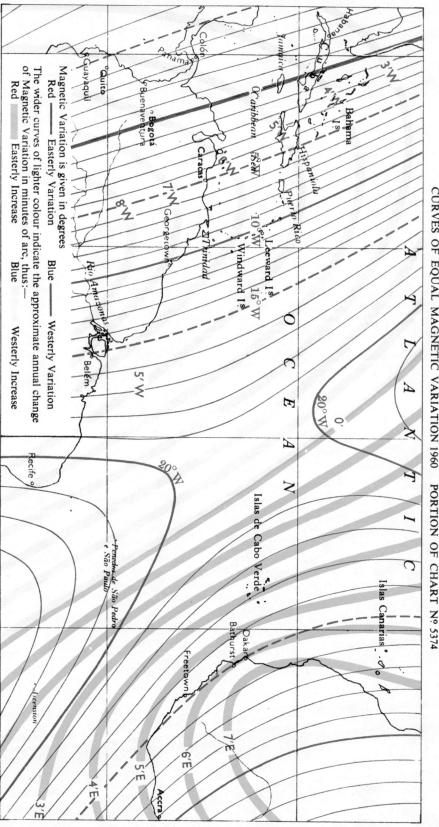

CURVES OF EQUAL MAGNETIC VARIATION 1960 PORTION OF CHART Nº 5374

The secular change is shown on the magnetic compass-roses on charts – for example:

'Variation 10° 25′W. (1954) *decreasing about 10′ annually.*'

It is always necessary to apply this change before using the magnetic rose, so that in this example, the corrected variation for 1962 would be 9° 05′W.

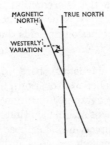

FIG. 193. Magnetic variation

The compass-roses are normally reprinted if the total change in variation has reached 2°, or if a major correction to the chart is made before this occurs.

The variation can also be found from the 'Variation Charts' on which are shown curves of equal variation called 'isogonic' lines and the annual value of the secular change. Chart 5374 covers the world. Charts 5375, 5376 and 5377 of a larger scale are available for specific areas.

The charts are reprinted every five years. In the case of any disagreement between the information shown on the compass-rose and that on the variation chart, the latter should be considered as more reliable.

Magnetic Disturbance

Certain disturbances of the Earth's magnetic field are encountered from time to time and may cause unknown errors of the compass. These fall generally under two headings:

(1) magnetic storms;
(2) local attraction.

Magnetic storms, often accompanied by displays of the Aurora Borealis, or Northern Lights, cause fleeting disturbances.

Local attraction occurs when a mass of magnetic ore, or possibly a wreck, lies sufficiently close to cause an error of the compass. Since the effect of one magnet on another varies inversely as the cube of the distance between them, this error is seldom caused by *visible* land, but more often by the ship passing over such masses lying in shallow water. It occurs in certain known localities, as set forth in the *Sailing Directions*, and is usually noted on the charts near the position. One of the most remarkable of these localities is off Western Australia, where, in 9 fathoms, the variation has been observed to vary from 56°E. to 26°W. in a distance of 200 yards.

SHIP'S MAGNETISM AND ITS CORRECTION

Disturbing Effect of the Ship on the Compass (Deviation)

As has been described, the compass-needle will lie in the magnetic meridian, provided that no disturbing influence is present. Unfortunately, disturbing magnetic fields are caused by the material of which a ship is constructed, and by fields set up by electrical apparatus[1].

The iron and steel used in the construction of ships consists of the three magnetic types previously described. Therefore at any moment the total field at the compass position is a combination of fields due to:

(a) the Earth's magnetism;
(b) the ship's permanent magnetism (hard iron);
(c) the ship's induced magnetism (soft iron), which depends on the direction of her head and her geographical position;
(d) the ship's sub-permanent magnetism (intermediate iron), which depends on the alteration in direction of her head, and on her past movements and vibrations, all of which are constantly changing quantities.

Of the above, (b), (c) and (d) comprise the ship's magnetic field, so that the forces acting on the compass at one particular moment may be shown as in Fig. 194.

The effect of the magnetic field of the ship is to cause the compass-needle to be no longer aligned in the magnetic meridian, but at an angle to this direction. This effect is called *deviation*.

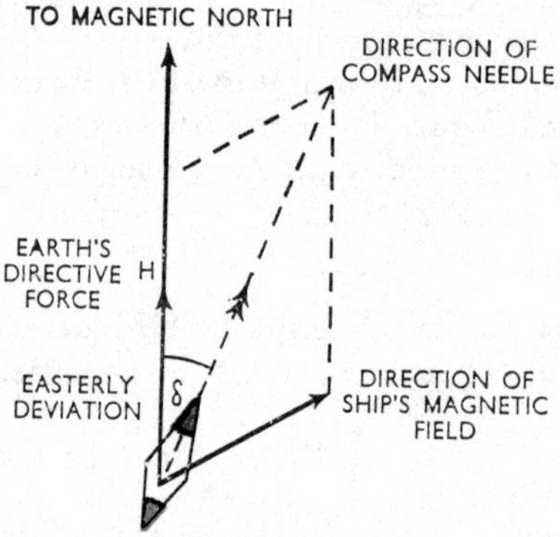

FIG. 194. Deviation

If the compass-needle points to the East of magnetic North, the deviation is called easterly (+), and if it points to the West, the deviation is called westerly (−).

The magnetic field of the ship changes its direction and amount, in part, as the ship alters her heading. Consequently, the deviation is different for different headings of the ship. As a result, bearings taken by compass have to be corrected for the deviation *for that heading* in order to give the magnetic bearings; and,

---

[1] The effect of fields set up by electrical apparatus that is liable to affect the compass, such as Degaussing gear, will be considered later.

conversely, magnetic bearings and courses have to be corrected for the deviation in order to give compass bearings and courses to steer.

Further, if the deviations differ on two headings, then, as the ship is brought from one heading to the other, the card is displaced to the position corresponding to the new deviation concurrently with the change of heading of the ship. Thus the change of headings by compass as read off the (moving) card against the lubber's point will not be the same as the change of magnetic heading (Fig. 195).

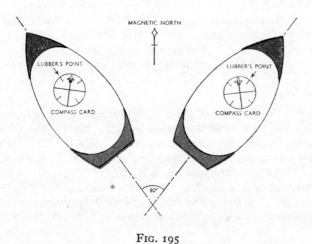

FIG. 195

CAUSES OF CHANGES IN DEVIATION OR IN APPARENT DEVIATION

A change of deviation may be caused by:

*(a) training of guns or directors from their normal positions;
(b) tools or other iron or steel objects left near the compass;
*(c) any alteration of electric leads; or by earths on electrical circuits;
*(d) the moving or installation of electrical instruments;
*(e) the slipping of stays or guys;
(f) the presence of boats alongside, or other ships within close distance;
*(g) movement of hawser reels;
(h) abnormal heating of the funnel;
(i) a list on the ship;
(j) rust on corrector magnets or Flinders bar, if of sufficient depth to diminish appreciably the area of the iron beneath it;
(k) induction;
(l) sub-permanent magnetism;
(m) lightning, particularly if it strikes the ship;
(n) magnetic storms;
(o) compass-card having excessive friction at the pivot;
(p) faulty azimuth circle;
(q) change of magnetic latitude;
(r) shocks, due to collision, grounding, gunfire, hits or near misses.

---

* These items are only likely to cause a change in deviation if the objects concerned are situated in the neighbourhood of the compass.

Compensation for the Ship's Magnetic Field

In order to ensure a reliable compass, it is necessary to counteract the effect of the ship's total magnetic field. A system of permanent and induced magnets, each creating opposite fields of the same strength as the different fields of the ship, would accomplish this. Because the field strength due to a short magnet varies inversely as the cube of the distance from the magnet, it is only necessary to place small correctors in and around the compass-binnacle to achieve this result.

The method of compensation adopted is to divide the effects of the disturbing fields into convenient components and to deal with each component separately. The components chosen are those related to the fore-and-aft, athwartship, and vertical directions in the ship, through the centre of the compass-needle system.

Permanent Magnetism

When a ship is building – and particularly during the fitting-out stage – her hard iron acquires permanent magnetism from the Earth's lines of force. This is increased by hammering, riveting, and other vibrations. The strength and nature of this magnetism depend largely on the direction in which the ship was heading, and on her magnetic latitude, at the time.

This permanent magnetism has the effect of turning the ship's hard iron into one large, complex, permanent magnet, whose polarity remains substantially in the same relative direction in the ship, no matter where the ship subsequently moves.

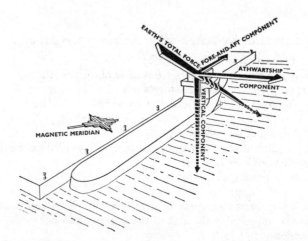

FIG. 196. Permanent magnetism acquired by a ship building on a N.W. heading in N. latitude

Fig. 196 shows a ship building on a north-westerly heading in North latitude. Here the Earth's total lines of force penetrate the ship from South to North in an oblique downward direction, inducing a blue pole near the stern and a red pole near the bow. The effect of this at the compass position can be resolved into three components in the directions previously mentioned. These components are described in Volume III.

Induced Magnetism

Now consider the magnetism acquired by the soft iron in the ship. This, as previously stated, is called 'induced' magnetism. By virtue of its particular properties, it produces at the compass position an effect of a magnet whose strength and polarity alter immediately the ship changes her heading or magnetic latitude.

The induced magnetism can also be resolved into components, for more convenient compensation. These are also described in Volume III.

Sub-permanent Magnetism

This is a very general term applied to that part of the ship's magnetism which is acquired in the intermediate iron when a ship has been heading in the same direction for a long period. The effect is accentuated by vibration, and the magnetism is not acquired immediately. All grades of magnetism between permanent and induced come under this general title of sub-permanent.

Sub-permanent magnetism has to be corrected initially with the permanent magnetism, and is thus the cause of changes in the deviation, since it does not subsequently behave like permanent magnetism. For example, after a dockyard refit or during an ocean passage the intermediate iron is magnetised and causes deviation when the direction of the ship's head is changed. Since the sub-permanent magnetism does not immediately disappear, the deviation will be of an amount diminishing with time. If not allowed for, this deviation is likely to cause, in the case of a well-placed upper-deck compass, a temporary inclination of course *towards* the heading on which the sub-permanent magnetism was produced (Fig. 197).

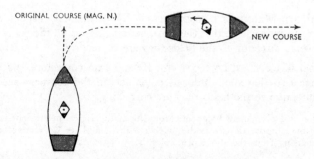

ORIGINAL COURSE (MAG. N.)

NEW COURSE

FIG. 197. Temporary deviation caused by sub-permanent magnetism after alteration of course

To eliminate errors caused by sub-permanent magnetism when the ship is swung to obtain her deviations, the rate of swinging should not exceed one complete turn of 360° in approximately 45 minutes. The error which results from swinging too quickly is sometimes known as 'Gaussin error'.

Effects of Lightning

Should a vessel be struck by lightning, her magnetism will probably be affected to an unknown degree. The effects are likely to be of a temporary nature, although it is not unusual for a ship to take several months before her magnetic state is at all stable again.

A rough and ready rule, which has been found effective, is to reverse the athwartship magnets at the compass of a ship that has been struck by lightning whilst the vessel is magnetically unstable.

Summary

Sub-permanent magnetism may be expected, and the deviation should therefore be checked frequently, when:

(a) the ship has been heading in the same direction for a long time;
(b) the ship leaves a dockyard after refitting;
(c) lightning strikes, or passes near to the ship;
(d) heavy gunfire has been carried out;
(e) heavy seas are experienced.

The effect of sub-permanent magnetism is greatest when course is altered from East or West, because the poles of the sub-permanent athwartship component are closer to the compass than those of the fore-and-aft component.

The amount of deviation caused by sub-permanent magnetism cannot be calculated, nor can it be corrected.

PRINCIPLES OF COMPASS CORRECTION

To remove deviation, the various effects of ship's magnetism are corrected in principle, as follows:

PERMANENT MAGNETISM COMPONENTS: By permanent magnet correctors, placed in the binnacle so that their magnetic fields act on the compass-needle in the reverse direction to the fields they are correcting.

INDUCED MAGNETISM COMPONENTS: By soft-iron correctors, placed around the binnacle so that their induced fields act on the compass-needle in the reverse direction to the fields they are correcting.

Note: Vertical permanent magnets correct for both vertical permanent and induced magnetism components (*see* under 'Heeling Error and its Correction', page 313), thus departing from the above principles.

SUB-PERMANENT MAGNETISM: Not corrected, but its effect may be expected on the occasions listed above.

Correctors

PERMANENT MAGNETS

These are supplied in various sizes from ½ to 9 inches long for different patterns of binnacle. They are painted red and blue; the latest pattern of corrector magnets is of harder steel and is distinguished by a green central band. Some are brass-cased, to resist rust. The magnets are inserted into fixed sockets underneath the compass in the three directions: fore-and-aft, athwartships, and vertical. In larger-pattern binnacles, the vertical magnets are placed in a movable bucket on a chain. When not in use, permanent magnets should be stowed with ends of opposite polarity adjacent, so that their magnetic strength is not diminished.

SOFT-IRON CORRECTORS

These consist of:

(1) a pair of soft-iron spheres, placed on athwartship brackets. At a 'badly-placed' compass these may be slewed from the athwartship line.

(2) a vertical soft-iron bar, called the 'Flinders bar'. This is mounted in a brass cylinder on the fore, or after, side of a compass. It is usually on the fore side of a compass placed forward in the ship. At a 'badly-placed' compass the Flinders bar may be slewed from the fore-and-aft line.

These correctors are supplied in various sizes. When shipped, they acquire induced magnetism from the Earth's field and thus have an effect on the compass[1]. Their required size and position can be calculated from tables, so that their effect will exactly compensate for the various components of the ship's induced magnetism. As induction in the soft iron of a ship varies with course and latitude, so will the induction in these correctors vary, and the correction therefore holds good wherever the ship goes. For this reason, spheres and Flinders bar, once in position, seldom require to be moved or altered.

HEELING ERROR AND ITS CORRECTION

Cause of Heeling Error

When a ship heels, the compass, being gimballed, remains horizontal. The forces acting vertically through the centre of the compass, though causing no deviation when the ship is upright, can then exert a horizontal pull on the compass-needles and so cause deviation. Such deviation is called 'heeling error'. This effect is shown in Fig. 198, where the resultant vertical component of the ship's magnetism (permanent and induced) is represented by a magnet, in this case with its blue pole uppermost. (If of the opposite polarity, the deviation would be to the low side, instead of to the high side, of the ship.)

When the ship rolls, this deviating force causes an oscillation of the compass card, which makes steering difficult. In the case of a permanent list, a steady

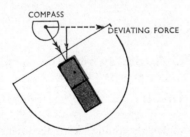
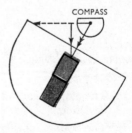

FIG. 198. Heeling error

---

[1] *See* also Volume III for the effect of the magnetism of the compass-needles on the soft-iron correctors.

deviation would be caused. In both cases the deviating force is proportional to the angle of heel[1].

Correction of Heeling Error

It is not practicable to compensate separately for the effects of the permanent and induced magnetism in the case of heeling error. Both types of magnetism are therefore corrected by vertical *permanent* magnet correctors, known as the 'H.E. correctors'. This correction of induced magnetic effects by permanent magnets violates the principles of compass correction already stated. The method of correction suffers, as a result, from the disadvantage that such correction only holds good in one latitude.

Heeling error is compensated, together with the other causes of deviation, when the compass is adjusted. Then, as the ship changes latitude, it reappears. In rough weather, where this manifests itself as an oscillating compass card, it is obviously desirable to reduce the heeling error at once. Where the form of correction consists of vertical magnets and a Flinders bar is in place, the following method of reducing heeling error at sea unfortunately introduces an appreciable deviation when the ship is upright, and must not therefore be used at the standard compass. It can, however, be used at the steering compass, where a steady card is of primary importance.

CORRECTION OF HEELING ERROR AT SEA (*Steering Compass only*)

If the compass cards are swinging wildly, it will be impossible to steady the ship exactly on a course, but her head should be held approximately North or South by compass, since it is on these headings that heeling error is a maximum.

The H.E. corrector magnets at the steering compass should then be moved until the compass card becomes steadier. If it is possible to take bearings from the steering compass, which is not usually the case, then a more accurate correction can be obtained by moving the corrector magnets until the bearing of a distant (stationary) object is steady by compass.

Having reduced heeling error on a course on which it has the maximum effect, it will then be correspondingly reduced on all other courses.

The original position of the correctors should be noted, so that, when the ship is no longer rolling, they may be replaced. Alternatively, the compass must be fully readjusted at the first opportunity.

SWINGING SHIP

The expression 'swinging ship' is used to describe the whole operation of adjusting the magnetic compass. This falls into two parts:

(1) The adjustment, during which correctors are placed to reduce the deviation.

(2) The 'swing', during which any deviation remaining after adjustment is observed and tabulated.

---

[1] In fact, the deviating force is proportional to the *sine* of the angle of heel, but for small angles this may be taken as the angle itself.

Occasions on which a Ship should be Swung

A ship should be swung to obtain deviations on the following occasions:

    (a) before sea trials of a new ship;
    (b) after extensive structural alterations near the compass;
    (c) after considerable change of magnetic latitude;
    (d) after refitting, or lying in one direction for a long period;
    (e) if any of the corrector magnets have been altered;
    (f) after modification or repair of D.G. equipment;
    (g) after wiping, flashing, or deperming treatment;
    (h) at least once a year.

Notes:

  (i) All adjustments other than (a) and (b) above should be carried out by a qualified Navigating Officer or naval swinging officer. These officers may also carry out the adjustment on occasion (b), if desired; but normally the adjustment on both occasions (a) and (b) is carried out by an officer of the Admiralty Compass Division. The services of a civilian adjuster should not be resorted to, in the case of H.M. ships, if this can be avoided, and even then only with the approval of the Senior Naval Officer. In this case, it is most desirable that a responsible officer should observe the adjustment of compasses, in order to satisfy himself that the whole procedure is carried out, that the heeling error is accurately corrected, and that all the compass-corrector coils are properly set.

     The procedure to be adopted is given in Volume III. Any departure from this procedure should be investigated, and if no satisfactory explanation is forthcoming a report of the circumstances should be forwarded to the Director, Admiralty Compass Division. It should be appreciated that local conditions may affect the operation to some extent, but the main principles set out should be common to all adjustments.

     Where a qualified Navigating Officer is borne, he should always carry out the swing of his own ship, except as indicated above.

  (ii) When a Navigating Officer is not available, the correctors are not to be altered without obtaining the permission of the Commanding Officer.

 (iii) When a ship is wiped, flashed or depermed, she should not be swung until at least 5 hours after completion of the operation. If possible, swinging should be deferred for 24 hours.

Unreliability of an Uncorrected Compass

Cases have occurred where small craft fitted only with a magnetic compass have sailed without having had it corrected, on the assumption that, although not corrected, it would be sufficiently accurate for navigation. In such circumstances the performance would almost certainly be such as to render it useless. It would possibly point vaguely in the direction of some large magnetic object near at hand – e.g. the funnel – merely deviating from side to side as the ship altered course.

The performances of the magnetic compasses of different classes of ship before correction are given below, as an indication of the results that may be expected.

Class of Ship	Deviation found before Correction
Aircraft carrier	up to 22°
Cruiser	up to 50°
Destroyer	up to 87°
Frigate	up to 29°
L.C.T.	up to 90°
L.C.A.	up to 30°

It does not follow that excessive deviation will always be found at an uncorrected compass. In exceptional cases very little correction may be required, particularly where the compass is well away from all steel structures.

Precautions before Swinging Ship

Before swinging ship the following precautions should be taken:

(1) The funnels to be at their normal sea-going temperature.
(2) The ship to be upright to avoid heeling error.
(3) The compass to be tested for friction.
(4) The lubber's point to be checked for coincidence with the fore-and-aft line.
(5) The azimuth prism to be checked for alignment.
(6) All movable iron to be in its sea-going position.
(7) Other ships to keep at least 3 cables clear during the swing.

Notes:

(i) To test a compass for friction, the card should be deflected about 2° by a magnet, and then released. If it comes to rest approximately in its original position the card is reasonably free from friction. This test should be carried out when there is no chance of the ship's head moving – i.e., the ship should be secured fore-and-aft.

(ii) The direction of the lubber's point can normally be observed against the jackstaff or some part of the bows which is known to be in the fore-and-aft line through the compass position. In ships where the compass is off the centre-line, there is normally an engraved plate showing the datum line; otherwise it will be necessary to set up a sighting staff by measurement from the centre-line.

(iii) Instructions for testing the azimuth prism are contained in the azimuth-circle stowage-box, together with a weighted thread. These instructions state that the thread should be stretched taut across the diameter of the circle in the engraved marks provided. When looking straight into the prism, the reflection of the thread should be in coincidence with the engraved line on the face of the prism. Keeping the eye steady, this coincidence should be maintained when the prism is tilted to its limits. If it is not, the azimuth circle should be returned to store as defective.

(iv) It may be objected that, as some methods of swinging ship involve the stern being towed round by a tug, precaution number (7) cannot then be observed. In fact, for small ships, the tug will normally be a wooden steamboat, and in other cases the possibility of the compass being adversely affected is accepted. In the latter case, care should be taken that the tug does not fall alongside the ship.

Preparations before Swinging Ship

Before swinging ship, the following preparations should be made:

Magnets. – Provide spare corrector magnets of appropriate sizes.

Keys. – Provide the binnacle keys; these are kept by the Navigating Officer. In addition, it should be ascertained that the various doors giving access to the correctors can be easily opened.

Flinders Bar. – As this is seldom altered, it should be ascertained that it can in fact be easily removed from its case, so that its length may be checked or altered as required.

Chart. – A chart of the area should be provided on the bridge, to ascertain and check magnetic bearings as required.

Communications. – Communications between the various compass positions, and with the D.G. operating panel, should be tested. A reliable rating should be stationed at each compass, other than the standard, for reading and reporting the ship's head.

Forms. – Two blank copies of Form S.374a, one of S.387, and the Form S.374a containing details of the last swing are required (*see* page 321).

Spanner. – This is required for moving the spheres. On some binnacles the 'B' corrector coils may require slackening in order to obtain access to the nut securing the spheres.

D.G. – The D.G. gear should be ready for operation, with an electrical rating standing by the switches. The covers should be removed from the corrector-coil resistance-boxes. The D.G. coils should be switched on for at least four hours before swinging to allow them to reach their operating temperature.

Methods of Swinging Ship

The ship proceeds to a place where there is some method of comparing compass bearings with magnetic bearings, so that direct values of deviation can be obtained. (This is not necessary for Method 5.)

It has been shown that the deviation changes with heading; the ship is therefore turned at rest, stopping to correct the deviation on the appropriate headings (normally the cardinal points only), and then swung through 360° to obtain the deviations remaining after correction.

There are five methods of swinging ship.

(1) By Bearings of a Distant Object

This method requires the ship's position to be known; the magnetic bearing of the distant object can then be obtained from the chart. Some charts give lines of bearing to distant objects.

In order to keep parallax errors within $\frac{1}{2}$° as the ship is swung, the following minimum distances between object and ship should be observed:

(i) if swinging at a buoy: 4 miles;
(ii) if swinging at single anchor: 6 miles;
(iii) if swinging under way: 10 miles, provided that the ship does not alter her position by more than 160 yards.

The ship should always be as close as possible to her buoy or anchor, and in these conditions the stern is usually towed round by a tug.

The minimum distances given are to some extent affected by the 'stem to standard' distance, and, if a buoy is used, by the state of the tide and depth of water. For accuracy, these factors should be taken into account.

If for any reason, such as bad visibility or scarcity of suitable objects, the above distances cannot be observed, the magnetic bearing must be corrected to allow for the radius of swing. *See* table on page 318.

(2) By Reciprocal Bearing

This normally involves taking bearings of a landing compass or bearing-plate set up ashore, the shore bearings being signalled off visually or by radio. Thus the reciprocal of the signalled bearing from ashore will be equivalent to the magnetic bearing from the ship, and comparison with the compass bearings

CORRECTIONS TO BEARINGS OF DISTANT OBJECT

RADIUS OF SWING	RELATIVE BEARING OF DISTANT OBJECT	DISTANCE OF DISTANT OBJECT					
		1 mile	2 miles	3 miles	4 miles	5 miles	6 miles
100 feet	45° or 135°	0° 40′	0° 20′	0° 15′	0° 10′	0° 05′	0° 05′
	90°	1° 00′	0° 30′	0° 20′	0° 15′	0° 10′	0° 10′
150 feet	45° or 135°	1° 05′	0° 30′	0° 20′	0° 15′	0° 10′	0° 10′
	90°	1° 25′	0° 45′	0° 30′	0° 20′	0° 15′	0° 15′
200 feet	45° or 135°	1° 20′	0° 40′	0° 25′	0° 20′	0° 15′	0° 15′
	90°	1° 55′	1° 00′	0° 40′	0° 30′	0° 25′	0° 20′
250 feet	45° or 135°	1° 40′	0° 50′	0° 35′	0° 25′	0° 20′	0° 15′
	90°	2° 25′	1° 10′	0° 50′	0° 35′	0° 30′	0° 25′
300 feet	45° or 135°	2° 00′	1° 05′	0° 40′	0° 30′	0° 25′	0° 20′
	90°	2° 50′	1° 25′	1° 00′	0° 45′	0° 35′	0° 30′
350 feet	45° or 135°	2° 20′	1° 10′	0° 45′	0° 35′	0° 30′	0° 25′
	90°	3° 20′	1° 40′	1° 05′	0° 50′	0° 40′	0° 35′

gives the deviation. In certain places there are 'magnetic huts', which contain a bearing-plate set up in the magnetic meridian. These are either manned by a party sent from the ship or, more generally, by a standing party provided by the Q.H.M.

Where the bearings are signalled by flags, it is necessary to arrange a system such as:

flag *close up:* 'STAND BY'
flag *dipped* : 'OBSERVE'

but lamp or voice signalling is generally preferred.

One advantage of the reciprocal-bearing method is that, within wide limits, the ship is not restricted in her movements, so that turning is facilitated.

A swing by this method may also be carried out between two ships, one of which has a recently corrected compass. She is then able to signal corrected magnetic bearings to the ship requiring adjustment.

An example of a completed Form S.374a for a swing by reciprocal bearings is given in Volume III.

(3) BY AZIMUTH OF A HEAVENLY BODY

The elevation of the body should be less than 30°, since the levelling of the compass bowl is only approximate; the rate of change of azimuth should be small. The sun is suitable for observation at rising and setting although, of course, the time is limited at setting.

True bearings can be obtained from the *Tables of Computed Altitude and Azimuth* (H.D.486) or from Weir's Diagram for the period of the swing, tabulated for intervals of about 4 minutes and converted to magnetic bearings.

An example of a completed Form S.374a for a swing by this method is given in Volume III.

Using this method the ship is not restricted in her movements.

If neither azimuth tables nor Weir's Diagram is available, the following method may be adopted, provided that there is no coefficient A or E present. (These are explained in Volume III. At a well-placed compass they should both be negligible.)

The bearing of the sun is observed on the normal number of headings, starting and finishing on the same heading, and the time of each observation is noted.

If the total change in azimuth is $x°$, and the total time taken is y minutes, then the rate of change of azimuth is $\dfrac{x°}{y}$ per minute.

From each observed bearing, deduct the calculated change in azimuth since zero time, and thus obtain a corrected bearing. The mean of these corrected bearings will then be the magnetic bearing at the time of the first observation. Subsequent magnetic bearings are then obtained, as required for each heading, by applying the calculated change in azimuth.

(4) By Transits

For this method, the ship turns at rest on the known bearing of two or more conspicuous objects in line.

Although this method has certain advantages, such as no possibility of parallax error, it is very often difficult to turn on a single transit if there is any wind, sea, or stream, and so this method is liable to take longer than others.

It may happen, however, that two or more transits are available. These may be quite separate, or a number of objects widely spaced may form transits with one common front or rear object. When this is the case, the ship may be positioned on any of the transits as convenient during the swing, and manoeuvring will thus be facilitated.

(5) By Gyro-compass

This is a convenient method to use while placing corrector magnets, but should only be used for obtaining deviations if no other method is practicable, since the accuracy of the deviations is dependent upon the accuracy of the gyro-compass.

Obtaining the Deviations of Between-deck Compasses

When a ship is being swung, the swinging officer must be informed of the positions of all the compasses in the ship. He must see that they are all adjusted, that good communication exists, and that a deviation table is produced for each.

The deviations of between-deck compasses are obtained by comparison of ship's head with the standard compass. An example (Form S.374a) is given in Volume III.

The deviations may be obtained by the following calculations:

EXAMPLE 1

On ship's head North by standard compass the deviation of the standard compass was found to be 1½°W.

Therefore, by definition, standard compass North is 1½° to the west of magnetic North (Fig. 199a).

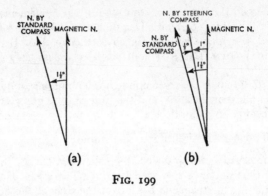

(a)   (b)

FIG. 199

Now, on this heading the steering compass was found to indicate a ship's head of $359\frac{1}{2}$°C. Therefore steering compass North will be $\frac{1}{2}$° to the east of this, which makes it only 1° to the west of magnetic North. In other words, the deviation of the steering compass is 1°W. (Fig. 199b).

The same result can be obtained mathematically by applying deviation to the standard compass according to the normal rule, to obtain the magnetic heading; then comparison between that and the heading of the steering compass gives the deviation of the latter, thus:

Standard compass heading	000°C.
Deviation of standard compass	$1\frac{1}{2}$°W.
Magnetic heading	$358\frac{1}{2}$°M.
Steering compass heading	$359\frac{1}{2}$°C.
Deviation of steering compass	1°W.

EXAMPLE 2

On ship's head S.W. by standard compass (225°C.) the deviation of the standard compass was found to be 2°E.

Therefore S.W. by standard compass is situated 2° away from magnetic S.W., as shown in Fig. 200.

Now, on this heading the steering compass was found to indicate a ship's head of $227\frac{1}{2}$°C. Therefore S.W. by steering compass will be $\frac{1}{2}$° away from magnetic S.W., i.e., deviation of the steering compass is $\frac{1}{2}$° West.

Mathematically, this can be calculated as follows:

Standard compass heading	225°C.
Deviation of standard compass	2°E.
Magnetic heading	227°M.
Steering compass heading	$227\frac{1}{2}$°C.
Deviation of steering compass	$\frac{1}{2}$°W.

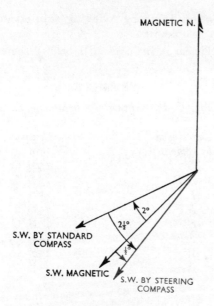

MAGNETIC N.

2°

2½°

S.W. BY STANDARD
COMPASS

½°

S.W. MAGNETIC

S.W. BY STEERING
COMPASS

FIG. 200

Procedure for Swinging Ship

The procedure is described, with examples, in Volume III.

During the operation, signals from the International Code are displayed.

Forms and Returns relating to the Magnetic Compass

(a) Form S.374a is supplied for the purpose of keeping a record of the deviations of all the compasses. It should be used whenever a ship is swung; one copy should be forwarded to the Director of the Compass Division, and the other kept in the ship's Navigational Data Book.

Anything likely to affect the compass which has occurred since the last occasion of rendering the form (such as alterations in the ship's structure or armament), or likely to affect the accuracy of the swing which is being recorded (such as the nearness of other ships, or the rapidity of the swing), should be noted in the 'Remarks' space of Form S.374a.

(b) Form S.387 is an abridged version of this form and is intended to be kept in the vicinity of the compass concerned.

(c) Whenever H.M. ships or craft are being swung by naval officers, the swinging officer is to make a careful examination of the compass, its equipment and surroundings, satisfying himself that the safe distances have not been infringed and that the equipment is in every way efficient. He should also inspect the compass-corrector coils, resistance-boxes, etc.

In the event of his finding any defects or any items which are improperly fitted or placed, he should report the matter to the Commanding Officer and note it in the 'Remarks' space when rendering the Form S.374a, a copy of which should on this occasion be forwarded to the administrative authority of the ship or craft.

Checking the Deviation Table by swinging ship on an object the true bearing of which is unknown

For this method coefficient A (*see Note* (i), below) should be zero, or of known account.

EXAMPLE

At a well-placed compass the bearings of a lighthouse, distant 16 miles, were found to be:

Ship's head (by compass)	Compass bearing
N.	156½°C.
N.E.	153½°C.
E.	151½°C.
S.E.	151½°C.
S.	151½°C.
S.W.	153½°C.
W.	156° C.
N.W.	156° C.

8) 1230

Mean =   153¾°

This mean bearing can be assumed to be the magnetic bearing of the lighthouse. Therefore the deviation table will be as follows:

SHIP'S HEAD (COMPASS)	MAGNETIC BEARING	COMPASS BEARING	DEVIATION (*if Coeff. A = 0*)	DEVIATION (*if Coeff. A = + ½*)
N.	153¾°M.	156½°C.	2¾°W.	2¼°W.
N.E.	153¾°M.	153½°C.	¼°E.	¾°E.
E.	153¾°M.	151½°C.	2¼°E.	2¾°E.
S.E.	153¾°M.	151½°C.	2¼°E.	2¾°E.
S.	153¾°M.	151½°C.	2¼°E.	2¾°E.
S.W.	153¾°M.	153½°C.	¼°E.	¾°E.
W.	153¾°M.	156°C.	2¼°W.	1¾°W.
N.W.	153¾°M.	156°C.	2¼°W.	1¾°W.

Notes:

(i) The coefficients are described in Volume III. A coefficient A of + ½° is equivalent to a deviation of ½°E. on all headings. It will thus increase the easterly and decrease the westerly deviations found by observation, as shown in the last column. Its value may be found on the back of Form S.374a.

(ii) In the above example, for the sake of brevity, only eight headings have been tabulated. In practice, the swing should be carried out on sixteen points.

OBSERVATION OF VARIATION AT SEA

In many parts of the world it is difficult to compute the probable position of the isogonic curves shown on Admiralty variation charts, and the correct value may be doubtful within several degrees. Instructions will be found in *Queen's Regulations and Admiralty Instructions* to the effect that observations of variation are to be made at every opportunity. These should be rendered to the Hydrographer on Form H.488, Record of Observations for Variation.

Observations at frequent intervals are desirable, particularly where the isogonic lines run close together and where the ship's track crosses them at a broad angle. Isolated observations are always of value, however.

Method of obtaining the Variation

Observations should be made with the standard compass on eight or sixteen equidistant headings, the ship being steadied for at least four minutes on each heading while bearings are obtained of the sun or other heavenly body, or of a distant object.

If the azimuth of the heavenly body is calculated, the difference between this true bearing and the compass bearing will give the total compass error.

The mean of the compass errors, corrected for Coefficient A if necessary, will give the variation.

Two sets of observations should be obtained – one set with the ship swinging to starboard and the other set with the ship swinging to port. The mean of the results should be used.

EXAMPLE

A ship was known to have Coefficient A of −1°. The following observations of the Sun were made:

Ship's head (compass)	Compass bearing	True bearing	Compass error
N.	250°C.	260°	10°E.
N.E.	250°C.	260½°	10½°E.
E.	250°C.	261°	11°E.
S.E.	251°C.	261¼°	10¼°E.
S.	251½°C.	261¾°	10¼°E.
S.W.	253°C.	262°	9°E.
W.	253½°C.	262¼°	8¾°E.
N.W.	254°C.	262½°	8½°E.

$$8 \,)\, 78\tfrac{1}{2}°$$

$$\text{Mean compass error} = 9\tfrac{3}{4}°\text{E.}$$
$$\text{Coefficient A} = 1°$$

$$\therefore \text{Variation} = 10\tfrac{3}{4}°\text{E.}$$

Note: In this example it is assumed that Coefficient A has been obtained as the result of a previous swing. Unless this swing was very recent, undue reliance cannot be placed on the variation obtained by this method.

OBSERVATION OF VARIATION ON LAND

Pattern 2 Landing Compasses (with calibration cards) and Pattern 41 Tripods are issued to Commanders-in-Chief at home and abroad for the purpose of obtaining observations of variation on shore. A theodolite fitted with an accurately-aligned magnetic needle is, however, a better instrument to use if it is available. The list of 'Spots suitable for Magnetic Observations' which previously appeared in the *Sailing Directions* will, in future, be omitted since any such observations, particularly abroad, may be of value.

Selection of Site

The site chosen for observations should be free from local magnetic influences such as iron drains, reinforced concrete, iron buildings or similar objects, and the observer must ensure that he has no magnetic material on his person. It is preferable that the position of the site should be known to within one minute of latitude and longitude, but sufficiently valuable data can be obtained if the position is known to within five miles.

Methods of making the Observation

By Theodolite. – Set up the instrument in the normal way and zero it accurately on magnetic north. Observe the magnetic bearings of one or more heavenly bodies at low altitude (preferably less than 30°), timing each observation. Several observations should be taken.

Work out the true bearings of the bodies at the time of observation, and thus obtain the variation.

By Landing Compass, Pattern 2. – Take care to set up the instrument truly level by the bubble. Observe the bearing of one or more heavenly bodies at less than 5° altitude, timing each observation. Several observations should be taken.

Apply the compass error, as tabulated in the calibration table, to the observations to obtain the magnetic bearings.

Work out the true bearings of the bodies at the times of observation, and thus obtain the variation.

Since no illumination is provided for this compass, observations are best made in daylight.

The value of the observations, in either of the above cases, will be enhanced if observations can be made over a period of days, and at different times of the day, in order to eliminate short period anomalies.

Reference: Admiralty Manual of Hydrographic Surveying.

COMPASSES AND BINNACLES

Descriptions of the principal types of non-transmitting compasses and binnacles fitted in H.M. ships are given below.

(a) Pattern 0195A Compass and Pattern 190 Binnacle

These are fitted in the majority of H.M. ships. The compass card (6 in. diameter) is made of mica and is secured to a nickel-silver float to which are attached two needles. The needles are cased in nickel-silver to prevent rust. The point of support is a sapphire cap inside the float. This rests on an iridium pivot, as shown in Fig. 201.

The compass bowl is made of brass, with a plain glass top and a frosted glass bottom to diffuse the artificial lighting placed beneath it. Between the frosted glass bottom and the sides of the bowl is the corrugated diaphragm which allows for expansion and contraction of the liquid filling of the bowl as the

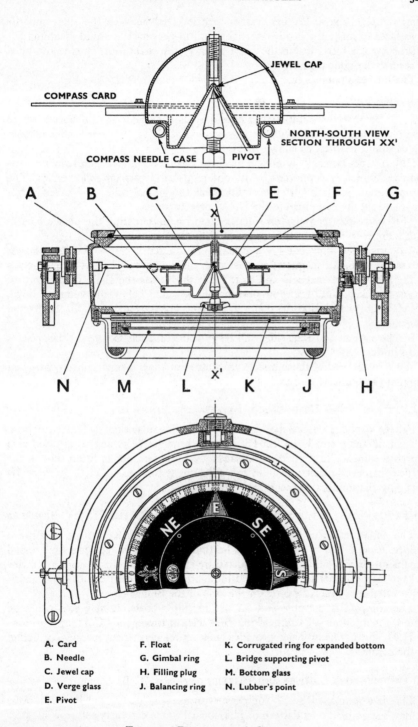

FIG. 201. Pattern 0195A Compass

A. Card
B. Needle
C. Jewel cap
D. Verge glass
E. Pivot
F. Float
G. Gimbal ring
H. Filling plug
J. Balancing ring
K. Corrugated ring for expanded bottom
L. Bridge supporting pivot
M. Bottom glass
N. Lubber's point

temperature changes. Rubber washers are inserted between the sides and the glass faces to make the bowl watertight, and to prevent the liquid escaping.

Brackets are fitted inside the bowl to carry the pivot, and outside the bowl to receive the gimbal pivots.

The lubber's point is fixed inside the bowl.

Suspension

In order that the compass card shall remain as near to the horizontal as possible, it is suspended with its pivoting point above the centre of gravity of the card and needles, as shown in Fig. 201.

Pattern 190 binnacle is shown in Fig. 202. The upper part contains the compass, which is supported by its outer gimbal-pivots on roller boxes. The compass may be lifted out after sliding back the gimbal roller-box cover-plates. Surrounding the compass are the D.G. corrector-coils.

The centre part contains an electric lamp for illuminating the compass card, with a dimmer switch on the after side of the binnacle.

A door on the after side gives access to numbered holes for the fore-and-aft horizontal corrector magnets; another door on the port side gives similar access to the athwartship magnets and to the clip that holds the chain of the vertical magnet bucket at its required position in the tube below the compass bowl. Wooden blocks fit inside the doors to prevent any movement of the horizontal magnets.

Brackets are fitted to the sides and front of the binnacle to support the spheres and Flinders bar.

Holes in the feet of the binnacle are slotted to allow a small movement when aligning the binnacle fore and aft.

(b) PATTERN 0188A COMPASS AND PATTERN 189 BINNACLE

Pattern 0188A Compass (3¼-in. card) is similar in design to Pattern 0195A, but considerably smaller. With Pattern 189 binnacle (Fig. 203) it is fitted as a portable compass in certain submarines. No Flinders bar is fitted, nor is the vertical magnet bucket movable; the adjustment for heeling error is made by changing the number of magnets.

(c) PATTERN 0183 COMPASS (BOAT'S COMPASS) AND PATTERN 1830V BINNACLE

The construction of the compass (4¼-in. card) is similar to that of Pattern 0188A, except that it has no glass bottom. The bottom consists of a metal expansion chamber that can be adjusted by a screw. The nut to work the screw is kept in the inside of the cover. Illumination of the card comes from an oil lamp fitted in a bracket casing on the side of the binnacle.

The compass is portable and for use in ship's boats. It may sometimes be found, mounted on a Pattern 1830V binnacle, in Emergency Conning Positions of H.M. ships. The binnacle provides facilities for permanent magnet correction of the compass.

(d) PATTERN 0919 COMPASS AND PATTERN 917 OR 917C BASEBOARD

This is a gimballed boat's compass, with a 3½-in. card, used in small craft. It may be mounted on a Pattern 917 baseboard which can carry soft iron spheres. Permanent magnet correction is provided by a Pattern 1135 corrector box fitted

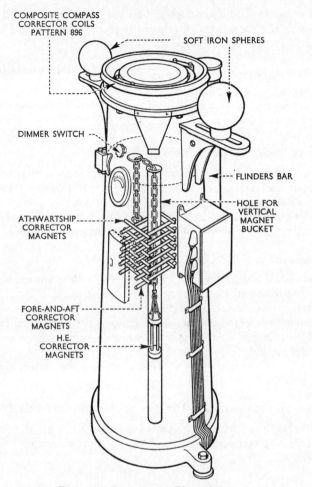

FIG. 202. Pattern 190 Binnacle

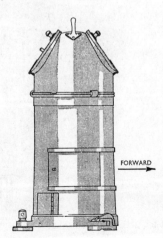

FIG. 203. Pattern 189 Binnacle

below the compass. Additional fore-and-aft magnets can be added in clips on the baseboard. If Pattern 917C baseboard is used, correction of D.G. can also be effected.

(e) Pattern 01151A Compass and Pattern 917 or 917C Baseboard

This compass, with a $3\frac{7}{8}$-in. card, is similar to Pattern 0919 compass, but it has a sprung instead of gimballed bowl and is intended for use in fast craft. It may be mounted and corrected in the same way as a Pattern 0919 compass.

Projector or Reflector Compasses

A projector compass is one in which the lubber's line and the relevant portion of the compass card are viewed as an image projected through a system of lenses upon a suitable screen adjacent to the helmsman's position.

A reflector compass is one in which the image of the compass card is viewed by direct reflection in a mirror adjacent to the helmsman's position.

(a) Pattern 29P and 33P Compasses

These projector compasses, fitted in a watertight tube known as a projector binnacle, are situated in the conning tower of some of the older submarines in order that the best available compass position, free of ferrous material and magnetic equipment, may be obtained. An image of the lubber's line and relevant portion of the compass card is projected down the tube to the steering position in the control room.

The Pattern 29P compass has a $3\frac{1}{4}$-in. card, and the Pattern 33P compass has a $2\frac{1}{2}$-in. card.

(b) Pattern 0921 Compass and Pattern 922Z series Binnacle (Fig. 204)

This compass, in a Pattern 922Z series binnacle, has a $4\frac{1}{4}$-in. card and is an overhead reflecting compass, used as a steering compass in small vessels up to about trawler size.

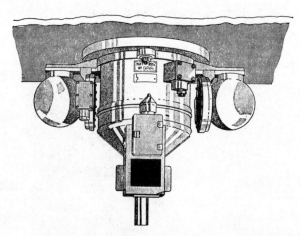

FIG. 204. Pattern 0921 Compass and Pattern 922Z series Binnacle

(c) A.C.O. PROJECTOR, TYPE 51

This consists of a Pattern 52 compass in a Pattern 53 binnacle and is a small Projector designed for fitting in certain Landing Craft. Adequate separation is thereby provided between the compass and the magnetic material of the hull, as well as the ferrous equipment that landing craft carry in operation. It is intended as a steering compass only and cannot be used for taking bearings.

(d) PROJECTOR OR REFLECTOR COMPASSES OF COMMERCIAL DESIGN

In ships designed with the Wheelhouse immediately below the Bridge, particularly R.F.A.s, compasses of this type may be found, mounted on the bridge, as the Standard Compass of the ship. The lubber line and relevant portions of the compass card are projected or reflected through a tube in the binnacle to the helmsman in the wheelhouse.

The advantages of this type of compass are as follows:

(1) Only one compass to correct instead of two. (A spare compass is always carried should the one in use become defective.)

(2) The design of the wheelhouse and its equipment is not restricted by the requirement to provide a good magnetic compass position for the steering compass.

(3) There is more space in the wheelhouse in the absence of a steering compass and binnacle.

(4) Reduction in compass corrector coil equipment and associated wiring from two sets to one.

Care and Maintenance

Paint. – Wooden binnacles should not in general be painted. Should painting become necessary, care must be taken that the various doors are free to open. Metal binnacles should be repainted only with the correct kind of corrosion-resisting paint.

Repairs. – The work of testing and repairing compasses is carried out mainly at the Admiralty Compass Observatory, Slough. Defective compasses and accessories must be returned through the Naval Store Officer and new items drawn to replace them. They are not to be sent to commercial compass firms or instrument makers for repair.

H.M. Dockyards undertake minor repairs to binnacles.

Keys. – The Navigating Officer is responsible for the binnacle keys. Binnacles should be kept locked.

ALTERATION OF POSITIONS OF BINNACLES

The positions of binnacles are not to be altered without Admiralty authority.

REMOVING A BUBBLE

A bubble generally indicates a leak and therefore a defective compass, which should be returned at the first opportunity and a new one drawn to replace it.

Compasses are supplied with their bowls filled with a mixture of alcohol and distilled water. The alcohol is added to reduce the freezing-point of the mixture.

If a bubble forms and it is not possible to exchange the compass, it is better to remove the bubble because it makes the compass less accurate and harder to read. Bubbles are removed as follows:

(1) *Compasses fitted with corrugated expansion chambers*

Unship the bowl from its gimbals and lay it on its side with the filling-hole uppermost. Remove the plug from the filling-hole and fill the bowl with distilled water. During this procedure rock the bowl from side to side to assist any air to escape. Unless the temperature is taken into account, movement of the expansion chamber may have injurious results, so this should not normally be pressed to assist the expulsion of air. When all the air has been removed, replace the filling plug.

(2) *Compasses fitted with nut-and-screw expansion chambers*

Take the nut from its stowage position and turn the compass so that the filling-plug is uppermost. Remove the filling-plug, place the nut on the expansion screw thread, and screw it hard up. Fill the bowl with distilled water, rocking it to assist the air to escape. When the water overflows, unscrew the nut about two turns. This will cause more water to overflow. Replace the filling-plug and unscrew and remove the nut. This leaves the bowl with a slight pressure inside it.

RULES FOR THE ARRANGEMENT OF STRUCTURES AND FITTINGS IN THE VICINITY OF MAGNETIC COMPASSES AND CHRONOMETERS

(*Extract from B.R. 100*)

'1. The magnetic compasses and associated equipment to be fitted in H.M. ships, together with the grading of the position in which each is to be fitted, are stated in the Staff Requirements. During the early stages of design the compass positions to fulfil these requirements are indicated on the drawings by the Director General, Ships, and, after concurrence by departments concerned, these positions are approved by the Board. When approval has been given the compass positions are not to be changed without Admiralty authority (vide Q.R. and A.I.).

2. The reliability and accuracy of magnetic and gyro-magnetic compasses are dependent to a great degree upon their position in the ship and upon the proximity of magnetic and electrical equipment to that position. Varying degrees of reliability and accuracy can be accepted, depending upon the function which a particular compass is intended to perform. Various grades of compass position can therefore be permitted.

Functions of Magnetic Compasses

3. The main functions of magnetic compasses in H.M. ships are defined as follows:

(a) The STANDARD COMPASS is a magnetic or gyro-magnetic compass which provides the primary means of navigation. It should be fitted in a

Grade I position. Such a compass, or a repeater from it, is to be sited at the position from which the vessel is ordinarily navigated, and the view of the horizon from this position is to be as uninterrupted as possible for the purpose of taking bearings.

(b) The SECONDARY COMPASS is a magnetic compass which provides a secondary means of navigating the ship. It should be fitted in a Grade II position or better.

(c) The STEERING COMPASS is a magnetic compass which provides the primary means of steering the ship. It should be fitted in a Grade II position or better.

(d) THE STAND-BY STEERING COMPASS is a magnetic compass which provides a secondary means of steering the ship. It should be fitted in a Grade III position or better.

(e) An EMERGENCY COMPASS is one fitted for the purpose of conning or steering the vessel after action damage and/or breakdown of all other means of doing so. It should be fitted in a Grade IV position or better.

Notes:

(i) A gyro-magnetic compass is on a par with a gyro-compass as a navigational aid and, if fitted, provides a primary means of navigating. It follows that such a compass should always be accorded a Grade I position.

(ii) (a), (b), (c) and (d) above are normally provided with correction for the effects of degaussing coils in ships so fitted.

Grades of Compass Position

4. The grading of each compass position in the ship is to be entered in the Navigational Data Book and is also to be indicated at the compass position by an engraved plate attached to the binnacle. Suitable plates will be supplied from the Compass Division at Slough. They are to be demanded by the Principal Ship Overseer or Dockyard Officers for new construction ships and fitted by the shipbuilder. For ships other than new construction, the plates will be supplied from Slough on demand and are to be fitted by ship's staff.

5. A GRADE I position is such that it is expected to remain magnetically stable within small limits over a period of several months, i.e., the compass in it, after adjustment, should be steady and the deviations over such a period should remain within 2° of the residual deviations as determined at the time of the adjustment.

A GRADE II position implies reasonable magnetic stability over a period of months. A compass in such a position, after adjustment, should be steady and the deviations over such a period should remain within 5° of the residual deviations as determined at the time of the adjustment.

A GRADE III position implies reasonable magnetic stability over a period of some weeks. A compass in such a position, after adjustment, should be steady and the deviations over such a period should remain within 5° of the residual deviations as determined at the time of the adjustment.

A GRADE IV position is such that the magnetic conditions are unlikely to change to such an extent as to render the compass useless. The deviations of a compass in such a position after adjustment, should remain for some weeks within 10° of the residual deviations determined at the time of the adjustment.

Rules concerning Ship's Structure and Fittings

6. In order to ensure that the various grades of compass position shall not be prejudiced by the proximity of magnetic material, or of magnetic or electrical equipment, the following rules are to be observed:

(a) MAGNETIC MATERIAL which may be regarded as part of the ship's structure must not be placed nearer to the compass position than is indicated in the following table:

	Grade I feet	Grade II feet	Grades III and IV feet
(i) Fixed material other than (ii) . .	10*	6	4
(ii) The deck above or below the compass may be made of magnetic material provided it does not pass closer to the compass than	10*	3½	2½
(iii) Magnetic material subject to movement	12	9	6
(iv) Large masses of magnetic material with variable fields such as turrets, launchers, funnels, etc.	20	15	—

Items of equipment such as mounting racks, shock mountings, pedestals, etc., which are normally bolted securely to the ship's structure, should be treated as part of the latter.

The vicinity of extremities of elongated masses of magnetic material should be avoided as a compass position.

(b) MAGNETIC OR ELECTRICAL EQUIPMENT fitted in the neighbourhood of a magnetic compass may produce a deviation of the compass. In order to prevent the introduction of an unacceptable deviation, after correction of the compass, due to the removal or replacement of any one item, it is laid down in general terms that at a Grade I compass position no one item of equipment must cause a deviation greater than ¼°. Similarly at a Grade II or Grade III position the deviation caused must not exceed 1°, and at a Grade IV position 2°. The distances which fulfil these requirements, and which are measured between the centre of the compass and the nearest point of the item of equipment, are known as 'SAFE DISTANCES' and are given in Appendices II and III of B.R. 100.

(c) MAGNETIC COMPASSES must not be placed nearer to one another than 6 feet, or 4 feet if corrector magnets not longer than four inches are used.

(d) CHRONOMETERS. – The minimum distances between chronometers and electrical fittings should be one-eighth of those laid down for a Grade I compass position.

(e) ELECTRIC WIRING in the vicinity of magnetic compasses must be arranged non-inductively and clips or conduits must be of non-magnetic material.

---

* In coastal and inshore craft with non-magnetic hulls these distances may be reduced to 8 feet.

7. It is possible that the combination of a multiplicity of electrical and magnetic equipment fitted at or near the safe distance specified for each of the various items, together, possibly, with that of the structural material, may prevent the compass from acting effectively in the role allocated to it. If such a case arises in service it will be necessary to take special measures to improve the compass position concerned. Conversely, in small vessels it may be impossible to avoid all infringements of safe distances. If, in the case of new construction or ships being modernised, it appears from an examination of the drawings that either of the above situations is likely to arise, it is the responsibility of the Director, Compass Division, after due consideration of the layout around the compass position as a whole, to suggest limited concessions either on behalf of the compass or on behalf of the equipment concerned, in order to ensure that the best compromise is reached and that the compass will remain effective within the limits stipulated for the grade of the position in which it is fitted.

8. When determining the 'safe distance' of large items of equipment such as radar sets, it is sometimes permissible to make a distinction between those parts which are readily interchangeable and those which consist of large masses, the exchange of which would entail a considerable amount of work. In such cases the 'safe distance' of any item which is readily interchangeable is laid down in the normal manner, so that it may be removed or exchanged without appreciably affecting the compass. The remainder of the equipment, comprising the 'large masses', is treated as part of the ship's structure (*vide* paragraph 6 (a)), and if it is removed or exchanged the compass affected must be re-adjusted.'

EFFECT OF DEGAUSSING ON THE MAGNETIC COMPASS

'Degaussing' is the term applied to methods of protecting shipping against the danger of magnetic mines. The subject is fully explained in the *Manual of Degaussing* (B.R. 825). In view of the fact that the technique is constantly changing, and is largely confidential, a description of the various types of installation will not be attempted here.

Although degaussing may neutralize the ship's magnetic field in the neighbourhood of a magnetic mine, the resultant field at the compass position may well be greater than would be the case if the ship were not degaussed. Some compensation will therefore be required in order to ensure that additional deviations of the compass are not introduced when the degaussing equipment is in operation.

In most cases this compensation is effected by fitting 'compass-corrector coils' to the magnetic compass binnacle. These corrector-coils are linked to the ship's degaussing coils so as to counteract at the compass the additional coefficients B and C, and Heeling Error, introduced when the degaussing coils are energized.

Responsibility for Compass Adjustment

In all ships, the responsibility for making final adjustments to compass-corrector coils lies with the officer or compass adjuster carrying out the adjustment.

During the inspection of D.G. equipment, before H.M. ships are swung for adjustment of compasses, the Admiralty D.G. representative (or the S.E.E. or E.E.M., as the case may be) attending the inspection is responsible that all compass-corrector coils are functioning correctly.

Full instructions for the testing and adjustment of compass-corrector coils are contained in B.R. 825.

CHAPTER X

Transmitting Compasses

WHEN it was becoming increasingly difficult to find a suitable position for a magnetic compass on the bridge, a transmitting magnetic compass was developed, the Admiralty Transmitting Magnetic Compass (A.T.M.C.). The master unit could be placed in a good magnetic position, and the repeaters where needed.

Any magnetic compass will suffer considerable disturbance if subjected to violent movements in a seaway, particularly if there is any uncorrected heeling error. It is for this reason that a magnetic compass does not make an entirely satisfactory datum, particularly in small ships. These disturbances are of short duration, depending on the periods of the compass card and the ship; they are equally disposed about a mean heading which, in a closely-corrected compass, is the magnetic meridian.

The Admiralty Gyro-Magnetic Compass (A.G.M.C.) uses this 'averaging' property of a magnetic compass combined with the short-term stability of a free gyroscope to enable true heading, which is free from unsteadiness, to be obtained from the magnetic compass. It also provides transmission to the ship's repeater system as does the gyro-compass.

General Principle of the A.G.M.C.

A free gyroscope is one which is not controlled in any way, and can wander in azimuth. If carefully balanced such an instrument can be made to have a low rate of wander and can, over a short period of time, be used to fix a datum in space. It can, for instance, serve admirably to determine the angle through which a ship turns and, if provided with a transmission system, it can show such an alteration of course on repeaters.

The free gyroscope in the A.G.M.C. is fitted with a small transmitter that feeds a receiver which, in conjunction with a simple follow-up system, an amplifier and a motor, drives a set of transmitters, M-type and magslip. These operate repeaters and provide a system stabilized in azimuth over a limited period of time.

The transmission from the gyro is also made to drive the *bowl* of the magnetic compass. This bowl, suitably inscribed with a 360° scale, remains fixed in azimuth as the binnacle outside it turns with the ship. The compass card, by virtue of its magnetic property, also remains stabilized in azimuth when the ship turns, so that the bowl and the card remain in the same position relative to one another.

The magnetic compass in the A.G.M.C. has a Wheatstone bridge arrangement whereby a correcting signal is generated if the north point of the compass card and the lubber's line on the compass bowl are not in alignment. The correcting signal feeds into the transmitting system through a reduction gear, and so gradually turns the whole of the repeater system, including the compass bowl, until the lubber's line is once more aligned on compass North. Thus, although the axis of the gyroscope may be pointing in any direction, the repeater system and the compass bowl become north-seeking. Moreover, when the gyroscope drifts, as it will, it will disturb the compass bowl and a correction will be applied to the transmission which will cancel the rate of drift. This is called Monitoring. Since the gyroscope has a very low random wander rate the correction rate can be kept very small and, as will be seen later, this is of considerable significance.

When the compass card is disturbed, a 'false' correction will be applied to the transmission system which will try to displace the repeaters from North. Owing to the fact that the rate of correction is small, the repeater system will be displaced by only a negligible amount during the few seconds that the card is deflected one way before the card crosses the meridian and the deflection is reversed.

We have then, in brief, a transmission and repeater system governed by a magnetic compass to make it north-seeking, and by a gyroscope to damp out the short period perturbations of the compass card. There is neither latitude nor speed error in the system, so that many of the chief drawbacks of both a gyro-compass and a magnetic compass are obviated.

A.G.M. 5 AND 6

These systems are practically the same, but the A.G.M. 5 can only provide 10-minute M-type transmissions, whereas the A.G.M. 6 provides 10-minute M-type transmissions for navigational instruments and coarse and fine magslip transmission to a Compass Retransmission Unit from which further magslip and M-type services are available. The A.G.M. 6 is thus a complete alternative to the gyro-compass.

The two systems have the following principal items of equipment:

	A.G.M.5	A.G.M.6
Master Unit	Pattern 8130	Pattern 8160
Binnacle	Pattern 8132	Pattern 8132
Gyro Unit	Pattern 8112	Pattern 8161
D.A.T.E.C.	Pattern 8136	Pattern 8164
Meter Panel	Pattern 8140	Pattern 8167

A.G.M. 6 is described in the next pages and, where the difference between A.G.M. 5 and A.G.M. 6 is significant, the details of A.G.M. 5 are also given.

Master Unit

This is a magnetic compass that is able to compare the direction indicated by the transmission system, which includes the free gyroscope, the compass bowl and the repeaters, with the magnetic meridian. It generates a signal when there is any discrepancy between these two headings so that the transmission is 'monitored' to the magnetic compass heading.

By providing a lubber's line in the binnacle and a scale on the bowl showing ship's head, the bowl of the compass acts as a repeater from the gyroscope.

In order to derive a correcting signal from a magnetic compass without imposing any reactive torque on the magnet system, the compass is modified in such a way as to make it part of an electrical resistance bridge. A set of platinum electrodes is fitted to the inside of the bowl and a thin strip of platinum is attached to the southern rim of the card, including about 180° of arc.

The compass liquid is made conducting by the addition of a small amount of lithium chloride.

Fig. 205. Admiralty Gyro-Magnetic Compass in Binnacle and with plinth

Any disturbance of the bowl and card relative to each other creates a small potential difference across the bridge which, when amplified, provides a usable signal to drive the bowl (and repeaters) into alignment with the compass card.

Binnacle (Fig. 205)

The binnacle is made of aluminium alloy and treated to resist corrosion from salt air. It is usually mounted on a plinth to bring the compass up to normal height. It is watertight and the cover should normally be in place.

The corrector-coil unit contains three sets of coils, B, C and H.E., which, when adjusted, counteract the effect of the ship's degaussing coils at the compass position.

The terminal cover carries a dimmer for the compass illumination and a switch marked ON, OFF and E.B. whereby the main low power supply or an emergency dry battery, fitted in the body casing, may be used to light the compass lamp.

In the lower part there are fore-and-aft and athwartship corrector-magnet racks and a bucket for the heeling error corrector-magnets.

The Flinders bar is usually fitted on the fore side of the binnacle and may be slewed up to 45°. The spheres can be slewed up to 10°.

Gyro Unit (Fig. 206)

The gyro unit, which consists of an a.c.-driven 4-inch gyroscope, may be sited in any convenient place, usually close to the console.

The Console

The Console, containing the electrical control gear, amplifiers, fuses and the D.A.T.E.C. panel, can be sited in any convenient place, usually the low-power room or gyro room.

D.A.T.E.C. (Fig. 207)

This is the Differential and Alignment Unit and Total Error Corrector.

DIFFERENTIAL UNIT

This is an electrical differential to overcome the drift of the gyroscope and to ensure that only a small part of the yaw of the compass card is transmitted to the repeaters. The rates (monitoring rates) are selected as follows:

(a) *A.G.M. 5.* – In the four-position control switch:

NORM. – This is the position in which the equipment must be operated in normal conditions. The monitoring rate is approximately 4°/min.

SET. – This position is used for quick settling with a monitoring rate of 40°/min.

(b) *A.G.M. 6.* – In the five-position control switch:

MONITORING 4·0. – This is used in the final stage of settling.

MONITORING 0·8. – This is the normal setting for small craft and a rough weather setting for larger ships.

MONITORING 0·4. – This is the calm weather setting for larger ships.

Notes:

1. For rapid settling when the gyro is started, a screw driver control is provided under plug ML.

2. The GYRO position on the D.A.T.E.C. panel is normally used only for testing.

FIG. 206. Gyro Unit

FIG. 207. D.A.T.E.C., Pattern 8164

ALIGNMENT INDICATOR

This is connected to the monitoring motor. When the system is lined up correctly with respect to the magnetic meridian the indicator rests in the central position. A signal applied to the motor deflects the indicator to show black or white in the window. Except in the calmest of weather the indicator will oscillate about the central position.

TOTAL ERROR CORRECTOR

Variation is applied manually. Deviation is fed to coils in the Master Unit, deflecting the card so that it gives *magnetic* and not compass headings. This is done through a potentiometer controlled by the position of a cam cut to the residual deviations after compass adjustment. The current in the deviation coils varies with the amount of deviation, but for a given deviation the effect of this current on the card will vary with magnetic latitude, due to the change in H (the horizontal component of the Earth's magnetic field).

Balancing Potentiometer (Fig. 208)

The function of the Balancing Potentiometer at the Master Unit is to enable the internal lubber's line to be lined up with 000° on the card by an adjustment of the potentiometer current.

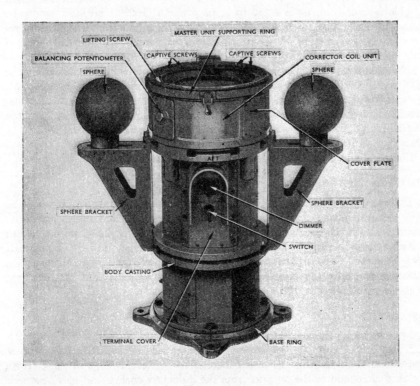

FIG. 208. Master Unit in Binnacle, Pattern 8132, with hood removed

Capabilities

ACCURACY. – Given a correctly-adjusted compass, a single observation of bearing or heading is unlikely to be in error more than $\frac{1}{2}°$.

TRUE HEADING. – True headings are supplied to the repeaters.

AVAILABILITY. – The equipment is ready for use about five minutes after switching on. No settling period is needed.

VERSATILITY. – If the gyro fails the compass can still be used as a transmitting magnetic compass by putting the D.A.T.E.C. control switch to MAG. If all power fails the compass can, of course, be used as a direct-reading compass when the bowl must be locked to ship's head.

A.G.M. 7

The Inductor Compass

In the Admiralty Gyro-Magnetic Compass, Type 7, the magnetic compass takes the form of what is known as an Inductor-type Detector Unit. This is a static device with no moving parts (except for the gimbals). Instead of having a pivoted magnetic system and card for determining the direction of the Earth's magnetic field, saturable inductors (magnetometers) are used to measure the strength of the magnetic field in the horizontal plane in two directions in the ship, namely fore-and-aft and athwartships.

This type of compass is fitted in ships where a Grade I position cannot be found on deck. It is mounted, with permanent magnet correctors and comprehensive D.G. correction, in a watertight binnacle which will normally be sited on a spur extending from one of the ship's masts.

The Detector Unit provides the angular measurement of the difference between ship's head and the magnetic meridian, hence the datum for the A.G.M. system. The gyroscope, providing the stabilizing element from which the transmission system to the repeaters originates, the Differential Alignment and the Total Error Corrector are substantially the same as in A.G.M. 6 and will not be described in this book.

Compass correction is novel and will be described later.

DETECTOR UNIT (Fig. 209)

This is the magnetically sensitive detector providing the datum to which the gyro transmission system is referred. It contains 'saturable inductors', sometimes known as 'Fluxgates', which are fixed magnetically-sensitive probes (about 3 inches long) which measure the strength of the magnetic fields along their own lengths. Two of these mounted fore-and-aft and two athwartships, measure two mutually perpendicular components of the Earth's magnetic field in the horizontal plane. They are energized electrically.

RESOLVER

By combining the two electrical outputs of the inductors in a resolver, which consists of two coils at right-angles, a position can be found for the rotor or search coil of the resolver in which there is no induced voltage in the coil. As the ship alters course the outputs from the inductors change and so a new zero position for the rotor has to be found. The angular position of the resolver rotor

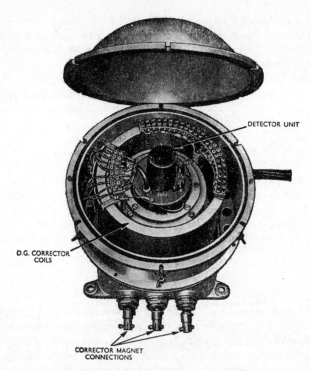

FIG. 209. Detector Unit in Binnacle

is therefore precisely related to the direction of the ship's head and can be connected to a compass card for indicating that direction.

TRANSMISSION

The gyroscope's transmission is coupled to the resolver rotor which is thereby stabilized in azimuth so that the ship appears to turn about it. If it is assumed that the rotor is in the balanced or null position, and the gyroscope has zero drift, the balanced or null position of the rotor will be maintained as the ship turns, since her heading alters by the same angular amount with respect to the resolver rotor and to the magnetic meridian. If for any reason the resolver rotor is not in the null position, a signal is generated in the rotor winding; it is fed into the transmission system through gearing, and gradually turns the whole of the repeater system, including the resolver rotor, until it is once more aligned on compass North. Thus, although the axis of the gyroscope may be pointing in any direction, the repeater system and the resolver rotor become north-seeking. Moreover, when the gyroscope wanders, as it will, it will disturb the resolver rotor and a correction will be applied to the transmission which will cancel the rate of drift.

Correction of the Compass

The permanent magnet correction follows the usual principles employed in conventional compass installations but, instead of separate moveable magnets, three pairs of rotatable magnets are used, so arranged that each pair can be set to provide a zero and a maximum field at the detector position by rotating a spindle connected by gearing to the magnets. For convenience, a Corrector Operating Unit is used coupled to the corrector mechanism by telescopic rods. Coefficients B and C and heeling error are each corrected by one pair of magnets.

To correct for heeling error, the heeling error magnets are set in the neutral position. A vertical inductor element in the detector, energized from the same supply as the horizontal inductors, measures the total vertical field at the compass position. This is indicated at the Electronic Heeling Error Instrument, which is plugged into the Corrector Operating Unit.

By means of a controlling knob on the Electronic Heeling Error Instrument, the charted value of the Earth's vertical field is fed back to the vertical inductor so that the indication of the Heeling Error Instrument is that of the ship's field.

The heeling error magnets are then rotated until the ship's field is cancelled as shown by zero reading on the instrument. H.E. is now corrected and the instrument unplugged.

Residual deviation is corrected by a cam in the Total Error Corrector.

A.T.M.C. 8

The A.T.M.C. 8 equipment consists of a conventional liquid-damped magnetic compass, having a 360° visible card, combined with a saturable inductor pick-up array attached to the underside of the bowl. The magnetic field from the compass magnets, acting upon the saturable inductors, gives rise to an electrical signal from the inductors which, when amplified, is used to drive a repeater.

The equipment provides a magnetic compass that can be used as a directly-read compass whether the power supply is on or off, combined with a transmitting system to a remote repeater when the power supply is switched on. It can be used in small vessels where only normal navigational accuracy is required and where gyro-stabilization is not considered necessary. It also provides an alternative to the projector compass in submarines with the advantage that only the cable between the binnacle and the amplifier, instead of the projector tube, needs to pass through the pressure hull.

COMPASS A.P. 160110

The compass is similar to Pattern 0188, but it has an improved magnet system with a higher moment, an improved expansion chamber, and the card, which is $3\frac{1}{2}$-in. diameter, is graduated every 2°. The compass is mounted in gimbals and fitted in a gunmetal pressure-tight binnacle.

BINNACLE A.P. 160111

The cover is secured by four clamps and it is tested to 600 lb. per sq. inch.

Horizontal corrector-magnets and spheres are located on the binnacle. Vertical corrector-magnets are carried in a separate magnet holder (A.P. 160112) secured below the binnacle. There is no lighting.

Compass Adjustment and Correction

The combination of an inductor system with a pivoted needle-type of magnetic compass has necessitated a somewhat unusual arrangement of corrector-magnets

FIG. 210. A.T.M.C.8 Binnacle and Compass

because the strength of the correcting field derived from the corrector-magnets and spheres should be the same at the inductors and the compass needle.

The magnets are placed in the horizontal plane that lies midway between the inductors and the compass needle. They are housed in four brackets, spaced at right-angles and projecting from the upper part of the binnacle. One pair of these brackets also carries the soft iron spheres.

The same consideration applies to heeling error correction. The separate magnet holder for the H.E. magnets is secured below the binnacle at such a distance that the difference in field between compass needles and Inductors is reduced to an acceptably small value.

A.T.M.C. 11 is similar to the A.T.M.C. 8 with the addition of D.G correction coils.

References

B.R. 1788 *Handbook of the Admiralty Gyro-Magnetic Compass, Type 5.*
B.R. 109 *Handbook of the Admiralty Gyro-Magnetic Compass, Type 6.*
C.D. Pamphlet No. 55 *Handbook of the Admiralty Gyro-Magnetic Compass, Type 7.*
C.D. Pamphlet No. 78 *Handbook of the Admiralty Transmitting Magnetic Compass, Type 8.*

CHAPTER XI

Chronometers, Watches and Time

Classification and Use

The following time-keeping instruments are supplied for navigational use in H.M. ships.

Description	Pattern No.
Chronometer	H.S.1
Chronometer watch	H.S.2
Deck watch	H.S.3
Dashboard watch	H.S.4
Sidereal stop-watch	H.S.7
Wristwatch chronograph	H.S.9

Chronometers are delicate and expensive instruments. They provide the most reliable means of time-keeping available, and are supplied mainly for the use of large vessels.

Chronometer watches are supplied to certain classes of vessel in lieu of chronometers. They are more compact, but should give results equal to those of chronometers.

Deck watches are supplied as the primary timepiece in a few vessels. In all other vessels they are used for conveying the time of observation to or from the chronometer or chronometer watch. When not being used for this purpose they should be kept in the stowage box.

Dashboard watches are supplied to surveying vessels for use in boats.

Sidereal stop-watches are supplied for use with the Rapid Sight-reduction Method.

Wristwatches are supplied for the use of aircrews, to surveying vessels and to the Commanding Officers of submarines.

Establishment

H.M. ships are supplied with chronometers and watches according to their class and the service on which they are employed. The establishment is laid down in the *Hydrographic Supplies Handbook* (H.51).

Chronometer Depots.

The head chronometer depot is situated at

Royal Greenwich Observatory,
Herstmonceux Castle,
Hailsham, Sussex.

All correspondence for this depot should be addressed to the Astronomer Royal. Packages should be addressed to The Officer-in-Charge, Chronometer Department. In addition, chronometers and watches are issued from chart and chronometer depots at home and abroad, a list of these depots being given in H.51.

Supply

First supply to ships in Home waters is usually made from the Chart and Chronometer Depot issuing the chart outfit, but surveying ships and ships commissioning at ports other than H.M. Dockyards are supplied from the Royal Observatory. Ships abroad are supplied from chart and chronometer depots as convenient. All demands for chronometers and watches by ships in Home waters should normally be addressed to the Hydrographer,

Hydrographic Supplies Establishment,
Creechbarrow House,
Taunton, Somerset

and, by ships abroad, to the Chart and Chronometer Depot on the station.

Because changing position and travelling upset a chronometer's rate, it is important to draw the chronometer several days before a ship sails, so that it can then settle down to a steady rate. When supplied, chronometers and watches are accompanied by Form H.62, which is the supply and receipt form also used for the chart outfit. When supplied from the Royal Observatory, Form R.O.192 takes the place of Form H.62.

The following information is given on these forms:

(a) Pattern Number;

(b) Name of maker;

(c) Number of the instrument.

Inside the instrument box, in addition, will be found:

(d) The date of issue from Royal Observatory;

(e) The error on G.M.T. (if supplied running);

(f) An abstract of rates (this is not always supplied, but may be demanded if required).

Transport

When supplied to a ship by hand from a chronometer depot, the chronometers and watches will be running. If forwarded by train or parcel post, the instruments will be wound, but stopped and with their balances wedged.

The Navigating Officer should always supervise the transport of chronometers which are running. Particular care must be taken to avoid their being given any rotary motion. Such motion has the effect of either causing the escapement to 'trip' or of stopping the chronometer. Tripping may easily result in considerable damage and will, in any case, cause the seconds hand to jump forward half a second or more. Chronometers should if possible be compared before and after transport, in order to ascertain whether stoppage or tripping has taken place. In such cases the subsequent rate of the chronometer affected should be carefully scrutinized for any indication of damage.

Chronometers should always be carried by hand, either in one of the special boxes kept for that purpose at the chronometer depots in Home Ports, or slung by means of a strap or handkerchief passed through the handles of the case. The use of a strap long enough to pass round the neck of the carrier, enabling the chronometer to be steadied against the front of the body by either hand, is recommended. If a short strap or a handkerchief be used, and the chronometer carried by one hand, great care must be taken, as previously explained, to avoid giving it a rotary motion or exposing it to any shock or violence.

When transporting chronometers in boats, they should be held, or rested upon the knee, and not allowed to be in contact with any portion of the boat's hull. Except on occasions of urgency, the transport of chronometers in bad weather should be avoided.

The gimbals should be locked before transport, and not unlocked until the final destination is reached.

Stowage

Chronometers, chronometer watches, and deck watches are normally stowed in the charthouse. Stowage boxes are provided, built in to the side of the chart table where space allows, or alternatively in a special cupboard. The type of stowage depends on the establishment of chronometers and watches laid down in H.51, and should comply with the regulations concerning safe distances from electrical instruments and D.G. coils. No electrical instrument should be allowed within one-eighth the distance given for Grade I Magnetic Compass positions.

The stowage box consists of soft iron, lined with thick rubber and wood, and a soft iron sheet is provided for insertion under the lid of the stowage box as required, for protection against magnetic fields. This can be removed, and the instruments viewed through a Perspex window which is flush with the top of the chart table. Where the soft iron screening is not provided, chronometers and watches should not be subjected to the effects of magnetic fields exceeding 1 gauss at the chronometer stowage position.

Chronometers and chronometer watches should never be moved from their stowage positions. Deck watches are supplied for taking the time of observations as required in various parts of the ship, and conveying this time to the chronometer or chronometer watch, or vice versa.

Action on Receipt

On receipt, the instruments and accompanying details concerning them should be compared with the supply and receipt note (H.62 or R.O.192) which should then be receipted and returned to the source of supply. The relevant details should then be entered on the first page of H.387, which is a book entitled *Daily Comparisons and Errors of Chronometers and Watches*.

Unpacking and Starting

1. *To unpack and start a Chronometer.* – Carefully remove the packing and dust inside the wooden box before taking the wrapping of thin paper from the chronometer. Find the packet of screws which fix the gimbal ring to the wooden box, then unscrew the glass face, grasp the brass case at the base with the right hand, and place the fingers of the left carefully round the edge of the metal face.

Now turn the chronometer over until it falls gently out of its case into the left hand. If it sticks at all, it can be pushed out by inserting the key and gently bearing down.

Remove the cork wedges from underneath the balance wheel by drawing them out in a direction parallel with the plate. Whatever pressure is exerted should act on the plate, not on the balance. Replace the chronometer in the brass case. Screw on the glass face. This operation should not start the chronometer. Screw the gimbal ring on to the chronometer, taking care that the slit for the locking apparatus is in its correct position. Then take hold of the chronometer with the left hand, the thumb being on the face and the fingers on the base, inclining it sideways in its gimbal ring, and screw it in its correct position in the wooden box. The chronometer is now ready to be started at any required time by a circular motion given to the box.

2. *To start a Chronometer Watch.* – To unwedge the balance of the watch, unscrew the bezel (glass face) in the same way as a chronometer. Lift the watch out of the brass box by the winding button. Great care must now be taken not to interfere with the hands of the watch. If the inner case of the watch is hinged, open in the usual way. In many instances, however, the cases are fitted with screw-on backs, the movement being uncovered by unscrewing the whole of the back of the inner case. Cut off the bent, narrow end of the paper wedge through the balance wheel, and then withdraw the remainder of the paper.

If the bent end of the paper is not cut off, it is apt to damage the balance wheel as it is withdrawn.

3. *To start a Deck Watch.* – Open the case and withdraw the paper wedge as described in 2.

4. *To start a Dashboard Watch.* – Unscrew ring and remove watch from bakelite holder. Slacken the locking screw of the rotating bezel. If the back of the case is milled it must be removed by unscrewing, otherwise open back by prising carefully with a thin knife-blade. Remove the paper wedge as in 2.

5. *Wristwatch Chronographs* are not supplied with the balance wedged, and the back of the case is tightened up before issue. Any interference with the back must be avoided, or the effectiveness of the watertight case will be impaired.

Winding, Setting Hands, etc.

Chronometers, both 2-day and 8-day, should be wound daily at approximately the same time. The former require about 7 and the latter $4\frac{1}{2}$ half-turns. A dial on the face shows whether a chronometer is wound, or the number of hours since it was last wound. Chronometers are wound by turning the key anti-clockwise. The key, called a 'tipsy key', is fitted with a ratchet so that if it is turned in the wrong direction no strain is brought on the winding mechanism.

To wind a chronometer, turn it over gently in the gimbal ring, face down, holding it firmly with the left hand. With one finger of the left hand open the dust cover and with the right hand insert the key and wind gently and evenly, counting the turns until the key is felt to butt and will wind no further. Be most careful not to force or jerk.

Having wound the chronometer, gently turn it over again, face up, and note that the hand on the winding indicator dial points to the 'up' position.

Watches should also be wound daily. Care should be taken that while the winding knob is turned the watch itself is kept motionless. Turning the latter in the opposite direction to the knob throws an unfair strain upon the mechanism, and may result in serious damage.

When setting chronometers and watches the hands must always be turned forwards, and never backwards, as damage may be caused to their mechanism if this is done.

Many watches are not fitted with push-pieces for use when setting the hands. In this case the winding knob should be pulled out to enable the hands to be set. Where any special method is involved, individual instructions will be issued with the watch.

When setting a watch, allowance should be made for any delay in 'pick-up' of the minute hand due to freedom in the train.

Replacement and Repairs

When ships are in Home waters, urgent replacements should be obtained from the nearest chart and chronometer depot. If replacement is not urgent, demands for instruments required should in all cases be forwarded to the Hydrographer, Taunton, the defective instrument being returned to the Royal Greenwich Observatory. Ships abroad should exchange defective instruments, or obtain replacements, from the nearest chart and chronometer depot.

Losses, through neglect or theft, should be fully reported in accordance with *Queen's Regulations and Admiralty Instructions*.

A reserve of two chronometer watches and two deck watches is supplied to Destroyer and Submarine Depot Ships and to Repair Ships for issue to ships in an emergency. Flagships may demand one of each of these additional if desired.

Chronometers and chronometer watches must never be placed in the hands of local watchmakers for adjustment or repair, except in the case of grave urgency abroad, in which event a special report of the circumstances is to be forwarded to the Hydrographer.

The same applies to other watches, except that abroad only, when replacements are not available, the watch may be entrusted to local watchmakers of standing for minor but urgent repairs. This should be interpreted to cover only the replacement of broken glasses or hands, or the refitting of winding buttons or stems.

When Unfit for Service

Chronometers, chronometer watches, dashboard watches, and deck watches are considered to be unfit for service if they
    (a) are broken down or damaged;
    (b) have run for over four years since the date of last issue from the Royal Observatory, which is shown on the label inside the box.

Other special reasons are:

    (c) Chronometer or chronometer watch – when daily rate exceeds 6 seconds or is irregular;
    (d) Dashboard, deck watch or wristwatch chronograph – when daily rate exceeds 12 seconds or is irregular.

Returning and Transferring

When chronometers and watches are time-expired they should be replaced as described above. Instructions for their disposal should be sought from the Hydrographer, and the instruments then despatched as directed. This will normally be to the Royal Greenwich Observatory, safe arrival being acknowledged on Form R.O.158. They should be accompanied by Form H.394 used as a supply note. If a ship is abroad the instruments should be exchanged on the first visit to a port where there is a chronometer depot. If the ship is not likely to visit such a port soon after the instruments become time-expired, application is to be made to the Hydrographer.

Transfers of chronometers and watches from one ship to another, or to a chronometer depot, should be accompanied by Form H.394. This form is also used as a receipt.   When transfer to another ship is effected, a copy of this form is to be sent to the Hydrographer, Taunton, for information.

Form H.394 is also to be completed and forwarded to the Hydrographer upon a ship paying off, or upon supersession of the Navigating Officer.

In the latter case, the receipt certificate on the form is also completed, and a duplicate of the return furnished to the officer taking charge of the instruments.

Packing and Transmission

If convenient, instruments may be returned by hand to a chronometer depot, whence they will be despatched as requisite. Otherwise the instructions given below should be followed.

CHRONOMETERS

(1) Take the brass case containing the chronometer out of its gimbals, unscrew the glass face, and remove the chronometer from the case. Secure the balance with two thin wedges of cork (which must be perfectly dry), placed as shown in Fig. 211. The wedging action should be divided between the cross bar and the arm of the balance, care being taken that the wedge, while placed as close as possible to the cross bar, does not touch the brass screws carried at its extremity. The placing of the two wedges should be symmetrical with regard to the axis of the balance, and while they must be inserted firmly enough to prevent any

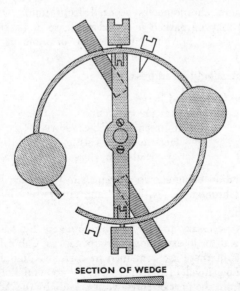

SECTION OF WEDGE

FIG. 211. Wedging the balance of a chronometer

motion of the balance, no attempt should be made to force them further. Replace the chronometer in the brass case, screw on its glass face, but do not put it again in its gimbals. Take out the screws which fix the gimbal ring to the wooden box; wrap the screws, with their circular brass nuts (if any), in paper; and lay the packet at the bottom of the wooden box. Place some clean, soft, packing material in the bottom of the box. Lay the gimbal ring upon the packing, seeing that the screws and nuts (if any) in the gimbal ring, used for fixing the chronometer to the ring, are screwed home. Place on the gimbal ring some more packing, then lay in the brass case containing the chronometer, first wrapping a sheet of thin paper round it to prevent contact with the packing material. Fill the space around the chronometer with soft packing, and likewise the space between the top of the chronometer and the glass lid. This should prevent the chronometer moving during transit.

(2) Close the wooden chronometer box and place it in a wicker basket or hamper, or in a box of partially yielding character, and pack (not too tightly) with soft packing. If no wicker basket is available, a wooden box, surrounded with packing material and enclosed in canvas, so that it cannot receive a jarring blow, may be used. *It is of the greatest importance that the outside packing case be soft and yielding.* When a wooden box is used, the lid of the box should be fixed by screws.

> *Note:* In order to guard against chronometers or watches being extracted from the hampers containing them, without removing the seals or cutting the cord, the lids should be secured by middling the cord and knotting it round the edge of the lid and the hamper, then crossing the parts and knotting them again in a similar manner at short intervals, the ends being finally sealed down on a card tacked to the lid of the hamper. The lid should be tied down with two or three short cords.
>
> In the case of a long hamper containing two of more chronometers, two pieces of cord should be used, working from the hinge on either side, the ends of each cord being separately sealed, as before, near the middle of the front of the hamper.

(3) Two or more chronometers secured from injury in their boxes (as explained in (1)) may be packed in a yielding case or basket, but all contacs between them must be prevented by the use of some packing material (at mentioned in (2)).

(4) The package should be addressed to:

> The Officer-in-Charge,
> Chronometer Department,
> Royal Greenwich Observatory,
> Herstmonceux Castle,
> Hailsham, Sussex,

the destination station being shown as Hailsham (Southern Region). It should also be marked 'Chronometer, with care' and always sent by passenger train – not by goods train.

(5) When it is necessary to convey chronometers by sea route, 'Lock up Stowage Category 1', or in exceptional circumstances 'Cabin Freight' should be employed. Details of these are contained in current Admiralty Fleet Orders – Stores section. This involves personal delivery to, and collection from, the ship. Collection from the port of entry will be made by the Admiralty. Chronometers are not to be shipped as mails.

(6) Each package should have on the outside some evidence as to whence it was despatched, and a letter should be sent by separate post to the Officer-in-Charge (address as above) giving information concerning the package, with the makers' names, the numbers of the instruments, and the route by which they have been sent.

CHRONOMETER WATCHES, AND OTHER WATCHES

These may be sent by post, if properly packed as explained hereunder.

In packing watches for transmission it is necessary to secure the balance, and for this purpose the back of the case must be opened. It is not necessary to wedge the balance of a wrist watch chronograph and no attempt should therefore be made to unscrew the back of the case.

The types of cases employed in the watches supplied to H.M. ships have either hinged, snap-on, or screw-on backs. Unless it is apparent that the case is hinged, an attempt should first be made to unscrew the back – this may require a little effort if the case is corroded at all. If the case cannot be opened in this manner, the back should be prised open carefully with a thin knife-blade. The case may have a small niche provided for the insertion of the blade.

Before the back of a dashboard watch is removed it is necessary to slacken off the locking screw of the rotating bezel.

Chronometer watches in brass mounting can be opened as described on page 347.

If the watch is in going order, it is advisable to let it run down before wedging the balance; otherwise it may be difficult to keep the latter still whilst wedging it.

When the case has been opened, the balance is to be wedged by drawing through it a narrow tapering strip of thin dry paper in the manner shown in Fig. 212.

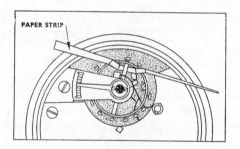

FIG. 212. Wedging the balance of a watch

The strip should be passed over the rims of the balance and underneath its cross bar. This operation requires considerable care, and is best performed with tweezers. The ends of the strip should be secured by snapping the inner back on to them.

When wedging the balances of watches with screw-on backs, however, the strip must be cut off at each end after insertion, sufficiently to ensure that these ends are clear of the screw thread. Should they become jammed in it while screwing on the back of the base, the balance may be strained and damaged. The friction caused by the paper is sufficient to keep the balance at rest.

When the balance has been secured, the watch should be placed in its wooden case, and if there is any play, covered with thin paper.

The case containing the watch is then to be placed in a strong cardboard or wooden box and well packed with soft material to prevent it being injured by jarring. If a wooden box is used the lid must be fixed by screws.

The package should be sealed, addressed as above to The Officer-in-Charge, Chronometer Department, and sent by post (registered parcel when sent from a port in the United Kingdom), unless some other safe and expeditious means offers. Provided that the postal limits are not exceeded, two or more watches may be enclosed in the same package if protected by sufficient packing material.

The outside wrapper is to show clearly from which ship the package was despatched, and both the Hydrographic Department, Taunton, and the Chronometer Department, Royal Greenwich Observatory, informed of its despatch.

Forms and Publications

H.51   The *Hydrographic Supplies Handbook* contains a section giving instructions for the supply, disposal, etc., of chronometers and watches, and an Appendix showing the Establishments for H.M. ships.

H.112   This booklet is contained in the small envelopes (H.137 and H.138), and gives instructions relating to the packing, transmission, use, and care of chronometers and watches.

H.394   Return showing chronometers and watches held, or transferred to another ship or chronometer depot. Also used as supply and receipt note in ships. It is contained in the small envelopes (H.137 and H.138).

H.387   This book, entitled *Daily Comparisons and Errors of Chronometers and Watches*, is supplied with the set of navigational publications to frigates and larger ships. Each book contains sufficient space for one year's comparisons. One page in the book is for keeping a record of all chronometers and watches received on board, and returned or transferred.

H.465   Chronometer depot report of the issue and recovery of chronometers and watches.

R.O.158   Receipt note, used by Royal Greenwich Observatory, for acknowledging safe arrival of instruments.

R.O.192   Supply and Receipt voucher for instruments supplied from R.G.O.

Obtaining Errors

Whenever possible, comparisons of the chronometer with G.M.T. should be obtained at intervals not exceeding 10 days:

The methods of obtaining the errors are:

1. Radio Time Signals.
2. Chronometer Depot clock.
3. Telephonic Time Signals (TIM).
4. Visual Time Signals.
5. Sextant observations of sun or stars.

1. Radio Time Signals

Many Radio Time Signals are operated automatically by mechanism connected to the standard clock of an observatory, which controls the emitting apparatus of the radio station broadcasting the time signal. At some stations the time signals are sent by hand. The different systems ('English', 'Onogo', 'Modified Rhythmic', etc.) are described in *Admiralty List of Radio Signals*, Vol. V. The B.B.C. Time Signal consists of the automatic transmission, by the standard clock at Royal Greenwich Observatory, of 6 pips, the final dot being the time signal. It should normally be accurate to 0·1 second.

To avoid possibility of errors, it is recommended that the Navigating Officer observe the time signals personally, the Wireless office being given warning of which signal is required. All details of these are given in the *Admiralty List of Radio Signals*, Vol. V. If the signal is obtained at a position remote from the chronometer, the error should be obtained by the deck watch, and a comparison, as explained later, made immediately before and after the time signal to obtain the error of the chronometer.

2. Chronometer Depot Clock

To find the error by this method, the deck watch must be taken ashore to a chronometer depot and compared with the depot clock. By making comparisons between chronometer and deck watch immediately before and after, as explained later, the error of the chronometer can be obtained. If there is much delay before making the second comparison, a mean comparison, also explained later, must be made.

3. Telephonic Time Signals

In the London telephone area and in the larger provincial centres it is possible to obtain the exact time by means of the telephone service. It is only necessary to dial the appropriate call letters or ask the operator for TIM or the Speaking Clock. The apparatus, which gives an accurate signal at every ten seconds, is controlled by the standard clock at the Royal Greenwich Observatory.

4. Visual Time Signals

At some ports, a visual time signal is made which usually consists of the automatic release of a ball from the yard arm of a signal station mast. The existence of these stations is noted on the charts and in the *Sailing Directions*. Full details are given in the *Admiralty List of Lights, Fog Signals and Visual Time Signals*. This method is, however, falling into disuse. The time required is the instant the ball begins to drop.

5. Sextant Observation of Sun or Stars

The facilities for obtaining errors by the foregoing methods are now so numerous, while the apparatus and calculations involved in obtaining errors by sextant observations are so complicated, that no description of this method will be given here.

Example of obtaining Error by Direct Comparisons

Just before going to observe the time by the method chosen, compare the D.W. with the chronometer, thus:

	h.	m.	s.	
D.W.T.	8	19	21·25	
Chronometer	6	16	00	
D.W. error	2	03	21·25	fast on Chronometer

Having made this comparison, find the error of the D.W. on G.M.T. by the method chosen, thus:

	h.	m.	s.	
G.M.T.	09	45	00	
D.W.	08	25	44	
D.W. error	1	19	16	slow on G.M.T.

As soon as possible afterwards, again compare the D.W. with the chronometer, thus:

	h.	m.	s.	
D.W.T.	8	28	21·25	at comparison
D.W. error	1	19	16	slow on G.M.T.
G.M.T.	9	47	37·25	at comparison
Chronometer	6	25	00	at comparison
Chronometer error	3	22	37·25	slow on G.M.T.

Should the difference between the chronometer and deck watch differ in the first and second comparison, repeat the comparison and check the working (*see* also page 356).

The Rate of a Chronometer

The difference between two errors of a chronometer is called the 'accumulated rate'. This, divided by the time elapsed between finding the two errors, is called the 'daily rate'. The time elapsed is called the 'epoch', expressed in days and decimals of a day, i.e. $\dfrac{\text{accumulated rate}}{\text{epoch}} = \text{daily rate.}$

The epoch should not exceed ten days, nor be less than five days. In practice, it is usual to take the errors of the chronometer every ten days, as this simplifies the working.

Always work in days and decimals of a day (to two places). Reduce all times to G.M.T. and so avoid the difficulties that may occur when Zone times are used or when the 'date line' is crossed.

Example of obtaining the Rate

At 1300 (Zone −4) on 10th January, on passage in the Indian Ocean, the D.W. was 04h. 59m. 43s. slow on G.M.T. by the 0900 ordinary (ONOGO modified) time signal from Shanghai (XSG). Comparison with the chronometer immediately afterwards gave:

	h.	m.	s.
C.	13	41	00
D.W.	04	03	47

At 0700 (Zone −8) on 17th January, the radio time signal from Wellington was taken and the chronometer was found to be 04h. 37m. 12s. fast on G.M.T.

Find the rate of the chronometer.

The Zone times are reduced to G.M.T. by applying the rule 'Zone East, Greenwich Time least: Zone West, Greenwich Time best', remembering that (−) Zones are Easterly and (+) Zones are Westerly.

10th January	Z.T.	1300
	Z.	− 4
	G.M.T.	0900/10th
17th January	Z.T.	0700
	Z.	− 8
	G.M.T.	2300/16th

These G.M.T.s are confirmed by consulting the times of the Radio Time Signals from Shanghai and Wellington in the *Admiralty List of Radio Signals*, Vol. V. On 10th January at 0900 G.M.T.:

	h.	m.	s.	
D.W.T.	04	03	47	at comparison
D.W.E.	04	59	43	slow on G.M.T.
G.M.T.	09	03	30	at comparison
C.	13	41	00	at comparison
∴ C.	04	37	30	fast on G.M.T.

On 17th January at 2300/16th G.M.T.:

Chronometer was 04h. 37m. 12s. fast on G.M.T.
G.M.T. of time signal on 16th January   2300
G.M.T. of time signal on 10th January   0900

∴ Epoch   =   6 days 14 hrs.
                   =   6·58 days.
Accumulated rate   =   18 secs. lost.

$$\therefore \text{Daily rate} = \frac{18}{6.58}$$

$$= 2.74 \text{ seconds, losing.}$$

Mean Comparison

It is sometimes impossible to compare the D.W. and the chronometer immediately after the error of the former has been obtained, as, for instance, when an error has been obtained from the depot clock.

Suppose the chronometer has a steady gaining rate of 3 seconds a day, and the D.W. a losing rate of 10 seconds a day. Clearly the comparison between them cannot remain constant even for one hour.

If the rates are steady, and comparisons are made before and after observing the error, it follows that, by interpolation, a comparison may be deduced which will be correct for any particular instant between the two comparisons actually taken. This calculated comparison is called a Mean Comparison.

Example of obtaining the Error by Mean Comparison

D.W. Error on Chronometer:

	Before observing				*After observing*		
	h.	*m.*	*s.*		*h.*	*m.*	*s.*
D.W.T.	8	24	07	D.W.T.	10	25	10
C.	8	39	00	C.	10	40	00
D.W. slow				*D.W. slow*			
on C.	0	14	53	on C.	0	14	50

The elapsed time between comparisons by the D.W. is 2h. 1m. 3s., or 121 minutes, approximately. Suppose that the D.W. showed 9h. 57m. 20s. when the time signal was received, and that it was made at 1145 G.M.T.

	h.	m.	s.
D.W.T. at which the error was observed	9	57	20
D.W.T. of last comparison	10	25	10
Elapsed time		27	50

In 121 minutes the D.W. has gained 3 seconds on the chronometer.

$\therefore$ In 27·8 minutes the D.W. has gained $\dfrac{27\cdot8 \times 3}{121} = 0\cdot7$s. on the chronometer.

By the last comparison the D.W. was 0h. 14m. 50s. slow on the chronometer.

Therefore at the time the error was observed the D.W. was 0h. 14m. 50·7s. slow on the chronometer; and at the time the error was observed, the chronometer must have been showing 10h. 12m. 10·7s.

	h.	m.	s.
G.M.T. at which error was observed	11	45	00·0
C. showed, when error was observed	10	12	10·7
$\therefore$ Chronometer is slow on G.M.T. at 1145	1	32	49·3

Greenwich Date (G.D.)

Since chronometers and watches record a series of 12h., they cannot distinguish between G.M.T. 3h., say, and G.M.T. 15h., and it is not always obvious from the 'time of day' in a ship whether the time is forenoon or afternoon at Greenwich. Should there be any uncertainty, it can be removed by comparing the G.M.T. obtained from the deck watch with the 'Greenwich Date' obtained from zone time.

EXAMPLE

Suppose that at Z.T. 0530 (−11) on 20th September the deck watch showed 6h. 28m. 43s. at the time of an observation, and that the deck watch was 31s. fast on G.M.T.

Then Z.T.		0530	20th September.	
Z.		−11		
G.D.		1830	19th September.	
		h.	m.	s.
D.W.T.		6	28	43
D.W.E.				31 fast
G.M.T.		18	28	12 19th September (*not* 6h. 28m. 12s.)

The Greenwich Date is, in effect, merely a term denoting approximate G.M.T.

The Deck Watch Error at any time

Since the deck watch is always used for taking times of sights, it is most necessary to know its accurate error at any time.

This can be found by finding the error of the chronometer on G.M.T. at the time required, on the assumption that its rate has been constant since the last time signal was received. Then, from comparison, the D.W. error on the chronometer can be obtained, giving the D.W. error on G.M.T.

The D.W. error obtained by applying its accumulated rate to the last error by time signal should never be used.

Example of obtaining the Deck Watch Error by Chronometer Comparison

At 2300 G.M.T. on 16th January the chronometer was found to be 04h. 37m. 12s. fast on G.M.T. and to have a daily rate of 4·25 seconds losing.

At about 1100 (Zone −9) on 20th January the following comparison was made before taking a sun sight:

	h.	m.	s.
C.	06	34	00
D.W.	01	55	18

What deck watch error should be used for this sight?

Z.T. of comparison	1100	20th January
Z.	− 9	
G.D.	0200	20th January

This confirms that D.W.T. was 01h. 55m. 18s. and not 13h. 55m. 18s.

Last error obtained on   16th Jan. at 2300 G.M.T.
Error required on   20th Jan. at 0200 G.M.T.

∴ Epoch = 3 days 3 hours
        = 3·12 days

Accumulated rate of chronometer 4·25 × 3·12
        = 13·3 sec. lost.

		h.	m.	s.
∴ On 20th, chronometer is		04	37	12 fast
				−13·3 losing
		04	36	58·7 fast on G.M.T.
At comparison	C.	06	34	00
G.M.T. of comparison		01	57	01·3
At comparison	D.W.	01	55	18
∴ D.W.E.		01	43·3 slow on G.M.T.	

UNIFORM TIME SYSTEM

Zone Time System at Sea

The following uniform system of time-keeping at sea has been adopted to ensure that all vessels within certain defined limits of longitude keep the same time, in a manner similar to that used on land. It is well known, for example, that London, Plymouth, and Dover all keep the same time and not the local time of each place. Similarly the ship's clock is set to show the time of a definite hourly meridian, instead of being set to an indefinite time selected by the ship.

The World is considered as being divided in respect of longitude into 24 zones of 15° each, the centre of the system being the meridian of Greenwich. The centre division therefore lies between the meridian of $7\frac{1}{2}°$ East and that of $7\frac{1}{2}°$ West, and is described as zone 0; the zones lying to the eastward are numbered in sequence up to 12 with a negative (−) prefix, and those lying to the westward are similarly numbered with a positive (+) prefix. The 12th zone is divided centrally by the 180th meridian, and both prefixes (+) and (−) appear in this zone, their position depending upon the 'Date Line'.

Modification of Zone Time System at Sea

A modification of this arrangement, adopted by France and Italy, consists in numbering the zones as 0 to 23, all eastward from Greenwich, and all positive; thus the signs of zones −1 to −12 are reversed, while zones +12 to +1 receive the numbers 13 to 23. In converting, therefore, from this to the British system, it is necessary:

(a) East of Greenwich, to change the sign from positive to negative;
(b) West of Greenwich, to deduct the time given from 24.

Standard Time on Land

The boundaries of time zones on land agree generally with those at sea (which are defined by the meridians of $7\frac{1}{2}°$, $22\frac{1}{2}°$, etc.), except when modified as necessary by the territorial limits of the countries concerned. Zone time on land is known as 'Standard Time'.

A Table of Standard Times kept in different countries is contained in the *Admiralty List of Radio Signals*, Vol. V, and the *Nautical Almanac*.

By this system the same time is therefore kept whether on land or sea throughout each zone (except during the periods of Summer Time), and in different zones the times differ from one another by an integral number of hours, the minutes and seconds in all zones remaining the same.

Conversion of Zone Time to G.M.T.

Greenwich Mean Time is kept in zone o. In zone -8, for example, the time kept is 8 hours in advance of Greenwich Mean Time, while in zone $+8$ it is 8 hours slow on that of Greenwich.

It will thus be seen that in order to obtain Greenwich Mean Time in any zone, the number of hours given by the Zone number $(+)$ or $(-)$ must be added to or subtracted from the ship's zone time. (*See* diagram on page 360.)

Zone Description

Zone time may also be indicated by referring to the letters attached to the zones and shown on the Time Zone Chart (*see* below). Greenwich Mean Time is Z (or Zero). Zones to the eastward are lettered A to M (J is omitted), those to the westward being lettered N to Y.

The 'zone description' of the time kept by a vessel is not necessarily the number of the zone in which she is. For example, if a vessel in British home waters is keeping Summer Time, the zone description of the time is '-1'.

A ship's domestic clocks will not, as a rule, be altered the moment she enters a new zone. The fact that she crosses a dividing meridian and enters a new zone does not alter the time she is keeping. Her clocks are altered to suit the convenience of those on board.

Time kept by Vessels in Harbour

The time kept by any vessel, if she is not in the open sea, will depend on local orders and arrangements. (*See* also page 362.)

Time Zone Chart

The Time Zone system is illustrated on chart No. D.6085 in the *Admiralty List of Radio Signals*, Vol. V, and on Admiralty Chart No. 5006, which is contained in folio H.92.

The Date or Calendar Line

This is a modification of the line of the 180th meridian, which is drawn so as to include islands of any one group on the same side of the line.

Full details of the date line are shown on the Time Zone Chart and described in the *Admiralty List of Radio Signals*, Vol. V, and the *Nautical Almanac*.

When the date line is crossed on an easterly course the date is put back a day; on a westerly course the date is put on a day.

DIAGRAM TO FACILITATE THE COMPARISON OF ZONE TIMES AT DIFFERENT PLACES

TIME \ ZONE	12	11	10	9	8	7	6	5	4	3	2	1	0	+-	+2	+3	+4	+5	+6	+7	+8	+9	+10	+11	+12
00		23	22	21	20	19	18	17	16	15	14	13	12	11	10	09	08	07	06	05	04	03	02	01	
01	01		23	22	21	20	19	18	17	16	15	14	13	12	11	10	09	08	07	06	05	04	03	02	01
02	02	01		23	22	21	20	19	18	17	16	15	14	13	12	11	10	09	08	07	06	05	04	03	02
03	03	02	01		23	22	21	20	19	18	17	16	15	14	13	12	11	10	09	08	07	06	05	04	03
04	04	03	02	01		23	22	21	20	19	18	17	16	15	14	13	12	11	10	09	08	07	06	05	04
05	05	04	03	02	01		23	22	21	20	19	18	17	16	15	14	13	12	11	10	09	08	07	06	05
06	06	05	04	03	02	01		23	22	21	20	19	18	17	16	15	14	13	12	11	10	09	08	07	06
07	07	06	05	04	03	02	01		23	22	21	20	19	18	17	16	15	14	13	12	11	10	09	08	07
08	08	07	06	05	04	03	02	01		23	22	21	20	19	18	17	16	15	14	13	12	11	10	09	08
09	09	08	07	06	05	04	03	02	01		23	22	21	20	19	18	17	16	15	14	13	12	11	10	09
10	10	09	08	07	06	05	04	03	02	01		23	22	21	20	19	18	17	16	15	14	13	12	11	10
11	11	10	09	08	07	06	05	04	03	02	01		23	22	21	20	19	18	17	16	15	14	13	12	11
12	12	11	10	09	08	07	06	05	04	03	02	01		23	22	21	20	19	18	17	16	15	14	13	12
13	13	12	11	10	09	08	07	06	05	04	03	02	01		23	22	21	20	19	18	17	16	15	14	13
14	14	13	12	11	10	09	08	07	06	05	04	03	02	01		23	22	21	20	19	18	17	16	15	14
15	15	14	13	12	11	10	09	08	07	06	05	04	03	02	01		23	22	21	20	19	18	17	16	15
16	16	15	14	13	12	11	10	09	08	07	06	05	04	03	02	01		23	22	21	20	19	18	17	16
17	17	16	15	14	13	12	11	10	09	08	07	06	05	04	03	02	01		23	22	21	20	19	18	17
18	18	17	16	15	14	13	12	11	10	09	08	07	06	05	04	03	02	01		23	22	21	20	19	18
19	19	18	17	16	15	14	13	12	11	10	09	08	07	06	05	04	03	02	01		23	22	21	20	19
20	20	19	18	17	16	15	14	13	12	11	10	09	08	07	06	05	04	03	02	01		23	22	21	20
21	21	20	19	18	17	16	15	14	13	12	11	10	09	08	07	06	05	04	03	02	01		23	22	21
22	22	21	20	19	18	17	16	15	14	13	12	11	10	09	08	07	06	05	04	03	02	01		23	22
23	23	22	21	20	19	18	17	16	15	14	13	12	11	10	09	08	07	06	05	04	03	02	01		23
ZONE	+12	+11	+10	+9	+8	+7	+6	+5	+4	+3	+2	+-	0	1	2	3	4	5	6	7	8	9	10	11	12

This diagram is self explanatory, but it must be noted that the date changes if the date-change line is crossed, advancing if crossed from left to right, and vice versa.

Example I. 03^h(3·0 a.m.) Jan. 2nd at Melbourne (Zone -10^h) corresponds to 12^h(Noon) Jan. 1st at New York (Zone $+5^h$).

Example II. 19^h(7·0 p.m.) Jan. 5th at Vancouver (Zone $+8^h$) corresponds to 11^h(11·0 a.m.) Jan. 6th at Perth (Zone -8^h).

That such an adjustment is necessary may be seen by considering an aircraft flying round the world in latitude 60° at 450 knots (the Sun's speed in longitude in that latitude).

If the pilot starts at noon on a Monday, when the Sun is on his meridian, and flies west, the Sun will remain on his meridian. He will thus experience no change of day at all. Wherever he is it will be noon, and people will be thinking about their midday meal. But when he arrives back at his starting point, the ground staff will be thinking about Tuesday's meal. Somewhere during his journey, therefore, Monday has suddenly become Tuesday. That somewhere is the date line, on one side of which people are calling the time noon on Monday, and on the other, noon on Tuesday.

A ship steaming round the world has a similar but less rapid, and therefore not so obvious, experience. She must adjust her clocks so as to keep the Sun approximately overhead at 1200, and when she crosses the date line she must make this further adjustment of one day.

Steaming *West*, a ship passes from a zone which is 12h. slow on G.M.T. to one which is 12h. fast the instant she crosses the date line. That is, she must *add* 24h. It is thus necessary to miss one day in the local time and to skip, for instance, from Tuesday to Thursday.

Steaming *East*, a ship goes from a zone which is 12h. fast on G.M.T. to one which is 12h. slow, and it is necessary to *repeat a day* in local time.

EXAMPLE

Consider a ship steaming from Vancouver to Sydney and arriving on the date line at 1345 on 2nd June, a Tuesday.

She passes from Zone (+12) to Zone (−12). At the instant she leaves Zone (+12), her Greenwich Date is:

$$
\begin{array}{ll}
\text{Z.T.} & \text{1345 Tuesday, 2nd June} \\
\text{Zone} + 12 & \\
\hline
\text{G.D.} & \text{0145 Wednesday, 3rd June} \\
\end{array}
$$

If she makes no adjustment of one day, her Greenwich Date at the instant she enters Zone (−12) is:

$$
\begin{array}{ll}
\text{Z.T.} & \text{1345 Tuesday, 2nd June} \\
\text{Zone} - 12 & \\
\hline
\text{G.D.} & \text{0145 Tuesday, 2nd June} \\
\end{array}
$$

She is therefore a day out on Greenwich time, and in order to bring herself into step again she must call her zone time 1345 (−12) Wednesday, 3rd June, so that:

$$
\begin{array}{ll}
\text{Z.T.} & \text{1345 Wednesday, 3rd June} \\
\text{Zone} - 12 & \\
\hline
\text{G.D.} & \text{0145 Wednesday, 3rd June} \\
\end{array}
$$

That is, she drops a day, and this she would probably do by keeping the time of Zone (+12) until midnight on Tuesday and then calling the next day Thursday (−12). If the example is worked with the ship steaming East, it is seen that she must repeat a day.

Rules for H.M. Ships

1. When a ship passes from one zone to another, the alteration of the ship's clocks other than signal clocks will be made as ordered by the Captain.

The following system is generally found convenient, in order that watch-keepers may share the difference of time:

When clocks have to be advanced, advance them 1 hour at 2330;

When clocks have to be retarded, retard them 1 hour at 1830.

2. Signal clocks should be kept at G.M.T. or at a specific zone time required for operations. The zone description of the time kept by these clocks should be marked by a conspicuous label.

3. When time is referred to in official correspondence, the zone description is to be added. For example, 'At Z.T. 1645 H....' or 'At Z.T. 1645 (−8)....'

4. When a ship is in harbour, or within the territorial limits of a country where the legal time differs half an hour from an exact zone time, the zone description with the hours and half hours is to be given. In a harbour where the legal time of the country is not in agreement with the zone system in any form, the exact amount in hours, minutes and seconds by which it differs from Greenwich Time is always to be given, together with its appropriate sign of (+) or (−).

Summer Time

Many countries adjust their clocks during the summer months so that an extra hour of daylight is added to the evening. Some countries have made this a permanent adjustment in force during the whole year. Details of Summer Time kept in different countries are given in the *Admiralty List of Radio Signals*, Vol. V.

British Summer Time (B.S.T.) is normally kept in Great Britain from April to October, details of the exact day of the change being promulgated as necessary. The zone description of B.S.T. is (−1).

Examples of the Zone System

When times of arrival and departure from places keeping different zone times are worked out, the best plan is to reduce the times to G.M.T. and thus avoid any chance of confusion, particularly when the date line is crossed.

EXAMPLE 1

A ship at San Francisco (California) is ordered to arrive at Hakodate (Japan) at 1200 on 20th January. She expects to make good a speed of 15 knots and proposes to allow 6 hours in hand for bad weather.

On what day and at what time should she sail from San Francisco?

San Francisco keeps Zone +8
Hakodate keeps Zone −9 } From *A.L.R.S.*, Vol. V, or *N.A.*

San Francisco to Hakodate   = 4,245 miles (from the *Admiralty Distance Tables* or *Ocean Passages of the World*)

Time taken on passage at 15 knots   = $\dfrac{4,245}{15}$ = 283 hours

Allowance for weather . . . . .   6 hours

Total steaming time . . . . .   289 hours or
                                  12 days 1 hour
Zone Time of arrival at Hakodate . . . 1200 (−9) 20th Jan.
Zone correction . . . . .   − 9

G.M.T. of arrival at Hakodate . . . 0300 (G.M.T.) 20th Jan.
∴ G.M.T. of departure from San Francisco . 0200 (G.M.T.) 8th Jan.
Zone correction . . . . .   + 8

∴ Zone Time of departure from San Francisco . 1800 (+8) 7th Jan.

EXAMPLE 2

A ship at Ascension Island proposed to sail for Cestos Bay in Liberia at 1800 (Zone 0) on 1st June. She expects to make good 10 knots and does not propose to make any allowance for bad weather or currents.

What will be her expected standard time of arrival at Cestos Bay?

Time kept at Ascension Island . . . G.M.T.
Time kept in Liberia . . . . . + 44 mins.
Ascension Island to Cestos Bay . . . 850 miles
Time on passage at 10 knots . . . 85 hours or 3 days 13 hours
Time of departure from Ascension Island . 1800 (G.M.T.) 1st June
Time on passage . . . . . 3 days 13 hours
G.M.T. of arrival at Cestos Bay . . . 0700 (G.M.T.) 5th June
    Time correction . . . . . − 44 mins.

Standard Time of arrival at Cestos Bay . . 0616 (+ 44 mins.) 5th June

CHAPTER XII

Tides and Tidal Streams

FROM earliest historical times men have associated the tides with the phases of the Moon, that is to say with the relative positions of the Sun and Moon. In order, therefore, to understand the fundamental causes of the tides it is first necessary to have some knowledge of the laws which govern the movements of these and other heavenly bodies.

These laws were originally stated by Newton. Although they are not capable of mathematical proof they are accepted because they explain the movements of the planets as they actually occur. The best test of their essential soundness is to be found in the accuracy of the data given in the *Nautical Almanac*.

The first law with which we are concerned states, *inter alia*, that any heavenly body in the universe will travel in a straight line at constant speed until some external force causes an alteration in its line of travel or of its speed.

The second law which concerns us states that for any two heavenly bodies a force of attraction is exerted by each one on the other, the force being:

(a) proportional to the product of the masses of the two bodies;
(b) inversely proportional to the square of the distance between them, and
(c) directed from the centre of the one to the centre of the other.

Finally there is a law which states that the entire mass of a solid body may be considered to be concentrated at its centre of gravity.

It will now be convenient to consider the Earth and the Moon as forming together an independent system, rotating about a common centre of gravity which lies on the line joining their centres. This rotation is in accordance with the laws of circular motion, one of which states that this motion occurs when a body moving at a steady speed is acted upon by a constant force which is always at right angles to the direction of motion. The 'constant force' in this case is the gravitational force exerted on the Moon by the Earth and vice versa. This Earth–Moon system is in a state of equilibrium whereby the speed of the Moon is never great enough to carry it out of its orbit into outer space and is never small enough to allow a collision between the Earth and the Moon; in other words, the speed is always exactly sufficient to maintain the Moon in its orbit round the Earth and to counteract the gravitational forces.

The Gravitational Forces

Since the tides consist of movements of water over the surface of the Earth, we must now consider the effect of the Moon's gravitational forces on the Earth and on the various parts of the Earth relative to the Earth as a whole. For this purpose we can consider the Earth as being stationary with the Moon moving in an almost circular orbit around it.

The gravitational forces act on the Earth as a whole, on the waters which are on or near the Earth's surface, and on the atmosphere. The physical properties of each of these are quite different and the forces therefore affect each in a different way.

The Earth as a whole is very dense and relatively rigid. The changes in the gravitational forces do, nevertheless, cause a distortion of the solid Earth (Earth Tides); this movement is, however, barely measurable and can be neglected for most practical purposes.

The atmosphere is neither dense nor rigid. The effect of a change in the gravitational force is measurable as a change in atmospheric pressure, and this too can be neglected.

The water on the Earth is relatively dense but non-rigid. Furthermore, in contrast to the solid Earth, the waters are concentrated on or near the surface of the Earth. The different effects of the gravitational forces on the Earth and on the waters of the Earth respectively will be described. These differences are of the greatest importance when considering the causes of the tides.

In Fig. 213 $M'M$ is the diameter of the Earth joining the centre of the Earth to the centre of the Moon. M is the point on the Earth's surface which is directly

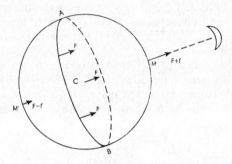

FIG. 213

under the Moon, i.e. which has the Moon in its zenith or, alternatively, at which the zenith distance is 0°. A and B are two points on a great circle whose plane is perpendicular to $M'M$ and which divides the hemisphere on which the Moon is shining (towards M) from the dark hemisphere (towards M'). At all points on this great circle the distance from the Moon may be considered as being the same as at the centre of the Earth (C in Fig. 213). Hence, if we denote the gravitational force exerted by the Moon on a small mass at C by F, the force exerted on a similar mass anywhere on the great circle AB will also be F. As one proceeds towards M, this force will increase to a maximum (corresponding to the minimum distance from the Moon) at M. We will call this maximum force $F + f$. As one proceeds towards M' it will decrease to a minimum ($F - f$) at M'. In all cases this force is directed towards the centre of the Moon but for all practical purposes it may be considered as being directed parallel to $M'M$.

The Tide-raising Forces

It is a fundamental and most important point that the tides are not caused *directly* by the pull of the Moon on the Earth or on the water as a whole. The cause of the tides is the difference between the gravitational force exerted on the Earth and that exerted on the water and, therefore, the difference between these differential forces at different points on the Earth's surface.

As the Earth is more or less rigid the force F can be considered to be concentrated, for the Earth as a whole, at the centre of the Earth. This force tends to move the Earth, as a whole, towards the Moon, i.e. it causes slight eccentricities in the Earth's orbit. At M there is a greater force $F + f$ tending to move the water on the light hemisphere towards the Moon. With a force of F acting on the Earth and a force of $F + f$ acting on the water, there is clearly a differential force $(+ f)$ tending to move water away from the Earth towards the Moon. At M' this differential force becomes $- f$, i.e. there is a greater force pulling the Earth towards the Moon than is pulling the water in the dark hemisphere. There is therefore a tendency for the water to be left behind. The maximum tide-raising force towards the Moon will be at M and the maximum away from the Moon at M'. At points A and B the tide-raising force will be nil.

If we now take any point P on the Earth's surface whose zenith distance is z, the tide-raising force becomes $f \cos z$. The sum of all the amounts $f \cos z$ over the surface of the Earth are collectively known as the tide-raising forces. The forces on the dark hemisphere balance those in the light hemisphere so that the total force over the Earth's surface is nil, i.e. the tide-raising forces do not move the Earth as a whole.

If we imagine the surface of the Earth to be entirely covered by water, the distribution of the tide-raising forces will be approximately as shown in Fig. 214. It will be observed that, except at the points M and M' the tide-raising force does not act at right angles to the Earth's circumference. At all other points the

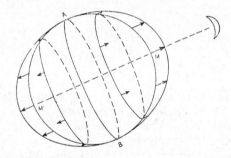

FIG. 214

tide-raising force can therefore be split up into (a) a vertical component directed at right angles to the Earth's surface and (b) a horizontal component directed toward the point on the Earth's surface directly under the moon (M or M'). *It is the horizontal component* which clearly tends to move water in the light hemisphere towards M and in the dark one towards M'.

Effect of Earth's Rotation

Fig. 215a represents the Earth with the Moon on the Equator, i.e. Declination 0°. Clearly, if the Earth and Moon were relatively stationary, there would be a permanent high water directly under the Moon at M and M' and permanent low water at the poles. The Earth, however, rotates, relatively, to the Moon, once in a lunar day of about 25 hours and the tide-raising forces undergo changes accordingly. If we consider the tide-raising forces at a point P in latitude $L°$ North, the force f will change as P is carried round by the Earth's rotation, so

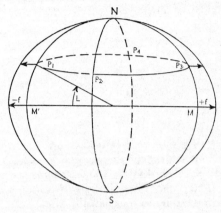

FIG. 215a

that, relative to the Moon, the point will move from P_1 through P_2, P_3 and P_4 back to P_1; the complete cycle taking exactly one lunar day. We have seen already that the force will be a maximum ($f \cos L$) in a southerly direction at P_3 and maximum again in the same direction and with the same magnitude at P_1 while at P_2 and P_4, on the plane at right angles to MM', it will be zero. The forces can therefore be represented as a simple cosine curve having two complete cycles per lunar day, as shown in Fig. 215b.

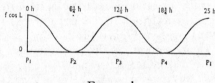

FIG. 215b

Such tide-raising forces, producing two equal maxima and two equal minima per lunar day, are termed semi-diurnal (i.e. one tidal cycle per half-day). When the Moon has zero declination, as shown in Fig. 215a, the tide-raising forces are semi-diurnal for all latitudes.

Effect of Moon's Declination

In Fig. 216a, where the Moon has declination D, the distribution of the tide-raising forces is shown by the dotted line, the maximum forces being, as before, at the points M and M'. Once again we will consider a point P in latitude $L°$ North as it is carried round, relative to the Moon, from P_1 through P_2, P_3 and P_4 back to P_1. The tide-raising force at P_1 is now $f \cos (L + D)$ and at P_3 it is $f \cos (L - D)$ while at P_2 and P_4 it is zero as before. It will be seen, however, that the distance from P_1 to P_2 is now less than from P_2 to P_3 and similarly the

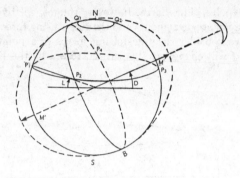

FIG. 216a

distance from P_3 to P_4 is greater than from P_4 to P_1. The effect of this is, firstly, to produce unequal intervals between successive maxima and minima and, secondly, to produce alternate maxima which are unequal in height, as shown in Fig. 216b. This effect is known as *diurnal inequality*, a phenomenon which is commonly found in the tides as they actually exist.

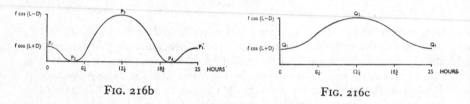

FIG. 216b   FIG. 216c

We will now consider a position Q in a latitude which is greater than $90° - D$. It will be seen that, as this position moves from Q_1 through Q_2 and back to Q_1, the tide-raising force never reaches zero (i.e. Q never cuts the plane AB). The minimum value of the force is at Q_1 and the force increases to a maximum at Q_2, falling again to a minimum at Q_1 after one complete rotation. The force has therefore only one maximum and one minimum in a lunar day and is therefore called *diurnal*. A typical curve is shown in Fig. 216c.

It can be shown that the curve shown in Fig. 216b can be reproduced as the sum of a diurnal curve such as Fig. 216c and a semi-diurnal curve such as Fig. 215b. The tides, as they exist in nature, always include, amongst others, a semi-diurnal and a diurnal component, though in some cases the diurnal is too small to be apparent while in other cases, rather less frequently, the semi-diurnal tide is hardly noticeable. The possible permutations are infinite and it can be said that there are no two places in the world, however close together, where the tides are exactly the same.

To sum up, the semi-diurnal tide-raising force is maximum when the Moon's declination is nil and minimum when the Moon's declination is at its maximum. The diurnal tide-raising force is nil when the Moon's declination is nil and maximum when the Moon's declination is maximum; the same is, of course, true of the effect of the Sun's declination but, whereas the Moon's declination attains a maximum value North or South of the Equator every 15 days or so, the Sun's declination changes much more slowly and attains a maximum only twice a year, in June and December, at the Solstices. These facts are of importance in dealing with the tides as they actually exist. In the waters round the British Isles the tides are mainly semi-diurnal and are therefore more influenced by the phases of the Moon than by declination. The large tides occur at Springs, near full or new Moon. The small tides occur at Neaps near the quarters. The largest tides of the year occur at Springs near the Equinoxes, when the Sun and Moon are on the Equator. The importance of the Spring tides is reflected in Admiralty Tide Tables, and for the British Isles the average heights of high and low water at Springs are normally given, as well as the average Neap values, corresponding to the average maximum range and the average minimum range over the year.

In some parts of the world, however, the diurnal part of the tide is the more important, so that the largest tides are associated with the greatest declination of the Sun and Moon. Maximum declination of the Sun occurs simultaneously with maximum declination of the Moon at Springs near the Solstices (around the middle of June and December).

Effect of changes in distances of Sun and Moon

As the orbits of the Earth round the Sun, and of the Moon round the Earth, especially the latter, are slightly elliptical, small changes in distance occur. The variation in the Moon's distance can cause a difference in the range of the lunar tide-raising force of from 15 per cent to 20 per cent. The variation in the Sun's distance can cause a difference of only about 3 per cent in the solar tide-raising force. Thus, there is a tendency for the tides to be larger at perigee than at apogee and a similar, but lesser tendency for the tides to be larger at perihelion than at aphelion.

The Tides as they exist

It has been shown that, if the Earth were covered completely with water, and if the water responded instantly to the forces acting on it, high water would occur directly under the Moon and directly opposite on the other side of the Earth. Under these fictitious conditions the time and height of high water or any other state of the tide could be predicted from astronomical theory for any point on the Earth's surface. The reality is, of course, quite different.

In order for an appreciable tide to be generated in a body of water, the dimensions of that body must be large enough for there to be an appreciable difference in the tide-raising forces between its extreme limits. The largest tides are therefore generated in the largest oceans such as the Pacific, Atlantic and Indian Ocean. These three main bodies of water each have different natural periods of oscillation and the tide-raising forces act upon each body of water as if it were water in a basin, causing a rhythmic but slightly irregular oscillation which varies according to the size, shape and general underwater topography of the basin. The natural period of oscillation of the basin is the decisive factor in determining whether the water responds to the diurnal rather than to the semi-diurnal forces, to the solar rather than to the lunar forces. The Pacific Ocean, for instance, is on the whole responsive to the diurnal forces and relatively unresponsive to the semi-diurnal forces. The Atlantic, on the other hand, is responsive to the semi-diurnal forces and relatively inert to the diurnal forces;

hence the tides on the shores of the Pacific tend to have a large diurnal component, while those on the shores of the Atlantic have a relatively small diurnal component.

The tide-raising forces set up oscillations of small amplitude in the deep oceans and these oscillations travel as waves towards the coast, into estuaries and up rivers. As the water becomes shallower the amplitude of the wave increases and further amplification occurs when the tidal wave travels up an estuary which, typically, gradually narrows from a wide entrance. The tide, as originally generated in the ocean, is always of small amplitude, probably not more than two feet; but under certain conditions it can be magnified to an amplitude of 20 feet or more on approaching the land. The large tides in the Bay of Fundy and in the Severn Estuary are closely related to their funnel-shaped approaches and a long fetch of relatively shallow water.

The effect of Shallow Water

The effect on a tidal wave entering shallow water is, besides increasing the amplitude of the wave, to distort it in the same way that an ordinary wave on the beach may be observed to become progressively distorted as it approaches the shore; it tends to acquire a steep front, that is to say that the period of rise becomes shorter than the period of fall. These shallow water effects are present to a greater or lesser degree in the tides of all coastal waters and they make the prediction of such tides more complex than for the simple oceanic tides.

Harmonic Constituents of the Tide

The tide-raising forces can be considered as the sum of an infinite number of constituent cosine curves, the periods and relative amplitudes of which can be calculated exactly from astronomical theory. Some 400 constituents have been calculated but, in practice, it is neither necessary nor practical to use so many. The largest number allowed for in any mechanical predicting machine is 62 and the smallest number 10.

Now it is a law of mechanics that if a periodic force is applied to a moving body, that body will eventually oscillate with the same period as the force applied. If no force is applied there can be no movement. As the period of each constituent of the tide-raising forces is known exactly, it can be seen that when these forces are applied to the water, the water will respond by oscillating with the same periods. The response of the water is, however, modified by topographical conditions which can retard or advance the time at which the tidal wave arrives and can increase or decrease the amplitude of the wave. The important fact, however, is that there is *some* response to all of the harmonic constituents of the tide-raising force, and *no* regular response to any other forces.

These constituents are given symbols from which the general significance of each can be deduced. Thus the letter M and, generally speaking, letters near M in the alphabet, indicate constituents associated with the movement of the Moon, while the letter S and letters near S indicate solar constituents. The approximate period is indicated by the suffix: namely $_1$ for diurnal constituents (having one complete cycle per day), $_2$ for semi-diurnal constituents (having two cycles per day), etc. There are four principal constituents which will be encountered by the navigator, as follows:

M_2 Principal Lunar constituent, moving at twice the speed of the mean moon.
S_2 Principal Solar constituent, moving at twice the speed of the mean sun.
K_1 Allowing for part of the effects of the Sun's and Moon's declinations.
O_1 Allowing for the remaining part of the Moon's declination.

The significance of other important constituents can be found in *Admiralty Tidal Handbook No. 1* and in the *Admiralty Manual of Tides*.

Principles of Harmonic Tidal Analysis and Prediction

In order that the tides may be predicted they must first be observed and analysed. It is not possible to make accurate predictions without previous observation. The longer the period of observation the better the analysis is likely to be. For Standard Port predictions in *TideTables* the general rule is for at least one complete year's observations to be analysed. For secondary port predictions, analysis of at least one month's observations is the aim.

Each tidal constituent has a 'speed', 'amplitude' and 'phase'.

The speed, which is known from astronomical theory, is given in degrees per hour. As one complete cycle is 360° and the S_2 constituent has two complete cycles per day, the speed of the S_2 constituent is 720° per day or 30° per hour. The speeds of M_2, K_1 and O_1 can similarly be calculated to be 28·98, 15·04 and 13·94 degrees per hour respectively.

The amplitude, which is unknown, is equal to half the range, the range being the difference in height between the maximum and minimum of each oscillation. The unit chosen is immaterial and can be in feet and decimals, metres, etc., according to the national unit of measurement.

The phase of a constituent, which is also unknown, is its position in time in relation to its position as indicated by astronomical theory. Owing to the fact that the tide-raising forces do not act instantaneously, each constituent has a time or phase lag. This can be observed in practice from the fact that Spring tides in the British Isles do not occur on days of full and new Moon, as theory would indicate, but two to three days later.

The object of tidal analysis is, therefore, to determine the unknown amplitude (H) and phase lag (g).

Tidal prediction by harmonic methods is simply the synthesis of the constituents for the particular astronomical conditions prevailing at the time.

Methods of Tidal Prediction

These can be divided into two groups, harmonic and non-harmonic. The harmonic methods are as follows:

(a) PREDICTION BY LARGE MECHANICAL OR ELECTRONIC COMPUTERS. – Although these machines appear intricate, the principle is very simple. In the mechanical type a number of cranks, revolving at a constant angular velocity, represent the movement of the different constituents, and the machine merely adds up the heights of each for any particular time. The number of constituents used varies with the complexity of the tide and may be anything from 12 to 62. Electronic tidal computers are not in use in this country but the construction of an electronic computer to do the same work would present no difficulties.

The predictions for the great majority of Standard Ports are computed on mechanical tide-predicting machines. In some cases, where the shallow water constituents are very complex, this method fails to produce predictions of the necessary accuracy and in such cases additional shallow-water corrections have to be applied. The methods by which the Standard Port predictions have been carried out are given in *Tide Tables*, Table V.

(b) PREDICTION ON THE SMALLER PORTABLE PREDICTING MACHINES. – The principle of these machines is exactly the same as for the larger ones but the number of constituents which they can use is generally smaller (from 10 to 16). These portable machines are not used for Standard Port predictions but are employed when a long series of predictions is required for a secondary port. They are also used for the prediction of tidal streams, as given in Admiralty Tide Tables.

(c) PREDICTION BY MATHEMATICAL COMPUTATION. – There are many ways in which the tide may be predicted by simple mathematics. The standard Admiralty Method (Form H.D.289) calculates the semi-diurnal and the diurnal tides separately and then combines them vectorially. Provision is also made for shallow water corrections. Mathematical methods take longer than mechanical ones and they are therefore used only for relatively short periods of prediction (say up to three days). This is the method of harmonic prediction most likely to be used by navigators where accurate prediction for secondary ports, or for Standard Ports at times between high and low water (foreign waters only) is required.

The non-harmonic methods of prediction involve the comparison of the tide at one place with the tide at another and the calculation of time and height differences (which may be variable) between the two. This method is used for the prediction of a few Standard Ports, mainly where there are several Standard Ports, relatively close together, in estuaries where the shallow water effects are considerable. In such cases, prediction by differences may give more consistent predictions than prediction from harmonic constants. This is also the standard method of predicting the times and heights of high and low water at secondary ports in the British Isles and other European waters. It should be noted, however, that in Vols. II and III of A.T.T., the differences given are much less reliable, owing to the relatively smaller number of Standard Ports and, in consequence, the greater differences in tidal characteristics between the Standard and the secondary ports. *Where accurate times and heights are required for secondary ports in foreign waters, Form H.D.289 should always be used if possible.*

Methods of Tidal Analysis

Tidal analysis can similarly be carried out using either harmonic or non-harmonic methods. For either method a complete and continuous record of one month's tidal observations is necessary if reasonably accurate results are required, though approximations can be made from shorter series. The standard Admiralty harmonic method smooths out the observations to remove the random effects of meteorological conditions; this is done by drawing contours of the tidal heights which, in the absence of disturbing meteorological effects, run smoothly from day to day. From this graph a number of selected heights are taken, and these heights are used for the mathematical calculation of the harmonic constants. The method is half graphical and half mathematical and is therefore known as the Admiralty Semi-Graphic Method of Harmonic Tidal Analysis. A complete description of the method, with instructions and an example, is to be found in H.D.505, *Admiralty Tidal Handbook No. 1.*

The analysis on one year's observations can be carried out by a similar but somewhat more elaborate process.

Non-harmonic analysis is simply the comparison of heights against heights and times against times, the results being plotted as simple graphs, from which average, maximum and minimum heights and time differences can be read off. This type of analysis is normally used for analysing observations for a period of one month at places destined to be included as secondary ports in Part II of A.T.T., Vol. I. The time differences given therein are average maximum and minimum and the tidal levels are values of Mean High Water Springs and Neaps, and Mean Low Water Springs and Neaps.

Tidal Streams and Currents

A careful distinction must be made between tidal streams (called, in some countries, 'tidal currents') and currents (called, in some countries, 'non-tidal currents').

Tidal streams are horizontal movements of the water in response to the tide-raising forces. The tidal streams do not cause any nett transfer of water. Mixed up with the tidal stream, however, are currents, some of which are more or less regular and some entirely random and capricious. Currents can be caused by oceanographic factors, such as water of differing salinity or temperature, by meteorological factors such as differing barometric pressure and wind, and by topographical factors such as irregularities in the sea bed.

Tidal streams are of two main types, rectilinear and rotatory. As the names imply, the first has only two directions (with perhaps small variations), which can be called the ebb and the flood streams, or preferably, east-going, west-going, etc. The rotatory tidal streams are continually changing in direction and rotate through 360° in a complete cycle.

Tidal streams, like tides, have semi-diurnal and diurnal components and can be analysed harmonically or non-harmonically. In the British Isles, the movement of the tidal streams is closely related to the tides in the vicinity. The rates of the stream are related to the range of the tide and the times of slack water are related to, though not necessarily identical with, the times of high and low water at the nearest Standard Port. The most convenient method of analysis and prediction is therefore the non-harmonic method, whereby the direction and rate is given for every hour before and after high water at the Standard Port.

In some parts of the world, however, the character of the tidal stream bears no relation to that of any nearby Standard Port. The streams in the Straits of Malacca are an example. In such places, therefore, it is necessary to analyse and predict the streams harmonically and predictions for a selected number of such places are given in A.T.T., Vols. II and III.

Where the tidal stream can be related to a Standard Port and when there are sufficient data, atlases are available showing simultaneous rates and directions over a wide area. Such atlases are provided for all the waters around the British Isles.

Observation of tidal streams presents greater difficulties than the observation of tides. Though the observation of the tide for a year at a Standard Port presents no insuperable difficulties, observation of tidal streams in the middle of some navigable channel could hardly be carried out for the same period without tremendous effort and expense. Fortunately, however, the degree of accuracy necessary for tidal predictions is unnecessary as well as impractical in the case of tidal streams. Because of the rapidly changing effects of the topography of the sea bed on the direction and rate of the tidal stream, it is often impossible to give more than an indication of how a ship will be affected by tidal streams in her passage. In a narrow channel, for instance, the stream may be running at 3 knots in the centre with virtually no stream, or even a stream running in the opposite direction, at the edges of the channel; the stream varying from nothing to three knots in the navigable part. Tidal stream predictions for any given position in the channel should be correct for that position, but may well be incorrect for a position a few yards either side. While, therefore, the tidal stream predictions must be accurate enough for navigational purposes, the methods of prediction do not have to be so complex as for tidal predictions. Tidal stream predictions can be carried out with sufficient accuracy by means of the portable (ten-component) predicting machine.

Eddies, Races and Overfalls

Eddies, tide-rips, overfalls and races are different forms of water turbulence caused by abruptly changing topography of the sea bed, the configuration of the coastline, the constriction of channels or by sudden changes in tidal or tidal stream characteristics.

An eddy is a circular movement of water, the diameter of which may be anything from a few inches to a few miles. For an example of the latter, see the Pocket Tidal Stream Atlas of the Approaches to Portland, where there is a permanent eddy to the east of Portland.

An overfall is another name for a *tide-rip* and is caused by a strong stream near the sea bed being deflected upwards by obstruction on the bottom, thus causing a confused sea on the surface.

A tidal race is an exceptionally strong stream, usually caused by the constriction of water passing round a headland or where tidal streams from different directions converge.

Where the effect of eddies, etc., are of a permanent nature, they are taken into account when predicting tidal streams.

Seiches, Bores, Seismic Waves

Seiches are sudden non-tidal fluctuations set in motion by sudden changes in meteorological conditions, such as the passage of a deep depression. The period between successive waves may be anything from a few minutes to a few hours and the height of the wave from a fraction of an inch to several feet.

A bore (in old English – *eagre*) is a phenomenon found in certain rivers where there is a large tidal range. The phenomenon usually occurs only at Springs, i.e. when the range of the tide is large. It occurs in rivers between points where the bed slopes fairly steeply and where, at low water, the channel is very restricted. In these conditions, by the time it is low water in the lower reaches, there is a considerable head of water in the upper channels trying to flow seawards. As the tide rises in the lower reaches its inward movement is resisted by the strong seaward flow down the sloping river bed. Eventually the water in the lower reaches acquires sufficient head to overcome that resistance and the water moves inward in the form of a wave, several feet high, the water on the up-river side still trying to move to seaward. At the instant before the arrival of the bore, the river level at that point is at its lowest; with the passage of the bore there is a very rapid rise in level. The bore is followed by a very strong inward flow of short duration called the 'after-rush'. Thereafter the level rises gradually and the inward flow continues at a much reduced rate until high water.

A *seismic wave* (often called, erroneously, a '*tidal wave*') is, as its name implies, the result of an earthquake, usually submarine, which sets up waves, entirely unconnected with the tides, in the same way that waves are set up by dropping a stone into a pond. These waves travel with great rapidity in the deep waters of the oceans, reaching speeds of about 400 knots. In common with other waves, on reaching shallow water they increase in height and often reach destructive proportions. Although there is reason to think that the heights of some seismic waves have been exaggerated, waves with an amplitude of 35 feet have certainly been recorded. The first destructive wave is usually preceded by a very rapid ebbing of the water and the arrival of the wave follows a few minutes later. The second and third waves are often higher than the first wave. Where the wave arrives at an island surrounded by very deep water, the seismic wave may be experienced only as a series of relatively rapid rises or falls; where, however, there is a stretch of shallow water near the coast, the wave may attain sufficient height to break and this type of wave is by far the most destructive.

Datum for Tidal Predictions

Soundings on Admiralty charts are given below the level of Chart Datum, an arbitrary level which should be so low that the tide will not frequently fall below it. The Navigator obtains the actual depth of water by adding to the sounding the height of the tide. Thus it is evident that the datum for tidal predictions must be the same as the datum for soundings and this principle is rigidly adhered to in Admiralty publications.

Admiralty Tide Tables

Admiralty Tide Tables are issued in three volumes with world-wide coverage. Vol. I covers the British Isles and provides the official predictions for the whole of that area. Vols. II and III are, for the most part, a compilation of the predictions of other countries, with a leavening of information obtained by H.M. Surveying Ships in foreign waters.

The predictions of the times and heights of high and low water for Standard Ports may be considered as being of a greater accuracy than is required for navigational purposes. The predictions do not, however, make any allowance for the effect of unusual weather conditions, such as excessively high or low barometric pressure or storm surges set up by high winds. Under perfect conditions the predicted height should not be in error by more than about 0·3 feet and the time of high water by more than ten minutes. Strong winds can, however, advance or retard the times by half an hour or so and storm surges can cause tidal heights to be very different from predictions. During an average year in the British Isles, there are several small surges which raise the height of high water by 2 to 3 feet. Under exceptionally severe conditions levels can be raised considerably higher; for instance, during the storms which caused extensive flooding and loss of life on the East Coast of the British Isles in January, 1953, high water on the Netherlands coast was at one time more than 10 feet higher than predicted.

The tidal data for the secondary ports are of more variable quality. At some places systematic observations have been taken but at others only a few random observations, taken perhaps many years ago, are available. At yet others, data have been interpolated from places on either side. In general the data are accurate enough for normal navigational needs, but are being continually improved by up-to-date observations where possible.

Tide Tables give the following information:

(1) Daily predictions of the times and heights of high and low water for a large number of Standard Ports.

(2) Data for Secondary Ports which enable the times and heights of high and low water to be calculated.

(3) Diagrams and tables for calculating the height of the tide at times between high and low water.

(4) Tidal stream predictions (Vols. II and III only) giving direction of flow, times of slack water and maximum rates.

(5) Data for Standard Ports, including tidal levels, method of prediction, etc.

(6) Details of chart datums and their connection to the Land Levelling System, where known. These are intended mainly for the use of Hydrographic Surveyors, Civil Engineers, etc., engaged on coast protection and other coastal engineering projects.

(7) Tidal angles and factors, being tables for use with Tidal Prediction Form H.D.289. (Vols. II and III only.)

(8) Table of Astronomical arguments, for use with the Admiralty Semigraphic Method of Harmonic Tidal Analysis, H.D.505 and with the ten component tide-predicting machine. (Vols. II and III only.)

(9) Vols. II and III also give the four principal harmonic constants for all places where they are known, and average seasonal variations in mean sea level. Also shallow water correction tables for use with Form H.D.289 where these are necessary and are known.

Definitions (Fig. 217)

TERMS IN GENERAL USE

Tides – The periodical vertical oscillations of the sea in response to the tide-raising forces of the Moon and the Sun.

Tidal Streams. – The periodical horizontal oscillations of the sea in response to the tide-raising forces of the Moon and Sun.

High Water. – The highest level reached by the sea during one tidal oscillation.

Low Water. – The lowest level reached by the sea during one tidal oscillation.

Maximum Rate. – The greatest rate reached in each of two more or less opposing directions by the tidal streams in one oscillation.

Slack Water. – The periods, preceding and succeeding maximum rate, when the tidal streams are at their weakest.

Chart Datum. – The low-water plane to which the depths of features permanently covered by the sea, and the heights of features periodically covered and uncovered by the sea, are referred. The tidal levels and predicted high and low water heights of the tide are also referred to this plane. By international

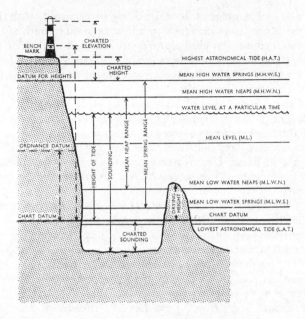

FIG. 217

agreement, chart datum should be a plane so low that the tide will not frequently fall below it. The heights of those features never, or rarely, covered by the sea are referred to a high-water plane.

Ordnance Datum. – The plane to which the heights of all features on maps are referred. It is the datum of the land levelling system and in most countries is based on mean sea level at the point of origin of that system.

Height of the Tide. – The vertical distance between the level of the sea at any instant and chart datum.

Range of the Tide. – The difference between the levels of successive high and low waters. (Amplitude = half the range.)

Mean Level. – The average level of the sea as calculated from a long series of observations. Mean Sea Level is the mean level of the sea at all stages of the tide. Mean Tide Level is the level midway between Mean High Water and Mean Low Water. If the tidal curve is distorted by the frictional effects occurring in shallow and restricted waters, Mean Sea Level and Mean Tide Level will differ.

Springs. – The range of the semi-diurnal tide varies mainly with the phases of the Moon, from new to full Moon and vice versa. Springs are those semi-diurnal tides of greatest range which occur in each of those periods.

Neaps. – Those semi-diurnal tides of least range which occur in each period from new to full Moon and vice versa.

Equinoctial Springs. – Spring tides which occur near the equinoxes. The semi-diurnal tides have their greatest range at those equinoctial springs when the Moon is nearest to the Earth.

Tropical Springs. – The range of the diurnal tide varies mainly with the declination of the Moon, from maximum north or maximum south of the equator to zero declination. Tropical Springs are those diurnal tides of greatest range which occur in each of these periods. 'Tropical' derives from the fact that when the Moon has its average maximum declination it is over the tropic of Cancer or Capricorn.

Mean High Water Springs (M.H.W.S.) and Mean Low Water Springs (M.L.W.S.). – The height of Mean High Water Springs is the average, throughout the year, of the heights of two successive high waters during those periods of 24 hours, in each semi-lunation, when the range of the tide is greatest. The height of Mean Low Water Springs is the average, throughout the year, of the heights of two successive low waters during the same periods of 24 hours.

Mean High Water Neaps (M.H.W.N.) and Mean Low Water Neaps (M.L.W.N.). – The height of Mean High Water Neaps (M.H.W.N.) is the average, throughout the year, of the heights of two successive high waters during those periods of 24 hours, in each semi-lunation, when the range of the tide is least. The height of Mean Low Water Neaps (M.L.W.N.) is the average, throughout the year, of the heights of two successive low waters during the same periods of 24 hours.

Highest Astronomical Tide (H.A.T.) and Lowest Astronomical Tide (L.A.T.). – The highest and lowest tides that it is possible to predict at Standard Ports. Unpredictable meteorological conditions may increase or decrease these figures.

Rectilinear Tidal Streams. – Those tidal streams, usually confined to rivers, estuaries and inshore waters, which flow only in two more or less opposing directions during an oscillation.

Rotatory Tidal Streams. – Those tidal streams which flow at their maximum rates in two more or less opposing directions, but which gradually turn from one to the other, and back to the original direction, during an oscillation.

Current. – The horizontal movement of the water due to causes, mainly meteorological and oceanographical, other than the tide-raising forces of the Moon and Sun. It may be a progressive or a fluctuating movement.

Flow. – The combination at any instant of tidal stream and current.

TERMS BECOMING OBSOLETE, BUT STILL FOUND ON CERTAIN CHARTS

High Water Full and Change (H.W.F. and C.). – This is the local mean time of high water on the day of full or new Moon, and the addition of 50 minutes for each subsequent day of the Moon's age gives an approximate time of high water on any day. A method of prediction which dated back hundreds of years.

Mean High Water Interval (M.H.W.I.). – This is the average interval between Moon's transit and the following high water, and will give a better average approximation to the time of high water than H.W.F. and C.

Flood Tide. – A loose term applied either to the rising tide or to the ingoing tidal stream. Strictly speaking, it would only be applicable in rivers where slack water coincides with high water.

Ebb Tide. – A loose term applied either to the falling tide or to the outgoing tidal stream. It also would only be strictly applicable in rivers.

CHAPTER XIII

Navigation in Ice

THE navigation of ships in or near pack ice is too extensive a subject for any detailed study to be attempted in a single chapter. Before proceeding to high latitudes, or areas where ice may be expected, the navigator is advised to study, in addition to the few hints given here, such of the undermentioned publications as may be applicable to the area of operations.

Terminology

Descriptive terms concerning ice and ice navigation are contained in the relevant *Sailing Directions*, and in the glossary of Hydrographic Terms contained in H.D. Professional Paper No. 11 (Part V).

Growth, Decay and Movement of Sea Ice

Remarks on the growth, decay and movement of sea ice are also contained in the *Sailing Directions*, with particular reference to the area covered by each individual volume.

Information on Ice Conditions

Information concerning the state of the ice in various areas throughout the year is contained in one or more of the following publications:

(a) *Sailing Directions.*
(b) U.S. Hydrographic Office *Sailing Directions.*
(c) *Monthly Ice Charts – Arctic Seas* (M.O.M. 390a).
(d) *Monthly Ice Charts – Western North Atlantic* (M.O. 478).
(e) *Monthly Ice Charts – North Pacific Ocean* (H.D. 416).
(f) *Ice Atlas of the Northern Hemisphere* (U.S. Hydrographic Office publication No. 550).
(g) *Manual of Ice Seamanship* (U.S. Hydrographic Office publication No. 551).
(h) *Oceanographic Atlas of Polar Seas* (U.S. Hydrographic Office publication No. 705).
Part I – Antarctic.
Part II – Arctic.
(i) *Pilot Chart of the North Atlantic Ocean.* – Issued monthly by the U.S. Hydrographic Office.
(j) Distribution of the Pack Ice in the Southern Ocean. *Discovery Reports, Volume XIX* (Cambridge). A summary of this report is contained in the *Antarctic Pilot.*
(k) *Lloyd's List*, published weekly, gives up-to-date information concerning the state of the ice on the North Atlantic shipping routes.

Not all these works are supplied to H.M. ships. The *Hydrographic Supplies Handbook* (H.51) and the *Meteorological Supplies Handbook* (W1) give the scale of distribution.

Other publications, and some useful reports, are available in the Hydrographic Department of the Admiralty.

Radio Reports of Ice Conditions in the North Atlantic

Radio reports available to ships are listed in the *Admiralty List of Radio Signals*, Vol. V, in the section headed 'Radio Navigational Warnings and Ice Reports – Service Details'. Ships may also ask the International Ice Patrol ships for reports at any time.

Recommended Routes clear of Pack Ice

When selecting a route which may take the ship near the limits of pack ice, the following should be consulted, in addition to those already mentioned:

(a) North Atlantic Route Charts (Admiralty Charts 2058b and 2058c).

(b) *Ocean Passages of the World.*

Occasionally the ice extends over a greater area than usual. When this occurs, amendments to the recommended routes are published in Admiralty Notices to Mariners.

A route which is clear of pack ice is not necessarily clear of icebergs and growlers.

The International Ice Patrol

The International Ice Observation and Patrol Services in the North Atlantic Ocean are conducted by the United States Coast Guard. The work is carried out by Coast Guard vessels and long-range reconnaissance aircraft operating from the U.S. Naval Station at Argentia, Newfoundland.

The objects of the service are to patrol the areas where ice is a menace to shipping, to keep track of ice and icebergs in these areas, to warn shipping accordingly, to destroy derelicts which are a danger to navigation, and to carry out scientific investigations relating to the formation and decay of sea ice.

Patrols start when the presence of ice begins to threaten shipping, normally in March each year, and continue until July. Ships on patrol are responsible for co-ordinating all reports from ships and aircraft and passing them to shore, whence they are re-broadcast to shipping at routine times. (*See Admiralty List of Radio Signals*, Vol. V.)

The ships patrol in the vicinity of the Grand Banks, and around the coasts of Newfoundland and Labrador.

Patrol ships also give assistance to ships in distress, and can render medical assistance.

The vessels employed on this service are designed for icebreaking, and are specially fitted for towing in ice.

During the period of the patrols, ships can assist, when between 39°N. and 49°N. and between 42°W. and 60°W., by reporting at four-hourly intervals their position, course and speed, water and air temperatures, visibility, wind and sea, and icebergs or obstructions, when sighted, giving date, time (G.M.T.), position, set and drift; when reporting an iceberg the temperature of the water should be included.

It should be remembered that fog and bad weather are common in this area, and there may therefore be dangers present which have not been detected by, or reported to, the patrols.

Reports from Ships sighting Ice or Icebergs

Reports should be made for the immediate information of ships in the locality, and for record purposes.

By the International Convention for the Safety of Life at Sea, 1948, ships sighting icebergs or ice dangerous to navigation are required to report the fact by radio to ships in the vicinity and to shore, by broadcast, giving the following particulars:

  (a) Kind of ice.
  (b) Position of the ice or iceberg.
  (c) Time (G.M.T.), and date, of making the sighting.

EXAMPLE: *TTT Ice – Large berg sighted in position 4600 North 4300 West at 0900Z May 13th.*

These reports may be amplified by giving the amount of ice in eighths of the sea covered, and the size of the floes:

  Large: over 1,000 yards in extent.
  Medium: 200–1,000 yards in extent.
  Small: less than 200 yards in extent.

Any reports made should be entered in the ship's log for record purposes, and where available, in Air Ministry Form 912 (Ice Report Form). These forms are issued on request to ships likely to encounter ice or icebergs.

Signs of the Proximity of Ice

Indications of the proximity of ice are mentioned in the appropriate *Sailing Directions*.

Remarks on the use of radar and asdics in or near ice will be found on page 383.

Ship Handling in Ice

A chapter on Ship Handling in Ice appears in the *Seamanship Manual*, Vol. III.

Some additional remarks are contained in the relevant *Sailing Directions*.

Accuracy of Charts of Polar Regions

Charts of polar regions are, generally speaking, very imperfect, and this must be borne in mind when fixing by terrestrial objects. It is advisable to keep to well-sounded tracks as far as possible.

In places where shallow water and rocks make accurate navigation essential, and when terrestrial objects are not available for fixing, it may be necessary to stop the ship to allow two astronomical position lines to be obtained. Otherwise single position lines only will be available during the period of no night, since with the run between sights so uncertain, transferred position lines produce only a very approximate result.

If radio aids are available under such circumstances, the problem is very much easier, but in remote areas such as the Antarctic, reliance must be placed on astronomical observations, radar when near the coast, and soundings. Soundings are of little value unless the ship is in one of the few well-charted areas, but will of course give warning of shallow water.

When fixing by astronomical observations, or with radio aids, it should be remembered that the ship's true latitude and longitude so obtained may not correspond accurately to her position in relation to charted objects or dangers.

Compasses

Consideration must be given to the possibility of compass errors due to high latitudes or local magnetic disturbances. While the gyro-compass may be expected to perform satisfactorily if the correct settings are applied (*see* appropriate handbook), the magnetic compass, owing to reduction in directive force, may develop large deviations in high latitudes unless accurately adjusted. The ship should be swung on the last possible occasion before entering the ice, and thereafter deviations should be obtained at frequent intervals. Provided the sky is not overcast, it is possible to obtain deviations on a wide range of headings as the ship manoeuvres through the ice.

Weather and Visibility

Fog, blizzards, and poor visibility are common in polar regions, and abnormal refraction often produces mirage effects.

The effects of abnormal refraction on astronomical observations are discussed in Volume III.

Keeping the Reckoning in Ice

Progress is generally slow, with constant alterations of course and speed to conform to the available leads.

It will seldom be possible to lay off a course and adhere to it.

Estimations of course and distance made good (rather than speed) must be made at very short intervals.

It is extremely difficult to estimate speed through ice. A Dutchman's Log is of little value as the speed is changing so frequently.

When estimating distance made good, progress relative to an iceberg or conspicuous ice floe should be noted. A radar or rangefinder range of an iceberg may be of assistance.

It should be remembered that ice floes move under the influence of wind and current, while icebergs are more influenced by currents than wind. Icebergs sometimes move against the wind and in the opposite direction to the ice floes, and these movements must be allowed for by taking into account the past and present winds and prevailing currents. The latter are described in the *Sailing Directions*.

In open pack where it is possible to maintain constant, or nearly constant speed, mean course and speed should be estimated at frequent intervals. Here a bottom log and A.R.L. plotting table may be of assistance, but arrangements must be made to enable the log to be housed at short notice should it be threatened by the ice.

Use of Radar in or near Ice

Radar can be of great assistance in giving warning of ice at night or in poor visibility, but it may also produce a false sense of security. A slight decrease in the performance of the set may well lead to dangerous growlers remaining undetected. Similarly, in anything except a flat calm sea, echoes from small floes and growlers may be lost in the wave clutter, while in very rough seas icebergs twenty or thirty feet in height may not be detected.

It should be remembered that ice does not give such a good echo as metal, so that, although a set may pick up navigational buoys at a certain range, it will not necessarily detect a growler of the same size.

Floes and leads show up well on a P.P.I., but no indication is given of the composition of the floes, so that radar by itself will not necessarily indicate the best course to follow.

The quality of the echoes received will depend on the surface of the ice rather than its thickness. Snow-covered floes will not produce such good echoes as those with a hard covering of ice.

At short ranges icebergs may be indistinguishable amongst the pack ice, but at longer ranges, where the beam is travelling more horizontally, they will show up.

In waters where shipping may be met, individual echoes should be plotted. This will indicate whether an echo is a ship, or a drifting berg or growler.

Confusion between a ship echo and an iceberg may result in avoiding action being taken too late. Even if the echo is classified as an iceberg it should be given a wide berth in order to avoid any growlers which may recently have calved from it.

When using radar in coastal waters it should be remembered that the appearance of coastlines may be greatly changed by the presence of fast ice or stranded icebergs.

While radar is a very valuable aid to navigation in ice, its limitations must constantly be borne in mind, and the fact that it is only *an aid* cannot be over-emphasized.

The Use of Asdics in Detecting Ice

In open water, asdics can be used to give warning of icebergs and growlers, and in the cold waters of the Antarctic good results can be obtained. In the relatively warm waters in which icebergs are met in the Northern Hemisphere results are not so good.

Icebergs rising and falling in a swell produce noise which can be detected by asdics keeping a listening watch.

The likelihood of damage to the equipment precludes the use of asdics in waters where pack ice or brash is present.

Preparation of Ships for Ice Navigation

Remarks on the preparation of ships prior to entering the ice are contained in the appropriate *Sailing Directions*.

Convoying in Ice

Notes on Convoying in Ice (H.D.394) deals with the convoying of ships by icebreakers.

CHAPTER XIV

Graphical Problems

IN NEARLY every problem that involves moving ships, it is essential to find the course and speed of one ship *relative* to another.

Consider two ships – O, steaming 085° at 12 knots, and A, steaming 030° at 10 knots (Fig. 218). At 1000 A bears 340°, distant 10 miles from O. O_1, O_2, O_3 ... etc. are the positions of O at intervals of 6 minutes after 1000, while A_1, A_2, A_3 ... etc., are the positions of A at similar 6-minute intervals. O_1A_1, O_2A_2, O_3A_3 ... are the ranges of A from O at 1006, 1012, 1018 ... respectively. To an observer on board O, therefore, the range of A is increasing while her bearing draws left.

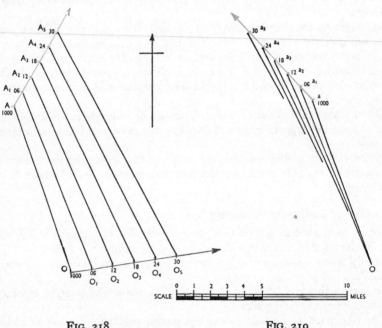

FIG. 218   FIG. 219

If the positions of A *relative to* O are plotted (Fig. 219), the apparent track of A as observed on board O is a, a_1, a_2, a_3, a_4 ... etc., where oa, oa_1, oa_2, oa_3 ... etc., are equal in length and parallel to OA, O_1A_1, O_2A_2, O_3A_3 ... etc., in Fig. 218; that is, an apparent course of 317° and an apparent speed of 10·2 knots.

Thus, if two ships are moving in different directions, then the movement of one as seen from the other will be different from the individual movements of either ship. The apparent movement of one as seen from the other is called its

384

'relative' movement; and in the example above, 317° is said to be the course of *A relative to O*, while 10·2 knots is the speed of *A relative to O*. This movement of *A* would be that observed on a P.P.I. or surface relative plot on board *O*.

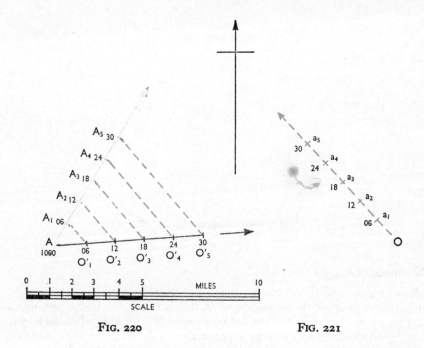

FIG. 220   FIG. 221

To Find the Course and Speed of a Ship Relative to Another Ship

Suppose the two ships in the above example are at the same point at 1000, say *A* (Fig. 220). Then O'_1, O'_2, O'_3 . . . etc. are the positions of *O* at subsequent 6-minute intervals, while A_1, A_2, A_3 . . . etc. are the positions of *A* at the same times. To an observer on board *O*, *A* is apparently opening on a steady bearing parallel to O'_1A_1 (or O'_2A_2, O'_3A_3 . . . etc.). Her apparent speed in knots along this bearing is found by dividing the distance O'_1A_1 by 6/60 hours. Fig. 221 shows this track of *A relative to O*.

In the triangle AO'_4A_4 in Fig. 222:

AO'_4 is proportional to the speed of *O*.

AA_4 is proportional to the speed of *A*.

O'_4A_4 is proportional to the speed of *A relative to O*.

Suppose now that *O* and *A* are in their former positions relative to each other, as in the lower half of Fig. 222 (that is, *A* bears 340°, 10 miles from *O* at 1000). After 24 minutes *O* will have moved to O_4 and *A* to A_4. If *O* had been plotted as stationary, as in Fig. 221, *A* would have apparently moved to a_4. Aa_4 is clearly equal and parallel to O'_4A_4 and is therefore equal to the movement over a 24-minute period of *A relative to O*.

The course and speed of one ship relative to another are therefore the same, regardless of the ships' actual positions.

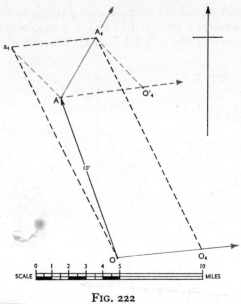

FIG. 222

The Speed Triangle

Relative course and speed can be found by constructing a 'speed triangle'[1].
In the above example the movement of O, that is to say, her course and speed
through the water, can be represented by a vector WO (Fig. 223a) whose length
is her speed measured on some convenient scale and drawn in the direction $085°$.
In the same way the vector WA in Fig. 223b represents the course and speed
of A through the water.

The point W is common to both vectors; if the triangle WOA is drawn
(Fig. 224), OA is obviously parallel to O'_4A_4 in Fig. 222. The ratio of OA to
O'_4A_4 is the same as the ratio of WO to AO'_4 and the length of OA measured
on the speed scale is therefore the speed of A relative to O. OA, in the direction
from O towards A, is thus a vector representing the movement of A relative
to O. It is conventionally marked by an arrowhead in a circle, the arrow pointing
towards the ship whose relative motion is represented. In Fig. 224, OA represents
the course and speed of A relative to O. The reciprocal vector AO represents
the course and speed of O relative to A.

WOA is a speed triangle. It is important to remember that, in any speed
triangle,

(a) *the arrowheads showing the true courses of the two ships must always
diverge from the point of intersection of the vectors* (W, in Fig. 224);

(b) *the arrows showing the true and relative courses of one ship converge to a
point* (A in Fig. 224).

Thus, when relative courses and speeds are considered, one ship can be plotted
at a point and kept there; the other can be plotted relative to that point by
moving her along a relative course at a relative speed.

---

[1] The Battenberg' course indicator is constructed to give a mechanical solution of the
speed triangle. Examples of its use are given at the end of this chapter.

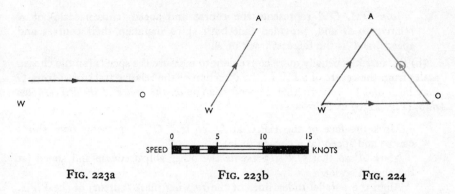

FIG. 223a   FIG. 223b   FIG. 224

In the past, relative velocity problems were solved by plotting the datum ship (Flagship, Senior Officer, ship on which station had been ordered, or the enemy) at a point, and keeping her there while initial and required positions of own ship were plotted in relation to her. However, in view of the increased use of the P.P.I., it has become desirable that the solution of relative velocity problems shall be based upon their 'P.P.I. Presentation', where own ship always appears stationary in the centre, and tracks developing always appear as tracks relative to own ship.

For example, another ship A bears 065°, distance 10 miles, course 080°, speed 10 knots. Own ship O is steering 030° at 16 knots.

(a) The relative track of A from O, which is the track seen on the face of a P.P.I., may be found by constructing a speed triangle *on the present position of the other ship* (Fig. 225a) as follows:

> Draw WA to represent 10 knots on any convenient scale in the direction 080°. This is the course and speed of the other ship relative to the water.
>
> Draw WO' to represent 16 knots on the same scale in the direction 030°. This is the course and speed of own ship relative to the water.

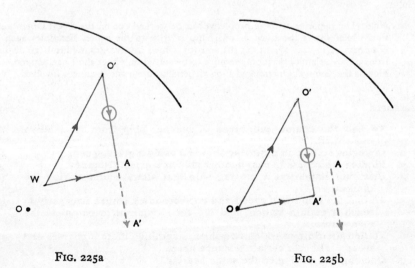

FIG. 225a   FIG. 225b

Join $O'A$. $O'A$ represents the course and speed (chosen scale) of A relative to O and, provided that both ships maintain their courses and speeds, AA' *is* the forecast track of A.

(b) Because it is usually more convenient to measure the speeds (on the chosen scale) from the centre of a P.P.I., the direction of the relative track of A from O may be found by constructing a speed triangle *on the centre of the P.P.I.* (*own ship*) (Fig. 225b) as follows:

Mark the face of the P.P.I. at O' so that OO' represents own ship's course and speed (at a chosen scale).

Mark A' so that OA' represents the other ship's course and speed (at the chosen scale).

Align the parallel index lines of the rotating mask (cursor) of the P.P.I. with $O'A'$; a parallel through A then gives the future track of A, and the length $O'A'$ gives the relative speed.

In the examples that follow, the lettering is made as consistent as possible, and the colour scheme adopted is as follows:

Course steered by own ship, O: red ⎫ In general, speed triangles are
Course steered by other ship, A: blue ⎪ drawn in full lines, and tracks
Relative courses: green ⎬ are shown by broken lines.
All other detail: black ⎭

The scale is necessarily varied.

In all problems of relative velocity the following factors are involved:

Course and speed of O.
Course and speed of A.
Relative course and relative speed of O or A.

If any four of the above are known, it is possible, by drawing a speed triangle to scale, to find the other two.

A number of examples illustrating the principles of speed triangles in various circumstances are summarized in the following table and explained in detail later.

Note: The majority of these problems can be worked out on the Local Operational Plot which shows the track of own ship relative to the water. Examples such as Numbers 4, 11, 12, 13, 14, 15 (b) and (c), which involve geographical (as distinct from purely relative) positions, require to be solved on either the Local Operational Plot or the General Operational Plot, depending upon the distances involved.

Example 1 – To find the Course and Speed of Another Ship from its Relative Movement

You are in a cruiser (O) steaming 340°, 12 knots. The following ranges and bearings of another ship (A) are obtained by radar.

Time	Bearing	Range (miles)
2300	330°	5·7
2306	338°	4·9
2312	350°	4·2
2318	005°	3·8
2324	020°	3·7
2330	039°	3·9
2336	055°	4·5

What is the true course and speed of the other ship? If she maintains this course and speed, when will she be 8 miles away?

In Fig. 226, the positions of the echo, a_1, a_2, a_3 . . . etc. are plotted relative to own ship O. A is the position of the other ship at the time of the last observation, 2336.

The relative course of the other ship is along $a_1 A$. Her relative speed is found by dividing the distance $a_1 A$ by the time taken for the echo to move from a_1 to A, that is, 7 miles in 36 minutes, or 11·7 knots.

Draw $O'A$ on a convenient scale to represent the course and speed of the other ship relative to own ship.

Draw WO' on the same scale to represent course and speed of own ship relative to the water. Join WA to complete the speed triangle WAO'.

The course of the other ship relative to the water (her true course) will be parallel to WA. Her true speed will be the length of WA measured on the speed scale.

If she maintains the same course and speed, her relative track will be along AM and she will be 8 miles away when she arrives at M. This will be after an interval of time equal to the distance AM divided by the relative speed, 11·7 knots.

Answer: Course: 041°.
        Speed: 10 knots.
        Eight miles away at 2359 (4·'5 at 11·7 knots).

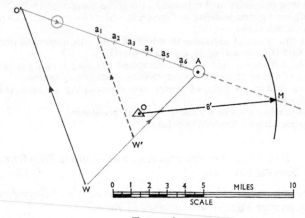

FIG. 226

Fig. 226 also shows that it is unnecessary to measure the actual relative course and speed of the other ship. a_1A is the relative track of the other ship between 2300 and 2336 and its length is proportional to the relative speed. If $W'a_1$ is laid off in direction 340° and equal in length to 36 minutes run of own ship, it will represent course and speed of own ship on the same scale as a_1A represents the relative speed, so that $W'A$ will represent the true speed of the other ship on that scale.

The triangles $AW'a_1$ and AWO' are similar, so that the direction of $W'A$ gives the true course of the other ship.

When the echo is being plotted on the Local Operational Plot, the true track of the other ship is obtained without further construction. This is because the position of own ship is shown moving relative to the water, and the plotted positions of the other ship give its movement relative to the water and not relative to own ship.

Example 2 – Changing Station on a Moving Ship and using a Given Speed

At 1315 the flagship (A) is steering 000° at 25 knots. Own ship (O) is stationed on the port beam (270°) distant 6 miles and is ordered to take station on the starboard quarter (135°) distant 8 miles. What is the course to steer at 25 knots? How long will it take?

To visualise this problem in terms of 'P.P.I. presentation' one must consider what the flagship's movement must be relative to own ship. In other words, 'What course must own ship steer to make the flagship appear to move from a position 6 miles 090° from me to a position 8 miles 315° from me?'

Fig. 227 shows the situation on the plot at 1315; the future position of the flagship relative to own ship must be A', and thus the future track of the flagship relative to own ship must be AA'.

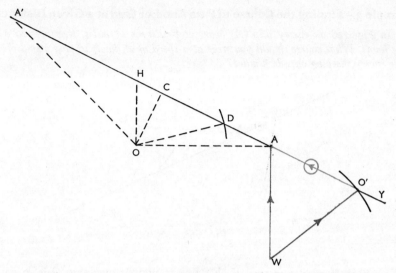

FIG. 227

CONSTRUCTION

Produce $A'A$ to Y. WA is a vector representing the flagship's true track, and is the last 30 minutes of the flagship's filtered track on the plot.

With centre W and radius 30 minutes' run at own speed 25 knots, cut AY in O', and complete a 30-minute speed triangle.

Then WO' is the course to steer – in this case 051°.

The flagship will then move at a speed of $O'A$ relative to own ship = $21\frac{1}{2}$ knots. The time taken to complete the manoeuvre will be the time taken by the flagship to move a relative distance AA' (13 miles) at $21\frac{1}{2}$ knots = $36\frac{1}{4}$ minutes.

> *Notes:*
> Other information can also be found from this figure.
> (1) 'How far astern of the flagship will we pass?' This is given by OH; when the flagship is at H, relative to own ship, we must be astern of the flag.
> Answer: 2·9 miles.
> (2) 'How close to the flagship will we pass?' This is given by OC, since the flagship's relative track AA' comes closest to O at C.
> Answer: 2·6 miles.
> (3) 'If the visibility is 4 miles, when and on what bearing should we sight the flagship?' Centre O, radius 4 miles, cut AA' in D. As the flagship proceeds along the relative track AA', when she gets to D she should be visible on a bearing $OD - 075°$.
> $$\text{Time taken} = \frac{AD}{21\frac{1}{2}} \times 60 = \frac{2\cdot3}{21\frac{1}{2}} \times 60 = 6\frac{1}{2} \text{ minutes.}$$
> She should be seen at $1321\frac{1}{2}$.

Note that in the speed triangle, true tracks diverge from the datum, W; and the flagship's relative track and her true track converge to her present position.

Caution: When the station-taking ship has a lower speed than the ship on which she is taking station, if the manoeuvre is capable of being performed at all there will normally be two courses which can be steered. Unless otherwise stated or for tactical reasons, the course required will be that giving the higher *relative* speed.

Example 3 – Finding the Course to Pass Another Ship at a Given Distance

In Fig. 228 an enemy ship (A) bears 263° distant 11 miles, steering 020°, 24 knots. What course should you steer at a speed of 28 knots to pass ahead of the enemy, keeping outside 5 miles?

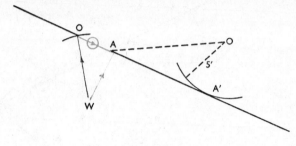

FIG. 228

This problem is similar to that of changing station. If own ship O is to pass ahead of the other ship keeping outside 5 miles, the other ship must be made to move relative to O to pass outside a circle of radius 5 miles, centred at O.

CONSTRUCTION

Lay off WA, the run of the enemy during the last 12 minutes, course 020°, speed 24 knots.

Draw AA', the tangent to the circle, centre O, radius 5 miles. This will be the relative track of A with respect to O, and must pass to the southward of O as shown.

With centre W and radius 12 minutes run at 28 knots, cut $A'A$ produced at O'.

Then WO' will be the course that own ship has to steer (350°) and $O'A$ will represent the relative course and speed of the enemy ship.

> *Note:* the caution appended to the previous example is also relevant to problems of this nature.

Example 4 – Changing Station on a Moving Ship that Alters Course during the Manoeuvre

In Fig. 229 the flagship (A) is steering 020° at 10 knots. At 1000, your cruiser (O), stationed 40 miles 270° from the flagship, receives the following signal: 'Take station 5 miles astern. Intend to alter course to 340° at 1200.' If you proceed at 15 knots, what course must you steer and when will you be in station?

Plot A_1, the position of the flagship at 1200, and from this position plot the imaginary position she would have been in at 1000 if she had steered 340° from 1000 to 1200, A_2.

From O, plot the relative position of the flagship after the change of station; that is, bearing 340°, distance 5 miles, A_3. It is now required to find the course you must steer at 15 knots so that the flagship appears to move from A_2 to A_3. This is the same problem as that illustrated in Example 2.

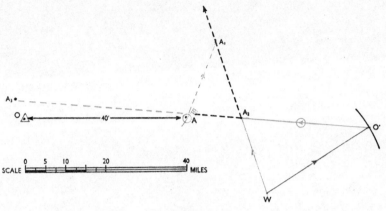

FIG. 229

Draw WA_2 to represent the flagship's course and speed relative to the water (340°, 10 knots). With centre W and radius representing your own speed, draw an arc cutting A_3A_2 produced in O'.

In the speed triangle A_2WO':

WA_2 = flagship's course and speed;

WO' = course of cruiser which, when she is steaming at 15 knots, will make the flagship appear to move from A_2 towards A_3;

$O'A_2$ = course and speed of flagship relative to the cruiser.

The relative distance, A_2A_3, divided by the relative speed of the flagship, gives the time taken to take up the new station.

Answer: Course to steer: 057°.

Time of arrival: 1326 (55 miles at 16 knots).

Example 5 – To find the Minimum Speed and Corresponding Course necessary to Reach a Certain Station, and the Time required to Complete the Manoeuvre

In Fig. 230, your submarine (O) observes an enemy ship (A) bearing 310° distant 4 miles. The enemy's course is estimated at 082° and her speed at 12 knots. It is desired to run submerged to a position for attack, ½ mile, 30° on her starboard bow and to proceed at the lowest possible speed.

(a) At what course and speed should you proceed?

(b) How long will it take you to reach the attacking position?

Plot relative position of the enemy when you are in position for attack, A_1.

Draw WA to represent the course and speed of the enemy relative to the water.

Clearly, if the submarine's speed is to be a minimum, the third side of the speed triangle must be the shortest possible. The shortest distance possible is the perpendicular from W on A_1A produced.

Draw this perpendicular, WO'.

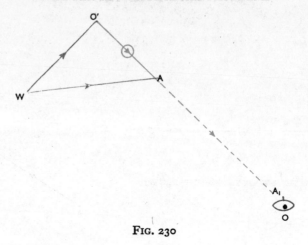

FIG. 230

In the speed triangle AWO':

    WA = enemy ship's course and speed;
    WO' = submarine's course and speed;
    $O'A$ = course and speed of enemy ship relative to submarine.

Answer: (a) Course to steer: 043°.
           Speed: 9·4 knots.
      (b) Relative distance AA_1 of 3'·5, at relative speed $O'A$ of 7·4 knots, will take 28 mins.

Example 6 – To find the Time at which Two Ships, Steaming Different Courses and Speeds, will be a Certain Distance Apart

In Fig. 231, own ship (O) is steering 000° at 16 knots. Another ship (A) bearing 301°, 15 miles away, is steering 040° at 12 knots. When will A be 5 miles away?

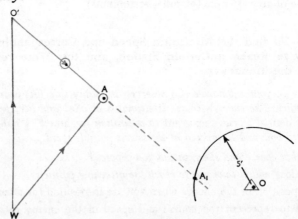

FIG. 231

Draw WA to represent the course and speed of the other ship; draw WO' to represent course and speed of own ship. $O'A$ is then the course and speed of the other ship relative to own ship, and her track relative to own ship will be AA_1.

With centre O and radius 5 miles draw an arc cutting $O'A$ produced in A_1. When the other ship has steamed the relative distance AA_1 she will be 5 miles from O, and the time taken will be equal to the distance AA_1, divided by the length of $O'A$ on the speed scale (10·5 miles at 10·2 knots).

Answer: Ships are five miles apart after 62 minutes.

> *Note:* If the arc of radius 5 miles does not cut $O'A$ produced, the two ships will not get within 5 miles of each other on their present courses and speeds.

Example 7 – Opening and Closing on the Same Bearing

In Fig. 232, your cruiser (O)*, stationed 2 miles on the port bow of the flagship* (A) *steering 328° at 11 knots, is ordered to open to 10 miles and preserve the bearing. Your available speed is 17 knots. Having opened to 10 miles, you are ordered to close to 4 miles on the same bearing. Find the course to open, the course to close, and the time taken.*

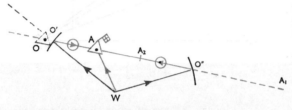

FIG. 232

From own ship, O, plot the relative position of the flagship when you have opened to 10 miles on the same bearing, A_1; and the position of the flagship when you have closed to 4 miles, A_2.

Draw WA to represent the course and speed of the flagship. With radius representing 17 knots and centre W draw arcs cutting AO in O' and OA produced in O''.

In the speed triangles $O'AW$ and $O''AW$:

    AW = course and speed of flagship;

    $O'A$ = course and speed of flagship relative to cruiser when opening;

    $O''A$ = course and speed of flagship relative to cruiser when closing;

    WO' = course of cruiser when opening;

    WO'' = course of cruiser when closing.

The time taken to open is the distance, AA_1, divided by the relative speed given by $O'A$: the time taken to close is the distance, A_1A_2, divided by the relative speed given by $O''A$.

Answer: Course to open: 310°.

           Time taken: 1 hour 5 minutes (8 miles at 7·4 knots).

           Course to close: 076°.

           Time taken: 16 minutes (6 miles at 22·5 knots).

Caution: When the station-taking ship has a lower speed than the ship on which she is taking station, if the manoeuvre is capable of being performed at all there will normally be two courses which can be steered. Unless otherwise stated or for tactical reasons, the course required will be that giving the higher *relative* speed.

Example 8 – To Close to a Given Distance as Quickly as Possible (OG – In)

(a) *In Fig. 233 an enemy ship (A) is steering a course AL. Own ship (O) wishes to close within d miles of A as quickly as possible.*

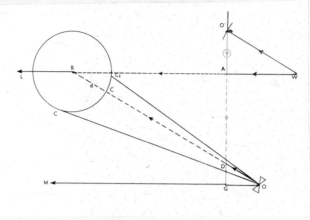

FIG. 233

Clearly, if A were stationary, O would steer directly towards A. But A is moving, and O must therefore steer for some point B ahead of A. O will come within the required distance after steaming for the shortest time if A is right ahead in position B when the range is d, that is, when own ship has arrived at C. Any other track from O to a circle of d miles radius and centre B, such as OC_1 or OC_2, will be longer than OC.

If own ship is now considered stopped, the enemy's relative track will be AD, where OD is equal to the required distance d.

From own ship draw OM parallel to AL. Let AD produced cut OM in G. The triangles ABD, DOG are similar.

$$\frac{OG}{OD} = \frac{AB}{DB} = \frac{AB}{OC} = \frac{\text{distance run by enemy}}{\text{distance run by own ship}}$$

$$= \frac{\text{enemy's speed}}{\text{own speed}}$$

$$\therefore OG = d \times \frac{\text{enemy's speed}}{\text{own speed}}.$$

To solve the problem, the procedure is as follows:

1. Calculate the length OG.
2. Lay off OG from O in a direction parallel to the enemy's course. Join GA and produce it.
3. Draw WA to represent the course and speed of the enemy ship. With centre W and radius own speed draw an arc cutting GA produced in O'. Then WO' is the course to steer.

This course, laid off from O, will cut GA in D and meet AL in B.

(*b*) *In Fig. 234, own ship* (*O*) *is a frigate 10 miles south of an unidentified ship* (*A*) *steaming 270° at 12 knots. Own ship wishes to close to visibility distance 3 miles as quickly as possible to identify. What course should own ship steer at her maximum speed of 18 knots, and when will she sight the other ship?*

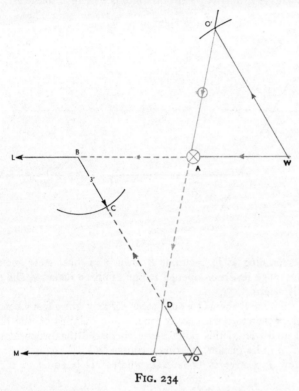

FIG. 234

$$OG = 3 \text{ miles} \times \frac{12 \text{ knots}}{18 \text{ knots}} = 2 \text{ miles.}$$

Lay off *OG* in direction 270° from *O*.

Join *GA* and produce it. This is the course the unidentified ship will have to make good relative to own ship.

At *A* draw *WA* to represent 270°, 12 knots.

With centre *W* and radius 18 knots on the same scale, draw an arc cutting *GA* produced in *O'*. *WO'* will be the course to steer.

Lay off this course from *O*, cutting *GA* in *D*, and *AL* in *B*. *OD* should equal 3 miles (*d*). Measure back along *BO*, *BC* = 3 miles.

Own ship should steer along *OC* and will be at 3 miles from the unidentified ship when she is at *C*.

$$\text{Time taken} = \frac{\text{relative distance } AD}{\text{relative speed } O'A} \text{ or } \frac{\text{distance } AB}{A\text{'s speed}} \text{ or } \frac{\text{distance } OC}{O\text{'s speed}}.$$

Answer: Course: 330°.

Time taken: 28 minutes (8'·4 at 18 knots, or 5'·6 at 12 knots).

Example 9 – To Open to a Given Distance as Quickly as Possible (OG – Out)

(a) In Fig. 235, own ship (O) wishes to open to a distance (d) from another ship (A) as quickly as possible. The other ship is steering a course AL.

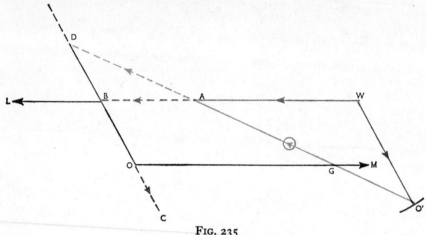

FIG. 235

By the same reasoning as in Example 8, own ship must steer such a course that, when the range has been opened to the required distance, the other ship will be directly astern.

If A were stationary, then O would steer directly away from her. But A is moving. O must therefore steer away from some point B on the line AL, at which A will arrive later, this point being so placed that when A reaches it, O will be at C, d miles distant, steering a course OC.

The track of A relative to O is AD, where OD is equal to the required distance (d).

From own ship, O, draw OM parallel but in the opposite direction to AL. Let DA produced cut OM in G.

The triangles BAD, DOG are similar. Therefore:

$$\frac{OG}{OD} = \frac{AB}{BD}$$

$$OG = OD \times \frac{AB}{BD} = BC \times \frac{AB}{OC} = d \times \frac{\text{distance run by enemy}}{\text{distance run by own ship}}.$$

$$= d \times \frac{\text{enemy's speed}}{\text{own speed}}.$$

To solve the problem the following procedure is adopted:

1. Calculate OG.
2. Lay off OG from own ship in the reverse direction to AL. Join GA and produce it in both directions.
3. Draw WA to represent the course and speed of the enemy. With centre W and radius own speed, draw an arc cutting AG produced in O'.

WO' is the course to steer.

The reciprocal of this course, laid off from O, will cut AL in B and GA produced in D.

> *Note:* It will be appreciated that, when O is within a certain area before the beam of A, the best course for O to steer will result initially in closing A. This will be the more marked,
> (i) the finer O is on A's bow;
> (ii) the greater the distance to which O wishes to open;
> (iii) the lower O's speed is in proportion to A's.

(*b*) *In Fig. 236, your destroyer* (O) *has carried out a torpedo attack from a position 3 miles on the starboard bow of an enemy cruiser* (A), *steering* 090° *at 24 knots; you wish to open to beyond the gun range of the enemy as quickly as possible. If your destroyer has 30 knots available, what course should you steer and when will you be out of range? The range of the cruiser's guns is 10 miles.*

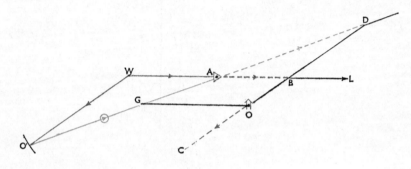

FIG. 236

$$OG = \text{10 miles} \times \frac{\text{24 knots}}{\text{30 knots}} = \text{8 miles.}$$

Lay off OG in direction 270° from O. Join GA and produce it in both directions. GA produced is the relative track which the cruiser will have to make good. At A lay off WA to represent 090°, 24 knots.

With centre W and radius 30 knots on the same scale, draw an arc cutting AG produced in O'. WO' is the course own ship must steer.

The reciprocal of this course, laid off from O, cuts AL in B, and GA produced in D. OD should equal 10 miles. The enemy cruiser will be at B when own ship has reached C, the required distance from the enemy.

Then the time taken $= \dfrac{\text{relative distance } AD}{\text{relative speed } O'A}$ or $\dfrac{\text{distance } AB}{\text{speed of cruiser}}$.

Answer: Course to steer: 234°.

Time taken: $12\frac{1}{2}$ minutes ($5'\cdot1$ at 24 knots).

Example 10 – To Remain within a Given Range of a Faster Ship for as Long as Possible

In Fig. 237, own ship (O) – *a cruiser – is engaging an enemy cruiser* (A) *steering* 180° *at 30 knots, bearing* 270° – *10,000 yards. Your available speed is 20 knots and you wish to keep the enemy under effective fire (range 18,000 yards) for as long as possible.*

If the enemy does not alter course, what course should you steer and how long will he be under fire?

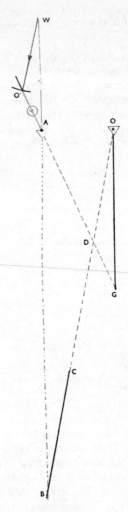

FIG. 237

This problem is exactly the same as the 'OG – In' (Example 8), but in reverse; that is, you start inside the distance and lose distance, instead of starting outside the distance and closing. You must steer a course so that the enemy is right ahead when the range has reached 18,000 yards.

The distance OG (9 miles $\times \dfrac{\text{30 knots}}{\text{20 knots}}$, or $13\frac{1}{2}$ miles) is laid off from O in the direction of the enemy's course.

AG is then the track of the enemy relative to you. Draw WA to represent 180°, 30 knots.

With centre W and radius 20 knots on the same scale, draw an arc cutting GA produced in O'. WO' is the course to steer. This course, laid off from O, will cut AG in D.

Draw AB along enemy's future track, so that AB meets OD produced in B. Measure BC along BO so that $BC = OD = 18,000$ yards.

When own ship has reached C, enemy will be at B, 9 miles ahead. The enemy will thus be within range for a time equal to the relative distance AD divided by the relative speed $O'A$.

Answer: Course: 191°.

Time within range: 49 minutes (16'·4 at 20 knots).

Example 11 – Crossing a Danger Area

A ship, shown in Fig. 238, wishes to cross a patrol belt from A to B as quickly as possible.

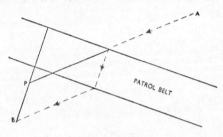

FIG. 238

From B lay off BP equal to the width of the zone and at right angles to it. Join AP, which will be the course to steer on either side of the zone.

Note: This problem would be worked on a geographical and not on a relative plot.

Example 12 – Scouting in a Given Direction and Returning in a Given Time

In Fig. 239, a frigate, in company with the flagship (A) at 0600, is ordered to investigate a DF report bearing 240°, and to rejoin the fleet at 1800, at 20 knots. Course and speed of the fleet 270° – 15 knots. At what time must the frigate alter course to rejoin, and what will be her course?

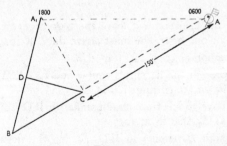

FIG. 239

From A lay off AB in direction 240° equal to 12 hours steaming at 20 knots. Plot A_1, the position of A at 1800.

Join BA_1 and draw CA_1 so that CA_1B is equal to CBA_1 (most conveniently done by drawing the perpendicular bisector of A_1B; C being the point where this cuts AB).

Then BC is equal to CA_1, and C is the turning-point.

Measure AC to find the time to alter course.

Answer: Time to alter course: 1330 (150′ at 20 knots).

Course to rejoin: 327°.

Example 13 – Proceeding to a Base and Rejoining at a Given Time

In Fig. 240, a cruiser (O), in company with a fleet (A) steering 100° at 10 knots, is ordered at 0800 to proceed to a base (B) that bears 180° distant 40 miles and to rejoin at 1500. What is the latest time she can part company if she proceeds to and from the base at 20 knots and remains at the base for one hour?

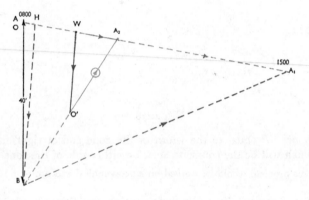

FIG. 240

Plot the flagship's position at 0800 and 1500, A and A_1 respectively.

Plot the base B. Measure A_1B (74′·25).

Calculate the time the cruiser will take to steam from B to A_1, at 20 knots (3h. 43m.).

This means that the cruiser must leave the base at 1117; and, if she is to remain at the base for one hour, she must arrive there at 1017.

Plot the fleet's position at 1017, A_2. Join A_2B.

Draw WA_2 to represent the flagship's course and speed. With centre W and radius 20 knots, draw an arc cutting A_2B in O'.

The cruiser will have to steer a course parallel to WO' to arrive at B when the flagship arrives at A_2, that is, at 1017.

Draw a line through B parallel to WO' cutting the flagship's track at H. Then H will be the point at which to part company.

AH, by measurement, equals 3 miles.

Answer: The cruiser must part company at 0818 (3′ at 10 knots).

Example 14 – Scouting on a Given Bearing at a Given Speed and Returning in a Given Time on the Same Bearing

At 1200 your cruiser (O) in Fig. 241, in company with the fleet, is ordered to scout on a bearing 145° from the fleet at 26½ knots and to rejoin by 1600 on the same bearing. Course and speed of the fleet 090° – 12 knots. What courses must the cruiser steer and when will she have to turn to rejoin?

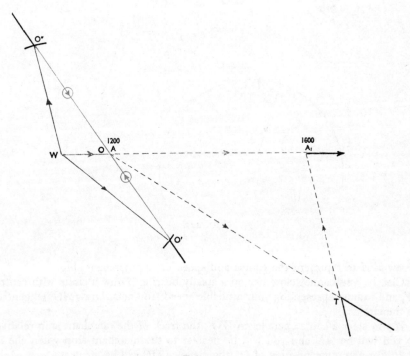

FIG. 241

A is the initial position of the fleet.

Draw *WA* representing the course and speed of the flagship. Draw the relative track *O″AO′* in the direction 325° – 145° through *A*. The courses to open and close are found exactly as in Example 7; the cruiser will open on a course parallel to *WO′* and close on a course parallel to *WO″*.

Plot the flagship's position at 1600 (A_1).

Draw a line through A_1 parallel to the cruiser's rejoining course *WO″*, and a line through *A* parallel to the cruiser's opening course, *WO′*. *T* will be the turning-point and the distance *AT* at 26½ knots will give the time of turning to rejoin.

Answer: Cruiser's course out: 123°.

        Cruiser's course to rejoin: 347°.

        Time of turning to rejoin: 1433 (67′·5 at 26½ knots).

Example 15 – To find the Shortest Distance to which a Ship can Approach Another Ship that is Proceeding at a Greater Speed

(a) In Fig. 242, own ship (O), with available speed 10 knots, sights a merchant ship (A) bearing 300° – 10 miles. You estimate the other ship's course and speed as 030°, 15 knots, and wish to close her. What is the shortest distance to which you can approach, and what course must you steer?

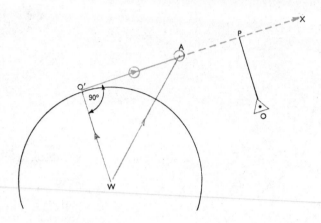

FIG. 242

Draw *WA* to represent the course and speed of the merchant ship.

Clearly, you cannot close her on a steady bearing. Draw a circle with centre *W*, and radius representing your available speed, 10 knots. Draw *AO′* tangential to the circle.

If you steer a course parallel to *WO′*, the track of the merchant ship relative to you will be *AX* and you will be nearest to the merchant ship when she is at *P*. For any other position of *O′*, the distance *OP* will be greater.

Answer: Course 342°.

Shortest distance: 7·4 miles.

(b) In Fig. 243, a cruiser (A) steering 195° at 25 knots is 064° – 25 miles from own ship (O), a destroyer, at 1000. The destroyer wishes to close to the least possible range and has an available speed of 12 knots until 1100, by which time she will have power for 20 knots. What course must the destroyer steer? What is the least range to which she can close, and when will she arrive at this range?

Plot *A*, the position of the cruiser at 1000. Draw *WA* to represent her course and speed.

With centre *W* and radius representing the destroyer's speed after 1100 (20 knots), draw an arc. Draw *AO′* tangential to this circle at *O′*. *WO′* will then be the course to steer at 20 knots to approach within the shortest distance of the cruiser, as in Example 15 (a). It will generally also be the course to steer at 1000 (*see* note opposite).

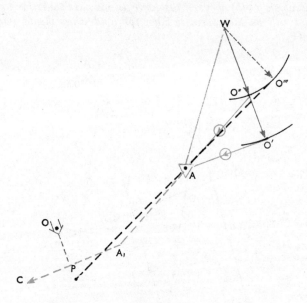

FIG. 243

With centre W and radius the destroyer's speed before 1100 (12 knots), draw an arc. Let this arc cut WO' at O''.

$O''A$ is the track of the cruiser relative to the destroyer before 1100. Produce $O''A$ to A_1 so that A_1 represents the cruiser's position relative to the destroyer at 1100, at which time the destroyer can increase speed.

Draw A_1C parallel to $O'A$. OP is at right angles to A_1C and is thus the least range to which the destroyer can close. The time taken to reach this position after 1100 is the relative distance A_1P at the relative speed represented by $O'A$.

Answer: Course to steer: 159°.

Shortest distance: 6'·5 at 1140.

Note: In examples of this nature it may sometimes be possible to reach a closer distance by steering the optimum course before speed can be increased, rather than the optimum course for the later speed. This can be tested (in the above example) by drawing AO''' tangential to the arc drawn with centre W and radius the destroyer's initial speed (12 knots). If $O''A$ produced passes closer to O than A_1C, then the course to steer at 1000 is WO''. In fact, if O is further from A than the bisector of the angle formed by the intersection of $O''A$ produced and A_1C, the course to steer at 1000 is WO''; if nearer, WO''. Any intermediate course will produce a 'composite' relative track passing farther from O than $O''A$ produced or A_1C (whichever is the nearer). If OP' is drawn at right angles to $O'''A$ produced, then OP' is the closest distance. The time taken to reach this position after 1000 will be the relative distance AP' at the relative speed represented by $O''A$.

Should the distance apart by both methods be the same, it will be reached soonest by steering the course WO''.

In either case the cruiser will be right ahead of the destroyer when the shortest distance is reached, but the destroyer will be finer on the cruiser's quarter if it is necessary to steer the course WO''.

(c) In Example 15 (b) above, if the destroyer will have power for 30 knots by 1115, what will be the course to intercept, and when should interception be achieved?

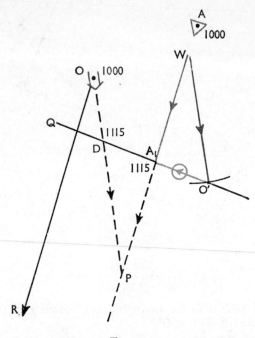

FIG. 244

In Fig. 244, O and A are the positions of destroyer and cruiser respectively at 1000; A_1 is the position of the cruiser at 1115.

At 1000, the destroyer must steer towards some future position of the cruiser, say P. Join OP.

Draw OR parallel to the track of the cruiser. Lay off OD representing the distance steamed by the destroyer before 1115, that is 15 miles, along the line OP. Join A_1D. Produce A_1D to cut OR in Q.

Since OR is parallel to A_1P, the triangles OQD and PA_1D are similar and:

$$\frac{OQ}{OD} = \frac{A_1P}{PD}$$

$$\text{i.e. } OQ = \frac{A_1P \times OD}{PD}.$$

OD is the distance steamed by own ship before increasing speed.

DP and A_1P represent own speed after 1115 and the cruiser's speed respectively. Therefore:

OQ = (distance steamed by own ship before increasing speed)

$$\times \left(\frac{\text{other ship's speed}}{\text{own speed after increasing}}\right).$$

To solve the problem, the procedure is as follows:

Obtain OQ as above. $OQ = 15 \times \dfrac{25}{30} = 12 \cdot 5$ miles.

Lay off OQ from O, parallel to AP. Join QA_1 and produce it.

At A_1 draw WA_1 to represent 195°, 25 knots. With centre W, and radius 30 knots on the same scale, draw an arc cutting QA_1 produced in O'.

Then WO' is the course to steer.

This course, laid off from O, will cut QA_1 in D, and AA_1 produced in P.

Answer: Course to intercept 169°.

The time taken is found by dividing the relative distance A_1D by the relative speed $O'A_1$.

Answer: Interception should be achieved by $1115 + (12 \cdot 7$ miles at $13 \cdot 3$ knots) $= 1211$.

Example 16 – Avoiding Action: a Ship of Greater Speed keeping outside a Certain Range of a Ship of Lesser Speed, that may steer any course

In Fig. 245, you are in a frigate (O) steaming at 25 knots when a damaged enemy cruiser (A) is sighted bearing 270° – 15 miles, steaming 15 knots. You wish to pass to the south-west of the cruiser. What is the most westerly course you can steer to keep outside a range of 10 miles from the cruiser?

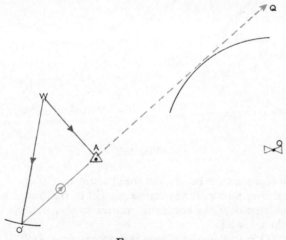

FIG. 245

If you wish to keep outside a range of 10 miles, the relative track of the cruiser must not pass within a circle whose centre is O and radius 10 miles. When the cruiser passes at a range of 10 miles, her track relative to you will be tangential to the 10-mile circle, that is AQ when the frigate wishes to escape to the south-west.

The best course the cruiser can steer to reduce the range at 15 knots is at right angles to AQ. Therefore, draw WA perpendicular to AQ with length equal to 15 knots to represent the course and speed of the cruiser.

With centre W and radius 25 knots on the speed scale draw an arc cutting QA produced in O'. Join WO'.

If the frigate steers a course parallel to WO' the relative track of the cruiser will be along AQ and she cannot approach closer than 10 miles.

Answer: Course 192°.

Example 17 – Avoiding Action: a Ship of Lesser Speed Escaping from a Ship of Greater Speed

In Fig. 246, you are in a damaged destroyer (O); your speed has been reduced to 10 knots. A battleship (A) steaming 15 knots bears 270°–15 miles. If the latter is steering a steady course 090°, what are the best courses for the destroyer to steer, and what will be the least distance apart of the ships on these courses?

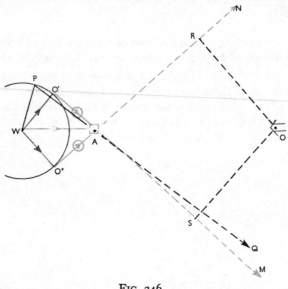

FIG. 246

Draw WA to represent the course and speed of the battleship.

Let the destroyer now steer any course parallel to WP, say. Then PA will be the course and speed of the battleship relative to you and she will appear to move along the track AQ.

The track AQ is furthest from own ship when angle APW is a right angle, that is, when AP is tangential to a circle drawn with centre W and radius representing own speed.

There are thus two possible courses, parallel to WO' and WO'', which make the battleship appear to move along the relative tracks AM and AN, respectively.

The least distance apart of the ships will be OS or OR, perpendicular to AM and AN respectively.

Answer: Destroyer's best course to north: 042°.

          Destroyer's best course to south: 138°.

          Least distance apart of the two ships: 10 miles.

Example 18 – Anti-Submarine Avoiding Action: Typical Problems

In Fig. 247, you are in a cruiser (O) steering 270° at 20 knots. At 1000 a signal is received saying that an enemy submarine (A) with a speed of 9 knots is 270° – 20 miles from you. You wish to proceed to the westward as quickly as possible, and you decide to avoid the submarine by 6 miles, passing north of her.

What course must you steer, and when can you alter course back to 270°?

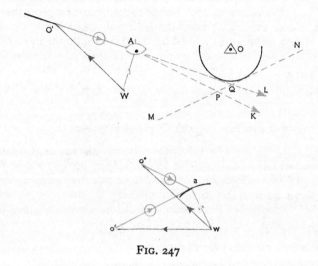

FIG. 247

There are two actions open to the submarine, and the cruiser must guard against both of them. The submarine can be considered as steering the best course to intercept the cruiser; or steering the best course to prevent the cruiser from altering course back to the west.

To find the amount that course must be altered

Plot the relative position of the submarine at 1000.

Draw AL tangential to the 6-mile circle of the cruiser. You must alter course so that the relative track of the submarine is along AL or south of it.

The best course for the submarine to intercept is at right angles to AL. Draw WA representing the speed of the submarine, 9 knots, on this course.

With centre W and radius the speed of the cruiser (20 knots) draw an arc cutting LA produced in O'. Join WO'.

If the cruiser steers a course parallel to WO', the relative track of the submarine will be along AL and she cannot approach within 6 miles of the cruiser.

To find the time the cruiser can alter back to the west

It must now be assumed that the submarine will steer at right angles to the relative course when the cruiser steers 270°. This will be her best action to prevent the cruiser from turning to the west.

Lay off wo' representing the cruiser's course and speed after turning back – 270°, 20 knots. With centre w, radius the submarine's speed of 9 knots, draw an arc (to the north-west). From o' draw the tangent o'a to this arc. Then wa will be the submarine's course to take her as close as she can get to the cruiser.

Draw MN tangential to the 6-mile circle and parallel to $o'a$. The cruiser can alter course to 270° once the submarine has crossed this line without fear of the submarine being able to get within 6 miles.

Now the submarine may have been steering a course parallel to wa throughout. In this case the track of the submarine relative to you would have been parallel to $o''a$ found by constructing the speed triangle $wo''a$ where wo'' is parallel to WO'.

Draw AK parallel to $o''a$. This is the relative track of the submarine when she is steering a course parallel to wa, and she will be able to close to within 6 miles if you alter course to 270° before the submarine crosses the line MN.[1] Any other course steered by the submarine will cause her to cross this line earlier, so course must not be altered by the cruiser until the interval, found by dividing the relative distance AP by the relative speed $o''a$, has elapsed.

Answer: Course to steer: 315°.

Time to resume original course of 270°: 1130 (17'·8 at 11·8 knots).

Example 19 – Submarine Attack: Typical Problem

In Fig. 248, you are in a submarine (O) and you receive a report that a troop transport (A) steering 135° at 15 knots, bears 000° – 20 miles from you at 1700. The submarine wishes to proceed to an attacking position, one mile on the starboard beam of the troopship steaming as slowly as possible whilst submerged. The visibility is 10 miles and the submarine will dive when the transport is sighted.

The submarine's maximum speeds are:

> *on the surface: 13 knots*
> *submerged: 9 knots*

Required:

- *(a) the submarine's course and speed on the surface*
- *(b) the time the submarine will dive*
- *(c) the bearing at which it is expected to sight the transport*
- *(d) the submarine's course and speed when submerged*
- *(e) the time of arrival in the position to attack.*

In order to steam as slowly as possible when submarged, the submarine must gain as much bearing on the transport as she can whilst still on the surface.

Plot the transport position at 1700, A. Draw WA to represent her course and speed. With centre W and radius 13 knots draw a circle. Draw AO' tangential to this circle; $O'A$ will be the relative track of the transport when the submarine is gaining bearing at the maximum rate. The submarine should steer a course parallel to WO' to achieve this.

Produce $O'A$ until it cuts the ten-mile range circle at A_1. When the transport reaches this point relative to the submarine she will be in sight. The time taken will be the relative distance, AA_1, divided by the relative speed $O'A$.

---

[1] Although AP is shorter than AQ, the submarine, by steering parallel to wa, will reach P later than she would reach Q by steering parallel to WA, as $\dfrac{AP}{o''a}$ gives a longer time than $\dfrac{AQ}{O'A}$.

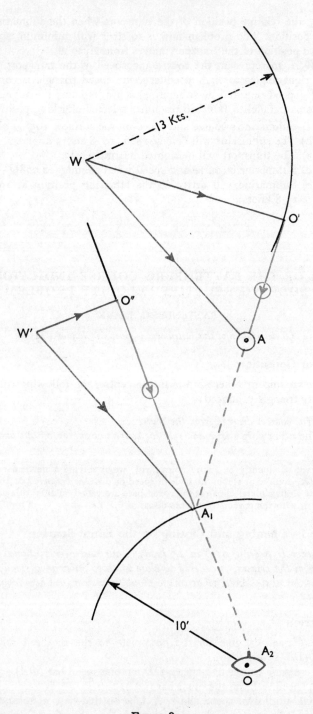

FIG. 248

Plot A_2, the relative position of the transport when the submarine is in the attacking position. The problem now is to steer with minimum speed so that the relative position of the transport moves from A_1 to A_2.

Draw $W'A_1$ to represent the course and speed of the transport. If $W'O'$ is drawn at right angles to A_2A_1 produced, the speed triangle is constructed so that $W'O''$ (speed required by submarine) is a minimum; the submarine would steer a course parallel to $W'O''$ to reach her selected attacking position, A_2.

Answer: (a) Submarine's course and speed on the surface: 105°, 13 knots.
       (b) The submarine will dive at 1826 (10′·8 at 7·5 knots).
       (c) The transport will be sighted bearing 344½°.
       (d) Submarine's course and speed when submerged 068½° – 6 knots.
       (e) Submarine will arrive in the attacking position at 1908 (9′·6 at 13·8 knots).

USE OF THE BATTENBERG COURSE INDICATOR IN SOLVING RELATIVE VELOCITY PROBLEMS

BATTENBERG, MARK 5

(A description of this instrument is given in Chapter VII)

Method of Operation

Whether own ship or other ship is in the centre, the following rules apply to the velocity triangle produced:

    (*a*) *True courses diverge from the centre;*
    (*b*) The other ship's *true and relative courses* converge *on one another.*

Notes:
    (1) It will frequently be found convenient, when solving a particular problem, to halve, double, or treble the scale of speed or distance engraved on the base-plate.
    (2) The sliding metal clips on the speed bars are called 'sliders' to avoid confusing them with the cursors (rotatable discs) of P.P.I.s.

Example 1 – Opening and Closing on the Same Bearing

A cruiser is steering 080° at 15 knots. Your destroyer stationed 190°, 12 miles, from the cruiser, is ordered to close to three miles on a steady bearing. If you steam at 24 knots, what course should you steer and how long should it take you?

CONSTRUCTION

Set the diametrical line on the base-plate to the required relative track, 010°–190° (BB_1 in Fig. 249).

Set the cruiser's course and speed, OD, on one speed bar (OA).

Set own speed, OE, on the other bar (OC).

Rotate OC until own speed slider, E, falls on that base-plate line parallel to the 010°–190° diameter which passes through the other ship's slider, D. There will be two possible positions of E.

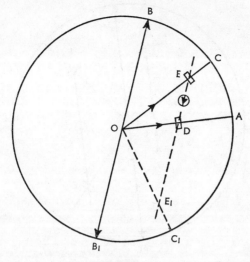

FIG. 249

One of these positions will give the course to steer to *close* on a steady bearing (OE = 045½°), and the other will give the course to steer to *open* on a steady bearing (OE_1 = 154°).

To find the time taken to close from 12 to 3 miles, measure the relative speed DE (14½ knots). Then the time taken = 9 miles at 14½ knots = 37 minutes.

Example 2 – Changing Station on a Moving Ship and Using a Given Speed

A cruiser is steering 050° at 20 knots. You are in a destroyer stationed 5 miles ahead of the cruiser and are ordered to change station to a position Green 120, 8 miles from her. If you proceed at 22 knots, what course should you steer and when should you be in station?

Construction

(a) Own ship at centre (P.P.I. Presentation)

Set the Perspex disc so that the 000° radial line coincides with the 000° line on the outer rose.

Plot on the Perspex disc the present position of the cruiser, F, and her final position, T, relative to your ship at the centre (Fig. 250).

Rotate the base-plate until the line joining F and T is parallel to the lines of the base-plate.

Set the cruiser's course and speed, OD, on one speed bar (OA); then set own speed, OE, on the other bar (OC).

Rotate OC until own speed slider, E, cuts the base-plate line passing through the other ship's slider, D. Then OE will give the course to steer (159°).

Note: When own speed is less than the other ship's speed there will be two possible positions for own speed bar. One of these positions will give a greater relative speed, ED, than the other, and this will be the solution usually chosen.

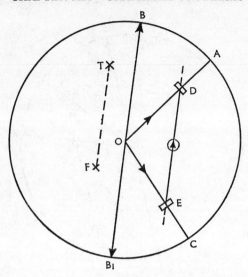

FIG. 250

Measure the relative distance FT, and the relative speed, ED. In this case, $FT = 11·4$ miles and $ED = 34·1$ knots. Then the time taken = $11·4$ miles at $34·1$ knots = 21 minutes.

(b) *Other ship at centre*

Plot on the Perspex disc *your* present position F_1 and *your* final position T_1, relative to the cruiser at the centre (Fig. 251).

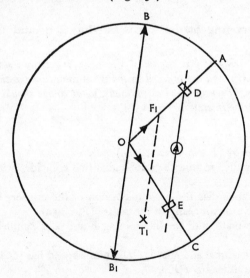

FIG. 251

Set the cruiser's course and speed, OD, on the speed bar OA.

Rotate the base-plate until it is parallel with the line joining F_1 and T_1.

Then proceed as before, the relative distance in this case being F_1T_1.

Observation of the Progress of a Manoeuvre

During the change of station described in Example 2, ranges and bearings of the other ship can be plotted on the Perspex plotting surface. If all goes well these should follow the relative track *FT*. Should they deviate, this will be due to one of two causes:

(a) inaccurate estimate of other ship's course and speed;
(b) inaccurate assessment of own ship's initial position and speed owing to the errors introduced when turning.

When the other ship's course and speed have not been signalled, (*a*) is likely to be the major source of error. In this case the base-plate should be re-aligned to the actual relative track, and the other ship's course bar (or speed) adjusted to complete the speed triangle. The problem can then be solved again, the required relative track now being the line joining the latest plotted position to *T*.

If errors in estimation of the other ship's course and speed are not suspected, and if own ship has now attained her correct speed, then the instrument only requires to be re-aligned for the new relative track from the latest plotted position.

Example 3 – Finding the Course to Pass another Ship at a Given Distance

At 1000 another ship bears 263°, distance 11 miles, course 020°, speed 24 knots. What is the course to steer at a speed of 28 knots to pass ahead of the other ship, keeping outside 5 miles? When will the two ships be closest?

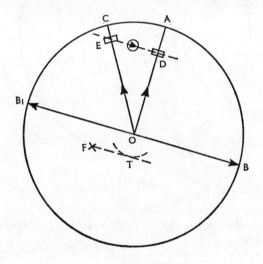

FIG. 252

CONSTRUCTION

Own ship is at the centre. Plot the position of the other ship on the Perspex, *F* (Fig. 252).

Relative to own ship, the other ship must move along *FT*, where *FT* is a tangent to the circle, centre *O*, radius 5 miles.

Rotate the base-plate so that the line through F touches the 5 miles circle on the Perspex disc.

Set the other ship's course and speed, OD, on one speed bar (OA); then set own speed, OE, on the other bar (OC).

Rotate OC until own speed slider, E, falls on the base-plate line passing through the other ship's slider, D.

In order that the relative track may be from F to T, there will be only one possible position for E, as shown. The course to steer will be OE (350°).

The two ships will be closest when the other ship is at T, and the time taken will be FT miles at ED knots = 9·8 miles at 14·5 knots = 40 minutes. The ships should therefore be closest at 1040.

Example 4 – Approaching as close as possible to a Faster Ship

At 1500 a ship bears 242°, distance 16 miles, course 320°, speed 32 knots. Own ship has 28 knots available. What is the course to steer to approach as close as possible, and how close will you get on this course?

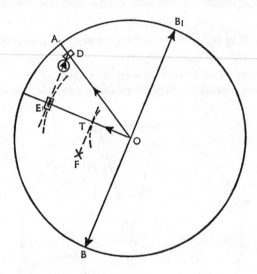

FIG. 253

CONSTRUCTION

Own ship is at the centre. Plot the other ship's 1500 position, F, using a half-scale (Fig. 253).

Set the other ship's course and speed, OD, on one speed bar (OA).

In order to be able to close on a steady bearing, the relative track ED would have to be parallel to FO, but since own ship is slower than the other ship this is not possible.

Set the base-plate so that a line through D is tangential to the 28 knot circle on the Perspex disc, and mark this point E.

Then OE will be the best course to steer (291°).

To find the nearest distance, find where the base-plate line through F cuts OE (in T). Then OT will be the distance required (10½ miles).

Example 5 – Closing to a Given Range as quickly as possible (OG – In)

An unidentified ship bears 000°, 10 miles from own ship (by radar), and is estimated to be steering 270° at 12 knots. Own ship has a maximum speed of 18 knots and wishes to close to 3 miles as quickly as possible in order to identify the other ship. What course should she steer?

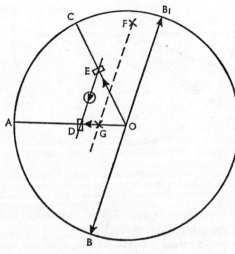

FIG. 254

CONSTRUCTION

To solve this problem we must first calculate the length OG (Fig. 254).

$$OG = \frac{\text{other ship's speed}}{\text{own speed}} \times \text{required range} = \frac{12}{18} \times 3 = 2 \text{ miles.}$$

Own ship is at the centre, O. Plot G, 270°, 2 miles from O (270° is course of other ship).

Plot F, the other ship's initial position.

Set the base-plate with its lines parallel to FG, which is the required relative track.

Set the other ship's course and speed, OD, on one speed bar (OA); then set own speed, OE, on the other speed bar (OC).

Rotate OC until own speed slider, E, falls on the base-plate line passing through the other ship's slider, D. Then OE will be the course to steer (330°).

Example 6 – Opening to a Given Range as quickly as possible (OG – Out)

Your destroyer has carried out a torpedo attack from a position 3 miles, Green 45, from an enemy cruiser which is steering 090° at 24 knots. You wish to open to beyond the gun range (10 miles) of the enemy as quickly as possible. If you proceed at 30 knots, what course should you steer?

CONSTRUCTION

Again here we must first calculate the length OG (Fig. 255).

$$OG = \frac{\text{other ship's speed}}{\text{own speed}} \times \text{required range} = \frac{24}{30} \times 10 = 8 \text{ miles.}$$

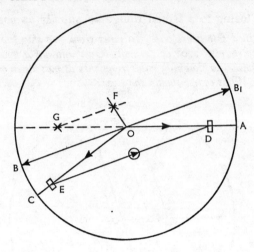

Fig. 255

With own ship at the centre, *O*, plot *G*, 270°, 8 miles from *O* (*OG* is plotted on the reciprocal of the other ship's course).

Plot *F*, the other ship's initial position, and proceed exactly as in Example 5 above. In this case *GF* produced is the required relative track.

The course to steer is 233°.

Example 7 – Laying Smoke on a Given Line

A destroyer covering a damaged merchant vessel decides to lay smoke along the line 085°–265°. The true wind is estimated to be blowing from 015° at 15 knots. If the destroyer steams at 20 knots, what two courses can she steer?

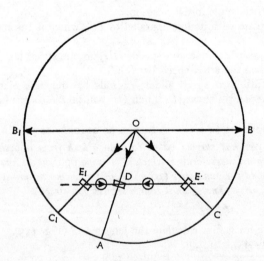

Fig. 256

CONSTRUCTION

Set the lines of the base-plate to the direction 085°–265° (BB_1 in Fig. 256). Set the true wind speed and direction, OD, on one speed bar (OA).

Set the destroyer's speed, OE, on the other bar (OC), and rotate it until the speed slider, E, falls on the base-plate line passing through the true wind slider, D.

This will give two possible courses, OE and OE_1, which the destroyer can steer (130° and 220°).

The course OE will give the higher relative wind speed ED, and will therefore produce a longer, thinner line of smoke than the course OE_1, which gives the lower relative wind speed E_1D.

USE OF RADAR IN FLEETWORK

Radar may be used to great advantage in solving many manoeuvring problems.

The modern radar, with its high aerial rotation rate and great accuracy, gives an up-to-date plot of other ships' positions, their bearings and ranges, and their approximate relative tracks from the afterglow tails on the P.P.I.

By fitting a rotatable disc carrying two speed arms and using the parallel lines engraved on the rotatable cursor of the P.P.I., all the relative velocity problems can be solved on the disc.

P.P.I. Manoeuvring Disc (Fig. 257)

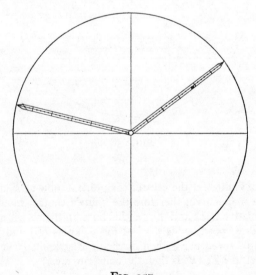

FIG. 257

The P.P.I. manoeuvring disc consists of a Perspex plotting surface that can be placed over the rotatable cursor of a Type 974 P.P.I.; two speed arms can be attached to the disc. Without the speed arms it can be used as a plotting surface or as a means of transferring information from a manoeuvring form (S.376) to the face of the P.P.I. (described later). With the speed arms in place, and used in conjunction with the parallel lines on the cursor, it becomes, in effect, a form of Battenberg.

With Type 978 radar all these facilities are incorporated in the Reflection Plotter.

USE AS A BATTENBERG

Relative Velocity problems are worked out in exactly the same way as on the Battenberg using the parallel lines on the cursor as the base-plate. The guide's position is always apparent, and any divergence of its contact from the intended relative track when changing station, can be seen at a glance.

EXAMPLE (Fig. 258). *Own ship is ordered to change station from 5 cables on the port bow to 5 cables on the starboard bow of the guide who is steering 000 degrees at 15 knots. Stationing speed is 25 knots. What is the course to steer?*

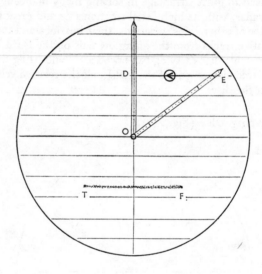

FIG. 258

Own ship *O* is, of course, at the centre; the guide is now at *F* and will be at *T* at the end of the manoeuvre; therefore the guide's contact must move from *F* to *T*. *FT* is the relative track and the parallel lines on the cursor are then aligned with it. The guide's speed bar is marked for 15 knots (*D*) and pointed to 000 degrees; own ship's speed bar is then marked for 25 knots (*E*) and adjusted so that *ED* is parallel to *FT*; *OE* is then the course to steer.

Use of Turning Data

For precise manoeuvres such as turning into the line or taking up close station on another ship, the position of 'wheel over' must be calculated accurately.

When using radar, not only can the position of the guide at 'wheel over' be plotted and the guide's contact be made to pass through it; but the path of the guide, relative to own ship during the turn, can be drawn on the face of the P.P.I. so that the guide's contact may be compared with the planned relative curve.

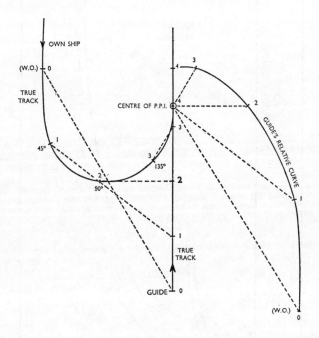

FIG. 259

Fig. 259 shows a suggested method of obtaining relative curves for varying speeds of own ship and guide. The positions of the guide during the turn are related to the position of own ship at the end of the manoeuvre, i.e. when in station astern of the guide (Position 4 – centre of P.P.I.).

The relative turning curves for turns of less than 180 degrees may be found in the same way and templates cut for use on the mask of the P.P.I. (Fig. 260).

Relative curves can also be obtained when in company at sea by plotting the guide on the mask of the P.P.I. while own ship is turning.

USE OF TEMPLATE (Fig. 260)

Plot the position of the guide when in station and determine the amount of the final turn. Set the parallel lines of the rotatable cursor to the guide's course and align the guide's course with them so that point Y is over the position of the guide. Mark the position of 'wheel over' for the appropriate final turn and the remaining curve on the mask of the P.P.I. with chinagraph pencil. Own ship is then steered so that the guide's contact passes through the selected 'wheel over' position.

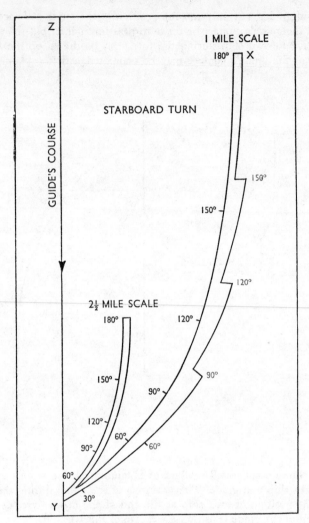

Note 1. The black figures show the positions of the guide at 'wheel over' and at intermediate positions *during a turn of 180 degrees.*

Note 2. The red figures show the positions of 'wheel over' for turns of 150, 120, 90 and 60 degrees

FIG. 260

ADJUSTMENT OF ERRORS (Fig. 261)

If the guide fails to pass through the planned 'wheel over' position (*X*), the speed and diameter of the turn must be altered. If the guide is outside (*A*), own ship must use less wheel to produce a larger transfer and turn earlier to compensate for the extra time of the turn. If the guide is inside (*B*), the turn must be quicker and later.

SAFETY

The safety distance can be applied by displacing the template laterally the required distance. When turning to take station in the centre of a column, the guide's contact must never be inside the adjusted position of 'wheel over'.

Relative Track Technique

The shortest distance between two points is a straight line and the shortest relative distance is a straight line. When solving the speed triangle, the speed used for own ship is the speed that will be used for the greater part of the manoeuvre and no allowance is made for acceleration and deceleration, with the result that the course to steer is correct only for the speed used.

INITIAL TURN OF LESS THAN 90 DEGREES

Fig. 262 shows the relative track of the guide, when own ship is changing station, during the period of increase of speed if course is altered before own ship gathers speed

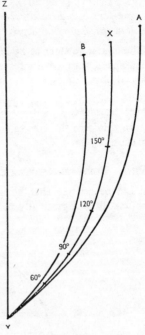

FIG. 261

(a curve starting in the direction $E'D$). It can be seen therefore that the traditional method of altering course immediately and then increasing speed may not necessarily be the best method.

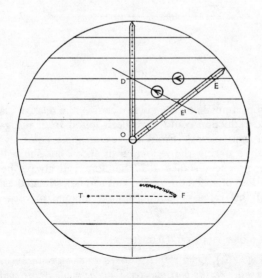

FIG. 262

EXAMPLE (Fig. 263). *Own ship is ordered to change station from 5 cables on the port bow F to 5 cables on the starboard bow T of the guide whose course and speed are 000 degrees, 15 knots. Stationing speed is 25 knots.*

The course to steer at 25 knots is *OE* but the course should not be altered until the speed starts to increase (for example, the ship's head should be *OC* at a speed of 20 knots) if the guide's contact is to remain on the line *FT*.

INITIAL TURN OF MORE THAN 90 DEGREES

In this case the course should be altered immediately the stationing signal is executed.

FINAL TURN OF LESS THAN 90 DEGREES

Let us assume that *T′* is the point at which speed should be reduced and course altered gradually to that of the guide (Fig. 263). Had the approach to

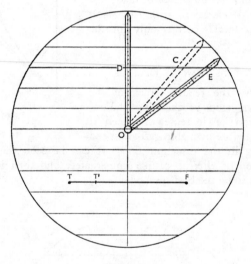

FIG. 263

the final position been made on the guide's course, the relative distance travelled during the speed reduction could have been found from the gain and loss of speed correction (yards/knot). From any other angle not only will the ship travel along a curve during the reduction of speed but she will lose speed in the act of turning. The distance *T′T* therefore will always be less than the relative speed × loss of speed correction and can be estimated as approximately three-quarters of this value depending on the amount of turn and the ship's turning data.

FINAL TURN OF MORE THAN 90 DEGREES

EXAMPLE (Fig. 264). *Own ship is ordered to change station from 1½ miles ahead F to two miles on the port quarter T of the guide whose course and speed are 000 degrees 15 knots. Stationing speed is 25 knots.*

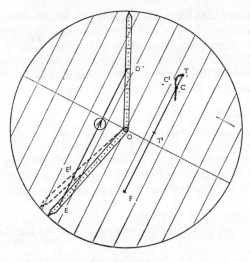

FIG. 264

Plot position T and, using the template, draw in the relative curve for a 180 degrees starboard turn. It is now necessary to make the guide's contact enter the relative curve at the appropriate point for the amount of own ship's final turn.

The first approximation gives a relative track FC. Align the cursor paralle to FC, complete the speed triangle OED, then OE is the course required for the change of station at 25 knots.

If it is intended to start the final turn at the speed of the guide plus the loss of speed during the turn (say 3 knots), speed must be reduced at T'. If the time taken to reduce speed from 25 to 18 knots is known, the relative distance $T'C$ can be calculated using this time and the relative speed ED.

During this reduction of speed, course must be adjusted so that $E'D$ remains parallel to FC and the amount of the final turn will be reduced; the guide's contact must now enter the relative curve at C' after which the turn is completed using the wheel for which the template was constructed.

Screening Problems

The Type 974 P.P.I. manoeuvring disc and the Type 978 Reflection Plotter, when used in conjunction with manoeuvring form (S.376), offer a simple and quick method of working screen problems with the advantage that all ships can be seen during the manoeuvre and their correct stations are shown.

The manoeuvring form (S.376) should be mounted between Perspex with one side on the 10-mile scale and the other on the 3-mile scale for Type 974, or $2\frac{1}{2}$ and 5-mile scales for Type 978. The parallel lines printed on the form are joined up to run through the spider's web of which 000 degrees depicts the screen on formation axis.

SETTING UP

Plot all ships' stations on the manoeuvring form relative to the screen axis. Then place the P.P.I. manoeuvring disc (or Reflection Plotter) over own ship's station on the manoeuvring form, aligning the axis line on the disc to the nearest parallel line on the form. Re-plot all ships on the disc emphasizing the position of the guide and taking care to avoid parallax errors (this is most important when using the Reflection Plotter). Now place the disc on the P.P.I. with the axis line on the correct true bearing. The positions of all the other ships when own ship is in station on the guide are now shown.

TAKING UP OR CHANGING STATION

Line up the cursor parallel to the guide's echo and the guide's plotted position on the disc, thereby completing the speed triangle (Fig. 265). Alter to the new course, plot the correct 'wheel over' position or reduction of speed position and adjust the course as necessary. (The calculated range and bearing of the guide should be set on the strobe and cursor as a check on the plot.)

EXAMPLES OF TYPICAL MANOEUVRING

Rotating the screen axis and formation axis whether or not the Guide is in Station Zero

Adjust the axis on the disc to the new heading and complete the speed triangle (Fig. 265).

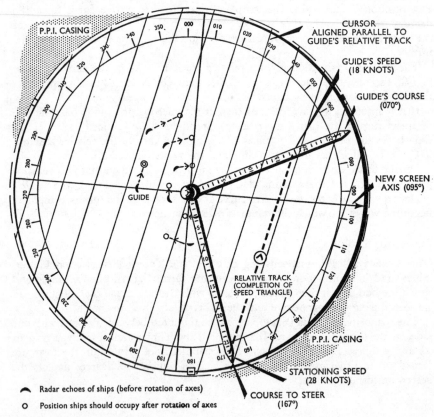

➤ Radar echoes of ships (before rotation of axes)

o Position ships should occupy after rotation of axes

--➤- Predicted relative tracks

FIG. 265

Rotation of the screen axis necessitating a change of station number

Ascertain the new station and, if necessary, adjust the axis on the manoeuvring form.

Place the disc over the new station on the manoeuvring form and re-plot.

Replace the disc, set to the new screen axis, on the P.P.I.

Complete the speed triangle.

Rotating the formation axis but not the screen axis

Re-plot the new formation axis and the main body on the manoeuvring form.

Plot the guide's and main body's new positions on the disc.

Replace the disc, set to the screen axis, on the P.P.I.

Complete the speed triangle.

Plotting and adjusting the centre of an eccentric screen

Place the disc over own station and plot the remainder of the screen and the station zero.

Move the disc so that the station zero, as plotted on the disc, is offset the required amount in the direction of the course (relative to the screen axis if other than north) and plot the position of the guide (and the main body).

On altering course move the station zero as plotted on the disc the required amount in the direction of the new course; re-plot the guide's new position.

Complete the speed triangle.

Notes:

(1) The manoeuvring disc should be aligned to north when being used for plotting except for screens requiring rotations of the axes. If the gyro fails a stabilized relative plot may be kept by aligning the axis line with own ship's course on the true bearing ring. (In an unstabilized picture the ship's head marker should be set to point up the face of the tube, i.e. at 000 degrees.)

(2) These screening manoeuvres show how to proceed directly from the old station to the new; they do not take into account either the preservation of an unbroken sonar front or any special instructions for screening vessels when re-orienting screens.

CHAPTER XV

Rule of the Road

An International Conference called by the Inter-Governmental Maritime Consultative Organization was convened in 1972 to revise and bring up to date the International Regulations for Preventing Collisions at Sea, 1960. The Regulations agreed by the Final Act of the Conference were called the International Regulations for Preventing Collisions at Sea, 1972.

The date of coming into force of the 1972 Regulations has been fixed for Noon, Local Time, 15th July 1977.

In this impression (1977) the 1972 Regulations are given in addition to the 1960 Regulations.

REPRINT OF CERTAIN BRITISH ADMIRALTY NOTICES TO MARINERS

(See Annual Summary)

Caution with regard to Ships approaching Squadrons, Convoys, Aircraft Carriers and other Warships at Sea and Aircraft Carriers at Anchor

Squadrons and Convoys

(1) The attention of shipowners and mariners is called to the danger to all concerned which is caused by single vessels approaching a squadron of warships, or merchant vessels in convoy, so closely as to involve risk of collision, or attempting to pass ahead of, or through such a squadron or convoy.

(2) Mariners are therefore warned that single vessels should adopt early measures to keep out of the way of a squadron or convoy.

(3) Although a single vessel is advised to keep out of the way of a squadron or convoy, this does not entitle vessels sailing in company to proceed without regard to the movements of the single vessel. Vessels sailing in a squadron or convoy should accordingly keep a careful watch on the movements of any single vessel approaching the squadron or convoy and should be ready, in case the single vessel does not keep out of the way, to take such action as will best aid to avert collision.

Aircraft Carriers

(4) Attention is also drawn to the uncertainty of the movements of aircraft carriers, which must usually turn into the wind when aircraft are taking off or landing.

(5) Furthermore, mariners are warned that by night aircraft carriers have:

    (a) their steaming lights placed permanently off the centre line of the ship, and at a considerably reduced horizontal separation,

(b) alternative positions for their side lights:

    (i) on either side of the hull,

    (ii) on either side of the island structure, in which case the port
bow light may be as much as 100 feet from the port side of
the ship.

(6) Certain aircraft carriers exhibit anchor lights as follows:

Four *white* lights located in the following manner:

In the forward part of a vessel at a distance of not more than
5 feet below the flight deck, two lights in the same horizontal plane,
one on the port side and one on the starboard side.

In the after part of the vessel at a height of not less than 15 feet
lower than the forward lights, two lights in the same horizontal
plane, one on the port side and one on the starboard side.

Each light visible over an arc of at least 180°. The forward lights
visible over a minimum arc from one point on the opposite bow to
one point from right astern on their own side, and the after lights from
one point on the opposite quarter to one point from right ahead on
their own side.

Replenishment-at-Sea

(7) British and Allied Warships in conjunction with auxiliaries frequently
exercise Replenishment-at-Sea. While doing so the two or more ships
taking part are connected by jackstays and hoses. They display the 'Not
Under Command' signals prescribed by Rule 4 of the International
Regulations for Preventing Collisions at Sea, 1960.

(8) Mariners are warned that while carrying out these exercises the
ships are severely restricted both in manoeuvrability and speed. Other
vessels are therefore advised to keep well clear in accordance with Rule 27
of the above Regulations.

Certain Warships—positions of steaming lights

(9) Certain other warships which, in accordance with Rule 13 of the
International Regulations for Preventing Collisions at Sea, cannot comply
fully with the requirements as to the number and positioning of lights,
comply as closely as possible.

The following vessels of 150 feet in length, or over, cannot be fitted with
a second steaming light owing to their special construction: Destroyers
(including 'Daring' class), frigates, ocean and coastal minesweepers and
boom working vessels.

(10) In addition, certain cruisers which cannot comply fully as regards
the position of the second steaming light have a slightly reduced vertical
separation between the two lights.

INFORMATION CONCERNING SUBMARINES

(Parts I and II only)

Part I – Warning Signals

(a) *Visual Signals*

1. Mariners are warned that considerable hazard to life may result by the disregard of the following warning signals, which denote the presence of Submarines:

> British vessels fly one of the two International Code groups HP or OIY to denote that Submarines, which may be submerged, are in the vicinity. Vessels are cautioned to steer so as to give a wide berth to any vessel flying either of these signals. If from any cause it is necessary to approach her, vessels should proceed at slow speed until warning is given of the danger zone by flags, semaphore or megaphone, etc., a good look-out being kept meanwhile for Submarines whose presence may be only indicated by their periscopes or snorts showing above water. A Submarine submerged at a depth too great to show her periscope, may sometimes indicate her position by releasing a 'smoke candle' which gives off a considerable volume of smoke on first reaching the surface. Her position may sometimes be indicated by red-and-white or red-and-yellow buffs or floats, which tow on the surface close astern.

(b) *Pyrotechnics and Smoke Candles*

2. The following signals are used by submerged Submarines in a Submarine exercise area.

SIGNAL	SIGNIFICATION
One *red* pyrotechnic light, or smoke, repeated as often as possible.	Keep clear. I am carrying out emergency surfacing procedure. Do not stop propellers. Ships are to clear the area immediately and stand by to render assistance.
Two *yellow* pyrotechnic lights, or two *white* or *yellow* smokes, 3 minutes apart.	Keep clear. My position is as indicated. I intend to carry out surfacing procedure. Do not stop propellers. Ships are to clear the immediate vicinity.

It must not be inferred from the above that Submarines exercise only when in company with escorting vessels.

3. Under certain circumstances warnings that Submarines are exercising in specified areas may be broadcast by a General Post Office radio station.

Part II – Navigation Lights

4. Submarines may be met on the surface by night, particularly in the vicinity of the following ports:

> Thames Estuary, Portsmouth, Portland, Plymouth, Barrow, Liverpool, Londonderry and Clyde Areas.

5. Hitherto the navigation lights of submarines have been exhibited from the conning tower which is near the centre of the vessel. The steaming light, bow lights and overtaking light have been necessarily low down and closely spaced with the result that they give no indication of the submarine's length nor of her exact course or change of course. Consequently they may be mistaken for the lights of a very much smaller vessel of the coaster type.

6. Special arrangements have now been made to fit H.M. Submarines with a second steaming light. The forward steaming light is placed in a special fitting in the fore part of the vessel between 1 and 6 feet above the hull. The main steaming light is fitted on the conning tower or fin. In submarines where the forward steaming light is appreciably less than 6 feet above the hull, and may in consequence be lower than the coloured side lights, the overall arrangement of lights as seen from other vessels may appear unusual. In addition, the vertical separation in some cases is less than 15 feet.

The overtaking light is placed on a special fitting near the stern of the vessel but may be at a height considerably less than that of the side lights.

NOTES ON FISHING VESSELS IN HOME WATERS

(Fuller details will be found in Form S.1176, Fishing Vessel Log)

The types of fishing vessels met with in home waters come under the four headings given below.

Trawlers

These vessels drag some form of net along the bottom and include fishing dredgers. They work under steam and under sail and will be found working alone or in company. The fact that when they are not getting their trawl in or out they are making way slowly through the water distinguishes them from drift-net vessels.

The trawl goes down to the bottom at an angle of 20° or more to the horizontal.

Trawlers can trawl at speeds up to six knots and should be passed at a distance of at least one cable astern, or well clear ahead. (*See* Rule 9 (a), (e), (f) and (h).)

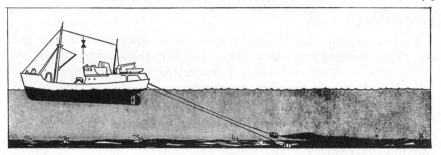

FIG. 266 – A trawler trawling

Drift-net Vessels (Drifters)

These vessels which usually fish in fleets lay about 80 oblong nets. The nets lie either on the surface or a fathom or two below it (depending on the type of fish netted). The nets are 35 – 40 yards apart from each other and are connected together by a long hawser.

The drifter lies at the leeward end of the nets either with its bows to the nets (in which case its mizzen is set and, if it is blowing, the foremast is lowered) or with its stern to them. The outer end of the hawser is buoyed and it is probable that every net will be buoyed as well.

A single drifter must be passed up to 4 miles to windward[1] but may be passed a cable or two to leeward (i.e., on the side of its higher light by night).

A fleet of drifters should be given a very clear berth. If it becomes necessary to pass through nets, they should be crossed at right angles midway between two buoys and with propellers stopped.

By keeping within the 10 fathom line, drifters may be avoided; they require over 10 fathoms in which to work their nets. (*See* Rule 9 (a), (c), (d), (f), (g) and (h).)

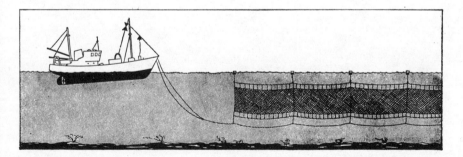

FIG. 267 – A drifter lying to her nets

---

[1] A drifter's nets may not lie directly to windward of her when she is getting up her nets.

Line Fishing Vessels

These vessels lay (i.e., 'shoot') lines with hooks along the bottom of the sea. When shooting these lines they move through the water at a fairly steady speed and act as ordinary power-driven or sailing vessels under way. When hauling in their lines they come under the heading of drift-net vessels.

The vessels may work under either steam or sail and may be the size of a deep sea trawler. If they work near the coast they are usually smaller. (*See* Rule 9 (a), (c) and (d).)

Seine-net Vessels

Seine-net fishing is usually done from the shore. It may also be done at sea, especially in the summer months. The net is long (600 – 1,000 fm.) and weighted at the bottom. One end is made fast to a buoy. The net is run out in a large circle by the vessel and is then hauled in. Seine-net vessels should be given a wide berth.

A SUMMARY OF SOUND SIGNALS

SIGNAL		MADE ON	INTERVAL	SIGNIFICATION	AUTHORITY
One prolonged blast	▬	Whistle	At least every 2 minutes	In fog – power-driven vessel making way through the water	Rule 15 (c) (i)
Two prolonged blasts	▬ ▬	Whistle	At least every 2 minutes	In fog – power-driven vessel under way but stopped and making no way through the water	Rule 15 (c) (ii)
One prolonged and two short blasts	▬ · ·	Whistle	At least every minute	In fog – (i) power-driven vessel towing (ii) cable-laying ship, etc., at work (iii) power-driven vessel not under command, whether making way through the water or not (iv) a power-driven vessel not able to manoeuvre as required by the Rules, e.g., a minesweeper with sweeps out (v) a power-driven vessel engaged in fishing when under way or at anchor	Rule 15 (c) (v) Rule 15 (c) (viii)
One prolonged and three short blasts	▬ · · ·	Whistle or Fog horn	At least every minute	In fog – a vessel being towed	Rule 15 (c) (vi)
One blast	▬	Fog horn	At least every minute	In fog – a sailing vessel under way on the starboard tack	Rule 15 (c) (iii)
Two blasts	▬ ▬	Fog horn	At least every minute	In fog – a sailing vessel under way on the port tack	Rule 15 (c) (iii)
Three blasts	▬ ▬ ▬	Fog horn	At least every minute	In fog – a sailing vessel under way with the wind abaft the beam	Rule 15 (c) (iii)

A SUMMARY OF SOUND SIGNALS—*continued*

SIGNAL	MADE ON	INTERVAL	SIGNIFICATION	AUTHORITY
▬ ·· One prolonged and two short blasts	Fog horn	At least every minute	In fog – (i) a sailing vessel towing (ii) a sailing vessel not under command, whether making way through the water or not (iii) a sailing vessel not able to manoeuvre as required by the Rules, e.g. becalmed or in irons (iv) a vessel engaged in fishing	Rule 15 (c) (v)
···· Four short blasts	Whistle	—	In fog—a power-driven pilot vessel, on duty, underway, stopped or at anchor, in addition to the normal signals	Rule 15 (c) (x)
5 seconds' ringing	Bell	At least every minute	In fog – a vessel at anchor	Rule 15 (c) (iv)
3 strokes followed by 5 seconds' rapid ringing, followed by 3 strokes	Bell	At least every minute	In fog – a vessel aground	Rule 15 (c) (vii)
· One short blast	Whistle	—	By a power-driven vessel in sight of another – 'I am altering my course to starboard'	Rule 28 (a)
·· Two short blasts	Whistle	—	By a power-driven vessel in sight of another – 'I am altering my course to port'	Rule 28 (a)
··· Three short blasts	Whistle	—	By a power-driven vessel in sight of another – 'My engines are going astern'	Rule 28 (a)

Signal	Morse	Instrument		Meaning	Reference
· · · · ·	Five or more short blasts	Whistle	—	By a holding-on power-driven vessel in sight of the giving-way power-driven vessel – 'I am in doubt whether you are taking sufficient action to avert collision'	Rule 28 (b)
— · ·	One prolonged blast and two short blasts	Whistle	—	In H.M. Dockyard Ports – 'Keep out of my way, because I cannot keep out of yours'	—
· · · · ·	Four short blasts followed by one short blast	Whistle	—	In H.M. Dockyard Ports – 'My ship is practically stopped, but turning to starboard'	—
· · · · · ·	Four short blasts followed by two short blasts	Whistle	—	In H.M. Dockyard Ports – 'My ship is practically stopped, but turning to port'	—
· · · — — — · · · S.O.S.		Whistle or Fog horn	—	A signal of distress	Rule 31
· — A		Whistle	—	I have a diver down; keep well clear at slow speed	International Code of Signals
· · — · F		Whistle	—	I am disabled; communicate with me	"
— — · G		Whistle	—	I require a pilot. When made by fishing vessels operating in close proximity on the fishing grounds it means 'I am hauling nets'	"
· — — — J		Whistle	—	I am on fire and have dangerous cargo on board; keep well clear of me	"

A SUMMARY OF SOUND SIGNALS—*continued*

SIGNAL	MADE ON	INTERVAL	SIGNIFICATION	AUTHORITY
K	Whistle	—	I wish to communicate with you	International Code of Signals
L	Whistle	—	You should stop your vessel instantly	,,
M	Whistle	—	My vessel is stopped and making no way through the water	,,
O	Whistle	—	Man overboard	,,
U	Whistle	—	You are running into danger	,,
V	Whistle	—	I require assistance	,,
W	Whistle	—	I require medical assistance	,,
Y	Whistle	—	I am dragging my anchor	,,
Z	Whistle	—	I require a tug. When made by fishing vessels operating in close proximity on the fishing grounds it means 'I am shooting nets'	,,

Morse signals:

- K — · —
- L · — · ·
- M — —
- O — — —
- U · · —
- V · · · —
- W · — —
- Y — · — —
- Z — — · ·

Rule of the Road (1960)

Scope of the Regulations

The thirty-one Rules are divided into six parts.

A – Preliminary and Definitions

B – Lights and Shapes

C – Sound signals and conduct in restricted visibility

D – Steering and Sailing Rules

E – Sound signals for vessels in sight of one another

F – Miscellaneous

The Steering and Sailing Rules provide for almost all occasions of two vessels or seaplanes approaching one another where risk of collision exists. They tell the seaman which vessel must give way, and describe the conditions under which he may expect the other vessel to keep clear of him.

The remaining Rules prescribe the means whereby vessels and seaplanes which are fully manoeuvrable may be identified by night or in low visibility; also the means whereby vessels or seaplanes with no power (or limited power) or with limited manoeuvrability may be distinguished by day or by night or in low visibility. By these means (i.e., the display of lights and shapes and the making of sound signals) the seaman may know instantly whether to expect another vessel to obey the Steering and Sailing Rules or whether she is unable to do so. The Rules include sound signals to be made by vessels in various circumstances, signals to be made by vessels in distress to attract attention or summon assistance, and precautions to be taken by all vessels.

Principles of the Steering and Sailing Rules

The rules for a power-driven vessel meeting another power-driven vessel depend upon the relative bearing of one ship from another; they

471

are quite separate from the rules for a sailing vessel meeting another sailing vessel, which are governed by the direction of the wind.

The main principles upon which the Steering Rules for power-driven vessels are based are as follows:

(i) When two vessels approach end on to one another, each must give way to the other.

(ii) In all circumstances where risk of collision exists one vessel (sometimes known as the 'privileged vessel') holds her course and speed while the other (sometimes known as the 'burdened vessel') gives way.

(iii) The vessel which is directed to give way does so by altering course, or reducing speed, or stopping, or going astern.

(iv) The vessel which is directed to give way should avoid crossing close ahead of the other.

(v) In a broad sense, vessels keep to the right.

(vi) Vessels should always keep a proper look-out (which includes operating radar in low visibility), exhibit the prescribed lights and shapes, make the prescribed sound signals, and be handled in a seamanlike manner with due caution and consideration for others, especially in conditions of low visibility.

(vii) If a collision appears to be unavoidable, each vessel must take whatever action is possible to avert it or to minimise the impact, even if such action involves a departure from the normal rules.

The principle on which the Sailing Rules are based is that the vessel which would lose more ground by an alteration of course is given the right of way.

Illustrations of Lights and Shapes

The coloured plates between pages 472 and 473 show the lights and shapes described in the various rules. A brief description is given against each illustration, but the illustration must be studied with the relevant Rule.

Power-driven vessel, less than
150 feet in length, under way at night

Rule 2 (a) (i). A power-driven vessel under way at night, *less than 150 feet in length*, carries one white steaming light and port and starboard bow lights.

Rule 10. In addition to the above lights, this Rule prescribes a white " overtaking " light for all vessels under way (not visible in the illustrations).

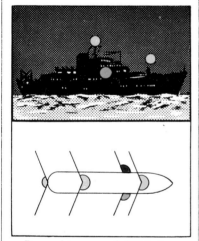

Power-driven vessel, 150 feet or
more in length, under way at night

Rule 2 (a) (ii). A power-driven vessel under way at night, *over 150 feet in length*, carries two white steaming lights and port and starboard bow lights.

Rule 10. In addition to the above lights, this Rule prescribes a white " overtaking " light for all vessels under way.

Rule 15. *In low visibility, day or night, power-driven vessels under way sound the following signals (on whistle or siren) at intervals of not more than two minutes:*
    if making way—one long blast ;
    if stopped—two long blasts.

Seaplane taxi-ing at night

Rule 2 (b). A seaplane under way on the water at night carries one steaming light and port and starboard bow lights on the wing tips.

Rule 10. Prescribes in addition an " overtaking " light.

The arcs of visibility differ slightly from those of power-driven vessels.

Rule 15. *In low visibility a seaplane on the water is not obliged to make the sound signals of other vessels or craft, but if she does not, she shall make some other efficient sound signal at intervals of not more than one minute.*

Vessel of under 150 feet towing
another at night: length of
tow is less than 600 feet

Vessel of over 150 feet towing
another at night: length of
tow is more than 600 feet

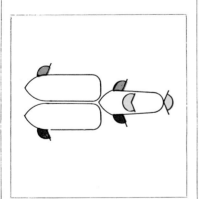

Vessel pushing two other
vessels at night

Rule 3. A power-driven vessel towing or pushing another vessel or seaplane carries her bow lights, overtaking light and steaming light.

If the length of tow is *less than 600 feet* an additional steaming light is carried above or below the white light of Rule 2 (a) (i).

If the length of tow is *more than 600 feet* a third steaming light is carried above or below the white light of Rule 2 (a) (i).

The overtaking light may be replaced by a small white light, not visible before the beam, for the tow to steer by.

By day a power-driven vessel towing, if the length of tow exceeds 600 feet, carries a black diamond shape.

(*See* " Towing Vessels—Second Masthead Light ", on page 494.)

Rule 5. The vessel being towed carries bow lights and an overtaking light. If more than one vessel is being towed, all but the last vessel in tow may carry, instead of the overtaking light, a small white light not visible before the beam.

By day the vessel being towed, if the length of tow exceeds 600 feet, carries a black diamond shape.

A vessel being pushed carries bow lights at the forward end. Any number of vessels pushed ahead in a group are lighted as one vessel.

Rule 15. *In low visibility, day or night, a power-driven vessel towing sounds the following signal on her siren or whistle at intervals of not more than one minute :*
one long blast followed by two short blasts.

A vessel towed (or, if more than one vessel is towed, only the last vessel in tow) sounds, if manned, on the whistle or foghorn immediately after the towing vessel :
one long blast followed by three short blasts.

Vessel not under command
and stopped, at night

Vessel not under command
but making way, at night

Vessel not under command, by day

Rule 4. A vessel under way at night, but not under command and stopped, hoists two all-round red lights, one above the other, visible two miles and switches off all other navigation lights.

If she is making way through the water she shows bow lights and overtaking light.

By day a vessel not under command hoists two black balls.

Rule 15. *In low visibility, day or night, a vessel not under command sounds, at intervals of not more than one minute:*

one long blast followed by two short blasts.

A cable-laying vessel making way, at
night

A vessel engaged in
replenishment, by day

Rule 4. A vessel engaged in laying or picking up cable or a navigation mark, surveying or underwater operations, or a vessel engaged in replenishment at sea or in the launching or recovery of aircraft carries, in lieu of her steaming lights, two all-round red lights with an all-round white light between them, each visible at least two miles.

If she is stopped she does not show her bow lights or overtaking light.

By day she hoists two round red shapes with a white diamond shape between them.

These lights and shapes indicate that she is unable to get out of the way of approaching vessels.

Rule 15. *In low visibility, day or night, she sounds, at intervals of not more than one minute:*

one long blast followed by two short blasts.

Minesweeper dangerous to
pass close on either side

Rule 4. A vessel engaged in minesweeping operations at night carries a green light, visible two miles, at the fore truck and at the end or ends of the fore yard on the side or sides on which danger exists, in addition to her normal steaming, bow and overtaking lights.

By day she carries black balls in the same positions as the green lights.

It is dangerous for other ships to approach closer than 3000 feet astern of the minesweeper or 1500 feet on the side or sides on which danger exists.

Rule 15. *In low visibility, day or night, when minesweeping, a vessel sounds, at intervals of not more than one minute :*
one long blast followed by two short blasts.

Sailing vessel under way
at night, bows on

Sailing vessel under way
at night, showing optional
fore masthead lights

Rule 5. A sailing vessel under way at night carries bow lights.

Rule 10. She also carries an overtaking light.

Rule 5. In addition she may carry on the top of the foremast a red light above a green light, visible two miles and showing from ahead to two points abaft the beam.

Rule 15. *In low visibility, day or night, sailing vessels under way sound the following signals at intervals of not more than one minute :*
one blast—vessel on the starboard tack ;
two blasts—vessel on the port tack ;
three blasts—vessel running with the wind abaft the beam.

Power-driven vessel of
less than 65 feet, at night
(using combined lantern)

Rule 7. Power-driven vessels of less than 65 feet in length carry one steaming light, bow lights and overtaking light (Rule 10). The bow lights may be combined in one lantern.

When towing or pushing another vessel, they carry an additional steaming light above or below the other steaming light; the overtaking light may be replaced by a small white light when towing.

Rule 15. *A power-driven vessel of 40 feet or more in length shall be provided with an efficient whistle.*

In low visibility the sound signals are the same as for larger power-driven vessels.

Rule 7. Vessels of less than 40 feet, under oars or sails, shall, if they do not carry bow lights, carry a combined lantern, either fixed or displayed in time to prevent collision.

Power-driven pilot-vessel
on duty and making
way, at night

Rule 8. A power-driven pilot-vessel on duty and under way carries bow lights, overtaking light and, at the masthead, a white all-round light above a red all-round light, both visible three miles.

She shows one or more flare-ups at intervals not exceeding 10 minutes or an intermittent white light visible all round.

A sailing pilot-vessel on duty and under way carries a white all-round light, visible three miles, at the masthead and an over-taking light; she shows one or more flare-ups at intervals not exceeding 10 minutes. Bow lights are used to indicate her heading on the near approach of or to other vessels.

A pilot-vessel on duty and not under way shows the masthead light or lights and flare-up. When anchored she shows, in addition, anchor lights (Rule 11).

Power-driven pilot-vessel
on duty at anchor

Rule 15. *A power-driven pilot-vessel on duty, in addition to the normal sound signals for power-driven vessels, may sound an identity signal of 4 short blasts.*

Pilot-vessel flag *

* This is not a provision of the regulations.

Trawler trawling and
making way, showing
optional steaming light

Fishing vessel making
way and having gear
extending more than 500 feet

Fishing vessel with
outlying gear extending
more than 500 feet

Rule 9. Vessels engaged in trawling show an all-round green light above an all-round white light, both visible two miles. They may carry in addition one steaming light, lower than and abaft the all-round green and white lights.

When making way through the water they show bow lights and overtaking light.

Vessels engaged in fishing, except trawling, show an all-round red light above an all-round white light. When making way through the water they show bow lights and overtaking light.

If outlying gear extends more than 500 feet an additional all-round white light shows the direction of the gear.

In addition, vessels engaged in fishing may use a flare-up or direct a searchlight in the direction of a danger to approaching vessels.

By day vessels engaged in fishing show a black shape consisting of two cones point to point. If less than 65 feet in length a basket may be shown instead of the black shape. If outlying gear extends more than 500 feet, a black cone, point upwards, indicates the direction of the gear.

Note: *Vessels fishing with trolling lines are not " engaged in fishing " as defined in Rule 1.*

Vessel of less than 150 feet,
anchored

Vessel of 150 feet
or more, anchored

Rule 11. A vessel of less than 150 feet, when at anchor, carries in the forepart a white all-round light visible two miles. She may also carry a second white light as for vessels of 150 feet and over, but the visibility is two miles.

A vessel of 150 feet or more in length, when at anchor, carries two white all-round lights, visible three miles: one near the stem, the other at or near the stern and 15 feet lower.

Vessel at anchor by day

Rule 11. Every vessel at anchor, by day, hoists one black ball in the forepart of the vessel.

Rule 15. *In low visibility, day or night, a vessel at anchor rings her bell rapidly for about 5 seconds every minute.*

In vessels of more than 350 feet in length, the bell is sounded in the forepart and a gong or other instrument similarly in the afterpart.

A vessel at anchor may in addition sound one short, one prolonged, and one short blast to give warning of her position and of the possibility of collision to an approaching vessel.

Vessel engaged in laying or picking up cable and at anchor, by night

Vessel engaged in laying or picking up a navigation mark and at anchor, by day

Rule 11. A vessel engaged in laying or picking up a submarine cable or navigation mark, surveying or underwater operations, when at anchor, carries the lights or shapes prescribed in Rule 4 (c) in addition to her anchor lights.

Vessel aground by night

Vessel aground by day

Rule 11. A vessel aground carries the light or lights for a vessel at anchor and the two red lights prescribed in Rule 4 (a). By day she carries three black balls, one above the other.

Vessel under sail and
propelled by machinery

Rule 14. A vessel proceeding under sail, when also being propelled by machinery, carries one black cone point downwards.

In low visibility she makes the sound signals for a power-driven vessel.

Clear both sides

Do not pass on the side
of the red light

Foul both sides

DREDGERS*

Lights and daymarks for dredgers are prescribed in local port regulations, and they may therefore differ from port to port.

The illustrations refer to dredgers working in H.M. Dockyard ports only.

Anchor lights are carried in addition to other lights.

By day black balls are hoisted in place of white lights, and red flags in place of red lights.

A light-vessel out
of station at night*

A light-vessel out
of station by day*

LIGHT-VESSELS*

A light-vessel when driven from her proper station strikes the distinguishing masthead marks if circumstances permit.

The characteristic light is not shown and the fog signals are not sounded. The following signals are made:

By night: A red fixed light at the bow and stern, and red and white flares shown simultaneously every 15 minutes. If the use of the flares is impracticable, a red and a white light are displayed simultaneously for about a minute.

By day: Two black balls, one forward and one aft, and the signal PC.

In fog or low visibility, a light-vessel out of position sounds the fog signal for a ship at anchor.

* This is not a provision of the " Collision Regulations ".

LIST OF RULES

RULE OF THE ROAD (1960)

Note: Additions and alterations to the 1948 Rules are shown in bold type.

PART A – PRELIMINARY AND DEFINITIONS

Rule 1

(a) These Rules shall be followed by all vessels and seaplanes upon the high seas and in all waters connected therewith navigable by seagoing vessels, except as provided in Rule 30. Where, as a result of their special construction, it is not possible for seaplanes to comply fully with the provisions of Rules specifying the carrying of lights and shapes, these provisions shall be followed as closely as circumstances permit.

(b) The Rules concerning lights shall be complied with in all weathers from sunset to sunrise, and during such times no other lights shall be exhibited, except such lights as cannot be mistaken for the prescribed lights or do not impair their visibility or distinctive character, or interfere with the keeping of a proper look-out. **The lights prescribed by these Rules may also be exhibited from sunrise to sunset in restricted visibility and in all other circumstances when it is deemed necessary.**

(c) In the following Rules, except where the context otherwise requires:

(i) the word 'vessel' includes every description of water craft, other than a seaplane on the water, used or capable of being used as a means of transportation on water;

(ii) the word 'seaplane' includes a flying boat and any other aircraft designed to manoeuvre on the water;

(iii) the term 'power-driven vessel' means any vessel propelled by machinery;

(iv) every power-driven vessel which is under sail and not under power is to be considered a sailing vessel, and every vessel under power whether under sail or not, is to be considered a power-driven vessel;

(v) a vessel or seaplane on the water is 'under way' when she is not at anchor, or made fast to the shore, or aground;

(vi) the term 'height above the hull' means height above the uppermost continuous deck;

(vii) the length and breadth of a vessel shall be her length **overall** and largest breadth;

(viii) the length and span of a seaplane shall be its maximum length and span as shown in its certificate of airworthiness, or as determined by measurement in the absence of such certificate;

(ix) vessels shall be deemed to be in sight of one another only when one can be observed visually from the other;

(x) the word 'visible', when applied to lights, means visible on a dark night with a clear atmosphere;

(xi) the term 'short blast' means a blast of about one second's duration;

(xii) the term 'prolonged blast' means a blast of from four to six seconds' duration;

(xiii) the word 'whistle' means any appliance capable of producing the prescribed short and prolonged blasts;

(xiv) the term 'engaged in fishing' means fishing with nets, lines or trawls but does not include fishing with trolling lines.

PART B – LIGHTS AND SHAPES

Rule 2

(a) A power-driven vessel when under way shall carry:

(i) On or in front of the foremast, or if a vessel without a foremast then in the forepart of the vessel, a white light so constructed as to show an unbroken light over an arc of the horizon of 225 degrees (20 points of the compass), so fixed as to show the light $112\frac{1}{2}$ degrees (10 points) on each side of the vessel, that is, from right ahead to $22\frac{1}{2}$ degrees (2 points) abaft the beam on either side, and of such a character as to be visible at a distance of at least 5 miles.

(ii) Either forward or abaft the white light prescribed in sub-section (i) a second white light similar in construction and character to that light. Vessels of less than 150 feet in length shall not be required to carry this second white light but may do so.

(iii) These two white lights shall be so placed in a line with and over the keel that one shall be at least 15 feet higher than the other and in such a position that the **forward light shall always be shown lower than the after one.** The horizontal distance between the two white lights shall be at least three times the vertical distance. The lower of these two white lights or, if only one is carried, then that light, shall be placed at a height above the hull of not less than 20 feet, and, if the breadth of the vessel exceeds 20 feet, then at a height above the hull not less than such breadth, so however that the light need not be placed at a greater height above the hull than 40 feet. In all circumstances the light or lights, as the case may be, shall be so placed as to be clear of and above all other lights and obstructing superstructures.

(iv) On the starboard side a green light so constructed as to show an unbroken light over an arc of the horizon of 112½ degrees (10 points of the compass), so fixed as to show the light from right ahead to 22½ degrees (2 points) abaft the beam on the starboard side, and of such a character as to be visible at a distance of at least 2 miles.

(v) On the port side a red light so constructed as to show an unbroken light over an arc of the horizon of 112½ degrees (10 points of the compass), so fixed as to show the light from right ahead to 22½ degrees (2 points) abaft the beam on the port side, and of such a character as to be visible at a distance of at least 2 miles.

(vi) The said green and red sidelights shall be fitted with inboard screens projecting at least 3 feet forward from the light, so as to prevent these lights from being seen across the bows.

(b) A seaplane under way on the water shall carry:

(i) In the forepart amidships where it can best be seen a white light, so constructed as to show an unbroken light over an arc of the horizon of 220 degrees of the compass, so fixed as to show the light 110 degrees on each side of the seaplane, namely, from right ahead to 20 degrees abaft the beam on either side, and of such a character as to be visible at a distance of at least 3 miles.

(ii) On the right or starboard wing tip a green light, so constructed as to show an unbroken light over an arc of the horizon of 110 degrees of the compass, so fixed as to show the light from right ahead to 20 degrees abaft the beam on the starboard side, and of such a character as to be visible at a distance of at least 2 miles.

(iii) On the left or port wing tip a red light, so constructed as to show an unbroken light over an arc of the horizon of 110 degrees of the compass, so fixed as to show the light from right ahead to 20 degrees abaft the beam on the port side, and of such a character as to be visible at a distance of at least 2 miles.

Rule 3 (*see 'Towing Vessels—Second Masthead Light', on page 494*)

(a) A power-driven vessel when towing or pushing another vessel **or seaplane** shall, in addition to her sidelights, carry two white lights in a vertical line one over the other, not less than 6 feet apart, **and when towing and the length of the tow, measuring from the stern of the towing vessel to the stern of the last vessel towed, exceeds 600 feet, shall carry three white lights in a vertical line one over the other, so that the upper and lower lights shall be the same distance from, and not less than 6 feet above or below, the middle light.** Each of these lights shall be of the same construction and character and one of them shall be carried in the same position as the white light **prescribed** in Rule 2 (a) (i). **None of these lights shall be carried at a height of less than 14 feet above the hull.** In a vessel with a single mast, such lights may be carried on the mast.

(b) The towing vessel shall also show either the stern light **prescribed** in Rule 10 or in lieu of that light a small white light abaft the funnel or aftermast for the tow to steer by, but such light shall not be visible forward of the beam.

(c) Between sunrise and sunset a power-driven vessel engaged in towing, if the length of tow exceeds 600 feet, shall carry, where it can best be seen, a black diamond shape at least 2 feet in diameter.

(d) A seaplane on the water, when towing one or more seaplanes or vessels, shall carry the lights prescribed in Rule 2 (b) (i), (ii) and (iii); and, in addition, she shall carry a second white light of the same construction and character as the white light prescribed in Rule 2 (b) (i), and in a vertical line at least 6 feet above or below such light.

Rule 4

(a) A vessel which is not under command shall carry, where they can best be seen, and, if a power-driven vessel, in lieu of the lights **prescribed** in Rule 2 (a) (i) and (ii), two red lights in a vertical line one over the other not less than 6 feet apart, and of such a character as to be visible all round the horizon at a distance of at least 2 miles. By day, she shall carry in a vertical line one over the other not less than 6 feet apart, where they can best be seen, two black balls or shapes each not less than 2 feet in diameter.

(b) A seaplane on the water which is not under command may carry, where they can best be seen, **and in lieu of the light prescribed in Rule 2 (b) (i),** two red lights in a vertical line, one over the other, not less than 3 feet apart, and of such a character as to be visible all round the horizon at a distance of at least 2 miles, and may by day carry in a vertical line one over the other not less than 3 feet apart, where they can best be seen, two black balls or shapes, each not less than 2 feet in diameter.

(c) A vessel engaged in laying or in picking up a submarine cable or navigation mark, or a vessel engaged in surveying or underwater operations, **or a vessel engaged in replenishment at sea, or in the launching or recovery of aircraft** when from the nature of her work she is unable to get out of the way of approaching vessels, shall carry, in lieu of the lights prescribed in Rule 2 (a) (i) and (ii), or Rule 7 (a) (i), three lights in a vertical line one over the other **so that the upper and lower lights**

shall be the same distance from, and not less than 6 feet above or below, the middle light. The highest and lowest of these lights shall be red, and the middle light shall be white, and they shall be of such a character as to be visible all round the horizon at a distance of at least 2 miles. By day, she shall carry in a vertical line one over the other not less than 6 feet apart, where they can best be seen, three shapes each not less than 2 feet in diameter, of which the highest and lowest shall be globular in shape and red in colour, and the middle one diamond in shape and white.

(d) (i) A vessel engaged in minesweeping operations shall carry at the fore truck a green light, and at the end or ends of the fore yard on the side or sides on which danger exists, another such light or lights. These lights shall be carried in addition to the light prescribed in Rule 2 (a) (i) or Rule 7 (a) (i), as appropriate, and shall be of such a character as to be visible all round the horizon at a distance of at least 2 miles. By day she shall carry black balls, not less than 2 feet in diameter, in the same position as the green lights.

(ii) The showing of these lights or balls indicates that it is dangerous for other vessels to approach closer than 3,000 feet astern of the minesweeper or 1,500 feet on the side or sides on which danger exists.

(e) The vessels and seaplanes referred to in this Rule, when not making way through the water, shall **show neither** the coloured side lights **nor the stern light,** but when making way they shall **show** them.

(f) The lights and shapes **prescribed** in this Rule are to be taken by other vessels and seaplanes as signals that the vessel or seaplane showing them is not under command and cannot therefore get out of the way.

(g) These signals are not signals of vessels in distress and requiring assistance. Such signals are contained in Rule 31.

Rule 5

(a) A sailing vessel under way and any vessel or seaplane being towed shall carry the same lights as are prescribed **in** Rule 2 for a power-driven vessel or a seaplane under way, respectively, with the exception of the white lights **prescribed** therein, which they shall never carry. They shall also carry stern lights as **prescribed** in Rule 10, provided that vessels towed, except the last vessel of a tow, may carry, in lieu of such stern light, a small white light as **prescribed** in Rule 3 (b).

(b) In addition to the lights prescribed in section (a), a sailing vessel may carry on the top of the foremast two lights in a vertical line one over the other, sufficiently separated so as to be clearly distinguished. The upper light shall be red and the lower light shall be green. Both lights shall be constructed and fixed as prescribed in Rule 2 (a) (i) and shall be visible at a distance of at least 2 miles.

(c) A vessel being pushed ahead shall carry, at the forward end, on the starboard side a green light and on the port side a red light, which shall have the same characteristics as the lights prescribed in Rule 2 (a) (iv) and (v) and shall be screened as provided in Rule 2 (a) (vi), provided that any number of vessels pushed ahead in a group shall be lighted as one vessel.

(d) Between sunrise and sunset a vessel being towed, if the length of the tow exceeds 600 feet, shall carry where it can best be seen a black diamond shape at least 2 feet in diameter.

Rule 6

(a) When it is not possible on account of bad weather or other sufficient cause to fix the green and red sidelights, these lights shall be kept at hand lighted and ready for immediate use, and shall, on the approach of or to other vessels, be exhibited on their respective sides in sufficient time to prevent collision, in such manner as to make them most visible, and so that the green light shall not be seen on the port side nor the red light on the starboard side, nor, if practicable, more than $22\frac{1}{2}$ degrees (2 points) abaft the beam on their respective sides.

(b) To make the use of these portable lights more certain and easy, the lanterns containing them shall each be painted outside with the colour of the lights they respectively contain, and shall be provided with proper screens.

Rule 7

Power-driven vessels of less than **65 feet in length,** vessels under oars or sails of less than **40 feet in length,** and rowing boats, when under way shall not be required to carry the lights **prescribed** in Rules 2, **3 and 5,** but if they do not carry them they shall be provided with the following lights:

(a) Power-driven vessels of less than **65 feet in length,** except as provided in sections (b) **and (c),** shall carry:

(i) In the forepart of the vessel, where it can best be seen, and at a height above the gunwale of not less than 9 feet, a white light constructed and fixed as prescribed in Rule 2 (a) (i) and of such a character as to be visible at a distance of at least 3 miles.

(ii) Green and red sidelights constructed and fixed as prescribed in Rule 2 (a) (iv) and (v), and of such a character as to be visible at a distance of at least 1 mile, or a combined lantern showing a green light and a red light from right ahead to $22\frac{1}{2}$ degrees (2 points) abaft the beam on their respective sides. Such lantern shall be carried not less than 3 feet below the white light.

(b) Power-driven vessels of less than 65 feet in length when towing or pushing another vessel shall carry:

(i) In addition to the sidelights or the combined lantern prescribed in section (a) (ii) two white lights in a vertical line, one over the other not less than 4 feet apart. Each of these lights shall be of the same construction and character as the white light prescribed in section (a) (i) and one of them shall be carried in the same position. In a vessel with a single mast such lights may be carried on the mast.

(ii) Either a stern light as prescribed in Rule 10 or in lieu of that light a small white light abaft the funnel or aftermast for the tow to steer by, but such light shall not be visible forward of the beam.

(c) Power-driven vessels of less than 40 feet in length may carry the white light at a less height than 9 feet above the gunwale but it shall be carried **not less than 3** feet above the sidelights or the combined lantern **prescribed** in section (a) (ii).

(d) Vessels of less than **40 feet in length,** under oars or sails, except as provided in section **(f)**, shall, if they do not carry the sidelights, carry, where it can best be seen, a lantern showing a green light on one side and a red light on the other, of such a character as to be visible at a distance of at least 1 mile, and so fixed that the green light shall not be seen on the port side, nor the red light on the starboard side. Where it is not possible to fix this light, it shall be kept ready for immediate use and shall be exhibited in sufficient time to prevent collision and so that the green light shall not be seen on the port side nor the red light on the starboard side.

(e) The vessels referred to in this Rule when being towed shall carry the sidelights or the combined lantern prescribed in sections (a) or (d) of this Rule, as appropriate, and a stern light as prescribed in Rule 10, or, except the last vessel of the tow, a small white light as prescribed in section (b) (ii). When being pushed ahead they shall carry at the forward end the sidelights or combined lantern prescribed in sections (a) or (d) of this Rule, as appropriate, provided that any number of vessels referred to in this Rule when pushed ahead in a group shall be lighted as one vessel under this Rule unless the overall length of the group exceeds 65 feet when the provisions of Rule 5 (c) shall apply.

(f) Small rowing boats, whether under oars or sail, shall only be required to have ready at hand an electric torch or a lighted lantern, showing a white light, which shall be exhibited in sufficient time to prevent collision.

(g) The vessels and boats referred to in this Rule shall not be required to carry the lights or shapes prescribed in Rules 4 (a) and 11 (e) **and the size of their day signals may be less than is prescribed in Rules 4 (c) and 11 (c).**

Rule 8

(a) A power-driven pilot-vessel when engaged **on pilotage duty and under way:**

    (i) Shall carry a white light at the masthead at a height of not less than 20 feet above the hull, visible all round the horizon at a distance of at least 3 miles and at a distance of 8 feet below it a red light similar in construction and character. If such a vessel is of less than 65 feet in length she may carry the white light at a height of not less than 9 feet above the gunwale and the red light at a distance of 4 feet below the white light.

    (ii) Shall carry the sidelights or lanterns prescribed in Rule 2 (a) (iv) and (v) or Rule 7 (a) (ii) or (d), as appropriate, and the stern light prescribed in Rule 10.

    (iii) Shall show one or more flare-up lights at intervals not exceeding 10 minutes. An intermittent white light visible all round the horizon may be used in lieu of flare-up lights.

(b) A sailing pilot-vessel when engaged **on pilotage duty and under way:**

    (i) Shall carry a white light at the masthead visible all round the horizon at a distance of at least 3 miles.

    (ii) Shall be provided with the sidelights or lantern prescribed in Rules 5 (a) or 7 (d), as appropriate, and shall, on the near approach of or to other vessels, have such lights ready for use, and shall show them at short intervals to indicate the direction in which she is heading, but the green light shall not be shown on the port side nor the red light on the starboard side. She shall also carry the stern light prescribed in Rule 10.

    (iii) Shall show **one or more** flare-up lights at intervals not exceeding 10 minutes.

(c) A pilot-vessel when engaged **on pilotage duty and not under way** shall carry the lights and show the flares prescribed in sections **(a) (i) and (iii)** or **(b) (i) and (iii), as appropriate, and if at anchor** shall also carry the anchor lights prescribed in Rule 11.

(d) A pilot-vessel when not engaged on pilotage duty shall show the lights or shapes for a similar vessel of her length.

Rule 9

(a) Fishing vessels when not **engaged in** fishing shall show the lights or shapes for similar vessels of their **length.**

(b) **Vessels engaged in fishing, when under way or at anchor, shall show only the lights and shapes prescribed in this Rule, which lights and shapes** shall be visible at a distance of at least 2 miles.

(c) (i) Vessels when engaged in trawling, by which is meant the dragging of a dredge net or other apparatus through the water, **shall carry two lights in a vertical line, one over the other, not less than 4 feet nor more than 12 feet apart. The upper of these lights shall be green and the lower light white and each shall be visible all round the horizon. The lower of these two lights shall be carried at a height above the sidelights not less than twice the distance between the two vertical lights.**

(ii) Such vessels may in addition carry a white light similar in construction to the white light prescribed in Rule 2 (a) (i) but such light shall be carried lower than and abaft the all-round green and white lights.

(d) **Vessels when engaged in fishing, except vessels engaged in trawling, shall carry the lights prescribed in section (c) (i) except that the upper of the two vertical lights shall be red. Such vessels if of less than 40 feet in length may carry the red light at a height of not less than 9 feet above the gunwale and the white light not less than 3 feet below the red light.**

(e) **Vessels referred to in sections (c) and (d), when making way through the water, shall carry the sidelights or lanterns prescribed in Rule 2 (a) (iv) and (v) or Rule 7 (a) (ii) or (d), as appropriate, and the stern light prescribed in Rule 10. When not making way through the water they shall show neither the sidelights nor the stern light.**

(f) **Vessels referred to in section (d) with outlying gear** extending more than 500 feet horizontally into the seaway shall **carry an additional all-round white light at a horizontal distance of not less than 6 feet nor more than 20 feet away from the vertical lights in the direction of the outlying gear. This additional white light shall be placed at a height not exceeding that of the white light prescribed in section (c) (i) and not lower than the sidelights.**

(g) In addition to the lights which they are required by this Rule to **carry,** vessels **engaged in** fishing may, if necessary in order to attract the attention of an approaching vessel, **use** a flare-up light, **or may direct the beam of their searchlight in the direction of a danger threatening the approaching vessel, in such a way as not to embarrass other vessels. They may also use working lights but fishermen shall take into account that specially bright or**

insufficiently screened working lights may impair the visibility and distinctive character of the lights prescribed in this Rule.

(h) By day **vessels when engaged in fishing** shall **indicate their occupation by displaying** where it can best be seen a **black shape consisting of two cones each not less than 2 feet in diameter with their points together one above the other.** Such vessels if of less than 65 feet in length may substitute a basket for such black shape. If their outlying gear extends more than 500 feet horizontally into the seaway vessels engaged in fishing shall display in addition one black conical shape, point upwards, in the direction of the outlying gear.

Note: Vessels fishing with trolling lines are not 'engaged in fishing' as defined in Rule 1 (c) (xiv).

Rule 10

(a) **Except where otherwise provided in these Rules,** a vessel when under way shall carry at her stern a white light, so constructed that it shall show an unbroken light over an arc of the horizon of 135 degrees (12 points of the compass), so fixed as to show the light $67\frac{1}{2}$ degrees (6 points) from right aft on each side of the vessel, and of such a character as to be visible at a distance of at least 2 miles.

(b) In a small vessel, if it is not possible on account of bad weather or other sufficient cause for this light to be fixed, an electric torch or a lighted lantern **showing a white light** shall be kept at hand ready for use and shall, on the approach of an overtaking vessel, be shown in sufficient time to prevent collision.

(c) A seaplane on the water when under way shall carry on her tail a white light, so constructed as to show an unbroken light over an arc of the horizon of 140 degrees of the compass, so fixed as to show the light 70 degrees from right aft on each side of the seaplane, and of such a character as to be visible at a distance of at least 2 miles.

Rule 11

(a) A vessel of less than 150 feet in length, when at anchor, shall carry in the forepart of the vessel, where it can best be seen, a white light visible all round the horizon at a distance of at least 2 miles. **Such a vessel may also carry a second white light in the position prescribed in section (b) of this Rule but shall not be required to do so. The second white light, if carried, shall be visible at a distance of at least 2 miles and so placed as to be as far as possible visible all round the horizon.**

(b) A vessel of 150 feet or **more** in length, when at anchor, shall carry **near the stem** of the vessel, at a height of not less than 20 feet above the hull, one such light, and at or near the stern of the vessel and at such a height that it shall be not less than 15 feet lower than the forward light, another such light. Both these lights shall be visible **at a distance of at least 3 miles and so placed as to be as far as possible visible all round the horizon.**

(c) Between sunrise and sunset every vessel when at anchor shall carry in the forepart of the vessel, where it can best be seen, one black ball not less than 2 feet in diameter.

(d) A vessel engaged in laying or in picking up a submarine cable or navigation mark, or a vessel engaged in surveying or underwater operations, when at anchor, shall carry the lights or shapes prescribed in Rule 4 (c) in addition to those prescribed in the appropriate preceding sections of this Rule.

(e) A vessel aground shall carry the light or lights prescribed in sections (a) or (b) and the two red lights prescribed in Rule 4 (a). By day she shall carry, where they can best be seen, three black balls, each not less than 2 feet in diameter, placed in a vertical line one over the other, not less than 6 feet apart.

(f) A seaplane on the water under 150 feet in length, when at anchor, shall carry, where it can best be seen, a white light, visible all round the horizon at a distance of at least 2 miles.

(g) A seaplane on the water 150 feet or upwards in length, when at anchor, shall carry, where they can best be seen, a white light forward and a white light aft, both lights visible all round the horizon at a distance of at least 3 miles; and, in addition, if the seaplane is more than 150 feet in span, a white light on each side to indicate the maximum span, and visible, so far as practicable, all round the horizon at a distance of 1 mile.

(h) A seaplane aground shall carry an anchor light or lights as prescribed in sections (f) and (g), and in addition may carry two red lights in a vertical line, at least 3 feet apart, so placed as to be visible all round the horizon.

Rule 12

Every vessel or seaplane on the water may, if necessary in order to attract attention, in addition to the lights which she is by these Rules required to carry, show a flare-up light or use a detonating or other efficient sound signal that cannot be mistaken for any signal authorised elsewhere under these Rules.

Rule 13

(a) Nothing in these Rules shall interfere with the operation of any special rules made by the Government of any nation with respect to additional station and signal lights for ships of war, for vessels sailing under convoy, **for fishing vessels engaged in fishing as a fleet** or for seaplanes on the water.

(b) Whenever the Government concerned shall have determined that a naval or other military vessel or waterborne seaplane of special construction or purpose cannot comply fully with the provisions of any of these Rules with respect to the number, position, range or arc of visibility of lights or shapes, without interfering with the military function of the vessel or seaplane, such vessel or seaplane shall comply with such other provisions in regard to the number, position, range or arc of visibility of lights or shapes as her Government shall have determined to be the closest possible compliance with these Rules in respect of that vessel or seaplane.

Rule 14

A vessel proceeding under sail, when also being propelled by machinery, shall carry in the daytime forward, where it can best be seen, one black conical shape, point **downwards,** not less than 2 feet in diameter at its base.

PART C – SOUND SIGNALS AND CONDUCT IN RESTRICTED VISIBILITY

Preliminary

1. The possession of information obtained from radar does not relieve any vessel of the obligation of conforming strictly with the Rules and, in particular, the obligations contained in Rules 15 and 16.

2. The Annex to the Rules contains recommendations intended to assist in the use of radar as an aid to avoiding collision in restricted visibility.

Rule 15

(a) A power-driven vessel **of 40 feet or more in length** shall be provided with an efficient whistle, sounded by steam or by some substitute for steam, so placed that the sound may not be intercepted by any obstruction, and with an efficient fog horn to be sounded by mechanical means, and also with an efficient bell. A sailing vessel of **40 feet or more in length** shall be provided with a similar fog horn and bell.

(b) All signals prescribed in this Rule for vessels under way shall be given:

    (i) by power-driven vessels on the whistle;
    (ii) by sailing vessels on the fog-horn;
    (iii) by vessels towed on the whistle or fog-horn.

(c) In fog, mist, falling snow, heavy rainstorms, or any other condition similarly restricting visibility, whether by day or night, the signals prescribed in this Rule shall be used as follows:

(i) A power-driven vessel making way through the water shall sound at intervals of not more than 2 minutes a prolonged blast.

(ii) A power-driven vessel under way, but stopped and making no way through the water, shall sound at intervals of not more than 2 minutes two prolonged blasts, with an interval of about 1 second between them.

(iii) A sailing vessel under way shall sound, at intervals of not more than 1 minute, when on the starboard tack one blast, when on the port tack two blasts in succession, and when with the wind abaft the beam three blasts in succession.

(iv) A vessel when at anchor shall at intervals of not more than 1 minute ring the bell rapidly for about 5 seconds. In vessels of more than 350 feet in length the bell shall be sounded in the forepart of the vessel, and in addition there shall be sounded in the after part of the vessel, at intervals of not more than 1 minute for about 5 seconds, a gong or other instrument, the tone and sounding of which cannot be confused with that of the bell. Every vessel at anchor may in addition, in accordance with Rule 12, sound three blasts in succession, namely, one short, one prolonged, and one short blast, to give warning of her position and of the possibility of collision to an approaching vessel.

(v) A vessel when towing, a vessel engaged in laying or in picking up a submarine cable or navigation mark, and a vessel under way which is unable to get out of the way of an approaching vessel through being not under command or unable to manoeuvre as required by these Rules shall, instead of the signals prescribed in sub-sections (i), (ii) and (iii) sound, at intervals of not more than 1 minute, three blasts in succession, namely, one prolonged blast followed by two short blasts.

(vi) A vessel towed, or, if more than one vessel is towed, only the last vessel of the tow, if manned, shall, at intervals of not more than 1 minute, sound four blasts in succession, namely, one prolonged blast followed by three short blasts. When practicable, this signal shall be made immediately after the signal made by the towing vessel.

(vii) A vessel aground shall give the **bell** signal **and, if required, the gong signal,** prescribed in sub-section (iv) and shall, in addition, give three separate and distinct strokes on the bell immediately before and after **such rapid ringing of the bell.**

(viii) A vessel **engaged in** fishing **when under way or at anchor** shall at intervals of not more than 1 minute sound **the signal prescribed in sub-section (v). A vessel when fishing with** trolling lines and under way shall sound the signals prescribed in sub-sections (i), (ii) or (iii) as may be appropriate.

(ix) A vessel of less than **40 feet in length,** a rowing boat, or a seaplane on the water, shall not be obliged to give the above-mentioned signals but if she does not, she shall make some other efficient sound signal at intervals of not more than 1 minute.

(x) **A power-driven pilot-vessel when engaged on pilotage duty may, in addition to the signals prescribed in sub-section (i), (ii) and (iv), sound an identity signal consisting of 4 short blasts.**

Rule 16

(a) Every vessel, or seaplane when taxi-ing on the water, shall, in fog, mist, falling snow, heavy rainstorms or any other condition similarly restricting visibility, go at a moderate speed, having careful regard to the existing circumstances and conditions.

(b) A power-driven vessel hearing, apparently forward of her beam, the fog-signal of a vessel the position of which is not ascertained, shall, so far as the circumstances of the case admit, stop her engines, and then navigate with caution until danger of collision is over.

(c) **A power-driven vessel which detects the presence of another vessel forward of her beam before hearing her fog signal or sighting her visually may take early and substantial action to avoid a close quarters situation but, if this cannot be avoided, she shall, so far as the circumstances of the case admit, stop her engines in proper time to avoid collision and then navigate with caution until danger of collision is over.**

PART D – STEERING AND SAILING RULES

Preliminary

1. In obeying and construing these Rules, any action taken should be positive, in ample time, and with due regard to the observance of good seamanship.

2. Risk of collision can, when circumstances permit, be ascertained by carefully watching the compass bearing of an approaching vessel. If the bearing does not appreciably change, such risk should be deemed to exist.

3. Mariners should bear in mind that seaplanes in the act of landing or taking off, or operating under adverse weather conditions, may be unable to change their intended action at the last moment.

4. **Rules 17 to 24 apply only to vessels in sight of one another.**

Rule 17

(a) When two sailing vessels are approaching one another, so as to involve risk of collision, one of them shall keep out of the way of the other as follows:

> **(i) When each has the wind on a different side, the vessel which has the wind on the port side shall keep out of the way of the other.**
>
> **(ii) When both have the wind on the same side, the vessel which is to windward shall keep out of the way of the vessel which is to leeward.**

(b) For the purposes of this Rule the windward side shall be deemed to be the side opposite to that on which the mainsail is carried or, in the case of a square-rigged vessel, the side opposite to that on which the largest fore-and-aft sail is carried.

Rule 18

(a) When two power-driven vessels are meeting end on, or nearly end on, so as to involve risk of collision, each shall alter her course to starboard, so that each may pass on the port side of the other. This Rule only applies to cases where vessels are meeting end on, or nearly end on, in such a manner as to involve risk of collision, and does not apply to two vessels which must, if both keep on their respective courses, pass clear of each other. The only cases to which it does apply are when each of two vessels is end on, or nearly end on, to the other; in other words, to cases in which, by day, each vessel sees the masts of the other in a line, or nearly in a line, with her own; and by night, to cases in which each vessel is in such a position as to see both the sidelights of the other. It does not apply, by day, to cases in which a vessel sees another ahead crossing her own course; or, by night, to cases where the red light of one vessel is opposed to the red light of the other or where the green light of one vessel is opposed to the green light of the other or where a red light without a green light or a green light without a red light is seen ahead, or where both green and red lights are seen anywhere but ahead.

(b) For the purposes of this Rule and Rules 19 to 29 inclusive, except Rule 20 (c) **and Rule 28,** a seaplane on the water shall be deemed to be a vessel, and the expression 'power-driven vessel' shall be construed accordingly.

Rule 19

When two power-driven vessels are crossing, so as to involve risk of collision, the vessel which has the other on her own starboard side shall keep out of the way of the other.

Rule 20

(a) When a power-driven vessel and a sailing vessel are proceeding in such directions as to involve risk of collision, except as provided for in Rules 24 and 26, the power-driven vessel shall keep out of the way of the sailing vessel.

(b) **This Rule shall not give to a sailing vessel the right to hamper, in a narrow channel, the safe passage of a power-driven vessel which can navigate only inside such channel.**

(c) A seaplane on the water shall, in general, keep well clear of all vessels and avoid impeding their navigation. In circumstances, however, where risk of collision exists, she shall comply with these Rules.

Rule 21

Where by any of these Rules one of two vessels is to keep out of the way, the other shall keep her course and speed. When, from any cause, the latter vessel finds herself so close that collision cannot be avoided by the action of the giving-way vessel alone, she also shall take such action as will best aid to avert collision (*see* Rules 27 and 29).

Rule 22

Every vessel which is directed by these Rules to keep out of the way of another vessel shall, **so far as possible, take positive early action to comply with this obligation, and shall,** if the circumstances of the case admit, avoid crossing ahead of the other.

Rule 23

Every power-driven vessel which is directed by these Rules to keep out of the way of another vessel shall, on approaching her, if necessary, slacken her speed or stop or reverse.

Rule 24

(a) Notwithstanding anything contained in these Rules, every vessel overtaking any other shall keep out of the way of the overtaken vessel.

(b) Every vessel coming up with another vessel from any direction more than $22\frac{1}{2}$ degrees (2 points) abaft her beam, i.e., in such a position, with reference to the vessel which she is overtaking, that at night she would be unable to see either of that vessel's sidelights, shall be deemed to be an overtaking vessel; and no subsequent alteration of the bearing between the two vessels shall make the overtaking vessel a crossing vessel within the meaning of these Rules, or relieve her of the duty of keeping clear of the overtaken vessel until she is finally past and clear.

(c) If the overtaking vessel cannot determine with certainty whether she is forward of or abaft this direction from the other vessel, she shall assume that she is an overtaking vessel and keep out of the way.

Rule 25

(a) In a narrow channel every power-driven vessel when proceeding along the course of the channel shall, when it is safe and practicable, keep to that side of the fairway or mid-channel which lies on the starboard side of such vessel.

(b) Whenever a power-driven vessel is nearing a bend in a channel where a vessel approaching from the other direction cannot be seen, such **power-driven vessel,** when she shall have arrived within one-half ($\frac{1}{2}$) mile of the bend, shall give a signal by one prolonged blast on her whistle which signal shall be answered by a similar blast given by any approaching power-driven vessel that may be within hearing around the bend. Regardless of whether an approaching vessel on the farther side of the bend is heard, such bend shall be rounded with alertness and caution.

(c) In a narrow channel a power-driven vessel of less than 65 feet in length shall not hamper the safe passage of a vessel which can navigate only inside such channel.

Rule 26

All vessels not engaged in fishing, **except vessels to which the provisions of Rule 4 apply,** shall, when under way, keep out of the way of **vessels engaged in fishing.** This Rule shall not give to any vessel engaged in fishing the right of obstructing a fairway used by vessels other than fishing vessels.

Rule 27

In obeying and construing these Rules due regard shall be had to all dangers of navigation and collision, and to any special circumstances, including the limitations of the craft involved, which may render a departure from the above Rules necessary in order to avoid immediate danger.

PART E–SOUND SIGNALS FOR VESSELS IN SIGHT OF ONE ANOTHER

Rule 28

(a) When vessels are in sight of one another, a power-driven vessel under way, in taking any course authorised or required by these Rules, shall indicate that course by the following signals on her whistle, namely:

One short blast to mean 'I am altering my course to starboard'.
Two short blasts to mean 'I am altering my course to port'.
Three short blasts to mean 'My engines are going astern'.

(b) Whenever a power-driven vessel which, under these Rules, is to keep her course and speed, is in sight of another vessel and is in doubt whether sufficient action is being taken by the other vessel to avert collision, she may indicate such doubt by giving at least five short and rapid blasts on the whistle. The giving of such a signal shall not relieve a vessel of her obligations under Rules 27 and 29 or any other Rule, or of her duty to indicate any action taken under these Rules by giving the appropriate sound signals laid down in this Rule.

(c) Any whistle signal mentioned in this Rule may be further indicated by a visual signal consisting of a white light visible all round the horizon at a distance of at least 5 miles, and so devised that it will operate simultaneously and in conjunction with the whistle sounding mechanism and remain lighted and visible during the same period as the sound signal.

(d) Nothing in these Rules shall interfere with the operation of any special rules made by the Government of any nation with respect to the use of additional whistle signals between ships of war or vessels sailing under convoy.

PART F – MISCELLANEOUS

Rule 29

Nothing in these Rules shall exonerate any vessel, or the owner, master or crew thereof, from the consequences of any neglect to carry lights or signals, or of any neglect to keep a proper look-out, or of the neglect of any precaution which may be required by the ordinary practice of seamen, or by the special circumstances of the case.

Rule 30

Nothing in these Rules shall interfere with the operation of a special rule duly made by local authority relative to the navigation of any harbour, river, lake, or inland water, including a reserved seaplane area.

Rule 31

Distress Signals

(a) When a vessel or seaplane on the water is in distress and requires assistance from other vessels or from the shore, the following shall be the signals to be used or displayed by her, either together or separately, namely:

(i) A gun or other explosive signal fired at intervals of about a minute.

(ii) A continuous sounding with any fog-signalling apparatus.

(iii) Rockets or shells, throwing red stars fired one at a time at short intervals.

(iv) A signal made by radiotelegraphy or by any other signalling method consisting of the group · · · — — — · · · in the Morse Code.

(v) A signal sent by radiotelephony consisting of the spoken word 'Mayday'.

(vi) The International Code Signal of distress indicated by N.C.

(vii) A signal consisting of a square flag having above or below it a ball or anything resembling a ball.

(viii) Flames on the vessel (as from a burning tar barrel, oil barrel, etc.).

(ix) A rocket parachute flare **or a hand flare** showing a red light.

(x) **A smoke signal giving off a volume of orange-coloured smoke.**

(xi) **Slowly and repeatedly raising and lowering arms outstretched to each side.**

Note: Vessels in distress may use the radiotelegraph alarm signal or the radiotelephone alarm signal to secure attention to distress calls and messages. The radiotelegraph alarm signal, which is designed to actuate the radiotelegraph auto alarms of vessels so fitted, consists of a series of twelve dashes, sent in 1 minute, the duration of each dash being 4 seconds, and the duration of the interval between 2 consecutive dashes being 1 second. The radiotelephone alarm signal consists of 2 tones transmitted alternately over periods of from 30 seconds to 1 minute.

(b) The use of any of the foregoing signals, except for the purpose of indicating that a vessel or seaplane is in distress, and the use of any signals which may be confused with any of the above signals, is prohibited.

ANNEX TO THE RULES

Recommendations on the Use of Radar Information as an Aid to Avoiding Collisions at Sea

(1) Assumptions made on scanty information may be dangerous and should be avoided.

(2) A vessel navigating with the aid of radar in restricted visibility must, in compliance with Rule 16 (a), go at a moderate speed. Information obtained from the use of radar is one of the circumstances to be taken into account when determining moderate speed. In this regard it must be recognised that small vessels, small icebergs and similar floating objects may not be detected by radar.

Radar indications of one or more vessels in the vicinity may mean that 'moderate speed' should be slower than a mariner without radar might consider moderate in the circumstances.

(3) When navigating in restricted visibility the radar range and bearing alone do not constitute ascertainment of the position of the other vessel

under Rule 16 (b) sufficiently to relieve a vessel of the duty to stop her engines and navigate with caution when a fog signal is heard forward of the beam.

(4) When action has been taken under Rule 16 (c) to avoid a close quarters situation, it is essential to make sure that such action is having the desired effect. Alterations of course or speed or both are matters as to which the mariner must be guided by the circumstances of the case.

(5) Alteration of course alone may be the most effective action to avoid close quarters provided that:

(a) There is sufficient sea room.

(b) It is made in good time.

(c) It is substantial. A succession of small alterations of course should be avoided.

(d) It does not result in a close quarters situation with other vessels.

(6) The direction of an alteration of course is a matter in which the mariner must be guided by the circumstances of the case. An alteration to starboard, particularly when vessels are approaching apparently on opposite or nearly opposite courses, is generally preferable to an alteration to port.

(7) An alteration of speed, either alone or in conjunction with an alteration of course, should be substantial. A number of small alterations of speed should be avoided.

(8) If a close quarters situation is imminent, the most prudent action may be to take all way off the vessel.

General Comments

The following comments are intended to assist in interpreting the Annex to the Rules.

The first half of paragraph (2) stresses the fact that, although radar information often allows a ship to go faster in restricted visibility, a clear radar screen should neither induce a sense of security, nor be regarded as a licence to proceed at any speed, nor incidentally should it lead to a neglect of other basic seamanlike precautions such as making the appropriate sound signals and keeping a sharp visual and aural look-out. Radar is always liable to miss potential hazards, especially in fog and rain, which, apart from frequently obscuring large areas of the screen, tend to reduce the range at which other objects are detected or may even obliterate them.

The second half of paragraph (2) implies that radar information sometimes enables a ship to appreciate that the situation is more complex then she would have realised without radar – and therefore that she should go still slower.

Paragraph (3) means that radar-fitted ships are not absolved, when they hear a siren forward of either beam, from acting strictly in accordance with Rule 16 (b) because:

(a) A radar range and bearing of another vessel do not necessarily positively identify that vessel as the one which sounded the siren.

(b) In any case, as the other vessel cannot be seen, there is no immediate means of telling what she is about to do.

In paragraphs (4) and (5) (d) the Close Quarters situation is not precisely defined, and it would be dangerous to attempt to do so. It suffices to say that if he is in any doubt, the prudent mariner will assume that a close quarters situation has arisen and act accordingly. In determining risk of collision the range is his prime consideration, but he should also take into account the possibility that the other vessel may not have radar, may not be as manoeuvrable as his own ship, and may be in charge of someone who is not as alert or as conversant with the rules as himself.

In paragraphs (5) (c) and (7) the meaning of 'substantial' alterations of course and speed cannot be laid down exactly. The main point here is that any alteration should be sufficiently bold to make it readily apparent to the other vessel, if she has radar. It should be remembered that few merchant ships are at present fitted with automatic plotting tables, and without them other ships' alterations may take longer to appreciate, especially at the greater ranges. Thus, as a general rule, alterations of course to avoid the close quarters situation should not normally be less than 20 degrees (and preferably greater).

TOWING VESSELS—SECOND MASTHEAD LIGHT

1. Some doubt has arisen whether the wording of Rule 3 of the International Regulations for Preventing Collisions at Sea 1960 requires vessels over 150 feet in length to carry a second masthead steaming light in accordance with Rule 2 (*a*) (ii) when towing or pushing another vessel. The Board of Trade has issued Merchant Shipping Notice No. M518 to clarify this issue, and the notice is · reprinted below.

INTERNATIONAL REGULATIONS FOR PREVENTING COLLISIONS AT SEA, 1960

Second masthead light to be exhibited by vessels of 150 feet or over when towing or pushing.

Notice to Shipowners, Shipmasters and Seamen and others concerned with foreign-going and home trade merchant ships and fishing vessels.

The Board have been considering a possible ambiguity in the wording of the International Regulations for Preventing Collisions at Sea 1960* concerning the second masthead light prescribed for vessels of more than 150 feet in length when towing or pushing.

According to Rule 2 (*a*) (ii), a vessel of more than 150 feet in length shall carry the second masthead light when under way. Rule 3, however, (which deals with lights and shapes to be exhibited by vessels when towing or pushing) by being explicit on the carriage of the sidelights, the towing lights (2 or 3 in a vertical line) and the stern light, and by omitting reference to the second white masthead light, creates an element of doubt about whether it needs to be shown. Thus, the question was raised whether a vessel of 150 feet or more in length, when towing or pushing another vessel or seaplane, was required to comply with Rule 2 (*a*) (ii).

This matter was raised with the Intergovernmental Maritime Consultative Organisation and after reference to their Sub-Committee on Safety of Navigation it was considered by their Maritime Safety Committee. An extract from the report of this Committee is appended below for the information of all concerned:

" The Committee, holding the view that the intention behind Rule 3 (*a*) of the International Regulations for Preventing Collisions at Sea seen in conjunction with Rule 2 (*a*) (ii) was that the second masthead light be carried by vessels of 150 feet or over in length when towing or pushing, wished to recommend that governments bring this to the attention of all concerned through the usual channels."

* Set out in SI 1965 No. 1525 (The Collision Regulations (Ships and Seaplanes on the Water) and Signals of Distress (Ships) Order 1965). (HMSO, 1*s*. 6*d*.)

2. H.M. Ships, R.F.A.s, Marine Services Vessels and P.A.S. craft over 150 feet in length that are fitted with a second masthead light in accordance with Rule 2 (a) (ii) of the Rule of the Road (1960) are to display this light in addition to the lights required by Rule 3 when towing or pushing another vessel.

Rule of the Road (1972)

Comes into force at Noon, Local Time, 15th July 1977

LIST OF RULES AND ANNEXES (1972)

The Regulations (1972) consist of 38 Rules arranged in 5 Parts (A to E), and 4 Annexes sub-divided into Sections.

LIST OF RULES

LIST OF ANNEXES

RULE OF THE ROAD (1972)

PART A – GENERAL
Rule 1

Application

(a) These Rules shall apply to all vessels upon the high seas and in all waters connected therewith navigable by seagoing vessels.

(b) Nothing in these Rules shall interfere with the operation of special rules made by an appropriate authority for roadsteads, harbours, rivers, lakes or inland waterways connected with the high seas and navigable by seagoing vessels. Such special rules shall conform as closely as possible to these Rules.

(c) Nothing in these Rules shall interfere with the operation of any special rules made by the Government of any State with respect to additional station or signal lights or whistle signals for ships of war and vessels proceeding under convoy, or with respect to additional station or signal lights for fishing vessels engaged in fishing as a fleet. These additional station or signal lights or whistle signals shall, so far as possible, be such that they cannot be mistaken for any light or signal authorized elsewhere under these Rules.

(d) Traffic separation schemes may be adopted by the Organization for the purpose of these Rules.

(e) Whenever the Government concerned shall have determined that a vessel of special construction or purpose cannot comply fully with the provisions of any of these Rules with respect to the number, position, range or arc of visibility of lights or shapes, as well as to the disposition and characteristics of sound-signalling appliances, without interfering with the special function of the vessel, such vessel shall comply with such other provisions in regard to the number, position, range or arc of visibility of lights or shapes, as well as to the disposition and characteristics of sound-signalling appliances, as her Government shall have determined to be the closest possible compliance with these Rules in respect to that vessel.

Rule 2

Responsibility

(a) Nothing in these Rules shall exonerate any vessel, or the owner, master or crew thereof, from the consequences of any neglect to comply with these Rules or of the neglect of any precaution which may be required by the ordinary practice of seamen, or by the special circumstances of the case.

(b) In construing and complying with these Rules due regard shall be had to all dangers of navigation and collision and to any special circumstances, including the limitations of the vessels involved, which may make a departure from these Rules necessary to avoid immediate danger.

Rule 3

General definitions

For the purpose of these Rules, except where the context otherwise requires:

(a) The word 'vessel' includes every description of water craft, including non-displacement craft and seaplanes, used or capable of being used as a means of transportation on water.

(b) The term 'power-driven vessel' means any vessel propelled by machinery.

(c) The term 'sailing vessel' means any vessel under sail provided that propelling machinery, if fitted, is not being used.

(d) The term 'vessel engaged in fishing' means any vessel fishing with nets, lines, trawls or other fishing apparatus which restrict manoeuvrability, but does not include a vessel fishing with trolling lines or other fishing apparatus which do not restrict manoeuvrability.

(e) The word 'seaplane' includes any aircraft designed to manoeuvre on the water.

(f) The term 'vessel not under command' means a vessel which through some exceptional circumstance is unable to manoeuvre as required by these Rules and is therefore unable to keep out of the way of another vessel.

(g) The term 'vessel restricted in her ability to manoeuvre' means a vessel which from the nature of her work is restricted in her ability to manoeuvre as required by these Rules and is therefore unable to keep out of the way of another vessel.

The following vessels shall be regarded as vessels restricted in their ability to manoeuvre

    (i) a vessel engaged in laying, servicing or picking up a navigation mark, submarine cable or pipeline;

    (ii) a vessel engaged in dredging, surveying or underwater operations;

    (iii) a vessel engaged in replenishment or transferring persons, provisions or cargo while underway;

    (iv) a vessel engaged in the launching or recovery of aircraft;

    (v) a vessel engaged in minesweeping operations;

    (vi) a vessel engaged in a towing operation such as severely restricts the towing vessel and her tow in their ability to deviate from their course.

(h) The term 'vessel constrained by her draught' means a power-driven vessel which because of her draught in relation to the available depth of water is severely restricted in her ability to deviate from the course she is following.

(i) The word 'underway' means that a vessel is not at anchor, or made fast to the shore, or aground.

(j) The words 'length' and 'breadth' of a vessel mean her length overall and greatest breadth.

(k) Vessels shall be deemed to be in sight of one another only when one can be observed visually from the other.

(l) The term 'restricted visibility' means any condition in which visibility is restricted by fog, mist, falling snow, heavy rainstorms, sandstorms or any other similar causes.

PART B – STEERING AND SAILING RULES

Section I. Conduct of vessels in any condition of visibility

Rule 4

Application

Rules in this Section apply in any condition of visibility.

Rule 5

Look-out

Every vessel shall at all times maintain a proper look-out by sight and hearing as well as by all available means appropriate in the prevailing circumstances and conditions so as to make a full appraisal of the situation and of the risk of collision.

Rule 6

Safe speed

Every vessel shall at all times proceed at a safe speed so that she can take proper and effective action to avoid collision and be stopped within a distance appropriate to the prevailing circumstances and conditions.

In determining a safe speed the following factors shall be among those taken into account:

(a) By all vessels:
  (i) the state of visibility;
  (ii) the traffic density including concentrations of fishing vessels or any other vessels;
  (iii) the manoeuvrability of the vessel with special reference to stopping distance and turning ability in the prevailing conditions;
  (iv) at night the presence of background light such as from shore lights or from back scatter of her own lights;
  (v) the state of wind, sea and current, and the proximity of navigational hazards;
  (vi) the draught in relation to the available depth of water.

(b) Additionally, by vessels with operational radar:
- (i) the characteristics, efficiency and limitations of the radar equipment;
- (ii) any constraints imposed by the radar range scale in use;
- (iii) the effect on radar detection of the sea state, weather and other sources of interference;
- (iv) the possibility that small vessels, ice and other floating objects may not be detected by radar at an adequate range;
- (v) the number, location and movement of vessels detected by radar;
- (vi) the more exact assessment of the visibility that may be possible when radar is used to determine the range of vessels or other objects in the vicinity.

Rule 7

Risk of collision

(a) Every vessel shall use all available means appropriate to the prevailing circumstances and conditions to determine if risk of collision exists. If there is any doubt such risk shall be deemed to exist.

(b) Proper use shall be made of radar equipment if fitted and operational, including long-range scanning to obtain early warning of risk of collision and radar plotting or equivalent systematic observation of detected objects.

(c) Assumptions shall not be made on the basis of scanty information, especially scanty radar information.

(d) In determining if risk of collision exists the following considerations shall be among those taken into account:
- (i) such risk shall be deemed to exist if the compass bearing of an approaching vessel does not appreciably change;
- (ii) such risk may sometimes exist even when an appreciable bearing change is evident, particularly when approaching a very large vessel or a tow or when approaching a vessel at close range.

Rule 8

Action to avoid collision

(a) Any action taken to avoid collision shall, if the circumstances of the case admit, be positive, made in ample time and with due regard to the observance of good seamanship.

(b) Any alteration of course and/or speed to avoid collision shall, if the circumstances of the case admit, be large enough to be readily apparent to another vessel observing visually or by radar; a succession of small alterations of course and/or speed should be avoided.

(c) If there is sufficient sea room, alteration of course alone may be the most effective action to avoid a close-quarters situation provided that it is made in good time, is substantial and does not result in another close-quarters situation.

(d) Action taken to avoid collision with another vessel shall be such as to result in passing at a safe distance. The effectiveness of the action shall be carefully checked until the other vessel is finally past and clear.

(e) If necessary to avoid collision or allow more time to assess the situation, a vessel shall slacken her speed or take all way off by stopping or reversing her means of propulsion.

Rule 9

Narrow channels

(a) A vessel proceeding along the course of a narrow channel or fairway shall keep as near to the outer limit of the channel or fairway which lies on her starboard side as is safe and practicable.

(b) A vessel of less than 20 metres in length or a sailing vessel shall not impede the passage of a vessel which can safely navigate only within a narrow channel or fairway.

(c) A vessel engaged in fishing shall not impede the passage of any other vessel navigating within a narrow channel or fairway.

(d) A vessel shall not cross a narrow channel or fairway if such crossing impedes the passage of a vessel which can safely navigate only within such channel or fairway. The latter vessel may use the sound signal prescribed in Rule 34 (d) if in doubt as to the intention of the crossing vessel.

(e) (i) In a narrow channel or fairway when overtaking can take place only if the vessel to be overtaken has to take action to permit safe passing, the vessel intending to overtake shall indicate her intention by sounding the appropriate signal prescribed in Rule 34 (c) (i). The vessel to be overtaken shall, if in agreement, sound the appropriate signal prescribed in Rule 34 (c) (ii) and take steps to permit safe passing. If in doubt she may sound the signals prescribed in Rule 34 (d).

(ii) This Rule does not relieve the overtaking vessel of her obligation under Rule 13.

(f) A vessel nearing a bend or an area of a narrow channel or fairway where other vessels may be obscured by an intervening obstruction shall navigate with particular alertness and caution and shall sound the appropriate signal prescribed in Rule 34 (e).

(g) Any vessel shall, if the circumstances of the case admit, avoid anchoring in a narrow channel.

Rule 10

Traffic separation schemes

(a) This Rule applies to traffic separation schemes adopted by the Organization:

(b) A vessel using a traffic separation scheme shall:
  (i) proceed in the appropriate traffic lane in the general direction of traffic flow for that lane;
  (ii) so far as practicable keep clear of a traffic separation line or separation zone;
  (iii) normally join or leave a traffic lane at the termination of the lane, but when joining or leaving from the side shall do so at as small an angle to the general direction of traffic flow as practicable.

(c) A vessel shall so far as practicable avoid crossing traffic lanes, but if obliged to do so shall cross as nearly as practicable at right angles to the general direction of traffic flow.

(d) Inshore traffic zones shall not normally be used by through traffic which can safely use the appropriate traffic lane within the adjacent traffic separation scheme.

(e) A vessel, other than a crossing vessel, shall not normally enter a separation zone or cross a separation line except:
  (i) in cases of emergency to avoid immediate danger;
  (ii) to engage in fishing within a separation zone.

(f) A vessel navigating in areas near the terminations of traffic separation schemes shall do so with particular caution.

(g) A vessel shall so far as practicable avoid anchoring in a traffic separation scheme or in areas near its terminations.

(h) A vessel not using a traffic separation scheme shall avoid it by as wide a margin as is practicable.

(i) A vessel engaged in fishing shall not impede the passage of any vessel following a traffic lane.

(j) A vessel of less than 20 metres in length or a sailing vessel shall not impede the safe passage of a power-driven vessel following a traffic lane.

Section II. Conduct of vessels in sight of one another

Rule 11

Application

Rules in this Section apply to vessels in sight of one another.

Rule 12

Sailing vessels

(a) When two sailing vessels are approaching one another, so as to involve risk of collision, one of them shall keep out of the way of the other as follows:

(i) when each has the wind on a different side, the vessel which has the wind on the port side shall keep out of the way of the other.

(ii) when both have the wind on the same side, the vessel which is to windward shall keep out of the way of the vessel which is to leeward;

(iii) if a vessel with the wind on the port side sees a vessel to windward and cannot determine with certainty whether the other vessel has the wind on the port or on the starboard side, she shall keep out of the way of the other.

(b) For the purposes of this Rule the windward side shall be deemed to be the side opposite to that on which the mainsail is carried or, in the case of a square-rigged vessel, the side opposite to that on which the largest fore-and-aft sail is carried.

Rule 13

Overtaking

(a) Notwithstanding anything contained in the Rules of this Section any vessel overtaking any other shall keep out of the way of the vessel being overtaken.

(b) A vessel shall be deemed to be overtaking when coming up with another vessel from a direction more than 22·5 degrees abaft her beam, that is, in such a position with reference to the vessel she is overtaking, that at night she would be able to see only the sternlight of that vessel but neither of her sidelights.

(c) When a vessel is in any doubt as to whether she is overtaking another, she shall assume that this is the case and act accordingly.

(d) Any subsequent alteration of the bearing between the two vessels shall not make the overtaking vessel a crossing vessel within the meaning of these Rules or relieve her of the duty of keeping clear of the overtaken vessel until she is finally past and clear.

Rule 14

Head-on situation

(a) When two power-driven vessels are meeting on reciprocal or nearly reciprocal courses so as to involve risk of collision each shall alter her course to starboard so that each shall pass on the port side of the other.

(b) Such a situation shall be deemed to exist when a vessel sees the other ahead or nearly ahead and by night she could see the masthead lights of the other in a line or nearly in a line and/or both sidelights and by day she observes the corresponding aspect of the other vessel.

(c) When a vessel is in any doubt as to whether such a situation exists she shall assume that it does exist and act accordingly.

Rule 15

Crossing situation

When two power-driven vessels are crossing so as to involve risk of collision, the vessel which has the other on her own starboard side shall keep out of the way and shall, if the circumstances of the case admit, avoid crossing ahead of the other vessel.

Rule 16

Action by give-way vessel

Every vessel which is directed to keep out of the way of another vessel shall, so far as possible, take early and substantial action to keep well clear.

Rule 17

Action by stand-on vessel

(a) (i) Where one of two vessels is to keep out of the way the other shall keep her course and speed.

(ii) The latter vessel may however take action to avoid collision by her manoeuvre alone, as soon as it becomes apparent to her that the vessel required to keep out of the way is not taking appropriate action in compliance with these Rules.

(b) When, from any cause, the vessel required to keep her course and speed finds herself so close that collision cannot be avoided by the action of the give-way vessel alone, she shall take such action as will best aid to avoid collision.

(c) A power-driven vessel which takes action in a crossing situation in accordance with sub-paragraph (a) (ii) of this Rule to avoid collision with another power-driven vessel shall, if the circumstances of the case admit, not alter course to port for a vessel on her own port side.

(d) This Rule does not relieve the give-way vessel of her obligation to keep out of the way.

Rule 18

Responsibilities between vessels

Except where Rules 9, 10 and 13 otherwise require:

(a) A power-driven vessel underway shall keep out of the way of:
  (i) a vessel not under command;
  (ii) a vessel restricted in her ability to manoeuvre;
  (iii) a vessel engaged in fishing;
  (iv) a sailing vessel.

(b) A sailing vessel underway shall keep out of the way of:
  (i) a vessel not under command;
  (ii) a vessel restricted in her ability to manoeuvre;
  (iii) a vessel engaged in fishing.

(c) A vessel engaged in fishing when underway shall, so far as possible, keep out of the way of:
  (i) a vessel not under command;
  (ii) a vessel restricted in her ability to manoeuvre.

(d) (i) Any vessel other than a vessel not under command or a vessel restricted in her ability to manoeuvre shall, if the circumstances of the case admit, avoid impeding the safe passage of a vessel constrained by her draught, exhibiting the signals in Rule 28.
  (ii) A vessel constrained by her draught shall navigate with particular caution having full regard to her special condition.

(e) A seaplane on the water shall, in general, keep well clear of all vessels and avoid impeding their navigation. In circumstances, however, where risk of collision exists, she shall comply with the Rules of this Part.

Section III. Conduct of vessels in restricted visibility

Rule 19

Conduct of vessels in restricted visibility

(a) This Rule applies to vessels not in sight of one another when navigating in or near an area of restricted visibility.

(b) Every vessel shall proceed at a safe speed adapted to the prevailing circumstances and conditions of restricted visibility. A power-driven vessel shall have her engines ready for immediate manoeuvre.

(c) Every vessel shall have due regard to the prevailing circumstances and conditions of restricted visibility when complying with the Rules of Section I of this Part.

(d) A vessel which detects by radar alone the presence of another vessel shall determine if a close-quarters situation is developing and/or risk of collision exists. If so, she shall take avoiding action in ample time, provided that when such action consists of an alteration of course, so far as possible the following shall be avoided:

    (i) an alteration of course to port for a vessel forward of the beam, other than for a vessel being overtaken;

    (ii) an alteration of course towards a vessel abeam or abaft the beam.

(e) Except where it has been determined that a risk of collision does not exist, every vessel which hears apparently forward of her beam the fog signal of another vessel, or which cannot avoid a close-quarters situation with another vessel forward of her beam, shall reduce her speed to the minimum at which she can be kept on her course. She shall if necessary take all her way off and in any event navigate with extreme caution until danger of collision is over.

PART C – LIGHTS AND SHAPES

Rule 20

Application

(a) Rules in this Part shall be complied with in all weathers.

(b) The Rules concerning lights shall be complied with from sunset to sunrise, and during such times no other lights shall be exhibited, except such lights as cannot be mistaken for the lights specified in these Rules or do not impair their visibility or distinctive character, or interfere with the keeping of a proper look-out.

(c) The lights prescribed by these Rules shall, if carried, also be exhibited from sunrise to sunset in restricted visibility and may be exhibited in all other circumstances when it is deemed necessary.

(d) The Rules concerning shapes shall be complied with by day.

(e) The lights and shapes specified in these Rules shall comply with the provisions of Annex I to these Regulations.

Rule 21

Definitions

(a) 'Masthead light' means a white light placed over the fore and aft centreline of the vessel showing an unbroken light over an arc of the horizon of 225 degrees and so fixed as to show the light from right ahead to 22·5 degrees abaft the beam on either side of the vessel.

(b) 'Sidelights' means a green light on the starboard side and a red light on the port side each showing an unbroken light over an arc of the horizon of 112·5 degrees and so fixed as to show the light from right ahead to 22·5 degrees abaft the beam on its respective side. In a vessel of less than 20 metres in length the sidelights may be combined in one lantern carried on the fore and aft centreline of the vessel.

(c) 'Sternlight' means a white light placed as nearly as practicable at the stern showing an unbroken light over an arc of the horizon of 135 degrees and so fixed as to show the light 67·5 degrees from right aft on each side of the vessel.

(d) 'Towing light' means a yellow light having the same characteristics as the 'sternlight' defined in paragraph (c) of this Rule.

(e) 'All round light' means a light showing an unbroken light over an arc of the horizon of 360 degrees.

(f) 'Flashing light' means a light flashing at regular intervals at a frequency of 120 flashes or more per minute.

Rule 22
Visibility of lights

The lights prescribed in these Rules shall have an intensity as specified in Section 8 of Annex I to these Regulations so as to be visible at the following minimum ranges:

(a) In vessels of 50 metres or more in length:
   —a masthead light, 6 miles;
   —a sidelight, 3 miles;
   —a sternlight, 3 miles;
   —a towing light, 3 miles;
   —a white, red, green or yellow all-round light, 3 miles.

(b) In vessels of 12 metres or more in length but less than 50 metres in length:
   —a masthead light, 5 miles; except that where the length of the vessel is less than 20 metres, 3 miles;
   —a sidelight, 2 miles;
   —a sternlight, 2 miles;
   —a towing light, 2 miles;
   —a white, red, green or yellow all-round light, 2 miles.

(c) In vessels of less than 12 metres in length:
   —a masthead light, 2 miles;
   —a sidelight, 1 mile;
   —a sternlight, 2 miles;
   —a towing light, 2 miles;
   —a white, red, green or yellow all-round light, 2 miles.

Rule 23

Power-driven vessels underway

(a) A power-driven vessel underway shall exhibit:

  (i) a masthead light forward;

  (ii) a second masthead light abaft of and higher than the forward one; except that a vessel of less than 50 metres in length shall not be obliged to exhibit such light but may do so;

  (iii) sidelights;

  (iv) a sternlight.

(b) An air-cushion vessel when operating in the non-displacement mode shall, in addition to the lights prescribed in paragraph (a) of this Rule, exhibit an all-round flashing yellow light.

(c) A power-driven vessel of less than 7 metres in length and whose maximum speed does not exceed 7 knots may, in lieu of the lights prescribed in paragraph (a) of this Rule, exhibit an all-round white light. Such vessel shall, if practicable, also exhibit sidelights.

Rule 24

Towing and pushing

(a) A power-driven vessel when towing shall exhibit:

  (i) instead of the light prescribed in Rule 23 (a) (i), two masthead lights forward in a vertical line. When the length of the tow, measuring from the stern of the towing vessel to the after end of the tow exceeds 200 metres, three such lights in a vertical line;

  (ii) sidelights;

  (iii) a sternlight;

  (iv) a towing light in a vertical line above the sternlight;

  (v) when the length of the two exceeds 200 metres, a diamond shape where it can best be seen.

(b) When a pushing vessel and a vessel being pushed ahead are rigidly connected in a composite unit they shall be regarded as a power-driven vessel and exhibit the lights prescribed in Rule 23.

(c) A power-driven vessel when pushing ahead or towing alongside, except in the case of a composite unit, shall exhibit:

  (i) instead of the light prescribed in Rule 24 (a) (i), two masthead lights forward in a vertical line;

  (ii) sidelights;

  (iii) a sternlight.

(d) A power-driven vessel to which paragraphs (a) and (c) of this Rule apply shall also comply with Rule 23 (a) (ii).

(e) A vessel or object being towed shall exhibit:
  (i) sidelights;
  (ii) a sternlight;
  (iii) when the length of the tow exceeds 200 metres, a diamond shape where it can best be seen.

(f) Provided that any number of vessels being towed alongside or pushed in a group shall be lighted as one vessel,
  (i) a vessel being pushed ahead, not being part of a composite unit, shall exhibit at the forward end, sidelights;
  (ii) a vessel being towed alongside shall exhibit a sternlight and at the forward end, sidelights.

(g) Where from any sufficient cause it is impracticable for a vessel or object being towed to exhibit the lights prescribed in paragraph (e) of this Rule, all possible measures shall be taken to light the vessel or object towed or at least to indicate the presence of the unlighted vessel or object.

Rule 25

Sailing vessels underway and vessels under oars

(a) A sailing vessel underway shall exhibit:
  (i) sidelights;
  (ii) a sternlight.

(b) In a sailing vessel of less than 12 metres in length the lights prescribed in paragraph (a) of this Rule may be combined in one lantern carried at or near the top of the mast where it can best be seen.

(c) A sailing vessel underway may, in addition to the lights prescribed in paragraph (a) of this Rule, exhibit at or near the top of the mast, where they can best be seen, two all-round lights in a vertical line, the upper being red and the lower green, but these lights shall not be exhibited in conjunction with the combined lantern permitted by paragraph (b) of this Rule.

(d) (i) A sailing vessel of less than 7 metres in length shall, if practicable, exhibit the lights prescribed in paragraph (a) or (b) of this Rule, but if she does not, she shall have ready at hand an electric torch or lighted lantern showing a white light which shall be exhibited in sufficient time to prevent collision.

  (ii) A vessel under oars may exhibit the lights prescribed in this Rule for sailing vessels, but if she does not, she shall have ready at hand an electric torch or lighted lantern showing a white light which shall be exhibited in sufficient time to prevent collision.

(e) A vessel proceeding under sail when also being propelled by machinery shall exhibit forward where it can best be seen a conical shape, apex downwards.

Rule 26

Fishing vessels

(a) A vessel engaged in fishing, whether underway or at anchor, shall exhibit only the lights and shapes prescribed in this Rule.

(b) A vessel when engaged in trawling, by which is meant the dragging through the water of a dredge net or other apparatus used as a fishing appliance, shall exhibit:

(i) two all-round lights in a vertical line, the upper being green and the lower white, or a shape consisting of two cones with their apexes together in a vertical line one above the other; a vessel of less than 20 metres in length may instead of this shape exhibit a basket;

(ii) a masthead light abaft of and higher than the all-round green light; a vessel of less than 50 metres in length shall not be obliged to exhibit such a light but may do so;

(iii) when making way through the water, in addition to the lights prescribed in this paragraph, sidelights and a sternlight.

(c) A vessel engaged in fishing, other than trawling, shall exhibit:

(i) two all-round lights in a vertical line, the upper being red and the lower white, or a shape consisting of two cones with apexes together in a vertical line one above the other; a vessel of less than 20 metres in length may instead of this shape exhibit a basket;

(ii) when there is outlying gear extending more than 150 metres horizontally from the vessel, an all-round white light or a cone apex upwards in the direction of the gear;

(iii) when making way through the water, in addition to the lights prescribed in this paragraph, sidelights and a sternlight.

(d) A vessel engaged in fishing in close proximity to other vessels engaged in fishing may exhibit the additional signals described in Annex II to these Regulations.

(e) A vessel when not engaged in fishing shall not exhibit the lights or shapes prescribed in this Rule, but only those prescribed for a vessel of her length.

Rule 27

Vessels not under command or restricted in their ability to manoeuvre

(a) A vessel not under command shall exhibit:

(i) two all-round red lights in a vertical line where they can best be seen;

(ii) two balls or similar shapes in a vertical line where they can best be seen;

(iii) when making way through the water, in addition to the lights prescribed in this paragraph, sidelights and a sternlight.

(b) A vessel restricted in her ability to manoeuvre, except a vessel engaged in minesweeping operations, shall exhibit;

(i) three all-round lights in a vertical line where they can best be seen. The highest and lowest of these lights shall be red and the middle light shall be white;

(ii) three shapes in a vertical line where they can best be seen. The highest and lowest of these shapes shall be balls and the middle one a diamond;

(iii) when making way through the water, masthead lights, sidelights and a sternlight, in addition to the lights prescribed in sub-paragraph (i);

(iv) when at anchor, in addition to the lights or shapes prescribed in sub-paragraphs (i) and (ii), the light, lights or shape prescribed in Rule 30.

(c) A vessel engaged in a towing operation such as renders her unable to deviate from her course shall, in addition to the lights or shapes prescribed in sub-paragraph (b) (i) and (ii) of this Rule, exhibit the lights or shape prescribed in Rule 24 (a).

(d) A vessel engaged in dredging or underwater operations, when restricted in her ability to manoeuvre, shall exhibit the lights and shapes prescribed in paragraph (b) of this Rule and shall in addition, when an obstruction exists, exhibit:

(i) two all-round red lights or two balls in a vertical line to indicate the side on which the obstruction exists;

(ii) two all-round green lights or two diamonds in a vertical line to indicate the side on which another vessel may pass;

(iii) when making way through the water, in addition to the lights prescribed in this paragraph, masthead lights, sidelights and a sternlight;

(iv) a vessel to which this paragraph applies when at anchor shall exhibit the lights or shapes prescribed in sub-paragraphs (i) and (ii) instead of the lights or shape prescribed in Rule 30.

(e) Whenever the size of a vessel engaged in diving operations makes it impracticable to exhibit the shapes prescribed in paragraph (d) of this Rule, a rigid replica of the International Code flag 'A' not less than 1 metre in height shall be exhibited. Measures shall be taken to ensure all-round visibility.

(f) A vessel engaged in minesweeping operations shall, in addition to the lights prescribed for a power-driven vessel in Rule 23, exhibit three all-round green lights or three balls. One of these lights or shapes shall be exhibited at or near the foremast head and one at each end of the fore yard. These lights or shapes indicate that it is dangerous for another vessel to approach closer than 1000 metres astern or 500 metres on either side of the minesweeper.

(g) Vessels of less than 7 metres in length shall not be required to exhibit the lights prescribed in this Rule.

(h) The signals prescribed in this Rule are not signals of vessels in distress and requiring assistance. Such signals are contained in Annex IV to these Regulations.

Rule 28

Vessels constrained by their draught

A vessel constrained by her draught may, in addition to the lights prescribed for power-driven vessels in Rule 23, exhibit where they can best be seen three all-round red lights in a vertical line, or a cylinder.

Rule 29

Pilot vessels

(a) A vessel engaged on pilotage duty shall exhibit:
  (i) at or near the masthead, two all-round lights in a vertical line, the upper being white and the lower red;
  (ii) when underway, in addition, sidelights and a sternlight;
  (iii) when at anchor, in addition to the lights prescribed in sub-paragraph (i), the anchor light, lights or shape.

(b) A pilot vessel when not engaged on pilotage duty shall exhibit the lights or shapes prescribed for a similar vessel of her length.

Rule 30

Anchored vessels and vessels aground

(a) A vessel at anchor shall exhibit where it can best be seen:
  (i) in the fore part, an all-round white light or one ball;
  (ii) at or near the stern and at a lower level than the light prescribed in sub-paragraph (i), an all-round white light.

(b) A vessel of less than 50 metres in length may exhibit an all-round white light where it can best be seen instead of the lights prescribed in paragraph (a) of this Rule.

(c) A vessel at anchor may, and a vessel of 100 metres and more in length shall, also use the available working or equivalent lights to illuminate her decks.

(d) A vessel aground shall exhibit the lights prescribed in paragraph (a) or (b) of this Rule and in addition, where they can best be seen:
  (i) two all-round red lights in a vertical line;
  (ii) three balls in a vertical line.

(e) A vessel of less than 7 metres in length, when at anchor or aground, not in or near a narrow channel, fairway or anchorage, or where other vessels normally navigate, shall not be required to exhibit the lights or shapes prescribed in paragraphs (a), (b) or (d) of this Rule.

Rule 31

Seaplanes

Where it is impracticable for a seaplane to exhibit lights and shapes of the characteristics or in the positions prescribed in the Rules of this Part she shall exhibit lights and shapes as closely similar in characteristics and position as is possible.

PART D – SOUND AND LIGHT SIGNALS

Rule 32

Definitions

(a) The word 'whistle' means any sound signalling appliance capable of producing the prescribed blasts and which complies with the specifications in Annex III to these Regulations.

(b) The term 'short blast' means a blast of about one second's duration.

(c) The term 'prolonged blast' means a blast of from four to six seconds' duration.

Rule 33

Equipment for sound signals

(a) A vessel of 12 metres or more in length shall be provided with a whistle and a bell and a vessel of 100 metres or more in length shall, in addition, be provided with a gong, the tone and sound of which cannot be confused with that of the bell. The whistle, bell and gong shall comply with the specifications in Annex III to these Regulations. The bell or gong or both may be replaced by other equipment having the same respective sound characteristics, provided that manual sounding of the required signals shall always be possible.

(b) A vessel of less than 12 metres in length shall not be obliged to carry the sound signalling appliances prescribed in paragraph (a) of this Rule but if she does not, she shall be provided with some other means of making an efficient sound signal.

Rule 34

Manoeuvring and warning signals

(a) When vessels are in sight of one another, a power-driven vessel under-way, when manoeuvring as authorized or required by these Rules, shall indicate that manoeuvre by the following signals on her whistle:

—one short blast to mean 'I am altering my course to starboard';

—two short blasts to mean 'I am altering my course to port';

—three short blasts to mean 'I am operating astern propulsion'.

(b) Any vessel may supplement the whistle signals prescribed in para-graph (a) of this Rule by light signals, repeated as appropriate, whilst the manoeuvre is being carried out:

(i) these light signals shall have the following significance:

—one flash to mean 'I am altering my course to starboard';

—two flashes to mean 'I am altering my course to port';

—three flashes to mean 'I am operating astern propulsion';

(ii) the duration of each flash shall be about one second, the interval between flashes shall be about one second, and the interval between successive signals shall be not less than ten seconds;

(iii) the light used for this signal shall, if fitted, be an all-round white light, visible at a minimum range of 5 miles, and shall comply with the provisions of Annex I.

(c) When in sight of one another in a narrow channel or fairway:

(i) a vessel intending to overtake another shall in compliance with Rule 9 (e) (i) indicate her intention by the following signals on her whistle:

—two prolonged blasts followed by one short blast to mean 'I intend to overtake you on your starboard side';

—two prolonged blasts followed by two short blasts to mean 'I intend to overtake you on your port side'.

(ii) the vessel about to be overtaken when acting in accordance with Rule 9 (e) (i) shall indicate her agreement by the following signal on her whistle:

—one prolonged, one short, one prolonged and one short blast, in that order.

(d) When vessels in sight of one another are approaching each other and from any cause either vessel fails to understand the intentions or actions of the other, or is in doubt whether sufficient action is being taken by the other to avoid collision, the vessel in doubt shall immediately indicate such doubt by giving at least five short and rapid blasts on the whistle. Such signal may be supplemented by a light signal of at least five short and rapid flashes.

(e) A vessel nearing a bend or an area of a channel or fairway where other vessels may be obscured by an intervening obstruction shall sound one prolonged blast. Such signal shall be answered with a prolonged blast by any approaching vessel that may be within hearing around the bend or behind the intervening obstruction.

(f) If whistles are fitted on a vessel at a distance apart of more than 100 metres, one whistle only shall be used for giving manoeuvring and warning signals.

Rule 35
Sound signals in restricted visibility

In or near an area of restricted visibility, whether by day or night, the signals prescribed in this Rule shall be used as follows:

(a) A power-driven vessel making way through the water shall sound at intervals of not more than 2 minutes one prolonged blast.

(b) A power-driven vessel underway but stopped and making no way through the water shall sound at intervals of not more than 2 minutes two prolonged blasts in succession with an interval of about 2 seconds between them.

(c) A vessel not under command, a vessel restricted in her ability to manoeuvre, a vessel constrained by her draught, a sailing vessel, a vessel engaged in fishing and a vessel engaged in towing or pushing another vessel shall, instead of the signals prescribed in paragraphs (a) or (b) of this Rule, sound at intervals of not more than 2 minutes three blasts in succession, namely one prolonged followed by two short blasts.

(d) A vessel towed or if more than one vessel is towed the last vessel of the tow, if manned, shall at intervals of not more than 2 minutes sound four blasts in succession, namely one prolonged followed by three short blasts. When practicable, this signal shall be made immediately after the signal made by the towing vessel.

(e) When a pushing vessel and a vessel being pushed ahead are rigidly connected in a composite unit they shall be regarded as a power-driven vessel and shall give the signals prescribed in paragraphs (a) or (b) of this Rule.

(f) A vessel at anchor shall at intervals of not more than one minute ring the bell rapidly for about 5 seconds. In a vessel of 100 metres or more in length the bell shall be sounded in the forepart of the vessel and immediately after the ringing of the bell the gong shall be sounded rapidly for about 5 seconds in the after part of the vessel. A vessel at anchor may in addition sound three blasts in succession, namely one short, one prolonged and one short blast, to give warning of her position and of the possibility of collision to an approaching vessel.

(g) A vessel aground shall give the bell signal and if required the gong signal prescribed in paragraph (f) of this Rule and shall, in addition, give three separate and distinct strokes on the bell immediately before and after the rapid ringing of the bell. A vessel aground may in addition sound an appropriate whistle signal.

(h) A vessel of less than 12 metres in length shall not be obliged to give the above-mentioned signals but, if she does not, shall make some other efficient sound signal at intervals of not more than 2 minutes.

(i) A pilot vessel when engaged on pilotage duty may in addition to the signals prescribed in paragraphs (a), (b) or (f) of this Rule sound an identity signal consisting of four short blasts.

Rule 36
Signals to attract attention

If necessary to attract the attention of another vessel any vessel may make light or sound signals that cannot be mistaken for any signal authorized elsewhere in these Rules, or may direct the beam of her searchlight in the direction of the danger, in such a way as not to embarrass any vessel.

Rule 37
Distress signals

When a vessel is in distress and requires assistance she shall use or exhibit the signals prescribed in Annex IV to these Regulations.

PART E – EXEMPTIONS

Rule 38
Exemptions

Any vessel (or class of vessels) provided that she complies with the requirements of the International Regulations for Preventing Collisions at Sea, 1960, the keel of which is laid or which is at a corresponding stage of construction before the entry into force of these Regulations may be exempted from compliance therewith as follows:

(a) The installation of lights with ranges prescribed in Rule 22, until four years after the date of entry into force of these Regulations.

(b) The installation of lights with colour specifications as prescribed in Section 7 of Annex I to these Regulations, until four years after the date of entry into force of these Regulations.

(c) The repositioning of lights as a result of conversion from Imperial to metric units and rounding off measurement figures, permanent exemption.

(d) (i) The repositioning of masthead lights on vessels of less than 150 metres in length, resulting from the prescriptions of Section 3 (a) of Annex I, permanent exemption.

(ii) The repositioning of masthead lights on vessels of 150 metres or more in length, resulting from the prescriptions of Section 3 (a) of Annex I to these Regulations, until nine years after the date of entry into force of these Regulations.

(e) The repositioning of masthead lights resulting from the prescriptions of Section 2 (b) of Annex I, until nine years after the date of entry into force of these Regulations.

(f) The repositioning of sidelights resulting from the prescriptions of Sections 2 (g) and 3 (b) of Annex I, until nine years after the date of entry into force of these Regulations.

(g) The requiremens for sound signal appliances prescribed in Annex III, until nine years after the date of entry into force of these Regulations.

ANNEX I TO THE RULES (1972)

Positioning and technical details of lights and shapes

1. Definition

The term 'height above the hull' means height above the uppermost continuous deck.

2. Vertical positioning and spacing of lights

(a) On a power-driven vessel of 20 metres or more in length the masthead lights shall be placed as follows:

(i) the forward masthead light, or if only one masthead light is carried, then that light, at a height above the hull of not less than 6 metres, and, if the breadth of the vessel exceeds 6 metres, then at a height above the hull not less than such breadth, so however that the light need not be placed at a greater height above the hull than 12 metres;

(ii) when two masthead lights are carried the after one shall be at least 4·5 metres vertically higher than the forward one.

(b) The vertical separation of masthead lights of power-driven vessels shall be such that in all normal conditions of trim the after light will be seen over and separate from the forward light at a distance of 1000 metres from the stem when viewed from sea level.

(c) The masthead light of a power-driven vessel of 12 metres but less than 20 metres in length shall be placed at a height above the gunwale of not less than 2·5 metres.

(d) A power-driven vessel of less than 12 metres in length may carry the uppermost light at a height of less than 2·5 metres above the gunwale. When however a masthead light is carried in addition to sidelights and a sternlight, then such masthead light shall be carried at least 1 metre higher than the sidelights.

(e) One of the two or three masthead lights prescribed for a power-driven vessel when engaged in towing or pushing another vessel shall be placed in the same position as the forward masthead light of a power-driven vessel.

(f) In all circumstances the masthead light or lights shall be so placed as to be above and clear of all other lights and obstructions.

(g) The sidelights of a power-driven vessel shall be placed at a height above the hull not greater than three-quarters of that of the forward masthead light. They shall not be so low as to be interfered with by deck lights.

(h) The sidelights, if in a combined lantern and carried on a power-driven vessel of less than 20 metres in length, shall be placed not less than 1 metre below the masthead light.

(i) When the Rules prescribe two or three lights to be carried in a vertical line, they shall be spaced as follows:

    (i) on a vessel of 20 metres in length or more such lights shall be spaced not less than 2 metres apart, and the lowest of these lights shall, except where a towing light is required, not be less than 4 metres above the hull;

    (ii) on a vessel of less than 20 metres in length such lights shall be spaced not less than 1 metre apart and the lowest of these lights shall, except where a towing light is required, not be less than 2 metres above the gunwale;

    (iii) when three lights are carried they shall be equally spaced.

(j) The lower of the two all-round lights prescribed for a fishing vessel when engaged in fishing shall be at a height above the sidelights not less than twice the distance between the two vertical lights.

(k) The forward anchor light, when two are carried, shall not be less than 4·5 metres above the after one. On a vessel of 50 metres or more in length this forward anchor light shall not be less than 6 metres above the hull.

3. Horizontal positioning and spacing of lights

(a) When two masthead lights are prescribed for a power-driven vessel, the horizontal distance between them shall not be less than one-half of the length of the vessel but need not be more than 100 metres. The forward light shall be placed not more than one-quarter of the length of the vessel from the stem.

(b) On a vessel of 20 metres or more in length the sidelights shall not be placed in front of the forward masthead lights. They shall be placed at or near the side of the vessel.

4. Details of location of direction-indicating lights for fishing vessels, dredgers and vessels engaged in underwater operations

(a) The light indicating the direction of the outlying gear from a vessel engaged in fishing as prescribed in Rule 26 (c) (ii) shall be placed at a horizontal distance of not less than 2 metres and not more than 6 metres away from the two all-round red and white lights. This light shall be placed not higher than the all-round white light prescribed in Rule 26 (c) (i) and not lower than the sidelights.

(b) The lights and shapes on a vessel engaged in dredging or underwater operations to indicate the obstructed side and/or the side on which it is safe to pass, as prescribed in Rule 27 (d) (i) and (ii), shall be placed at the maximum practical horizontal distance, but in no case less than 2 metres, from the lights or shapes prescribed in Rule 27 (b) (i) and (ii). In no case shall the upper of these lights or shapes be at a greater height than the lower of the three lights or shapes prescribed in Rule 27 (b) (i) and (ii).

5. Screens for sidelights

The sidelights shall be fitted with inboard screens painted matt black, and meeting the requirements of Section 9 of this Annex. With a combined lantern, using a single vertical filament and a very narrow division between the green and red sections, external screens need not be fitted.

6. Shapes

(a) Shapes shall be black and of the following sizes:
  (i) a ball shall have a diameter of not less than 0·6 metre;
 (ii) a cone shall have a base diameter of not less than 0·6 metre and a height equal to its diameter;
(iii) a cylinder shall have a diameter of at least 0·6 metre and a height of twice its diameter;
(iv) a diamond shape shall consist of two cones as defined in (ii) above having a common base.

(b) The vertical distance between shapes shall be at least 1·5 metre.

(c) In a vessel of less than 20 metres in length shapes of lesser dimensions but commensurate with the size of the vessel may be used and the distance apart may be correspondingly reduced.

7. Colour specification of lights

The chromaticity of all navigation lights shall conform to the following standards, which lie within the boundaries of the area of the diagram specified for each colour by the International Commission on Illumination (CIE).

The boundaries of the area for each colour are given by indicating the corner co-ordinates, which are as follows:

(i) *White*

| x | 0·525 | 0·525 | 0·452 | 0·310 | 0·310 | 0·443 |
| y | 0·382 | 0·440 | 0·440 | 0·348 | 0·283 | 0·382 |

(ii) *Green*

| x | 0·028 | 0·009 | 0·300 | 0·203 |
| y | 0·385 | 0·723 | 0·511 | 0·356 |

(iii) *Red*

| x | 0·680 | 0·660 | 0·735 | 0·721 |
| y | 0·320 | 0·320 | 0·265 | 0·259 |

(iv) *Yellow*

| x | 0·612 | 0·618 | 0·575 | 0·575 |
| y | 0·382 | 0·382 | 0·425 | 0·406 |

8. Intensity of lights

(a) The minimum luminous intensity of lights shall be calculated by using the formula:

$$I \times 3 \cdot 43 \times 10^6 \times T \times D^2 \times K^{-D}$$

where I is luminous intensity in candelas under service conditions,

T is threshold factor 2×10^{-7} lux,

D is range of visibility (luminous range) of the light in nautical miles,

K is atmospheric transmissivity.

For prescribed lights the value of K shall be 0·8, corresponding to a meteorological visibility of approximately 13 nautical miles.

(b) A selection of figures derived from the formula is given in the following table:

RANGE OF VISIBILITY (LUMINOUS RANGE) OF LIGHT IN NAUTICAL MILES D	LUMINOUS INTENSITY OF LIGHT IN CANDELAS FOR K = 0·8 I
1	0·9
2	4·3
3	12
4	27
5	52
6	94

Note: The maximum luminous intensity of navigation lights should be limited to avoid undue glare.

9. Horizontal sectors

  (a) (i) In the forward direction, sidelights as fitted on the vessel must show the minimum required intensities. The intensities must decrease to reach practical cut-off between 1 degree and 3 degrees outside the prescribed sectors.

    (ii) For sternlights and masthead lights and at 22·5 degrees abaft the beam for sidelights, the minimum required intensities shall be maintained over the arc of the horizon up to 5 degrees within the limits of the sectors prescribed in Rule 21. From 5 degrees within the prescribed sectors the intensity may decrease by 50 per cent up to the prescribed limits; it shall decrease steadily to reach practical cut-off at not more than 5 degrees outside the prescribed limits.

  (b) All-round lights shall be so located as not to be obscured by masts, topmasts or structures within angular sectors of more than 6 degrees, except anchor lights, which need not be placed at an impracticable height above the hull.

10. Vertical sectors

  (a) The vertical sectors of electric lights, with the exception of lights on sailing vessels shall ensure that:

    (i) at least the required minimum intensity is maintained at all angles from 5 degrees above to 5 degrees below the horizontal;

    (ii) at least 60 per cent of the required minimum intensity is maintained from 7·5 degrees above to 7·5 degrees below the horizontal.

  (b) In the case of sailing vessels the vertical sectors of electric lights shall ensure that:

    (i) at least the required minimum intensity is maintained at all angles from 5 degrees above to 5 degrees below the horizontal;

    (ii) at least 50 per cent of the required minimum intensity is maintained from 25 degrees above to 25 degrees below the horizontal.

  (c) In the case of lights other than electric these specifications shall be met as closely as possible.

11. Intensity of non-electric lights

Non-electric lights shall so far as practicable comply with the minimum intensities, as specified in the Table given in Section 8 of this Annex.

12. Manoeuvring light

Notwithstanding the provisions of paragraph 2 (f) of this Annex the manoeuvring light described in Rule 34 (b) shall be placed in the same fore and aft vertical plane as the masthead light or lights and, where practicable, at a minimum height of 2 metres vertically above the forward masthead light, provided that it shall be carried not less than 2 metres vertically above or below the after masthead light. On a vessel where only one masthead light is carried the manoeuvring light, if fitted, shall be carried where it can best be seen, not less than 2 metres vertically apart from the masthead light.

13. Approval

The construction of lanterns and shapes and the installation of lanterns on board the vessel shall be to the satisfaction of the appropriate authority of the State where the vessel is registered.

ANNEX II TO THE RULES (1972)

Additional signals for fishing vessels fishing in close proximity

1. General

The lights mentioned herein shall, if exhibited in pursuance of Rule 26 (d), be placed where they can best be seen. They shall be at least 0·9 metre apart but at a lower level than lights prescribed in Rule 26 (b) (i) and (c) (i). The lights shall be visible all round the horizon at a distance of at least 1 mile but at a lesser distance than the lights prescribed by these Rules for fishing vessels.

2. Signals for trawlers

(a) Vessels when engaged in trawling, whether using demersal or pelagic gear, may exhibit:
  (i) when shooting their nets:
      two white lights in a vertical line;
  (ii) when hauling their nets;
      one white light over one red light in a vertical line;
  (iii) when the net has come fast upon an obstruction:
      two red lights in a vertical line.

(b) Each vessel engaged in pair trawling may exhibit:
  (i) by night, a searchlight directed forward and in the direction of the other vessel of the pair;
  (ii) when shooting or hauling their nets or when their nets have come fast upon an obstruction, the lights prescribed in 2 (a) above.

3. Signals for purse seiners

Vessels engaged in fishing with purse seine gear may exhibit two yellow lights in a vertical line. These lights shall flash alternately every second and with equal light and occultation duration. These lights may be exhibited only when the vessel is hampered by its fishing gear.

ANNEX III TO THE RULES (1972)

Technical details of sound signal appliances

1. Whistles

(a) *Frequencies and range of audibility*

The fundamental frequency of the signal shall lie within the range 70–700 Hz.

The range of audibility of the signal from a whistle shall be determined by those frequencies, which may include the fundamental and/or one or more higher frequencies, which lie within the range 180–700 Hz ($\pm$ 1 per cent) and which provide the sound pressure levels specified in paragraph 1 (c) below.

(b) *Limits of fundamental frequencies*

To ensure a wide variety of whistle characteristics, the fundamental frequency of a whistle shall be between the following limits:

(i) 70–200 Hz, for a vessel 200 metres or more in length;

(ii) 130–350 Hz, for a vessel 75 metres but less than 200 metres in length;

(iii) 250–700 Hz, for a vessel less than 75 metres in length.

(c) *Sound signal intensity and range of audibility*

A whistle fitted in a vessel shall provide, in the direction of maximum intensity of the whistle and at a distance of 1 metre from it, a sound pressure level in at least one 1/3rd-octave band within the range of frequencies 180–700 Hz ($\pm$ 1 per cent) of not less than the appropriate figure given in the table below.

LENGTH OF VESSEL IN METRES	1/3RD-OCTAVE BAND LEVEL AT 1 METRE IN DECIBELS REFERRED TO 2×10^{-5} N/m²	AUDIBILITY RANGE IN NAUTICAL MILES
200 or more	143	2
75 but less than 200	138	1·5
20 but less than 75	130	1
Less than 20	120	0·5

The range of audibility in the table above is for information and is approximately the range at which a whistle may be heard on its forward axis with 90 per cent probability in conditions of still air on board a vessel having average background noise level at the listening posts (taken to be 68 dB in the octave band centred on 250 Hz and 63 dB in the octave band centred on 500 Hz).

In practice the range at which a whistle may be heard is extremely variable and depends critically on weather conditions; the values given can be regarded as typical but under conditions of strong wind or high ambient noise level at the listening post the range may be much reduced.

(d) *Directional properties*

The sound pressure level of a directional whistle shall be not more than 4 dB below the sound pressure level on the axis at any direction in the horizontal plane within ± 45 degrees of the axis. The sound pressure level at any other direction in the horizontal plane shall be not more than 10 dB below the sound pressure level on the axis, so that the range in any direction will be at least half the range on the forward axis. The sound pressure level shall be measured in that 1/3rd-octave band which determines the audibility range.

(e) *Positioning of whistles*

When a directional whistle is to be used as the only whistle on a vessel, it shall be installed with its maximum intensity directed straight ahead.

A whistle shall be placed as high as practicable on a vessel, in order to reduce interception of the emitted sound by obstructions and also to minimize hearing damage risk to personnel. The sound pressure level of the vessel's own signal at listening posts shall not exceed 110 dB (A) and so far as practicable should not exceed 100 dB (A).

(f) *Fitting of more than one whistle*

If whistles are fitted at a distance apart of more than 100 metres, it shall be so arranged that they are not sounded simultaneously.

(g) *Combined whistle systems*

If due to the presence of obstructions the sound field of a single whistle or of one of the whistles referred to in paragraph 1 (f) above is likely to have a zone of greatly reduced signal level, it is recommended that a combined whistle system be fitted so as to overcome this reduction. For the purposes of the Rules a combined whistle system is to be regarded as a single whistle. The whistles of a combined system shall be located at a distance apart of not more than 100 metres and arranged to be sounded simultaneously. The frequency of any one whistle shall differ from those of the others by at least 10 Hz.

2. Bell or gong

(a) *Intensity of signal*

A bell or gong, or other device having similar sound characteristics shall produce a sound pressure level of not less than 110 dB at 1 metre.

(b) *Construction*

Bells and gongs shall be made of corrosion-resistant material and designed to give a clear tone. The diameter of the mouth of the bell shall be not less than 300 mm for vessels of more than 20 metres in length, and shall be not less than 200 mm for vessels of 12 to 20 metres in length. Where practicable, a power-driven bell striker is recommended to ensure constant force but manual operation shall be possible. The mass of the striker shall be not less than 3 per cent of the mass of the bell.

3. Approval

The construction of sound signal appliances, their performance and their installation on board the vessel shall be to the satisfaction of the appropriate authority of the State where the vessel is registered.

ANNEX IV TO THE RULES (1972)

Distress signals

1. The following signals, used or exhibited either together or separately, indicate distress and need of assistance:

(a) a gun or other explosive signal fired at intervals of about a minute;

(b) a continuous sounding with any fog-signalling apparatus;

(c) rockets or shells, throwing red stars fired one at a time at short intervals;

(d) a signal made by radiotelegraphy or by any other signalling method consisting of the group · · · − − − · · · (SOS) in the Morse Code;

(e) a signal sent by radiotelephony consisting of the spoken word 'Mayday';

(f) the International Code Signal of distress indicated by N.C.;

(g) a signal consisting of a square flag having above or below it a ball or anything resembling a ball;

(h) flames on the vessel (as from a burning tar barrel, oil barrel, etc.);

(i) a rocket parachute flare or a hand flare showing a red light;

(j) a smoke signal giving off orange-coloured smoke;

(k) slowly and repeatedly raising and lowering arms outstretched to each side;

(l) the radiotelegraph alarm signal;

(m) the radiotelephone alarm signal;

(n) signals transmitted by emergency position-indicating radio beacons.

2.   The use or exhibition of any of the foregoing signals except for the purpose of indicating distress and need of assistance and the use of other signals which may be confused with any of the above signals is prohibited.

3.   Attention is drawn to the relevant sections of the International Code of Signals, the Merchant Ship Search and Rescue Manual and the following signals:

(a) a piece of orange-coloured canvas with either a black square and circle or other appropriate symbol (for identification from the air);

(b) a dye marker.

APPENDIX I

Aide-memoire for the Navigating Officer

This Aide-Memoire is arranged in the approximate order in which the headings occur during a commission. It must be remembered that these lists and the references are by no means complete nor do they cover every situation.

GENERAL REMARKS

The duties of the Navigating Officer are defined in *Queen's Regulations and Admiralty Instructions*, Chapter 34.

The ship is normally handled by the Captain, but the Navigating Officer must study the subject of ship handling in the *Manual of Seamanship*, Vol. III, and the performance of his own ship in the Navigational Data Book and the *Admiralty Manual of Navigation*, Vol. IV.

Notes on exercising command from the bridge or the operations room and the functions of the command team are given in the *Admiralty Manual of Navigation*, Vol. IV.

ON COMMISSIONING A SHIP

1. Draw Naval stores and books.
2. Draw and check the chart outfit and navigational publications (Chapter II).
3. Draw the chronometer(s) and watches (Chapter XI).

   Note: Application for (2) and (3) should be made in good time, stating the date on which they are required (normally about two weeks before sailing).

4. Correct the charts and publications and rate the chronometer(s).
5. Make yourself thoroughly acquainted with all the alternative steering arrangements, and bridge and steering communications.
6. Study the procedure to be adopted between steering positions and the engine room regarding telegraphs (normally included in the Captain's Standing Orders), and make sure that there can be no misunderstanding.
7. In a new ship start the Navigational Data Book (Chapter II). If recommissioning, draw the book from the office of the Admiral Superintendent of the Dockyard where it has been lodged for safe custody between commissions.
8. Check the operation of Radio Navigational Aids, echo-sounding equipment, plotting tables, bottom log and warning radar.
9. Study the arrangements for switching on D.G. circuits and the positions and functions of the corrector boxes. Obtain the latest records of D.G. ranging (Navigational Data Book).
10. Check the positions of all correctors at magnetic compasses with the latest deviation tables. Make arrangements for compass adjustment.
11. Make arrangements with the Electrical Officer concerning the starting and stopping of the gyro-compass, and the settings for latitude and speed.
12. Ensure that all quartermasters know their duties (steering orders, change-over steering procedure, writing up the ship's log, etc.) and exercise all Navigational Special Sea Dutymen.

13. Check that the hand lead lines are marked correctly (*Q.R. and A.I.*).
14. In a new ship, check the arcs of visibility of the navigation lights (*see* Vol. III).
15. Write the ND Departmental Orders.

IN HARBOUR

1. Correct the charts and publications from the latest Notices to Mariners (temporary and preliminary for the area only) and Radio Navigational Warnings.
2. Wind and compare the chronometer(s) and watches daily.
3. Rate the chronometer(s) at least every ten days.
4. Supervise the daily checking of ship's clocks.
5. Change the barograph paper (weekly) if no meteorological officer is borne.
6. Supervise the quartermasters.

BEFORE GOING TO SEA

Planning

1. Consider the overall distance from port to port (*Admiralty Distance Tables*) and estimate the time on passage, making allowances for exercises. Calculate suitable times for departure and arrival, bearing in mind the following:

    (a) The times of departure and arrival may be subject to tidal considerations, e.g. Dockyard Ports (*Tides and Tidal Streams in Dockyard Ports*).
    (b) A passage through narrow or ill-lit channels may be more safely accomplished in daylight.
    (c) Shipping lanes may be avoided by a slight change in route, or crossed in daylight rather than in darkness (*Ocean Passages of the World*).
    (d) Concentrations of fishing vessels may be avoided (*Monthly Fishing Atlas* and *Fishing Vessel Log*).
    (e) NEMEDRI or Admiralty Notices to Mariners No. 1 may require the ship to traverse certain channels in dangerous waters.
    (f) The time of arrival may be influenced by dockyard working hours, ship's company meals and courtesy to the country being visited (e.g. gun salutes and official calls).
    (g) Ascertain the Standard Time kept at the port of arrival (*A.L.R.S.*, Vol. V, and *N.A.*).

2. Having established suitable times for departure and arrival, plot the intended track of the ship throughout the voyage on a small-scale chart, taking into consideration whether a great-circle route can be followed with advantage, and allowing for tidal streams in tidal waters (*Tidal Streams Atlas* or *Pocket-Atlas*) and currents (*Atlas of Surface Currents*). Mark the track at suitable time intervals and show the times of alterations of course, sunrise, sunset, moonrise, moonset, also the positions where changes of Decca Chain will occur.

3. Extract all the largest-scale charts required for the voyage (Chart Catalogue or *Sailing Directions*), number them consecutively, and plot the intended track and times on individual charts. It is advisable to mark also the distances *from* the destination at every 100 miles or less (depending on the length of voyage).

4. Draw the arcs of ranges (for height of bridge) of the major coastal lights that may be seen in the dark hours.
5. Study the appropriate *Sailing Directions*, the *Radio Navigational Warnings* and the *Station Guide Book*.
6. Study the coverage of Radio Aids to Navigation; Decca (Data Sheets), Loran (Index Chart), Consol (*A.L.R.S.*, Vol. V), MF DF (*A.L.R.S.*, Vol. II).
7. Plan the dates and times of alteration of the clocks.
8. Study the weather to be expected on passage, the radio forecasts available, the times and frequencies of Fleet Forecasts, Synoptics, Coded Analysis Messages, Home Station Gale Warnings, and the weather reports to be made by the ship (*A.L.R.S.*, Vol. II, *A.L.R.S.*, Vol. III, Area forecast chartlets, Code Sheet and *Meteorological Services Handbook*).
9. Study the chart and publications for the port of arrival. It is most advisable to do this before sailing, you may not have adequate time on passage.
10. Prepare a sailing signal, if required.
11. Show the plan to the Captain and advise him on the writing of the Night Order Book.

Practical

1. Give the necessary instructions for starting the gyro-compass (with latitude setting), for warming through radar and Decca, and switching on D.G. circuits if passing through danger areas (NEMEDRI).
2. Test bridge communications, echo sounding, bottom log and check all navigational gyro repeaters (including lubber's lines).
3. Make sure that all the necessary instruments (binoculars, rangefinder, distance meter, Battenberg, etc.) and publications are available on the bridge.
4. Make arrangements for the training of unqualified officers in watchkeeping and navigation.
5. Make arrangements for the assistance of berthing (unberthing) parties and tugs, if required.

ON LEAVING HARBOUR

1. Check the gyro-compass error and the compass deviation by transits.
2. See that the correct speed setting is applied to the gyro-compass.
3. Note the direction and strength of the tidal stream when passing buoys, etc.
4. Check the buoys as you pass them, remembering that shape is more important than colour.
5. Advise the Captain about shutting down boilers not required for operational speed.

Note: When first proceeding to sea at night make sure that the regulations concerning lights showing outboard are being observed (*Q.R. and A.I.*).

COASTING AND IN LOW VISIBILITY

1. The present position of the ship must always be on the chart.
2. Check the ship's position by every available means.
3. Brief the operations room fully concerning the state of the weather.

4. Ensure that all shipping is plotted and that courses, speeds and closest approach are reported to the bridge.
5. Ensure that the periods of all lights are carefully checked.
6. Advise the Captain about connecting up more boiler power.

ON OCEAN PASSAGE

1. The last fix on leaving land (the 'departure fix') is important; if the visibility is poor, remember the principle explained in Chapter V – 'Outward bound, don't run aground'.
2. Take every opportunity of fixing the ship's position astronomically and by radio navigational aids. Morning and evening stars, sun sights a.m. and p.m. and a meridian altitude should invariably be taken if possible.
3. If the horizon is bad, do not take sights that you cannot trust. Remember that the horizon may be improved by going down to a lower deck level.
4. Adjust the clocks for zone time.
5. Plot a daily analysis chart (if no Meteorological Officer is borne), and make weather reports (*Meteorological Services Handbook*).
6. Check compasses by azimuths of heavenly bodies at least every twelve hours.
7. Make the necessary routine Hydrographic observations (e.g. observation of variation) listed in current Admiralty Fleet Orders.

ON MAKING LAND

The precautions to be observed on making land are laid down in *Q.R. and A.I.*

Before making a landfall
1. Prepare the chart(s), giving the range arcs of the more powerful lights.
2. Study the soundings.
3. Give the operations room personnel a full description of what they may expect to see on radar and the reports that are required from them.

On approaching land
1. Take soundings.
2. Operate radar.
3. Have anchors cleared away.
4. Advise the Captain about extra boiler power.

ENTERING HARBOUR

This section is a resumé of some of the points to consider before and during the entrance to a harbour.

Before
1. Study the chart and sailing directions until you have a picture of what the place will look like and all the main features are familiar.
2. Using any transits and conspicuous objects, prepare the chart so that all courses, positions of 'wheel-over' and reductions of speed are clearly shown. Draw in clearing bearings for dangers and outline the areas where soundings

are insufficient for your draught. Transfer all this information from the chart to your note book (with sketches), then show the chart and your plan to the Captain. The plan should be equally effective in good or bad visibility (*see* Chapter VI).

3. Study any local traffic regulations (*Sailing Directions*).
4. Ascertain whether pilotage is compulsory or not (*Payment of Pilotage, Sailing Directions* and *Station Guide Book*); if it is, study *Q.R. and A.I.* and prepare the Pilotage Form with the correct tonnage (Chapter II).
5. Advise the Captain about extra boiler power.

Entering

1. Close up special sea-dutymen in plenty of time.
2. Sound continuously.
3. Follow your plan of entry, making bold corrections for cross tidal sets to regain your intended track.
4. Note the points mentioned in 'On Leaving Harbour'.

ANCHORING AND MOORING

See Chapter V.

AT OPEN ANCHORAGE

1. Make arrangements to receive weather reports to plot a daily analysis chart and obtain weather forecasts (if no Meteorological Officer is borne).
2. If there are few charted objects for fixing the ship, 'shoot up' uncharted marks to assist in fixing if the weather deteriorates.
3. Mark the bridge circle on the chart.
4. Take steps to ensure that you are always informed by the Officer of the Watch or quartermaster on the first signs of the approach of bad weather.
5. On the approach of bad weather:

   (a) Consider recommending an alteration to the notice for steam.
   (b) Start the gyro-compass.
   (c) Warm up a radar set.
   (d) Put the chart of the anchorage on the bridge and check the ship's position.
   (e) Set anchor watch.
   (f) Consider shifting berth or putting to sea or letting go second anchor to reduce the yaw.

ON RETURN TO HARBOUR

1. Analyse the passage and enter any data of interest in the Navigational Data Book, i.e.:

   (a) Speed by engine revolutions for the time out of dock.
   (b) Log errors.
   (c) Leeway experienced for different wind strengths and directions.

    (d) Alteration in compass deviations.

    (e) Unusual results obtained from radar and radio aids.

    (f) Complete the narrative of ship's movements and the record of distances steamed.

2. Demand replacements for worn or damaged charts.

TESTS AND CALIBRATIONS

1. Correction of magnetic compasses (Chapter IX).
2. Calibration of bottom log (on first commissioning, and periodically thereafter).
3. Calibration of DF (Chapter VI).
4. Calibration of A.R.L. tables (on first commissioning and periodically thereafter).
5. D.G. ranging (*D.G. Manual* and *Admiralty Manual of Navigation, Vol IV*).
6. Calibration of navigational rangefinders (Chapter VII).
7. Marking of hand lead lines.
8. Establishing details of ship's performance (*Q.R. and A.I.*).
9. Checking of aneroid barometer.

ON BEING RELIEVED

1. Prepare plan of turnover to make sure that your successor obtains all the information about the ship.
2. Make sure that all your knowledge of the ship is recorded in the Navigational Data Book.
3. Check Naval stores and books on loan and obtain your successor's signature for them.
4. Prepare supply, receipt and transfer notes for the chart outfit and chronometers.
5. Forward the returns laid down in Appendix II.
6. Sign the ship's log.

PAYING OFF

1. Prepare supply and receipt notes; return chart outfit and chronometers.
2. Return Naval stores and books on loan.
3. Bring the Navigational Data Book up to date and send it to the office of the Admiral Superintendent of the Dockyard for safe custody until the ship recommissions.
4. Forward the returns laid down in Appendix II.

APPENDIX II

List of Returns to be rendered by the Navigating Officer

WHEN	SUBJECT	FORM	TO WHOM	AUTHORITY
Weekly	Ship's Log	S.322 S.325	Captain, for signature	Q.R. & A.I.
Monthly	Ship's Log	S.322 S.325	Captain, for signature	Q.R. & A.I.
Quarterly	Pilotage Return	S.454	D.N.D., Admiralty	B.R. 2030
Periodically	Deviation of compasses	S.374a	Director, Compass Department, Slough (on each occasion of swinging ship)	B.R. 45(1), Chapter IX
,,	Hydrographic Notes	H.102	Hydrographer, Taunton (copy to C.-in-C. of station): (a) on receipt of new navigational information, (b) with reports of proceedings, if appropriate	(a) Q.R. & A.I. (b) Q.R. & A.I.
,,	Ship's Performance Trials	S.347	Admiralty (within six months of first commissioning)	Q.R. & A.I.
,,	Radio . Navigational Aids: Operational Report	H.434	Admiralty through admin. authority (if results are exceptional or unusual)	A.F.O.
,,	Ship's Log	S.322 S.325	Head of Record Office, Admiralty (in batches of 12 two years after the date of the first log in the batch)	Q.R. & A.I.
On Supersession	Pilotage Return	—	See Quarterly Return	
,,	Chronometer Return	H.394	The Hydrographer, Taunton	
,,	Transfer of Chart Folios	H.11	The Hydrographer, Taunton	H.51
On Paying-off	Pilotage Return	—	See Quarterly Return	

WHEN	SUBJECT	FORM	TO WHOM	AUTHORITY
On Paying-off	Transfer of Chart Folios	—	*See* On Supersession Return	
,,	Ship's Log	—	*See* Periodical Return	
,,	Fishing Vessel Log	S.1176	Secretary of the Admiralty (N.L. Branch)	S.1176
,,	Navigational Data Book	Manuscript	Supt. of Dockyard, for custody	*Q.R. & A.I.*

Notes

1. Other returns may be required by Administrative Authorities, e.g. Ship's Log (monthly) for inspection.
2. Particulars of, and regulations for, Secret and Confidential charts and other Hydrographic publications are contained in the appropriate 'H' form.

Index

Printed in England for Her Majesty's Stationery Office by UDO (Litho) Ltd., London.

Dd 585884 K80 6/77